THE MAKING OF THE
MODERN AGE

THE MAKING OF THE
MODERN AGE

Europe and the West Since the Enlightenment

SECOND EDITION

ARTHUR HABERMAN

Associate Professor of History and Humanities
York University

Consulting Editor:

Sydney Eisen
Professor of History and Humanities
York University

 EDUCATIONAL PUBLISHING COMPANY
A DIVISION OF CANADA PUBLISHING CORPORATION
TORONTO ONTARIO CANADA

Arthur Haberman is Associate Professor of History
and Humanities in the Faculty of Arts, and Master
of Founders College at York University. He
completed his B.A. at the City College of New York
and received his M.A. and Ph.D. from New York
University. Professor Haberman has served as
Associate Dean of the Faculty of Education at York
and has extensive experience working with teachers
and students in secondary schools. He has also
worked on History and Social Studies curricula
with the Ministry of Education of the Province of
Ontario and the National Faculty of Humanities,
Arts and Sciences.

Sydney Eisen is Professor of History and
Humanities at York University. He received his B.A.
from the University of Toronto and his Ph.D. from
The Johns Hopkins University, and he has taught at
Williams College and the City College of New York.
At York, he served as Chairman of the Department
of History and Dean of the Faculty of Arts. He has
been associated with the Advanced Planning
Program of the College Entrance Examination
Board and with the National Humanities Faculty,
and he has worked with teachers and students in
secondary schools.

Cover design by Susan Weiss

Cover photograph from the collection of the
National Museums, Paris, *''Pont de chemin de fer
à Argenteuil''* by Claude Monet

Maps by Robert Garbutt and James Loates *illustrating*

Study material by
Jim Christopher
Leaside High School
East York Board of Education

The publisher acknowledges the contributions
of Robert Remnant to the study material
contained in the first edition of *The Making of the
Modern Age*.

Canadian Cataloguing in Publication Data

Haberman, Arthur, 1938—
   The making of the modern age

Bibliography: p.
Includes index.
ISBN 0-7715-8344-3

1. History, Modern—19th century. 2. History,
Modern—20th century. I. Title.

D358.H28 1986   909.8   C86-094521-9

Written, Printed, and Bound in Canada

   2 3 4 5 JD 91 90 89 88 87

ISBN 0-7715-8344-3

To Lisa, Jennifer, and Rebecca

Acknowledgments

For permission to reprint copyrighted material grateful acknowledgment is made to the following:

Executors of the Estate of Mrs. Elsie Bambridge and The Macmillan Company of London and Basingstoke for the excerpt from "The White Man's Burden", taken from *The Five Nations* by Rudyard Kipling.

The Bobbs-Merrill Company, Inc. for the excerpt taken from *Europe in the Nineteenth Century*, Vol. 1, edited by E. N. Anderson, S. J. Pincetl, Jr., and D. J. Ziegler. Copyright 1961 The Bobbs-Merrill Company, Inc.

Angel Flores for "Correspondences" by Charles Baudelaire, translated by Kate Flores, taken from *An Anthology of French Poetry from Nerval to Valéry in English Translation with French Originals*, New Revised Edition, edited by Angel Flores, published by Doubleday & Company, Inc., copyright © 1958 by Angel Flores.

The Hamlyn Publishing Group Limited for the excerpts taken from *Hitler: A Study in Tyranny* by Alan Bullock, © 1952 Odhams Press Limited. Reproduced by permission of The Hamlyn Publishing Group Limited.

Harcourt Brace Jovanovich, Inc., for "Grass" from *Cornhuskers* by Carl Sandburg, copyright, 1918, by Holt, Rinehart and Winston, Inc., copyright 1946, by Carl Sandburg. Reprinted by permission of Harcourt Brace Jovanovich, Inc.; the excerpt from *The Origins of Totalitarianism*, 2nd edition, by Hannah Arendt, reprinted by permission of Harcourt Brace Jovanovich, Inc.

Little, Brown and Company for the excerpts taken from *The Complete Letters of Vincent van Gogh*.

Reproduced by permission of Little, Brown and Co. in association with the New York Graphic Society.

McClelland and Stewart Limited for the excerpts from *The War Speeches of the Rt. Hon. Winston S. Churchill*, Vol. 1, compiled by Charles Eade, reprinted by permission of The Canadian Publishers, McClelland and Stewart Limited, Toronto.

The New York Times Company for the excerpt from George C. Marshall's Speech—June 5, 1947; the excerpt from the Cominform Agreement between the Soviet Union and Its Allies—October 6, 1947; the excerpt from Nikita Khrushchev's Speech—June 5, 1956, © 1947/1956, copyrights renewed, by The New York Times Company. Reprinted by permission.

The Owen Estate and Chatto and Windus Ltd. for the first two verses from "Apologia Pro Poemate Meo" from *The Collected Poems of Wilfred Owen*.

Oxford University Press Canada for the excerpts from *The Speeches of Adolf Hitler, April 1922–August 1939*, Vol. 1, edited by Norman H. Baynes, published 1942; *Documents on International Affairs, 1935*, Vol. 1, edited by John W. Wheeler-Bennett & Stephen Heald, published 1936. *The Communist International 1919–1943 Documents*, Vol. 1, selected and edited by Jane Degras, published 1956. All issued under the auspices of the Royal Institute of International Affairs, published by Oxford University Press, London. Reprinted by permission of Oxford University Press, Canada; excerpt and poem "Loushan Pass" from *Mao and the Chinese Revolution* by Jerome Ch'ên. © 1965 Oxford

Contents

Introduction

This book explores the origins and development of the time span (1789 to the present) in Europe and the West that has come to be known as the "modern" period. The French Revolution and the Industrial Revolution mark the beginnings of the great social, political, and intellectual upheavals that have characterized this age, which has seen the rise of both modern democracy and totalitarianism, a transformation in the method of the production of goods, the growth of cities, the increasing importance of the middle class and the masses, and the vast expansion of our knowledge of nature and of human beings. Many of these developments are traced back to their origins, but, of course it is difficult to find the "beginning" of anything in history. Elements of the modern age can be found in the days of the Italian Renaissance, but it is not until the eighteenth century that all the ingredients of the modern age are present. The examination of this time period, known as the Enlightenment, brings an appreciation for the ideas and events which brought the modern age into being.

What features are peculiar to the people living in the modern age? We can think of several that distinguish them from their medieval ancestors, for example, their high degree of self-consciousness, their deep interest in analysing and understanding human nature, and their belief that people are masters of their fate — that they make their own history and create their own world.

The sentiment of nationalism, the sense of being or aspiring to be a citizen of a nation is central to individuals in the modern age. This may well be the strongest and most enduring motive force of the period, replacing family, tribal, and religious loyalties of an earlier time.

Revolution and violence have been ever-present in the modern age — perhaps no more so than in other periods, but on a vastly greater scale and for different reasons. Political change in the modern age has often come about by revolution, whether in the name of nationalism, democracy, anti-colonialism, or simply "the people". With the decline of monarchies and aristocratic authority, politics became the affair of the many (usually a combination of the middle class and the masses) rather than of the few. Mass politics, involving mass electorates, mass revolutions, and mass armies, has resulted in a raising of the level of political violence. Wars in the modern period have been fought between whole peoples, not simply between rulers and states.

The new masses who emerged with the Industrial Revolution have also become literate. This represents a significant feature of the modern age, since only a small fraction of the population prior to the mid nineteenth century could read or write. Political and social institutions, literature and art, and even the nature of warfare, all have been transformed by these developments in production, population, and literacy.

The modern period has been both optimistic and pessimistic about human nature and the future of the human species. Most people in the nineteenth century believed that humanity was progressing, life was getting better, and knowledge about the world was increasing. In the twentieth century, prolonged wars, persistent violence, the continuing starvation of millions of people, and the realization that pollution and the problem of energy may put a limit on industrial and technological growth, have all tempered earlier expectations. In place of certainty about progress, there is now a good deal of doubt and perplexity about the future. One thing seems clear: all is change in the modern world, and the rapidity of change is its most notable characteristic.

This book discusses the modern age from the perspective of the West. It is important, therefore, to understand the broad meaning of ''West'' and ''Western'' as they appear in this work. The concept of the West used here denotes the attitudes, ideas, and institutions coming out of Europe, and the extensions of European civilization throughout the globe. But it is not a static concept. With the passage of time and in the course of events the idea of ''the West'' changes, just as the geographic area covered by ''the West'' does not remain the same. In this book the West is studied as a dynamic entity — ideologically, geographically, and historically.

The emphasis is on Western history and culture, particularly that of Europe, while other civilizations are touched upon only briefly in relation to the West. It is important to note that this approach in no way implies a judgment as to whether the influence of the West was for good or for ill, nor does it suggest that the flow of influence was in only one direction. It does suggest, however, that in order to understand the modern age, the study of the West and its relation to the world is essential. It is hoped that students in search of such an understanding will find their efforts well rewarded.

CHAPTER **1**

The Origins of the Modern Age

THE CONCEPT OF A MODERN ERA FIRST arose in the West during the early Renaissance when the Italian poet Francesco Petrarca (1304–74) made the distinction between the idea of humanity in his own time and that of the preceding age. That age, the centuries between the end of the classical world (generally put at the fall of Rome in 476 A.D.) and the Renaissance, was labelled medieval, or the Middle Ages. The term implied a period of cultural decline between two periods of cultural greatness. During the Renaissance, or "rebirth," in Italy and then in northern Europe, people perceived of themselves as "modern." While they admired the Greek and Latin classics, they took a renewed interest in contemporary culture and society, became more secular in outlook, and turned to exploring the world around them.

Modernity has also been defined in a religious sense, both with respect to ideas and institutions. Some think of the modern age as rooted in the events and ideas that emerged from the Protestant Reformation of the early sixteenth century. Sparked by the German cleric Martin Luther (1483–1546), the Reformation redefined humanity's relationship to the divine. In doing so, more emphasis was placed upon the individual and the direct relationship between human beings and God rather than the role of the Church. The Protestant Reformation ended the unity of Western Christendom, as new churches emerged which broke up the Roman Catholic Church, whose ideological and institutional structure had been at the center of Western civilization since the fourth century.

In attempting to trace the origins of the modern age, historians have found different points to emphasize. The growth of the modern state in the early modern period is regularly cited as a fundamental institutional novelty, which forever changed our patterns of political and diplomatic organization, as well as our loyalties. Social historians point to the shift from an aristocratic society to one based upon commerce and money, which resulted in the rise of new classes. Economic historians discuss the modern society in terms of trade, technology, and new modes of production and distribution, and intellectual historians refer to the rise of modern science, with its view of an orderly universe and the ability of human beings to understand it.

All critics place the beginnings of modernity sometime in the period between the Renaissance and the Enlightenment. Whenever the break between the pre-modern and the modern is seen to occur, modern science and the modern state are never ignored. It is in the changes occurring in these areas that we can clearly see the foundations of the modern age.

Whatever the basis cited, it is agreed that by the eighteenth century, in what came to be called the period of the Enlightenment, the West had acquired most of the ingredients that went into making the modern age. Not only was the Enlightenment self-consciously modern, but its concept of the universe, its social philosophy, and its system of knowledge all were fundamentally important in shaping the world in which we live and the ways we understand that world.

A. THE SCIENTIFIC REVOLUTION

Much of the optimism of the modern age was based first on what came to be known as the scientific revolution, a series of breakthroughs in our understanding and interpretation of

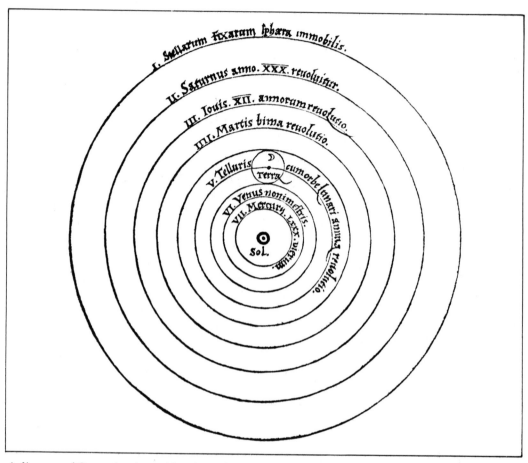

A diagram of Copernicus' new idea about the universe, from his work On the Revolutions of the Heavenly Bodies. *The sun is at the center, and the plants are pictured as revolving around it. (The Pierpont Morgan Library)*

the heavens and the earth. It took place mainly in the seventeenth century, and it brought changes in humanity's view of itself, nature, and God. It heralded great progress in knowledge and in humanity's capacity to comprehend and control nature. By the time Isaac Newton published his *Principia Mathematica* (*The Mathematical Principles of Natural Philosophy*) in 1687, a new cosmology (a theory of the structure of the universe) and a new epistemology (a theory of knowledge) were part of the outlook of educated people.

THE INHERITED THEORY OF THE HEAVENS AND EARTH

The old view of the cosmos, held in medieval and early modern times, was one adopted mainly from the works of the Greek philosopher Aristotle and the ancient astronomer Ptolemy, with an overlay of Christian perceptions. The universe was seen to be made up of a series of concentric and ever larger spheres. The earth, the innermost sphere, was a motionless hard solid substance. The other spheres were transparent and on them hung the heavenly bodies, the stars and planets. The earth was thought to be composed of four basic elements — earth, air, fire, and water. Each element had its own characteristics and its proper place in the system: earth and water had gravity, for they fell; fire and air had levity, for they rose. In the medieval view, the earth's geographical center was thought to be Jerusalem, the most holy city, and often maps made in the Middle Ages placed Jerusalem at the hub of the earth. Apart from the earth, the remainder of the universe was composed of a fifth element, a quintessence, a perfect kind of material.

In this model the heavenly spheres were thought to revolve about the immobile earth; to each sphere were attached heavenly bodies which moved about the earth with them. In the medieval period people believed there were ten spheres, each "higher" or more perfect than the previous one; the last was the home of God. Thus, the cosmology was a hierarchy, a universe in which the heavens were qualitatively different from, and purer than, the earth. Though the earth was made of base material, human beings were, nevertheless, at the center of the universe, having a special relation to God. The motion of the spheres was seen as circular, and this movement was thought to be perfect. All things were presumed to have a purpose, an end or goal, which caused them to act as they did.

NEW IDEAS ABOUT THE UNIVERSE

It was Nicolas Copernicus (1473–1543) who issued the first substantive challenge to the cosmology of the Middle Ages, which by the fifteenth century had become very complex. All kinds of special motions had to be assumed in order to retain the principle of circularity and the centrality and stillness of the earth. Copernicus suggested in his *On the Revolutions of the Heavenly Bodies* (1543) that the Ptolemaic system was wrong in its model of the universe. Offended by the overly complicated old view, Copernicus substituted a cosmos which was heliocentric (sun-centered) for one which had been geocentric (earth-centered). He proposed that it was simpler to hypothesize that the earth rotated on its axis, as did the other planets, and that the sun was the stationary body around which the whole universe moved. Copernicus' system was an hypothesis, a new model of interpretation; it did not provide quantities of evidence from observation in support of its claims.

Although Copernicus continued to accept the concept of circular motion as "true" movement, as well as other assumptions of the old model, his work was controversial, and it did not win immediate acceptance. A wealth of observation was needed to test the theory and refine it. New observations were made by the Danish astronomer Tycho Brahe (1546–1601), who assembled data and proposed a model which amounted to a compromise. He suggested that all the planets except the earth circled the sun, and that the whole system could be understood to be circling the earth.

The search was now on for the laws of celestial motion, and greatly improved instruments permitted more accurate observation. Tycho Brahe's assistant Johannes Kepler (1571–1630) made the breakthrough. What Kepler wished to discover was mathematical regularity, and his laws of planetary motion were a great advance in that direction. His first two laws state: 1) the movement of the planets is a regular elliptical orbit, with the sun as one focus; 2) the planets move in a velocity in which equal areas are swept out in equal times. These two laws, Kepler claimed, were true for all planets. His third law, which states that the square of the period of the orbit of a planet is proportional to the cube of that planet's mean distance from the sun, was the one which proclaimed that all the heavens were bound in a single mathematical relationship. To Kepler the universe was a lawful mechanical system, expressed in mathematics. The proposal put forth by Copernicus now had acquired greater status.

GALILEO AND THE NEW SCIENCE

The most dramatic moments in the development of modern science occurred in the career of the Italian Galileo Galilei (1564–1642). Galileo, in 1609, borrowing an idea from the Dutch, designed and built a telescope in order to see the heavens more closely. As he said in an essay directed to the Grand Duchess Christina of Tuscany, "I discovered in the heavens many things that had not been seen before our own age." He discovered the moons of Jupiter and used that self-contained system to reflect upon the solar system as a whole. He also gazed more closely than anyone before him at those ancient and revered heavenly symbols, the sun and the moon; he found that the sun had changing spots and that the moon seemed to have mountains.

The telescopes of Galileo.
(*Reproduction permission courtesy Istituto E Museo Di Storia Della Scienza, photograph courtesy Metropolitan Toronto Library Board*)

Galileo was certain that his observations supported the heliocentric view of the solar system. His view of the heavens, however, was not only contrary to the accepted authority of Ptolemy, it was also seen to be a challenge to the authority of the Bible and the Catholic Church. Theologians and philosophers were angry with Galileo for putting forth a view of the world which seemed to contradict the Bible and the dogmas of the Church. What was central for them was the revelation of God as it was understood in that age. Galileo defended himself by claiming that the Bible itself was open to interpretation and by appealing directly to scripture and to St. Augustine's writings. He also proclaimed the soundness of his method:

I think that in discussions of physical problems we ought to begin not from the authority of scriptural passages, but from sense-experiences and necessary demonstrations; for the holy Bible and the phenomena of nature proceed alike from the divine Word, the former as the dictate of the Holy Ghost and the latter as the observant executrix of God's commands. . . . But I do not feel obliged to believe that the same God who has endowed us with senses, reason, and intellect has intended to forgo their use and by some other means to give us knowledge which we can attain by them.[1]

In 1633 Galileo was brought before the Inquisition and tried for heresy. He was accused of holding "the doctrine—which is false and contrary to the sacred and divine Scriptures—that the Sun is the center of the world and does not move from east to west and that the Earth moves and is not the center of the world; and that an opinion may be held and defended as probable after it has been declared and defined to be contrary to the Holy Scriptures." Galileo was forced to acknowledge publicly that he had made an error, and to recant his theories and observations. The story is told that as he left the courtoom Galileo said: "And yet it moves."

Galileo's controversial opinions on the heavens did not stop another aspect of his scientific work which contributed to the new view of nature. His discoveries in the area of motion helped to develop the modern science of mechanics. The prevailing theory, based on Aristotle, was that bodies in motion came to rest, and thus a force was always required to keep a body moving. Galileo formulated a new hypothesis, which suggested that bodies in motion would continue unless some form of resistance was introduced. He now worked on a mathematical explanation of the movement of falling bodies. His laws of terrestrial motion complemented Kepler's laws of celestial motion.

At this time there were many theories in vogue, as people searched for a comprehensive model based upon the new data. Moreover, Galileo, in his letter to his Duchess, was expressing the sense of the times: scientists now trusted explanations which found mathematical expression and could be demonstrated by observation. The old authorities, be they the ancient philosophers of Greece and Rome, or those steeped in Christian learning, no longer possessed the intellectual prestige that they had in the past. Mathematics itself began to develop in new ways, with the invention of analytic geometry and calculus. It was the English poet John Donne who best captured the ambiguity of the time when the "new philosophy," what then was called natural philosophy, was being developed:

And new philosophy calls all in doubt;
The element of fire is quite put out;
The sun is lost, and th'earth, and no man's wit
Can well direct him where to look for it.[2]

The challenge to old models introduced uncertainty, a sense that the old order was disappearing and that the fixed truths of the inherited culture were no longer reliable.

NEWTON AND THE NEW MODEL OF THE UNIVERSE

It was Isaac Newton (1642–1727), an English physicist and mathematician, who provided the synthesis which became the new model of science for the next several centuries. Newton worked on the problem of motion as a youth, and he developed in his twenties a theory of gravity which claimed that the planets moved in the manner described by Kepler because they were drawn to the sun by a force which could be calculated. Newton then worked on a unified theory — an attempt to unite Kepler's and Galileo's laws. He managed this feat in his famous law of gravity. The movement of all bodies, he proclaimed, followed a formula: the force of gravity between two bodies was inversely proportional to the square of the distance between them. The force which held the planets in orbit, said Newton, was the same as that which caused bodies to fall to earth. The new cosmos was one system, understood as a whole.

Newton's achievement was acknowledged by his contemporaries, and his name has become synonymous with a whole new worldview. Like Galileo, Newton realized that he was challenging more than theories about the movement of the earth. The perception of the relationship between man and God was at stake as well. Newton, who spent much time on theology, affirmed at the end of his scientific masterwork of 1687, *The Mathematical Principles of Natural Philosophy*, that the world was organized by a beneficent and wise God:

This most beautiful System of the Sun, Planets, and Comets could only proceed from the counsel and dominion of an intelligent and powerful Being. . . .

This Being governs all things, . . . as Lord over all. . . . And from his true dominion it follows, that the true God is a Living, Intelligent and Powerful Being. . . . He is Eternal and Infinite, Omnipotent and Omniscient. . . . He endures for ever, and is every where present; and by existing always and every where, he constitutes Duration and Space.[3]

The English essayist Alexander Pope wrote a famous epitaph for Newton, which celebrated his achievements:

Nature and nature's laws lay hid in Night:
God said, 'Let Newton be!' and all was Light.[4]

The picture of the world put forth by Newton and his contemporaries was that of the universe as a machine. This mechanistic model saw the universe as orderly, coherent, and natural. God was viewed as the creator of this machine, the Prime Mover, who brought into being the world in its lawfulness, regularity, and beauty. This was the image of God as a master-builder who created a perfect machine and then let it run. This view of God as the creator who stood aside from his work and did not get involved directly with humanity was called Deism, and was accepted by many who supported the "new philosophy."

There were a number of assumptions of the new science which came to play a role in humanity's understanding of itself. With the acceptance of the Newtonian cosmology, it was agreed that the universe was orderly, and the function of the investigator was to discover that order. Nature had a new status, and to be "natural" came to be associated with the lawfulness of the universe. Mathematics had a new status as a means of expressing laws. To describe something mathematically was thought to get at its reality; quantitative explanations came to be trusted not only for their accuracy, but as a reflection of reality. Finally, though humanity was seen by some to be diminished because human beings were no longer at the center of the cosmos, others saw humanity as raised higher than ever.

Many believed that humanity was now asserting its independence of tradition and old authority.

NEW IDEAS ABOUT KNOWLEDGE

A new theory of knowledge was at the center of the quest for order in the heavens and earth. Two individuals, Francis Bacon (1561–1626) and Rene Descartes (1596–1650), were associated with efforts to arrive at a new understanding of the nature of knowledge.

Bacon claimed that the only way to obtain knowledge was through experience and observation. This approach to knowledge came to be called empiricism, which is an insistence on accumulating information, after which generalizations might be made. Bacon emphasized induction, a form of reasoning from the particular to the general. Repeated instances of the same phenomena build up a body of knowledge which permits us to generalize and, ultimately, to formulate laws. Bacon wished to provide a method for the development of a new science and believed that in humanity's rational capacity he had found the key. In his *Novum Organum* (1620) he wrote: "men have been kept back by a kind of enchantment from progress in the sciences by reverence for antiquity, by the authority of men accounted great in philosophy, and then by general consent."[5] His new method yielded results in all areas and became the basis for great advances in the sciences.

Descartes in his *Discourse on Method* (1637) advocated a new theory of knowledge based on humanity's reasoning ability combined with intuitive powers, an approach which emphasized the importance of the human mind. "*Cogito ergo sum*," (I think, therefore I am), he proclaimed, defining human beings as mind endowed with reason. He developed rules of logic for achieving certainty: first, to seek clarity — "never to accept anything for true which I did not clearly know to be such"; second, to strive for economy and simplicity of complex matter; third, to move from the simple to the complex because of a belief that the rules for the simple hold true for the complex as well; fourth, to be comprehensive.

Descartes' rationalism was based on seeking clear self-evident truths, reasoning from those axioms, and obtaining solutions through deduction — reasoning from the general to the particular. It is a skepticism tempered by a willingness to trust the mind to find order, or to grasp it intuitively. As well, Descartes trusted the proofs of those he called the "geometers," the mathematicians, for he believed that mathematical reasoning was the path to a secure theory of knowledge. Descartes had enormous confidence in humanity's ability, once the right *method* was established, to penetrate the mysteries of nature. Descartes' emphasis on rationalism and deduction is to be contrasted with Bacon's stress on empiricism and induction. Yet, both methods were used by scientists to advance knowledge.

To the Enlightenment the scientific revolution and the thinkers associated with it had performed a heroic task, and had displaced the ancient wisdom of Greece and Rome, as well as of the scriptures, in the study of nature. Order had been constructed out of chaos. Nature was coherent and was governed by laws. Humanity saw itself as capable of solving problems of cosmology and epistemology in new ways without reference to ancient or theological authority. "Go, wondrous creature!," said Pope in his *Essay on Man*, "mount where science guides,"

Go, measure earth, weigh air, and state the tides
Instruct the planets in what orbs to run;
Correct old time, and regulate the Sun;

And a bit later:

Take Nature's path, and mad Opinion's leave;
All states can reach it, and all heads conceive;
Obvious her goods, in no extreme they dwell;
There needs but right thinking and meaning well.[6]

There was a new confidence that human beings could master the universe.

B. THE STYLE OF ABSOLUTISM

In the West, in the modern era, the issue at the heart of political discourse has been the question of the legitimacy of authority. The arguments generally center on the concepts of order, authority, and rights. In the last half of the seventeenth century and through the early eighteenth century, the major new idea in government was absolutism, which was introduced in its most elaborate form in France.

CLASSICISM IN THE SEVENTEENTH CENTURY

The development of absolutism in the seventeenth century is related to the new classicism which was in vogue at the time. Classicism in culture was an expression of admiration for the achievements of the ancient Greeks and Romans. Absolutism was one aspect of classicism, looking particularly to the Roman Empire. The supporters of absolutism valued certainty, stability, order, and fixed standards. Classicists believed that the quality of life had been at its peak during the ancient period.

In the latter part of the seventeenth century, in the political world, it was Rome — not the Rome of the Republic, but the Rome of the Empire, the Rome of the Emperor Augustus who brought stability, order, and peace to a republic torn apart by revolution — which was admired. The supporters of absolutism believed that there existed fixed standards, eternal truths, which in the sphere of government were most closely approximated by the political genius of ancient Rome, and that those standards should provide the model for their own political structures.

CLASSICISM AND ABSOLUTISM

The classicism which was so admired by the absolutists assumed that the good life was one which was lived in accordance with clearly set out rules of behaviour, and with stable institutions and structures. At the courts of the absolute rulers life was dominated by codes of etiquette, elaborate dress, and good manners. There was a belief in an ordered society and an understanding of place based upon birth. Socially, one's career could be made or broken by knowing the appropriate courtesies, and by a sense of what was proper at any given time. To be civilized at the court of Louis XIV of France (1643–1715) meant to engage in an elaborate social and personal ritual, to know the rules of protocol, and to understand one's place in the world.

Politically, as socially, the new classicism of the absolutist regimes meant order and obedience to established rules. These rules were institutionalized by kings in an attempt to substitute stability for the chaos and irrationality of feudalism, and to set up common norms through a centralized authority, in place of the incoherence of many local jurisdictions.

In the late seventeenth century, then, the social and political forms taken by absolutism were a challenge to the old feudal order. Absolute rulers wished not only to centralize political authority, but to introduce and enforce a national language, and to foster and manage a national economy. Often faced with entrenched local authority, many provincial dialects, an old-fashioned agricultural economy, and different economic codes, absolute rulers attempted to modernize, that is, to wrest their sovereignty out of this medieval world.

ABSOLUTISM AS A STYLE OF GOVERNING

This rationalism of absolute government was in the spirit of the scientific revolution of the same period. It was an attempt to discover an order underneath the seeming chaos of external events. For Louis XIV, this meant that the entity we now call France was to be given a central organization, that regulations from the center replaced local custom, that a bureaucracy responsible to the king came into being where it had never existed before, and that the monarchy took the initiative to create national wealth and a national armed force.

The Bourbon monarchy of France, most especially the strong rule of Louis XIV, led in the development of absolutism as a system. Louis XIV during his long and powerful reign became the archetypal absolutist whose style in war, economics, culture, and architecture was emulated by lesser rulers throughout the European continent. Louis came to be called "Le Roi soleil," the Sun King, and as the planets were seen to revolve around the sun in the new cosmology of the scientific revolution, so too Louis saw himself as the center of affairs in his kingdom and in the West.

Louis XIV governed as well as reigned. During his childhood, and before he assumed control, France, like most states, was organized in a feudal manner, and the king was under the sway of powerful ministers. When Cardinal Mazarin, who had been the main minister to the crown of France for over a decade, died in 1661, Louis, then twenty-three

A portrait of Louis XIV by Pierre Mignard, painted in 1674. Hung originally at Versailles, the painting commemorates a French military victory.
(From the book A Pageant of Canada, *published by the National Gallery of Canada)*

years old, assembled his advisors and proclaimed: "I shall in the future be my own first minister. You will aid me with your counsel when I ask for them." And Louis never faltered until his death fifty-four years later. Seeing his fortunes and those of France as synonymous, he took hold of and guided the government apparatus.

In order to gain control of France, Louis had to curb the authority of the old nobility and to establish a system of government responsible to him throughout the realm. He created a new set of civil servants, his *intendants*, who held office at the pleasure of the king. They were ordinarily recruited from the upper middle classes, and their position and status were entirely dependent on the authority of the monarch. They were responsible for the collection of taxes and administration of the regions to which they were dispatched to represent the crown. No intendant was permitted to serve in the area in which he was born; as a result, they were always seen to be dispassionate emissaries of the king, and not local officials tied to local affairs.

ABSOLUTISM AND THE ECONOMY
The economy and its control was a major concern of the absolute rulers. Louis collected old taxes, such as the *taille*, or land tax. He also introduced new measures throughout the kingdom, including a head tax on everyone. The civil servants of the king made every effort to collect indirect taxes, such as those on salt, tobacco and wine. In every case, often successfully, the representatives of the king were given the authority to override local autonomy and opposition. This centralization of authority did much to break down the localisms entrenched in the laws and customs of the Middle Ages, but much remained of the old system.

Louis worked with his economic minister Jean Baptiste Colbert (1619–83) to make France a great economic power, as part of a plan to enhance his authority and to provide himself with the revenues to pursue his diplomatic policies and support a strong army. The policy of the centralization of the economy was pursued as France challenged the colonial authority and wealth of the British and the Dutch.

The production and export of manufactured goods was encouraged in order to give France a favourable balance of trade which would provide it with the gold needed to sustain the ambitious foreign policy of the monarch.

Colbert worked mightily to reform the internal economy of France. As a loose feudal confederation of territories, France had a system of internal tariffs which hampered trade within the kingdom. Colbert managed to institutionalize the Five Great Farms, a unit roughly half the size of France in its northern part, into an area in which goods could circulate tax free. A more efficient system of tax collection was also inaugurated. In order to aid the general economy of the kingdom, Colbert followed a policy, very modern in conception, of having the state build and encourage the infrastructure of the economy: roads and canals were built; new industry was sponsored; and in the areas of glass, tapestries, and silk Colbert encouraged the manufacture of goods which had heretofore been imported and which could now be exported because they were so desirable. The idea was to increase exports and restrict imports.

The centralization of the armed forces was part of the same trend. Louis XIV abandoned the old practice of having a fighting force assembled by many semi-independent chieftains, each of whom had authority over a mixed bag of private soldiers. In 1661 France had an army of 20 000; in 1667 it was 72 000; in 1688 it was 290 000 and still growing. Louis followed a policy designed to encourage a career in the service of the state and of having a professional standing army. The army was disciplined, wore uniforms, and had a pay scale akin to that of the civil service. His army drilled and practiced with the newest weapons; in the late seventeenth century that meant a gun with a bayonet attached. Military strategy was given great attention as fighting became more sophisticated.

Louis XIV sought religious conformity as well. The vast majority of the French were Roman Catholic, and Louis believed that all his subjects should share the same religion as part of a unity of belief. In France, in 1598, King Henry IV had issued the Edict of Nantes, which gave French Protestants, called

Huguenots, religious liberty and protection under law. During Louis XIV's reign pressure was placed upon Huguenots, numbering about five per cent of the population, to convert. Finally, in 1685, Louis XIV revoked the Edict of Nantes in an effort to secure religious unity. Many Huguenots emigrated to England, the Germanies, Holland, and America, and they took with them their skills and wealth.

THE PALACE OF VERSAILLES

The visual symbol and architectural manifestation of Louis XIV's absolutist temperament and the model of classical aesthetics was the monumental palace of Versailles, which the Sun King had built for himself and his court. Louis disliked Paris. In his childhood he had experienced a rebellion in the city and he feared its mobs. As king, he was unhappy living in the palace of the Louvre in the middle of the city. He also wanted to satisfy his grand theatrical sense: the monarchy, he believed, should be surrounded with glory and ritual. It needed a home that would place it at the center of all events in France and in the civilized Western world.

The palace at Versailles, about fifteen kilometres south of Paris, was begun in 1669. Louis and his court moved to it in 1682, prior to its full completion in 1701. It was given the same status that a great cathedral might have had several hundred years earlier, or that of the pyramids in ancient Egypt. The best talent of France — its architects, designers, landscape gardeners, and artisans of all sorts — was hired for its construction. It began by costing about three per cent of the yearly state budget, and in some years used over ten per cent of the annual expenditure. Up to 35 000 people worked on it at any one time. They built a great palace in the classical style, improving on nature, so it was thought, by imposing perfection on it. A marshy swampland was thus transformed into the architectural wonder of the age.

Rooms were vast and symmetrical, named after classical gods and goddesses — salons of Venus, Diana, Mercury, Mars, and Apollo. The Grand Hall of Mirrors was seventy-three metres in length, full of Venetian mirrors, its ceilings painted by Charles Lebrun to celebrate the age of Louis XIV. Beautiful parks were created, as grown trees were assembled from all over France, arrayed in geometrical order, and tailored precisely to classical notions of proportion.

At Versailles Louis lived and governed, and it was impossible to draw a clear line between the two. With nobles gathered round, he went riding in the parks and hunted in the daytime, gave magnificent balls and staged cultural events at night, all the while acting as his own first minister and conducting the affairs of the kingdom. All of Louis XIV's ordinary movements became celebrated rituals, from his rising in the morning to going to bed at night. Life was full of rigid etiquette and formalism. Louis' daily life was to be a work of classical art, measured, proportioned, and stylized — all part of the theatricality of the modern ruler and the modern state.

ABSOLUTISM AND THE SOCIAL SYSTEM

One result of Louis' policies was that the old nobility lost a good deal of its political power. Often, in place of power, the nobles retained their social and economic privileges, for the Sun King did not wish to do away with the class. Thus, in the time of Louis XIV, the nobility ceased to have control of the army, lost much of its power and functions in local government, and had little to do in the way of public service. Yet nobles paid modest taxes and had the rights of a special class. They provided an entourage appropriate for a Sun King.

The nobility was expected to be at the court, in attendance on the king, as part of the grandeur with which Louis surrounded himself. Now, instead of putting on armour, nobles indulged in luxurious living in the presence of the king; instead of governing a local area, they manoeuvred for favour and position in the eyes of the king. The Duc de Saint-Simon (1675–1755) gave a glimpse into court life at Versailles:

In everything [Louis XIV] loved splendor, magnificence, profusion. He turned this taste into a maxim for political reasons, and instilled it into his court on all matters. One could please him by throwing oneself into fine food, clothes, retinue, buildings, gambling. These were occasions which enabled him to talk to people. The essence of it was that by this he attempted and succeeded in exhausting everyone by making luxury a virtue, and for certain persons a necessity, and thus he gradually reduced everyone to depending entirely upon his generosity in order to subsist.[7]

Absolutism, as Louis XIV practiced it, did much to transform the feudal system into a modern one. In the feudal era one's loyalty was to a locality and only distantly to a dynasty; in the modern era one's loyalty was directed to a state, which a dynasty might symbolize. Louis transformed the mixture of territories that make up the area of France into the state of France. And for all his extraordinary ego, Louis XIV tried to change the loyalty of a people to its ruler into a loyalty directed to the institution of kingship.

The checks on power which had existed in the feudal period—the essentially contractual mutual arrangement between lord and vassal, the traditional limitations on authority, the freedom of being part of a loose system which was not centrally organized—all these began to be eroded under the self-conscious policy of a king who wanted mastery over his kingdom. Louis desired, and to an extent managed, to be politically free, to organize France under his authority, and to create an order similar to that of the first Roman Emperor Augustus out of the chaos he inherited. Louis' motto was *Nec pluribus impar*, meaning ''None is his equal.'' It is not likely that he actually said the one thing universally attributed to him, ''*L'état c'est moi*'' (I am the state), but there is no question he believed it: for Louis, all roads led to his splendid palace at Versailles.

LOUIS XIV, EUROPE, AND THE WIDER WORLD

Though Louis dominated Europe, and the culture of France was seen as pre-eminent during much of the Enlightenment, he could never control the continent to the extent he desired. Louis devised a foreign policy designed to extend the power, glory, and authority of France, and he fought a series of wars which gained some of his ends. Still, he did not manage to compel Europe into accepting French domination.

Louis followed an expansionist policy, believing, as many did, that states must continually add to their power if they wished to prosper. In 1667 his armies marched west into territories controlled by Spain in the Netherlands and the Franche-Comté. A coalition was soon formed by the Dutch, English, and Swedes, which Louis recognized as more powerful than France. When hostilities ceased in 1668, France did manage to retain some of the Flemish territory it had conquered. Louis next warred with the Dutch in 1672. Yet another coalition stopped him, but in the treaty of Nimwegen in 1678 Louis did gain the Franche-Comté from Spain. In 1688 he invaded Austria, starting what has come to be called the War of the League of Augsburg. The League was an alliance created by Holland, Sweden, Austria, Spain, and some German princes in 1686 to prevent French expansion. England joined the alliance and the war against France in 1689. Louis overextended himself in this war, and by its end, in 1696, he was facing domestic problems associated with bad harvests and the constant drain on the French economy. The Treaty of Ryswick in 1697 forced Louis to recognize William of Orange (a Dutch prince whom the British had recently placed on the throne after ousting the Catholic pro-French James II) as the legitimate king of England and to return some territories taken during the war. Louis also had to make some commercial concessions to the Dutch.

In the last years of his long reign Louis XIV made one last attempt at expansion. The result was a major European war conducted over the important issue of the succession to the Spanish throne. The last Hapsburg ruler of Spain, the feeble Charles II, had no heirs, and there had been long speculation over the inheritance and the disposition of the powerful kingdom. Charles made a complicated will and died in 1700. Louis XIV decided that he would choose the option in the will of having Spain and its territories be inherited by his grandson. The danger to the rest of Europe was clear, for if that occurred France would now control Spain and its possessions. To fight the War of the Spanish Succession, William III of England founded a Grand Alliance in 1701, which included Holland and the Austrian Empire, in addition to some smaller sovereignties.

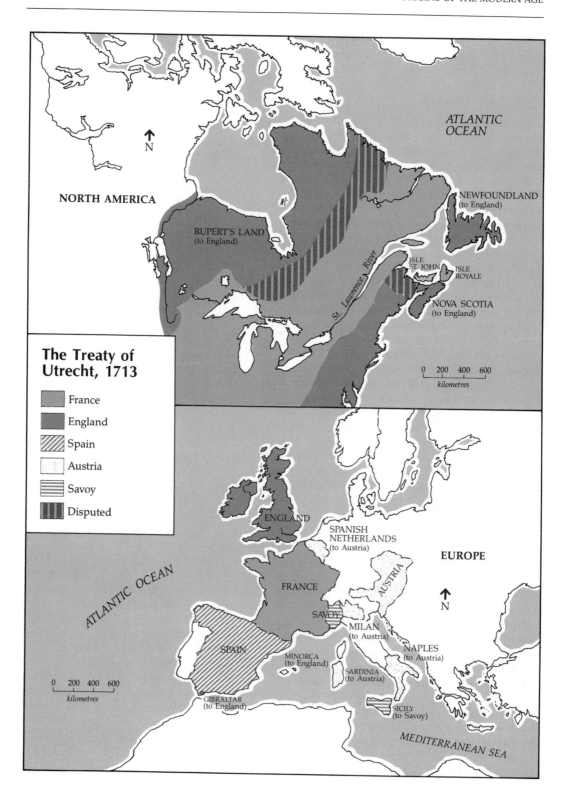

NORTH AMERICA

ATLANTIC OCEAN

NEWFOUNDLAND
(to England)

RUPERT'S LAND
(to England)

St. Lawrence River

ISLE
ST. JOHN

ISLE
ROYALE

NOVA SCOTIA
(to England)

**The Treaty of
Utrecht, 1713**

France
England
Spain
Austria
Savoy
Disputed

0   200   400   600
kilometres

ENGLAND

SPANISH
NETHERLANDS
(to Austria)

EUROPE

FRANCE

AUSTRIA

SAVOY

MILAN
(to Austria)

NAPLES
(to Austria)

ATLANTIC OCEAN

SPAIN

MINORCA
(to England)

SARDINIA
(to Austria)

0   200   400   600
kilometres

GIBRALTAR
(to England)

SICILY
(to Savoy)

MEDITERRANEAN SEA

It was a long war, now fought by professional armies with modern weaponry. Though neither side won, the war was an affirmation that Louis XIV's attempt to dominate Europe would not succeed. The Peace of Utrecht in 1713 was the major treaty signed by the war-weary parties. It was agreed that France and Spain were never to be united under a single ruler. Spain was forced to give up Gibraltar and the island of Minorca to England, and to cede its possessions in Italy and the Netherlands to Austria. In addition, Spain ceded the *asiento* to England, the valuable right to slave trading in Spanish America. The English, in addition, received from France two colonies in North America, Newfoundland and Acadia, and France recognized English control of Hudson's Bay.

France neither won nor lost the war, though England gained much in the settlement. It still remained the major power on the European continent. Louis XIV's ultimate ambition, to extend his dominion to all of the West, could not be achieved. Yet, when he died in 1715 he left France the most powerful state in Europe, a country whose style and culture were at the center of Western civilization.

ANALYSIS AND DISCUSSION

1. "Galileo's ideas and observations were significant not for what they proved, but for what they disproved. The idea of a heliocentric universe contrasted sharply with the prevailing Roman Catholic view of the world." Discuss this statement with specific reference to both the new theories of Copernicus, Kepler and Galileo, and the teachings of the Church.

2. "The Scientific Revolution introduced order where before there had only been chaos." Evaluate and analyse this statement in terms of the ideas of Descartes, Newton, and Bacon.

3. "Perhaps the greatest challenges to existing institutions during the Enlightenment were the concepts of *empiricism* and *rationalism*." Do you agree? Discuss.

4. Many parts of France's overseas empire, including Canada, were deeply affected by the policies of Louis XIV. What was the impact of his policies of mercantile control and foreign expansion upon France's colonial possessions?

5. The memoirs of the Duc de Saint-Simon make fascinating reading if you are interested in the inner workings of court life under the "Sun-King." Re-read the excerpt from the writings of Saint-Simon on pages 12–13. After examining it closely:

a) Explain the way in which Louis exercised control over his court.

b) Consider Saint-Simon's point of view. To what extent do you think that he approved of Louis' methods? What literary device does he employ to make his point?

CHAPTER **2**

The Enlightenment

IN 1784 THE GERMAN PHILOSOPHER IMMANUEL Kant wrote an essay in which he asked: "Do we live at present in an enlightened age?" His reply to his rhetorical question reveals much about the way in which the eighteenth century thought of itself. "No," Kant stated, "but in an age of enlightenment."[1] The major thinkers of the eighteenth century thought themselves to be enlightened in comparison with previous eras. Yet, they also believed they had a considerable amount to accomplish before humanity might claim to be living in an enlightened era.

The Enlightenment, as the eighteenth century came to be called, was an age of optimism, tempered by the realistic recognition of the sad state of the human condition and the need for major reforms in government and society. Progress was a keynote of the age, and new values which stressed freedom, rights, and equality were emphasized, but these were in sharp contrast to the political and social realities of the time. The Enlightenment was a period in which scientists, social thinkers, and philosophers believed that humanity, through the employment of reason, was truly beginning to gain mastery over the world. Scientists were confident they were uncovering the laws of nature; social philosophers developed secular ideologies designed to transform traditional beliefs, structures of government, and economic systems. The ambiguity of Kant's answer was appropriate to the age: there was a great gulf between enlightened aspirations and political, intellectual, and social realities.

A. CONTRACT AND RIGHTS: COMMUNITY AND THE INDIVIDUAL IN THE ENLIGHTENMENT

Authority in the modern era came to be secularized. Whereas during the Middle Ages the Church and other ecclesiastical bodies had claimed some authority over princes and the lives of people on earth, in the Enlightenment most theories of power and authority were grounded in the relationship between human beings and the secular sovereignty in which they lived. This trend was enhanced by the practice of absolutism, which on occasion hid behind a divine right theory, but in reality was about the increase in the power of the central state. Absolutists attempted to hold the church in check in order to enhance state authority.

Major political philosophers also developed formulations about power which were secular and concerned with the justification and limits of authority, as well as the relationship between the individual and the community. If absolutism was one side of the debate about authority, the notion of rights based on nature or contract was the other.

Contract theory presupposes some formal and necessary relationship between ruler and ruled. Oddly enough, though it was a modern construct, it had its roots in the Middle Ages, in the feudal contract which was the theoretical basis of the relationship between lord and vassal. The vassal swore loyalty to a lord, and agreed to perform certain services, while the lord in turn was responsible for the protection of the vassal. The arrangement between lord and serf, though based on tradition, was also contractual in nature. In a sense, the absolutism of Louis XIV was an attempt to substitute central authority, a single sovereign, for a mass of local arrangements.

Custom sometimes placed sovereignty in institutions. In the Enlightenment the most common and cited institutional arrangement based upon custom was the model provided by the British Parliament. In Britain sovereignty resided in Parliament. It was understood that the term Parliament referred to the king and the two houses of Lords and Commons. Britain was said to have a mixed constitution, one in which the king represented the monarchical authority, the House of Lords the aristocratic, and the House of Commons the democratic elements. When an English king tried to subvert this division and the mutual dependence it involved, as did James II in 1688, he was forced into exile, and the new monarchs, his daughter Mary and her husband William III of Holland, agreed to be constitutional rulers in accordance with the understanding of the relationship between the institution of monarchy and the houses of Parliament. This was a recognition of a contractual arrangement based upon custom.

HOBBES AND THE PROBLEM OF AUTHORITY
Earlier in England, during a civil war in the 1640s, Thomas Hobbes (1588–1679) wrote *Leviathan* (1651), a work of political theory which was concerned with the issues of freedom and authority. Hobbes, in search of a principle of order, rejected divine right ideas and even history as bases for forming a political community. He wished to pursue the path the natural scientists were using in their speculations about the physical universe, and to construct a political science based upon rational thought and the observation of humanity. Hobbes began with a thought-experiment which later became common during the Enlightenment. He imagined humanity in a "state of nature," a time when there was no society or civilization, as a way of determining first whether power was necessary and secondly where it should preferably rest.

For Hobbes the supposed state of nature would reveal the most important axiom he needed: a picture of human nature unfettered by authority, what we really would be like if there were no restraints upon us of law and custom. Hobbes claimed that there was "a general inclination of all mankind, a perpetual and restless desire of power after power, that ceaseth only in death." People were never content, he stated, and they therefore constantly competed and sought glory. The result

was war, a condition in which civilization and its benefits were not possible. In what has become one of the most quoted statements of political philosophy, Hobbes said that in the state of nature there were "no arts; no letters; no society; and which is worst of all, continual fear, and danger of violent death; and the life of man, solitary, poor, nasty, brutish and short."[2]

This state of nature had to be abandoned. A political sovereignty needed to be established, and its main function was to preserve life, society, and property. This, according to Hobbes, required a kind of contract made by all the people to establish a sovereign over themselves and to obey the sovereign. Hobbes' pessimism about human nature led him to say that the sovereign — the commonwealth or state — was not limited in authority; for to limit the sovereign was to open a new quest for power which would result in yet more war. Other rules were deduced, the main one being that among individuals in a sovereignty "covenants must be kept," for it was in the interest of all to do so, or there would be no force of law. In Hobbes' state sovereignty was absolute.

Hobbes' formulation of the modern state, using the image of the Leviathan, a beast recounted in the biblical book of Job, was one which came down on the side of the absolute sovereign. His sovereign could be an institution, a parliament, as well as a monarch. Yet there were a number of assumptions in the Hobbesian formulation which made him thoroughly modern. All people were equal in Hobbes' new state. There was in Hobbes a thrust towards egalitarianism, which ignored the highly aristocratic class structure of the age, because it was not rational. Hobbes abandoned feudalism and divine right, and although he was an authoritarian, his was a political philosophy which made humanity responsible for its own laws and for its own destiny.

LOCKE AND THE IDEA OF NATURAL RIGHTS
John Locke (1632–1704) was an English empiricist, whose philosophy was based upon the mind receiving sensations from outside and whose theory of knowledge was essentially

"Some of the Principal Inhabitants of Ye Moon: Royalty, Episcopy and Law," by William Hogarth. This print of 1724 satirically attacks the king, bishops, and lawyers as empty symbols interested only in their own gain and welfare.   (Dover Publications, Inc.)

inductive. Yet in his political philosophy, expounded mainly in his *Two Treatises of Government* (1690), Locke proceeded along rationalist lines, though he did not ignore history and custom, as had Hobbes. Locke's main experience was in an England full of dissension, recovering from civil war, determined to limit authority yet keep the peace. In his formulation Locke also began with a theory of humanity in a state of nature. But, unlike Hobbes, he believed that the state of nature was a relatively peaceful place. People would not be at war all the time, nor would self-interest always dictate acquisitive selfish behaviour. "The state of nature has a law of nature to govern it, which obliges every one: and reason, which is that law, teaches all mankind, who will but consult it, that being all equal and independent, no one ought to harm another in his life, health, liberty, or possessions.''[3] Still, Locke believed that a state of nature would be unsatisfactory. Human beings would in fact fight, and they needed to establish a power to settle disputes impartially and to set up a system of government that would guarantee life, freedom, and protection of property.

In establishing a sovereign authority, Locke claimed, people retained their ''natural rights,'' which they had in the state of nature. This meant that we could not alienate our life, liberty, and property; rather, government existed in order to protect these rights, and therefore only limited powers were to be given to it. Hence, for Locke, a contract was made between individuals to establish an authority, and then a contract was also made between the governing authority and the people, which limited the power of the government. The agreement was usually in the form of a constitution. Should the government of the day either violate natural rights or exceed the authority given to it by the constitution, then the contract between it and the people was no longer valid. Power returned to the people, who then established a new sovereignty.

Locke, in advancing the doctrine of civil liberty and in appealing to both reason and history, put forth the concepts that became central for the whole of the modern age in the debate over the notion of the state and its authority. Locke was clear that in England the historic power of the state rested in Parliament, in the division among king, lords, and commons, because this division worked against tyranny by preventing any individual or an oligarchy from obtaining absolute authority. Civil liberty also meant a constitutional recognition and certification of what were called ''liberties,'' or civil rights, which had been shared by all in a state of nature and which were retained when the political community was established.

While a civil egalitarian, Locke did not propose, and did not agree with, political democracy. ''Life, liberty, and property'' were natural rights and property meant that the propertied class was protected and had the right to exercise political authority. Contract theory, as Locke formulated it, was a doctrine which was concerned with the protection and disposition of property. Locke included civil liberty among the ''properties.'' In England, for nearly 200 years after Locke, only men of property had full political rights, though all were equal under law.

The right of revolution was part of Locke's beliefs. Since government was limited by history and nature, if the ruler or rulers were to break the contract made with the people, if the polity became a tyranny, then individuals had the right to rebel, to bring down the sovereign in the name of liberty. Locke, like Hobbes, desired order, but he was determined to establish that authority had its limits.

MONTESQUIEU AND THE RELATIVITY OF SOCIAL SYSTEMS

The French thinker, the Baron Charles de Montesquieu (1689–1755), in *The Spirit of the Laws* (1748), tried to use the empirical and historical method exclusively, in his considerations on government and society. Rather than approach political philosophy via a state of nature, or axioms about human behaviour, Montesquieu's work was an attempt to show that customs, geography, and history were variables in determining the nature of law and government in any territory. In this sense, he was among the first of the social scientists. In asking about the relationship between individuals and communities, and whether there was some basic regularity which could be discerned, he was following the path of science. Montesquieu tried to get at many variables, and while his conclusions were based upon limited data, the approach was sociological and anthropological and would later be borrowed by others.

For Montesquieu there were three types of government: republics, despotisms, and monarchies, each appropriate to specific places and times. Republics belonged to small city-states, like ancient Athens or, in his day, modern Geneva, but Montesquieu believed that the size of modern political structures meant that the heyday of republicanism was over. Despotism, he thought to be peculiar to large empires, while in the Europe of his day monarchy, as it had developed historically, was the most appropriate form. The kind of monarchy he supported was one which had the quality of honour, and in which the nobility governed well according to precedent and tradition. No supporter of royal absolutism, Montesquieu placed the liberty of Frenchmen in institutions which by custom tempered the authority of the Crown and supported the rule of law. He was, in principle, a supporter of an idealized version of what he understood to be the English constitution, a balance between freedom and authority.

The categories used by the seventeenth century and the Enlightenment in politics were thus new and potentially revolutionary. Philosophers argued about sovereignty and were interested in a definition of human nature. Some worked by Descartes' method, beginning with axioms clear to the mind. Others were more empirical, like Montesquieu. All wished for a universal theory to hold true for everyone, everywhere. None of these philosophers were democrats, all supported institutional restraint and wanted authority to be lodged in a special class. Hobbes would accept virtually no restraint on sovereign power, while Locke and Montesquieu sought balance and limits within a necessary order. Liberty was an issue, and property was accepted as part of liberty. Equality was discussed and defended in terms of civil life, though not in terms of political participation or political action.

ROUSSEAU: FREEDOM AND COMMUNITY

In the works of Jean-Jacques Rousseau (1712–78) a shift occurred in political thinking about the community and the individual. In the opening words of *The Social Contract* (1762) he announced: "Man was born free, and everywhere he is in chains." For Rousseau civilization had its drawbacks, and he ascribed the evil in society to the institutions which it supported. In an earlier work, his *Discourse on the Origin of Inequality* (1755), Rousseau suggested: "above all things let us beware of concluding with Hobbes that man, as having no idea of goodness, must be naturally bad." Rather, Rousseau believed that people in a state of nature had what he termed "natural pity," a feeling of empathy with others. It was civilization, claimed Rousseau, especially the invention of private property, which made us selfish and egotistical, and destroyed natural goodness.[4]

Rousseau's challenge to civilization as he knew it did not mean an abandonment of community. Since civilization existed, he was determined to give it legitimacy by restoring that lost sense of community. He redefined power and sovereignty by placing them in the hands of the people, who themselves were the ultimate judges of the public interest. Human beings, for Rousseau, needed both liberty and society. They entered into a social contract through an arrangement among themselves, but they retained sovereignty in themselves, even when they established a government.

Rousseau focussed on the important question of the nature of community. He believed that as individuals we needed civil society; alone, we would lose our human qualities. Sociability was part of our nature. Thus, we entered into a community not simply to protect liberties and rights, but to assert our humanness; for Rousseau claimed that being in a civil community meant that justice would be substituted for instinct. Yet, he recognized that the community was more than the sum of the individuals in it and more than their individual wishes. A community had an identity and a will, what Rousseau referred to as the General Will, which represented the larger interest. This was not the will of the majority or even the will of all, for these could will evil. The state was thus the political manifestation of a community in which individuals were citizens rather than lone self-seeking atoms. In entering a community, claimed Rousseau, an individual gave up his private interest to "the common cause," for the General Will was the community interest, not one's special interest. Liberty, in Rousseau's system, related to the community's rather than the individual's interest.[5]

The thrust of Rousseau's formulation was to challenge the dichotomy between liberty and authority presented by earlier Enlightenment thinkers. For him, we were political beings, individuals who lived in, and needed, a community. Indeed, our identity, our "moral" being, was at least in part nurtured and determined by the community. Hence, to join a community meant duties as well as

A detail from Hogarth's "Canvassing for Votes," in which he depicts the election process as full of bribery, and the candidates as vain and deceitful.   (Dover Publications, Inc.)

rights, but, if dissatisfied, one could also decide to leave. Rousseau was the most ruthlessly egalitarian thinker to date in the West. He believed in direct democracy, and he disliked any governmental structure which separated the individual from the source of authority. The people remained sovereign.

Though a believer in liberty and a passionate critic of the arbitrary and aristocratic mode of life during the eighteenth century, Rousseau, has also been accused of being an authoritarian. "Whoever refuses to obey the General Will," he said, "shall be constrained to do so by the whole body." The community was given ultimate authority by Rousseau; once we join a community our own interests and those of the community should naturally coincide. Rousseau, who lived at a time when the modern state was being formed, favoured abandoning contemporary notions of authority. He acknowledged that his concept of sovereignty could only be attained in a small polity, where all citizens would participate. Yet the size of states was getting bigger, not smaller. Many earlier thinkers, Rousseau recognized, were talking about liberty, but their defense of property meant they supported a structure of unjust authority; they spoke about equality, but they accepted the power of special classes and interests. Rousseau insisted that community and equality were essential ideals in working out issues of sovereignty and liberty.

B. KNOWLEDGE, PROGRESS, AND SOCIAL CRITICISM

In France in the eighteenth century a group of writers came into being who referred to themselves collectively as *philosophes*. They were men who were critical of the evils of society and supported universal toleration. They were liberal in spirit, curious about the world, and "enlightened" in outlook. Among their most prominent figures were Montesquieu, Voltaire, and Diderot. Rousseau can be included among them, although, because of his suspicion of knowledge, some doubt if he really belonged. While they formed no single school of thought, they shared a belief in the progress of knowledge and in using their critical understanding of society to help make the world better.

BAYLE AND SKEPTICISM

The philosophes all accepted the scientific method, be it empiricism or rationalism, as the basis of the new knowledge. Though they had their own set of axiomatic moral truths, they had great faith in the power of reason. They also tended to be skeptics, refusing, like Bacon and Descartes, to accept anything as true unless proof was clear and verifiable. This skepticism was learned from the philosopher Pierre Bayle (1647–1746), whose *Historical and Critical Dictionary* (1697) was the foundation for critics of the next two generations. Bayle adapted the methods of rationalist and empirical science to historical material: nothing was to be accepted as real or true unless evidence for the statement could be substantiated, and all knowledge was to be put to the same test.

Bayle angered authorities both in Catholic France and Protestant Holland. He saw the Bible as a source which could no longer be treated with special consideration; biblical figures were attacked, and contradictions were pointed out. In his article on "David" in his *Dictionary*, he attacked many of David's acts on grounds of morals. Bayle said: "the profound respect we ought to have for this great Prince, this great Prophet, should not hinder us from disapproving the Blemishes that occur in his life." David's acts were put to the same moral tests as those of any other human being.

Bayle inaugurated a new intellectual attitude of making no distinction between the sacred and the secular in his historical and social criticism: ". . . none can be well qualified to write a good History, unless he be such an enemy to lying, that his conscience does not

permit him to tell lies even to the advantage of his religion, and dearest friends. . . ."[6] Bayle quite correctly saw himself as making a breakthrough toward a new kind of history and criticism of society — skeptical in its attitude towards authority and religion, seeking a pattern based on empirical data, and using the test of reason in place of revelation, tradition, and custom. His *Dictionary* was enormously influential.

THE *ENCYCLOPEDIA*

The philosophes were inspired by Bayle's work to produce an *Encyclopedia*, which was to show the interrelationship of all knowledge and to enlighten the public. They were led by Denis Diderot (1713–84), who proclaimed in the *Prospectus* for the *Encyclopedia* that it was desirable to show in one work all advances of human knowledge:

Putting all that concerns the sciences and the arts into one dictionary was even more a question of making evident the mutual light they throw on one another. [We want] to make use of the links to reveal the [underlying] principles more forcefully and the results more clearly; to indicate the close or distant connections [that exist] between the beings which form nature, and which have concerned men; to show by the interweaving of roots and branches how impossible it is to know well some parts of the whole without going up or down many others; to form a general map of the efforts of the human mind in all activities, over all the centuries. . . .[7]

To the philosophes in the Enlightenment, as to Francis Bacon, knowledge was indeed power. Knowledge was needed to better society, to undo evil, to reform laws, to educate, to put into practice the new values. Diderot claimed the true philosophe was dispassionate in the search for truth, but motivated by a desire to improve the lot of humanity. He was a new type: "Reason is to a philosopher what grace is to a Christian. Grace impels the Christian to act, reason impels the philosopher."[8] The philosophes, it has often been remarked, were interested in this world, in directing attention to the present and in the amelioration of existing social and political conditions.

VOLTAIRE: HISTORIAN AND CRITIC OF SOCIETY

The name of Voltaire, the pen name of François Marie Arouet (1694–1778), is synonymous with the rationalism and social criticism of the philosophes. His pen was the most eloquent and prolific of the age, and he took a critical and witty stance on a wide variety of subjects throughout his lifetime. His first major intellectual encounter was with English thought, and his *Philosophical Letters* (also called the *English Letters*), begun in 1726, was the result of several years' stay in England. Voltaire contrasted France with England and used the comparison to praise English liberty and attack French absolutism, to challenge the Catholic Church in France, and to implicitly attack the political structure of France: "the English are the only people on earth," he said, "who have been able to regulate the power of kings by resisting them. . . ."[9] The English had liberty, and they were right to war with the absolute monarch, Louis XIV, to prevent him from realizing his imperial ambitions. Voltaire found his early culture heroes in England — Bacon, Locke and Newton — and he praised the English for honouring philosophers of merit by giving them public awards and recognition.

Such criticism was resented by the French authorities, who had Voltaire's book burned by the public hangman. Voltaire found it necessary to outwit the authorities to protect his own interests and, if necessary, his person: he made himself independently wealthy, and a good part of his life was lived in exile in Switzerland. He became the model of the "man of letters," whose writings were feared by established powers.

Voltaire criticized his countrymen, and while he seemed to condemn his own age he found much to admire in it compared with other ages. His major work of history was *The Age of Louis XIV* (1751). In it he claimed that the period marked by the life and work of Louis XIV was one of the four great ages of humankind, to be compared with Athenian Greece, the Roman Empire, and the Italian Renaissance. The measure of greatness for Voltaire was culture, and he proclaimed that during the fourth age "human reason in general was brought to perfection." Voltaire gave full credit to all of Europe, especially Louis XIV, for advances in literature, the arts, and the sciences, and at the end of his work he claimed that his aim had been to show "that during the past century mankind, from one end of Europe to the other, has been more enlightened than in all preceding ages."[10]

THE IDEA OF PROGRESS

During the eighteenth century there grew a sense among learned people, who formed academies of the arts and the sciences, that the "moderns" were in advance of the "ancients." This was a unique moment for the West, for since the fall of the Roman Empire the culture of the West had looked to ancient civilization for guidance and instruction. Even in the Renaissance of the fifteenth century, scholars and artists viewed themselves as part of the continuity of an ancient tradition which had been interrupted by centuries of barbarism. And the myths of a classical golden age of perfection, which preceded ages of silver and even baser metals, had long been part of the tradition in the West. No longer so for Voltaire and his friends.

This new belief in progress began to be formulated systematically in the middle of the eighteenth century. The young aristocrat A.R.J. Turgot (1727–81) in a lecture in 1750 on "A Philosophical Review of the Successive Advances of the Human Mind," formulated one of the earliest and most important notions of the idea of progress. Turgot began with what would become an important distinction in reflections on the philosophy of history. Nature is governed by laws, he stated, but these were recurrent; they formed a cyclical pattern in which things remained the same. The human pattern had its order too, but unlike the natural order this was part of "an ever changing spectacle," and it had its own logic, understood as the progress of the species.

To Turgot progress meant the advancement and improvement of civilization. He attacked war and self-interest, and he claimed that eventually "manners are softened, the human mind becomes more enlightened, and separate nations are brought closer to one another."[11]

Why do people progress? Turgot believed genius—grasping what is new and using it to transform society — was part of the reason. However, genius was related to particular societies. Some societies, for example tolerant and rational ones, presented favourable conditions for its development, and it was these societies which contributed to progress. One of the functions of society was to put the human talent available to it to best use. Turgot believed that liberty and commerce stimulated the development of free thought and genius. Thus, the idea of progress began as a social philosophy which was on the side of change.

VOLTAIRE: HERO OF THE AGE

Voltaire's pen grew more acid as the century wore on. The event which affected him most was an earthquake in the Portuguese city of Lisbon in November, 1755, which caused great tidal waves and resulted in the death of many people. This natural event had to be understood, Voltaire believed, in light of religious belief. He took as his object of attack Alexander Pope's *Essay on Man* (1734) and its most quoted line, "whatever is, is right." He wrote his own poem which claimed:

All may be well; that hope can man sustain,
All now is well; 'tis an illusion vain.[12]

In his preface to the poem Voltaire acknowledged that there was evil in the world, and philosophy was sometimes not able to explain it. It was the arbitrariness of the earthquake which Voltaire ranted against. Its meaningless destruction forced him to reconsider the view of a rational, perfectly ordered world organized by a creator, an outlook which the philosophes had often adopted and defended.

In *Candide* (1759) Voltaire used the form of the philosophical tale to express his doubts about all being for the best. His main character, an innocent youth, journeyed through the world, encountering ideas and experiences which held up to ridicule the philosophy of optimism. The reader could see that Candide experienced the corruption and meanness of contemporary institutions — the aristocracy, the church, and the military. With humour, Voltaire attacked many prevailing beliefs.

One character, Pangloss, who was Candide's teacher, kept telling him in the face of misfortune and injustice that this was "the best of all possible worlds," as Voltaire reminds us of the ravages of the Lisbon earthquake. Another character, Martin, is a gloomy pessimist who believed that the devil was in control of the world, and that we had been left by the deity to our own devices. It was Candide who chose neither optimism nor pessimism, but told his friends: "we must cultivate our garden." Candide, in the middle of the book, found the fabled Eldorado, a utopia, the land of gold. This, too, he resisted, because it stifled change and human development. Voltaire was asking the Enlightenment to do what was possible to improve the lot of humanity; he asked that people not seek the garden of Eden, but work in a garden of our own making.

Voltaire's attacks on existing institutions in France often centered on the organized Catholic Church, which he viewed as corrupt and a preserve of the aristocracy. He popularized the slogan "*Ecrasez l'infame*" (crush the infamous thing). In 1763 he published a "Treatise on Tolerance" which had as its opening sentence: "The murder of Jean Calas, committed in Toulouse with the sword of justice, the 9th of March, 1762, is one of the most singular events that calls for the attention of the present age and of posterity."[13] Calas was a Protestant merchant accused of murdering his son in order to prevent him from converting to Catholicism. He was tortured on the wheel and found guilty, with no real evidence in support of the accusation. It was, Voltaire claimed, a triumph of "fanaticism . . . over reason." He wrote to condemn religious hatred and in support of universal tolerance. The case became notorious, and in 1765 Calas' name was cleared.

Voltaire did not support democracy. He was at one with many in his time who believed that enlightened despotism, combined with an institutionalization of tolerance and liberty, was the best form of government. Like many later liberals, Voltaire feared giving too much power to the masses, whom he viewed as uneducated and unenlightened. He was not without his own prejudices, including an irrational and virulent anti-Semitism. He was

The first of a series of eight prints on "A Rake's Progress," by Hogarth, 1735. This print has Tom Rakewell at the center, having just inherited his miserly father's wealth, rejecting a life of industry and middle-class values for one which is modelled on aristocratic show and pretention. On the right is Sarah Young, Tom's betrothed, whom he now rejects. Tom is eventually ruined by his own actions and goes mad.   (Dover Publications, Inc.)

nevertheless accepted as a hero by the people who saw him as representing the best of the temper of the times.

ROUSSEAU AND SENTIMENT

As in politics, so in the analysis of human nature, Jean-Jacques Rousseau introduced a new element into Enlightenment thought. His concern was with the sentiments rather than the rational features of civilization. Rousseau was unhappy with the posture of the philosophes and attacked the artificiality of his contemporary society, in favour of a return to a more natural, instinctive life. *Emile* (1762) was a work on education, one which claimed that the child was a special person who had to be carefully nurtured to develop naturally. To

Rousseau "everything is good as it comes from the hands of the Maker of the world; but degenerates once it gets into the hands of man."[14] Children were innocent; thus he advocated an education which was rustic and which would develop natural goodness. Rousseau was seen by the philosophes as proposing a kind of primitivism, which they believed was social regression. But Rousseau's plea for a life of sentiment and passion, his concern with the natural environment, and his rejection of the artificiality of civilization had broad appeal. His views became the basis of the Romantic movement in the next generation.

SATIRE: HOGARTH AND SWIFT

Satire was a major weapon of the Enlightenment, a means of exposing some of the follies of society and holding them up to ridicule. In England, William Hogarth (1697–1764) and Jonathan Swift (1667–1745) took this form of social criticism to its highest level, Hogarth in his art and Swift in his writings. Hogarth developed a new popular art form, the engraving, which narrated a tale, often in a series, and which was designed to be a criticism of contemporary customs and attitudes. His themes included politics, the class structure in England, the houses of Parliament, the courts, and the Anglican Church. Printed in many copies, Hogarth's studies combined narrative literary form with clever and sophisticated draftsmanship. In "The Rake's Progress" he attacked the aristocracy, the institution of arranged marriage, the corruption of greed and wealth, and the consequences of a life dedicated solely to furthering one's own ambition. In "Industry and Idleness," a moral tale designed to teach proper behaviour, he contrasted the responsible worker with the idler. Hogarth recorded the lives of the middle class and the poor, and was a supporter of the new merchant class and its social values.

Swift's social and political satire was designed, as he put it, "to vex the world rather than divert it. . . ."[15] Unlike the philosophes, Swift distrusted abstract reasoning, and believed that without a realistic view of the world and human nature, abstract thought alone would create its own rigidity and injustice. Swift lived most of his life in Ireland and supported the Irish in their attempts to humanize English rule over their island. In his short satire, *A Modest Proposal*, Swift presented the logic of empire in its most grotesque form — the "civilized" Englishman, unaware of the evils of his own behaviour, arguing that the cure for Ireland's economic troubles lay in the Irish destroying their own children.

Swift's *Gulliver's Travels* (1726) was the greatest satire of the age, a book which attacked politics, society, and the idea of a benign human nature. Gulliver (the name means a true fool) was an average man, who took four voyages. The first voyage, to Lilliput, was to a thinly disguised England in which the small stature of the Lilliputians reflected their moral qualities. They chose leaders in silly ways, were full of their own self-impor-

tance, and asked Gulliver to help them obtain raw power. In the second voyage, to Brobdingnag, Gulliver met huge people, whose rulers were moral giants as well. Here Gulliver, representing a typical Englishman, took pains to explain the English system to the king of Brobdingnag, naively outlining its social injustices, pretentions, and irrationalities. The king was horrified at Gulliver's recounting of the events of European history in the last century, "protesting it was only an Heap of Conspiracies, Rebellions, Murders, Massacres, Revolutions, Banishments; the very worst Effects that Avarice, Faction, Hypocricy, Perfidiousness, Cruelty, Rage, Madness, Hatred, Envy, Lust, Malice, and Ambition could produce." Gulliver could not accept the negative verdict, and then, in order to impress the king, offered him power through the ability to make gunpowder, which was refused. Gulliver thought this was the result of "narrow principles and short views."[16]

The character of Gulliver was used by Swift to challenge some of the prevailing views of his time. Swift believed that English political institutions, the very ones praised by Voltaire, needed reform. In an age of moral optimism, he tempered his hopes with reality. He stressed that human beings were full of excessive greed and pride, and believed that these blinded them to their own deficiencies. To Swift, the emphasis of the philosophes on the corruption of institutions was too narrow a view; human nature was itself problematic. He did not think that humanity was rational, only capable of reason, and he thought it necessary to recognize the limitations of humanity in order to bring about a healthy society.

Finally, Swift challenged and parodied some of the intellectual optimism of the Enlightenment. Gulliver, in the third of his four journeys, travelled to lands in which scientific experiments lost their human values, where humanity's most fervent and selfish desires, such as eternal life, resulted in horror. Like all great satirists, Swift focussed on moral dilemmas which were appropriate to all societies: how to deal with power, how to manage resources, how to handle our differences. He was a lifelong supporter of diversity, liberty, and toleration.

In the last journey of Gulliver, Swift inverted reality. It was the animals who created a rational society, but one so full of pride in themselves that the rational horses practiced genocide against human ''Yahoos,'' and destroyed others in the name of progress. Swift was telling his age that values came before rationality, that rationality could create its own distortions and moral crises. His work was prophetic, and was adapted in the twentieth century by many major political satirists, including Yevgeny Zamiatin, Aldous Huxley, and George Orwell. Swift, characteristically, wrote his own epitaph in Latin, which was translated in the following way by the twentieth century Irish poet William Butler Yeats:

Swift has sailed into his rest;
Savage indignation there
Cannot lacerate his breast.
Imitate him if you dare,
World-besotted traveller; he
Served human liberty.[17]

The political philosophers, the philosophes, and the satirists all saw themselves serving human liberty. The issue of the age was the freedom of the individual as part of a just community and state. Taking the work of Voltaire, Swift and Locke into account, it is clear that the Enlightenment thinkers, while hopeful, were not so optimistic as to think reform was easy. They saw much potential in humanity, but this was tempered by a concern for our ability to handle our own vanity, pride, and quest for power. They were, however, believers in progress, even if it was hard won. No starry-eyed optimists, the reformers of the Enlightenment did turn away from the afterlife in favour of the here and now. Like Kant, they knew they were not living in an age of enlightenment, but they saw themselves and their programs as enlightened.

C. FROM ABSOLUTISM TO ENLIGHTENED DESPOTISM

THE IDEA OF ENLIGHTENED DESPOTISM

The program of the philosophes had its effect on the conduct of politics in many European states. In particular, in the last half of the eighteenth century there arose a new form of absolutism known as enlightened despotism. These monarchs were expected to be en-

lightened or, at minimum, choose advisors who would pursue enlightened policies. Thus, enlightened despotism was a notion that rulers ought to be philosophers as well, and that they should establish just laws and practices in their domains.

Enlightened despotism was not constitutional rule, though it had about it the hint of a contract theory. Monarchs still had virtually unlimited power. But they believed, in their own self-interest, that through enlightened policies they should foster greater prosperity and social progress. Sovereignty lay in the hands of the monarch, as Frederick II of Prussia stated, but that also entailed a great responsibility:

. . . such a system can flow but from a single brain, and this must be that of the sovereign. Laziness, hedonism and imbecility, these are the causes which restrain princes in working at the noble task of bringing happiness to their subjects . . . [a] sovereign is not elevated to his high position, supreme power has not been confined to him in order that he may live in lazy luxury, enriching himself by the labor of the people, being happy while everyone else suffers. The sovereign is the first servant of the state. He is well paid in order that he may sustain the dignity of his office, but one demands that he work efficiently for the good of the state, and that he, at the very least, pay personal attention to the most important problems.[18]

Frederick did proclaim that the ruler was expected to govern on behalf of the people.

Those who followed a policy of enlightened despotism did so out of their own self-interest, and with a clear intent of increasing the power of their sovereignty. It was useful and advantageous for a state to modernize, as that concept was then understood: to be efficient in administration, centralize decision making, increase production, grow more food, and enhance the health and welfare of subjects.

ENLIGHTENED DESPOTISM IN PRACTICE

The main enlightened despots emerged in the large eastern European states — Frederick II (the Great) of Prussia (1740–86), Joseph II of Austria (co-ruler with his mother Maria Theresa from 1765–80, ruler 1780–90), and Catherine II (the Great) of Russia (1762–96). All had intellectual pretensions. Though they practiced an authoritarianism from the center, they courted philosophes and artists and musicians and flirted with liberal social principles. They were interested in legal reform and were eager to eliminate religious influences in their states. As players in the game of international power, there was often a discrepancy between their espousal of Enlightenment principles and their practice of war and diplomacy. They thought of themselves as wise philosopher-monarchs, advancing culture, protecting society, and creating a better state. The model despot, Frederick the Great, was a poet, musician, composer of distinguished works for the flute, and a philosopher who corresponded with Voltaire; he was also an indefatigable worker on behalf of his state, and he helped to propel Prussia into a position of greater power and authority in Europe.

Governmental reform meant a further centralization of power, a carrying out of policies and goals like those of Louis XIV. The virtue of a single integrated administration was discussed by Joseph II. ''Uniform principles'' must exist in a state, and all people were to be ''subject to impartial guidance,'' and to be ''joined in a common enterprise.'' All three monarchs placed themselves at the center of a new administrative structure, and regularly sent agents to localities to inspect what was being done.

Legal reform followed. The monarchies of the eighteenth century had often come into being as a result of patchwork additions over the centuries. Law, usually based in custom, differed from region to region. A single law code for the entire state was the ideal. A Prussian civil procedure was put forth in 1781, and an Austrian criminal procedure in 1788. Work begun by Frederick II resulted in a complete civil, criminal, and constitutional law code in Prussia in 1794; initiatives by Joseph II resulted in an Austrian civil code in 1812.

The law codes reflected Enlightenment attitudes. All people were declared citizens under the law of a single state administered from the center. The state was viewed as a community which secured rights and established the duties of its citizens. No other institution,

even the family or the church, was to be independent of it. Torture was restricted, there was a sense that punishment should fit the crime, and prison reform was introduced. Yet, the class structure of the monarchical state remained in place, and the practice of serfdom was retained in each state.

Religious reform had two aspects: toleration, and control of religious institutions in the kingdom. Frederick II had a clear sense that subjects were citizens, no matter what their religious beliefs. He wrote:

Catholics, Lutherans, Reformed, Jews and other Christian sects live in this state, and live together in peace: if the sovereign, actuated by a mistaken zeal, declares himself for one religion or another, parties will spring up, heated disputes ensue, little by little persecutions will commence and, in the end, the religion persecuted will leave the fatherland and millions of subjects will enrich our neighbors by their skill and industry.[19]

Toleration was seen to be both good policy and good philosophy. To drive individuals out of the state meant a loss of human resources, in Frederick's case a serious matter because his state had a lower population at that time than any of the other major powers. His toleration was enlightened and humanitarian; it was influenced by a genuine sense that religious differences were less important than the need to foster good citizenship. Joseph II also followed this policy. In Austria, a mainly Catholic state, full civil rights were given to Jews, Protestants, and Greek Orthodox, and they could worship as they chose in a private manner.

Frederick took action to regulate the Lutheran Church, the major religious body in his kingdom, to make certain it conformed to civic policy. Joseph II had an established Catholic Church, and he made great efforts to place it under the authority of the state, by making the monarch the means of communication between the Papacy and the Austrian Catholic Church, requiring bishops to take an oath of allegiance to the monarch, and regulating many church activities. In Russia, Catherine II nationalized the properties of the Russian Orthodox Church and made the clergy into paid state officials.

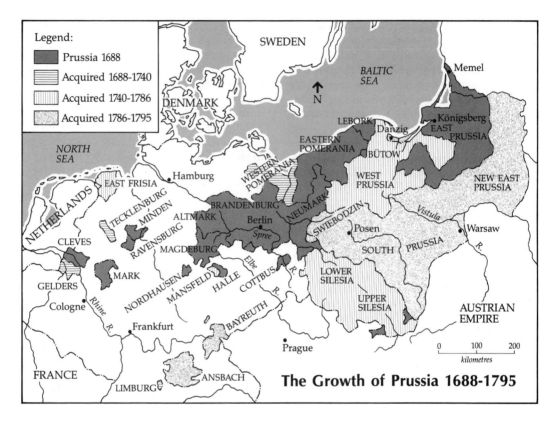

The Growth of Prussia 1688-1795

Legend:
- Prussia 1688
- Acquired 1688-1740
- Acquired 1740-1786
- Acquired 1786-1795

The enlightened despots tried to turn the state into a more unitary organization than it had ever been. Their sovereignty extended to all aspects of the kingdom, including religion. As part of this increase of activity by the state, enlightened rulers supported cultural institutions and state schools.

There was as well some attempt at social reform. In Austria the personal servitude of peasants was limited. On his own crown lands, Frederick II gave his peasants hereditary tenure and reduced their labour and financial obligations to him as landlord. Peasants often supported enlightened despotism because the intervention of the centralized state usually meant a better life. Local lords could no longer behave arbitrarily, and there was less physical punishment and less illegal expulsion from the land.

Economic reform was a key to the policy of the enlightened despots, especially for Frederick II. Frederick made salt, coffee, and tobacco into state enterprises. He attempted

to modernize agricultural techniques by the use of new machinery and better management of the land. Swampy areas were drained and new settlers attracted to cultivate the reclaimed land. There were attempts at tax reforms. The policy generally followed by Frederick II and his fellow monarchs was that of mercantile protectionism and intervention by the state. The monarchs were not at all interested in *laissez-faire* in their economic policies. Rather, they wanted to extend the authority of the state into all areas, guiding public policy to further the interests of their realm.

Frederick II, as "enlightened" as he was, knew that the modern state was founded on power. He kept a large standing army; it grew from 83 000 in 1740 to 200 000 at the end of his reign in 1786. When he thought it in his interest to do so, he would wage war and disregard treaties, as in 1740 when he invaded Austria in order to gain the valuable territory of Silesia. Frederick was a self-interested realist. Insofar as the reform program of the philosophes accommodated his aspirations for power, he would follow it; when it would not, the state and its authority were his primary considerations.

THE NEW VIEW OF THE STATE

Enlightened despotism in practice was part of the transition from the old feudal kingship to the modern secular state. The monarchs of the eighteenth century, as a result of the Enlightenment, had lost some of their traditional sources of authority. In the West divine right was no longer to be taken very seriously. Simple absolutism, based upon the notion that the will of the monarch and the interests of the kingdom were one and the same thing, could no longer be adequately defended. Hence, the sensitive monarchs, using the ideas and language of the time, constructed, in theory and practice, a new defense of their authority. The legitimacy of government was now to be based upon its necessity and utility: it provided security and protection for life and property.

The role of the state was changing in the eighteenth century. It was beginning to subsume other interests, such as those of the churches and the localities, and it was seen now to be at least partially responsible for the well-being of the people living within it. To make this possible, authority was centralized, and thus the old local authority of the privileged was limited. Now, too, there was a distinction between the person of the monarch and the state. The state had a clear existence and a legal form, separate from the individual who headed it. Frederick the Great loved power and had a well-developed ego, but he never made the mistake of thinking he was Prussia itself. Power, in the end, belonged to the state of which Frederick was the head and which he administered.

Enlightened despotism was a phase in which monarchy was adjusting to the ideas of the time. It was, however, a program more honoured in rhetoric than in practice, especially in the case of Catherine II of Russia. Some monarchs, Louis XV and Louis XVI of France, and George II and George III of Great Britain, were not interested in the programs of the Enlightenment. Yet in all states power was

becoming more centralized, and institutions and laws were being restructured.

D. POLITICAL ECONOMY: MERCANTILISM AND *LAISSEZ-FAIRE*

THE MERCANTILE SYSTEM

The prevailing economic policy of major states in the early modern period goes under the name of mercantilism, a system (though by no means uniform) in which governments intervened in the economy in order to increase the wealth of the state. Mercantilism focussed on trade and markets as a way of expanding the economy and increasing wealth. States organized the economy and passed statutes regulating activity. One of the features of the mercantilist period was the attempt to move beyond that to the acquisition of great empires in order to add to the wealth of the mother state.

Economic success in the mercantilist period was defined in terms of the amount of actual wealth on hand, which explains the concern with amassing large supplies of gold and silver. In international trade, bullion was the unit of currency and support for paper money. In order to obtain bullion, states believed they needed a favourable balance of trade, which would provide them with surplus wealth. Mercantilists believed that states were competing for a fixed amount of wealth in the world.

Self-sufficiency in a state was a major economic goal, the idea being that the less dependent a state was on imports, the more wealth it would amass. Surplus wealth was to be used for reasons of state, including war, which was viewed as inevitable. One of the ways of acquiring self-sufficiency was to establish colonies overseas, to become an imperial power. There was always the hope that colonies would yield precious metals, as did those of Spain. But colonies were viewed as part of a system tied to the mother state; they would supply raw materials for manufacture, and provide markets to which manufactured goods could be exported. Self-sufficiency was usually defined in an imperial sense rather than a national one.

The system came to be called commercial capitalism. It was through the manipulation and expansion of trade that wealth was accumulated, and merchants became prosperous in the process. States and merchants encouraged manufacture at home and export to colonies and other countries. One consequence of this policy was to discourage too much consumption at home, because it was believed that this would decrease the quantity of manufactured goods available for export. Wages were kept low and hours of labour were long. This system meant luxuries should not be imported. Louis XIV and Colbert were behaving as mercantilists in founding industries in silk, tapestries, and china. They not only protected their local market, but these goods became so desirable that other countries wanted them and gave up their currency to France. In the eighteenth century the British were also following a mercantile policy in discouraging their colonies from doing business with the French.

Banks grew on a grand scale and were important in supporting expanding economies. Private banks increased in number, but some countries also founded national institutions in order to regulate the supply of money and the debt. The Bank of England was founded in 1694. A central banking system gave England an advantage in being able to fund debts incurred by war and to have a system which supported national policy.

Commerce also encouraged a money economy and the growth of new types of business organizations. Merchants would band together in joint ventures to develop trade in new areas. Joint-stock companies were formed, in which individuals owned shares of capital. Governments encouraged investment and often chartered new companies granting a monopoly of trade in an area. Private enterprise could also be used as an arm of government policy. The Hudson's Bay Company, the Dutch East India Company, and the British East India Company were founded for these purposes.

Risks came with the new mercantile policy. Economies went through cyclical periods, depending upon a state's fortunes in war, the success of its colonial policy, its ability to manufacture goods, and the status of its agricultural sector. Also, in the early days of joint-stock companies there was much speculation in new enterprises, with an eye to greater

profits. Inflation in stocks was the result of such speculation, and in 1720 two "bubbles" burst on investors in England and France. The South Sea Company of England and the Mississippi Company of France both suffered from wildly over-optimistic speculative activity. The crashes wiped out many investors, as the dangers of such economic activity were discovered with a vengeance.

Traditional absolutist rulers, enlightened despots, parliamentary governments, all adopted the mercantilist ideas, as Britain, France, Spain, Austria, Prussia, and Holland vied for trade and the accumulation of wealth. Colonies were an extension of the state, as imperial wars were an extension of state interests. The early modern state was a political economy. Economics was one of the ways that states pursued their interests, centralized their power, and modernized. Those states which could not keep up, Spain in the eighteenth century for example, ceased to be world powers.

THE IDEA OF *LAISSEZ-FAIRE*

In the middle of the eighteenth century the economic theory of mercantilism was challenged by the spirit of reform introduced by the philosophes. In France a group of thinkers, calling themselves Physiocrats, led by François Quesnay (1694–1774) and A.R.J. Turgot, worked to develop a science of economics. Their name implied what they proposed to do: build a science of wealth based upon a method derived from the natural sciences, and arrive at laws of economic behaviour. The Physiocrats agreed that the economic system needed reform in the direction of freedom. If that were accomplished, they believed that there would be a healthy competitive marketplace in which trade would no longer be hampered by regulations. Land, the Physiocrats argued, was the basis of wealth, and they sought to emphasize increased agricultural productivity. This, they suggested, would produce the surplus which would allow for the development of a national economy. Commerce was to be free. It was Turgot who invented the slogan of economic liberalism: *"Laissez-faire, laissez passer."*

Adam Smith's *An Inquiry into the Nature and Causes of the Wealth of Nations* (1776) was the

Hogarth's ''An Emblematical Print on the South Sea Scheme,'' 1721. A commentary on the South Sea ''bubble'' in which many were ruined in a frenzy of economic speculation. (Dover Publications, Inc.)

most important and influential economic work of the eighteenth century. Strongly supporting the idea of economic liberty, Smith claimed: ''Nothing . . . can be more absurd than this whole doctrine of the balance of trade. . . .''[20] He believed that the mercantilist theory was founded on a mistaken idea of value. Rather than bullion, he insisted, it was labour which gave goods value. Nor was the quantity of wealth static, as the mercantilists believed. The system was one which could expand by producing more goods. Mercantilism had emphasized the wrong end of the economic process:

Consumption is the sole end and purpose of all production; and the interest of the producer ought to be attended to only so far as it may be necessary for promoting that of the consumer. The maxim is so perfectly self-evident that it would be absurd to

attempt to prove it. But in the mercantile system the interest of the consumer is almost constantly sacrificed to that of the producer; and it seems to consider production, and not consumption, as the ultimate end and object of all industry and commerce.[21]

Smith wished to encourage free trade and competition in order to create more wealth. He believed that the economy should be a self-regulating system based upon the law of supply and demand. If individuals would pursue their own enlightened self-interest, wealth would be increased and the economy would work according to natural laws, like those put forth by Newton in the physical world. A division of labour would result in greater efficiency, and free trade would force industries and states to operate only in those areas where they could compete. To complete the analogy with the physical sciences, he imagined a free economy working harmoniously as if regulated by an "invisible hand": the deist god of nature was also the guardian of the liberal economy.

Smith was a moral philosopher as well as an economist. He wished to get rid of some of the restraints on individual action and to permit people to determine their own self-interest. An artificial economic system, he claimed, "retards, instead of accelerating, the progress of the society towards real wealth and greatness. . . ." The moral value of a system without restraint was that "the obvious and simple system of natural liberty establishes itself of its own accord. Every man, as long as he does not violate the laws of justice, is left perfectly free to pursue his own interest his own way, and to bring both his industry and capital into competition with those of any other man, or order of men."[22] This system Smith called "natural liberty." The state was not going to disappear, far from it. It would now have different functions: to protect society in case of war; to administer justice and protect individuals; and to create and maintain public works and institutions.

The Wealth of Nations was the seminal work of modern economic theory, one which the new industrial capitalism would cite as its theoretical base. It was another illustration of how deeply the scientific method penetrated the thought of all areas of knowledge during the Enlightenment. It was also a plea for liberty, joining an ever more vocal chorus.

E. EMPIRE AND REVOLUTION

WAR AND DIPLOMATIC CHANGE

The wars of the mid-eighteenth century, following a period of relative peace and stability after the Treaty of Utrecht in 1715, were part of the quest for political and economic advantage among states. The first major one was the War of the Austrian Succession, begun by the young Frederick II in 1740 in an attempt to expand Prussian power at the expense of Austria. France joined Prussia in this period, while Britain typically supported the enemies of France, its major rival in world affairs. The Treaty of Aix-la-Chapelle in 1748 settled that conflict, Austria ceding Silesia to Prussia,

though the issues which were behind the war, the place of Austria and Prussia in middle Europe, and the rivalry between Britain and France in the world, remained open.

What was viewed at the time as a "diplomatic revolution" occurred in 1756 in January. It was an English-Prussian agreement, based upon their mutual interests in the House of Hanover (the German lands of the British crown), which unlocked the old arrangements. Traditionally, Britain had been allied with Austria and Prussia allied with France. In May, 1756, Austria signed a defensive agreement with France, which was joined by Russia. In world terms, Britain and France had exchanged allies — Britain now sided with Prussia, France with Austria. As a means of symbolizing the new union, the Empress of Austria, Maria Theresa, gave her daugher, Marie Antoinette, in marriage to the heir of the throne of France, the man would later rule as Louis XVI.

The new French-Austrian alliance was immediately viewed as a threat by Frederick II. He went on the offensive and in August 1756, invaded Saxony on the road to Austria. In the Seven Years' War, Prussia fought France, Austria, and Russia. Though Prussia was always in a position of weakness, Frederick's military genius, yet another side of his "enlightened" brilliance, enabled it to survive the war, although the army was reduced from 150 000 in 1756 to 90 000 by 1760. Events elsewhere also helped Prussia. In 1762 the Empress Elizabeth of Russia died. Her successor, Peter III, was on the throne only for a matter of months, but he was an admirer of Frederick II and withdrew from the coalition against Prussia. Britain sent financial assistance to Frederick, and by 1762 British success in the war with France in the colonial world was stretching French resources to their limit. In 1763 hostilities were ended with the Treaty of Hubertusburg, which acknowledged the balance of power stalemate in central Europe and kept the continent much as it was in 1756.

It was overseas that things changed. Fighting between Britain and France occurred in North America, India, and the West Indies. Here, British naval power was the dominant influence; France could remain the dominant power on the European continent, but it could not at

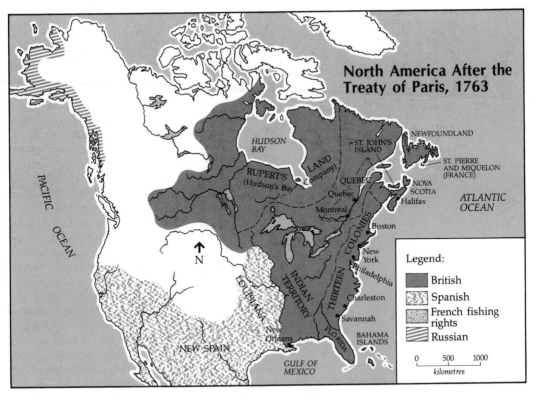

North America After the Treaty of Paris, 1763

the same time control the supply routes to its overseas empire. In North America Britain won the Battle of Quebec on the Plains of Abraham in 1759; in the West Indies and in India Britain was also victorious. The result was the Treaty of Paris in 1763. France ceded all its possessions in Canada to Britain, except for St. Pierre and Miquelon, two tiny islands off the coast of Newfoundland, and the British now controlled virtually all of North America east of the Mississippi River. India was firmly in British hands. Thus Britain achieved imperial dominance.

GREAT BRITAIN AND THE AMERICAN COLONIES

The victory of Britain in 1763 was a prelude to a colonial revolution which had major repercussions in the world. Colonial culture in America was itself part of the culture of the Enlightenment. The colonies were peopled by Britishers who had emigrated for a variety of reasons: some for religious freedom, others for opportunity, some for both. They were thirteen separate colonies, each with its own

legislature and each ruled by a governor appointed by the king. The colonies were part of the British Empire, and responsible to the king, but with an ambiguous relationship to the houses of Lords and Commons in London. For a long time, especially during the war, they had become increasingly accustomed to doing things their own way.

Yet they were part of an empire and were expected to follow mercantilist policies developed at the center. The Navigation Act of 1660 was the major statute which regulated their trade. It required that the trade of the colonies be conducted via English ships and that the crews be mainly English. Some goods made in the colonies could not be sold outside the empire — sugar, tobacco, and cotton among them. In 1663 another act stated that all European goods which were to go to areas of the empire must first pass through British ports. These were only a few of the regulations. Mercantilist policies were common at the time, and England viewed its empire as a self-sufficient unit. It planned its economy and became the "warehouse" for a vast worldwide commercial enterprise. Britain itself was to be the manufacturer and the colonies were to be suppliers of raw materials and to provide buyers. When an opportunity arose in the colonies for a wider free market with other countries, it was resisted by the British because it was seen as taking wealth away from the realm.

The settlers in America were mainly artisans and yeoman farmers, and included people from dissenting (that is, non-Anglican Protestant) religious groups, such as Puritans and Quakers. They were literate and shared British culture. In Europe the American colonists were often viewed unrealistically as innocents who were experimenting with the natural North American environment, or as people living an egalitarian existence, which was to be admired. Land was free, the individual could pursue his own interest, and laws were created without the burden of European institutional restraints; or so it was believed by Voltaire and the philosophes. European reformers everywhere saw the American colonies as unspoiled, and this image was reinforced by the intellectual qualities of prominent Americans, such as Benjamin Franklin, a scientist, literary man, and diplomat, accepted by the philosophes as one of their own.

In the Americas the colonies had a governmental structure mirroring that of Britain. All but one had two-house legislatures that conducted themselves in the manner of the British Parliament. Power in this arrangement favoured the representative assemblies of the colonies, because the governors appointed by the king were paid by taxes raised in the colonies, not directly by the Crown. Being so far away from the center of the empire, the governors had to listen to the concerns of the local legislatures.

After the wars of empire ended in 1763, Britain, in order to raise money to pay for the war, began to tighten its imperial controls. In 1764 the British Parliament passed the Sugar Act, heavily increasing taxes on imports to the Americas, such as sugar, coffee, and wine, and doubling taxes on goods sent to the colonies from Europe through Britain. There was anger in the colonies, the colonists claiming that no one had the right to tax property without the consent of those who were directly

affected. Citing the arguments surrounding the Glorious Revolution and taking a leaf from John Locke, the colonists suggested that as Englishmen they must be directly represented in matters of taxation.

To the people of Great Britain this seemed an odd position. The British Parliament, after all, was sovereign, and the colonists were merely being asked to assume their share of the imperial enterprise. American colonists, they said, were represented in Parliament in the sense that there were always members who presented their case. Parliament was governed by men of virtue, it was claimed, who governed disinterestedly with the whole of the empire in mind. In Britain itself few had the vote, and Parliament, though a two-house body, was aristocratic in its composition and outlook. To many colonists this argument of "virtual" representation did not reflect their practice; by the mid-eighteenth century there had developed a tradition of direct representation in colonial assemblies. For them, the immediate issues were trade and wealth, and the principle on which they fell back was "no taxation without representation." Some claimed, with precedent, that the British Parliament had no sovereignty over the colonies; they were the king's lands and the colonists appealed directly to the crown to end what they considered a policy of tyranny.

Other provocative laws were passed by Britain through the decade of the 1760s. One, the Stamp Act in 1765, taxing printed paper in the colonies, was repealed after merchant protests and boycotts. In 1767 the Townshend Acts imposed new duties on glass, lead, paints, paper, and tea. The protest in the colonies ranged from attempts to negotiate a solution, to clear statements by some colonists that the British Parliament had no constitutional right to legislate for the colonies. Protest in the colony of Massachusetts resulted in resistance which made it impossible for customs officials to enforce the regulations. Britain sent troops in 1768 and occupied the port of Boston. In 1770 British troops fired on a crowd, killing five civilians. This "Boston Massacre," as it was called, was publicized by Paul Revere's engraving. Though Revere exaggerated the circumstances, the event and the publicity did much to contribute to the alien-

Paul Revere's "The Bloody Massacre," an engraving published in 1770.   (Library of Congress)

ation of the colonists from British authority. In 1773 a tax on tea was levied which resulted in violent resistance. Anger at this economic policy coincided with the feeling that the British Parliament was corrupt, that it was exceeding its authority, and that it was destroying the colonists' rights as Englishmen.

Many in Britain believed that imperial rights were at stake. Moreover, the mercantile system had been in operation for over a century. In 1774 the British Parliament passed the Coercive Acts, a set of laws directed against the colony of Massachusetts, which took the lead in the resistance. American colonists referred to these laws as the Intolerable Acts.

Massachusetts then organized the First Continental Congress. At that meeting, colonists argued that the British Parliament did not have sovereignty over the colonies, and, therefore, it could not legislate for them. The Congress challenged Britain's authority and called for the people to take up arms.

THE AMERICAN REVOLUTION
In 1775 at Concord in Massachusetts the first battle occurred. It was a small skirmish, but it was an armed fight between "Patriots" and British troops, local militia against the uniformed and trained defenders of the empire. A Second Continental Congress followed,

forming a revolutionary army. Yet there was still hesitation to turn the resistance into a movement for independence. The colonies, many claimed, needed Britain; resistance was being undertaken because they wished their rights as Englishmen restored.

Thomas Paine (1737–1809), in his *Common Sense* of January 1776, articulated the argument for independence. The monarchy was corrupt, he claimed, and the king a "Royal Brute." He appealed to natural rights: "A government of our own is our natural right,"[23] and he called for independence. The pamphlet went through twenty-five printings in one year, and was read throughout the colonies. Paine spoke in plain language and appealed to the common people to govern themselves.

The Congress decided to move towards independence. It appointed a group of people to draw up a statement which would justify this momentous action, one unprecedented in world history. Thomas Jefferson (1743–1826) was the main draftsman of the Declaration of Independence, a clear expression of the spirit of the Enlightenment and a justification of revolution that could be traced to Locke. Jefferson began with a statement of rights:

We hold these truths to be self-evident: That all men are created equal; that they are endowed by their Creator with certain unalienable rights; that among these are life, liberty, and the pursuit of happiness; that, to secure these rights, governments are instituted among men, deriving their just powers from the consent of the governed; that whenever any form of government becomes destructive of these ends, it is the right of the people to alter or to abolish it, and to institute new government. . . .

Then the complaints: "The history of the present king of Great Britain is a history of repeated injuries and usurpations, all having in direct object the establishment of an absolute tyranny over these states." Jefferson catalogued the "tyranny" by showing the king to have assented to acts which broke the contract between him and his subjects. Jefferson wrote that the Congress "in the name and by the authority of the good people of these colonies, solemnly publish and declare, that these United Colonies are, and of right ought to be,

FREE AND INDEPENDENT STATES."[24] Sovereignty was declared to belong to the people, who now returned to a state of nature to reconstitute authority and make another contract to form a new legitimate government.

The war with Britain effectively took five years. The new United States of America was aided by France, Britain's rival, in an effort to weaken British supremacy of the seas and to undermine the British Empire. The Peace of Paris was made in 1783 between Great Britain and the new United States of America, and the world recognized the new sovereign state.

THE MAKING OF THE CONSTITUTION OF THE UNITED STATES

By the time of the signing of the Peace of Paris, the Americans already had a governing document, the Articles of Confederation, agreed to by the Continental Congress in 1781. The Articles established a political entity to conduct the war, but in its concern for limiting centralized power, it left the question of sovereignty ambiguous, reserving much authority for the separate states. Morever, it was difficult to change the Articles because unanimous consent of the thirteen participants was required for all amendments. It was, therefore, agreed to hold a constitutional convention in 1787.

The document produced by the representatives gathered in Philadelphia became the Constitution of the United States. It reflected a number of diverse viewpoints, all in the tradition of Enlightenment thinking. The group of people gathered together, led by George Washington, James Madison, and Alexander Hamilton, had a view of rights which was in accord with the Declaration of Independence. They believed in natural rights — life, liberty, and property — and they thought that individuals should be free, as far as possible, to pursue their own self-interests. Yet, they also believed that human nature was far from benign. Left to their own devices, they feared, individuals would destroy the community and one another. It was, therefore, necessary to limit freedom by checking the ability of people to do evil.

"Factions," meaning groups of individuals with special interests who wished to gain and manipulate power on their own behalf, were especially feared. This reflected the view that the British Parliament in the eighteenth century had become "corrupt" because it became dominated by an oligarchy. Thus, factions needed to be controlled. This was to be done in two ways: first, by building in safeguards to make it impossible for a faction to dominate the legislative and executive branches of government; secondly, by making the central government large enough so that factions would check one another.

Republicanism was supported, democracy was feared. The constitution-makers believed that rights were in danger in mass democracies because the people might choose badly. They wished to establish a representative government that would be stable and that could temper the dangers of liberty.

As Englishmen, the makers of the Constitution were in favour of mixed government along the lines theorized earlier by Montesquieu. They wanted a monarchical element, an aristocratic one, and a democratic one, all in proper balance. Power would check power, no single element would dominate. While the individual states were to retain some power, the framers of the system recognized the need for a central government which could conduct war, diplomacy, and trade, and pursue the national interest. The formula was one of a balance between liberty and authority.

The conservative nature of the Constitution became evident when it dealt with slavery, which existed in several of the individual states. The institution was both racist and contradictory to the essential premises of the Declaration of Independence and the new Constitution. Slavery did not become a major issue at the convention. How to count the slaves for purposes of representation was discussed, and a compromise stipulated that they be counted as "three-fifths" for purposes of taxation and representation. Slavery existed in the Bible as well as in the Athens of Socrates. That Americans did not see a contradiction in their eloquent appeal to rights and the existence of slavery is extraordinary in retrospect. This issue would not go away, and the subsequent history of the United States is filled with its consequences.

The new Constitution more nearly resembled that of the England the Americans left than it did anything else. Three branches of government were established. The executive was a president chosen by "electors," who were chosen by the states. The legislative branch had two houses. A Senate reflected the interests of the individual states — each state legislature chose two senators for six year terms; this was the aristocratic element. The House of Representatives, with seats assigned according to population, and chosen by the people, was the democratic element. The Constitution reflected the British parliamentary system of king, lords, and commons. A judicial branch of government was established and kept separate from the others. All this was part of an elaborate mechanism, designed to express the will of the majority and to prevent a concentration of authority. This was a system of "checks and balances," which allowed each branch of government both independence and some power over the others. It included a veto power of the president; it gave the Senate the right to ratify treaties and to approve executive appointments; it gave the judiciary authority over constitutional matters; and it reserved the right to originate money bills for the House of Representatives. In the preamble to the Constitution sovereignty was declared to be in the hands of the people: "We the people of the United States . . . do ordain and establish this CONSTITUTION for the United States of America."

Added to the Constitution was a "Bill of Rights," ten amendments passed in 1791, detailing the basic rights of Americans. The first amendment states: "Congress shall make no law respecting an establishment of religion, or prohibiting the free exercise thereof; or abridging the freedom of speech, or of the press; or the right of the people peaceably to assemble, and to petition the government for a redress of grievances."[25] The Americans attempted to implement some of the ideas of natural rights in their basic law.

The American Constitution thus embodied the major ideas of the Enlightenment. It was a document reflecting a belief in progress, yet tempered in its view of human nature. While claiming to give sovereignty to the people, it established a universe of politics which had a Newtonian balance and harmony as its model. However, it did proclaim individual rights as its central core. European reformers now looked to the new world to teach the old.

F. THE ARTS

THE FINE ARTS

From the time of Louis XIV, Classicism and the classical world dominated the visual arts in the seventeenth and eighteenth centuries. The ancient past was admired; its themes were the sources of inspiration for the content of paintings, and its idea of beauty was the model for the age. The French artist Nicolas Poussin (1594–1665) claimed: "My nature forces me towards the orderly." He painted scenes from classical mythology and biblical themes, and depicted an external nature which was static and harmonious. This uniform style, symmetrical in form and line, was encouraged by Louis XIV.

The art of Classicism was a quest for an ideal, an attempt to paint nature and human beings not as they were, but as they ought to be. Poussin's work was a search for the order and truth he found in the ancients. His paintings have a geometrical harmony, reflecting a sense of architectural unity in the universe, and his work set the artistic tone for the period dominated by the taste of Louis XIV, the Sun King.

A modification in style occurred after the death of Louis XIV. Antoine Watteau (1684–1721) in 1717 submitted his painting "The Embarkation of Cythera" to the French Academy, and on its strength he was admitted to the society. The painting had no profound allegorical or didactic meaning. It was lush and charming, celebrating a dreamlike mood. The style he represented, and which was popular to about 1760, was called Rococo, a modification of the Baroque of a century earlier. The Rococo had movement and delicacy in contrast to the Classical stability and weightiness. It was light and airy, almost whimsical, appealing to the senses rather than to the mind, opening up painting and architecture to the imagination of the creative artist. The Rococo, like the Baroque, stressed movement. But the Baroque had emphasized power, whereas the Rococo was more delicate and fragile. An attempt to move away from the more ponderous qualities of Classicism, the Rococo often descended into sentimentality and, while popular at the time, did not halt the return of the classical ideal after 1760.

In 1755 the art critic Johann Winckelmann (1717–68) proclaimed: "There is but one way for the moderns to become great, and perhaps unequalled; I mean, by imitating the ancients."[26] Neo-classicism as a style of art became the vogue, taking hold of the public until well into the period of the French Revolution. It is an indication of the hold of the past on painting, and an expression of the continued tension in the visual arts between the contemporary and the traditional. Jacques-Louis David's (1748–1825) "The Oath of the Horatii" of 1784 was the definitive statement of this style and was immensely popular. The theme was civic duty and family; the painting was organized geometrically, almost as a set of sculptures; and it had a lesson to teach derived from an ancient event. Stable and orderly, it was considered a masterpiece from the moment it was shown.

CLASSICAL MUSIC

Classical music had nothing to do with the musical composition or performance of ancient times. It is called classical because in the eighteenth century music sought to incorporate the values of Classicism — order, harmony, stability, and symmetry. Classical musicians adopted structured rules of composition and harmony, and they developed musical forms which evolved into sonatas, concertos, and symphonies. This Classical form, best exemplified in the works of Franz Joseph Haydn (1732–1809) and Wolfgang Amadeus Mozart (1756–91), was, in the main, "absolute" music, composed as relations of sound without reference to a story or a moral lesson. In the symphony it reached its most sophisticated development, and the fundamentals of classical musical form dominated composition and taste in the West through the nineteenth century.

Music could also be "programmatic," written to convey a special mood or feeling, or to help tell a story. Opera was the most sophisticated development of this sort, combining theatre and music. Mozart, who is probably the greatest musical genius of Western culture, wrote forty-one symphonies, which extended that form, and also composed several operas, including *The Marriage of Figaro, Don Giovanni,* and *The Magic Flute*, which contributed to the popularity and importance of opera as an art form.

Mozart's last complete major work was *The Magic Flute*, written in 1791 while he was ill and also writing his unfinished Requiem mass. In it, he and his librettist, Schikaneder, reflected and supported many of the values of the Enlightenment while drawing on both musical tradition and folk-culture. *The Magic Flute* was in that favoured form used by Voltaire and Swift, and very popular in the Enlightenment, the imaginary voyage. The journey was taken by a prince, Tamino, who was on a rite of passage to becoming a wise and virtuous human being. He and his princess, Pamina, both were tested for courage and fortitude by a group of people who belong to a fraternal brotherhood, resembling the world of the philosophes, and whose symbols of wisdom were the sun and light. This fraternal order had some of the rites and practices of the contemporary society of Freemasons, to which Mozart and Schikaneder belonged. This order was a supporter of a universal brotherhood of humanity and drew upon the values of the major thinkers of the Enlightenment.

Mozart wrote the opera as a *singspiel*, a song-tale, which was part of the folk culture of his day. He adapted folk-tale elements, including a magical instrument which would help save Tamino and Pamina, and a character, Papageno, who represented the child of nature introduced by Rousseau. Yet, it also had strong classical elements. The journey to enlightenment resembled the tale of the Greek hero Orpheus in the underworld; the ancient four elements of earth, air, fire, and water were used throughout; there were biblical resonances to Adam, Moses, and Jesus; and Egyptian myths of the sun and moon were important to the piece.

The main character, Tamino, underwent several trials in order to display his maturity and his capacity to live a life of reason. He reached his goal using a combination which included an ancient sage who represented wisdom, Pamina who was love, Papageno who was a child of nature, and the flute which represented art. Hence, it was a moral allegory of universal reason, based on the premises of the Enlightenment. There was also the egalitarian thrust so prevalent in the later Enlightenment: the prince was worthy not because of his hereditary position, but because he displayed character and virtue; the princess herself underwent the trials, an early example in a major composition of women having a role equal to that of men.

All the above was accomplished by Mozart while he wrote classical operas which conveyed in an orderly way plot, emotion, character, and relationships. Certain key signatures were used for individual characters or to indicate a state of feeling: for example, E flat major represented solemnity, enlightenment, and perfected love; its musical relative minor, C minor, was the key of death. Hence, the music itself had unity and order and reflected what was going on in the plot. What Mozart was doing was inventing a musical language — just what writers and artists did in their own areas.

G. THE STUDY OF THE PAST

The major figures of the Enlightenment embraced the past while trying to improve upon it. During the Enlightenment historical studies grew in importance. The past was seen as a source of wisdom and inspiration, as a way of learning about humanity, and as a means of understanding society and moving it in desired directions. The values of the Enlightenment permeated the study and understanding of the past.

The masterpiece of historical literature of the time, reflecting and shaping every Enlightenment value, was Edward Gibbon's (1737–94) massive *The Decline and Fall of the Roman Empire*. Gibbon admired the classical period and its writing. The Greece of Athens and the Rome of the later Republic were for him the highpoints of human accomplishment. But history was, for Gibbon, a succession of periods of light and darkness. As much as he revered the societies of Greece and Rome, he disliked the introduction of barbarism and the culture of Christianity. He was writing, he supposed, in an age of reason, and he passionately believed in the secular, rational values of his time: ''I had likewise flattered myself, that an age of light and liberty would receive, without scandal, an inquiry into the human *causes* of the progress and establishment of Christianity.''[27]

Most criticism of Gibbon was directed to his famous Chapters 15 and 16, which discussed the introduction of Christianity. He was a firm rationalist, and refused to give any credence or special treatment to any supernatural belief. The result was a scholarly discussion of the institutional growth of the Catholic Church, which angered some and scandalized others. Gibbon defended himself by citing the available documentation in every case, and routed his critics. He saw it as his task to record successive changes in politics and social policy. He wrote of ''the experience of history,'' meaning that we could learn from the study of the past.

The Enlightenment view of history was didactic, and Gibbon's purpose was to teach. He taught lessons — about behaviour, public events, the relations between rulers and ruled, against tyranny, and in favour of tolerance and moderation. He clearly stated that the decline and fall of Rome was an ''awful revolution'' in human affairs, and it ''may be usefully applied to the instruction of the present age.''[28] He was writing what he termed ''philosophical history,'' and he adopted a reasoned, dispassionate stance, which, he believed, gave perspective and lent weight to his judgments.

If history was written in order to instruct mankind, it was also meant, especially in the hand of Gibbon, to be pleasing in style and to entertain. Gibbon's prose was itself classical, as ordered as a painting by Poussin or David, or a symphony by Mozart. It had rhythm, measure, and symmetry, as well as a sense of balance and harmony.

The style of an author should be the image of his mind, but the choice and command of language is the fruit of exercise. Many experiments were made before I could hit the middle tone between a dull chronicle and a rhetorical declamation. Three times did I compose the first chapter, and twice the second and third, before I was tolerably satisfied with their effect.[29]

Progress was also part of Gibbon's message. Much of the past Gibbon viewed with a pessimistic eye: human beings often did evil; the ''good'' periods were followed by ''bad'' ones, and barbarism was ever at the gates of civilized Europe. Alas, ''reason'' in Greece and Rome was destroyed by superstition. Still, there was progress, a ''source of comfort and hope.''

The discoveries of ancient and modern navigators, and the domestic history or tradition of the most enlightened nations, represent the *human savage* naked in both mind and body, and destitute of laws, of arts, of ideas, and almost of language. From this abject condition, perhaps the primitive and universal state of man, he has gradually arisen to command the animals, to fertilize the earth, to traverse the ocean, and to measure the heavens.[30]

Thinkers in the Enlightenment viewed the present with hope; the golden age was not simply in the past, but would also appear again in the future. Voltaire had already argued that the great age of Louis XIV was the equal of those of the past. The Enlightenment was secure in its feelings that with the application of reason things were getting better. Gibbon spoke for many when he stated in the conclusion of his work: ''Since the first discovery of the arts, war, commerce, and religious zeal have diffused among the savages of the Old and New World these inestimable gifts: they have been successively propagated; they can never be lost. We may therefore acquiesce in the pleasing conclusion that every age of the world has increased and still increases the real wealth, the happiness, the knowledge, and perhaps the virtue, of the human race.''[31]

ANALYSIS AND DISCUSSION

1. It has been stated that the ideas of the nature of humanity and the role of government described by Thomas Hobbes are thoroughly modern. Select a modern state and discuss how Hobbes' ideas might apply to it.

2. Assume that you are either Thomas Hobbes or Jean-Jacques Rousseau. Write a short rebuttal of the ideas of the other person on the topic of "humanity in the state of nature."

3. Voltaire's *Candide* and Swift's *Gulliver's Travels* are two excellent examples of the use of ridicule and satire as tools for social criticism. Explain, in your own words, the aspects of European society that they were criticizing and comment on the effectiveness of this literary approach.

4. "Although Frederick the Great and Louis XIV were both effective absolute rulers, their approach to governing was vastly different." Explain this statement with reference to ideas of government in the early modern period.

5. Briefly explain the basic ideas contained in Adam Smith's *The Wealth of Nations* and contrast them with the concept of mercantilism.

6. "It has been said that the American Revolution was the child of the Enlightenment and the parent of the French Revolution." Discuss this statement with specific reference to the impact of the ideas of writers such as John Locke upon political thought in the Thirteen Colonies.

SYNTHESIS AND EVALUATION   CHAPTERS 1 AND 2

1. "[The] rationalism of absolute government is its justification." Explain this statement through an analysis of the political and economic advantages of absolute rule as practised by Louis XIV in France.

2. "Just as the Scientific Revolution freed humanity from the conventions of the past, so too the writings of Enlightenment philosophers shook the foundations of accepted political and social beliefs." Discuss this statement with reference to the impact of these new ideas upon the dominant beliefs of Europeans from the sixteenth to the eighteenth century.

3. The practice of Enlightened Despotism was an attempt made by an old institution to adjust to new ideas. Examine Enlightened Despotism in terms of the characteristics and degree of success of this adjustment.

4. "Montesquieu applied the methods of empiricism to a study of government and society. In this he was the first 'social scientist'." Analyse this statement in terms of Montesquieu's investigation of political systems.

5. "To the proponents of social contract and natural law there was no greater triumph prior to 1789 than the adoption of the Constitution of the United States." Analyse the American constitutional experiment in terms of the ideas of the Enlightenment.

CHAPTER **3**

The French
Revolution

July 14, 1789	Storming of the Bastille
1789–91	National (Constituent) Assembly writes first French Constitution
August 26, 1789	Declaration of the Rights of Man and Citizen
1790	Civil Constitution of the Clergy
	Edmund Burke publishes *Reflections on the Revolution in France*
1791 and 1792	Thomas Paine publishes *The Rights of Man*
October 1791– August 1792	Legislative Assembly
April 1792	France declares war on Prussia and Austria
1792–94	The Convention: First French Republic
January 1793	Louis XVI guillotined
1793–94	The Reign of Terror
July 1794	Fall of Robespierre; end of Jacobin Rule and the Terror
1795–99	The Directory

ON JULY 14, 1789, A CROWD OF PARISIANS stormed the Bastille, an imposing prison in Paris and a symbol of the absolute authority of the King of France. This event helped to set in motion the French Revolution, which in turn inaugurated a new period in Western, and perhaps even in world, history. For twenty-six years, from the fall of the Bastille in 1789 to the defeat of Napoleon in 1815, all of Europe and large parts of the world were absorbed in the political and intellectual repercussions of this upheaval.

The Revolution introduced important changes on the Western scene. Before it was over, the *bourgeoisie*, or middle class, had replaced the old aristocracy as the dominant political class in France. The terms "liberalism" and "conservatism" were coming into use throughout Europe as political designations, while "democracy" emerged as a new goal and a new hope for the masses. And wars were being fought between peoples-in-arms, and not simply between kings with professional armies. Very few events have changed the quality of peoples' lives as much as the French Revolution.

THE "OLD REGIME" IN FRANCE

France was governed prior to 1789 by an "absolute" monarchy. The famous statement attributed to King Louis XIV, "*L'état, c'est moi*" (I am the state), was correct in the sense that the king alone symbolized the union of the different parts of France and that he controlled the armed forces and made the laws of the French state in his own name. He was in fact responsible to no man, and all servants of the central government were accountable to him.

However, in spite of the claims of the king to absolutism, France was also a state with a long history and many ancient traditions. Its law was not simply the word of the king, but also the custom of the community. Since it was still an aristocratic and partly feudal state, considerable power rested with the nobility and was exercised in the local areas. And, as France was a large country with poor communications, bad roads, an inefficient and underdeveloped civil service, and complex laws and traditions which sometimes limited the king, it was impossible for the monarch to exercise absolute authority in the modern sense.

Legally, everyone was part of one of the three "estates" of French society. The first estate was the clergy, the second the nobility, and the third was made up of all those who were not included in the first two categories. This third estate was huge, encompassing over ninety-seven per cent of the people of France, and there were important social and civil divisions within it. Most members of the third estate were peasants working in the countryside, some on their own plot of land. A minority worked in the towns and cities. Some did menial service jobs, some were artisans or labourers, and others were small shopkeepers or owners of small pieces of property from which they drew a living. And, finally, the third estate also included the *bourgeoisie* of France—professionals such as lawyers, doctors, writers, wealthy merchants, and owners of large amounts of capital. This group was an influential part of the population.

There were important social, political, and

Cette fois ci, la justice est du côté du plus fort.

A caricature of the French estates at the time of the Revolution. Justice is on the side of the representative of the third estate.   (Musée Carnavalet, Paris—Flammarion)

economic implications in belonging to one estate or another. France was a "corporate" society, composed of separate estates with varying rights and responsibilities, and a person in France possessed his status of citizenship by virtue of being a member of one of these estates. Laws, social privileges, and the kind and amount of taxes one paid were different for each estate. Rather than attempting to abolish this structure, kings in the seventeenth and eighteenth centuries often tried to alter it by asserting central authority over local tradition and special privilege. There was much to divide Frenchmen, but they were united in loyalty to the monarchy.

The clergy was an important estate be-cause France, legally and socially, was a Catholic country. The upper clergy, particularly the bishops, were mostly nobles, while the lower clergy—the parish priests—were ordinarily of lower-class origin and had great influence in the countryside. The foundations of the old regime were supported by the clergy who were a privileged order and looked to the monarch to uphold the exclusive authority of the Catholic Church. The Church was wealthy, and the tithe, a tax levied on Frenchmen to support the Church, was still collected. It has been estimated that the Church owned from twelve to twenty per cent of the land in France. Moreover, religion was an important influence in the lives of the vast majority of the people.

Whether devout or not, Frenchmen, especially in the countryside, organized their lives around the activities of the Church—its holidays, its worship, and its social functions.

The nobility was composed of two groups: nobles of the sword and nobles of the robe. The nobles of the sword were the old, traditional, feudal nobility, the descendants of the nobles of the medieval period, who had been warriors, local rulers, and administrators. In exchange for their services, the medieval nobility had received many privileges, including tax exemptions. These privileges had remained, despite the fact that by the eighteenth century the central administration of the king had become much more important and local nobles had ceased to perform administrative functions. Hence many of the nobles of the sword did very little for the French state, even though they had great hereditary advantages. However, some of them pursued careers in the Church, and as a result there were many nobles of the sword in high Church offices. Others held important positions in the army and at court.

The nobles of the robe, on the other hand, were a more recent group, having been created by the French kings in the century or so prior to the Revolution. They often performed civil service functions akin to those in our day; many, however, had purchased their offices and had no specific duties. They dominated the *parlements* (law courts), the most influential of which, by tradition, was the *Parlement* of Paris. They also sat on the provincial estates, which were ancient deliberative bodies established in some provinces. These local assemblies usually played a minor role under the absolute monarchy of France, but when the monarch and the central state were weak they could become a threat to the power of the French king. This occurred prior to the French Revolution; indeed, the nobles were the first rebels against the authority of the king.

The third estate was not a privileged order. It paid most of the taxes and did much of the work of the nation. Although it was far from rebellious, it harboured deep grievances against the privileged estates. It participated in only one major political institution, the Estates-General, a national body which originated in the Middle Ages and was composed of representatives of the three estates. The Estates-General had not met since 1615, and there was no requirement that the King summon it.

By the standards of that time, France under the old regime was an advanced state, and the cultural leader of Western civilization. Though it had fewer colonies than England, France's population was double that of its rival, and its land was among the most fertile of Europe. The Frenchmen of the third estate, in spite of their grievances, were still much better off than their contemporaries in eastern or southern Europe (the peasants, in fact, owned forty per cent of the land). France's achievements in medicine, philosophy, and literature were well ahead of the rest of Europe. To be sure, there was deep discontent in 1789, but, in seeking out and analysing the causes of the French Revolution, we must remember that this revolution occurred in a relatively advanced country and not in a backward area.

THE INFLUENCE OF ENLIGHTENMENT THOUGHT

All the leaders who came to the fore after the fall of the Bastille were influenced by the ideas of the Enlightenment. French Enlightenment thinkers firmly believed that life could be made better, that human misery was created by social and political systems which should be changed, not endured. According to Voltaire:

There is no good code of laws in any country. The reason is evident. . . . Laws were established in nearly all states through the selfish interests of the legislator, to meet the need of the moment, through ignorance and superstition.[1]

Many philosophes in the eighteenth century sought the establishment of a better society— perhaps a heaven on earth—for all humanity.

The philosopher who most clearly reflected this attitude during the French Revolution was the Marquis de Condorcet (1743–94). Though a noble, he placed himself on the side of those who wished to overthrow the old regime, giving up his title at the time of the Revolution. When the Jacobins gained control of the government of France in 1793, Condorcet was outlawed, as he was suspected of not being sympathetic to the government. While in hiding in 1794, he finished his *Sketch for a Historical Picture of the Progress of the Human Mind*, a remarkable work, considering the conditions under which it was written. According to Condorcet:

All errors in politics and morals are based on philosophical errors and these in turn are connected with scientific errors. There is not a religious system nor a supernatural extravagance that is not founded on ignorance of the laws of nature. . . .

Thus all the intellectual activities of man, however different they may be in their aims, their methods, or the qualities of mind they exact, have combined to further the progress of human reason. Indeed, the whole system of human labour is like a well-made machine, whose several parts have been systematically distinguished but none the less, being intimately bound together, form a single whole, and work towards a single end.[2]

As for his own fate:

How consoling for the philosopher who laments the errors, the crimes, the injustices which still pollute the earth and of which he is often the victim is this view of the human race, emancipated from its shackles, released from the empire of fate and from that of the enemies of its progress, advancing with a firm and sure step along the path of truth, virtue and happiness! It is the contemplation of this prospect that rewards him for all his efforts to assist the progress of reason and the defence of liberty. He dares to regard these strivings as part of the eternal chain of human destiny; and in this persuasion he is filled with the true delight of virtue and the pleasure of having done some lasting good which fate can never destroy by a sinister stroke of revenge, by calling back the reign of slavery and prejudice. Such contemplation is for him an

asylum, in which the memory of his persecutors cannot pursue him; there he lives in thought with man restored to his natural rights and dignity, forgets man tormented and corrupted by greed, fear or envy; there he lives with his peers in an Elysium created by reason and graced by the purest pleasures known to the love of mankind.[3]

The ideas of the Enlightenment did much to undermine the foundations of the old regime. The old system had assumed social and political inequality and was based on loyalty to an absolute monarch and on the legitimacy of tradition. Enlightenment thinkers asked if the old traditions and institutions were "rational," or if they were consistent with the "natural rights of man." Clearly the old regime left much to be desired, and the philosophes were always ready with plans for a new order.

THE AMERICAN REVOLUTION AND EUROPE
The American Revolution was seen by Europeans as a major world event. American diplomats such as Benjamin Franklin, John Adams, and Thomas Jefferson were stationed in Europe and spread the new revolutionary ideas, while those Europeans who had fought in the American Revolution brought back stories of their experiences and a newly acquired political outlook. Societies were formed in Europe to discuss the American constitution, and many people viewed the events in America with envy. Europe was provided with an example of revolution-making and proof that a revolution could be successful. Moreover, Europeans noted that the colonists had not simply overthrown an old state, but had united to set up the institutions for a new one. When the Americans drew up a new constitution in 1787 proclaiming the principles of government by which they chose to live, they seemed to be creating a social contract. Thus, the American Revolution was thought by Europeans to be a model for the establishment of a new rational order based on the sovereignty of the people.

Actually, the Europeans were far too optimistic about the American experience

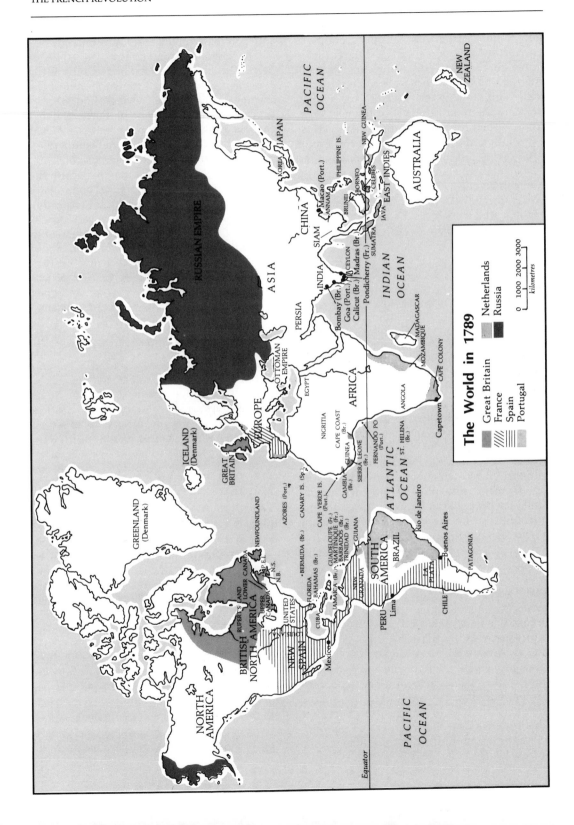

The World in 1789

- Great Britain
- France
- Spain
- Portugal
- Netherlands
- Russia

0 1000 2000 3000
kilometres

PACIFIC OCEAN

NEW ZEALAND

AUSTRALIA

NEW GUINEA

EAST INDIES

BORNEO
CELEBES
JAVA
SUMATRA
PHILIPPINE IS.
BRUNEI
ANNAM
Macao (Port.)
KOREA
JAPAN

CHINA
SIAM
INDIA
Madras (Br.)
Pondicherry (Fr.)
CEYLON
Calicut (Br.)
Goa (Port.)
Bombay (Br.)

PERSIA

INDIAN OCEAN

MADAGASCAR
MOZAMBIQUE

RUSSIAN EMPIRE

ASIA

OTTOMAN EMPIRE
EGYPT

EUROPE

GREAT BRITAIN

ICELAND (Denmark)

AFRICA

NIGRITIA
CAPE COAST
GUINEA (Br.)
SIERRA LEONE
GAMBIA (Br.)
FERNANDO PO (Port.)
ANGOLA
ST. HELENA (Br.)
CAPE COLONY
Capetown

AZORES (Port.)
CANARY IS. (Sp.)
CAPE VERDE IS. (Port.)

ATLANTIC OCEAN

GREENLAND (Denmark)

NORTH AMERICA

BRITISH NORTH AMERICA
RUPERT'S LAND
LOWER CANADA
UPPER CANADA
NEWFOUNDLAND
P.E.I.
N.S.
N.B.
BERMUDA (Br.)
UNITED STATES
FLORIDA
BAHAMAS
CUBA
JAMAICA (Br.)
GUADELOUPE (Fr.)
MARTINIQUE (Fr.)
BARBADOS (Br.)
TRINIDAD (Br.)
NEW GRANADA
GUIANA
NEW SPAIN
Mexico

SOUTH AMERICA
BRAZIL
Rio de Janeiro
PERU
Lima
LA PLATA
Buenos Aires
CHILE
PATAGONIA

PACIFIC OCEAN

Equator

providing a pattern for Europe. Conditions in North America were very different from those in Europe. The Americans had not started out with a corporate society, with a nationally established religion, or with a long tradition antagonistic to the new order they wished to establish. But the American Revolution did give Europeans the notion that revolution-making was possible, and it made many believe that the ideas of the Enlightenment could be realized without great difficulties. It was an illusion which disappeared very quickly once the French Revolution was under way.

THE FAILURE OF ABSOLUTE MONARCHY

Revolutions seldom break out as a result of poverty and oppression alone. They are complex political, intellectual, social, and economic movements which usually occur when a system of government fails to cope with its own difficulties. Moreover, "social forces" and "ideology" are seldom sufficient explanations for the outbreak of revolutions, for revolutions are made by individuals against other individuals, and are not simply the battle of one system against another.

From the beginning of his reign in 1774, Louis XVI of France faced one crisis after another. These crises often stemmed from the financial difficulties of the government, and they brought out tensions within the old privileged order in France. Throughout the eighteenth century the nobility had been trying to gain a greater share of power in the French state. What the nobles objected to was the continuing centralization of the state, which had gone on since the time of Louis XIV. The King, in sending his agents into the countryside and asserting his authority over legal and fiscal matters, was taking away what they considered their "rights" and "privileges." In effect, the nobles claimed that France had an ancient inherited constitution, based on custom and tradition, and that the King could not arbitrarily change this system. Thus the resurgent nobility, including most of the leading churchmen, came

into conflict with the absolute monarchy.

The first and second estates asserted themselves through traditional bodies such as the *parlements*, which had grown up out of the medieval law courts. These bodies, and especially the *Parlement* of Paris, claimed that according to custom the *parlements* had to register edicts of the King before they could become law. In the reign of Louis XVI, the royal government often bypassed the *parlements*, and the nobility continually complained that the King was not respecting the "ancient hereditary rights" of Frenchmen. Indeed, the first two estates claimed to be the defenders of traditional law in France and the guardians of the ancient "constitution." They did not attack the old order; rather, they accused the King of abandoning it in favour of a centralized "royal despotism."

The struggle between the King and the nobility frustrated any attempts made by the central government to reform the system. Realizing that France was in need of reform, especially in its inequitable and inefficient system of taxation, Louis XVI and many of his ministers tried to establish new institutions, such as provincial assemblies of all Frenchmen who owned property, and drew up new fiscal measures to reduce the inequality of taxation. These measures were always thwarted or vetoed by the first two estates, theoretically on the basis of guarding the "constitution" against the monarch's ambitions, but actually to protect their old privileges and to gain new powers for themselves.

Part of the reason for this opposition to royal reforms was the change that was taking place within the upper class in the years before the Revolution. In the early eighteenth century there had been a considerable amount of movement between classes. The kings often selected their civil servants from the third estate, and sometimes rewarded them with titles; a wealthy man could purchase a patent of nobility and the Church provided an opportunity for talented Frenchmen to rise within the system. But by 1788 French society was becoming increasingly less mobile. Both old and new members of the nobility were determined to keep certain state and Church offices for themselves. Thus, by the eve of the Revolution, all the bishops of the Church were of the noble class, and the officer corps of the army was restricted to the old nobility. It was becoming more and more difficult for Frenchmen in the third estate, no matter how intelligent, talented, or wealthy, to rise within the system. The social structure of France in 1788 resembled a pyramid with a few privileged nobles at the peak and the mass of Frenchmen at the bottom, and these masses had less hope than ever of moving toward the top.

THE CALLING OF THE ESTATES-GENERAL AND THE ESTABLISHMENT OF A NATIONAL ASSEMBLY

The immediate crisis which precipitated the Revolution of 1789 was economic — the French state had slowly been going bankrupt and all attempts at reform had failed. Louis XVI, though not a man of great intelligence or ability, was well-meaning, generally liked, and took his responsibilities as king seriously. He recognized that France was weakened because it was unable to tax the resources of some of the wealthiest elements of the kingdom.

Several attempts to change the tax structure and to rationalize the organization of the state were rejected by the *parlements*, who accused the King of tampering with the ancient laws of France. In 1787 he and his finance minister, Calonne, called together an Assembly of Notables, a body which had not met since 1626, in the hope that it would support a reform of the tax structure. The Assembly, dominated by nobles, refused to put through any program of tax reform which did not give it, in exchange, some governmental power. Hence nothing was accomplished. Then, in May 1788 Louis tried to destroy the power of the *parlements* by issuing the May Edicts, abolishing the right of *parlements* to approve new taxes. But the May Edicts antagonized everyone, including the third estate which did not want a more powerful king. In July 1788, under continuing financial pressure, Louis XVI gave in to the demands of many vocal Frenchmen and summoned the Estates-General for a meeting to be held in May 1789. Calling the Estates-General was an admission that traditional absolutism had failed to deal with the problems that France was facing.

The King's announcement led to the first public discussion of politics in the history of France. In line with French tradition, Louis invited the people to draw up lists of grievances (*cahiers de doléances*). Most of the *cahiers*, including many from the first and second estates, asked for constitutional government, and freedom of speech and the press. Some members of the first and second estates even asserted that they were willing to give up their tax privileges. The *cahiers* of the third estate often went further, many calling for a new constitution embodying the ideas of the Enlightenment about the nature of individual freedom and social equality.

It is impossible to generalize about the *cahiers*, but it is worth noting that those of the third estate often included a list of grievances about daily life and not simply comments on the government or statements of political philosophy. One member of the Estates-General recalled how a group of villagers composed their *cahier*:

I had trouble enough at first in making my good villagers understand that the States-General could not occupy itself with details peculiar to their commune; they understood at last that they must concern themselves, for the moment, with what was of universal interest and with general reforms.... They eagerly seized upon my proposal to demand that priests be chosen by the parishioners, that the celibacy of priests be abolished, that all cults be given equal freedom, and, lastly, to assure the success of these changes, prevent new abuses, and regulate the expenses of the nation, that there be a yearly assembly of representatives, etc.[4]

Many *cahiers* attacked privilege and waste and called for an end to corruption in administration. The villagers of Erceville, in the region of Orléans, complained that they alone have been charged with the mass of the taxes, while their seigneur, who farms much of the land in the parish, enjoys total exemption, although he has had a great part of the land planted with woods, which are populated by game that devastates the rest of the countryside; and that the woods, as well as the avenues he has had planted in great quantity, damage and almost destroy the neighboring lands, so that these lands, even in the better years, yield no harvest. Wherefore they ask that, concurrently with them and without any distinction of title or rank, the said seigneur be taxed like them.[5]

The discussion of reform during the period between the calling of the Estates-General in July 1788 and its meeting in May 1789 led to a break between the third estate and the privileged groups. While virtually all agreed that the old system of government had to be changed, they did not agree on either the means to do it or the ends to be achieved. The nobility wanted the Estates-General to meet as the Estates-General of old: each estate would sit separately and vote by estate and not by individual representative. Thus the first two estates could always outvote the third. On the other hand, the third estate wanted the representatives of the Estates-General to meet together, to have as many representatives in the third estate as in the first two combined, and to vote as individual representatives, not by estate. We see a clash here between a corporate view of France and the Enlightenment idea of the autonomy of the individual.

The most radical position at that time was taken by the Abbé Sieyès (1748–1836), a churchman of bourgeois background. He was one of many churchmen who attacked the privileges of their estate and joined with the voices of reform. In *What Is the Third Estate?*, written in early 1789, Sieyès proclaimed:

1) What is the third estate? Everything.
2) What has it been in the political order up to the present? Nothing.
3) What does it demand? To become something....

Who would dare to say ... that the third estate does not contain in itself all that is necessary to constitute a complete nation? ...

What is a nation? A body of associates living under a *common* law and represented by the same *legislature*.

Is it not all too certain that the noble order has privileges, exemptions, and even rights separated from the rights of the great body of citizens? It departs in this respect from the common order, from the common law. Its civil rights make it already a people apart in the nation at large....

The third estate ... includes everything that belongs to the nation; and everything that is not the third estate cannot be regarded as being of the nation. What is the third estate? Everything.[6]

The King, alone in a position to arbitrate between the differing views on how the Estates-General would meet and how voting should be conducted, compromised. He gave the third estate twice as many members as each of the others and decided that the Estates-General would meet and vote by estate. When the Estates-General met formally on May 4, 1789, the third estate tried to persuade the other estates to join it. A number of the clergy, mainly parish priests, moved over to the third estate, but the upper clergy and most of the nobility did not.

The vast majority of representatives of the third estate, it must be noted, were *not* peasants or workers. They were generally members of the *bourgeoisie*—lawyers, government officials, businessmen, doctors, or people of wealth who lived off property. Thus the third estate was represented by a literate, articulate, well-informed body, one which had a great deal of political awareness. They were angered by the social and economic privileges of the first and second estates, and they demanded equality and a share of political power in exchange for their support of the regime. Their hostility was not directed towards Louis XVI or even the institution of kingship. They wanted a monarchical regime restrained and limited by a constitution.

On June 17, firm in their belief that they

represented the great body of Frenchmen, the representatives of the third estate, along with some of the lower clergy, declared themselves a National Assembly. They agreed with some of the implications of Sieyès' statement—that France was not only a state, but a nation, and that this nation included all of the French people as equals under the law. Hence no group of people could claim to legislate for France without showing that they represented the nation as a whole. The King responded to this declaration by locking the third estate out of its meeting hall. The representatives, in the midst of great confusion, then moved to a nearby indoor tennis court and vowed that the National Assembly would continue to meet until France had a constitution. The Tennis Court Oath was a momentous event, for this was the first extra-legal action taken by the third estate. Some scholars regard this moment as the true beginning of the Revolu-

tion, the symbol of the alienation of the third estate from the legal structure of the old regime.

In the meantime tension was mounting throughout the land. There was apprehension that the King would dismiss the Estates-General. The economic situation was so bad in 1789 that bread riots became common in cities. There were also uprisings in the rural areas, and an atmosphere of fear spread throughout the country. In Paris, on July 14, a mob stormed the Bastille and killed several soldiers. The city hall was captured and the mayor of Paris was killed. When the King was told of these events by the Duc de Liancourt, there was, according to one witness, "a few moments silence." Then Louis XVI said, "It is then a revolt," to which de Liancourt replied, "No, Sire, it is a revolution."[7]

As violence increased and France seemed to be falling into chaos, Louis had little alter-

Triomphe de l'Armée Parisienne réunis au Peuple à son retour de Versailles à Paris le 6.º Octobre 1789

The court of Louis XVI was forced to move from the Palace of Versailles to the city of Paris on October 6, 1789. A group of citizens and soldiers leads the triumphal march. (Bibliothèque Nationale, Paris)

native but to recognize the existence of the National Assembly. He then ordered the first two estates to join the third, and thus the third estate achieved its goal. But the life of the National Assembly had been saved by violence, and henceforth violence or the threat of violence was an ever-present element in the Revolution.

THE CONSTITUTION OF 1791 — THE REFORM OF FRANCE

The National Assembly set out to restore order and to provide France with a written constitution. Its first act, on the night of August 4, was to abolish the remnants of feudalism. This meant that the French peasants were freed of all remaining seigniorial obligations—such as labour service, manorial dues and tithes—and became free persons. The privileges of the nobility, such as the hunting rights mentioned in many *cahiers*, were ended.

On August 26 the Assembly promulgated the major document of the Revolution—the Declaration of the Rights of Man and Citizen. It was a statement of principle and of hope, reflecting the political ideas of the Enlightenment, and became the creed of the Revolution.

I   Men are born and remain free and equal in rights. Social distinctions may be based only on common utility.

II   The aim of all political association is to preserve the natural and imprescriptible rights of man. These rights are liberty, property, security and resistance to oppression.

III The principle of all sovereignty rests essentially in the nation. No body and no individual may exercise authority which does not emanate from the nation expressly.

VI   Law is the expression of the general will. All citizens have the right to take part, in person or by their representatives, in its formation. It must be the same for all whether it protects or penalizes. All citizens being equal in its eyes are equally admissible to all public dignities, offices and employments,

according to their capacity, and with no other distinction than that of their virtues and talents.

XVII Property being an inviolable and sacred right, no one may be deprived of it except for an obvious requirement of public necessity, certified by law, and then on condition of a just compensation in advance.[8]

Thus, at one stroke, some central features of the legal and social structure of the old regime were rejected and a new era of liberty and the rule of law was proclaimed. As French ideas and, later, French troops spread throughout Europe, the Declaration, along with the revolutionary slogan "Liberty, Equality, Fraternity," became the new gospel of the oppressed.

The Declaration was made the "preamble" to the Constitution of 1791, drawn up and approved by the National Assembly. France became a centralized state without feudal remnants. Power resided in a one-house legislature, elected by about two-thirds of all Frenchmen. These voters were called "active" citizens because they paid a certain sum in taxes; "passive" citizens were not given the franchise. The king had a suspensive veto, which meant that he could delay legislation but not nullify it. All Frenchmen were declared equal before the law, and a new judicial system was instituted. A more equitable system of taxation was also established.

The Constitution did not place all Frenchmen on an equal footing, and it has been called (with some justification) a bourgeois document. Property was protected and full citizenship was granted only to those who paid above a certain level of taxation. None the less, the Constitution of 1791 was by far the most democratic political and social instrument in Europe.

The National Assembly also undertook the reform of the Church, and in July 1790 passed the Civil Constitution of the Clergy. The lands of the Church were nationalized, not only for financial reasons—the state was able to raise money by issuing bonds on the security of this new wealth—but also on social and ideological grounds. The priests of the Church were to be paid by the state and were required to take an oath of loyalty to France and to the new constitution. Many priests who had worked for the Revolution were torn between loyalty to Paris and to Rome. The Civil Constitution thus split the lower clergy, and the tensions aroused throughout France by this issue remained one of the unsolved problems of the Revolution.

One of the most important features of the French Revolution was the emergence of the idea that in the modern state there was only *one* loyalty—to the nation itself. In the past, many loyalties had been recognized—loyalty to one's king, to one's church, to one's lord, to one's locality. Such divided allegiance was no longer possible in the new state, which was to be centralized and secular, and demanded the total loyalty of the people. In the Middle Ages the great sin had been heresy: disloyalty to the Church. The modern heresy would be treason: disloyalty to the state.

ROYAL, ARISTOCRATIC, AND EUROPEAN RESPONSES

Although Louis XVI called the Estates-General and had recognized the National Assembly, he was far from happy with events from 1789 to 1791. As King, he saw his traditional powers and prerogatives limited in the name of the people of France; as a devout Catholic, he saw the Revolution undermine the Church. In a desperate move, on June 20, 1791, he tried to flee to Austria. By taking this action he was deserting a state of which he was the executive head to seek temporary refuge in a country known to be totally unsympathetic to the actions of the National Assembly. But Louis was apprehended at the French border station of Varennes and taken back to Paris. Thus it was clear that France had a chief executive who refused to accept the principles of the new constitution. Public opinion, which earlier had been willing to accept and even love the King as a con-stitutional monarch, now began to turn against him.

The Revolution lost the support of many devout Catholics. The Pope condemned both the Civil Constitution of the Clergy and the Revolution itself, and the clergy were forbidden to take the oath required of them by the state. As a result, revolutionary France had two bodies of clergymen—one which took the oath, called the "constitutional" clergy; the other which refused, called the "refractory" clergy. This division of loyalty among the clergy caused difficulties in many parishes throughout France. In some areas violence broke out as a result of the unwillingness of some of the local population to accept a new "constitutional priest" in place of a familiar "refractory" one. From this moment the Catholic Church officially opposed all manifestations of revolutionary activity.

While some of the nobility, like some of the lower clergy, helped to construct the new society in France, others became active opponents of the Revolution. A number of nobles left France and fled to more conservative European countries. Known as *émigrés*, many plotted to overthrow the Revolution and restore the old order.

The European reaction to the Revolution was mixed. Initially, especially among the more literate elements where the ideas of the Enlightenment had spread, the reaction was highly favourable. In England, in some of the German states, and in the Hapsburg lands, many people thought that France would provide the model for a new European society. But favourable response was often short-lived. When in 1792 the Revolution became associated with violence and war, a number of prominent Europeans ceased to support it. European governments, in contrast to their people, opposed the Revolution from the start and saw it as a threat to their own authority.

The most interesting response to the Revolution was that of the Englishman Edmund Burke, who published his *Reflections on the Revolution in France* in 1790.

Burke claimed that the Revolution had gone astray by attempting to overthrow old institutions and establish new ones overnight. In his view, society was not a rational organization but an organic, ever-changing body held together by a complex network of traditional institutions and customs. To try to change these institutions and customs too quickly would disrupt the whole organism and bring about a state of chaos. This in turn would breed violence and lead to a dictatorship in order to restore order. Burke believed that tradition and custom represented the accumulated wisdom of the ages and reflected the many-sided nature of humanity. By eliminating tradition and by trying to establish a state on the rational principles of the Enlightenment, the revolutionaries had condemned the country to anarchy. Burke was not against change, but because society was so complex, he thought that change should only come slowly. He did not oppose all of the aims of the Revolution, but he warned that the means chosen could not result in the desired end.

Burke's analysis of the French Revolution is the beginning of modern conservative ideology, even though his conservatism is peculiarly English. He had supported the American Revolution because he felt that the colonists were fighting for their traditional rights as Englishmen. He opposed the French Revolution because he believed that tradition was being undermined. But the problem in France, which he recognized yet refused to deal with, was that tradition had failed to cope with the political, economic, and social problems of French society.

Burke was challenged by Thomas Paine, whose *The Rights of Man* was published in two parts in 1791 and 1792. Paine defended the Enlightenment view of human nature: "Man, were he not corrupted by governments, is naturally the friend of man, and ... human nature is not of itself vicious." He insisted that while Burke had sympathy for the French monarchy, he cared little for the ordinary person:

Not one glance of compassion, not one commiserating reflection ... has he bestowed on those who lingered out the most wretched of lives. ... He is not affected by the reality of distress touching his heart, but by the showy resemblance of it striking his imagination. He pities the plumage, but forgets the dying bird.[9]

The debate between Burke and Paine aroused great contemporary interest and many thousands of copies of each work were sold.

1792 — WAR AND THE SECOND REVOLUTION

The National Assembly completed its work with the making of the Constitution of 1791. In the new Legislative Assembly which met in October 1791, a number of groups appeared which were not formal political parties but were united in aims and goals. On the right were the Feuillants, a conservative group, representing allegiance to the ideals of the Constitution of 1791 and the constitutional monarchy. A large group of people of the upper *bourgeoisie* collectively called the Marsh took a middle position. On the left were the Girondins and Jacobins. The Girondins (many of whom came from the Gironde in Southern France) became the dominant single group and wished to transform the Revolution into an international force. In accord with the ideals of the Enlightenment, they felt that the new order ought to be universal, not just limited to France. The Jacobins (named after a monastery in which they met) were discontented with what they considered the halfway nature of the Revolution and wished to turn the new constitutional monarchy into a republic. They were not so attached to the idea of private property as the other groups in the Assembly and were more interested in social reform. Thus we see that while some elements in the Legislative Assembly thought that the Revolution was at an end, others felt that it had just begun. It is not surprising that there was a good deal of conflict within the Assembly.

The Legislative Assembly had many additional problems to face. The economy was in severe disorder, and food shortages existed in many areas. As a result, the peasants and urban workers were still discontented. The monarchs of Europe were making threatening statements against France, and many members of the Assembly felt that the *émigrés* were planning a war to overthrow the Revolution. In this tense situation the Girondins found more support for their position than any other group, and in April 1792, in an atmosphere which resembled a crusade, France declared war against the enemies of the Revolution. Paradoxically, France was fighting under the nominal authority of a King who would be restored to absolute power if France lost, for the European powers, especially the Hapsburgs and the princes of the German states, stated openly that they were determined to restore the old order.

France was militarily unprepared for the war and faltered at first. Frustration and defeat, along with the economic and social problems of the Revolution, produced an atmosphere of tension in France. People feared that France would lose, that the King would be restored as an absolute monarch, and that the Revolution would be undone. Frenchmen who had committed revolutionary acts or who had acquired some of the lands confiscated from the Church could not afford to see a return of the old order. In other words, once the war began, supporters of the Revolution realized that military defeat meant the loss of all the gains made since 1789.

Leaders of the Jacobins and Girondins began to preach that all who opposed the war were enemies of France and the revolutionary ideals. At the same time, it became apparent that the Legislative Assembly was not governing well. Confidence and morale were deteriorating, especially in Paris. On August 10, 1792, the Parisians revolted against the constitutional monarchy, arrested the King, and demanded that a Convention be established to write a new constitution

based on the principle that all people are equal. This "second revolution" used the same basic political premise as the Revolution of 1789, the idea of the sovereignty of the people, but its leaders were prepared to push its application further than the Constitution of 1791.

Though led by the middle-class Jacobins, the second revolution was brought about by urban workers, the *sans-culottes,** who represented a small minority of all France. This uprising brought home the fact that it is no easy matter to create new institutions and a new stable government, and that a major upheaval in society puts in motion political and social passions that are hard to control. The third estate was now in a position to govern France, but it was divided within itself. In 1789 the members of the third estate agreed that the old order must go; by 1792 they could not agree on the nature of the new order. For the moment, the outcome of the second revolution was the suspension of the monarchy and the convoking of a National Convention to write yet another constitution.

JACOBIN CONTROL AND THE TERROR

When the National Convention met in September 1792, the constitutional monarchists were no longer a significant political force. The Girondins, who were more moderate on the question of private property and had the support of the countryside, were the party of stability; the Jacobins, who had become the leaders of the urban group, were the party that wished to extend the Revolution to the lower classes. The Girondins, as the party responsible for a war which was going badly, were weakened, while the Jacobins were gaining in strength.

The National Convention had to decide what to do with the King, and the issue divided the representatives along party lines— the Jacobins wished to execute him, while

---

* "Without breeches." The workers wore trousers rather than breeches which were the fashion of the day.

Louis Capet étant monté sur l'échafaud les mains liées derrière le dos, considéra pendant quelques minutes les objets qui l'environnoient, son confesseur lui dit allez fils ainé de S.t Louis, le ciel vous attend. Cette exécution eut lieu place de la Revolution. ci-devant place Louis XV

A 10 heures 10 minutes la tête de Louis Capet fut séparée de son Corps, et ensuite montrée au peuple, à l'instant les cris de vive la république se firent entendre de toutes parts. Cette exécution se fit place de la Revolution. ci-devant place Louis XV,

The execution of Louis XVI, January 21, 1793   (Bibliothèque Nationale, Paris)

the Girondins wanted to delay a decision. The King was tried in the Convention, and in January 1793 he was convicted of treason against the French state. On January 21 Louis XVI was guillotined. With the execution of the monarch there was no turning back; if the war was lost, the revolutionaries would be tried and executed themselves. People were now, more than ever, fighting for their lives and not simply for the implementation of their political ideas.

The trial had been a struggle between the Jacobins and Girondins for power. The Jacobins had won; by the summer of 1793, with the support of the Parisian working class, they secured control over the Convention.

The Jacobins were led by a number of men who had risen to prominence after 1789 as defenders of the ideals of the Enlightenment

and the Revolution. If a single person stood out among them, it was Maximilien de Robespierre (1758–94), a lawyer from Arras who came to Paris in 1789 as a representative to the Estates-General for the third estate, and who became prominent in the National Assembly. Robespierre believed in republicanism with a fanatical zeal. Known as the "incorruptible," he proclaimed that it was necessary to establish a "republic of virtue" and was willing to use nearly any means to achieve his lofty ends.

In order to cope with the war and with those who opposed their regime, the Jacobins suspended constitutional government and ruled by "emergency decree." They set up a Committee of Public Safety and a Committee of General Security in order to protect the state and make decisions. They reorgan-

"The Death of Marat", July 13, 1793, a painting by Jacques Louis David (1748–1825) depicting the assassination of the revolutionary Marat by Charlotte Corday to avenge the wrongs against the Girondins (Brussels: Musées Royaux des Beaux Arts—Giraudon)

Playing cards of 1794. The one on the left is the symbol of Justice, holding the scales and the sword. The other depicts the philosopher Jean-Jacques Rousseau holding his influential work The Social Contract.   *(Musée Carnavalet, Paris—Hachette)*

ized local governments and put them in the hands of Jacobin supporters. They took over the law courts, initiated food and price controls, and requisitioned grain and property in order to feed Paris and the army. To get more troops, they decreed a *levée en masse* (general conscription) and ordered all Frenchmen to assist in the war effort:

The young men shall go to battle; the married men shall forge arms and transport provisions; the women shall make tents and clothing and shall serve in the hospitals; the children shall turn old linen into lint; the aged shall betake themselves to the public places in order to arouse the courage of the warriors and preach the hatred of kings and the unity of the Republic.[10]

One of the major reasons for the ultimate success of France in waging a long war against Europe was this democratization of the war effort. While other states were still fighting with mercenary armies in the eighteenth-century manner, France was able to raise huge armies, train them, and inspire soldiers with a zeal to win. In revolutionary France the citizen-soldier replaced the professional soldier; it took the rest of Europe until the end of the Napoleonic period to match the new armies and tactics of France.

With Jacobin control came the "Terror," which lasted from September 1793 to June 1794. The Terror, which was an attempt to destroy the internal enemies of the Revolution, was a response to fear, particularly of losing the war, and reflected the willingness of the Jacobins to go to extremes in order to

HYMNE À L'ÊTRE SUPRÊME.

Par T. H. DESORGUES. Musique de GOSSEC. No. I.

The Festival of the Supreme Being, a civic festival organized by the Jacobins in Paris on June 8, 1794. The hymn was one of several songs sung by the participants. (Painting by De Machy: Musée Carnavalet, Paris—Flammarion; Music: Bibliothèque Nationale, Paris—Flammarion)

save the Revolution. Even though they were concerned with social reform—they made it easier for peasants to purchase land, they tried to establish a national education system, and they abolished slavery in the colonies of France—the Jacobins felt that they could not afford to tolerate any opposition. In their zeal to establish an ideal society on earth, they crushed opposition and would not tolerate neutrality on the part of others. Robespierre, a member of the Committee of Public Safety, told the National Convention:

If we have to choose between an excess of patriotic zeal and the empty shell of bad citizenship, or the morass of moderatism, we will not hesitate. A vigorous body suffering from an overabundance of sap is a richer source of strength than a corpse.[11]

In a sense the French Revolution had the spirit of a "religious" movement, and this is clearest in the Jacobin period. The Jacobins set up a new national educational system to indoctrinate as well as to educate. In order to establish their "Republic of Virtue," they devised a new calendar designating the year in which the Republic was established as the "year one." They demanded conformity on all levels—in clothes, in books, and even in songs. A new flag, the Republican tricolour, was introduced, replacing the Bourbon fleur-de-lis; statues were put up to Enlightenment heroes; people were now addressed in the familiar *tu* rather than the more formal *vous*; and everyone was designated as *citoyen*—"citizen." The Jacobins inaugurated a cult of the "worship of the supreme being," and tried to formulate a vaguely deist religion. The guillotine, which they used to kill eighteen thousand people, became the instrument of a new, modern Inquisition.

The idealism and martial spirit of the Revolution is best summed up in the "Marseillaise," sung by the revolutionaries who overthrew the constitutional monarchy and inaugurated the Republic in 1792:

Allons, enfants de la patrie,
Le jour de gloire est arrivé!
Contre nous de la tyrannie
L'étendard sanglant est levé!
Entendez-vous dans ces campagnes
Mugir ces féroces soldats?
Ils viennent jusque dans nos bras
Égorger nos fils, nos compagnes!
Aux armes, citoyens, formez vos bataillons!
    Marchons! marchons!
Qu'un sang impur abreuve nos sillons!

Come, children of our homeland,
Our day of glory now has come!

French Society during the Directory, after the fall of Robespierre and the Jacobins (Bibliothèque Nationale, Paris—Bulloz)

Against us hateful tyranny
Has raised its bloody banner!
Do you hear throughout the land
The fierce soldiers bellow?
They are coming here to us
To slaughter our sons and our companions!
  March on! March on!
Until our furrows are drenched with their impure
    blood!

The Jacobins had gained control during a period when France was in serious danger. In order to save the Revolution and bring an ideal democratic state into existence, they had been willing to suppress the rights of individuals and execute thousands. Thus, on a basic principle, the French Revolution bequeathed a mixed legacy to the Western tradition. The Jacobins were the first political movement to inaugurate a totalitarian regime in the name of liberty and democracy.

The extraordinary tension of life under the Jacobins was the result of a crisis situation. Yet the success of the Jacobins in meeting that crisis led to their downfall. Once France was holding its own against its enemies, Frenchmen were less inclined to accept the continuation of the Terror and the rule of the Committee of Public Safety. Robespierre, deserted by his supporters, was overthrown in June 1794, and Jacobin rule ended with Robespierre's execution on the guillotine.

THE DIRECTORY

With the fall of the Jacobins, it was possible that France would have a "third revolution," but there was no support for such a movement. France was now controlled by the republican centre—the *bourgeoisie* who remained quiet or went underground during the Jacobin period. A new constitution, favouring the educated property-owning citizens, was drawn up and went into effect in 1795. It was called the rule of the Directory, for at the top were five Directors chosen by two houses of parliament. This constitution provided for a complicated balance of powers between all parts of the government, and was designed to avoid the problems arising from a single-legislature system.

From the start, the government of the Directory lacked strength. It had enemies on all sides—royalists and the Church to the right, radical republicans to the left. One of its major preoccupations was holding onto power, and more than once it had to rely upon the army. In one case it called upon a young general named Bonaparte for assistance. Beset by internal coups and external enemies, it is a wonder that the Directory was able to survive.

In fact, a Party of Order—a large group of powerful people at the centre—was appearing in France. Though these people believed in democracy, they feared that it would degenerate into mob rule. They believed in equality, but still wanted to retain the distinctions among citizens, between those who had property and those who did not. Above all, they wanted to avoid a repetition of the chaos and terror of the last five years. Supported by people of this kind, the Directory was able to retain control until 1799. It fought the war successfully, was moderate in its policies at home, and, though not an innovative government, maintained many of the constitutional and civil gains made since 1789.

RETROSPECT 1789-99

Some historians have said that in ten years France did away with a thousand years of history. While this is too sweeping a statement, it does indicate how deep were the changes brought about by the Revolution. Between 1789 and 1799 four elections had taken place and three constitutions had been written. In 1788 France was a corporate state with many feudal relics and an inequitable and inefficient system of taxation. By 1799 it was becoming a centralized state with one judicial, social, political, and economic system. In this manner the Revolution, without the restraint of tradition, accomplished what no absolute monarch had been able to do.

As the political and social structure of France changed, so did the demands upon the citizens: now everyone was expected to give his loyalty to the state. Even warfare was democratized; it was no longer confined to the mercenary armies, and everyone was required to contribute to this new kind of war—"total war." The state now demanded love and obedience, and in a time of crisis insisted that everything be subordinated to its interests. In effect, nationalism was becoming a secular religion.

Unlike the American Revolution, the French Revolution was exported. As France gained success in war and its armies invaded other countries, the Declaration of the Rights of Man and Citizen was posted in every town square. The Revolution, its ideals, and its consequences became part of the Euro-pean political tradition. Later generations of Europeans used the Revolution as a model, in the hope of freeing their peoples while avoiding the pitfalls of the French experience. Even in the twentieth century, the French Revolution has had an enormous impact, not only because of the actual changes it has brought about, but because of what people *thought* it did. Revolutionaries from Lenin to Castro were students of the French Revolution, and the direction they gave to their own movements was shaped in part by their interpretations of what happened in France between 1789 and 1799.

ANALYSIS AND DISCUSSION

1. "The French Revolution inaugurated a new period in Western history." Citing specific examples, indicate in what ways Western civilization was changed during the French Revolution.

2. The rebelliousness of the French aristocracy is one of the most intriguing aspects of the French Revolution. *Explain* clearly why this privileged class rebelled against the system which gave it a special status.

3. Because of our intense curiosity to understand why people act as they do, the causes of an historical event provide some of the most fruitful ground for historical analysis.
The following questions focus attention on some important aspects of the causes of the French Revolution:

a) "By the standards of that time, France under the old regime was an advanced state...." Account for the fact that the first great revolution of modern times occurred in a relatively advanced nation, rather than in a more backward one.

b) The ideas of the Enlightenment contributed significantly to the outbreak of the French Revolution. In what ways did the Enlightenment function as a cause of the Revolution?

c) The French Revolution is generally regarded as the pivotal event in the emergence of the *bourgeoisie* as the dominant class in Western society. Why did the *bourgeoisie* revolt and what role did they play in bringing about the Revolution?

4. What is the third estate?
It is like a strong and robust man whose arms are still in chains. If the privileged order were removed, the nation would not be something less but something more. So, what is the third estate? Everything, but an "everything" shackled and oppressed. What would it be without the privileged order? Everything, but an "everything" free and flourishing.

Outline the social, political, and economic conditions existing in France in 1789 which would account for the widespread popularity of Abbe Sieyès' ideas.

5. "A major upheaval in society puts in motion political and social passions that are hard to control." Show to what extent this was true of the French Revolution from the

Constitution of 1791 to the establishment of the Directory in 1795.

6. Edmund Burke and Thomas Paine wrote their conservative and liberal analyses of the French Revolution in the years prior to the Reign of Terror. In light of their views, discuss how each might have reacted to the events of the decade following 1789.

7. In many ways, France under Robespierre and the Jacobins was the first European example of a modern "totalitarian" state. Discuss this idea with reference to the organization and functioning of a totalitarian state of the twentieth century.

CHAPTER **4**

Napoleonic Europe

THE FRENCH REVOLUTION CHANGED not only the political and religious institutions of France, but also its social structure. Prior to 1789, advancement in society was usually determined by the accident of birth; the success of the Revolution meant that persons of ability, intelligence, and ambition could make their own way, even to the highest levels of power. There is no better example of the opportunities opened up by this social revolution than the career of Napoleon Bonaparte (1769–1821) who, within a dozen years after the fall of the Bastille, became ruler of France and master of much of Europe.

THE RISE OF NAPOLEON

Napoleon was born in 1769 on Corsica, an island off the coast of Italy, into an undistinguished noble family of Italian ancestry. Since Corsica had been acquired by France in 1768, Napoleon was sent to France at the age of ten for his education. He prepared for a career in the French army and chose the artillery as his specialty because it was among the branches of the army least dominated by the aristocracy and consequently more open to promotion. Until 1793 he was a minor officer, but the seizure of power by the Jacobins gave him opportunities to display his extraordinary talents.

Unlike most army officers, Napoleon's political sympathies were with the left. He was attracted to the Jacobins with their policies of social democracy and centralization of power, and when they were in power Napoleon was given command of artillery units in France and Italy and appointed a Brigadier-General. With the fall of the Jacobins in 1794, General Bonaparte's posi-

tion became insecure, but he quickly overcame this problem by rendering valuable services to the Directory. In 1795 he helped to disperse a royalist demonstration in Paris, giving evidence of his loyalty to the regime and thereby winning its gratitude.

In 1796 Napoleon was given the command of an army to challenge Austrian power in Italy. France had been at war since 1792, and though it had fought against many states, its major enemy on land at this time was Austria. Napoleon took his army across the Alps and defeated the Austrians. Since he had been given only vague directions by the French government, he operated as an independent authority. He set up a new administration in northern Italy which he called the Cisalpine Republic, supplied and fed his soldiers from the surrounding countryside, and negotiated a treaty with Austria. The Treaty of Campo Formio, signed in October 1797, gave France control over the Austrian Netherlands and extended its eastern border to the Rhine River. As this was accomplished at a time when the war was not generally going well for France, Napoleon became a national hero and the government was forced to recognize his arrangements and ratify the treaty.

The position and power of General Bonaparte were further consolidated in September 1797 when he was asked by the Directory to help put down a new royalist plot in France. The action against the plotters was successful, but the civilian constitutional government of France was now becoming increasingly dependent upon the military to defend it against internal enemies. Plagued by financial instability, an ineffective constitution, enemies on the left who

*Napoleon as a student in
1785   (Malmaison—Bulloz)*

wanted a more republican and democratic government, and enemies on the right who were royalist, the Directory stumbled from crisis to crisis. Unable to win popularity with domestic measures, it relied more and more on the success of its foreign policy to hold the loyalty of the people. This made Napoleon's position as a successful and popular general all the more important.

After returning from his victories in Italy in 1797, Napoleon was given the command of an army for the invasion of England. He decided, however, that such an invasion was premature, and that it would be better to attack English interests in the Middle East where the opportunity for success was far greater. He wrote on January 29, 1798:

I will not remain here [in France]; there is nothing to be done. They will listen to nothing. I realize that if I stay my reputation will soon be gone. All things fade here, and my reputation is almost forgotten; this little Europe affords too slight a scope; I must go to the Orient; all great reputations have been won there. . . . The Orient awaits a man![1]

Consequently, he took his troops to Egypt. But Napoleon's Egyptian Campaign of 1799 was a failure, for while the French army was able to advance through Egypt, the French navy was defeated by the English fleet under Admiral Horatio Nelson. Napoleon's plan to use Egypt as a base for an invasion of India did not materialize, but these setbacks did not diminish his popularity in France, for the French people were not aware of them.

Meanwhile the political situation in France was increasingly deteriorating, and there were numerous plans in Paris for overthrowing the Directory. The most important group threatening the government was headed by one of the Directors, the Abbé Sieyès. Sieyès had been one of the early revolutionary leaders in 1789, but by 1799 he had changed from a democrat into an advocate of authoritarian rule. He attributed the failure of the Revolution to the inability of any government since 1789 to retain authority, and he now believed that reform must come from above—France must first have order before it could achieve the goals of 1789. Thus Sieyès combined with others, including Lucien Bonaparte (Napoleon's brother), to overthrow the Directory and establish a strong new regime. They looked to Napoleon, who was still in Egypt, for military support and leadership, and when he learned of their plans he hurried back to France in October 1799. Napoleon agreed to the proposed *coup*, for he was now ready to make his move from general to political leader.

The destruction of the Directory was a *coup d'état*—the replacement by force of one ruling group by another. It was not a revolution, because its authors did not offer a coherent program of reform, at least not until they were in power. What the new regime did offer, in the manner of modern authoritarian regimes that seize power illegally, was stability and security. The leaders of the *coup* claimed that the Directory was floundering about both at home and abroad, and they appealed to Frenchmen to support them on behalf of the nation.

The *coup* was relatively simple in execution. Sieyès and his followers convinced the legislature that a Jacobin revolution was under way, and the legislature moved from Paris to a suburb, giving the trusted Napoleon control of the Parisian militia. After some hesitation, the soldiers who were expected to protect the government joined Napoleon in overthrowing it. A self-constituted group in the Directory then assumed authority and delegated power to a provisional government of three consuls, in which Napoleon took the title of First Consul. The Consuls promised to implement the ideals of the Tennis Court Oath, to provide France with a sound administrative organization, just laws, and order and good government. They used the rhetoric of the Revolution to justify their *coup*.

CONSOLIDATION IN FRANCE

Napoleon's ascent to power was spectacular. He always claimed he was "a child of the Revolution," and in one sense this was true, for without the opportunities offered by the Revolution, a man like Napoleon would likely have been a minor functionary in the French army, honourably pensioned off at the end of his career. The circumstances of the Revolution, however, enabled him to become a General at twenty-four, a French national hero at twenty-eight, and ruler of the nation at thirty. Yet his career after 1799 was even more spectacular, for within the next decade he became Emperor of the French and master of much of Europe.

One of Napoleon's greatest accomplishments was the consolidation of his position as ruler of France, for the Revolution had demonstrated repeatedly that it was much easier to obtain power in a revolutionary situation than to hold on to it. Since the fall of Robespierre in 1794, no leader in France had a great national following. Most French politicians had compromised themselves or had become identified with a particular position at one stage or another during the turbulent decade from 1789 to 1799. Napoleon's greatest advantages in 1799 were his military popularity and his lack of political identity. Though he had been associated with the Jacobin group in 1793–94, he had left this far behind by 1799 and was regarded as a hero in the midst of a multitude of corrupt political intriguers. Therefore, he could be, and was for a time, all things to all people.

The first task of his government was to write yet another constitution. Drawn up in six weeks, it appeared to guarantee representative institutions, although it placed most of the power of the state in the hands of Napoleon. He was to control the initiation of legislation, foreign affairs, and the courts. There were representative institutions, called the Legislative Body and the Tribunate, and these gave the illusion of democracy, but they had no real power and could not direct or check the power of the executive. When the constitution was submitted to the French people for ratification, it won overwhelming support. Clearly, the people of France were willing to accept the authority of Napoleon over the insecurities of the last decade.

Napoleon worked to unite the French nation and to establish himself as the symbol of unity. He continued the policy of his French predecessors, whether kings or republicans, of transforming the semi-feudal France of the eighteenth century into a centralized nation-state. He appealed for stability while maintaining many of the popular gains of the Revolution, such as the equality of all under the law. Much of the internal chaos of the decade from 1789 to 1799 was ended, and most Frenchmen welcomed the change.

Many Frenchmen had been unhappy with the changes brought by the Revolution, especially the attacks on the traditional church. Local insurrection and civil war had broken out, most notably in the areas of the Vendée and Brittany. Napoleon was determined to end such disruptive and wasteful fighting, which was hurting France and tying up soldiers badly needed in the struggle against foreign enemies. He did so by promising a general amnesty for political crimes and by offering religious liberty to those who did not support the constitutional church as established by the Civil Constitution of the Clergy in 1790.

Napoleon set out to make France prosperous and efficient as well as politically stable. He created a central bank, standardized the coinage of France, and even, for a time, balanced the budget. Indeed, he displayed in all his domestic measures the administrative gifts for which he became renowned, and proved to be as skilful at civilian administration as he had been as a general. With the appearance of constitutionality, but without real restraints, he could accomplish by decree in a few days what would take a democratic government many months to debate and implement.

The two basic components of Napoleon's domestic policy were his reform of the law and his agreement with the Church. The first, intended to unify the nation and to give France a just and stable regime, was begun when Napoleon established a commission in 1800 to draft a civil law code. The "system" during the old regime was based on a confused mass of feudal and local traditions, and the various governments since 1789 had created a patchwork of legislation rather than a thorough reorganization of the law. The Napoleonic Code, completed in 1804, was the first uniform set of laws that the French nation ever had, and it influenced the laws of much of continental Europe which was occupied and administered at one time or another by Napoleon and his armies.

The *Code Napoléon* preserved many of the principles of 1789. It affirmed freedom of conscience, the supremacy of the state, the equality of all citizens before the law and the right of individuals to choose their own profession. It sought to maintain social order by protecting the institutions of property and the family; property rights were held to be sacred, and the husband was given absolute authority over the family. Thus Napoleon adopted a conservative view of social order which held that certain institutions had to be safeguarded because they cemented society and prevented social disorganization. Yet, compared with the rest of Europe, which was still aristocratic and semi-feudal, the *Code Napoléon* upheld many of the liberal ideas of the *philosophes*. The Code was in many ways a compromise between old and new, and reflected the wishes of the large majority of the former third estate without alienating the other classes.

Napoleon's religious policy was motivated by practical goals rather than religious beliefs. He assumed that the Catholic Church in France must be pacified if order was to be established quickly. He realized that many Frenchmen were more willing to forget the Bourbon monarchy than to discard their priest or abandon their church. In 1800 he began secret negotiations with Pope Pius VII, and when France won major military victories in Italy in 1800 and 1801, the Pope felt he had to come to terms with Napoleon.

The agreement between Napoleon and the Church, known as the Concordat of 1801, was a compromise, but one that favoured Napoleon. The French state was obliged to pay the clergy, Catholic seminaries were allowed to reopen, and the clergy again became responsible to the Papacy. In return,

Napoleon as the heroic warrior crossing the Alps in a military campaign in 1800, painted by Jacques Louis David. Actually, Napoleon rode a mule.   (Malmaison—Giraudon)

the Papacy recognized that property seized from the Church during the revolutionary period was legally the property of those Frenchmen who had purchased it. It also gave the state the right to select French bishops, subject to the veto of the Pope. What Napoleon received, by implication, was Papal recognition of his regime, for the Papacy had refused to negotiate with the Jacobins or any of the other revolutionary regimes that had preceded Napoleon. The Concordat meant that Catholics in France could, with a clear religious conscience, give their support to the Napoleonic regime, in-

Napoleon the Emperor, a sketch for a painting by David (Versailles: Musées Nationaux)

cluding many of its more liberal policies. On the other hand, in order to appease the large number of Frenchmen who viewed the Church as an evil institution opposed to the principles of toleration, democracy, and republicanism, Napoleon insisted upon the right to exclude Papal Bulls from France and upon the end of special privileges for the clergy.

His success with the Concordat, the *Code Napoléon*, and the pacification of France enabled Napoleon to revive the principle of one-man rule. As a result of a referendum held in 1802, he became "First Consul for Life." In another referendum of 1804, Frenchmen overwhelmingly approved his assumption of the position of hereditary Emperor. As an Emperor with strong popular support, Napoleon seemed to combine the mutually exclusive principles of hereditary monarchy and responsibility to the popular will. His success had been extra-

ordinary, and he had no doubt that he was a "man of destiny."

PEACE IN EUROPE

To retain the loyalty of Frenchmen, Napoleon needed to overcome France's enemies. Defeat on the battlefield would have brought social disorder and possible foreign occupation of the country, and Napoleon's popularity in France was in part based on the sense of security he gave to Frenchmen. Ultimately, however, only peace would enable him to consolidate whatever gains he made at home and abroad.

When Napoleon seized power in 1799, France was still at war. French armies had already defeated a collection of states — the First Coalition — which had included Austria, Prussia, and England. A new grouping, the Second Coalition, including England, Austria, and Russia, was formed in 1799 with the aim of stopping France from gaining more territory and spreading the ideas of the Revolution throughout Europe. It was these countries that Napoleon had to face.

Napoleon pursued the land war in Europe with great success. He easily defeated the Austrians and, in February 1801, signed the Treaty of Lunéville with the Hapsburg Empire. The treaty gave France legal control of Italy and enabled Napoleon to reorganize the numerous German states into a series of larger, more powerful states based on the French model; it also effectively terminated the Holy Roman Empire which had been founded in the year 962.

Once peace had been made with Austria, the Second Coalition was destroyed as an effective alliance. Russia withdrew from the war, feeling that its major interests lay in the Near East and the Mediterranean. The only holdout was Britain, and here Napoleon negotiated the Peace of Amiens, which was signed by both nations in March 1802. This settlement gave England control of the seas, but left the French victories on the continent intact. Thus, for the first time in a decade, Europe enjoyed peace. In the ten years of war, the French had defended the Revolution and made great gains on the European continent. After Amiens the French Foreign Minister, Charles Maurice de Talleyrand, who had survived many changes of government, said that France was in the best position in its history and that it could not wish for more.

WAR AGAIN

Up to 1802 it could be said that Napoleon still worked within the system of statehood and sovereignty as it had evolved in Europe since the Renaissance. Though he added territory to France, he recognized that Europe was composed of a number of large entities, each independent, each with the right to exercise power within its territories and to make war and peace. After 1802 his vision changed. "My power," he said on December 30, 1802, "proceeds from my reputation, and my reputation from the victories I have won. My power would fail if I were not to support it with more glory and more victories. Conquest has made me what I am; only conquest can maintain me. . . . A man must be firm, have a stout heart, or else leave on one side war and government."[2]

Napoleon now began to think in terms of a universal empire with France at the centre. This ambition was not new in France and in Europe—it can be seen in the careers of some earlier French monarchs, notably Louis XIV, and in the actions of other European rulers, including many Holy Roman emperors— but such ambitions had failed, and a large portion of Europe, had slowly evolved into a system of nation-states. Napoleon now wished to transform this state system into a single imperial organization with France at its head and with himself as a world emperor.

The instrument on which this quest for empire depended was the revolutionary army. The Revolution introduced into France the first mass armies of modern times. Whereas wars in the eighteenth century had been fought with professional armies, the French Revolutionary armies were the first in Europe to demonstrate the potential of the citizen-soldier. The eighteenth-century professional army fought in order to gain tactical advantage, not to

kill or be killed, for such armies were both small and very expensive to recruit and train. Often, an eighteenth-century army spent a good deal of time trying to occupy a strategic point, and warfare was very much like a chess game, with emphasis on manoeuvre and tactics. Into this formal, stylized, regulated system, Napoleon and the generals of the French Revolution introduced the unskilled, unprofessional mass soldier, who could not drill as well as his professional counterpart, but who could move much more quickly and whose sole aim was to defeat the opposing force.

Recruited through conscription, the new armies were much larger and much more committed to victory than the old. Napoleon was particularly adept at leading such an army. He was not a skilled planner, and he often made up his strategy and tactics as he went along; but no one was his match at improvisation on the battlefield. He ignored the old rules in order to surprise and demolish his opponent, and he inspired his soldiers to heroic deeds. In Napoleon's early years as Emperor, his battles were examples of a new military style and a new, spontaneous kind of leadership.

The peace of Amiens did not last, and war was resumed in 1803 as a result of a dispute between France and England. This was the beginning of a long sporadic war, which lasted until Napoleon's defeat in 1814. In broad terms the war was fought over antagonistic conceptions of Europe and the world. While Napoleon sought to establish a universal empire with France at the centre, Britain was determined to continue the state system of Europe, keep control of the seas, and dominate world trade. Other European states, in their own self-interest and in order to keep their independence and sovereignty, generally had to combine with England against France. Therefore, Napoleon knew that he had to defeat England to realize his imperial dream, and from 1803 to 1805 he massed soldiers on the French coast and threatened to invade England. However, under the leadership of Admiral Nelson, England maintained its naval superiority and at Trafalgar, in 1805, destroyed a large part of the French navy. Thus the invasion of England never materialized.

THE NAPOLEONIC ORGANIZATION OF EUROPE

A series of stunning victories on land enabled Napoleon to reorganize Europe. The empire of Napoleon, at its height, included Holland, Belgium, the left bank of the Rhine, part of Germany on the North Sea, the west coast of Italy down to the city of Rome, and the west coast of modern-day Yugoslavia. There were a number of satellite states: the Duchy of Warsaw, the rest of Italy, the Confederation of the Rhine, and Spain. By 1812 only Russia, Great Britain, and the Ottoman Empire held European territory that was not controlled by or allied with France.

Wherever Napoleon gained control, he introduced some measure of reform, and many of the ideas of the Revolution spread throughout Europe as a result of his conquests. He reorganized governments, making them more rational and efficient. His greatest influence, however, was in the area of law. The Napoleonic Code was introduced into every conquered state, establishing equality under the law and increasing the possibility of social mobility. It had a lasting effect on the legal systems of the low countries, Italy, and western Germany. Outside of Europe, many Latin-American countries, as well as Louisiana and Quebec, were under French influence during this period and absorbed some of the principles of the Enlightenment through the Napoleonic Code.

Napoleon was a major force in abolishing the feudal structure throughout Europe. Against the traditional view that each person was essentially a member of a guild or class, the French armies proclaimed the idea of citizenship and spread the view that all citizens were members of a unified nation. The new state would be centralized and secular rather than feudal and religious. Napoleon introduced toleration for all religions and took away the right of the Church to collect tithes and hold special courts. In many areas of Europe, in fact, the corporate feudal structure of society was ended forever by French conquest.

In some parts of Europe, especially in Italy, Napoleon was first viewed as a liberator. In contrast to the other monarchs of the continent, he was progressive and enlightened, and for many years the lower classes of Europe welcomed French victories. However, as time went on his subjects found his rule oppressive; they came to resent the French presence and the demands made on them to supply Napoleon with goods and men for his wars. The spirit of nationalism, which had been fostered by the Revolutionary armies and Napoleon, was now turned against the French conquerors.

THE CONTINENTAL SYSTEM

Napoleon's major competitor for power was still England. If he was to dominate Europe, England had to be defeated, or at least weakened. The plan that he adopted, known as the Continental System, was introduced in 1805 and was designed to impose a continental boycott by all of France's subjects and friends on English trade in order to decrease English exports, thereby ruining English industry. Napoleon expected that the Continental System would enable France to replace England as the major trading partner of all European nations, and that England's economic ruin would make it easier for France to become the master of continental Europe.

The Continental System failed to achieve its goals. England developed other markets, especially in Latin America, and used its enormous wealth, gained from the Industrial Revolution, to finance anti-French schemes in Europe. In addition, the Continental System was not a "common market"; Napoleon's tariff policy favoured French goods over those of other European countries and this caused resentment within the system. In the end, Napoleon failed to impose his policy on his reluctant partners.

THE RESPONSE TO NAPOLEON

As the Napoleonic conquests in Europe continued, resentment began to mount against French ideas and institutions. The argument was put forth, especially in the German states, that different peoples had their particular characteristics deeply rooted in their past and that their *own* traditions, not those of France, should determine the character of their society and the basis of change and reform. This reaction was a manifestation of modern nationalism.

Enlightenment thinkers had viewed the individual both as an independent being and as part of a common humanity. The proponents of nationalism, however, saw the individual as an integral part of the community. Nationalists argued that people received their identity from the special historical and cultural group to which they belonged. They felt that differences between human groups were far more significant than any universal qualities common to all people. The spirit of modern nationalism evident in the early years of the French Revolution had combined both the universalism of the Enlightenment and love of country. However, some of the later forms of nationalism cared little for or rejected the notion of a common humanity.

The roots of nationalism run deep in European history. The first major work setting forth this new idea was J. G. Herder's *Ideas on the Philosophy of the History of Mankind* (a multi-volumed work published from 1784 to 1791). Herder, who had lived in several German states, believed that each people had a unique spirit or genius, manifested in folkways, customs, institutions, and ideas. Thus, while the Enlightenment philosophers proclaimed the idea of a common human nature and therefore the desirability of a universal solution to social and political problems, Herder stated that there is no absolute standard in the universe, but only particular standards that depend on the character of each national group. Herder thought that each people or culture had its own unique and valuable contribution to make to world civilization. Should any group be destroyed by another, the whole world would be the loser.

The response to the new idea of nationalism was particularly strong in the German states and in the Austrian Empire. The peoples of middle Europe wanted their own strong state and their own intellectual life, free from French or other foreign domina-

tion. In the various German states, a conscious national identity began to develop that cut across existing political boundaries. A similar frame of mind can be seen in other areas, especially Italy and Spain.

THE CAMPAIGN IN RUSSIA

In eastern Europe a treaty between France and Russia, which Napoleon had negotiated, gradually broke down, and Russia and France drifted into war. Czar Alexander I had abandoned the Continental System in December 1810 and was not happy with Napoleon's attempts to re-establish an independent Polish state on Russia's borders, while Napoleon was angry with the Czar's lack of co-operation in the Continental System. The military and diplomatic preparations for war against Russia were begun in 1811. Napoleon assembled a huge army of French and allied troops—the "Grand Army"—and made treaties with Prussia and Austria in order to obtain their neutrality. These treaties, made under threat, were only good as long as Napoleon could continue his military domination of eastern Europe. In order to turn English attention away from Europe to the Atlantic, Napoleon fostered enmity between England and the United States, and in June 1812 England and the United States went to war. Thus, with Russia diplomatically and militarily isolated, and England distracted, Napoleon, in the early summer of 1812, with an army of over 600 000 men, invaded Russia.

The Russian strategy was to retreat, and to try to deprive Napoleon of his supplies as he was drawn into the vastness of Russian territory; a direct encounter with Napoleon's army was to be avoided. The Russians, like many of the other powers, learned from Napoleon; in order to defeat him, they now began to adopt his own military tactics of swift movement and living off the land. His enemies had superior numbers, and time was not on his side. If he could not defeat the Russians quickly, especially before the harsh winter set in, he would be in serious difficulty.

Napoleon raced through the country in the summer of 1812, while the Russians continued to retreat. As the Russians moved backwards, they adopted a "scorched earth" policy—destroying crops so that Napoleon's army could not easily live off the land. His armies reached Moscow on September 14, but the Russians set the city ablaze, leaving Napoleon with a worthless prize. He had mistakenly assumed that once he reached Moscow, Czar Alexander I would have to sue for peace, but Alexander made no such move. Meanwhile winter was approaching.

Finally, in October, Napoleon realized that he could not spend the winter in a deserted city in the middle of Russia, and he ordered his army to retreat. The winter of 1812 came early and was especially hard, and the Russians did everything in their power to deny Napoleon any supplies. The retreat became a long nightmare. Exhausted, hungry, and freezing, the Grand Army straggled back. Its members were decimated; out of 600 000, about 50 000 of Napoleon's soldiers lived through the experience. One of Napoleon's generals, the Marquis de Caulaincourt, described the retreat in his memoirs:

Cossacks kept up perpetual raids along the road, which they constantly crossed between one division and another—or even, when there was a gap, between one regiment and another....Wherever there was no shooting to fear, wherever transport waggons were moving along in disorder or unarmed stragglers were making their way as best they could, the Cossacks improvised sudden attacks, killing and wounding, robbing all those whose lives they spared, and looting waggons and carriages when they came upon them.

It is not difficult to imagine the perturbation spread by such tactics and their effect on the army's morale. What was worse, they made communication extremely difficult, not only between one corps and another, but between one division and another....

The cold was so intense that bivouacking was no longer supportable. Bad luck for those who fell asleep by a campfire! ... One constantly found men who, overcome by the cold, had been forced to drop out and had fallen to the ground, too weak or too numb to stand.... Once these poor wretches fell asleep, they were dead. If they resisted the craving for sleep, another passerby would help them along a little farther, thus prolonging their agony for a short while but not saving them; for in this condition the drowsiness

Napoleon as the enemy. A Russian satire depicts Napoleon as a wolf posing as a liberator. The Czar, dressed as a peasant, holds Napoleon, exposing him for what he is. (*Slavonic Division, the New York Public Library—Astor, Lenox, and Tilden Foundations*)

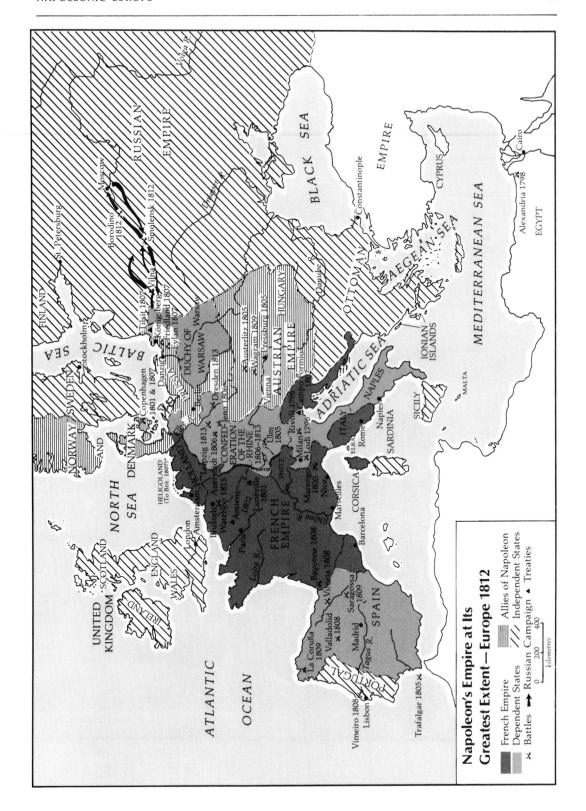

FINLAND

RUSSIAN EMPIRE

St. Petersburg
Moscow
Borodino 1812 ✗
Smolensk 1812 ✗
Vilna
Tilsit 1807
Königsberg
Eylau 1807 ✗
Friedland 1807 ✗
Danzig

NORWAY

SWEDEN

Stockholm

BALTIC SEA

DENMARK

Copenhagen 1801 & 1807

PRUSSIA

Berlin

DUCHY OF WARSAW

Warsaw

Dresden 1813 ✗

Jena 1806 ✗

Leipzig 1813 ✗

CONFEDERATION OF THE RHINE 1806–1813

Auerstädt 1806 ✗

Vienna

AUSTRIAN EMPIRE

HUNGARY

Austerlitz 1805 ✗

▲ Wagram 1809
▲ Pressburg 1805

Dnieper R.

Dniester R.

Danube R.

BLACK SEA

OTTOMAN EMPIRE

Constantinople

AEGEAN SEA

CYPRUS

EMPIRE

Alexandria 1798

Cairo

EGYPT

MEDITERRANEAN SEA

MALTA

IONIAN ISLANDS

SICILY

Naples

NAPLES

ADRIATIC SEA

Campo Formio 1797

Rivoli 1797 ✗

ITALY

Rome

Milan ▲
✗ Lodi 1796
Marengo 1800 ✗

SWITZ.

Ulm 1805 ✗

ELBA

SARDINIA

CORSICA

Nice

Marseilles

Barcelona

FRENCH EMPIRE

Paris

Brussels
Amiens 1802 ▲
Waterloo 1815 ✗
Lunéville 1801 ▲

HOLLAND

Amsterdam

HELIGOLAND (To Brit. 1807)*

NORTH SEA

London

UNITED KINGDOM

ENGLAND

SCOTLAND

WALES

IRELAND

ATLANTIC OCEAN

Loire R.

Bayonne 1808 ✗

Vitoria 1808 ✗

Saragossa 1809 ✗

Valladolid 1808 ✗

Madrid

La Coruña 1809 ✗

SPAIN

Tagus R.

PORTUGAL

Lisbon

Vimeiro 1808 ✗

Trafalgar 1805 ✗

Rhône R.

Volga R.

Napoleon's Empire at Its Greatest Extent — Europe 1812

▓ French Empire	‖ Allies of Napoleon
▒ Dependent States	∕∕∕ Independent States
✗ Battles ➤ Russian Campaign	▲ Treaties

0 200 400
kilometres

engendered by cold is irresistibly strong. Sleep comes inevitably; and to sleep is to die. I tried in vain to save a number of these unfortunates. The only words they uttered were to beg me, for the love of God, to go away and let them sleep. To hear them, one would have thought this sleep was their salvation. Unhappily, it was a poor wretch's last wish; but at least he ceased to suffer, without pain or agony. Gratitude, and even a smile, were imprinted on his discoloured lips. What I have related about the effects of extreme cold and of this kind of death by freezing is based on what I

Napoleon as the Devil, a German caricature of 1813   *(British Museum—John R. Freeman)*

saw happen to thousands of individuals. The road was covered with their corpses.[3]

It was clear that the Emperor was no longer invincible. Another coalition was formed as Prussia and Austria hastened to join Russia in a union supported by English subsidies. Moved by national sentiment, many youths in the German states joined anti-Napoleonic armies to fight for "liberation." Napoleon managed to raise yet another army, but he could not carry the day against the combined forces of the nations of Europe, and he was defeated at the "Battle of Nations" at Leipzig, in Germany, in October 1813. On another front, British and Spanish forces, fighting under the Duke of Wellington since 1808, crossed from Spain into France. Six months later, on March 31, 1814, the coalition armies took Paris. Napoleon was dethroned and his dream of empire shattered.

THE RESTORATION IN FRANCE

The immediate problem in Europe was what to do with France and Napoleon. The diplomat Talleyrand, who had served Napoleon but had changed sides at the right moment, was now at the head of the royalist group. He persuaded the allies to restore France's "legitimate" government, the Bourbon dynasty, which had been deposed during the Revolution. Fearing another revolutionary outbreak in France and yet another European war, the four coalition powers accepted Talleyrand's principle. They invited the older of the two brothers of the executed Louis XVI to assume the throne of France. As Louis XVI's son (who would have been Louis XVII) had died in 1795, the new monarch called himself Louis XVIII.

The lessons of the revolutionary period had not been lost on the new King. Having left France twenty-five years before, he did not wish to be driven out again. With the agreement of the allied powers, he became a constitutional monarch and issued the Charter of 1814, a document which contained many of the Napoleonic reforms, particularly the principles of the Napoleonic Code. It established a parliamentary form of government, provided for an independent judicial system, and declared the sale of much national property in the last twenty-five years to be final and irrevocable. Louis XVIII had the wisdom not to try to restore the old order, and thus, although a Bourbon was once again the hereditary monarch of France, the old notions of absolute power and divine right were not revived.

The allies negotiated peace terms with the new government of France. The First Peace of Paris, signed in May 1814, was exceptionally moderate under the circumstances. France was given its extended boundaries of 1792 (not the pre-revolutionary boundaries of 1789) and was not asked to reimburse the allies for the damage and devastation of the war. Napoleon was sent into exile on the small island of Elba off the Italian coast and, as a cruel joke, given the title of Emperor of Elba. All further details of the European settlement were left for an international conference to be held in Vienna.

THE CONGRESS OF VIENNA

The gathering in Vienna in September 1814 was the greatest assembly of diplomats, statesmen, kings, major and minor princes, and ecclesiastics that Europe had ever seen. Outwardly a diplomatic conference, it often resembled an enormous party. There was great joy over the defeat of Napoleon and a feeling of relief that the "revolutionary" menace that had haunted Europe for the last twenty-five years was finally overcome.

Although representatives of nearly every European sovereignty were present, decisions were made by the statesmen who spoke for the great powers: Prince Metternich of Austria (the dominant personality of the meeting), Czar Alexander of Russia, Hardenberg of Prussia, and Lord Castlereagh of England. These statesmen represented the major members of the coalition which had defeated Napoleon, and they believed that they had the responsibility for maintaining stability on the European continent. The Congress of Vienna effectively recognized one of the important principles of the modern nation-state system—that the great powers must agree on important decisions. Small states counted little because they could not change the balance of power without the support of at least one of the major powers.

One other state took part in the deliberations—France. At the beginning of the negotiations, France was excluded, but the shrewd diplomatic efforts and sense of reality of Talleyrand soon gave France a place in the discussions. He pointed out that Europe needed France as much as France needed Europe. If France were excluded from the major decisions, it could not be held responsible for supporting the new order. On the other hand, if France were invited to participate in the agreement, it could be expected to support the forces of stability and order. Talleyrand's logic was persuasive. Since the other great powers supported a "state system," they could not deprive such a powerful state as France of a voice in the settlement. They wished France to become a partner in the new Europe and not, as it had been in the last twenty-five years, a force for revolution. The "big four" thus became the "big five."

The "principle of legitimacy" was constantly employed by the big powers in their settlement. Legitimacy meant that each state had a legal ruler—the one who had ruled prior to 1789. Looking back with nostalgia, some diplomats envisaged a wholesale restoration of the Europe of the old regime. Others, however, prepared to make reasonable compromises. They understood that the realities of power were no longer what they had been prior to 1789, and that the "legitimate" ruler would not always be acceptable. As disagreements over territory developed, it became evident that no large power was prepared to endorse legitimacy at the expense of its own self-interest.

The most divisive issue at the conference was the question of the territories of Poland and Saxony. Alexander I wanted to control Poland, and Prussia was willing to give it to him in exchange for the kingdom of Saxony, a German principality whose ruler had not abandoned Napoleon until the last moment. Neither Austria nor England were willing to accept this, for fear of upsetting the balance of power in middle Europe. Again, Talley-

rand entered the scene. He signed an agreement with England and Austria in January 1815, pledging to go to war should Prussia and Russia force the issue. Thereafter, a compromise was quickly reached; Alexander received part of Poland and Prussia annexed part of Saxony.

Once the Poland-Saxony question was settled, the way was cleared for agreement on central Europe. Austria received territory in nothern Italy to be added to its empire, and members of the Hapsburg ruling family were put in control of other areas of Italy. The German lands were organized into thirty-nine separate sovereignties (there had been more than three hundred states before Napoleon), and a German confederation of these states was established, even though it had no real authority. In dealing with the Italian and German problems, the Congress ignored the powerful desire for national unity and independence that had burst forth in both these areas, especially in the German states, in the war against Napoleon.

One difficulty in any reorganization of the German states was the fact that both Prussia and Austria had some claim to German leadership. Prussia, with its capital in Berlin, was an old German state with a strong military tradition. Since the mid seventeenth century, a remarkable ruling family, the Hohenzollerns, had added to the strength and territory of Prussia until it had become a force in Europe as well as among the German states. During the Napoleonic years, Prussia underwent major political reform and reorganization; serfdom was abolished, and the middle class was given the right to own property and to serve in the army. Prussia had thereafter played a major role in rousing German sentiment against Napoleon and ultimately in defeating him. It was also becoming the centre of German culture.

On the other hand, the Austrian Empire, with its capital in Vienna, was a conglomeration of different groups of peoples speaking many languages. The ruling family, the Hapsburgs, had been Holy Roman emperors for centuries and traditionally laid claim to the leadership of the German peoples. But as their empire developed, it came to include

Hungary, Bohemia, and parts of Italy. To recognize the right of a national group, like the Germans, to form their own state would have meant the end of the Austrian Empire, and Metternich therefore did his utmost to suppress the spirit of nationalism.Both Austria and Prussia wished to prevent the other from leading Germany, and a national German state uniting all peoples of German nationality was regarded by both France in the west and Russia in the east as a menace. Thus, after the Congress of Vienna, central Europe, though not as chaotic as in pre-1789 days, was still a patchwork of separate principalities, and not a group of nation-states.

The rest of the peace settlement was reached without discord. All agreed that a number of buffer states should be established on France's frontier. Holland and Belgium were united into the Kingdom of the Netherlands. Prussia received much of the left bank of the Rhine. Switzerland was restored, and the kingdom of Sardinia-Piedmont was given additional territory.

While the diplomats were hammering out a final agreement, they were again faced, as if in a bad dream, with the threat of Napoleon. In March 1815 Napoleon escaped from Elba, landed in France, and marched with a small army to Paris, proclaiming the renewal of his empire. Some Frenchmen flocked to join Napoleon, for although the restoration of the monarchy had brought to the throne a reasonable king, many of the royalists and clergy who returned with Louis XVIII had attacked all the reforms that had come into effect since 1789. Nor had the magic of Napoleon's name and the glory of his rule been forgotten.

The return of Napoleon united the powers at Vienna as nothing else could, and they agreed to raise an army under the British general, the Duke of Wellington. On June 18, 1815, near the town of Waterloo in Belgium, the allied army won a decisive victory. Napoleon surrendered to the English, who exiled him to the island of St. Helena in the South Atlantic, where he lived until his death in 1821.

Napoleon's last military interlude, called "The Hundred Days," proved costly for France. In a new treaty, the Second Peace of Paris, France lost more territory and was assessed an indemnity of 700 million francs. Until the indemnity was paid, France was to be occupied by an allied army. The changes did not substantially transform the Vienna agreements; if anything, "The Hundred Days" made the European powers more wary of change, of revolution, of liberalism, and of anything which might endanger the internal stability of regimes or the new balance of power.

The accord at Vienna was the most significant diplomatic agreement of the nineteenth century. It laid a foundation for a long period of relative peace among the European powers by creating something of a balance of power and thus limiting the possibility of major wars. Its weakness was the assumption that the status quo could be maintained, since it either ignored or sought to suppress the forces of change, most especially the principles of nationalism and liberalism. Thus it virtually guaranteed that new revolutionary situations would develop. For all the verbiage about the idea of legitimacy, it was not a peace which attempted a complete restoration of the old regime; on the other hand, it did nothing to satisfy the aspirations of peoples to form nation-states and to live by the principles of 1789. Yet it was durable; for a century after Vienna, there were no world wars. If the diplomats lacked vision, they did at least have a sense of the possible.

THE NAPOLEONIC MYTH

Napoleon was a product of the Revolution, but was he "a child of the Revolution" as he claimed? He certainly had no sympathy with liberty or nationalism when these clashed with his ambitions. At the same time, he was a defender of the secular state, the equality of people under law, and the social principle of "careers open to talent." His own career is difficult to evaluate when one considers the means which he used to achieve his ends. If he believed in equality, he also believed in imposing it from above. He preferred artillery to persuasion, and, in the end, force was his means of government.

Napoleon on his way to exile on St. Helena after "The Hundred Days", as portrayed by a British officer on board   (British Museum—John R. Freeman)

And the principle of equality did not cover Napoleon himself, or his family, for he became an emperor and they princes and kings. At the height of his success, he could claim more power than any of the divine-right rulers of France.

Napoleon's support came from the same people who, in 1789, attacked the old regime. The peasants, workers, and middle classes responded to him, preferring the enlightened despotism of a Napoleon to the chaos of a revolutionary democracy or the divine-right authority of a traditional king. He created the illusion of representative government while transforming himself into an absolute emperor. His great achievement was administrative—he organized the French state and rationalized its laws. By his ability to govern France, he solidified much of the egalitarian impetus of the revolutionary period. The Revolution had brought years

of political instability and uncertainty; Napoleon offered stability and order.

By introducing a system which combined absolute rule and popular will, Napoleon added one more alternative for the French political tradition. This alternative has been called Caesarian Democracy, and though it harks back to Roman practices it is peculiar to modern times. Like Caesar, Napoleon took the reins of government in a chaotic situation and imposed order. Like Caesar too, he was able to win the loyalty of the people, though he had a deep contempt for democratic forms. He was neither the first nor the last ruler to demonstrate that absolutism could have a popular base.

On St. Helena, writing his memoirs, Napoleon rearranged and coloured his exploits and his life to make it appear to posterity that he had stood for order against chaos and for the people against the forces of reaction. Thus grew the Napoleonic legend, aided by some writers of the Romantic movement who saw Napoleon as a hero and liberator thwarted by the forces of evil. On St. Helena Napoleon wrote:

I sealed the gulf of anarchy, and I unravelled chaos. I purified the revolution, raised the people, and strengthened monarchy. I stimulated every ambition, rewarded every merit, and pushed back the bounds of glory! All that amounts to something! . . .

Had I succeeded, I would have died with the reputation of the greatest man that ever existed. As it is, although I have failed, I shall be considered as an extraordinary man: my elevation was unparalleled, because unaccompanied by crime. I have fought fifty pitched battles, almost all of which I have won. I have framed and carried into effect a code of laws that will bear my name to the most distant posterity. I raised myself from nothing to be the most powerful monarch in the world. Europe was at my feet. I have always been of opinion that the sovereignty lay in the people. In fact, the imperial government was a kind of republic. Called to the head of it by the voice of the nation, my maxim was [that careers are open to talents] without distinction of birth or fortune, and this system of equality is the reason that your oligarchy hates me so much.[4]

The legend in some ways was mightier than the man. In the period after 1815, those who longed for national liberation from traditional monarchies associated Napoleon with the ideas of freedom and liberty. He was seen as the prophet of Italian liberation

Napoleon romanticized, a medallion by Pierre-Jean David d'Angers, dated 1832   (Bibliothèque Nationale, Paris—Giraudon)

The return of the ashes of Napoleon to Paris, December 15, 1840   (Bibliothèque Nationale, Paris—Hachette)

from Austrians, and of Polish liberation from Russians. His kind of leadership—an absolute ruler supported by popular will—was seen as an answer to the aspirations of the middle and lower classes, who were fighting for social and political reform against reactionary and privileged rulers and aristocracies. The cost of Napoleon's wars was often forgotten.

EUROPE AND THE WORLD IN 1815

The Vienna settlement, though a compromise between the old and the new, recognized the changing structure of power within Europe and the world. Russia had emerged as a great force in Europe, while Prussia had become a powerful modern state. Austria continued to exist as a large empire. Guided by the conservative policies of Metternich, Austria tried to defeat any liberal or national movement which might threaten her stability and internal organization.

By far the most powerful state to emerge

from the defeat of Napoleon was Great Britain. The colonial rivalry with France, culminating in the Wars of Empire in the eighteenth century, had long ago ended in the humiliation of France. After Vienna, France had neither a large navy nor significant colonial enterprises, while the other colonial empires—the Spanish, Portuguese, and Dutch—were on the wane. But the British Empire, spurred on by the Industrial Revolution and British control of sea power, had yet to reach its height. The British did not wish to acquire land on the European continent, but they energetically moved across oceans and added to their possessions. In 1815 they ruled British North America and asserted claims in other areas on that continent, such as the Oregon Territory. The West Indies were under British control, and Britain carried on the brisk trade with Latin-America that had begun during the French Revolution and the Napoleonic Wars. In the East they governed India and other territories, including Ceylon, Mauri-

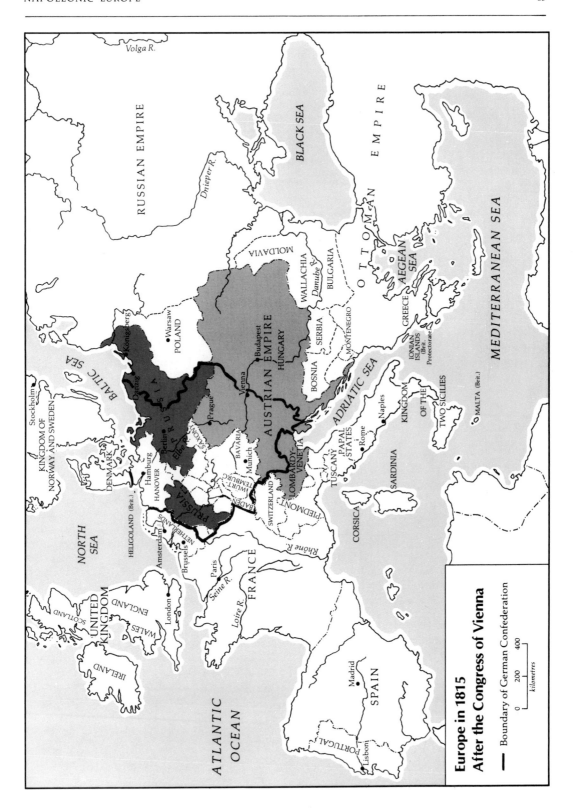

**Europe in 1815
After the Congress of Vienna**

— Boundary of German Confederation

Volga R.

RUSSIAN EMPIRE

Dnieper R.

BLACK SEA

OTTOMAN EMPIRE

MEDITERRANEAN SEA

AEGEAN SEA

GREECE

IONIAN ISLANDS (Brit. Protectorate)

MALTA (Brit.)

ADRIATIC SEA

MOLDAVIA

WALLACHIA

Danube R.

BULGARIA

SERBIA

BOSNIA

MONTENEGRO

Budapest

AUSTRIAN EMPIRE

HUNGARY

Vienna

Prague

LOMBARDY-VENETIA

PIEDMONT

PAPAL STATES

Rome

TUSCANY

Naples

KINGDOM OF THE TWO SICILIES

SARDINIA

CORSICA

BALTIC SEA

Königsberg

Danzig

POLAND

Warsaw

P R U S S I A

Berlin

Elbe

SAXONY

BAVARIA

Munich

WÜRTTEMBERG

BADEN

SWITZERLAND

Rhône R.

Stockholm

KINGDOM OF NORWAY AND SWEDEN

DENMARK

HELIGOLAND (Brit.)

Hamburg

HANOVER

PRUSSIA

Amsterdam

NETHERLANDS

Brussels

NORTH SEA

UNITED KINGDOM

SCOTLAND

IRELAND

WALES

ENGLAND

London

Paris

Seine R.

FRANCE

Loire R.

ATLANTIC OCEAN

SPAIN

Madrid

PORTUGAL

Lisbon

0 200 400
kilometres

"The Apotheosis of Napoleon" by Jean Auguste Dominique Ingres (1780–1867), dated 1853. Napoleon is depicted as a classical hero ascending to heaven.   (Musée du Louvre—Giraudon)

tius, and the Cape of Good Hope. The Atlantic and Indian oceans were British seas in the early nineteenth century.

In terms of wealth and power, Europe continued its domination of the globe in the early nineteenth century. The United States remained isolationist, fearing European influence and desiring to expand its own frontiers to the west rather than playing a role in European power politics. Other peoples of the world seemed unable to compete with the intellectual advances, or to withstand the military power, of Europeans. As Europe began to industrialize and create wealth unprecedented in human history, the feeling among Europeans of superiority over all other peoples seemed to be further confirmed.

ANALYSIS AND DISCUSSION

1. "The Revolution had demonstrated that it was much easier to obtain power in a revolutionary situation than to hold on to it." Explain Napoleon's success in consolidating his power whereas earlier leaders had failed.

2. Napoleon's domestic policy combined a conservative view of the social order with many of the liberal ideas of the philosophes. Illustrate this combination of conservatism and liberalism in Napoleon's domestic policy.

3. Despite his military successes and his strong hold on the French people, Napoleon was eventually toppled from power by a combination of personal weaknesses and external forces beyond his control. Explain clearly the combination of factors which led to Napoleon's downfall.

4. "Although a political dictator, Napoleon more than anyone else preserved the ideals and accomplishments of the Revolution." Defend or refute this statement with reference to the social, legal, and religious reforms of the period and the degree of military security won by Napoleon's armies.

5. "Enlightened leaders in France may have believed in the concept of a world community but the example of the French Revolutionary citizen army and resistance to the Napoleonic Empire gave birth to the idea of the modern nation state." Analyse this statement as an explanation of the growth of nationalism in Europe in the early nineteenth century.

6. In Napoleonic Europe, one effective way of influencing public opinion was through the arts. With a highly controversial figure such as Napoleon the propagandists were hard at work on both sides of the issue. Examine and compare the illustrations selected for this chapter. What are the various images of Napoleon which are being portrayed? What motives might each artist have had? What might have been the impact of each of these depictions of the Emperor?

7. "If the diplomats [at the Congress of Vienna] lacked vision, they did at least have a sense of the possible." Explain this comment in terms of the Vienna accord and its long-term effect upon Europe.

SYNTHESIS AND EVALUATION   CHAPTERS 3 AND 4

1. Thomas Jefferson was a follower of Locke's belief that society has a responsibility to protect the "life, liberty and pursuit of happiness" of the individual while Maximillien Robespierre was the heir of Rousseau's belief that the idea of "liberty . . . related to the community's rather than the individual's interest." Apply these ideas to the progress of the American and French Revolutions.

2. "Revolutions seldom break out as the result of poverty and oppression alone. They are complex political, intellectual, social and economic movements which usually occur when a system of government fails to cope with its own difficulties." Examine the causes of the French Revolution in the light of this statement.

3. A major historical event such as the French Revolution exerts immense influence on the lives of people. After a careful examination of the results of the Revolution, assess to what extent it resulted in an improvement or a decline in the quality of life for Frenchmen and their European neighbours.

4. "The great man is always representative either of existing forces or of forces which he helps to create by way of challenge to existing authority. But the higher degree of creativity may perhaps be assigned to those great men who helped to mould forces which carried them to greatness rather than to those who rode to greatness on the back of already existing forces." (E.H. Carr, *What Is History?*) After a careful examination of Napoleon's career, assess his greatness in the light of this statement.

CHAPTER **5**

Industrialism and Ideologies

1733 Kay invents "flying shuttle"
1764 Hargreaves invents "spinning jenny"
1769 Watt patents steam engine
1779 Crompton invents steam-driven loom
1798 Publication of *Lyrical Ballads* by Wordsworth and Coleridge
1807 Fulton makes first steamboat
1814 Stephenson uses steam-engine for railroad
1820s Utopian Socialism— Saint-Simon, Fourier, Owen

THE DEFEAT OF NAPOLEON AND THE reorganization of Europe at the Congress of Vienna did not guarantee future stability. Industrialization, which began in Great Britain, increasingly affected both the economic and social structure of Europe. New ideologies and attitudes, especially socialism, liberalism, and romanticism, challenged the old ways of thinking about human beings and society. And nationalism, while submerged by the settlement at Vienna, grew more intense and widespread. Rapid change became part of the motif of the century.

THE INDUSTRIAL REVOLUTION

The reorganization of industry and the extraordinary increase in the production of goods in the late eighteenth and early nineteenth centuries is generally called the Industrial Revolution. Some historians have objected to the use of the term "revolution," claiming that "evolution"—a slow change coming over a long period of time—is a more apt description. All agree, however, that a great change in industry did occur, that this change transformed the quality of life for masses of people, and that wealth and productivity were enormously increased. It has been suggested that a "dual revolution"—the French and the Industrial, making their initial impact about the same time—transformed the nature of Western society.

The Industrial Revolution began in Great Britain in the latter part of the eighteenth century. From there it spread to other parts of Europe and the world, and by 1900 nearly every country in Europe (the Balkan areas excepted) was involved in the process. The transformation of industry from handicraft to machine production came at different times in different areas. Some British industries, for example textiles, were highly mechanized by 1850 and were already characterized by large plants, masses of factory workers, and professional managers. Belgium and France began to industrialize after the Napoleonic Wars, the German states followed in the 1850s, the United States in the late 1860s, Italy and Austria in the 1870s, and Russia by the end of the century. Thus the progress of industrialization was uneven—more rapid in western Europe than in eastern and southern areas.

In Great Britain the quantity of goods and services grew enormously during the first half of the nineteenth century. Between 1796 and 1830 cotton manufacturing increased threefold, and by 1850 that industry directly employed 500 000 people. The output of coal increased from 16 000 000 tons in 1815 to 50 000 000 in 1848, and the output of iron doubled from 1 000 000 tons in 1835 to 2 000 000 in 1848. Transportation also expanded rapidly. In 1838 there were 540 miles of railway; by 1850 there were 6621 miles. Shipping tonnage also grew from 2 500 000 tons in 1827 to 4 000 000 in 1848. Napoleon, in the day of his glory, had contemptuously called England "a nation of shopkeepers." By 1848 people enviously called it "the workshop of the world."

THE ROLE OF TECHNOLOGY

The Industrial Revolution was made possible by advances in technology. Inspired by curiosity and motivated by the prospect of financial rewards, inventors discovered ways of tapping new sources of power and introduced new methods of increasing the production of goods. Machinery began to replace manpower and the factory began to replace the cottage as the major elements in production.

The first important change came in textiles, particularly in cotton manufacturing. England had relied for centuries on wool as its main type of cloth, and the wool industry was protected by a law passed in 1700 making it illegal to import printed cotton fabrics. However, demand for cotton arose because the fabric was light, pleasant to touch, easy to wash, and more suitable for warm weather than wool, and in the eighteenth century a native cotton industry grew up in Lancashire. There was also a significant demand throughout the globe for clothing made of the lighter material.

New inventions in the eighteenth century speeded up the processes of spinning and weaving, the two essential steps in the finishing of cotton goods. In 1733 John Kay invented the "flying shuttle," a device which was pushed from one side of a loom to the other and allowed a weaver to more than double his production of cloth. There was now an increased demand for cotton thread, and before long the "spinning jenny," invented by James Hargreaves in 1764, enabled one person to spin many threads at a time. Other inventors found ways of running the new machines by mechanical power, and the steam-driven loom of Samuel Crompton, invented in 1779, was used by a major portion of the industry by 1820.

The vast increase in the manufacture of cotton goods which resulted from these inventions produced, in turn, a greater demand for raw cotton. English manufacturers who had formerly been supplied with raw cotton from India turned to the United States, where cotton growing underwent its own Industrial Revolution in 1793 with the invention by Eli Whitney of the "cotton gin." This machine speeded up the separation of cotton from its seeds, making it possible for the southern plantations of the United States to supply much of the cotton which the English finished in their mills and exported around the world.

In the past, people, animals, water, and wind provided the main sources of power for the making of goods. Steam engines existed in the early eighteenth century, but they consumed too much fuel and had limited practical use. In 1769 James Watt patented an improvement, an engine with a condenser, which made the use of steam power more economical. Watt's steam engine produced revolutionary changes in the production of goods. It became the major source of power and also revolutionized transportation. In the first two decades of the nineteenth century, Robert Fulton of the United States made the first steamboat, and George Stephenson of England adapted the steam engine to the railway. The steamship and steam locomotive carried people and goods faster and more efficiently than ever before. Manufactured products could be produced in quantity and quality as never before, and they could be transported much more quickly to large markets.

The Industrial Revolution changed the way people looked at distance and time. Heretofore, a journey of 200 km usually required days; now it could be accomplished comfortably by railway in hours. The rapid advance of frontiers in the Americas, Asia, Africa, and parts of Europe was made possible by the laying of railway tracks, the shipment of people and goods to new areas, and the maintenance of lines of communication. The railway thus allowed old and new countries to exploit their resources more extensively. The railway track and the steam locomotive became the universal symbol of progress for people in the West in the nineteenth century.

GREAT BRITAIN

There are many reasons why industrial development took place first in Great Britain. Britain had a wealthy mercantile class which was both willing and able to invest large sums of money in new ventures. The central Bank of England, established in 1694, had long experience in controlling the money market and could provide credit for new industrial enterprises. Britain's colonial empire ensured ready markets for the products of the new factories. Thus the availability of capital, the experience of merchants, and the vast markets protected by the British navy, all contributed to the early and rapid industrialization of a number of industries.

The attitude of the British aristocracy was also significant for the new industrial enterprise. Though governed by an aristocracy, England's political and social structure was more flexible than that of France in the old regime, and, while the English aristocracy controlled parliament, it also paid taxes. Further, English society was much more mobile than other European societies, and its aristocracy included many newcomers with large economic resources and recently acquired titles. The English upper classes did not sneer at "new money" as did their continental counterparts. Intermarriages between old noble families and those of the new rich were common. Moreover, many English aristocrats, when they spotted a good thing, moved into the new business world and helped to develop industry as well as the natural resources on their own estates.

As England became the leading producer of goods in the world and lost any fear of trade rivals, traditional economic attitudes based on government regulation of trade and industry (including protective tariffs) no longer served its interests. Therefore, English economic policy began to change and, throughout the first half of the nineteenth century, it was increasingly guided by the theories of Adam Smith and his followers. Smith, who wrote during the Enlightenment (see Chapter I), argued that the principle of laissez-faire—a free market place, guided by supply and demand—should be the basis of government policy. Jeremy Bentham (1748–1832), one of the philosophical heirs of the Enlightenment and one of the great reformers of his day, stated that if one wished to increase the national wealth "the general rule [was] that nothing ought to be done or attempted by government." Governments, he believed, ought to be guided by the motto "Be quiet."[1] Both Smith and Bentham thought that each individual would contribute to the welfare of the community by pursuing a natural self-interest and that government interference would hinder the growth of wealth and resources.

Many agreed with both Smith's idea of an economy guided by the laws of supply and demand (he used the term "invisible hand") and Bentham's plea for "quietism." Yet, while a large number of economic regulations were removed, British governments never adopted a policy of total laissez-faire. They allowed certain monopolies (especially in transportation) to continue, used the navy to help private shippers, and in general fostered the growth of British industry. And from 1833 onwards the government undertook to regulate the hours and working conditions first of women and children and ultimately of men who laboured in the factories and mines.

THE SPREAD OF INDUSTRIALIZATION

Once there was peace on the continent, other countries began to use the English experience in order to increase their own wealth. Belgium, which became independent from Holland in 1830, was the first continental country to undergo heavy industrialization. France lagged behind Belgium because France began to develop major credit and marketing facilities only in the mid nineteenth century. While the English pound had been stable and supported by the government since about 1700, the French franc, as a result of political unrest and government debt, was an unstable currency. Among the German states, Prussia led the way in industrialization and railway building. It eliminated all internal tariffs in its own territory, and in 1834 it spearheaded the formation of the Zollverein, a tariff union that included many of the German states. When Germany was unified in 1871, the wealth of Prussia and the Zollverein provided the basis for further industrial growth. Other European states were slower to develop an industrial base.

With the growth of industrialization the gulf between rich and poor nations became wider. The Congress of Vienna had distinguished between "greater" and "lesser" military powers. By the end of the century, the Industrial Revolution created another kind of distinction based on production and trade, and the three large powers that

A commentary on German customs before the establishment of the Zollverein, which ended many of the complicated internal duties. "You see, sir, that I have nothing to declare, for the things on the back of the waggon haven't crossed the Lippe border yet, there is nothing in the middle, and what's up front is already over the border." (Ullstein)

had industrialized—England, France, and Germany—almost completely controlled events in Europe and much of the world. Large states which had limited industrialization—Russia, Austria, and Italy—had become middle powers. Those states which failed to industrialize—Spain, Portugal, and Turkey among them—remained on the sidelines.

SOCIAL EFFECTS OF THE INDUSTRIAL REVOLUTION

Combined with the impetus provided by the French Revolution and the Napoleonic wars, the Industrial Revolution produced important changes in Western politics, society, and ideology. Prior to industrialization, production had been organized on a local basis. A merchant purchased raw material, handed it out to his labourers in various localities, picked up their finished work, and then marketed the goods. This has been called the "putting-out" system. Many labourers were farmers who made articles in their spare time to increase their income. The period from about 1500 to the start of the Industrial Revolution was an age of handicraft work.

A new form of economic organization was introduced during the Industrial Revolution. Machine production was quick and efficient, for machines generally performed a single function on a mass scale. At the same time, a worker at a machine now performed a single task. Moreover, large machines could be placed only in a central location—a factory—where power was supplied and where all the workers assembled at regular hours, each to perform one task. Masses of people working with machines and performing specialized functions in one factory could produce many times more goods than these same people working in their homes. This assembling in factories on a daily basis of such masses of workers who were dependent on the same market conditions for their livelihood, who endured the same hardships while at work, and who suffered the same privations when out of work, brought into existence a new working class with ideas and interests peculiar to itself.

The growth of factories increased the number and size of cities. In England the population of Manchester, the centre of the cotton industry, grew from 77 000 in 1801 to 303 000 in 1850. While the transition was

"London going out of Town—or The March of Bricks & Mortar", a view on the expansion of urban life in the Industrial Revolution by the English caricaturist George Cruikshank (1792-1878)

often slow—even in 1900 more continental Europeans lived in rural areas than in urban areas—there was a clear shift of population from the country to the city in both Europe and North America. The new urban environment meant that one's neighbour was next door, perhaps upstairs, perhaps in the next room, sometimes in the same room.

The common experience for many people became the factory, not the farm. The factory was generally a large building holding machines, and machine production demanded regularity, order, and discipline as never before. People who had lived in the country, risen with the sun, and carried out their tasks in accordance with the needs of the day and the season now lived in crowded cities and operated by the clock.

The machine altered the employer-employee relationship which had existed for centuries. Prior to the nineteenth century, most people, whether peasants or craftsmen, knew their employers well and had some sort of personal relationship with them. Now labour became depersonalized—in a factory one was usually directed by a foreman, not the owner. Employers were engaged in a cut-throat competitive struggle; they often worked themselves to the limits of endurance and expected their employees to do the same. Frequently, the hired foremen were tougher than the owners because they were responsible for increasing production. The individual worker was but a pair of hands to be used when needed, or cast away when not.

Conditions of labour in the new factories were often deplorable. Men, women, and children worked in crowded stuffy factories, sometimes with dangerous machinery, for very long hours. Governments took little action until the early 1830s when the British Parliament ordered an investigation of work in the factories. The results were published in the Sadler Report, named after the chairman of the parliamentary committee. Here is one example of the interviews conducted by the committee:

What age are you? —Twenty-two.

What is your occupation? —A blanket manufacturer.

Have you ever been employed in a factory? —Yes.

At what age did you first go to work in one? —Eight.

How long did you continue in that occupation? —Four years.

Will you state the hours of labour at the period when you first went to the factory, in ordinary times? —From 6 in the morning to 8 at night.

Fourteen hours? —Yes.

With what intervals for refreshment and rest? —An hour at noon.

Then you had no resting time allowed in which to take your breakfast, or what is in Yorkshire called your "drinking"? —No.

When trade was brisk what were your hours? —From 5 in the morning to 9 in the evening.

Sixteen hours? —Yes.

With what intervals at dinner? —An hour.

How far did you live from the mill? —About two miles.

Was there any time allowed for you to get your breakfast in the mill? —No.

Did you take it before you left your home? —Generally.

During those long hours of labour could you be punctual; how did you awake? —I seldom did awake spontaneously; I was most generally awoke or lifted out of bed, sometimes asleep, by my parents.

Were you always in time? —No.

What was the consequence if you had been too late? —I was most commonly beaten.

Severely? —Very severely, I thought.

"Over London by Rail", an etching by Gustave Doré of the slums of London which appeared in 1871

In whose factory was this? —Messrs. Hague & Cook's, of Dewsbury.

Will you state the effect that these long hours had upon the state of your health and feelings? —I was, when working those long hours, commonly very much fatigued at night, when I left my work; so much so that I sometimes should have slept as I walked if I had not stumbled and started awake again; and so sick often that I could not eat, and when I did eat I vomited.

Did this labour destroy your appetite? —It did.

In what situation were you in that mill? —I was a piecener.

Will you state to this Committee whether piecening is a very laborious employment for children, or not? —It is a very laborious employment. Pieceners are continually running to and fro, and on their feet the whole day.[2]

The first effective factory act was passed in 1833. It limited the hours of child labour in textile mills and, most important, appointed factory inspectors to administer it.

In 1880–81 Arnold Toynbee (a young scholar at Oxford who died in 1883 at the age of thirty-one) delivered his *Lectures on the Industrial Revolution*. These lectures were the first scholarly assessment of the Industrial Revolution and became the basis of an historiographical controversy which lasts to this day. Toynbee condemned the human cost of industry—low wages, long hours, unsafe conditions, no guarantee of employment, no provisions for old age, a discipline determined by machine, and whole families working because the income of one or two people was not sufficient. In his view, "the effects of the Industrial Revolution prove that free competition may produce wealth without producing well-being."[3]

Yet many historians have noted that life in the countryside or in the small towns was not particularly charming for most people, and a school of thought led by T. S. Ashton has insisted that the workers were better off in the nineteenth century than before:

One of the merits of the factory system was that it offered, and required, regularity of employment and hence greater stability of consumption. During the period 1790–1830, factory production increased rapidly. A greater proportion of the people came to benefit from it both as producers and as consumers. The fall in the price of textiles reduced the price of clothing. Government contracts for uniforms and army boots called into being new industries, and after the war the products of these found a market among the better paid artisans. Boots began to take the place of clogs, hats replaced shawls, at least for wear on Sundays. Miscellaneous commodities, ranging from clocks to pocket handkerchiefs, began to enter into the scheme of expenditure, and after 1820 such things as tea and coffee and sugar fell in price substantially. The growth of trade-unions, friendly societies, savings banks, popular newspapers and pamphlets, schools and nonconformist chapels—all give evidence of the existence of a large class raised well above the level of mere subsistence.[4]

Historians do agree that a new class of workers came into being and that problems between the masses and their employers grew more intense. Karl Marx called this new class the "proletariat." The proletariat did not own the means of production—tools, plants, or raw material; they owned only their labour, and thus were at the mercy of employers and the market. But these urban factory workers began to be aware of their collective power and tried to use it as a force for change and betterment. By mid-century, especially in western Europe, the cities and their inhabitants, whether poor labourers or wealthy employers, were providing the impetus for social and political change.

RESPONSES TO THE NEW AGE

The problems bred by the Industrial Revolution brought a variety of responses. While many industrialists saw no reason for changing the system, some realized that the machine and the new technology were producing their own form of inhumanity. Thus there were some members of the middle and upper classes who believed that the state must intervene. The extent of state intervention was a hotly disputed issue, even among those who agreed on the principle.

Many workers and intellectuals wanted a complete restructuring of society which would eliminate inhumanity and exploitation while establishing a sense of community

The membership certificate of the United Machine Workers' Association, established in England in 1844. The symbols of modern industry and labour are used to portray the new style of work during the Industrial Revolution.   (Trades Union Congress, London— John R. Freeman)

among all people. Their new ideology was called socialism and was the opposite of *laissez-faire* and "individualism." The early socialists felt that solutions to industrial problems did not lie merely in political reforms such as giving the vote to all citizens, but in a wholesale reconstruction of the economic and social system. Some of the most important early socialists—Saint-Simon, Fourier, Owen—were labelled "utopians" by Karl Marx because they believed that they could create a socialist society by persuasion or by going off and establishing ideal communities. In contrast to the "utopian socialists," Marx saw himself as a "scientific socialist" who understood the real nature of class conflict. He thought that revolution was necessary to bring about economic and social change.

One of the most interesting of the utopians was the Comte de Saint-Simon (1760–1825), who felt that humanity was entering a new age as a result of progress in science. He thought that humanity had advanced in a

A view of the Crystal Palace in London, opened in 1851 to house a vast industrial exhibition, sometimes referred to as the first world's fair

"Pit, boxes, and gallery", a view of the social classes by Cruikshank

series of alternating periods of construction and destruction. Social institutions were established as a response to the prevailing culture of the time, and, as knowledge advanced and conditions changed, old institutions became less useful. Thus, at some point in time, social organization had to be changed because it no longer reflected the progress of knowledge. Saint-Simon pointed to the Church as an institution which was progressive in the medieval period, but which now

was regressive, because it failed to change in accord with the ideas of the Enlightenment. Periods of destruction were characterized by the elimination of regressive institutions, and Saint-Simon said that the French Revolution had performed such a task when it destroyed the obsolete old regime.

Saint-Simon wanted to provide a plan for a new social order based on scientific knowledge. He insisted that the old privileged class must give way and that scientists, among others, must reorganize society for the good of "the most numerous and poorest class."

The scientists, artists, and artisans, the only men whose work is of positive utility to society, and cost it practically nothing, are kept down by the princes and other rulers who are simply more or less incapable bureaucrats. Those who control honours and other national awards owe, in general, the supremacy they enjoy, to the accident of birth, to flattery, intrigue and other dubious methods. . . .

Ignorance, superstition, idleness and costly dissipation are the privilege of the leaders of society, and men of ability, [who are] hardworking and thrifty, are employed only as inferiors. . . .

To sum up, in every sphere men of greater ability are subject to the control of men who are incapable. From the point of view of morality, the most immoral men have the responsibility of leading the citizens towards virtue; from the point of view of distributive justice, the most guilty men are appointed to punish minor delinquents.[5]

Saint-Simon recognized no basic and permanent hostility between industrialist and worker—it was the existing system that made for this hostility; but, in the new order, both would perform their tasks with dignity and both would strive for the common good.

Saint-Simon was the first to see economic organization as the important factor in shaping society, and he therefore stressed economic planning rather than politics. In his work *On Social Organization* (1825) he wrote:

The men who brought about the [French] Revolution, the men who directed it, and the men who, since 1789 and up to the present day, have guided the nation, have committed a great political mistake. They have all sought to improve the governmental machine, whereas they should have subordinated it and put administration in the first place.[6]

Saint-Simon's contribution to socialism was this stress on economic organization combined with his deep moral commitment. His vision of an ideal society was guided by a profound desire to end the injustices of a bad system.

Charles Fourier (1772–1837), another French utopian socialist, had less faith in the possibilities of industrial society. He was one of the first of the modern socialists to want a perfect community set apart from the rest of society. Fourier introduced the idea of the self-sufficient, co-operative community, free from the constraints and trials of the new urban industrial civilization. This community was to be based on agriculture and craftsmanship rather than on industrialization, and all members would share equally in the communal life.

Fourier deplored the amount of unhappiness in society; part of the blame, he thought, must be attributed to the fact that most labour was "unattractive." In order to cope with this problem, Fourier proposed that labour be "associative":

It is necessary, in order that it become attractive, that associative labour fulfil the following seven conditions:

1. That every labourer be a partner, [paid] by dividends and not by wages.
2. That every one, man, woman, or child, be [paid] in proportion to [their contributions of] *capital*, *labour*, and *talent*.
3. That the [daily routine of workers] be varied about eight times a day, it being impossible to sustain enthusiasm longer than an hour and a half or two hours in the exercise of agricultural or manufacturing labour.
4. That [work] be carried on by bands of friends, united spontaneously, interested and stimulated by very active rivalries.
5. That the workshops and husbandry offer the labourer the allurements of elegance and cleanliness.
6. That the division of labour be carried to the last degree, so that each sex and age may devote itself to duties that are suited to it.
7. That in this distribution, each one, man, woman, or child, be in full enjoyment of the right to labour or the right to engage in such branch of labour as they may please to select, provided they give proof of integrity and ability.

Finally, that, in this new order, people possess a guarantee of well-being, of a minimum sufficient for the present and the future, and that this guarantee free them from all uneasiness concerning themselves and their families.[7]

Rather than have the individual adjust to society, Fourier wished to create a community which responded to individual needs. A number of co-operative communities were formed in Europe and the United States on the principles outlined by Fourier; all were ultimately unsuccessful.

The English utopian socialist Robert Owen (1771–1858) was a self-made, successful businessman and a reformer. In 1797, at his factory in New Lanark, he set up model living conditions for his workers—hours of labour were limited, schools were established, and decent housing was introduced. Though Owen's factory made a profit, he had difficulty in persuading his partners that his schemes were sound.

Owen was an environmentalist; he believed that the character of an individual was formed by the environment in which he lived, and he devoted his energy and his future to plans that would change the environment of the workers. In order to put his schemes into practice in an ideal setting, he founded a colony in New Harmony, Indiana. After the failure of this scheme, he returned to England and became involved in a movement for establishing co-operative factories and stores. He was also a leader in the trade-union movement, which was intended to unite the workers in order to force owners to improve conditions. Thus, although he started out as a utopian, Owen eventually became involved in the class struggle. Yet Owen always felt, unlike Marx, that capitalism did not have to produce class antagonisms.

"New Harmony", an engraving based on Robert Owen's plan for his utopian experiment (Historical Pictures Service, Chicago)

"New Harmony—all owin', no payin' ". Cruikshank satirizes Owen's vision.

The early socialists were a mixed group with very different ideas. Yet they all felt that the "social issue" was the key to the problems of the day. They deplored excessive individualism and called for a greater co-operation and concern for the community. None regarded private property with the same kind of sanctity as did classical liberal thinkers like Adam Smith and those who followed him. Property, the socialists felt, had to be controlled to make certain that it was used for worthwhile social ends. None of them were revolutionaries; they did not wish to overthrow society by violent means, but to transform it through education and political activity. While they were concerned for the rights of the individual, they did not believe that any individual was autonomous, or that people should be considered apart from the society in which they lived. The utopians were the first thinkers to introduce an ideology which recognized the widespread social and economic consequences of the Industrial Revolution and proposed solutions for dealing with them.

RESPONSES TO THE NEW AGE— LIBERALISM AND CONSERVATISM

In the first half of the nineteenth century, socialism was not the dominant political and social outlook. At this time individuals of influence and power tended to be either "liberal" or "conservative." These terms did not indicate party labels so much as differing views of human beings and the nature of social and political organization.

Liberalism generally accepted the eighteenth-century view of humans as rational beings. It considered society as the sum of the interests and needs of the individuals who composed it. Therefore, the role of the state (as Smith and Bentham proposed) was to protect the freedom of the individual so that all persons could rationally pursue their own happiness and self-interest. Liberals assumed that the combined happiness of all individuals would create the best society. They opposed absolute and arbitrary rule and subscribed to constitutional forms of government, whether they were monarchies or republics. Since they believed that sover-

"Over population" by Cruikshank

eignty was vested in the people and not in a ruler, they insisted that individual rights must be protected. But at this time they were generally not democrats and sought to limit the vote to property owners. The early liberals feared that basic human rights would be lost if governments intervened in domestic affairs.

Conservatives, on the other hand, believed in the value of tradition and the need for more, rather than less, government. They viewed society as a combination of ancient and diverse institutions which had to be preserved and protected; and they believed that anarchy would result if the complex organism of society was subjected to the rational process of reformers. Conservatives had a less optimistic view of human nature than liberals. In their opinion, people were incapable, without guidance, of knowing or pursuing their own self-interest. Thus they tended to be more paternalistic and authoritarian than liberals, and emphasized order. Since the primary duty of the state was, in their view, to prevent society from falling apart, they favoured a strong central government which would ensure social stability and intervene when the forces of change seemed to threaten the forces of order.

States at this time tended to be characterized as more or less liberal or conservative. Of the great powers of Europe, England and France were generally thought of as liberal in form and attitude, while the eastern states—Austria, Prussia, and Russia—were considered to be conservative. Though it is difficult to draw clear lines, it may be said that liberalism was the outlook of the urban middle class while the landed upper class was usually conservative. Thus liberals were strong in the western states which began to industrialize early, but were weak in eastern Europe. In the east they were the political opponents of the ruling elite and, sometimes, even revolutionaries.

Later in the century the terms "liberal" and "conservative" most often became labels referring to one's attitude towards change. To be liberal meant to be willing to change to meet new needs. To be conservative meant either to be unwilling to change—to be committed to the social and political *status quo*—or, like Burke, to desire slow change, fearing the disorganization which might result from a quick transformation of social and political institutions.

ROMANTICISM

The first half of the nineteenth century cannot be understood without taking into account the beliefs and attitudes included under the general label of Romanticism. Romanticism was not a political ideology, but a way of looking at life, and it influenced all the political doctrines of the time, in-

"Scarcity of Domestic Servants; or, Every Family their own Cooks!!!" Cruikshank's comment on the domestic scene.

cluding the various forms of socialism, liberalism, and conservatism. It was also closely tied in with the nationalism of this period. It represented a new way of looking at humanity and, as such, was one of the most important and influential movements of the whole modern period.

Even in the eighteenth century there had been a reaction against Enlightenment ideas about people and society. Many believed that the attitudes of the *philosophes* were too rational and too orderly, and that they failed to take into account the emotional side of human nature. After all that happened during the French Revolution, it seemed unlikely that a mere rational adjustment of political and social institutions would make people eternally happy. The Enlightenment view of humanity persisted after the French Revolution, but Romanticism grew up alongside of it, contesting its assumptions and adding a new dimension to the understanding of human beings.

The faith of the Enlightenment had grown out of a combination of the ideas of classicism and of modern science. Classicism stood for order, and those who espoused it had laid down rules of architecture, literature, painting, and music which had to be followed to produce an acceptable work. Science from the time of Newton had assumed the existence of a mechanistic, orderly universe, working according to laws which could be discovered through observation and expressed in mathematical formulae. As a result, eighteenth-century thinkers tended to see things in terms of all-embracing generalizations rather than in terms of uniqueness or individuality. For example, political assumptions, as in the American Declaration of Independence, began with the words "All men ..."; scientific assertions began with the statement: "In X condition, all bodies . . . " Eighteenth-century literary guides gave the rules for the construction of all poems, while the French Revolution itself produced a Declaration of the Rights of Man and Citizen, thought to be true for *all* people.

Romanticism was a reaction against such an ordered, rational mode of thought. While most Enlightenment thinkers had conceived of the rational and natural as one, the Romantics divorced nature and reason. They emphasized the emotional side of people— feelings and sentiments—rather than their rationality. And they believed that emotion might reveal profound truth. For the Romantics, movement and change became more important concepts than universal harmony. In place of the Enlightenment concept of the universal character of humanity, they stressed human diversity and, in fact, revelled in it.

Romanticism began as a literary movement, for the ideals of the Romantics found more response in the poet than in the scientist. In Germany, Herder was the leading eighteenth-century figure. He was joined by Johann Wolfgang von Goethe (1749–1832), who wrote *The Sorrows of Young Werther* (1774), beginning a new trend in literature. Goethe's hero was a boy in love; his method of exposition was to describe states of emotion; his message was that personal sentiment—what came to be called the heart— was the true guide to a meaningful life.

Among the most important results of Romantic literary criticism was the reassertion of Shakespeare's genius. Friedrich von Schlegel (1772–1839) in Germany and Samuel Taylor Coleridge (1772–1834) in England both felt that Shakespeare had not been appreciated in the eighteenth century because the Enlightenment had adopted a narrow classical view of drama. In fact, Voltaire had asserted that Shakespeare's "genius was at once strong and abundant, natural and sublime, but without the smallest spark of taste, and without the slightest knowledge of the rules."[8] Schlegel and Coleridge pointed to the quality of Shakespeare's vision—"natural and sublime"—and stated that had he used the eighteenth-century rules of drama he would never have written such overpowering plays.

Literary Romanticism reached its height in English poetry. The *Lyrical Ballads* (1798), published by Coleridge and William Wordsworth (1770–1850), pictured nature as idyllic, beautiful, and ever-changing. The poems also explored the action of people in natural settings where, according to Wordsworth, people acted less artificially and revealed the intensity of their emotions. In his "Lines Written in Early Spring" Wordsworth expressed one of the moods of English Romanticism:

> I heard a thousand blended notes,
> While in a grove I sate reclined,
> In that sweet mood when pleasant thoughts
> Bring sad thoughts to the mind.
>
> To her fair works did Nature link
> The human soul that through me ran;
> In much it grieved my heart to think
> What man has made of man.
>
> Through primrose tufts, in that sweet bower,
> The periwinkle trailed its wreaths;
> And 'tis my faith that every flower
> Enjoys the air it breathes.
>
> The birds around me hopped and played,
> Their thoughts I cannot measure: —
> But the least motion which they made,
> It seemed a thrill of pleasure.
>
> The budding twigs spread out their fan
> To catch the breezy air;
> And I must think, do all I can,
> That there was pleasure there.
>
> If this belief from heaven be sent,
> If such be Nature's holy plan,
> Have I not reason to lament
> What man has made of man?[9]

As a result of the emphasis on the emotional and the irrational, the Romantic movement did not develop an absolute standard of truth or beauty. Indeed, many Romantics consciously avoided an attempt to impose fixed standards for fear they would be substituting new rules for old. Thus the movement contained elements that defied accurate definition and even contradicted one another. In many ways the avoidance of a categorical truth was a strength, for it meant that any serious attempt to define the nature of reality was given an open hearing.

The Romantics reintroduced religion and mysticism to the European intellectual scene, and in contrast to Enlightenment thinkers they embraced the unknown, glorified faith based on feelings, and encouraged emotional commitment. The most important Romantic work on religion was *The Genius of Christianity* by René de Chateaubriand (1768–1848) in which Christianity was held up among all religions as "the most poetic, most human, the most conducive to freedom, to the arts and literature. . . ."[10] He contrasted religion with science, and found science wanting.

The Romantic period produced a new interest in the Middle Ages. Enlightenment thinkers had viewed the Middle Ages with disdain, because they believed that life was dominated by the Church and there was little scientific progress. Romantic historians and poets, on the other hand, viewed the Middle Ages as a creative period when true feelings and emotions could find expression, and people had a sense of order and community, living close to nature and the soil.

Tradition and custom, sneered at in the Enlightenment and the Revolutionary period, were revered by Romantics because of people's long adherence to them. There was a renewed interest in folk customs, in the early literature of peoples, and in the formative years of a nation's growth. If the Romantics had any political bias, it was probably conservative (though many Romantics were active in liberal and radical and nationalist movements) because Romanticism emphasized the value of tried political institutions and the beauty of custom, rather than the need for rational reform.

While English and French Romantics were mainly poets, artists, and historians, German Romanticism found expression in philosophy, particularly in the publications of G. W. F. Hegel (1770–1831). Rejecting the rationalist philosophy of the eighteenth century, Hegel advocated philosophical "idealism"—that is, he defined reality in terms of the importance of ideas, not in terms of the material world. For example, in Hegel's view the French Revolution began when Enlightenment thinkers introduced the idea of revolution and not when fighting actually broke out in 1789. Hegel believed that "Reason" governed the universe, but for him "Reason" referred to a changing, developing universe, not a rational, unchanging, harmonious universe. Hegel's "Reason" manifested itself in the progress of human history, which he pictured as the unfolding of "the Spirit," sometimes interpreted by him as the Will of Providence. According to Hegel, people and society developed through conflict and struggle; ideas clashed and from this clash emerged new, more progressive ideas that continued the development of the Spirit.

Hegel developed his own view of freedom. Unlike Enlightenment thinkers, who saw freedom in terms of the rights of the individual, he saw it in terms of "law, morality, the state." Freedom resided in the group, in peoples, in a collective unit, rather than in individuals. This meant that the individual must work to promote the collective development of the people and the formation of the national state. This form of nationalism, with its strong romantic flavour, was rooted in the veneration of the *Volk.* For Hegel and those who followed him, the individual is free only if the group

is free, because people find their identity in terms of their ancestry, their tradition and the norms of the people of which they are a part. Hegel's Romanticism, then, justified the growth of nationalism in nineteenth-century Europe and, indeed, gave it an intellectual basis.

Romanticism, however, had no single philosophical base and was not a coherent movement. It is best looked upon as an attitude which inspired a reinterpretation of human nature, and introduced new ideas about the good, the true, and the beautiful. However, Romanticism deeply affected the behaviour of people. It supported the various nationalist movements of the time, justified revolution where the *status quo* prevented free expression, and encouraged the lower classes to take action against the more privileged. Hence it was not simply an intellectual and emotional attack on the Enlightenment; it was also an attempt to develop new answers to practical problems.

ANALYSIS AND DISCUSSION

1. The Industrial Revolution occurred first and most strikingly in Britain. Using Britain as a model, explain the conditions needed for successful industrialization.
2. "The commercial benefits of industrialism were obvious in mid-century Europe. It was the human cost which was often ignored." Discuss this statement with reference to the contrast between the European achievement of industrialization and the realities of factory life.
3. "The image of the Crystal Palace and the etching 'Over London by Rail' by Gustave Doré convey two contrasting views of the industrial revolution. While both are accurate, neither give a complete picture of the period." Discuss this statement with specific reference to both images and their relationship to the reality of industrialization.
4. "The railway track and the steam locomotive became the universal symbols of progress for people in the West in the nineteenth century." What developments contributed to

the emergence of the railway and the steam engine as the pre-eminent symbols of nineteenth-century progress?
5. Compare the ideas of utilitarians such as Jeremy Bentham with those of Utopian socialists such as Saint-Simon, Fourier, and Owen. What impact would such ideas have had upon the industrialist and working classes during the industrial revolution?
6. "The terms 'liberal' and 'conservative' did not indicate party labels so much as differing views of men and nature of social and political organization."
a) Identify the main components of liberalism and conservatism, and indicate the major differences between the two approaches to political action.
b) Compare and contrast the effects you think each view would have on (i) the way government and society would be organized (ii) the way individuals would be treated.

CHAPTER **6**

Conservatism, Liberalism, and Nationalism: 1815-1848

THE INDUSTRIAL REVOLUTION, THE French Revolution, and the new ideologies all contributed towards a change in political and social attitudes throughout Europe. While the conservatives defended the *status quo*, others wanted the revolutionary trend to continue. The period from 1815 to 1848 is characterized by a conscious struggle between conservatives like Prince Metternich of Austria who preferred that things remain the same, and people like the Italian philosopher, nationalist, and rebel Giuseppe Mazzini who were dedicated to upsetting the assumptions and realities of the Vienna settlement.

THE CONGRESS SYSTEM IN ACTION— SPAIN, GREECE, BELGIUM

When the Congress of Vienna ended, the four major victorious powers tried to systematize their diplomatic relations by establishing a Quadruple Alliance in November 1815. England, Austria, Prussia, and Russia inaugurated what has been called the "congress system." They agreed to meet periodically in order to sort out international problems and maintain peace among the great powers. At the first of these meetings, at Aix-la-Chapelle, in September 1818, France was invited to join, thus creating a Quintuple Alliance. At the same time the other four powers ended their occupation of France, and France was recognized as an equal in the congress system.

A second agreement had been made at Vienna by the conservative states of eastern Europe. Spurred on by Alexander I of Russia, who associated his form of autocracy with the will of God, and who viewed himself as having a special mission, Russia, Prussia, and Austria joined in a Holy Alliance in September 1815. Although the purpose of the Holy Alliance was publicly stated as the protection of the Christian principles of "religion, peace and justice," the agreement was actually a kind of mutual assistance pact among monarchs united by a common fear of liberal and national revolutions.

Indeed, members of the alliance seemed to believe that all change was dangerous and that a revolutionary threat to one was a threat to all, because revolution was contagious. The Holy Alliance was later signed by most other European states, since it cost little to take a pledge in favour of religion, peace, and justice, without being required to act. However, the three original signatories continued an informal alliance that was based on shared conservative attitudes. This group was dominated by Prince Metternich of Austria who tried to use both the congress system and the Holy Alliance to prevent drastic social and political change in Europe.

England refused to join the Holy Alliance and refused to subscribe to the idea that the great powers should intervene in the affairs of other states. At the next congress, at Troppau in 1820, the question of intervention came up. A revolution in Naples in 1820 threatened Austrian authority and Metternich proposed that the congress system undertake to suppress it. Neither Great Britain nor France agreed to this, but Metternich got Prussia and Russia to endorse armed Austrian intervention. The liberal revolution was crushed, and the reactionary regime was restored by force.

A more important revolution took place in Spain. In early 1820 a group of liberals rebelled against the reactionary King

Ferdinand VII. They declared Spain a constitutional republic, with a constitution based on the Napoleonic Constitution established in Spain in 1812, which itself was based upon the principles of the French Revolution. The Spanish revolt aided the cause of Latin Americans who wanted independence from Spain's colonial empire. The question of Spain was taken up by yet another congress, this time at Verona in 1822. England still resisted intervention, but Bourbon France, fearful of a republican Spain on its borders, agreed that the revolutionaries must be overthrown. With the approval of the three conservative powers, France sent an army into Spain; in 1823 Ferdinand VII was restored to his throne.

The question of intervention in Latin America now came to the fore. This time British interests were directly at stake, for English trade with Latin America had increased greatly and England was prepared to use its sea power to support the new Latin American states. The United States, as well, wanted to resist European intervention and in December 1823 President James Monroe issued the statement which has become known as the Monroe Doctrine. It asserted that any attempt by an outside power to intervene in any area of the western hemisphere would be viewed as an act which endangered the United States. The U.S. doctrine was a bluff, because the Americans could not have enforced their threat. But American and English interests coincided at this time, and until the United States had sufficient sea power to enforce the doctrine European nations were kept out of the western hemisphere by the strength of the British fleet.

The rebellions in Spain and in Naples were unsuccessful, but there was a successful nationalist revolution in Greece. The Ottoman Empire of Turkey was both a European and an Asian power. Within Europe, it controlled the Balkan peninsula, bordered on both Austria and Russia, and like Austria was a multi-national state. When the Greeks rebelled to gain their independence, there was much European sympathy for them. Greece had been the cradle of Western civili-

zation, and many Romantics believed that Greek glory would rise again from the ashes of the Turkish Empire. The Greeks were encouraged, not only by the liberal powers, France and England, but by a conservative power, Russia, for Russia saw the Greek revolution as an opportunity to gain influence in some of the Slavic areas of the Balkans. Russia, France, and England entered into a treaty in 1827 in order to guarantee Greek independence. Faced with such a force, Turkey could do nothing but accede, and Greece was granted independence in 1830. By this time, then, the congress system was no longer operating as a stabilizer of Europe, as Metternich had hoped it would. The meeting at Verona proved to be the last of the post-Vienna congresses; it seemed clear that national self-interest had replaced the idea of European co-operation.

In its attitude towards the establishment of new states, Europe was divided into a liberal west and a conservative east. The revolt in Belgium in 1830 made this clear. United with Holland in 1815, the Belgians resented the rule of the Dutch king imposed by the Vienna powers. The French and British were sympathetic to this liberal nationalist revolt and intervened on behalf of the Belgians, who were finally successful in 1831. The European powers then recognized the existence of a separate Belgian state. In a treaty signed by all the major powers, Belgium was recognized as a neutral state whose sovereignty was guaranteed by mutual agreement. Belgium adopted a liberal-constitutional monarchy and, because of its advanced industrial capacity, became one of the more important smaller powers on the continent.

THE CONSERVATIVE STATES

Prince Metternich managed to dominate the policies of the conservative states up to 1848. He was a man of the old order, opposed to the Industrial Revolution and to new ideas of constitutional democracy, socialism, and nationalism. The Austrian Empire, whose foreign policies he controlled, was a multinational entity dominated by its German-speaking nobility. To give in to any of the forces of change meant, in Metternich's view, the end of the multi-national empire. He strongly upheld the *status quo*, not only domestically, but internationally as well, for he believed that revolution was not a matter which concerned only the particular state involved. Aware of how the ideas of the French Revolution had spread, he believed that political borders could not stop revolutionary activity, and he thought that the states of Europe were all in danger if they did not band together. Furthermore, as an aristocrat who valued European civilization and culture, Metternich, like Burke, viewed the forces of revolution as the forces of barbarism.

Metternich was skilful and unscrupulous in diplomacy. In an instruction to the Austrian ambassador in Paris in 1834, he wrote:

Whenever King Louis-Philippe tells you that his intentions are not being carried out by his own agents, do not believe a word of it but give the appearance of never doubting it.[1]

Viscount Melbourne, the British Prime Minister in 1841, declared: "It is difficult to say what Prince Metternich's real sentiments are."[2] But Metternich's persuasiveness became so legendary that the British Ambassador in Vienna in 1820 felt it necessary to send the following message, in code, to his superior in London:

I hope you will not imagine I am led or over persuaded out of my instructions or your sentiments by Count Metternich.... You know, although I render him complete justice for his great talents and extraordinary union of agreeable qualities, I am fully aware of his political chicanery.[3]

Metternich in a portrait in the neo-classical tradition, extolling him as a man of order (Österreichische National-bibliothek)

But Metternich saw himself in a very different light:

My mind is not narrow in its conceptions. I am either short of or beyond the preoccupations of most statesmen. I cover a much wider ground than they either want to or are capable of seeing. I cannot help telling myself twenty times a day: "O Lord! how right I am and how wrong they are!"[4]

There was no doubt in his mind that he was playing a constructive, even a prophetic, role in European history.

In 1820 Metternich drew up what he called his "confession of faith." A secret document, it was written at the request of Czar Alexander I of Russia, who had worked closely with Metternich since 1815. In it he set out his view of the post-Revolutionary world:

Kings have to calculate the chances of their very existence in the immediate future; passions are let loose, and league together to overthrow everything which society respects as the basis of its existence; religion, public morality, laws, customs, rights, and duties, all are attacked, confounded, overthrown, or called in question. The great mass of the people are tranquil spectators of these attacks and revolutions, and of the absolute want of all means of defence. A few are carried off by the torrent, but the wishes of the immense majority are to maintain a repose which exists no longer, and of which even the first elements seem to be lost....

The scenes of horror which accompanied the first phases of the French Revolution prevented the rapid propagation of its subversive principles beyond the frontiers of France, and the wars of conquest which succeeded them gave to the public mind a direction little favourable to revolutionary principles. Thus the Jacobin propaganda failed entirely to realize criminal hopes.

Nevertheless the revolutionary seed had penetrated into every country and spread more or less. It was greatly developed under the *régime* of the military despotism of Bonaparte....

The evil exists and it is enormous. We do not think we can better define it and its causes at all times and in all places than we have already done by the word 'presumption,' that inseparable companion of the half-educated, that spring of an unmeasured ambition, and yet easy to satisfy in times of trouble and confusion.

It is principally the middle classes of society which this moral gangrene has affected, and it is only among them that the real heads of the party are found.

For the great mass of people it has no attraction and can have none. The labours to which this class—the real people—are obliged to devote themselves, are too continuous and too positive to allow them to throw themselves into vague abstractions and ambitions. The people know what is the happiest thing for them: namely, to be able to count on the morrow, for it is the morrow which will repay them for the cares and sorrows of to-day. The laws which afford a just protection to individuals, to families, and to property are quite simple in their essence. The people dread any movement which injures industry and brings new burdens in its train....

We are convinced that society can no longer be saved without strong and vigorous resolutions on the part of the Governments still free in their opinions and actions.

We are also convinced that this may yet be, if the Governments face the truth, if they free themselves from all illusion, if they join their ranks and take their stand on a line of correct, unambiguous, and frankly announced principles.[5]

Metternich tried to suppress the liberal and nationalist aspirations of those who wanted to unite Germany, for this too would disrupt the empire and reduce the influence of Austria. After the defeat of Napoleon, a number of students in German universities claimed that the German states had fought a "War of Liberation," and did not wish to see the reestablishment of traditional regimes. When disturbances occurred throughout central Europe in 1819, Metternich got a number of German princes to agree to a series of repressive measures called the Carlsbad Decrees. A commissioner was to be appointed for each university whose duty was "to watch over the most rigorous observation of the laws and disciplinary regulations." The Decrees also dealt with press censorship and proposed a commission "to make careful and detailed inquiries respecting the facts, the origin and the [various facets] of the secret revolutionary activities"[6] believed to exist in the German states. Metternich was successful in his policies to the extent that the Austrian Empire survived despite the liberal, constitutional, and national sentiments of the time. However, from 1815 to 1848 revolutionary activity in the Empire grew more intense while the bureaucracy of the state grew more repressive.

The structure of government in Prussia resembled that of Austria, with an absolute monarchy and a central bureaucracy. But the reforms begun during the Napoleonic era continued and Prussia began to change socially and economically. Religious toleration was practised. With the abolition of serfdom, every person in Prussia acquired the rights of citizenship. Increased social mobility, the new economics of the customs union, and the fostering of industry meant the emergence of a middle class, although the *Junkers*, the traditional Prussian nobility, continued to dominate the army and agriculture. The monarchy in Prussia set a middle course. Unlike the Bourbons in the French Revolution and the Hapsburgs in nineteenth-century Austria, the Hohenzollerns of Prussia made it possible to transform the state into a constitutional monarchy.

Russia was a powerful state, but so large that it was difficult to govern. It remained a serf society ruled by autocratic monarchs. Alexander I, who had occasionally proclaimed liberal principles before the Congress of Vienna, recanted afterwards and reintroduced oppressive measures. However, one significant change occurred. While Russia was not Western in a commercial or industrial sense, and had virtually no middle class, Russian intellectual life became more integrated with the rest of Europe. In the eighteenth century French was spoken at the Russian court, and some Russians knew and subscribed to the ideals of the Enlightenment. After the Napoleonic Wars, a number of the Russian nobility went to western Europe to be educated and returned with Western liberal ideals. Reacting to the autocracy of Alexander, a group of "Westerners" —that is, Russian nobles and intellectuals who wished Russia to emulate the liberal

West—formed clubs and secret societies to foster their ideals.

When Alexander I died in 1825, there was a crisis over who was to succeed him, and some of the nobility tried to use the occasion to establish a constitutional monarchy. An uprising in December 1825, known as the Decembrist Revolt, was quickly suppressed. This first Russian revolution suggested that the liberal ideals of the Enlightenment had penetrated Russia much more successfully than Napoleon's soldiers. After the failure of the uprising, Nicholas I, Alexander's younger brother, became Czar. He ruled until 1855 as the most reactionary monarch in Europe.

THE LIBERAL STATES

In England the Industrial Revolution provided the impetus for reform. Until 1830 England was governed by the Tory (Conservative) Party, which generally stood for the aristocratic quality of English life. In the first years after Napoleon's defeat, a serious internal crisis developed as large numbers of unemployed former soldiers and new machines which threw craftsmen out of work combined to produce an economic slump. There was a considerable amount of restlessness, and the first response of the Tories, who like their counterparts on the continent feared revolution, was repression. In 1819, after a number of disturbances, the Six Acts were passed limiting the right of public assembly and giving the state great powers to suppress dissent.

However, not all Tories were reactionaries, and in the 1820s a group led by George Canning and Robert Peel attempted to introduce a series of reforms. Tariffs were lowered and inquiries were made into the laws that restricted workers' organizations. Working people obtained limited rights to form associations for collective bargaining. Various political disabilities suffered by those who did not belong to the established church, the Church of England, were ended, and both non-Anglican Protestants and Catholics were given the right to sit in parliament and to hold other public offices. Thus the Tories were not bound rigidly to the *status quo*, and in the international field they

*"The Peterloo Massacre" of August 1819 in Manchester, England. Troops are shown
dispersing a gathering calling for political reforms.   (Mansell Collection)*

refused to support the policies of Metternich and the conservative powers.

But the great issue in England was the reform of parliament. The House of Commons of 1830 was a mixed representative body under aristocratic control. No new ridings had been created since 1688, and the shifts in the population and the growth of large urban centres in the north of England as a result of the Industrial Revolution had not been reflected in the distribution of seats. There had been many voices of reform—as early as 1776 John Wilkes claimed that parliament was not organized to represent the people and that parliamentary debates should be published in the newspapers. Over the years a number of schemes had been advanced to reform the system, but the Tories saw the Constitution as a hallowed institution which should not be disturbed, lest it be destroyed. Reformers pointed to innumerable parliamentary ridings in which very few people were represented (rotten

boroughs) and to other ridings which were virtually the property of the wealthy and landed aristocracy (pocket boroughs). Property qualifications for voting limited the size of the electorate, and, because members of parliament were not paid, only the well-to-do could afford to seek office.

Jeremy Bentham, the leading liberal thinker of the time, sought to establish a principle by which the value of institutions and laws could be tested, and by which change could be accomplished in a peaceful, orderly manner. The "proper end of government in every political community," he said "is the greatest happiness of all the individuals of which it is composed, [or,] in other words, the greatest happiness of the greatest number."[7] This was the principle of utility, and his philosophy was called Utilitarianism, because the test for the value of an institution or law was its usefulness in contributing to the greatest happiness of all. Bentham and his followers attacked the institution of par-

*"Pity the sorrows of a poor old Man!"
The French painter Théodore
Géricault commented in 1821 on
poverty in London. A beggar is
shown fainting outside a bakery.
(Bibliothèque Nationale, Paris)*

liament as it existed because it represented the few, not the many. It must be reformed, they insisted, and each person must have an equal voice in the election of members.

The movement to reform the House of Commons was taken up by the opposition party, the Whigs (Liberals), under the leadership of Lord Grey. In 1830 the Whigs took office for the first time since the Napoleonic Wars and immediately introduced a reform bill which was rejected by the Commons. A second bill was passed in the Commons but voted down by the House of Lords. The great masses in the country, however, made clear their support of the measure, sometimes by agitation and threats, and, since revolution prevailed in Europe at the time, it seemed that England would have its own revolution if the reform was not accepted. This is one of the early instances in modern England of the effect of public opinion on politics; while the masses of England were not yet represented in the Commons, they had made their position clear. Finally, in 1832, the bill was passed.

The First Reform Act did not democratize England, although it made parliament somewhat more representative. The electorate was increased from about one half to three quarters of a million men. Property qualifications for voting were altered to include

some persons whose wealth was not based on land, but voting was still restricted to property owners. Some of the less populated towns and rural areas lost seats, while industrial areas with a greater density of population made gains.

The Reform Act was a major step on the road to truly representative parliamentary government in England. It meant that the importance of the new urban population had been recognized, that industrial areas would help to shape the future of the country, and that industrial wealth had been brought more directly into the English political system. The Reform Act of 1832 benefited the middle class and not the working class, as the centre of gravity of English politics began to shift away from the aristocracy. Most important, an old hallowed institution had been changed peacefully—and this became an important precedent. The middle class in England did not need a revolution in order to achieve its political objectives.

Reform continued after 1832. Slavery was ended in the British Empire in 1833. Various bills were passed regulating hours and conditions of employment in industry, culminating in the Ten Hours Act in 1847, which forbade the employment of women and children for more than ten hours a day. Regulations were adopted to protect those who worked in the coal mines. The government began contributing funds to education, took an interest in health and sanitation, and set up inspection systems to enforce the new regulations.

For many workers, however, the Reform Act of 1832 had been far too moderate. Hence, in order to press for further change, a group of artisans in 1836 founded the London Working Men's Association. The organization was led by William Lovett, who wrote the "People's Charter," which was the political program of the group. The Charter called for universal manhood suffrage, electoral districts with equal numbers of inhabitants, the end of property qualifications for members of parliament, payment for members of parliament, annual elections of parliament, and the secret ballot. The Charter quickly became the rallying-cry for many different working-class groups. Thus the Chartist movement was born.

Almost from the first, the movement was divided between those wanting peaceful, moderate reform and those who were militant. In 1839 a Chartist Convention was held near the Houses of Parliament. A petition embodying the program, signed by about one million people, was presented to the House of Commons, only to be rejected. Militants under the leadership of Fergus O'Connor rioted, but Lovett and his group continued to press for non-violent agitation. Though violence and rebellion were in the air, moderation won the day. Chartism continued as a movement through the 1840s and into the early 1850s, but with no immediate effect on parliamentary reform.

The Charter was never accepted by parliament, yet five of its six points (all except annual parliaments) were eventually written into law. According to one historian:

Chartism ... left a deep and permanent mark on English history. It was the first widespread and sustained effort of working-class self-help; it was directed to the cause of parliamentary democracy and constitutional reform; and the impetus it gave to eventual political reform on one hand and to trade union organization on the other was never wasted.[8]

In France after 1815 the substance of the reforms of the Revolutionary and Napoleonic periods were allowed to stand. Louis XVIII, who returned in 1814 and ruled until his death in 1824, was a constitutional monarch, and his regime is notable for the active participation of the French *bourgeoisie* and upper classes in French politics. All Frenchmen had civil rights and were equal before the law, but political rights, as in England, were restricted to the propertied and landed classes.

Towards the end of his reign, Louis had difficulty with the reactionaries in France, many of whom had returned from exile when he was restored to the throne. This group of "Ultras"—short for ultra-royalists —was "more royalist than the King." Led by Louis's brother Charles, they wanted to end constitutional and parliamentary government, to re-establish monarchical authority, and to return land taken away from the privileged groups during the Revolution and now owned by the middle class and peasants. In short, they wanted to restore the old institutions of France—absolute monarchy, the privileged nobility, and the Church.

Louis XVIII was succeeded in 1824 by his brother, who became Charles X. The new King had little understanding of the social and economic problems of France, and continued his open support of the Ultras. He adopted many of the rituals of the old regime and tried to play the role of the benevolent, divine-right, absolute monarch. In 1830 the various liberal opposition groups in the French parliament coalesced and voted "no confidence" in the government. Charles legally dissolved parliament and called for new elections. Although the franchise was highly restricted, the Ultras lost much of their support. Fearful of the further liberalization of French politics, Charles X, on July 25, 1830, issued an edict that directly challenged the liberals. These July Ordinances dissolved parliament again and called for an election with an even more restricted franchise. At the same time, the edict asserted that "the liberty of the periodical press is suspended."[9]

The response to the Ordinances was im-

July 1815—royalists dance at the Tuileries in Paris in celebration of the defeat of Napoleon and the beginning of the restoration of the Bourbon monarchy in France.

mediate and nearly unanimous—rebellion against the monarchy by all but the most privileged classes. Many French soldiers refused to support Charles. In a few days the government was overthrown and the King was in exile. It appeared that France might now be bitterly divided over the nature of a new regime, but the Marquis de Lafayette, an old hero of both the American and French revolutions, unified the diverse elements that had made the Revolution of 1830. He proposed that the Duke of Orleans (a cousin of Charles X), who had fought on the side of the Revolution and who had always proclaimed constitutional principles, become France's king under a new constitution. This was acceptable to all sides, and with surprising speed France settled down under the constitutional rule of King Louis-Philippe, known as the "bourgeois monarch"

and the "citizen-king." His reign is called the July Monarchy.

The Revolution of 1830 reconfirmed that the people of France still supported the principles of 1789. The new King reflected this spirit; he did not call himself Louis XIX, King of France, but Louis-Philippe, King of the French. The fleur-de-lis of the Bourbons was abandoned for the tricolour flag of the Revolution, and the King was often seen dressed in middle-class clothes, carrying an umbrella. In his social life, he associated with the new monied class of France.

The Charter of 1814 was revised by the new monarch. Voting rights were extended, although a property qualification remained in force, and the power of the King was clearly limited. Though he was "head of the State," he did not have power "either to suspend the laws themselves, or dispense with

The July Revolution of 1830 in France   (Musée Carnavalet, Paris—Lauros-Giraudon)

their execution." Moreover, the Charter required "the King and his successors ... to swear, on their accession, in [the] presence of the assembled Chambers [Parliament], to observe faithfully the Constitutional Charter."[10] Much power was vested in the parliament, which was dominated by wealthy citizens.

Though French workers had been deeply involved in the Revolution of 1830, they obtained very little from it. In 1841 child labour was restricted in factories employing more than twenty people, but there was no inspection system established to police this measure. The poor were still left to the care of the Church or private charities, and little was done to improve public health or alleviate the distress of the growing industrial class in the cities. Discontent within the working class mounted over the years.

England and France, when compared to other large European states, were liberal and progressive. The French Revolution had been a political victory for the *bourgeoisie*, and the Industrial Revolution gave it great financial power. In 1788 both states had been aristocratic; by the 1830s the upper middle class was the dominant group in France and was sharing political power and social position with the aristocracy in England.

NATIONAL MOVEMENTS: ACTION AND FRUSTRATION

Liberalism in the west, conservatism in the east, and nationalism virtually everywhere: that is the political keynote of the early nineteenth century in Europe. Before 1848 nationalist movements existed, but few had any measure of success. Only Greece and Belgium became independent in this period, and both had received support from some

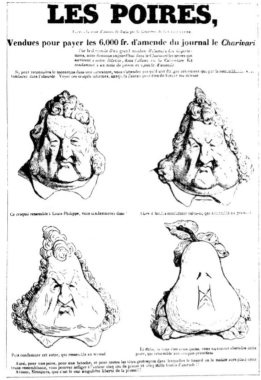

LES POIRES,

Vendues pour payer les 6,000 fr. d'amende du journal le *Charivari*

"The Pears". Charles Philipon drew this caricature of Louis-Philippe in 1832, viewing him as a pear, a reference to a simpleton in French. From that time on, Louis-Philippe was saddled with the image. (Prints Division, The New York Public Library— Astor, Lenox, and Tilden Foundations)

of the great powers. Among the long-established states, England, France, Spain, Portugal, and Holland all had a strong cultural tradition and a sense of national identity. Nationalism for these states meant an attachment to their traditions, a sense of separateness, and a pride in their achievements.

The most important areas in which peoples wanted to create new national states were southern and central Europe, but up to 1848 all of these aspirations were frustrated and forced underground by the existing authorities. Germans, Hungarians, Bohemians, Italians, and other groups were part of the Austrian Empire. In the Balkan Peninsula, Bulgarians, Rumanians, Serbians, and other groups were controlled by the Turkish Ottoman Empire. Most Poles were under Russian domination.

The creation of new nation states was not a simple matter of one group throwing off the control of another. In middle Europe and the Balkans, it was virtually impossible, even with supreme goodwill, to sort out various cultural groups as distinct "nations." How large must a group be to be considered a nation? Were people who had immigrated from one area of Europe to another doomed forever to be outsiders in a nation-state with strong feelings of nationalism? Should a new state be created only if it could be economically viable? And what are the rights of minorities? All these questions became important as nationalism became a vital force in European politics.

The major premise of nationalism is the belief that cultural groups have the right to determine their destiny: that is, they have the right to self-government in a separate state. Nationalism is not necessarily connected with any political ideology. It can take many forms—liberal, conservative, socialist, monarchist, republican. But up to 1848 nationalists in southern and middle Europe united with liberals and adopted liberal principles in opposition to conservative states. The union of nationalism and liberalism was artificial, for some of their principles are mutually contradictory. For example, liberalism espouses individualism and equal rights; nationalism looks on people primarily as members of an historical, cultural, and linguistic group, and proclaims that all groups are different. The union between liberalism and nationalism came about only because they had the same enemies.

The leading European proponent of nationalism was Giuseppe Mazzini (1805–72), an Italian patriot who lived most of his life in exile. In 1835 Mazzini attempted to define a nation:

The essential characteristics of a nationality are common ideas, common principles and a common purpose. A nation is an association of all those who are brought together by language, by given geographical conditions or by the role assigned them by history, who acknowledge the same principles and who march together to the conquest of a single definite goal under the rule of a uniform body of law.

The *life* of a nation consists in harmonious activity (that is, the employment of all individual abilities and energies . . . within the association) towards this single goal.[11]

Mazzini believed that if the world were organized as a group of national units, according to the principle of the self-determination of peoples, political problems would be solved.

Yet Mazzini also illustrates the distinction between nationalism and liberalism. In his most important work, *The Duties of Man*, he expressed his devotion to nationalist states, organized democratically under the principles of liberalism; but whereas the liberals emphasized rights, Mazzini emphasized duties. And while Mazzini shared the liberal belief in a universal kinship, he did not believe in a universal human nature. He believed that all people belonged to one family, but that each human being's personality was shaped by the national group to which that person belonged. Each group, he insisted, should cultivate its own personality. Mazzini envisioned a world of separate

co-operating nations, with liberal governments.

Mazzini's view of freedom was different from that of liberals. Liberals defined freedom in terms of the individual; people were free if their basic rights as individuals were protected. Mazzini saw freedom, however, in terms of the nation; freedom was achieved if a nation gained the right to govern itself and was free from outside interference. Mazzini saw people primarily as citizens of nation-states, not as individuals with natural rights.

Since the rulers of European empires did not recognize the principle of nationalism and sought to crush any nationalist manifestations, Mazzini, like many liberal nationalists, advocated revolution against conservative governments. In the 1830s he founded Young Italy, a society dedicated to lead Italian youth in a revolution against their Austrian masters. Many similar societies were formed throughout Europe with the aim of creating revolutions. Until 1848, despite national fervour and revolutionary activity, Prince Metternich's policies generally succeeded and the three large conservative powers kept the forces of change at bay. In 1848, however, liberalism and nationalism combined in a series of revolutions that upset the stability of Europe.

ANALYSIS AND DISCUSSION

1. The congress system which emerged after the Congress of Vienna is regarded by many as a highly successful example of international co-operation and control.
a) Draw up a list of criteria by which such a system could be judged.
b) On the basis of your list, assess the extent to which you believe the congress system was successful.
2. Metternich's "confession of faith" reflects a view of human beings and society with which most of the leaders of his time would have agreed. Indicate the extent to which you would agree or disagree with Metternich's view and explain the reasons for your position.

3. "The middle class in England did not need a revolution in order to achieve its political objectives."
a) What were the political objectives of the English middle class?
b) How can we account for the peaceful achievement of these objectives?
4. "Liberal reform in the early nineteenth century meant an increase in rights and power for the middle class but left workers outside of the decision-making process. Such an omission was bound to end in confrontation." Discuss this statement with reference to the position of the working class as reflected in both the Chartist Movement and the disillusionment with the July Monarchy in France.

5. "England and France, when compared to other large European states, were liberal and progressive." Identify the characteristics which made England and France comparatively liberal and progressive at this period in history.

6. In this chapter, there is a definition of nationalism by the Italian nationalist Giuseppe Mazzini. To what extent do you agree or disagree with his definition? Give the reasons for your position.

SYNTHESIS AND EVALUATION   CHAPTERS 5 AND 6

1. "Some historians have objected to the use of the term 'revolution' [with respect to the process of industrialization], claiming that 'evolution' — a slow change occurring over a long period of time — is a more apt description." Discuss this statement with reference to the arguments which might be used on both sides of the issue.

2. "It has been said that the Industrial Revolution, with its emphasis upon wages earned outside of the home, set back the cause of equal rights for women immeasurably. The equal status of the farm wife with her husband disappeared in the industrial town." Evaluate this idea in terms of the role of women in industrial and pre-industrial societies.

3. Metternich grew up during the era of the French Revolution. His attitudes and values were shaped by the excesses of that period. Study the excerpt from Metternich's "Confession of Faith" on page 110. Outline the influences of the revolution upon Metternich's thinking and, in your own words, summarize his view of the role of government in society.

4. Three of the most important early socialist thinkers were Saint-Simon, Fourier, and Owen.
a) By combining their ideas, prepare a single statement of the basic principles of "utopian" socialism.
b) Assess the extent to which these principles constituted a valid answer to the problems created by industrialization.

5. The text suggests a number of questions raised by the growth of nationalism:
a) How large must a group be to be considered a nation?
b) Should a new state be created only if it can be economically viable?
c) What should be the rights of minorities in a state?
Answer these questions first by preparing a definition of nationalism which satisfies you, and then by applying your definition to the questions.

CHAPTER **7**

Nationalism and National Movements: 1848-1871

Europe
1848   Revolutions in France, Austria, Hungary, Italy, Prussia
1852   Cavour becomes Prime Minister of Piedmont
1854–56 Crimean War
1859–60 Italian Wars; the Unification of Italy
1862   Bismarck becomes Prime Minister of Prussia
1864   Danish War
1866   Austro-Prussian War
1867   The *Ausgleich* in Austria-Hungary
1870   Franco-Prussian War
        Rome annexed to Italy
1871   Proclamation of German Empire at Versailles
                    Other Areas
1861–65 United States Civil War
1867   Dominion of Canada established by British North America Act
1868   Meiji Era begins in Japan

I N 1848 LIBERAL AND NATIONALIST sentiments in Europe erupted in a series of revolutions. New ideas, institutions, and classes that had been contained by the conservative powers seemed to be about to triumph over all that was traditional. But the revolutions of 1848, after a brief moment of success, ultimately failed. Liberals throughout Europe proved unable to establish and consolidate political power, and conservatives in the end retained control of most states. But national feeling grew more intense after 1848, in spite of the collapse of the revolutionary movements, and by 1871 both Italy and Germany came into being as new nation-states.

Outside Europe, national issues were also of primary importance. The United States, in the early 1860s, was torn apart by a prolonged and bloody civil war, which was in part fought over different concepts of nationhood. Canada came into being in 1867 by a British act of parliament, but the new state faced the problem of having to integrate French and English elements with widely different traditions. Japan, long a state with a homogeneous population, faced the problem of attempting to adopt Western industrialism with extraordinary speed without losing its own identity.

It was a new age—of revolutions, limited wars, changing ideologies, and nation-building.

THE REVOLUTIONS OF 1848

Metternich had feared that revolution in one European state would inspire other uprisings. Hence he wanted to stamp out all revolutions and was willing to prop up even the weakest European regime as long as it was a so-called "legitimate" one. He had special fears for the multi-national Austrian Empire, and he attempted to suppress the national aspirations of all groups, lest the empire disintegrate.

Metternich's fears were justified by events. When a revolution did break out, it usually sparked others; this occurred in the 1820s and the 1830s, and ultimately on a grand scale in 1848, the most revolutionary year in the history of the West. Only England and Russia escaped serious uprisings in 1848— England because its upper and middle classes were united in their desire for stability and because it had already embarked on a program of political and social reform; and Russia because its autocracy was strong and the potential revolutionary forces, the middle class and the industrial working class, were very sparse and weak.

In 1848 a revolution in France once again gave the lead to Europe. King Louis-Philippe and his ministers represented the views of the upper and upper-middle classes. Little industrial reform took place as discontent mounted both among the lower middle class and the growing body of workers. Opposition to the regime arose particularly among republicans who sought participation for more people in the political life of the nation. Under the July Monarchy, political societies were illegal, and in 1847 Louis-Philippe and his Prime Minister, François Guizot, suspended the right of political assembly. The republicans, among them many opposition members of parliament, responded by holding "banquets" in order to demand a wider franchise. On February 22, 1848, a "banquet" was cancelled by the King and Guizot in an attempt to silence the opposition. Here is how one participant described the events that followed:

All that evening, all that night of the 23rd to 24th February, had a sinister aspect. The work of the insurrection went on with an extraordinary activity, in silence, and without any military force intervening to oppose it. Paris was filled with barricades, from the Boulevard de Gand up to the Bastille, from the Porte Saint-Denis to the Seine. The insurgent people had come down into the streets with their working tools, waiting until they could take up rifles on the next day. They cut down, alas, the beautiful trees of the boulevards; they demolished the railings of the monuments, the lamp-posts, fountains and sheds, and everything that might serve to hinder the passage of troops; they carried on to the pavements, materials from houses under construction, beams, blocks of stone, planks and carts; and all this was built round with formidable walls of paving-stones. One heard nothing but the blows of axes and the sounds of trees which, in falling, broke their branches; sometimes, a clashing of weapons and a few detonations lost in the shadows; almost all the time, like a monotonous accompaniment, the sound of the tocsin; and soon the barricades were manned and guarded by their sentinels, and one saw, around sparkling braziers, groups of squatting men, casting bullets, and smoking their pipes peacefully, in this strange bivouac in the middle of the great city which was being tilled for the planting of freedom.[1]

The pattern of revolution, established in

"The Gamin in the Tuileries" by Honoré Daumier (1808–1879). This political cartoon was based on an incident following the success of the February Revolution of 1848 in France. A crowd went to the palace to celebrate the end of the monarchy. Many people lined up for an opportunity to sit on the royal throne. (British Museum—John R. Freeman)

1789, was repeated. The army, ordered to fire on the revolutionaries, refused, and within three days Louis-Philippe abdicated and left the country. All the revolutionaries agreed on a republican form of government, and a provisional government was established until elections could be held in April. The February Revolution in France raised the hopes of nationalists and liberals all over Europe.

Within a month the Austrian Empire was shaken by national and liberal uprisings. In Vienna the revolutionaries challenged the conservative policies of the Austrian state. In Hungary revolutionaries led by Louis Kossuth demanded a constitution and autonomy for the Magyar people. In Italy, King Charles Albert of the independent state of Piedmont declared war on Austria in the hope of creating a united Italy. Throughout the Italian peninsula people rose in revolt, and by mid-1848 the revolutionaries apparently controlled large areas. Other peoples in the Austrian Empire soon demanded national autonomy.

The Vienna revolution was at first successful. In March 1848 Emperor Ferdinand dismissed Metternich and granted a constitution to Austria. In April Hungary obtained its own constitution but not full autonomy. In June the Emperor, like Louis-Philippe, was forced to flee his capital. Throughout the empire several constitutional bodies were meeting; like their French predecessors of 1789, they all voted to abolish the feudal rights of the nobility and to end serfdom by giving the peasants equality under the law.

In the German states revolution was directed against Austria, the state which had the most to lose from German unification. The German nationalist revolutionaries turned to Prussia for leadership. In Berlin, Prussian revolutionaries, following the lead of Paris and Vienna, demanded constitutional government, and in March 1848 the Prussian King, Frederick William IV, promised a constitution. Other revolutions followed in the smaller German states, and demands for reform were heard everywhere. A National Assembly of representatives from all the German states, elected by uni-

A caricature of Metternich, showing him in flight from Vienna during the 1848 revolution in Austria   (John Webb)

versal manhood suffrage, met in the city of Frankfurt in May 1848. Here, it was hoped, plans could be made by representatives of the people to establish a liberal, constitutional, and a unified German state.

The revolutionary forces varied in their composition from one area to another. In Paris workers joined with intellectuals. In Vienna students and intellectuals led the way. In Hungary the revolutionaries were aristocrats who fought for autonomy from Austria. In Italy some members of all classes, including peasants, supported insurrections and backed the attempt of Piedmont to unite Italy. In the German states 1848 was, as one historian has called it, a "revolution of the intellectuals."

By mid-1848 Europe was convulsed by revolutions; a year later, most of these revolutionary movements had failed. One reason for this failure was the inability of the revolutionaries to remain united. While people could agree to overthrow the old regimes, they could not agree on the shape of the new order. Some intellectuals and industrial workers wanted to see radical social change that would include establishing democracy and socialism. Middle-class liberals were suspicious of socialism and of too much democracy; they wanted freedom, political power, order, and the protection of property. The peasants of Europe—the vast majority of people—remained conservative in temperament and were usually loyal to their rulers, traditional church, and local lord. Hence not everyone greeted revolution with joy. The professional armies of Europe often continued to support the old regimes. Moreover, nationalities who sought freedom and autonomy for themselves denied the same freedom to others. For example, Germans fighting for national unity were unwilling to extend the same right to Poles living in German states.

The divisions within the revolutionary party are clearest in France. The provisional government that took power after the February Revolution was composed of varied elements—liberals, socialists, constitutional monarchists. Faced with poor harvests and massive unemployment, this government set up National Workshops which, in the end, became public works projects to provide work for the unemployed. However, when the liberals won a majority in the elections of April 1848, they decided to do away with these National Workshops on the ground that they were too much of a financial drain on the *bourgeoisie* and peasants. In June the National Workshops were closed.

The workers responded by mounting a second revolution, recalling the Jacobin uprisings of 1792–93. They set up barricades in an attempt to seize power. But the provisional government called in the army, led by General Cavaignac, to suppress this new attempt at revolution. Whereas in 1789 and in February 1848 the troops had hesitated to fire on citizens, in June 1848 they supported the liberal government of the middle classes and peasants against the radical aims of the Parisian workers. From June 24 to 26, 1848, Paris was involved in a civil war fought among the members of the old Third Estate. Victor Hugo (1802–85), one of the best-known writers of France, described his experience at that time:

The insurgents were firing throughout the whole length of the Boulevard Beaumarchais from the tops of the new houses. Several had ambushed themselves in the big house in course of construction opposite the Galiote. At the windows they had stuck dummies—bundles of straw with blouses and caps on them.

I distinctly saw a man who had entrenched himself behind a barricade of bricks in a corner of the balcony on the fourth floor of the house which faces the Rue du Pont-aux-Choux. The man took careful aim and killed a good many persons.

It was 3 o'clock. The troops and mobiles fringed the roofs of the Boulevard du Temple and returned the fire of the insurgents. A cannon had just been drawn up in front of the Gaîté to demolish the house of the Galiote and sweep the whole boulevard.[2]

The bloody "June Days" shook Paris, France, and Europe; the defeat of the workers, or "Social Republicans," marked the first step back to conservatism.

The results of the election in December 1848 reflected the change in mood. Running for the office of president of the new French republic were General Louis Cavaignac, the hero of the repression; Alphonse de Lamartine, a liberal poet; Alexander Ledru-Rollin, a radical; and an unknown man with a famous name, Louis Napoleon Bonaparte, the nephew of Napoleon. About 5 500 000 people voted for Bonaparte, 1 500 000 for Cavaignac, 370 000 for Ledru-Rollin, and only 21 000 for Lamartine. The election showed that a large majority of Frenchmen opposed radicalism; they preferred the "order" and "glory" which were associated with the name of Napoleon.

Before becoming President, Louis Napoleon had had a pathetic career. His several attempts to enter politics had failed. He had written a few works in which he claimed to be the representative of the imperial, paternal state established by his uncle, but no one had paid much attention to them. He had been in jail after 1840, when he had tried to overthrow the government of Louis-Philippe in a farcical uprising. In 1846 he escaped from prison, fled to England, and did not return to France until mid-1848.

A barricade in Paris during the street fighting of June 1848.   (Radio Times Hulton Picture Library)

As President of the Second Republic, Louis Napoleon proceeded to liquidate the republican regime. In December 1851 he used the army to overthrow the constitution. In December 1852 he declared himself Emperor, and called a plebiscite asking for public approval. The country voted overwhelmingly in his favour; France thus chose to have both its second Napoleon and its Second Empire. Another republican experiment had failed.

In the Austrian Empire, even though one Emperor abdicated, the Hapsburgs managed to regain control. The army continued to support the central regime, which played off one nationality against another and kept the liberals quiet by promising a constitution. King Charles Albert of Piedmont was defeated in July, and Austria regained control of its Italian possessions. In Hungary difficulties between Hungarians and other national groups, such as Slovaks, Serbs, and Croats, divided the revolutionaries and allowed the Austrian forces to restore order.

The promised constitutions never went into effect, and by 1849 all the revolutionaries had been defeated.

One of the revolutionary outbursts had occurred in the Papal States, the territory in Italy under the rule of the Pope. These lands were protected by French troops according to an agreement made by Napoleon I with the Papacy in the Concordat of 1801. Yet Rome was the centre of one of the republican movements, led by Mazzini and Giuseppe Garibaldi. Pope Pius IX (1846–78) had a reputation as a liberal, but he turned more conservative as the revolutions of 1848 unfolded, and he left Rome in November because of the strength of the republicans and the chaos in the city. A constituent assembly was called by the revolutionaries, and in February 1849 Mazzini's group proclaimed the establishment of a democratic Roman Republic.

As other European states began to restore stability, they turned their attention to Rome. France sent troops against Mazzini in

Pope Pius IX is portrayed as a reactionary underneath the mask of compassion in this caricature made after the defeat of the revolutions of 1848–49. In 1848 Pope Pius said of the Roman Republic, "in Rome . . . there does not exist, nor can arise, any legitimate authority which is not derived from us." (British Museum—John R. Freeman)

April 1849, and Austria, Spain, and the kingdom of Naples—all Catholic areas—joined forces to defeat Mazzini and restore the Pope, who returned to Rome in 1850. However, Italian nationalists would never let him or the rest of Italy forget that he was brought back by foreign troops fighting against Italians.

In the German states, while the Frankfurt Assembly was talking, the princes were regaining control. By the time the Assembly drew up a liberal constitution in May 1849, the local sovereigns were back in power. Frederick William IV of Prussia refused the crown of a united Germany offered by the Assembly. He replied that he would accept the crown from his fellow princes, but not

from an illegal body. Soon the delegates in Frankfurt went home, and all seemed to be as it was before.

CONSEQUENCES OF THE FAILURE OF 1848

If intellectuals and ideas—especially liberalism and nationalism—helped to make the revolutions of 1848, they were also partly responsible for their failure. Liberalism stood for rational discourse, freedom, and constitutional government. The nationalism of the pre-1848 period put its faith in a mass uprising which would somehow overthrow regimes like that of Austria. After that, all people would group into nations, draw up constitutions, and live together in peace. Before 1848 many persons thought that once the message penetrated, the deed would be accomplished. In 1848, however, it became clear that intellectuals and ideas would not by themselves make a successful revolution. For example, in the German states it was felt that the Frankfurt Assembly talked too much and did too little. A strong current of anti-intellectualism appeared in central Europe after 1849.

Many, though not all, nationalists abandoned liberalism as an ideology for change and adopted a new "realistic" policy. If nationalism was to succeed, they thought, it could not rely on liberal methods, but must adopt a policy of force. In response to the failures of 1848, nationalists reoriented themselves—realism and power were viewed as the way of the future. Nationalists were ready to ally with anyone who could help them to achieve their ends.

Liberalism, however, remained the political philosophy of the middle class and a powerful force where that class was numerous. After 1848 it became a respectable political stance concentrating on constitutional and legal reform. Liberalism was particularly strong in England, France, the United States, Belgium, and Piedmont, all of which already had some form of representative institutions and democracy, and it made inroads into the German states and the Austrian Empire. But the working classes of the Industrial Revolution often rejected the *laissez-faire* eco-

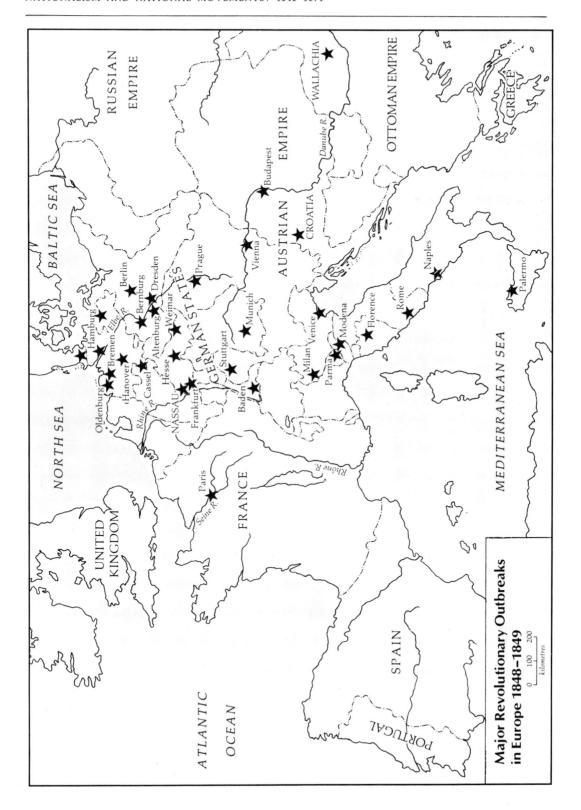

RUSSIAN EMPIRE

OTTOMAN EMPIRE

GREECE

BALTIC SEA

WALLACHIA

Danube R.

AUSTRIAN EMPIRE

Budapest

CROATIA

Vienna

Prague

Naples

Berlin

Dresden

Rome

Palermo

Hamburg

Bernburg

Weimar

Munich

Florence

Bremen

Altenburg

Modena

Oldenburg

Hanover

Cassel

GERMAN STATES

Stuttgart

Milan Venice

Parma

Hesse

NASSAU

Frankfurt

Baden

Elbe R.

Rhine

NORTH SEA

MEDITERRANEAN SEA

Paris

Rhône R.

FRANCE

Seine R.

UNITED KINGDOM

ATLANTIC OCEAN

SPAIN

PORTUGAL

**Major Revolutionary Outbreaks
in Europe 1848–1849**

0   100   200
kilometres

nomics of liberalism. Labourers blamed the failure of 1848 on the middle class, and many turned from liberalism to revolutionary socialism.

The failure of the revolutions of 1848 also created a community of exiles. Some fled their homeland; others were banished because of their revolutionary activity. A number of the best minds in Europe migrated to London—Britain was the only land which tolerated them—in order to continue their activities and begin preparations for the overthrow of established governments.

THE UNIFICATION OF ITALY AND GERMANY

What moved the great majority of people in the mid nineteenth century was not socialism or liberalism, but nationalism. The nationalist revolts of 1848 ended in failure, but national aspirations did not disappear. Rather, they became more intense in Italy, in the German states, in the Hapsburg lands, and in the Balkans.

In 1850 "Italy" was a geographical area, not a state; "Germany" was a group of many sovereignties; and "Austria" was an empire of many peoples. In a few decades all this changed radically. The map of Europe was reconstructed by nationalist movements. By 1871 Italy and Germany were nation-states and the Austrian Empire had been transformed.

THE CRIMEAN WAR

The Crimean War of 1854–56, by revealing the weakness of the conservative powers, cleared the way for the restructuring of both Italy and Germany. There had been no conflicts between major European powers since 1815, but this calm was broken in 1854 by a war between Russia and Turkey which drew in other states. It began as a dispute over the area now known as Rumania, then under the control of the Ottoman Empire. Russia had been pursuing an expansionist policy since the seventeenth century, absorbing Slavic areas on its border. In the eighteenth century the policy had been generally successful in the west and in the north, but not in the south, where Russia was eager to secure an

outlet to the Mediterranean Sea. Russian ambitions had been checked by England and France, both of which did not want naval competition in the Mediterranean area, and thus, when the war broke out, England and France joined Turkey in order to check Russian expansion in the south. Austria, unable to make up its mind, finally mobilized against Russia, but did so too slowly and too late to make any difference. The war did not last long and it was not very bloody. Russia was decisively defeated.

The Congress of Paris in 1856 arranged the peace. The Russians were prevented from sending warships through the Black Sea into the Mediterranean and agreed "to respect the independence and the territorial integrity of the Ottoman Empire."[3] For the first time in centuries, Russia had lost a European war, while Austria had mobilized with the speed of a turtle, displaying its military weakness. Although England and France had not covered themselves with glory, they had been more effective. For those with nationalist ambitions, the weakness of the conservative states of Europe was a good omen.

The war showed the European powers that international conflicts were not a thing of the past, and general rearmament began throughout Europe. The growth of industry and the development of new technology resulted in the production of new weapons, such as machine guns, which made killing more grisly and efficient. The competition in war technology of the last half of the nineteenth century actually began in the period after the Crimean War.

CAVOUR AND ITALY

One other state joined in the Crimean War. The small Italian principality of Piedmont-Sardinia sent troops to fight Russia, but not because of any special feelings of friendship for Turkey. Count Camillo di Cavour (1810–61), who led the parliament of the constitutional monarchy under King Victor Emmanuel, understood that only those who take part in a war can participate in the peace. The Piedmontese soldiers fought well and Cavour earned a place at the conference table when peace came. At Paris in 1856

Piedmont did not demand land, but did raise the question of Italian national ambitions, reminding England, France, and Austria of Piedmont's contribution to the victory.

National unification had been a passion in the Italian peninsula since the time of Napoleon. Revolutionary secret societies committed to a republican solution, such as Mazzini's Young Italy, began to appear in the 1830s and 1840s. Among the many revolutionary military leaders, the most famous and the most dashing was Giuseppe Garibaldi (1807–82), a liberal soldier of fortune who had fought in Latin America in the 1830s and had joined Mazzini in Rome in 1848. On the other hand, a group of Italian theologians and laymen had looked for leadership to the Papacy, which controlled middle Italy; they proposed a loose federation with the Pope at the head.

Cavour was a hard-headed, practical man, with a liberal outlook. He admired England, and had organized Piedmont as a parliamentary constitutional monarchy on the English model. He had a strong sense of the possible—he was not willing to take great risks for fear of losing what he had gained. He was both a Piedmontese patriot and an Italian patriot, but was afraid that if Italy were unified Piedmont would be swallowed up. Thus his aim was to extend Piedmontese institutions into Italy.

Cavour recognized the importance of the Industrial Revolution in changing the lives of peoples and states. As Prime Minister of Piedmont from 1852, he helped to reorganize the economy on modern lines, encourage financial growth, and stimulate the building of railways, which he knew would play an important role in centralizing power. As he wrote in 1846:

The influence of railroads will extend all over the world. In the nations which have reached a high level of civilization they will furnish immense impetus to industry; their economic results will be impressive from the beginning, and they will accelerate progress. But the social results which should take place, greater to us than the material results, will be especially remarkable in those nations which have remained backward. For

them the railroads will be more than a means of self enrichment; they will be a powerful ally, with whose help they will triumph over the forces holding them in a dismal state of industrial and political immaturity. We are convinced that the locomotive is destined to diminish, if not abolish altogether, the humiliating inferiority to which many branches of the great Christian family are reduced. Thus considered, it fills a providential role; perhaps this is why we see it triumph so easily and so quickly over obstacles which have long prevented it from penetrating into certain regions.

If this is true, no nation has more right than Italy to place great hope in the potential of the railroads. The extensive political and social consequences which should result from them will testify better in this beautiful country than elsewhere to the great role they will play in the world's future.[4]

Having witnessed the failures of 1848, Cavour distrusted sentimental nationalist uprisings. He did not think Mazzini's ideas and methods could succeed or create anything lasting. He hesitated to try to do too much, such as uniting Italy all at once, because he knew he might end up with nothing. Only diplomacy and war, he believed, could bring about the national revival of Italy, the *Risorgimento*, as it was called. Cavour was the first practitioner of *Realpolitik*—the politics of reality—which Bismarck in Germany would make into a fine art. Like all of the "realists" of the time, he subordinated means to ends. He also knew that Italian unification could not take place unless the great powers (as in the case of Belgium and Greece) were willing to accept the change in the map of Europe that Italian unification implied.

The real enemy of Italy in 1848 was Austria. Searching for an ally among the great powers, Cavour found Louis Napoleon, now the Emperor Napoleon III of France.* Louis Napoleon thought he would continue the Napoleonic tradition by supporting Italian nationalism, and perhaps win glory for

*Napoleon Bonaparte's only son, the Duke of Reichstadt, died without heirs in 1832. He had been called Napoleon II by his followers.

France in the process. In July 1858 Piedmont and France signed the Pact of Plombières, agreeing to make war on Austria so that Lombardy and Venetia, the two other northern provinces of Italy, might be annexed to Piedmont. Cavour agreed to cede Nice and Savoy to Napoleon in exchange for French help. Thus the agreement was limited to the unification of northern Italy. The pact was the first offensive treaty of modern times: the parties signing it agreed to bring about a war and even divided the spoils before the war actually occurred.

The first step in the plan was to provoke Austria. Cavour did this by protecting draft-dodgers fleeing to Piedmont from the Austrian areas and by mobilizing his troops on the border of the Austrian lands. Austria actually declared war first on April 20, 1859. From the outset, the war went well for Piedmont. Napoleon III came under pressure from many French Catholics who opposed the war as a threat to the Papal States and who were not sympathetic to the nationalist cause of Italy. Moreover, he feared that Piedmont's rapid success would inflame nationalist sentiment throughout the Italian peninsula. Hence he abruptly ended his active military support of Piedmont on July 11, 1859. Though Lombardy was annexed by Cavour, Venetia remained in the hands of Austria.

But neither Cavour nor Napoleon III had foreseen the effect of local Italian uprisings and the intervention of Garibaldi. While Piedmont fought in the north, revolutionary assemblies in central Italy threw out local rulers and voted for unity with Piedmont. Thus all of Italy north of the Papal States, with the exception of Venetia, was united. In 1860 Garibaldi used the success of Piedmont in the north to unite the south. He invaded the island of Sicily with his "red shirts," a group of guerilla soldiers, and in April 1860 issued a proclamation of aims:

The misfortunes of Italy arise from the indifference of one province to the fate of the others. The redemption of Italy began from the moment that men of the same land ran to help their distressed brothers. Left to themselves the Sicilians will have to fight not only the mercenaries of the Bourbon, but also of Austria and the Priest of Rome.

Let the inhabitants of the free provinces lift their voices on behalf of their struggling brethren, and impel their brave youth to the conflict. Let the Marches, Umbria, Sabina, Rome, the Neapolitan, rise to divide the forces of our enemies.

Where the cities suffice not for the insurrection, let them send bands of their bravest into the country. The brave man finds an arm everywhere. Listen not to the voice of cowards, but arm, and let us fight for our brethren, who will fight for us tomorrow....

To arms! Let us put an end, once for all, to the miseries of so many centuries. Prove to the world that it is no lie that Roman generations inhabited this land.[5]

Garibaldi took control of Sicily in July 1860 and then moved on to the mainland. On September 8, 1860, he entered the city of Naples, uniting the south of Italy.

Cavour feared that Garibaldi would invade Rome and that France would join Austria to protect the Papacy as it was obliged to do under the Concordat of 1801. If this occurred, all gains might be dissipated. Therefore, he sent the Piedmontese army south in order to check Garibaldi, after assuring Napoleon III that Rome would not be affected. Although he was a staunch republican, Garibaldi, in a patriotic and sublimely idealistic gesture, surrendered his conquests to King Victor Emmanuel of Piedmont. Cavour's sense of "realism" had won the day. The parliament of the north agreed to annex southern Italy, including part of the old Papal States, but not the area around Rome. An Italian parliament met at Turin in 1861 and declared Italy a constitutional monarchy with Victor Emmanuel as King.

Cavour died in 1861 at the moment of his greatest success. His legacy is a strange one, for though he callously disregarded international law and made the ends justify the means, his views always had a liberal tinge because of his admiration of England. But his methods raised enormous problems. To force an Austrian declaration of war against Piedmont may have been clever, but it was

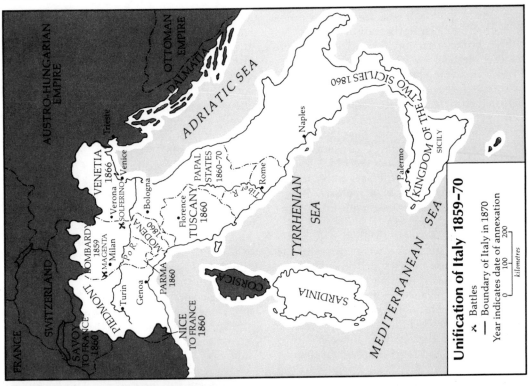

Unification of Italy 1859–70

× Battles
— Boundary of Italy in 1870
Year indicates date of annexation

0   100   200
kilometres

AUSTRO-HUNGARIAN EMPIRE

OTTOMAN EMPIRE

DALMATIA

ADRIATIC SEA

TWO SICILIES 1860

SWITZERLAND

FRANCE

SAVOY TO FRANCE 1860

VENETIA 1866

Trieste
•Venice
Verona•
×SOLFERINO
LOMBARDY 1859
×MAGENTA •Milan
Po R.
MODENA 1860
PARMA 1860
•Turin
Genoa•
NICE TO FRANCE 1860

PIEDMONT

TUSCANY 1860
Florence•
•Bologna

PAPAL STATES 1860–70
Tiber R.
•Rome

Naples•

TYRRHENIAN SEA

CORSICA

SARDINIA

MEDITERRANEAN SEA

KINGDOM OF THE TWO SICILIES
Palermo•
SICILY

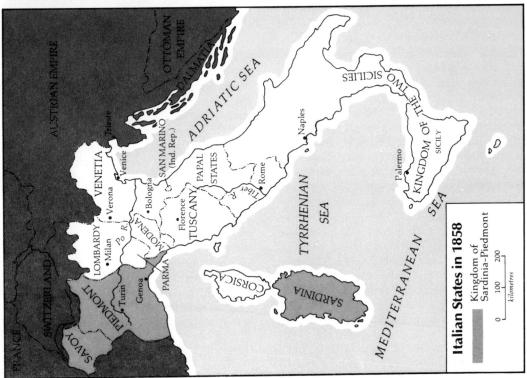

Italian States in 1858

Kingdom of Sardinia-Piedmont

0   100   200
kilometres

AUSTRIAN EMPIRE

OTTOMAN EMPIRE

DALMATIA

ADRIATIC SEA

THE TWO SICILIES

SWITZERLAND

FRANCE

SAVOY

PIEDMONT
•Turin
Genoa•

LOMBARDY
•Milan
Po R.
PARMA
MODENA

VENETIA
Trieste
•Venice
Verona•

SAN MARINO (Ind. Rep.)

•Bologna
TUSCANY
Florence•
PAPAL STATES
Tiber R.
Rome•

Naples•

TYRRHENIAN SEA

CORSICA

SARDINIA

MEDITERRANEAN SEA

KINGDOM OF THE TWO SICILIES
Palermo•
SICILY

also deceitful. A war was instigated simply to further the cause of the nation-state.

The completion of Italian unity took another decade. In 1866 Italy united with Prussia in a war against Austria. The Italian military effort was unsuccessful, but Prussia defeated Austria, and Italy obtained Venetia. During the Franco-Prussian War of 1870, French armies were too busy losing to Prussia to protect Rome; consequently, Italian troops walked into the old Imperial City and annexed it to the new Italy. Italy's success was the result of a realistic, tough policy used against equally realistic, tough, and determined enemies.

Not all Italians were thrilled to join the united nation-state, nor were all problems solved. Immense poverty continued. Many in the south feared domination by the more economically advanced north. Some sought a high degree of local independence and now feared the encroachments of the central authority. The Papacy was antagonistic to the new Italy, and large numbers of devout Catholics did not give their support to the liberal, constitutional regime.

BISMARCK AND GERMANY

Austria, fearful of breaking up its empire, had always refused to take the lead in German unification. As a result, Prussia became the centre of German nationalism. The Prussian state also seemed to be moving in the direction of liberalism. Though the revolution of 1848 had failed, Prussians did obtain a constitution and a two-house legislature; the executive power of the King, however, was unchecked by parliament.

King William I, who became Regent for his ailing father in 1857 and ruler in his own right in 1861, had occasionally espoused liberal principles, although his liberalism was more like that of enlightened despotism than parliamentary government. In 1862 he asked his parliament for funds in order to re-build the army. The Progressive Party, the liberal group, was not happy with this plan, first proposed in 1860, but voted the funds both in that year and in 1861. In 1862, however, the liberals refused to grant the money

requested. A deadlock resulted, since the monarch was responsible for maintaining the army, while parliament was responsible for voting money to finance it. The constitution had no quick remedy in case of a deadlock, and a contest for supremacy arose between parliament and the crown. William legally dissolved the parliament in 1862, but new elections brought a more liberal parliament to Berlin. At this moment, close to abdication, the King asked Otto von Bismarck (1815–98) to be his First Minister.

Bismarck was a *Junker*, a member of the Prussian aristocracy. He had served as Prussian ambassador to Russia and France, but had not had an outstanding public career to this point. He believed in monarchical principles and had little use for republican, liberal, or socialist ideas. But he was not dogmatic and not opposed to reform as long as it came from above and contributed to the strength of the state. As a Prussian nationalist, he did not want German unification to submerge Prussia. He believed that Germany must be an extension of Prussian government and institutions. Though he was determined to uphold the power of the monarchy, he was also a realist who did not attempt to do away with the Prussian constitution; he knew that if he went too far, he could produce a revolutionary situation.

Bismarck responded to the constitutional deadlock by claiming that all powers not specifically given by the constitution to parliament belonged to the King. He advised the King to ignore the deadlock and ask the civil service to carry on and collect taxes as before. Parliament was incensed, but it did not resort to revolutionary action. Bismarck demonstrated that, though Prussia had a constitution, the King's powers were decisive, and though Prussia had a parliament, the King and his ministers could defy it. He showed, moreover, that a minister chosen by the King did not need the confidence of parliament in order to govern in Prussia.

Having collected the taxes and put the army on a sound basis, Bismarck began to pursue an expansionist foreign policy in order to point the way to German unity and to silence his critics by winning glory for the state. In 1862 he stated how this was to be accomplished:

The eyes of Germany are fixed not upon Prussia's liberalism, but upon her armed might. Bavaria, Württemberg, and Baden may indulge in liberal experiments; therefore, no one will assign to them Prussia's role. Prussia must harbor and maintain her strength for the favorable moment—a moment which has already, on one occasion, slipped by; Prussia's boundaries, as drawn by the Vienna treaties, are not suitable for a healthy state life. The great questions of the day will not be decided by speeches or by majority decisions— that was the mistake of 1848 and 1849—but by blood and iron![6]

In 1864 Bismarck joined with Austria in a war against Denmark over the German-speaking provinces of Schleswig and Holstein, which had been governed by the Danish king. Denmark was quickly defeated, and the war demonstrated the success of the new Prussian army provided for in the enlarged budgets.

Keeping aloof from all political parties, Bismarck used the desire for a German nation-state and Prussia's dominant economic position to unite some of the German states against Austria. While liberals and conservatives in Prussia had different concepts of nationalism, they were all swept along by the feeling for unity. German intellectuals were more willing to support Bismarck after the failures of 1848. Many of them were such ardent nationalists that once Bismarck became successful, they dropped their liberalism in favour of a policy which emphasized the power of the state. But not all the smaller German states looked with approval on Prussia's growing strength. Some wanted to maintain their autonomy and not be absorbed by the larger Prussia. Religious differences existed as well; many southern German states, most notably Bavaria, were Catholic, and felt closer to Austria than to Protestant Prussia.

Bismarck was aware of the obstacles to German unification. He realized he would have to defeat Austria and silence its claims to German leadership in order to enable Prussia to bring about German unification.

To accomplish his end, he embarked on a most extraordinary demonstration of *Realpolitik*. Militarily, he prepared for war with Austria by making certain that the Prussian army was better trained, better equipped, and more easily mobilized. Diplomatically, he prepared by isolating his enemy: he brought about an alliance with Italy by promising Italy control of Venetia; he pacified France with vague promises of territory; he hinted to Russia that Prussia would support its Mediterranean claims, recently thwarted by the Crimean War; and he calculated that England would not intervene as long as he did not challenge its empire. Bismarck wanted a short and decisive war with Austria, for he knew that if the war was a long one, other powers might enter. He also knew that Prussia should not annex too much too fast, for what was won on the battlefield might be lost at a conference table with the great powers present.

Bismarck brought on the Austro-Prussian War of 1866 by provoking a disagreement between Austria and Prussia over the occupation of Schleswig-Holstein. The war lasted only seven weeks and ended in a great victory for Prussia. It was a quick, surgical operation which astounded the world. When the Prussian generals said they could continue on to Vienna and totally defeat Austria, Bismarck said no, for he had brought about the war to unite Germany, not to crush Austria. Bismarck's uncanny sense of limits meant that victory was an accomplished fact almost before the world knew that war had begun.

The Seven Weeks War resulted in the creation in 1867 of the North German Confederation composed of twenty-two of the thirty-nine German sovereignties. The Confederation was a political union with the Prussian king as president and the constitution based on the Prussian model. Bismarck had succeeded in creating the largest German entity since the middle ages.

As a result of war and defeat, the Austrian Empire was weakened. The government in Vienna, which was dominated by the German-speaking group within the Empire, was forced to give in to some of the demands of

Daumier: "Let us embrace"   (Bequest of W. G. Russell Allen. Courtesy, Museum of Fine Arts, Boston)

the large Hungarian minority. In what is known as the *Ausgleich*, or compromise, the Hungarians were given internal self-government, and Austria-Hungary became a dual monarchy under the Hapsburgs. However, the other national minority groups received no such concessions, and began to feel they would never gain their national freedom without a struggle. Like Italy before them, they began to look for allies among the great powers.

The Seven Weeks War was a great diplo-matic defeat for France and Napoleon III. For centuries France had successfully resisted the creation of a strong power on its borders. Now, with Prussia leading a large German confederation, all that was changed. Bismarck realized that if he wished to unify the rest of Germany, he must defeat France, for France would never permit the peaceful union of the northern and southern German states. And he also felt that he must frighten the southern states into the union as they were less than eager to enter a Germany dominated by Prussia. Thus, as he had done before, Bismarck manufactured a crisis in order to start a war.

The crisis was precipitated in 1870 by the question of succession to the Spanish throne. Spain had been without a monarch since 1868 and the most likely candidate for the throne was a member of the Hohenzollern family, a cousin of King William I of Prussia. France did not want to have members of the Hohenzollern family ruling on both her eastern and south-western borders. Therefore, Napoleon III instructed his ambassador to Prussia, Count Benedetti, to prevail on William I to persuade his cousin to withdraw from candidature to the throne of Spain. The King agreed, but a few days later Napoleon asked that William guarantee that the candidacy would not be renewed. This last demand made by Benedetti while the King was staying at Ems, a health resort, was refused. William had a summary of the conversation telegraphed to Bismarck, merely to keep him informed. Bismarck, however, shortened this "Ems Dispatch" in such a way as to make it seem that the two countries had insulted one another.

Here is the original telegram received by Bismarck from one of the King's aides:

His Majesty writes to me: "Count Benedetti spoke to me on the promenade, in order to demand from me, finally in a very importunate manner, that I should authorize him to telegraph at once that I bound myself for all future time never again to give my consent if the Hohenzollerns should renew their candidature. I refused at last somewhat sternly, as it is neither right nor possible to undertake engagements of this sort à tout jamais [for ever]. I told him that I had as yet received no news, and as he was earlier informed from Paris and Madrid than myself, he could see clearly that my government had no more interest in the matter."

His Majesty has since received a letter from Prince Charles Anthony. His Majesty, having told Count Benedetti that he was awaiting news from the Prince, has decided, with reference to the above demand, on the suggestion of Count Eulenburg and myself, not to receive Count Benedetti again, but only to let him be informed through an aide-de-camp: "That his Majesty has now received from the Prince confirmation of the news which Benedetti had already received from Paris, and had nothing further to say to the ambassador." His Majesty leaves it to your Excellency [Bismarck] to decide whether Benedetti's fresh demand and its rejection should be at once communicated to both our ambassadors, to foreign nations, and to the Press.[7]

Bismarck released this version:

After the news of the renunciation of the hereditary Prince of Hohenzollern had been officially communicated to the Imperial Government of France by the Royal Government of Spain the French Ambassador further demanded of His Majesty, the King, at Ems, that he would authorize him to telegraph to Paris that His Majesty, the King, bound himself for all time never again to give his consent, should the Hohenzollerns renew their candidature. His Majesty, the King, thereupon decided not to receive the French Ambassador again, and sent the aide-de-camp on duty to tell him that His Majesty had nothing further to communicate to the ambassador.[8]

The text which Bismarck released to the newspapers stirred nationalist sentiment in each country to a fever. This is an early example of the manipulation of public opinion through modern communications, in this instance the newspaper. It is also an early example of the role public opinion played in a European diplomatic decision, for both Germans and Frenchmen put immense pressure on their governments to avenge national honour. France actually attacked first. Consequently, sentiment in Europe, especially in England, was with Prussia and Germany.

The Franco-Prussian War, begun in July 1870, was effectively ended on September 2 with the defeat of Napoleon III at Sedan. When the conflict broke out, the south German states sided with Prussia, and, due to superior mobilization and an effective war plan, the German armies completely shattered the French. This in itself was extraordinary. It had taken virtually all of Europe to defeat Napoleon I, and for centuries France had been the first land power on the

Daumier: "The Dream of the Inventor of the Needle-Gun"

*Daumier: "Horrified at the Heritage"
(Courtesy of the Fogg Art Museum,
Harvard University. Gift of Philip
Hofer.)*

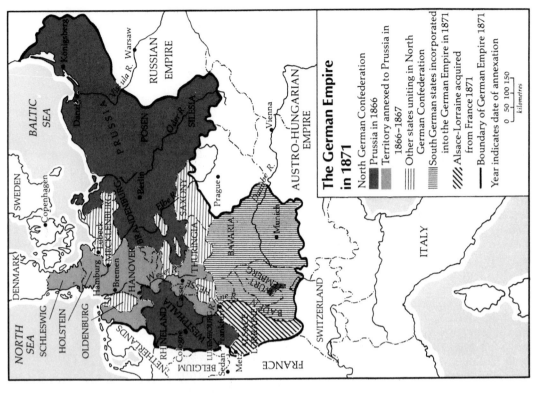

The German Empire in 1871

The German Empire in 1871

North German Confederation
Prussia in 1866
Territory annexed to Prussia in 1866–1867
Other states uniting in North German Confederation
South German states incorporated into the German Empire in 1871
Alsace-Lorraine acquired from France 1871
Boundary of German Empire 1871
Year indicates date of annexation

0 50 100 150
kilometres

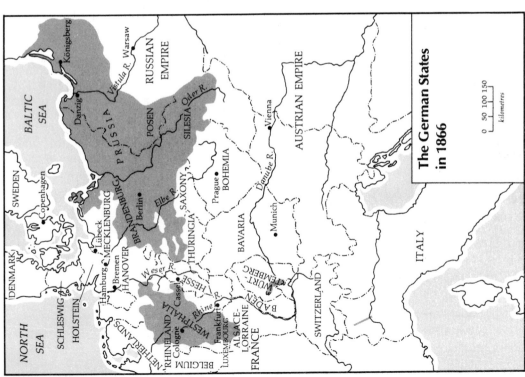

The German States in 1866

0 50 100 150
kilometres

continent. Now the balance of power had clearly shifted, and every European power had to rethink its military position.

The defeat of France resulted in the fall of Napoleon III, who fled to England and died in exile there in 1873. The political vacuum in France was filled by a provisional government which proclaimed the Third Republic. France fought on after Sedan, but in vain as the German armies encircled Paris. Frenchmen, sharply divided on the nature of the new French regime, fought each other for control of the government while they continued to fight the Germans. Officially, France surrendered in early January 1871.

Before a treaty was signed with France, Bismarck took the final step in German unification. The south German states joined the North German Confederation to create the German Empire, now comprising all of the old German states with the exception of Austria. The King of Prussia was proclaimed hereditary Emperor of the German Empire on January 18, 1871, at Versailles, the palace built by Louis XIV in the seventeenth century to symbolize the unity of France and French domination of the European continent. The proclamation at Versailles was thus a symbolic gesture as well as a political event, for it signalled the end of French primacy in Europe.

THE PERIPHERY OF THE WEST: NATIONAL PROBLEMS

In the decades of the 1850s and 1860s national issues were also important in some areas outside Europe. In 1850 the United States was at the beginning of a constitutional battle which threatened its existence as a nation. In British North America tension persisted between peoples of English and French origin. Japan, a tradition-oriented, non-Western state, had been deliberately closed to outsiders for several centuries; but it was now under pressure to change from both inside and outside forces. By 1870 the United States had gone through a civil war and survived as one entity, Canada had come into existence as a nation, and Japan was transforming itself into a Western state and a world power. Thus events outside

Europe as well as changes in the map of Europe itself brought new powers and new power relationships into existence.

THE UNITED STATES: SECTIONALISM, NATIONALISM, AND CIVIL WAR

The division in the United States, while centring on the specific issue of slavery, was over the larger question of state sovereignty. The northern portion of the country had developed industrially while the South had become a one-crop agricultural region, relying on cotton and slavery for its prosperity. Those who defended the existence of slavery based their argument on the principle of "states' rights" and a belief in a weak federal government. Southerners such as Senator John C. Calhoun of South Carolina argued that the United States was created as a federal government with limited powers. Each of the states, he said, had the right to make its own laws unfettered by others. He insisted on local autonomy at the expense of strong centralizing forces.

Abraham Lincoln (1809–65) came to represent those who defended a strong central government. Lincoln, a self-educated lawyer, received the presidential nomination of the Republican Party in 1860. He was a moderate, talking of the injustice of slavery, but accepting its existence in the South. In the 1850s he said that he accepted what he regarded as a present evil in order to preserve the country, but he was opposed to the spread of slavery into new territories as they became part of the United States. Southerners feared that his election would lead to the end of the kind of local autonomy they desired.

The divisions within the country were brought to a head with Lincoln's election to the presidency in November 1860. Lincoln was to assume office in March 1861, but on December 20, 1860, South Carolina seceded from the federal union of the United States. Other southern states followed, believing that their values, culture, and social structure would be preserved only if they created an independent nation. The secessionist states united to form the Confederate States of America, with a constitution which protected states' rights. Lincoln appealed to these states to rejoin the union, promising that he would accept slavery as long as it was not extended; at the same time he insisted that he could not allow secession, for it would mean an end to the country. The South had stood firm and attempted to seize forts which were the property of the federal government. Federal authorities regarded this as an act of rebellion, and civil war began.

From 1861 to 1865 the United States suffered through the bloodiest war in its history. The country was ravaged and hundreds of thousands were killed. Though the South mustered large forces and had able generals, in the end the more heavily industrialized North overwhelmed the Confederacy. Lincoln's plans to "bind up the nation's wounds" were ended by an assassin's bullet only a few days after the end of the war. Like Cavour, he died at the moment of his greatest success. Though the northern victory solved few of the problems that brought on the war, it ended slavery in the United States. Moreover, it enabled the country to survive and grow as a single nation.

CANADA:
UNITY AND DOMINION STATUS

To the north of the United States lay a series of British colonies with origins in early French and English settlements. Following a colonial rebellion in 1837 the Whig government in England, which had passed the first Reform Bill, sent John Lambton, first Earl of Durham, to investigate conditions and report to the British parliament. Arriving in 1838, Durham found that the French still felt very strongly about their old traditions and civilization. He wrote: "I expected to find a contest between a government and a people; I found two nations warring in the bosom of a single state; I found a struggle, not of principles, but of races."[9] Durham recommended that all Canadians—English and French—be united under one government, and hoped that from such a state a nation would evolve. The British government accepted Durham's report, and in 1840 an Act of Union brought together Lower Canada, which was mainly French, and Upper Canada, which was mainly English, into one political unit. However, friction between the two groups continued.

In the early 1860s a number of leaders in British North America turned to the idea of a federal system of government in which some colonies would be united, but local autonomy would be maintained in important matters, such as education. General discussions for such a confederation were begun in 1864; the result was the passing of the British North America Act by the British parliament in 1867. The act established a new country, the Dominion of Canada, which included Lower and Upper Canada—Quebec and Ontario—and two of the maritime provinces—New Brunswick and Nova Scotia. A federal parliament was established to govern the whole country, and each province was given its own legislature. Manitoba and British Columbia joined the Confederation as provinces in 1870 and 1871, respectively; Prince Edward Island in 1873; Alberta and Saskatchewan in 1905; and Newfoundland, as the tenth province, in 1949.

Without a revolution, a group of colonies had become a state. Though the animosity between English and French continued, the importance of the Canadian example was worldwide. A precedent was set by England in allowing and encouraging colonies to become a state and run their own internal affairs. Canada remained part of the British Empire closely linked to Britain in economic, cultural, and diplomatic affairs. This model of "dominion status" was later applied to Australia, New Zealand, and South Africa.

JAPAN:
TRADITION vs. WESTERNIZATION

Europeans knew little about Japan in 1850. From about 1600 Japan had been governed by "shoguns," lords who ruled in the name of the Emperor. In an effort to achieve stability after centuries of chaos and civil war, these shoguns had systematically excluded all external influences on Japan. Only one foreign port was tolerated—the Dutch trading post of Dechima, founded in 1641.

Though Christian missionaries had entered Japan in the sixteenth century, they were excluded by 1630, and the persecution of Japanese Christians resulted in a virtual end to Western influence.

However, though Japanese society was highly traditional, some contact with the West did occur. The Japanese learned such skills as smelting and shipbuilding, and in the nineteenth century they built furnaces and steam engines. Urban population grew and medical practices became more advanced. Moreover, there were small groups of Japanese who were "Westerners"—that is, people who criticized the policies of the shoguns and wanted Japan to become a significant world power. By 1850 there were two potent forces of change in Japan: first, domestic discontent with policies of the shogunate; second, American and European pressures forcing Japan into diplomatic relations with the rest of the world.

On July 8, 1853, Commodore Matthew C. Perry of the United States sailed into Tokyo Bay with four warships. The government of Japan was not powerful enough to expel Perry and was forced to negotiate with him. Treaties were soon made with the United States which opened ports for American trade and provided for an exchange of diplomats. The prohibition against foreigners, which had held for over 250 years, disappeared, as ships from seventeen other nations sailed into Tokyo Bay and negotiated similar treaties.

The intrusion of these foreigners had major domestic consequences. Many Japanese lords did not like the treaties, and the Emperor, until now a symbolic figure who took no part in government, refused to sign them, thereby dividing Japanese opinion between himself and the shogun. A show of strength by foreign nations forced the Emperor to approve the treaties in 1865, but in 1868 the power struggle between shogun and Emperor came to a climax. The court announced the restoration of powers to the Emperor, and after some fighting, the shogun was forced to give in. Mutsuhito, the new fifteen-year-old Emperor, took the name Meiji (Enlightened One), and the Meiji Era,

which lasted until his death in 1912, began.

The policy of the new Emperor was to develop Japan both industrially and militarily. He was determined to build a state which could compete with and stand up to the world powers that had humiliated Japan. Thus Japan consciously began to "Westernize." In 1868 the Emperor issued the "Charter Oath," a statement of the new policy;

1. Deliberative assemblies shall be widely established and all matters decided by public discussion.
2. All classes, high and low, shall unite in vigorously carrying out the administration of affairs of state.
3. The common people, no less than the civil and military officials, shall each be allowed to pursue his own calling so that there may be no discontent.
4. Evil customs of the past shall be broken off and everything based upon the just laws of Nature.
5. Knowledge shall be sought throughout the world so as to strengthen the foundations of imperial rule.[10]

Though strong localisms persisted, many feudal privileges were ended, and government became more centralized.

As part of his reforms, the Meiji ruler gave Japan a constitution in 1889. The Emperor retained great powers, his traditional position of divinity was continued and enhanced, and he held control of the army and foreign affairs. A Diet (parliament) of two houses was created: the upper house, the House of Peers, was aristocratic; the lower house, the House of Representatives, was elected by all males over twenty-five who paid a fixed amount of taxes. In effect, this restricted the right to vote to a tiny part of the population. A prime minister, chosen by the Emperor, and a privy council, consisting of twenty-six members selected by the Emperor on the advice of the prime minister, were to assist the Emperor in ruling the country.

The constitution of Japan, which lasted until the end of the Second World War, was ambiguous in certain areas. It did not state clearly whether the Diet had the right to approve the budget; nor did it specify how much control the Diet was to have over the military. In addition, the constitution left so much in the hands of the Emperor that Japan seemed to be a paternalistic state governed by a benign father. The Emperor had no real responsibility to the Diet. Yet this was the first constitution adopted by a state whose roots were non-European.

Economic growth was fostered by a combination of government initiative and private enterprise, a system sometimes called "hothouse capitalism." The government attempted to provide political stability and a sound financial atmosphere, and to encourage industrial development. It also sponsored railways, telegraph lines, and shipbuilding. At this time, family-business enterprises, called *zaibatsu*, grew up and became very powerful institutions. Between 1883 and 1890 Japan's railway lines expanded from 393 km to 2332 km; between 1887 and 1892 cotton production increased tenfold; between 1904 and 1914 coal production nearly tripled; between 1902 and 1912 the amount of capital invested in sugar refining increased five times, in machine production nine times, in gas companies eleven times, in electricity fifteen times. In some enterprises Japan began to compete with the major industrial countries.

Economic growth at home was accompanied by expansion overseas. In the 1880s Japan established relations with Korea, an area which had long been part of the Chinese sphere of interest. Consequently, a series of minor clashes broke out between China and Japan. When an internal uprising occurred in Korea in 1894, Japan and China both sent in troops to suppress it. Rather than firing on Koreans, Japanese and Chinese ships fired at each other, and war began. The Sino-Japanese War ended after nine months, with Japan the clear victor. In the treaty of Shimonoseki of 1895, Japan received Formosa, the Liaotung Peninsula, and the Pescadores. Korea obtained its independence from China, only to come under the influence of Japan.

Shimonoseki made the West sit up and take notice of Japan; but the Japanese victory in the Russo-Japanese War of 1904–05 startled the world. The war was fought over the difficulties that arose between Russian interests in Manchuria and Japanese interests in neighbouring Korea. Japan tried to negotiate the issue but Russia refused, and in February 1904 war began. On the sea the Japanese demolished the Russians, though on land neither won a decisive victory. President Theodore Roosevelt of the United States mediated between the warring countries and in 1905 helped to negotiate the Treaty of Portsmouth by which Japan received part of Sakhalin and Russia obtained leases in the Kwantung Peninsula and south Manchuria. Russia also recognized Korean "independence."

By 1905 Japan was competing successfully with European powers. In only a few decades Japan had undergone an industrial revolution. Moreover, Japan was now a world power, not with the mighty status of England, France, and Germany, but certainly the equal of Italy and definitely above Spain and Portugal. The Japanese humiliation in Tokyo Bay in the 1850s had been turned into a great national triumph by the beginning of the twentieth century.

THE END OF FRENCH CONTINENTAL ASCENDENCY— THE NEW BALANCE OF POWER IN 1871

Bismarck's Europe began in 1871. With the defeat of France and the creation of the new German Empire, Germany now became the single most important state on the European continent. It was large in territory and population, had great industrial potential, a strong armed force, and a vibrant culture. France, by no means finished, could no longer set the pace for the European continent. In the meantime England expanded its empire; Austria-Hungary stumbled along, a major power that was in danger of collapse and division; and Russia, though potentially a great power, was held back by slow economic development and reactionary governments. And, while the new Italy took its place alongside the great powers, many doubted that it belonged there.

The map of Europe in 1871 more closely reflected national groupings than ever before. But the methods used to create the new nation-states—the *Realpolitik* of Cavour and Bismarck—were now being imitated by others. Mazzini's dream had not come true—nationalism did not increase the harmony among peoples, but often increased antagonisms and created an atmosphere of animosity, suspicion, and revenge. Europe became an armed camp in the name of national defence, and everyone feared the possibility of a general European war.

Technology strengthened national units and gave the central governments of all states the ability to control their hinterland, particularly through the building of rail-roads. Italy had few railroads from north to south before it was unified, but quickly attempted to build links between areas with different traditions, dialects, and economies; Prussia's railways and industry had been vital for the unification of Germany, and after 1871 Germany became a major industrial power. After the Civil War the United States built vast railroads and expanded westwards, while Canada incorporated British Columbia in 1871 on condition that the federal government build a railroad to the west coast. Japan, in the meantime, expanded its own railroad network and demonstrated that the capacity for modern industry and technology did not exist solely in people of European origin.

Daumier: "The Charms of Railway Travel"   (*Bequest of William F. Babcock. Courtesy, Museum of Fine Arts, Boston*)

ANALYSIS AND DISCUSSION

1. "The revolution of 1848, after a brief moment of success, ultimately failed."
a) Explain the factors which led to the initial success of the 1848 revolutions.
b) Account for the eventual failure of the 1848 revolutions, illustrating your general points with examples from specific revolutions.

2. The unification of Italy was done through a combination of the ideology of nationalism and clever politics and diplomacy.
a) To what extent would you describe the Italy of 1860 as a liberal state?
b) To what extent did the unified Italy live up to the expectations of Mazzini, Cavour, and Garibaldi?

3. "The great questions of the day will not be decided by speeches or by majority decisions—that was the mistake of 1848 and 1849 — but by blood and iron!"
a) Illustrate the extent to which Bismarck applied this principle in engineering the unification of Germany.

b) Show how the unification of Germany depended on other factors than simply "blood and iron."

4. "Cavour was the first practitioner of *Realpolitik* — the politics of reality — which Bismarck in Germany would make into a fine art." Explain this statement with reference to the philosophy of *realpolitik* and its application in Italy and Germany.

5. While nationalism was a powerful force in every state, its effects varied according to the political, social, and economic conditions. Compare the effects of nationalism on the development of Canada, the United States, and Japan in the years before 1900.

6. Not all Europeans were impressed with Bismarck's successes in Germany. The French cartoonist Daumier illustrated his sentiments in his cartoon "Let us embrace." Analyse Daumier's view and using any of his other pieces contained in the chapter speculate on the artist's opinion of European life in the late nineteenth century.

CHAPTER **8**

Expanding Liberalism
and Socialism:
1871-1914

THE NINETEENTH CENTURY WAS A time of optimism in the West. Industrialization was spreading and wealth and productivity were increasing. After 1848 middle-class liberals and socialists, particularly in western Europe, ceased to be revolutionaries and were hopeful that their ideas would be implemented by peaceful, democratic means. The revolutionary tradition, however, did not die, particularly among those who became adherents of the socialism of Karl Marx.

JOHN STUART MILL AND LIBERALISM

Despite the setbacks of 1848 and the strength of both conservative and radical forces, liberalism was the dominant political creed of the nineteenth century. It stood for freedom, constitutionalism, and self-determination. While it was generally associated with western European states and the middle class, it recognized no national or class boundary in the extent of its influence. The leading spokesman of liberalism was John Stuart Mill (1806–73), a disciple of Bentham.

Mill was deeply concerned with the preservation of freedom in the political and economic spheres; at the same time he understood the plight of the workers. Faced with the social abuses of industrial England, he saw the need for government legislation to improve the lot of working people. While he supported an extension of the franchise to the workers and to women on the same basis as men, he nevertheless feared that the uninformed voter would be subject to manipulation by powerful interests. Mill placed great value in the process of education and thought that the general public would have

to be educated if the principles of liberty and equality were to be protected.

Mill's most influential work, *On Liberty*, was published in 1859. In it he stated that in order for the individual to lead a free life power must be checked, especially the power of the majority. Minorities and free speech had to be protected, because society benefited from talented individuals and from new ideas. Mill set down a principle as a guideline for government intervention in the affairs of individuals:

That principle is, that the sole end for which mankind are warranted, individually or collectively, in interfering with the liberty of action of any of their number, is self-protection. That the only purpose for which power can be rightfully exercised over any member of a civilized community, against his will, is to prevent harm to others. His own good, either physical or moral, is not a sufficient warrant. He cannot rightfully be compelled to do or forbear because it will be better for him to do so, because it will make him happier, because, in the opinions of others, to do so would be wise, or even right. These are good reasons for ... reasoning with him, or persuading him, or entreating him, but not for compelling him, or [punishing him] ... in case he do otherwise. To justify that, [it is necessary that] the conduct from which it is desired to deter him, must be calculated to produce evil to someone else. The only part of the conduct of anyone, for which he is [responsible] to society, is that which concerns others. In the part which merely concerns himself, his independence is, of right, absolute. Over himself, over his own body and mind, the individual is sovereign.[1]

Mill was disturbed by the implications of bureaucracy, which he believed added unnecessarily to the power of the state. Here he was influenced by the French social thinker Alexis de Tocqueville (1805–59), whose works dealt with the role of institutions and legal systems in maintaining freedom. Tocqueville, in a study of the United States, *Democracy in America* (1835), claimed that democracy flourished in New England because it had institutions through which many people participated in government and a legal system that made certain that government was not arbitrary. Mill sought a compromise between the need for centralized power and the evils resulting from a large bureaucracy:

I believe that the practical principle in which safety resides . . . may be conveyed in these words: the [widest distribution] of power consistent with efficiency; but the greatest possible centralization of information, and diffusion of it from the centre. Thus, in municipal administration, there would be, as in the New England States, a very minute division among separate officers . . . of all business which is not better left to the persons directly interested; but besides this, there would be, in each department of local affairs, a central superintendence, forming a branch of the general government.[2]

Above all, Mill was wary of any philosophy which focussed upon the group, rather than individuals, as the important political unit. "The worth of a State," he said, "in the long run, is the worth of the individuals composing it."[3] Liberalism, for Mill, meant a continued concern for the rights, freedom, and importance of the individual. He recognized the importance of the group, but felt it could only be justified when it advanced the interests of the individuals in it.

(10)

THE NEW LIBERALISM

In the second half of the nineteenth century, governments adopted liberal legislation in order to counter the more radical ideas of socialism, anarchism, and Marxian communism. As a result, revolutionary movements found it difficult to maintain their following. Especially in western Europe, many radicals became convinced that social reform could be accomplished by means of

the vote and through organizing labour into unions and political parties. Liberals, in fact, had become more democratic on the question of the franchise, and as the vote was extended to larger numbers of people, revolution seemed to many no longer necessary—the system could now be changed from within.

At the same time economic liberalism was undergoing a transformation. Liberals began to abandon their belief in *laissez-faire* and their old fear of government intervention in the affairs of individuals and groups. In the past liberals had stressed free and unhampered economic competition. Towards the end of the nineteenth century, however, they recognized that freedom for the individual depended to a large extent on conditions of labour and life. Thus, although they still defended individual rights, they found themselves increasingly involved in social-welfare measures. Liberal governments began to tamper with the economy in order to create more wealth. Some liberals adopted attitudes of the moderate socialists and appealed to governments to correct social inequities and evils stemming from the Industrial Revolution.

Yet many radicals refused to believe that society could ever undergo a basic change without a revolution; tinkering with the prevailing system was not enough while property and wealth remained in the hands of a few individuals, and governments represented the rich and powerful. Even the vote, they believed, would not solve the problems of inequality and oppression; only a drastic redistribution of wealth would do this, and the rich would hardly give up their property without a violent upheaval. Some radicals became anarchists and called for the complete destruction of all authority; others became followers of the revolutionary philosophy of Karl Marx.

KARL MARX AND THE GROWTH OF SOCIALISM

No political philosopher has had more influence in the world of the last hundred years than Karl Marx (1818–83). Marx studied philosophy in Germany, then became a journalist and lived most of his adult life in England. His most popular work was the *Manifesto of the Communist Party*, written with the collaboration of his friend Frederick Engels (1820–95) and published a few weeks before the French revolution of 1848. In the *Manifesto* and in other writings, Marx declared that modern history could be understood only in terms of "the class struggle," and that social change could take place only by means of a revolution in which the oppressed class overthrew the oppressors.

Marx believed that the most important features which determined a person's ideas and beliefs were one's environment and one's relationship to the economic system. Thus he felt that social and economic conditions were more important than ideas for an understanding of human beings and society. According to Marx, the French Revolution was not the end product of the ideology of the Enlightenment. It occurred in 1789 because social and economic conditions were ripe for revolution.

Marx based his analysis on his own interpretation of history, for he believed that through history one could discover laws of social change. He distinguished four types of society that had appeared in the West—the primitive, the ancient, the feudal, and the modern (or bourgeois, as he often called it). What determined their distinctive characteristics was the way they produced goods, that is, their economic life, and the social relations resulting from it. Each of these societies was different in the development of technology and the ownership of the means of production, and each became transformed as economic conditions changed. Thus feudal society became bourgeois when industrial production became more important than agriculture. The owners of industry—the *bourgeoisie*—replaced the owners of land— the aristocracy—as the dominant class, while the "exploitation" of the proletariat replaced that of the serfs.

The social organization of each society, Marx thought, was based on the nature of its economic life. Feudalism had existed because people were needed to cultivate the land, some owning it and some working on it, and

this had produced two distinct classes: the nobility and the serfs. With the introduction of industrial society, the dominant class changed, although the principle remained the same—the major social distinction now was between the owners of the means of production and the workers. The proletariat, according to Marx, was exploited by the middle class, as the serf had been exploited by the nobility.

Marx believed that economic change occurs with technology. Social change, however, is produced by class conflict, that is, conflict between those who control and those who do not control the means of production. "The history of all hitherto existing society," he said, "is the history of class struggles."[4] Classes engage in a conflict which ultimately creates a new social organization. For Marx the French Revolution was the "bourgeois" revolution, for it resulted in the victory of the middle class over the aristocracy. But class conflict continued:

The modern bourgeois society that has sprouted from the ruins of feudal society has not done away with class antagonisms. It has but established new classes, new conditions of oppression, new forms of struggle in place of the old ones.

Our epoch, the epoch of the bourgeoisie, possesses, however, this distinctive feature: it has simplified the class antagonisms. Society as a whole is more and more splitting up into two great hostile camps, into two great classes directly facing each other: Bourgeoisie and Proletariat.[5]

According to Marx, change occurs as a "dialectical process," a conflict of opposites. For example, the capitalist class in pursuit of its economic ends produces its opposite, the exploited proletariat. The interests of the two classes cannot be peacefully reconciled, and the result is conflict, revolution, and a new social organization. Thus capitalism must die, said Marx, because it "produces its own gravediggers," the proletariat. Marx predicted that after the proletariat overthrew their masters a transition period would ensue. This would be followed, in turn, by communism, in which there would be no exploitation, because the means of production would be owned by society. In a communist society with only one class—the workers—there would be no conflict because there would be no individual owners of the means of production. Hence, the dialectical process would come to an end. In the words of Marx:

When, in the course of development, class distinctions have disappeared, and all production has been concentrated in the hands of a vast association of the whole nation, the public power will lose its political character. Political power, properly so called, is merely the organized power of one class for oppressing another. If the proletariat during its contest with the bourgeoisie is compelled, by the force of circumstances, to organize itself as a class, if, by means of a revolution, it makes itself the ruling class, and, as such, sweeps away by force the old conditions of production, then it will, along with these conditions, have swept away the conditions for the existence of class antagonisms and of classes generally, and will thereby have abolished its own supremacy as a class.

In place of the old bourgeois society, with its classes and class antagonisms, we shall have an association, in which the free development of each is the condition for the free development of all.[6]

Marx stated that social revolution will occur when finally the owners of the means of production and the proletariat become polarized. Before that happens those who are marginal to both classes—the small shopkeeper, the craftsman, the person who lives on a small income from property—will disappear. Because capitalism generates competition, the large capitalist will devour the small one, and the members of marginal classes will either become part of the proletariat or, more rarely, large capitalists. The reason the revolutions of 1848 failed, Marx later said, was that Europe was not ready for the socialist revolution. Too many marginal people existed, such as the lower middle class and the propertied peasants, who failed to realize that their interest lay with the workers and not the *bourgeoisie.* The process of polarization had to continue; eventually, the revolution would come.

Marx recognized that some areas were economically less developed than others.

According to his theory, the revolution would first transform the more highly industrial states and then spread to the less developed ones. He believed that England and Germany would take the lead in the development of world socialism.

Marx's thought, like that of the Enlightenment, was cosmopolitan. Though nationalism was a strong motive force in nineteenth-century Europe, Marx insisted that class and not nation must unite people. "The workingmen have no country," he said. French proletarians and German proletarians were not primarily Frenchmen or Germans, but proletarians. All workers who had to sell their labour would be "alienated" from the system, no matter what their nationality. Their interests and desires were similar because the industrial process was the same everywhere. To promote these interests, they had only to develop "consciousness," to become aware of their common cause and their common enemies; workers should not be deluded by nationalism, religion, or other doctrines which, according to Marx, supported the tyranny of the *bourgeoisie* over the proletariat. "The ruling ideas of each age," he wrote, "have ever been the ideas of its ruling class."[7]

Marx challenged the ability of capitalism to transform itself into a better system. He did not believe that the state was neutral; it was controlled by whoever had economic power. Marx thought that it was useless for the proletariat to try to take political action within a parliamentary system, because capitalists would not give up control of the state without a fight. Thus, while earlier socialists—for example, Saint-Simon and Owen—had expected the state to remedy social ills and reorganize the economic system, Marx looked upon the state as an institution of the enemy. The state must be overthrown: "Let the ruling classes tremble at a communistic revolution. The proletarians have nothing to lose but their chains. "They have a world to win. WORKING MEN OF ALL COUNTRIES, UNITE!"[8]

In the *Communist Manifesto* Marx derisively called some of the earlier socialists "utopians" because they believed that the lower classes could, through reason and an appeal to humanism, convert the owners of the means of production to a more humane view towards the proletariat; this only proved to Marx that these early socialists did not understand history and were talking about some mythical utopia, not the real world. Engels, who outlived Marx and often tried to clarify what he said, claimed that the Marxian analysis was "scientific," not utopian. He felt that Marx had discovered a fundamental law of history:

It was precisely Marx who had first discovered the great law of motion of history, the law according to which all historical struggles ... political, religious, [or] philosophical ..., are in fact ... the ... clear expression of struggles of social classes, and that the existence and thereby the collisions, too, between these classes are in turn conditioned by the degree of development of their economic position, by the mode of their production.... This law ... has the same significance for history as the law of the transformation of energy has for natural science.[9]

This emphasis on "science" sometimes obscures the ethical and emotional content of the writings of Marx and Engels. They were in fact pleading for the oppressed and the down-trodden—expressing an almost romantic view of the nature of the working class and the ultimate end of society. The goal, as Marx put it, was to free people from the burdens of capitalism and allow them to become self-creative, free to develop their potential in society. Socialism, Engels stated in 1880, offers

The possibility of securing for every member of society, by means of socialised production, an existence not only fully sufficient materially, and becoming day by day more full, but an existence guaranteeing to all the free development and exercise of their physical and mental faculties— this possibility is now for the first time here, but it is here.[10]

It was the moral content as well as the "scientific" aspects of Marxism which has, in some quarters, given the writings of Marx and Engels the same status that the Bible has for many Christians.

Marx was in the end the greatest synthesizer of ideas of the nineteenth century. From the Enlightenment he inherited the idea of progress, a scientific method, and an optimistic, cosmopolitan outlook. From Hegel he took "the dialectic"—the idea of change through the conflict of opposites. Romanticism provided the impulse of seeking an historical explanation for social change. And he fused all of these diverse influences into a uniquely forceful doctrine.

The appeal of Marx was enhanced by the failures of the 1848 revolutions. Most of the middle class *did* side with order. The workers *were* fired upon in the streets of Paris. The professors of the Frankfurt Assembly *did* refrain from acting on their theories of constitutional government and went on teaching in the universities of authoritarian states. In short, the Marxist analysis seemed to be borne out.

THE NEW SOCIALISM

In the second half of the nineteenth century the revolution anticipated by Marx did not materialize. In the industrial nations, particularly England and Germany, the state took an ever-increasing interest in the conditions of labour. Working people also became greater participants in political life, and nationalism was far from a dying sentiment among them.

In the light of changing social and economic conditions, socialists were compelled to reconsider their views. Socialists found themselves in serious disagreement, and socialism developed innumerable splits among its adherents in the late nineteenth century. The major division was between those who continued to espouse Marx's idea that capitalism would fall through violent upheaval, and those who were convinced that there had been certain errors in Marx's analysis and that, in the political climate of their age, less revolutionary strategies were called for. The latter were called "revisionists"; they believed that it was possible to change society through the organized pressure of labour unions and by means of parliamentary tactics.

Eduard Bernstein (1850–1932), a German

socialist who spent a good deal of his adult life in England, was the leading revisionist. His major work, *Evolutionary Socialism* (1899), argued that the pattern of historical and economic development as outlined by Marx was not being realized. Bernstein maintained that with the extension of the franchise the democratic state need not be controlled by capitalists and that state action to benefit the workers was possible. Bernstein also believed that the nature of capitalism was changing: far from producing only two classes, the few rich and the masses of poor, the middle class was expanding and more workers were becoming property owners. Moreover, the workers were making great gains by putting political pressure on the capitalists. Thus, he claimed, it was not necessary to use violent revolutionary means to destroy the capitalist system, as Marx had argued; it was being transformed through peaceful means into a socialist system.

Bernstein set out to revise and update Marx:

The adherents of this theory of a catastrophe [that is, the collapse of bourgeois society] base it especially on the conclusions of the *Communist Manifesto*. This is a mistake in every respect....

In all advanced countries we see the privileges of the capitalist bourgeoisie yielding step by step to democratic organisations. Under the influence of this, and driven by the movement of the working classes which is daily becoming stronger, a social reaction has set in against the exploiting

"Justice" by Ernst Barlach, a protest against misguided justice   (Simplicissimus, *Aug. 26, 1907*)

tendencies of capital, a counteraction which, although it still proceeds timidly and feebly, yet does exist, and is always drawing more departments of economic life under its influence. Factory legislation, the democratising of local government, and the extension of its area of work, the freeing of trade unions and systems of co-operative trading from legal restrictions, the consideration of standard conditions of labour in the work undertaken by public authorities—all these characterise this phase of the evolution.[11]

Bernstein's stress was on political evolution, through gradual and peaceful change, not revolution. In nearly all European societies, revisionists and Marxists battled for control of socialist movements.

In politics the revisionists were often known as "democratic socialists" or "social democrats." Groups of this type developed in Germany, Britain, and France. The German Social Democratic Party was divided between revisionists, who talked about "gradualism" and saw Eduard Bernstein as their guide, and orthodox Marxists, who talked of overthrowing the existing state. This division within the German socialist party was often papered over during elections. In 1912 the socialists won 110 seats in the election and became the largest single party in the Reichstag, the lower house of parliament.

In Britain the Labour Party was founded in 1900. It was a federation of organizations which included the trade unions and the Fabian Society. The latter was a group of intellectuals who favoured the gradual transformation of England into a welfare state. The Labour Party won 29 seats in the House of Commons in the election of 1906.

In France the leading revisionist, Jean Jaurès, was a social philosopher and historian whose socialism was founded on humanitarian principles. Socialism, according to Jaurès, was not inevitable, but desirable. He organized a political party in order to gain control of government democratically and thereby implement his program. In the election of 1910 his party won 76 seats in the French Chamber of Deputies. Other socialist parties were also represented and

French socialism was a major political force by 1914.

Thus, in western Europe, and in the states which were most "advanced" both socially and industrially, socialism and liberalism began to come closer together. Socialists accepted democratic means of promoting their program and liberals recognized the need for welfare legislation. In eastern and southern Europe, where governments were less willing to change, where industrialism made fewer gains, and where the old aristocratic tradition continued to be strong, socialists were more revolutionary. In Russia, for example, where the czarist government resisted demands for more democratic institutions and social change, many socialists could not conceive of working within the system to achieve reform.

The varieties of socialism and the many splits among socialists produced tensions in the international socialist movement. The First International—a union of all socialists—was founded in London in 1864. The group accepted the Marxist idea that only co-operation among workers of all nationalities would bring about international socialism. It advocated the socialization of all industry and the take-over of state organizations by the workers. But unity did not prevail and the tendency of socialists to quarrel and split continued.

The First International ended in 1876 as a result of doctrinal differences between Marxist socialists and anarchists. Led by Michael Bakunin (1814–76), the anarchists stressed the desirability of destroying all authority and insisted that the peasant as well as the proletarian must be considered in the theories and practices of the socialists. Bakunin and his followers regarded the state as an evil to be destroyed entirely and rejected the Marxist idea that the institutions of a society should be seized by the workers during a period of transition to socialism.

The Second International, founded in 1889, was composed of both Marxists and democratic socialists, and the two groups quarrelled endlessly. Jaurès insisted that socialists must take part in governments in order to obtain better conditions for the

"The Landlord" by R. Roubille, attacking the wealthy property-owners   (L'Assiette au Beurre,
*Sept. 23, 1905. Reproduced by General Research and Humanities Division, The New York
Public Library—Astor, Lenox, and Tilden Foundations)*

"The Strikers", *a French print that appeared in 1904 in the magazine* L'Assiette au Beurre

workers, but the large majority of representatives from the less industrialized and less liberal states opposed co-operation with existing governments and declared that revolution was the only solution. The difference that emerged in the Second International between those socialists who supported parliamentary democracy and gradual change and those who advocated violent revolution marks the beginning of the twentieth-century division between western European democratic socialism and eastern European totalitarian communism. In the west, where governments were more democratic and where the trend to universal suffrage was clear, socialists hesitated to advocate revolution against a representative government. In the east, where governments were authoritarian and reluctant to grant any constitutional concession, socialists remained revolutionaries, aiming to overthrow the existing authority and take power. Socialist activities were usually regarded as illegal in eastern Europe and many socialists

could see no way to work within the existing system without totally giving up their beliefs.

The development of democratic socialism accounts, to some extent, for the waning of liberalism in the twentieth century. As liberals began to see a need for government intervention, many became democratic socialists. Others moved towards the conservative position, for the conservatives now tended to adopt the old liberal view that the government which governs least governs best. Those who remained liberals found themselves in a middle position, between democratic socialism and conservatism; to go in either direction often meant, for a liberal, joining another party.

THE DEMOCRATIC STATES

Great Britain

Both major political parties in England, the Liberals and the Conservatives, adopted programs of political and social reform. The Conservatives, under the leadership of

Benjamin Disraeli (1804–81), made an effort to become a popular, vote-winning party. Disraeli deplored class warfare and sought to avert it. It was his idea to involve Conservatives in reform in order to build a union between the monarchy, the aristocracy, and the lower classes. He was a nationalist and was convinced that a responsible aristocracy could provide the most humane government for England. Yet he realized that his party would not survive unless it had some appeal for the masses. In 1867 he persuaded the Conservatives to pass the Second Reform Bill, which gave the vote to a million working men. As head of a Conservative government from 1874 to 1880, he introduced legislation which gave greater power to unions, improved working conditions, and provided better housing for workers.

William Ewart Gladstone (1809–98), the leader of the Liberal Party, was Disraeli's great rival. He formed four governments in the period from 1868 to 1894 and attracted strong support from workers and middle-class voters. Under his leadership, the Liberals passed the Third Reform Bill in 1884, extending the vote to agricultural workers. In addition, his party reformed the civil service and established a system of public elementary education.

Both Disraeli and Gladstone believed in constitutional government and parliamentary democracy, but they differed in their political attitudes. Gladstone sought to knock down barriers that, he believed, stood in the way of people helping themselves. Disraeli was a far more paternalistic reformer, and wished to retain ancient privileges and institutions.

After Disraeli's death the Conservatives placed less emphasis on social reform and pursued the aggressive imperial policy which he had initiated; the Liberals, under pressure from their working-class supporters and fearing the growth of the Labour Party, became more socialist. In 1906 the Liberals were elected by a great majority, largely as a result of their promise of a reform program. Led by Prime Minister Herbert Asquith and Chancellor of the Exchequer David Lloyd George, they passed legislation which included old-age pensions, insurance against work injuries, and a minimum-wage law. To pay for these measures, it was necessary to increase taxes, and in the 1909 budget prepared by Lloyd George a new concept of social reform was introduced. Lloyd George promised a heavy tax on inherited wealth and a graduated income tax. A Conservative called it "a budget with a vengeance"; Lloyd George styled it "a war budget." The Liberals, in using the power of taxation to bring about social reform, took an important step towards the establishment of a welfare state.

The opposition to the budget of 1909 was centred in the artistocratic and conservative House of Lords. The Lords refused to pass the budget after it had been accepted in the Commons and this led to a constitutional battle. The Lords could theoretically reject a budget, but tradition and public opinion were against them, and ultimately they had to give in. In a period when democracy was making great gains, many resented the power and the audacity which this hereditary body demonstrated in flouting the will of the elected representatives.

Once the budget was passed, the Liberals set out to limit the power of the House of Lords. After an intense battle and two elections, they pushed through the Parliament Act of 1911, which stated that the House of Lords could not alter money bills or delay passage of any other bill for more than two years. Thus bills passed by the Commons in three successive sessions would automatically become law. The victory over the House of Lords and the inauguration of the welfare state showed that the British system was flexible and was adjusting to the needs of the time.

One of Britain's greatest problems was "the Irish question." Ireland was part of Great Britain from 1801, but the Irish desired their own government. The question was further complicated by the religious issue since most of Ireland was strongly Catholic, while six counties in the North, known as Ulster, were mainly Protestant. The Ulstermen were determined to remain within the British Empire, fearing that Irish independence would make them a minority in a state dominated by Catholics. Hatred and violence were nearly always present in English-Irish relations.

Despite other successes, Gladstone was unable to get parliament to pass a Home Rule Bill giving Ireland autonomy over its own internal affairs. Ireland did receive Home Rule in 1914, but Ulster was unhappy. The country was on the verge of civil war when the First World War broke out. Home Rule was suspended for the duration of the war. Finally, in the 1930s, after years of strife with England and civil war among the Irish, southern Ireland became independent as the republic of Eire. Northern Ireland remained attached to Great Britain and continued to be troubled by hostility between Catholics and Protestants.

France

France's Third Republic was launched in the midst of a disaster. After defeat by Bismarck in the Franco-Prussian War of 1870-71, the French set up a provisional republic which negotiated the Treaty of Frankfurt, officially bringing an end to the fighting. Bismarck demanded a war indemnity of five billion francs and the annexation of the border areas of Alsace and Lorraine, areas which were in part German-speaking but whose inhabitants regarded themselves as French. The first election of the Third Republic, in February 1871, resulted in a National Assembly dominated by monarchists of various sorts—Bonapartists, Bourbonists, Orleanists—and it was this Assembly which ratified the treaty.

In the meanwhile a mixed group of republicans, socialists, and workers established the Paris Commune, which refused to recognize the National Assembly and rebelled. The government of the Third Republic, whose temporary headquarters was at Versailles, sent in troops to suppress this uprising. In a rush of support, the old aristocracy, the Catholic Church, the middle class, and the peasants stood behind the Assembly. In May 1871, after a series of bloody battles, the revolutionaries were defeated. Some were either killed or arrested; others fled into exile.

Led by Prime Minister Adolphe Thiers, the provisional government seemed to have little chance of surviving. No real political parties existed in the early years of the Third Republic. For every measure proposed by the government, Thiers and others had to put together a precarious coalition in order to assure passage in the Assembly. The monarchists were so divided that they could not band together behind a single candidate, and an attempt at a Bourbon restoration in 1873 did not succeed. No formal constitution was drawn up. On the grounds that "a republic is the form of government which divides us least," the Assembly passed a number of laws in 1875 which gave some structure to the state. The laws provided for two legislative chambers—one elected by universal suffrage, the other by indirect election—and a weak president elected by both houses. Real power was in the hands of the prime minister whose cabinet was drawn from the legislature.

France was governed by a succession of coalitions, and the coalitions were so weak and artificial that cabinets lasted an average of less than one year. What kept France from total chaos was its civil service and the bureaucracy originally set up by Napoleon I. The Third Republic, despite its sketchy framework and obvious weaknesses, lasted until 1940—longer than any other form of government in France since 1789.

The Republic followed a cautious policy, for republicanism was still suspect in France and the mood of the country was conservative. Hence reforms which would offend major conservative interests were avoided. The rejection of an income tax reassured the middle class and property owners. The Catholic Church continued to be very influential in French life and the Concordat of 1801 was continued, although by 1880 legislation had been introduced which reduced the role of the Church in education. In response to the nationalist fervour against Germany after the humiliation of the Franco-Prussian War, the army was reconstructed and given authority independent of civilian control. However, as the Third Republic gained stability, Frenchmen developed trust in the republican form of government. But the Dreyfus affair at the turn of the century sharply divided the country and nearly destroyed the Republic.

Captain Alfred Dreyfus, a member of the general staff and a Jew, was arrested in 1894 on a charge of treason; he was accused of giving secret military documents to Germany. Dreyfus was tried in a military court. The evidence used against him was a document, allegedly written in his own handwriting, although the experts could not agree on this. Dreyfus was convicted and sent off to a penal colony on Devil's Island.

By 1896 new evidence had been discovered which seemed to indicate that Dreyfus was innocent. The army, however, refused to reopen the case, and it was supported by the monarchists and the Church, who hated the Republic and were intent on protecting the honour of the general staff of the army. These groups used every available means to stir up anti-Semitism against Dreyfus and other Jews.

Dreyfus's cause was taken up by a number of intellectuals, including the aging Emile Zola, whose pamphlet *J'Accuse* (1898) created a sensation by attacking the army for a deliberate miscarriage of justice:

I accuse the War Office of having led a vile campaign in the press . . . in order to misdirect public opinion and cover up its sins.

I accuse . . . the first court-martial of having violated all human rights in condemning a prisoner on testimony kept secret from him. . . .

The action I take here is simply a revolutionary step designed to hasten the explosion of truth and justice.[12]

The army and the conservatives claimed that Dreyfus was guilty and that, if the case was reopened, secrets important for the security of France would be made public.

The "affair" captivated France, Europe, and North America. There were Dreyfusards and anti-Dreyfusards everywhere. The crisis polarized French politics: those arguing for Dreyfus generally were in the middle and the left of French politics, strongly anti-clerical, and favouring civil liberties and the republican regime. Those arguing against Dreyfus were on the right, the monarchists and the pro-Catholic element, who were still hoping to see an end to the Republic and the establishment of a traditional authoritarian regime. The Dreyfusards claimed that justice for one individual was more important than the needs of the state. The anti-Dreyfusards insisted that the individual did not matter, that the state came first and, therefore, that the army must not be endangered because of one individual. The case was finally reopened in 1899, and a military court, by a five to two vote, again found Dreyfus guilty. The world was shocked, for it was clear beyond any doubt that he had been deliberately framed by respectable army officers. The French government took the case away from the military and pardoned Dreyfus later in that year. He was finally exonerated in 1906.

Politically, the Dreyfus affair strengthened the republicans and weakened the monarchists, the military, and the Church. The blatant miscarriage of justice and the hate campaign of the right backfired. The army lost its independence and was put under the control of a civilian, constitutional authority. At the same time, the close association between Church and State that had existed since the Concordat of 1801 was ended. In 1905, in the law which separated Church and State, it was stated:

1. The Republic assures liberty of conscience, and guarantees the free practice of religions, subject only to the restrictions hereinafter enacted in the interest of public order.

2. The Republic neither recognizes nor salaries nor subsidizes any religion. Consequently, on and after the first day of January next after the promulgation of the present law all expenses connected with the practice of religions will be omitted from the budgets of the State, of the departments and of the communes. . . . The public religious establishments are hereby suppressed. . . .[13]

Few people now took the monarchists seriously and they ceased to be a major political force. The Dreyfus affair was thus a watershed in the history of the Third Republic, for it made the republicans stronger and opened the way for a degree of social reform.

Germany

The new German Empire, founded in 1871, was dominated until 1890 by Bismarck. The Empire was a federation, with the Upper House (*Bundestag*) representing the individual states and the Lower House (*Reichstag*), elected by universal suffrage, representing the people at large. Prussia was the dominant power—the Prussian king was Emperor of Germany, and the Prussian bureaucracy had become the bureaucracy of the German Empire. In the legislature the Prussian representatives, voting as a block, could veto amendments to the constitution. Bismarck, the Prussian Prime Minister, was Chancellor of the Empire.

The empire gave the *appearance* of being a democracy and a limited monarchy, but the power of the executive branch of the government was virtually unchecked. The Emperor could choose his ministers without having to consult with or gain the approval of the German parliament. As a result, the man in whom the Emperor had confidence, Bismarck, ruled without any clear legislative restraint. The constitution contained no statement of rights or guarantees of liberty. The Emperor was supreme commander of the army and navy; he could declare war and make peace, and he could convene or dismiss the two Houses of Parliament. The Lower House had the right to pass legislation, but could not initiate bills. It could refuse to approve the budget, but the precedent of 1862 in Prussia, when the executive overcame the unwillingness of the legislature to pass a budget, was in everyone's mind. In any case most of the revenue of the German Empire was derived from taxes which the Reichstag did not control—fixed customs and excise taxes, rather than income taxes. Thus, in Germany, democracy was in part dependent on the willingness of the Emperor to follow democratic procedures and not exercise power in an arbitrary fashion.

After his striking military and diplomatic successes, Bismarck's power was greater than ever. In the 1870s he was careful to get the approval of the legislature for most of his domestic policies, and found a willing ally in the National Liberal Party, which gave him large army budgets in exchange for favourable economic policies, such as his support of free trade.

None the less, he became fearful of the growth of German socialism. In 1875 the moderate socialists and Marxists joined to form the Social Democratic Party whose program was more egalitarian and democratic than Bismarck could tolerate. In 1878 he got the Reichstag to pass an anti-socialist law which made it extraordinarily difficult for all socialists to organize public meetings. In addition, it decreed that "all printed matter, in which social-democratic, socialistic, or communistic tendencies appear . . . is to be forbidden."[14]

Bismarck realized that repressive measures alone would not halt the growth of socialism. In order to counteract the appeal of the socialists, and because he had a paternalistic view of the role of the state, he initiated a program of social legislation which included sickness and unemployment insurance, and an old-age pension scheme. Germany was the first European state to introduce such a broad scheme from above, and for the time it was the most comprehensive program of social legislation in existence. Bismarck's plan won much popular support: while keeping power securely in the hands of the Emperor, he had given Germans the feeling that the paternal state was concerned with social welfare. This paternalism, however, did not halt the growth of the Social Democratic Party. In 1890, realizing that his policy had been a failure, Bismarck supported a repeal of the anti-socialist law restricting socialist activities.

The major issue uniting Germans of all political persuasions was nationalism. Nationalist sentiment became stronger now that Germany was a nation-state of over forty million people, capable of challenging English industry and defeating French arms. Although Germany was a late-comer in the nation-state system, Germans thought that their country deserved to rank among the great nations of the world. Many of them believed that a German empire should be established in order to compete successfully with the other large states. Bismarck was opposed to any further foreign adventures, having already achieved his aims, but in 1884, to satisfy his critics, he yielded to imperialist sentiment and gave government approval to the founding of colonies.

William II, who began his rule in 1888, was both a nationalist and an imperialist. He forced the aging Bismarck to resign in 1890; officially, the break occurred over a disagreement on government policy and the role of the Chancellor. But it would appear that William, who was a young man when he came to the throne, believed in using his authority as Emperor to the full. He could

not tolerate Bismarck, who, he felt, was restraining him. Bismarck had fashioned the constitution of the German Empire for a sensible monarch who would rely on an adviser such as himself; nothing, however, prevented a headstrong monarch from trying to rule on his own.

Upon dismissing Bismarck, William launched into a policy of *Weltpolitik*—a policy aimed at making Germany into a great world power. He constructed a large navy, thereby threatening English naval supremacy, and he allowed the German military to develop its weapons and strategy unhampered by civilian authority. He sought markets for Germany's new industrial products by establishing colonies and extracting trade concessions from other nations. All

A huge hammer in the Krupp works, designed to shape hot metal. The Krupp factories produced many armaments in Germany.   (Fried. Krupp GMBH, Essen)

this required military power, and William made it clear that Germany was prepared to use it if he thought it necessary.

Germans gradually became disenchanted with his arrogant style, if not with his policies. Once the restrictions on the socialists were dropped, the Social Democratic Party grew until, in 1914, it was the largest party in the Reichstag. Though the Emperor was not mentioned personally, the Social Democrats and other parties began to talk about the need for some sort of restraint on the central government and for clear constitutional bounds to its power. The lack of such restraint was apparent in 1913, when the Reichstag voted "no confidence" in the government, and the government did not resign, but continued in power. Thus, despite democratic elements in the German constitution, the question of ultimate power and responsibility in Germany was still not settled.

The United States

Having emerged from the Civil War as a united country, the United States grew into one of the great industrial nations of the world. From 1865 to 1900 large industrial monopolies emerged unhampered by government interference or control. Working conditions were often bad, and there was a good deal of labour unrest, but large businesses easily suppressed efforts by the workers to form effective unions. Federal and local laws protected big business, and federal and state governments supported anti-union actions.

The advance of the frontier continued as the United States expanded westwards, and by 1890 there were few frontiers left. The old image of America—a new world inhabited by pioneers—was transformed by urban growth and rural settlement. At the same time, the United States accepted large numbers of Europeans escaping from the hardships and oppression of their own society. Great waves of newcomers—Irish, Germans, Jews, Scandinavians, and others— came to the United States. The United States had a population of 23.2 million in 1850, and in the next decade alone, received nearly 3 million immigrants. In the century between

1840 and 1940, nearly 35 million Europeans entered the country.

Though many immigrants brought radical political ideas with them, socialism did not find a congenial home in the United States. Robert Owen failed to establish a socialist community at New Harmony, Indiana. Several groups tried to build model communities on Fourier's plan, but these did not last. Workers leaving Europe soon found jobs or land for themselves, and no socialist movement of major consequence developed. A distinctly American socialist party did, however, appear in the early twentieth century. It was moderate in its tactics, and related ideologically to the democratic socialists of Europe. Led by Eugene Debs, the party helped to create an atmosphere for reform, but was never a serious contender for national power.

Despite the victory of the forces of unity in the Civil War, the office of the president was not strong until the turn of the century. Congress dominated politics. It took most of the initiative for the expansion of the frontier, maintaining a policy of *laissez-faire* within the country and setting up high protective tariffs to shield domestic goods against foreign competition.

The tradition of a weak executive and a strong legislature was reversed by two presidents in the early part of the twentieth century. Theodore Roosevelt (1858–1919) came to office in 1901 as the result of the assassination of his predecessor, William McKinley. Roosevelt declared that the government was responsible for regulating economic affairs in the interests of the nation as a whole, and made efforts to control trusts and monopolies in order to preserve fair competition and limit excess profit. Moreover, he extended government regulations to labour practices, railroad rates, food and drugs, and the conservation of natural resources.

Roosevelt ended the traditional American foreign policy of non-involvement in world affairs. He realized that the United States was becoming a world power and believed it should exercise an influence on world events. He was especially interested in Latin America, an area which the United States regarded as its "sphere of influence." In order to make the construction of the Panama Canal possible, he sponsored a revolution in Colombia and the establishment of an "independent" state of Panama. He intervened in the Dominican Republic, a country heavily in debt to Europeans, in order to keep Europeans out; he intervened in Cuba to restore order; he kept European powers from intervening in Venezuela in 1902 in order to collect their debts; and he mediated in the Russo-Japanese War, helping to negotiate the Treaty of Portsmouth which ended it in 1905.

Woodrow Wilson (1856–1924), who became president in 1913, carried state intervention much further. He spoke of the need for a "New Freedom" in which government would mediate between conflicting interest groups, rather than representing one of them. In order to increase competition he revised the tariff to allow importation of more goods. He introduced a graduated income tax and undertook banking and currency reform. The Federal Reserve Act of 1913 helped to centralize banking policy and gave the government great power in controlling interest rates and the flow of money. While the power of big business was being limited, unions were given freedom to organize; the state no longer placed itself and its power solely on the side of the manufacturers.

In foreign policy Wilson followed Roosevelt by intervening in the affairs of Latin America. After the outbreak of the First World War in Europe, he also played an important role in world diplomacy, even though the United States did not enter the war until 1917. Roosevelt and Wilson were the first American presidents whom European statesmen considered as equals.

Italy

Italy was a constitutional monarchy based on the English model, and by 1912 a democracy with universal manhood suffrage. Nevertheless, after achieving unification Italy lacked stability and seemed to be unable and unwilling to deal with the many problems that beset the new state. Unification had brought under one government

areas which had little relationship to one another. Literacy was low and poverty severe, particularly in the south. At the same time, population was fast increasing and many Italians were leaving for better opportunities in other lands.

Italy was also being torn apart by a dispute between the new state and the Roman Catholic Church. When Rome was annexed to Italy in 1870, Pope Pius IX refused to recognize the Italian state and forbade Italian Catholics (over ninety-nine per cent of the population) to take part in state elections. His successors generally continued these policies, and, while most Catholics ignored the papal sanctions against the state, many felt uneasy in the face of Church hostility. Not since the French Revolution had a modern secular state faced such a challenge from the Church.

The parliamentary system as it developed in Italy was unable to cope with these problems. In England the two major parties gave voters an opportunity to choose between alternative policies. If the party in power was unable to deal with a problem, its opponent was willing and indeed eager to take office. No such party system developed in Italy; instead, parliamentary instability encouraged what was called *trasformismo*— "transformism." This involved putting together a coalition of interest groups that would be willing to support a given measure; once the issue had been settled, however, the coalition was dissolved. When no coalition could be formed—as was usually the case with serious problems—nothing was done. Hence, solutions to the nation's difficulties were postponed while governments manufactured coalitions in order to stay in power.

In this atmosphere various leftist and rightist groups fought one another. A Socialist Party was founded in 1892. In the first decade of the twentieth century it was led by moderates; but with the democratic process becoming more and more discredited, orthodox Marxists took control of the party in 1912. Anarchism became fashionable, especially in rural areas, which resented taxation by the central government. On the right, a

Nationalist Party was founded in 1910. Like the French right, it was anti-republican, monarchist, and talked of the need to build up state power.

Yet Italian democracy had some strength and seemed to be gaining stability under the leadership of Giovanni Giolitti (1842-1928), the most important member of the Chamber of Deputies from 1903 to 1915. Though a master of *trasformismo*, Giolitti did deal with important matters. Under his regime, universal manhood suffrage was introduced, factory legislation was passed, unions were legalized, and some attempt was made to cope with the poverty of the peasant, which was particularly serious in the south.

THE PERSISTENCE OF THE OLD EMPIRES

A map of eastern Europe in 1871 shows three old empires: the Austro-Hungarian, the Russian, and the Ottoman. All were governed in authoritarian or semi-authoritarian fashion, and all faced problems trying to adjust to an age of liberalism and socialism. Each was destined to be transformed during the First World War.

Austria-Hungary

After the *Ausgleich* of 1867 Austria-Hungary had a constitution, but the empire was still a very traditional regime ruled by the Emperor, Franz Joseph, who reigned from 1848 to 1916. While the Hungarians had the right of internal self-government and the Poles and Czechs were granted language rights and some cultural autonomy, the remaining Slavic areas were controlled by Vienna. The Austro-Hungarian Empire was a patchwork of peoples and languages, which continued to exist because it was convenient and even useful.

Once Prussia had created a united Germany, Austria focussed attention on its Slavic and Balkan lands to the east. Austrian policies were a holding operation—an attempt to control and subdue nationalist interests. They worked for a time, but the basic problem persisted: national groups continued to demand autonomy or independence. Yet had their wishes been granted,

it would have been difficult to sort out all these national groups and draw acceptable boundaries around them. These groups were so intermingled that, no matter what boundaries would have been established, there were bound to be dissatisfied minorities in the new states. For this reason, some people liked the idea of a multi-national state and believed that it could work if reforms came quickly enough from within.

Unlike England, France, and Germany, Austria lacked a large middle class. It was still mainly an empire of aristocrats and peasants, and, as a power, it grew continually weaker relative to the industrial states. A sizable *bourgeoisie* existed only in the city of Vienna, and what little impetus there was for liberal reform came from them. However, these Austrian liberals were strong nationalists who wanted constitutional government for themselves but were unwilling to grant rights of local self-government to other nationalities within the empire.

Austria-Hungary did, to some degree, move along the path of western European states when it introduced universal manhood suffrage in 1907. Two socialist parties emerged in this period. The Christian Socialists helped to secure legalization of unions and a social insurance scheme, but after 1907 they turned to the right towards ardent nationalism and anti-Semitism. The Social Democratic Party, led by Viktor Adler, was a moderate Marxist party which pressed for reforms through parliamentary means. It proposed internal autonomy for the various nationalities.

Despite the fact that Austria ruled many different groups, the Austrian regime often discriminated against minorities. Jews had received civil rights in 1867 and had become a large part of the Viennese bourgeois class. But, as in France, they were often regarded as outsiders and blamed for the shortcomings of the regime; after 1900 anti-Semitism became more intense and widespread in Austria. There were attempts to pass laws forbidding Jews and "foreigners" from participating in governmental affairs, and the Viennese municipal government began to exclude people on the basis of cultural origin.

In reaction to such policies, political Zionism, a movement to establish a national homeland for Jews, began in Vienna under the leadership of Theodore Herzl, a Jew who had been assimilated into Austrian culture. Herzl proposed that, in the face of such hatred, a homeland for the Jews should be established as a sanctuary from racism and anti-Semitism.

When it was faced with the challenge of the First World War, the Austro-Hungarian Empire was incapable of putting a modern army into the field, and the weakness of its economy and its governmental structure was revealed. In 1916 the regime collapsed to the cheers of many of its own citizens. But there was no easy solution to the problem of how such a vast area, including so many nationalities, would now be restructured and governed.

Russia

The defeat of Russia in the Crimean War in 1856 provided the impetus for internal reform. For a century and a half before, Russia had been successful in diplomacy and war, and this success had been a powerful argument against reform. It was said that Russia required an autocratic government and that Russian serfdom must be maintained if the state were to survive. However, the new Czar, Alexander II, who ruled from 1855 to 1881, realized that Russian society had to be changed if Russia was to compete with other nations and maintain a place among the great powers. He turned his attention to the institution of serfdom.

Russian serfdom had developed about 1500. While other European states were making the transition from a medieval serf society to a modern one, Russian society in the eighteenth and nineteenth centuries became more rigidly divided between nobles and serfs. In its legal aspect Russian serfdom resembled slavery in the United States more than it did the earlier serfdom of other European states, for Russian serfs were owned by their masters and could not leave the land.

Early in the nineteenth century the arguments for reform came from the "Westerners," that group of the nobility who wanted to see Russia emulate Western society. They argued that Russia must be liberalized and given a constitutional base. They were opposed by Slavophiles, a group of traditionalists who felt that Russia was different from the West and should preserve its society and culture. The Westerner-Slavophile argument involved only some nobles and a small group of writers and, in fact, Russia was in some ways already becoming "Westernized" by the mid nineteenth century. Many of the nobility were now educated in the West, and Russian writers, such as Turgenev and Dostoevsky, had adopted such typically Western forms of literature as the novel.

Alexander II was no liberal, but he did feel after 1856 that to preserve Russia he must change the basis of its society. "It is better to abolish serfage from above," he said to his nobility in a speech in 1856, "than to await the time when it will begin to abolish itself from below."[15] In 1861, after many meetings with influential nobles, he decreed the end of serfdom in Russia. The serfs became peasants, subject to the authority of the government, rather than their local masters. The nobility was given land and fees to compensate them for the loss of their "property." Moreover, peasants were obliged to pay over a forty-nine-year period for the land they received. Alexander II inaugurated a new legal system, so that Russian peasants now came to the representatives of the Czar's court for justice, not to their nobles. And, finally, local representative institutions, the Zemstvos, were established in 1864. Thus even Russia underwent major changes in the 1860s. Reform was initiated by the Czar rather than from the society itself.

Industrialization in Russia began in the 1890s in the reign of the very conservative Alexander III (1845–94). The movement to industrialize received its impetus and leadership from Count Witte, Finance Minister from 1892 to 1903. Coal production increased tenfold from 1890 to 1910. Railways and telegraph lines were built, and exports quadrupled from 1880 to 1913. Foreign investment was encouraged, and large sums of money and a good many industrial managers were brought from western European countries. Czar Nicholas II (1868–1918) and his advisers were more wary of industrialization because they feared the political consequences of creating a large urban working class. In general the government favoured agricultural, rather than industrial, interests; none the less, the beginnings of Russia's industrial might are to be found in Witte's work.

In spite of reform and the beginnings of an industrial program, Russia suffered a defeat in the Russo-Japanese War of 1904–05. This humiliation helped to bring on a revolution in 1905. The revolution did not overthrow the Czar, but forced him to grant a constitution, which included a Duma (parliament). To this extent Russian liberalism was victorious, though after 1906 the Czar and his advisers persistently tried to revoke many of their concessions. None the less, from 1906 onwards, Russia was going through an experiment that might ultimately have established a limited constitutional monarchy on the western European model, had not war and revolution intervened.

Socialism also made inroads in Russia in this period. The Russian Social Democratic Party was founded in 1898 by Marxists. In 1903 it divided along lines similar to those of other European socialist parties—one group believed in gradualism and wished to work through parliamentary democracy, the other felt that revolution was the only way to establish a socialist society in czarist Russia. Though socialists played a part in the revolution of 1905, many were in exile during this period.

Russia thus underwent great changes during this time. The general trend, as in Germany and Italy, was towards liberalization and constitutionalism. It remained to be seen whether the traditional rulers could adjust to the problems which came with the end of serfdom, the beginnings of industrialization, and the political demands of liberals and socialists.

Turkey and the Balkans

The Ottoman Empire, like Austria-Hungary, was a weak, divided, multi-national state ruled from a central capital (Constantinople).

Known as "the sick man of Europe," the empire in 1871 still controlled most of the Balkan peninsula with the exception of independent Greece. These Balkan territories were troubled by innumerable nationalist movements, and, as in the case of the Austrian Empire, it would have been difficult to make clear territorial divisions between the national groups. Moreover, both Austria-Hungary and Russia wished to gain an outlet to the Mediterranean Sea and to acquire a dominant position in the Balkans; hence they manoeuvred for control of these territories. Any Balkan peoples who could free themselves from the Turks would thus face problems from Vienna or St. Petersburg.

In view of these external pressures and an internal reform movement, the Sultan, in 1876, granted a constitution based on the German model. Although this was, in theory, a great advance over the existing system, in practice very little changed. The constitution reserved great powers for the Sultan, and from 1876–1909 Abdul-Hamid II continued to rule as an autocrat. He was, however, challenged by those who wished to Westernize Turkey and the empire.

In 1877 war broke out between Russia and Turkey over the Balkans. Turkey lost the war in 1878 and, as a result, Serbia, Rumania, and Bulgaria were given their independence as nation-states. It was a great victory for Russia, which saw itself as the protector of the Slavic peoples.

The Turkish army, disgusted with backward internal policies and the loss of part of the empire, rebelled in 1908 and forced the Sultan to adopt a measure of reform. In 1909 a counter-revolution by Abdul-Hamid II failed, and he was deposed. The army now held the key to power. But the Ottoman Empire continued to disintegrate. A series of Balkan wars in 1912–13 resulted in the independence of Albania and the annexation of Macedonia to Greece. As Turkey failed to establish any kind of parliamentary government, the army stepped into the power vacuum, attempting to shore up the crumbling state by using authoritarian and repressive methods. But it failed to hold the empire together.

The three empires of eastern Europe—
Austria-Hungary, Russia, and Turkey—
were thus weak and divided. All were
governed ineffectively. In a period of nationalism, liberalism, democracy, and industrialization, they increasingly seemed to be
anachronisms.

LIBERALISM, SOCIALISM, AND NATIONALISM BY 1914

During the period from the Franco-Prussian
War to the First World War, all European
states, even the empires of the east, moved
towards constitutional government. Many
of them established universal manhood suf-

frage, and their parliaments passed social
legislation and legalized unions. The trend
towards social democracy was clearer in the
west than the east, but the movement towards egalitarianism was evident everywhere. By the end of this period liberalism
had become a middle-of-the-road position;
this in itself was an indication of how far
European politics had moved since the French
Revolution.

Socialism gained ground throughout the
period, although Marx was not accepted as
a prophet by all socialists. Many socialists,
especially in western Europe, became revisionists, adopting the political methods of

"Outbreak" by Käthe Kollwitz, 1903   (Kupferstichkabinett, Staatliche Muséen Preussischer
Kulturbesitz, Berlin (West))

the liberals in order to produce socialist ends. When socialist parties worked through parliamentary channels, it became clear that socialism had great appeal for the masses, as socialists were voted into legislatures in large numbers.

Though liberalism and socialism were doctrines which crossed national boundaries, nationalism remained an extraordinarily powerful ideal. Socialists could persuade Frenchmen and Germans to vote socialist, but they could not persuade most of them to forget that they were Frenchmen or Germans. And the peoples of the Austrian or Ottoman empires were more interested in obtaining their national freedom than participating in a socialist or liberal revolution.

In reviewing the state of Europe in early 1914, most commentators were optimistic about the future, despite ever-present international tensions. Wealth was increasing and internal reform was the order of the day. Few realized that Europe was on the brink of a long and terrible world war.

ANALYSIS AND DISCUSSION

1. The political philosophies of John Stuart Mill and Karl Marx were among the most influential philosophies of the last half of the nineteenth century. Summarize the main ideas of each man and identify the differences between each set of ideas.

2. According to Marxian theory, revolution would first transform the more highly industrialized states and then spread to less developed ones. Explain the reasons why this important expectation in Marx's theory failed to materialize.

3. "In the second half of the nineteenth century . . . in the industrial nations, particularly England and Germany, the state took an ever-increasing interest in the conditions of labour. This gradual improvement in the life of the working class gave rise to the concept of democratic socialism." Explain the philosophy of democratic socialism as outlined by support-

ers such as Eduard Bernstein and examine its electoral success in the early twentieth century.

4. "The Dreyfus affair was a watershed in the history of the Third Republic." Explain, citing specific evidence, in what respects this statement is true.

5. "In 1871, three old empires — the Austro-Hungarian, the Russian, and the Ottoman — were all governed in authoritarian or semi-authoritarian fashion, and all faced problems trying to adjust to an age of liberalism and socialism." Identify the problems faced by each empire. What general problems were applicable to all three empires?

6. One of the most striking changes in the United States in the early twentieth century was the growth in power and prestige of the office of the president. Evaluate the roles of Theodore Roosevelt and Woodrow Wilson in bringing about this change.

SYNTHESIS AND EVALUATION   CHAPTERS 7 AND 8

1. "Revolutionaries such as Thomas Paine or Garibaldi are essential for making a revolution but have no place in the country once the battles have been won." Discuss this statement with reference to the fate of revolutionary leaders.

2. "Bismarck's answer to socialism was a form of benevolent paternalism. In many ways it was a natural successor to the enlightened despotism of Frederick the Great in the previous century." Evaluate this quotation in terms

of the philosophy and goals of both systems.

3. Compare Mill's ideas on freedom as expressed in On Liberty with those of John Locke on natural rights.

4. The forces of conservatism, liberalism, and socialism competed for adherents in the late nineteenth and early twentieth centuries. Select one western European country to represent the continent and examine the interplay of these forces within its boundaries.

CHAPTER **9**

Towards a
New Universe:
The Transformation
of Thought,
1850–1914

c. 1830–57	Comte publishes his works on the "Positive Philosophy"; development of "Sociology"
1830s and 1840s	Balzac writes *La Comédie Humaine*
1835	Strauss' *Life of Jesus*; Biblical criticism
1850s	Baudelaire begins Symbolist Movement in Literature
c. 1850–1900	Spencer publishes social and philosophic works; Social Darwinism
1859	Darwin's *Origin of Species*
1864	Pope Pius IX issues Syllabus of Errors
c. 1870–90	Nietzsche probes human nature and society
1878–1903	Reign of Pope Leo XIII
1880	Zola writes "The Experimental Novel" to explain his work
1880s	Van Gogh and Gauguin challenge traditional representational art
1883	Dilthey publishes his *Introduction to the Human Studies*
c. 1900–20	Weber develops new attitudes towards a "Science of Society"
1900	Freud publishes his *Interpretation of Dreams* Planck's Quantum Theory
1905	Einstein's "Special Theory of Relativity"

IN MANY WAYS, PEOPLE IN THE nineteenth century continued the quest of Enlightenment thinkers, who had searched for truths about the universe and human beings that could be confirmed by observation and deduction. Above all, they continued to believe in Newton's vision of a harmonious machine-like universe, working according to laws that could be expressed in mathematical formulae. This approach to science seemed to offer hope for an ever-increasing understanding of nature, and the fact that it was successful in the physical sciences convinced many people that the same method could be applied in other areas, for example, in investigations of society and even of the nature of beauty and of the meaning of good and evil. Hence we have social philosophers in the nineteenth century who claimed to have discovered "scientific" socialism, artists who proclaimed the rise of the new "realist" school of art and literature, and scholars who developed the "social sciences." By the end of the century the very word "science" had become synonymous with the idea of truth.

In the Enlightenment the advance of science was associated with faith in progress. Enlightenment thinkers believed that people by the use of their intellect had advanced from barbarism to civilization, and that this process would continue indefinitely. This belief in continuing progress through the application of science and reason persisted in the nineteenth century, and people saw everywhere around them evidence that seemed to confirm their faith. Methods of communication were vastly improved, largely by the railway, steamboat, and telegraph. The invention of the light bulb

changed daily habits which had persisted since the beginning of the human species. Great industrial fairs and exhibitions—in Paris, London, Philadelphia—were organized to illustrate the continued progress of humanity. On all fronts it seemed as if Condorcet's vision of the future was coming true—that the world was ever progressing through the advances of science.

Some believed that the new world of liberalism and science would usher in an era of international co-operation, and the fact that there had been no major international war since the Napoleonic Wars seemed to support this hope. People cared more about the welfare of others. Enormous charitable and scientific enterprises were undertaken to contribute to human well-being, and from 1850 to 1914 there was a great deal of optimism about the possibilities of life and the future of the human species.

NEW QUESTIONS ABOUT THE NATURE OF THE BIOLOGICAL UNIVERSE—DARWIN

The idea that the universe operated as a harmonious balanced machine was challenged in the second half of the nineteenth century by Charles Darwin (1809–82), who saw change and development to be the pattern of nature. In 1859, after more than a quarter of a century of gathering evidence and pondering nature, Darwin published a work with the long title *The Origin of Species by Means of Natural Selection, or the Preservation of the Favoured Races in the Struggle for Life*. Though Darwin did not use the term "evolution," the issues raised by his book at once became the source of great controversy in England and throughout the West. Darwin set out to prove that species of animals, and by implication the human species, were not special creations of God, but that all had evolved from common ancestors through a long process of gradual change. Species had come into existence and had ceased to exist in a process that was still continuing. This view seemed to place human beings among the apes, not the angels, and it challenged the traditional Christian conception of God's special creation of all living beings, particularly humans

The idea of evolution was connected with changing views of the age of the earth. Scholars had generally thought that the earth was young, basing the belief on what they saw and on the chronology of the Bible. One Anglican bishop, using Biblical clues, had dated the origins of humanity and God's creation of the universe at 4004 B.C. But geology, which made great strides in the 1830s with the works of Charles Lyell, was beginning to extend the time scale, and Lyell postulated that the earth was, in fact, millions of years old. In the eighteenth century people's consciousness of space had changed through advances in astronomy, and now in the nineteenth century their consciousness of time changed through discoveries in geology. Darwin seized on this new time scale, which showed that there had been sufficient time on earth for life to evolve. He insisted that species developed very slowly, through an evolutionary process, by adapting to their environment. Those species which could adapt survived, and those with physical or mental characteristics which could not adapt passed out of existence. Darwin spoke of "favoured races," meaning those which were more suited to their environment.

According to Darwin, the selection process through which species survived or disappeared was "natural," which implied both that it was a normal process and that it was not controlled by a deity. Because all species tended to increase in number and food supplies were limited,

Darwin thought of life as a constant "struggle for existence." Through "natural selection" some survived and others did not, and those that survived could develop into a new species. The term "survival of the fittest," though first used by one of Darwin's contemporaries, Herbert Spencer, was adopted by Darwin and became associated with his ideas.

Unlike some of his contemporaries, Darwin was not horrified by the process he described. He found it fascinating and beautiful:

It is interesting to contemplate an entangled bank, clothed with many plants of many kinds, with birds singing on the bushes, with various insects flitting about, and with worms crawling through the damp earth, and to reflect that these elaborately constructed forms, so different from each other, and dependent on each other in so complex a manner, have all been produced by laws acting around us. These laws, taken in the largest sense, [are] Growth with Reproduction; Inheritance which is almost implied by reproduction; Variability from the indirect and direct action of the external conditions of life, and from use and disuse; a Ratio of Increase so high as to lead to a Struggle for Life, and as a consequence to Natural Selection, entailing Divergence of Character and the Extinction of less-improved forms. Thus, from the war of nature, from famine and death, the most exalted object which we are capable of conceiving, namely the production of the higher animals, directly follows. There is grandeur in this view of life ... having been originally breathed by the Creator into a few forms or into one; and that, whilst this planet has gone cycling on according to the fixed law of gravity, from so simple a beginning endless forms most beautiful and most wonderful have been, and are being, evolved.[1]

In presenting this theory of evolution, Darwin was talking as a biologist trying to explain the development of living organisms. But, as with other important scientific ideas, the philosophical implications of his theory were very significant. He had challenged the Newtonian and Biblical picture of a static universe, for he conceived nature to be in a state of flux. He also suggested that nature was not necessarily benign. Both Enlightenment and Romantic thinkers believed that to be "natural," to be at one with "nature," was a good thing. But for Darwin "nature" was *neutral*; it was natural to struggle—some lived and some died.

If one accepted Darwin's view of nature, peace and harmony were not necessarily the "natural" way of the world. The Darwinian idea of the necessity, the inevitability, and even the ultimate benefits of struggle was transferred by many, though not by Darwin himself, to politics, ethics, and economics. Those who practised the "politics of reality" or the ethics of selfishness or the economics of rugged individualism claimed that evolutionary thought justified their actions. The latest scientific theory seemed to be on their side. Socialists often felt, for example, that Marx's idea of the necessity of class conflict and Darwin's "struggle for existence" were parallel; Marx himself thought that Darwin was one of the great original thinkers of the age.

There was a concept of progress in Darwin, although it differed from the Enlightenment idea of progress. By progress Darwin meant more than simply the process of evolution, for he saw "higher" species emerging from "lower" ones through a struggle within the environment and with other species. Human beings were now at the highest level in the evolutionary ladder, and there was nothing to say the process ended here. Darwin's theories, often distorted, were used by those who wished to argue that struggle among people and nations was essential for the achievement of progress. This idea could be used, for example, to justify imperialism abroad and the neglect of poverty at home.

SOCIAL DARWINISM

One of the major intellectual influences on Darwin was the *Essay on Population* by Thomas Malthus (1766–1834). Appearing in 1798, this essay had a great influence on nineteenth-century thought. Writing only a few years after Condorcet's enormously optimistic vision of the future, Malthus asserted that nature was not benign and that progress was not inevitable. The increase in population, he believed, would always outrun people's limited resources; thus human beings were doomed to a wretched existence. The capacity of people to reproduce, he thought, was always greater than their capacity to increase their food supply, since the food supply increased arithmetically (1, 2, 3, 4), while population increased geometrically (1, 2, 4, 8). The consequence of this "law" of increasing population was that suffering would increase despite social and political improvements, because not enough food could ever be produced to sustain life. Malthus' contribution to nineteenth-century thought is this idea of scarcity and struggle. Marx also assumed that scarcity and struggle were part of the history of humanity, while Darwin applied the idea of struggle for survival in the face of a limited supply of food to all creatures.

The application of Darwinian ideas to human affairs has been called "Social Darwinism." Herbert Spencer (1820–1903) was the most important social Darwinist, and his ideas had a great vogue which lasted into the late nineteenth century. He had, in fact, been an evolutionist in social matters before Darwin published *The Origin of Species.* He believed that everything evolved from the simple and uniform to the complex and specialized. For example, life began with a group of similar cells, and from these evolved all the complex specialized living creatures in nature including human beings. Spencer believed that this principle of development, from the "homogeneous" to the "heterogeneous," could explain all social, political, and intellectual movements, and he devoted his life to writing a philosophic synthesis based on this theory. He accepted the struggle for existence and the survival of the fittest as normal and good.

Spencer did not believe that governments should try to change the social environment because it would hamper the processes of nature and interfere with individual liberty. He thought that evil would disappear when "every man may claim the fullest liberty to exercise his faculties,"[2] providing that every other person had similar liberty. If this principle were operative, Spencer felt that only the fit would survive, for he also assumed the inevitability of scarcity. Competition was therefore necessary in order to allow those who were "fit" to emerge on top in the economic and social struggle. Spencer was the last major thinker in the old *laissez-faire* tradition.

Spencer's ideas gained many advocates throughout the world, particularly in the United States, which was industrializing very quickly after its Civil War, and where a "rugged individualism" was being preached. Many believed that governments existed only to make certain that the economic market place operated smoothly. Industrialists fostered the idea of *laissez-faire* and preached the necessity of competition. But towards the end of the century, as socialist ideas were more widely accepted, Spencer's popularity waned. Spencer himself hated socialism and regarded it as the curse of the age—he went so far as to deplore public education and public management of the post office.

Social Darwinism was also used to support racial theories which had preceded the development of evolutionary biology. Romantics and nationalists had stressed the differences between peoples rather than the unity of humanity. Some thought that certain groups of peoples were naturally superior to others because of what they had accomplished, and that technological and scientific progress was an indication of a higher species. Naturally, the standards employed to judge "progress" were those of Western society — industrialization, scientific advance, and technological innovation. Thus many Europeans began to feel superior to other peoples and used racism to justify imperialism—the control over less "advanced" areas of the globe.

Some Europeans claimed that imperialism, far from having only economic or power motives, was also intended to civilize and Christianize so-called "backward peoples." This latter idea was celebrated in a famous poem by the Englishman Rudyard Kipling (1865–1936):

Take up the White Man's burden—
Send forth the best ye breed—
Go bind your sons to exile
To serve your captives' need;
To wait in heavy harness
On fluttered folk and wild—
Your new-caught, sullen peoples,
Half devil and half child.
. . .
Take up the White Man's burden—
Ye dare not stoop to less—
Nor call too loud on Freedom
To cloak your weariness;
By all ye cry or whisper,
By all ye leave or do,
The silent, sullen peoples
Shall weigh your Gods and you.[3]

Others believed that the expansion of European rule would demonstrate the virility and survival capacity of superior people and would rid the world of misfits. Struggle and conquest would be of great benefit to humankind.

In the era of Bismarck, *Realpolitik*—the politics of reality—was admired because it was openly based on power. Those who praised *Realpolitik* thought that the progress of a people was measured by the strength of its army or industrial machine, and they saw nothing immoral in a state using war to achieve its goals. In his discussion of politics, the German historian Heinrich von Treitschke (1834–96) stated that:

The State is not an Academy of Arts. If it neglects its strength in order to promote the idealistic aspirations of man, it repudiates its own nature and perishes. . . .

The entire development of European [politics] tends unmistakably to drive the second-rate Powers into the background, and this raises issues of immeasurable gravity for the German nation, in the world outside Europe. Up to the present Germany has always had too small a share of the spoils in the [division] of non-European territories among the Powers of Europe, and yet our existence as a State of the first rank is vitally affected by [our ability to] . . . become a power beyond the seas. If [we do] not, there remains the appalling prospect of England and

Russia dividing the world between them, and in such a case it is hard to say whether the Russian [club] or the English money bags would be the worst alternative. . . .

Without war no State could [exist]. All those we know of arose through war, and the protection of their members by armed force remains their primary and essential task. War, therefore, will endure to the end of history, as long as there is [a large number] of States. The laws of human thought and of human nature forbid any alternative, [nor] is one to be wished for. The blind worshipper of an eternal peace falls into the error of [ignoring] the [national] State, or dreams of one which is universal, which we have already seen to be [contrary to] reason.[4]

RELIGIOUS THOUGHT

Religious belief and religious institutions were still very strong in the mid nineteenth century. But just as Darwin challenged the view of nature held by many scientists, so in the early nineteenth century a new type of Biblical study raised fundamental issues of religious faith among theologians. The study of ancient languages had grown more sophisticated with the development of philology as a "scientific" discipline. Texts could now be understood more clearly in the manner and spirit in which they were originally written. After studying the variations in language used in the original texts, some scholars concluded that the Bible, and most notably the five books of Moses in the Old Testament, was written by several people at different times. This was a challenge to the old belief that the Bible was revealed truth.

The New Testament underwent similar analysis. David Strauss' *Life of Jesus*, which appeared in 1835, argued that the story of Jesus was largely an imaginative creation and that none of the supernatural events surrounding Jesus' life actually occurred. Later in the century studies by archaeologists and anthropologists raised further questions about the origins and uniqueness of Judaism and Christianity. Such studies suggested that religions are created by people as a way of comprehending their place in the universe.

All this provided a major challenge to religious traditions.

In this atmosphere Darwinian ideas were a fresh challenge to faith. As soon as *The Origin of Species* was published, unbelievers and rationalists added evolutionary arguments to their continued assault against traditional religion. The Darwinian challenge to religion was greater than that of Newtonian physics. Religion and Newton could accommodate one another because Newton saw God as the creator of the mechanical universe; nor were questions of ethics and salvation directly affected by Newton's thought. However, if Darwin was right, life was a process of constant change not an act of special creation; species emerged and were destroyed in random fashion and God did not seem to care. Darwin's universe was always in flux, and the outcome of the process of evolution was not certain. If one accepted Darwin, many asked, what were the goals of people in life? How should they behave? What was their relationship to God?

Debates and discussions were held on the origins of the human species and on human nature, and treatises were written on the questions raised by scientific Biblical criticism and Darwinian thought. Most notably, the idea that the human species was a special creation of God was seriously challenged. Those Protestants in England and the United States who looked to the Bible for literal truth regarded Biblical criticism as heresy and Darwin as the devil.

The "warfare between science and theology," to use the words of one historian, was not universal. Some religious thinkers were willing to take geology and Darwin at face value. If what the geologists and Darwin were saying was *true*, then their views could not be contradictory to revealed truth, for one kind of truth would not disagree with another. These people felt that evolution could be part of God's plan and found beauty in the idea that all living things were interrelated. Later in the century some expressed the belief that human beings were active participants in the completion of God's plan, and found comfort and inspiration in this vision of the world.

While not all scientists were unbelievers, and some were deeply religious people, there were others like Thomas Henry Huxley, Darwin's chief defender, who were "agnostics"—in fact, Huxley created the term "agnostic" when he could find no other label to describe his attitude to religion. Agnosticism maintained that ultimate truths about nature and God were not knowable; therefore one should not waste time arguing about these things, but suspend judgment and pursue knowledge in those areas where knowledge was possible. Darwin himself was an agnostic but had no interest in making a public stand on the issue.

THE CATHOLIC CHURCH IN TRANSFORMATION

The Catholic Church attempted to resist Darwin's influence, but there was some hesitation to confront evolution directly. It did not wish to condemn Darwin officially, as it had done with Galileo. Moreover, the Church was never "fundamentalist"; it traditionally relied on a large body of interpretation, and therefore was not overly dependent upon the literal meaning of the Bible. In the eyes of a number of Catholic intellectuals, Biblical criticism and evolution in themselves did not challenge basic Catholic dogmas.

Nevertheless, with the introduction of modern liberalism, nationalism, and socialism, the Church found itself on the side of the conservative forces in the competition for the hearts and minds of people. The initial response of the Church was to attack the modern world. Pope Pius IX, who witnessed all of the new trends in his long reign from 1846 to 1878, turned from a moderate liberal into an arch-conservative. In 1864 he issued a Syllabus of Errors which denounced all of the major ideas of the nineteenth century—liberalism, nationalism, socialism—as errors in thought and defended the right of the Church to interfere in all matters, including politics, when the Church's conception of salvation was involved. In essence he damned the whole period since 1789 in the Syllabus:

[It is wrong] that every man is free to embrace

and profess the religion he shall believe true, guided by the light of reason. . . .

. . . [It is wrong] that the Church ought to be separated from the State, and the State from the Church. . . .

. . . [It is wrong] that it is allowable to refuse obedience to legitimate princes; nay more, to rise in insurrection against them. . . .

. . . [It is wrong] that in the present day, it is no longer necessary that the Catholic religion be held as the only religion of the State, to the exclusion of all other modes of worship. . . .

. . . [It is wrong] that the Roman Pontiff can, and ought to, reconcile himself to, and agree with, progress, liberalism, and modern civilization.[5]

In 1870 Pius IX in his beleaguered state called the First Vatican Council, the first ecumenical council for over three hundred years. The major act of the Council was to proclaim the doctrine of Papal Infallibility as dogma in matters of faith and morals. Some liberal Catholics objected to this theological position. They also tried to get the Church to recognize that, since it was no longer a political power, it was in a better position to serve the spiritual needs of people. Theologically, the conservative position triumphed, but the First Vatican Council ended in September 1870, as Italian troops were occupying Rome and annexing most of the city into the new state of Italy.

The trend set by Pius IX was broken by his successor, Leo XIII, who was Pope from 1878 to 1903. Leo XIII tried to seek a new path for the Church, since he realized that clinging to old positions put the Church at a serious disadvantage in the modern world. He believed that the Church had an important social role and tried to reconcile Catholicism with social action. For a time he gave his approval to the involvement of the Church in the great social questions of the day, particularly those relating to conditions of the working class. Leo XIII also looked to the works of the thirteenth-century theologian St. Thomas Aquinas, who had attempted to reconcile reason and faith. It should be noted that neither secular philosophy nor the secular state, which did not accept Catholic principles and did not protect the Church, had any appeal for the Pope. Nevertheless, Leo XIII paved the way for the Catholic Church to begin the process of modernization.

REALISM IN LITERATURE

Literature in the mid nineteenth century reflected an interest in scientific method and scientific accomplishment. Beginning in the 1830s, at its height in the 1850s and 1860s, and still flourishing in 1890, the new trend was called "the literature of realism." Realism was expounded in France by Honoré de Balzac (1799–1850), who rejected the fanciful, poetic, escapist, mystical literature of Romanticism and began to write "social novels." Balzac's social novels, collectively entitled *La Comédie Humaine*, were an attempt to render life as he saw it, not as he or others wanted it to be.

Balzac was an acute observer of society and felt that one ought to depict it vividly, objectively, and almost photographically. He was less interested in nature than the Romantics, and more concerned with people and society. The function of the novelist, he thought, was to give a picture of the human condition without sentimentalism. In introducing one of his novels, *Le père Goriot*, Balzac said: "You may be certain that this drama is neither fiction nor romance. *All is true*, so true that everyone can recognize the elements of the tragedy in his own household, in his own heart perhaps."[6] The result of Balzac's approach was a new kind of "realistic" novel. Here is a passage from his novel *Eugénie Grandet* which describes the death of Eugénie's father, a miser who has hoarded all his money and mistreated Eugénie, her mother, and all others with whom he had contact:

Whenever he was capable of opening his eyes, in which his whole life had now taken its last refuge, he would promptly turn them toward the strong-room door, behind which his treasure lay, and say to his daughter, "Are they there? Are they there?" And there would be a kind of panic in his voice.

"Yes, Father."

"Look after the gold. . . . Put some gold in front of me!"

Eugénie would spread some golden louis for him on the table, and he would sit there for hours on end, gazing at them, like a baby staring blankly at the one same object as soon as it begins to see; and, like the baby, he would produce a feeble smile.

"That makes me feel warm," he would occasionally murmur, and there would be a blissful expression on his face.

When the parish priest came to administer the last sacraments, Grandet's eyes, which had been apparently lifeless for some hours past, suddenly brightened at the sight of the cross, the candlesticks, and the silver holy-water sprinkler. He stared hard at them, and his wen twitched for the last time. As the priest lowered the gilded crucifix to his lips for him to kiss the image of Christ, he made a terrifying effort to take hold of it, and this final exertion cost him his life. He called to Eugénie, whom he could not see, although she was on her knees before him, and her tears were dropping onto his already-cold hand.

"Give me your blessing, Father," she said.

"Take good care of everything! I shall expect a full account when we meet in the beyond," he said, proving by these last words that Christianity is unquestionably the miser's religion after all.[7]

Throughout the nineteenth century the reading public steadily increased. The middle class had the leisure to read books and the money to buy them. As literacy grew and education slowly became universal, workers also began reading more and more books. Cheap "penny pamphlets" appeared, and novels were serialized in magazines. People did not wish to read only about the aristocracy or the world of kings and chivalry, but also, as Balzac understood, about themselves and the world in which they lived. Hence the "social novel" reflected its readers and their world. Novelists had considerable influence in shaping public opinion and arousing interest in reform.

The realistic novel reached its heights in the writings of Emile Zola (1840–1902), who thought that the intellectual principles of the physical and biological sciences could also be applied to the novel. In an essay entitled

"The Experimental Novel" (1880), Zola spoke of using the "experimental method" in the novel, just as it was being used in other areas of knowledge:

I shall try to prove in my turn that, if the experimental method leads to the understanding of physical life, it must also lead to the understanding of emotional and intellectual life. This is only a question of degree, in the same direction, from chemistry to physiology, then from physiology to anthropology and to sociology. At the end of this we find the experimental novel.[8]

To Zola, the writer was part observer and part experimenter. The observer looks at life in order to discover the facts of existence, the nature of the characters, and the environment in which they will move. The experimenter then takes these basic facts and makes the story move along in the "determined" way demanded by the facts. Zola believed that predictions of human behaviour could be made in the same way as we can predict the moon's movement around the earth, if we know the facts and the scientific laws involved. For example, if we wished to write about life in the mines, we should first go to the mines. Then we would choose characters and establish the hereditary and environmental influences that work upon them. If the characters are put in the environment of mining life, the story will automatically move along according to the nature of the characters and the nature of the environment. "At the end," stated Zola, "there is knowledge of man, scientific knowledge, in its individual and social operation."[9] Taking into account the variables of heredity and environment, an investigator could successfully predict human behaviour. There was little room in Zola's scheme for free will.

POSITIVISM AND SOCIOLOGY

With the advance of science in the nineteenth century, the scientific spirit permeated all areas of thought, and society itself was considered an appropriate subject for scientific analysis. The most fertile thinker in the scientific study of society in the first half of the nineteenth century was Auguste Comte (1798–1857). Comte constructed a theory which he called "The Positive Philosophy"— "positive" meaning "scientific." The aim of positivism was to achieve a total scientific synthesis of all knowledge, and Comte's ultimate purpose was to reform and restructure society on the basis of the "scientific principles" he discovered. Throughout the century the term positivism became synonymous with the scientific spirit.

Comte felt that humanity had progressed through three stages of knowledge. In the past, people had first used the notion of supernatural forces (the Theological stage) and then abstract ideas (the Metaphysical stage) for example the idea of "nature" to explain the world. Now, according to Comte, people explained things on the basis of scientifically discovered laws (the Positive stage). Just as the physical sciences had shown the world to be subject to fixed, invariable laws, the scientific study of society, he felt, would eventually accomplish the same task for social phenomena. Comte believed that the laws of society were to be discovered by the study of history.

Comte coined the term "sociology" to designate the new science of society. Sociology was to be the study of both "social statics" and "social dynamics" and was to use the methodology of science. "Statics" was a study of the workings of society, that is, the co-existence of customs, institutions, legal codes, and other elements which make up a society. "Dynamics" was a study of social change for the purpose of formulating scientific laws of social development. Comte was certain from his study of history that humanity was constantly progressing. Consequently, he predicted a world of peace and harmony in which co-operation would replace competition. He constructed a "Religion of Humanity"—a "scientific" religion that would honour all those in the past who had contributed to the advancement of civilization—in order to inspire contemporaries to bring such a world into being.

THE CHALLENGE TO THE RATIONAL UNIVERSE

In the last two decades of the nineteenth century a number of thinkers, writers, and artists began to challenge the positivist approach to knowledge and the centrality of rationality in understanding human nature.

In the areas of philosophy and history, Wilhelm Dilthey (1833–1911) wrote his *Introduction to the Human Studies* in 1883, a work in which he rejected the positivist model of the natural sciences as the appropriate means of studying humanity, society, and the past. Dilthey insisted that human beings were not to be understood by using the methods of the natural sciences. Rather, it was necessary for the investigator to use imagination to reconstruct the reality of any past age. In order to truly understand a culture, Dilthey proposed that the historian seek out what he called "spontaneous expressions" of past societies, ways in which people related and communicated with one another and expressed their beliefs and values, instead of basing research solely on formal political and diplomatic documents. Dilthey wished to probe the inner life of a people, and he tried to develop a method which would reliably get at the core of human reality underneath external appearances.

The Italian philosopher and historian, Benedetto Croce (1866–1952) raised the question of the impossibility of complete objectivity in investigating the past. In 1893 he stated that history was more akin to art than it was to science, and later he coined the aphorism "every true history is contemporary history," indicating that the researcher not only chooses a topic out of personal and current interest, but that we never fully escape our own times. We use the past, claimed Croce, both to understand it and to deal with contemporary concerns.

In sociology, many students of society thought that Comte had an over-simplified view of both the discovery and application of scientific laws relating to people and society. Among these was Max Weber (1864–1920), the German sociologist who argued that there were limits to what the social sciences could do. Weber claimed that Comte confused the propositions "what is" and "what ought to be." He asserted that while the social sciences, like the physical sciences, could tell us "what is," it was a serious error to derive a set of values from this research. Science did not give

us a philosophy of life, and if something is "scientific," this did not mean that it is desirable. Therefore, Weber claimed science cannot answer all questions—it cannot tell us how to act, it can only clarify what may happen if we commit a particular act.

The fate of an epoch which has eaten at the tree of knowledge is that it must know that we cannot learn the *meaning* of the world from the results of its analysis, be it ever so perfect; it must rather . . . create this meaning itself. It must recognize that general views of life and the universe can never be the products of increasing [scientific] knowledge, and that the highest ideals, which move us most forcefully, are always formed only in the struggle with other ideals which are just as sacred to others as ours are to us.[10]

Weber was wary of turning science into a faith and insisted that people had the choice, the free will, to direct their own lives.

Towards the end of the century Zola's naturalistic view of literature, based on grounds which he believed were scientific, began to be questioned. The observer began to be seen as at least equal in importance to that which was being observed. A number of literary and artistic movements grew up which attempted to take this into account. Careful observation and prediction were no longer held up as the only ideals. People were viewed as more complex creatures than the realists had recognized. Many writers turned back to the work of Charles Baudelaire (1821–67) for guidance. Baudelaire was a "symbolist," who maintained that literature should not try to imitate nature but should attempt to get at the hidden meanings of things.

Nature is a temple from whose living columns
Commingling voices emerge at times;
Here man wanders through forests of symbols
Which seem to observe him with familiar
  eyes.

Like long-drawn echoes afar converging
In harmonies darksome and profound,
Vast as the night and vast as light,
Colors, scents and sounds correspond.

There are fragrances fresh as the flesh of
  children,

Sweet as the oboe, green as the prairie,
 — And others overpowering, rich and corrupt,
Possessing the pervasiveness of everlasting
   things,
Like benjamin, frankincense, amber, myrrh,
Which the raptures of the senses and the
   spirit sing.[11]

Baudelaire's followers stressed the mysterious and the wonderful in life. Reality, they claimed, went deeper than mere observation, and the writer should not be a photographer, a reflector of external reality. He should evoke the unconscious and the profound in human nature.

Artists too sought to explore the inner life of human beings, in an effort to comprehend fully a human nature which was now seen as more varied than that suggested by the rationalist thinkers of the Enlightenment and their nineteenth century successors. The paintings of the Dutch artist Vincent van Gogh (1853–90) were an expression of his own world and his own psyche. He used colour and line as means of suggesting mood, and attempted through an exploration of his inner life to make a statement about the basic nature of all of humanity. His friend, the Frenchman Paul Gauguin (1848–1903), rejected the European tradition entirely, and moved to Tahiti. Gauguin believed European civilization to be artificial and oversophisticated, and he thus purposely placed himself on its margin, in order to try to return to a more primitive condition of existence and to develop an art which dealt with essentials. He experimented with colours and symbols, in which he found more profound meaning than traditional representational art.

PSYCHOLOGY AND THE QUESTION OF THE IRRATIONAL

One of the most startling and fruitful results of the new probings into human nature at the turn of the twentieth century was the development of modern psychology by the Austrian doctor Sigmund Freud (1856–1939), who attempted to understand people by probing the workings of the individual mind. Freud stands alongside Darwin, Marx, and Einstein as one of the great innovators of modern thought. Although he started out in medicine, he realized by the 1890s that some of his patients'

symptoms were not the results of physical ailments, but had their origins in the mind. In order to treat these symptoms he developed the method of psychoanalysis, by which the mental history of each patient was carefully analysed. Sometimes he was quite successful. As a result of his research, Freud rejected the view that people are basically rational creatures. He developed a highly complex theory of human behaviour which has changed our whole attitude towards human nature.

Freud first made a distinction between the conscious and the unconscious. He theorized that, in each person, there were at least two levels of mind in operation, with the unconscious often playing a primary role, as in the case of hysterical patients. Thus the actions of a person may be the result of a non-rational motive which cannot be explained in conventional ways or by rational ideas. Freud stressed the importance of childhood experiences in forming and influencing the actions of the mature person. He recognized the significance of dreams and published *The Interpretation of Dreams* in 1900. Dreams, Freud said, are the way people mentally act out events and desires which cannot be fulfilled in society.

In developing a theory of human nature, Freud claimed that people had certain instincts, such as sexual desires and aggression, which have to be repressed in a civilized world. These instincts, sometimes referred to as the libido, were included in the part of a person's personality which Freud called the "id," a term for one's basic desires. The id, however, is held in check by the "super-ego," which is the conscience acquired by all people as a result of participating in and learning from any society. The face one presents to the world is the "ego"—the personality or the self which is constantly caught between the desires of the id and the repression of the super-ego. When the tensions between the id and super-ego become unbearable, an individual may cease to be able to function effectively.

Freud's work opened up new areas of knowledge. Above all, he challenged the Enlightenment view that people were guided by reason and substituted a notion of people guided by unconscious motives, unfulfilled desires, and levels of the mind which are difficult to understand. He also made a great advance in the study of motivation. He saw behaviour as a complex problem not to be explained simply in terms of economic gain or social satisfaction. People wear many masks, and the job of the psychologist, according to Freud, was to penetrate them and to understand what was underneath.

The study of the irrational and the challenge to current assumptions about people and society predated Freud. For example, the French poet Baudelaire had stressed the symbolic and the unconscious. But perhaps the most influential thinker in this area was Frederick Nietzsche (1844-1900), a German philosopher who questioned many of the assumptions of Western philosophers about human nature and society. Nietzsche rejected the notion of a common humanity and stressed the differences between types of people. He argued that it was essential for the individual, especially the superior individuals, to develop their own talents in their own way. He refused to accept the values of the West: for Nietzsche, Christianity was the religion of the weak, because it made people subordinate themselves to myths and preached a morality of self-sacrifice; democracy, because of its impetus towards equality, inevitably meant mediocrity and the crushing of genius; nationalism, with its emphasis on the demands of the group, meant the end of the individual.

Nietzsche made a distinction between the "noble man" and the "common man": the "noble man" is one who follows his own rules and determines his own destiny, while the "common man" follows others. He feared the development of mass society because he thought that the masses would subordinate culture, which had been achieved through the efforts and genius of the few, to economic desire, and that a sterile civilization would be the result. He called for a new kind of philosophy:

The falseness of a given judgement does not constitute an objection against it, so far as we are concerned. . . . The real question is how far a judgement furthers and maintains life, preserves a given type, possibly cultivates and trains a given type. We are, in fact, fundamentally inclined to maintain that the falsest judgements . . . are the most indispensable to us, that man cannot live without accepting logical fictions as valid, without measuring reality against the purely invented world of the absolute. . . . Getting along without false judgements would amount to getting along without life, negating life. To admit untruth as a necessary condition of life . . . implies, to be sure, a perilous resistance against customary value-feelings. A philosophy that risks it nonetheless, if it did nothing else, would by this alone have taken its stand beyond good and evil.[12]

Nietzsche called for a new morality which rejected the values of science and materialism and allowed superior individuals to develop their full potential.

NEW QUESTIONS ABOUT THE NATURE OF THE PHYSICAL UNIVERSE

Although Darwin had challenged the view that life forms remain unchanged, the controversy which he had set off over the nature of the biological universe had not affected physics. People continued to think of the physical universe moving in a mechanical order, much as Newton had explained it. This view was under serious challenge by 1914, especially by Albert Einstein (1879-1955) and Max Planck (1858-1947).

Einstein's "special theory of relativity" was introduced in 1905 in a brief paper which made the concept of relativity the keynote of twentieth-century physics. Einstein claimed that the observer—that is, the "subjective" element—was extremely important in describing the movement of bodies in space. Using trains as his example, Einstein stated that an observer who is standing in a meadow sees a train from a very different position from that of an observer who is looking at it while travelling on another train. The observer in the meadow and the observer on the other train will measure the speed differently. The Newtonian system had assumed that the observer did not enter into the calculation while Einstein's system included the frame of reference of the observer as an essential part of any calculation.

COLLECTION NATIONAL MUSEUM
VINCENT VAN GOGH, AMSTERDAM

△

Vincent van Gogh (1853–1890). Van Gogh was a post-impressionist painter who had great influence on succeeding generations of painters. He wrote letters to his brother Theo and others which are statements about being a creative artist in modern times. The quotations from Van Gogh accompanying the illustrations of his works are taken from his letters.

The illustration is from one of Van Gogh's letters of 1883.

If you hear a voice within you saying, "You are not a painter," then by all means paint, boy, and that voice will be silenced. . . . One must undertake [work] with confidence, with a certain assurance that one is doing a reasonable thing, like the farmer who drives his plow, or like our friend in the scratch below, who is harrowing, and even drags the harrow himself. If one hasn't a horse, one is one's own horse —

Letter 336, Volume II, The Complete Letters of Vincent van Gogh *(New York Graphic Society, 1958)*

△

*Van Gogh, "Carpenter's Workshop and a
Laundry", 1882.*

*... If you became a painter, one of the things
that would astonish you is that painting and
everything connected with it is really hard
work from a physical point of view; besides
the mental stress, the worry of mind, it requires
a rather great exertion of strength, and this day
after day.*

Letter 182, Volume I

*... Strolling on wharves and in alleys and
streets and in the houses, waiting rooms, even
saloons, is not a pleasant pastime,* except for an
artist. *As such, one would rather be in the
dirtiest place where there is something to draw
than at a tea party with charming ladies. Unless
one wants to draw ladies—then a tea party is
all right even for an artist. . . .*

Letter 190, Volume I, The Complete Letters
of Vincent van Gogh *(New York Graphic
Society, 1958)*

Van Gogh, "Head of a Peasant", 1884. In 1882, Van Gogh had commented on the process of painting:

In a certain way I am glad I have not learned

painting. . . . Now I say, No, this is just what I want—if it is impossible, it is impossible; I will try it, though I do not know how it ought to be done. I do not know myself how I paint it. I sit down with a white board before the spot that strikes me, I look at what is before my eyes, I say to myself, That white board must become something; I come back dissatisfied—I put it away, and when I have rested a little, I go and look at it with a kind of fear. Then I am still dissatisfied, because I still have that splendid scene too clearly in my mind to be satisfied with what I made of it. But I find in my work an echo of what struck me, after all. I see that nature has told me something, has spoken to me, and that I have put it down in shorthand. In my shorthand there may be words that cannot be deciphered, there may be mistakes or gaps; but there is something of what wood or beach or figure has told me in it, and it is not the tame or conventional language derived from a studied manner or a system rather than from nature itself.

Letter 228, Volume I, The Complete Letters of Vincent van Gogh *(New York Graphic Society, 1958)*

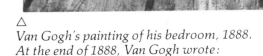

△

Van Gogh's painting of his bedroom, 1888.
At the end of 1888, Van Gogh wrote:

*Christ alone—of all the philosophers, Magi,
etc.—has affirmed, as a principal certainty,
eternal life, the infinity of time, the
nothingness of death, the necessity and the
raison d'être of serenity and devotion. He lived
serenely, as a greater artist than all other
artists, despising marble and clay as well as
color, working in living flesh. That is to say,
this matchless artist, hardly to be conceived of
by the obtuse instrument of our modern,
nervous, stupefied brains, made neither statues
nor pictures nor books; he loudly proclaimed*

that he made . . . living men, immortals.

*This is serious, especially because it is the
truth.*

*Science—scientific reasoning—seems to me
an instrument that will lag far, far behind. For
look here: the earth has been thought to be
flat. It was true, so it still is today, for instance
between Paris and Asnières. Which, however,
does not prevent science from proving that the
earth is principally round. Which no one
contradicts nowadays.*

*But notwithstanding this they persist
nowadays in believing that life is flat and runs
from birth to death. However, life too is
probably round, and very superior in expanse
and capacity to the hemisphere we know at
present.*

*Future generations will probably enlighten
us on this so very interesting subject; and then
maybe Science itself will arrive—willy-nilly—
at conclusions more or less parallel to the
sayings of Christ with reference to the other
half of our existence.*

◁ *Van Gogh, "The Potato Eaters", 1885.*

*I have tried to make it clear how those people,
eating their potatoes under the lamplight, have
dug the earth with those very hands they put
in the dish, and so it speaks of manual labour,
and how they have honestly earned their food.*

Letter 404, A. H. Barr, Vincent van Gogh
(Museum of Modern Art, 1936)

Letter B 8 [11], Volume III, The Complete
Letters of Vincent van Gogh   *(New York
Graphic Society, 1958)*

△

Van Gogh, "Road with Cypresses", 1890.

I still have a cypress with a star from down there, a last attempt—a night sky with a moon without radiance, the slender crescent barely emerging from the opaque shadow cast by the earth—one star with an exaggerated brilliance, if you like, a soft brilliance of pink and green in the ultramarine sky, across which some clouds are hurrying. Below, a road bordered with tall yellow canes, behind these the blue Basses Alpes, an old inn with yellow lighted windows, and a very tall cypress, very straight, very somber.

On the road, a yellow cart with a white horse in harness, and two late wayfarers. Very romantic, if you like, but also Provence, I think.

Letter 643, Volume III, The Complete Letters of Vincent van Gogh *(New York Graphic Society, 1958)*

◁ *Van Gogh, "Self-Portrait", 1886–88. In 1886, Van Gogh wrote:*

*This one thing remains—*faith; *one feels instinctively that an enormous number of things are changing and that everything will change. We are living in the last quarter of a century that will end again in a tremendous revolution.*

But suppose both of us see its beginning at the end of our lives. We certainly shall not live to see the better times of pure air and the rejuvenation of all society after those big storms. . . .

And to say, We are still in the closeness, but the following generations will be able to breathe more freely.

Letter 451, Volume II, The Complete Letters of Vincent van Gogh   *(New York Graphic Society, 1958)*

Einstein defined space relatively, not absolutely. There can be no accuracy in describing where a planet is in space, for example, without stating where the observer who is doing the measuring is standing. Mars looks different to a person on earth than it would to a person on the moon. Space is "relative," meaning that it can only be defined as the *relation* between things in an otherwise empty universe.

Einstein also redefined time, speaking of it as an order of events related to the observer. The reason we can talk to one another about time is that we agree on a similar reference system: for example, the year 1905 means something to us because we have defined what a "year" is and "1905" is one thousand and nine hundred and five "years" after something else happened. Thus time is not objective, but subjective. Our clock is related to our position in space in relation to the sun and the rotation of the earth around its axis. One can conceive of another clock on another planet working in accordance with another set of relationships. A "year," the amount of time taken by the earth to rotate around the sun, would be different for someone on another heavenly body with a different rotation.

While Einstein was redefining the meaning of universal space and time, other physicists were presenting new concepts regarding the behaviour of the tiny particles of matter. Scientists had noted that atoms did not seem to give off heat or light energy at a consistent rate at all temperatures. In order to explain this phenomenon Max Planck, in 1900, introduced the quantum theory, which asserted that the energy content of atoms seemed to change discontinuously, in bundles or quanta, rather than gradually and smoothly. Thus it was not possible to measure the behaviour of any single electron, but only the mass behaviour of a number of electrons. The laws that were developed from this insight were different from the laws of Newtonian mechanics, which had assumed that one could predict perfectly the behaviour of all bodies. These new "laws" were statements of probability and statistics, not of objective certainty.

The physics introduced by Einstein and Planck formed the basis of nuclear physics, which ultimately enabled people to harness power and build a new technology. The new physics, it should be noted, did not "prove Newton wrong." Rather, Newton's formulae were found to be inadequate for describing certain things, particularly minute particles of matter.

Atomic physics has a different idea of "objectivity" than does the Newtonian model. As Werner Heisenberg stated: "The science of nature does not deal with nature itself but in fact with the *science* of nature as man thinks and describes it."[13] He meant that nature is not observed by the scientist in its purity, but that our idea of nature is in part determined by what we are and the method of questioning we use. The nineteenth-century physicists felt that they were photographing nature, telling us what was "out there." The twentieth-century physicists claim that they are giving order to a part of nature, and that this order is based on their understanding of certain controlled conditions. Further, the Newtonian world was understandable to our senses. Science since the early twentieth century is abstract and difficult to visualize and discuss in the old familiar terms. In physics the observer is as important as the thing observed. Reality is no longer "out there," but is the combined interaction of the observer and the observed. This is what is meant by relativity: not that everything is relative, but that everything is relative to the frame of reference of the observer.

In the nineteenth century the Newtonian view of the universe was thought to be final, a perfect picture lacking only some details. In the twentieth century scientists know a good deal more about the universe than ever before, but do not claim to have such a perfect picture. Many state that it is impossible to get one at all. The new science is forcing a thorough revision of ideas about human beings and the universe that have existed since Newton, and because of the complexity of the new ideas, this revision has come about very slowly. Many of us still see the world in Newtonian terms.

TOWARDS AN UNCERTAIN UNIVERSE— THE NEW REALITY IN 1914

There were two types of culture in the West by 1914. On the public level, in what we call mass culture, the old ideas of the universe, society, and human nature did not automatically die with the writings of Weber, Freud, Nietzsche, and Einstein. Rather, they persisted, partly because of a feeling on the part of most people that they were still true, partly because very few read the works of these thinkers. The new ideas did not filter down to the level of public discussion until after the First World War. Among those intellectuals who did read these works, however, there was a revolt against traditional views of science and society as they had been formulated in the eighteenth and nineteenth centuries. Most people in the West prior to the First World War believed that modern technology was creating a better life for all.

However, underneath the optimism of the vast majority and its belief in progress, the ideological foundations of Western culture were slowly being eroded. The belief in a rational human nature no longer seemed tenable, and the optimism based on the idea of progress, which had characterized the West since the Enlightenment, was evaporating. It seemed that all social norms, all standards of behaviour and of worth, were being seriously questioned; but no new standards were on the horizon to take their place. At the turn of the century this was not yet regarded as a serious problem: Europe and the West were prospering, and again a liberal spirit seemed to permeate the world. But as the twentieth century wore on, the new ideas slowly became diffused through society until they, along with the disillusionment created by two world wars, brought about the reorientation in our outlook.

ANALYSIS AND DISCUSSION

1. Darwin's *Origin of Species* raised important questions which challenged many traditional ideas about human nature and society. Summarize Darwin's main ideas and show how they constituted a challenge to traditional ideas.

2. "Social Darwinism" describes the attempts to apply Darwinian ideas to human affairs. Illustrate the ways in which Darwin's ideas were applied to (a) government, (b) economics, (c) foreign policy.

3. Re-read the section from Rudyard Kipling's "The White Man's Burden" on page 170. In your own words write a commentary on the idea of imperialism based upon the attitudes expressed in the poem.

4. "The warfare between science and theology, to use the words of one historian, were not universal. Some religious thinkers were willing to take geology and Darwin at face value." Discuss the varying responses of Christian theologians to the "Darwinian revolution" in the late nineteenth century.

5. Compare Emile Zola's approach to the writing of a novel with that of experimenters in the sciences.

6. The years from 1850 to 1914 saw the development of many new ideas about human beings and their world. Select one of the prominent intellectuals of the period (e.g. Comte, Weber, Freud, Nietzsche, or Einstein) and examine the ways in which the ideas of that individual represent this change.

7. Read, study and reflect upon the words and images left to us by Vincent van Gogh between pages 178 and 183. Write a "letter to Van Gogh" expressing your personal feelings with regard to his ideas and his art.

CHAPTER **10**

Diplomacy and World War: 1871-1919

TOWARDS THE END OF THE NINETEENTH century the major nation-states—England, France, Germany, Russia, Italy, the United States, and Japan—seemed to be on the road to solving their domestic problems. Foreign relations, however, went from crisis to crisis, and in August 1914 Europe plunged into a major war. The First World War, also known as the Great War, lasted until November 1918. Though the First World War was proclaimed at the time as "the war to end all wars," it was really the beginning of an era of violence, and its shadow continues to haunt the twentieth century. The rise of communism and fascism and the emergence of the non-European world were all connected with the war and its effects. The First World War marked the beginnings of the decline of Europe as the centre of world affairs. It was the first large-scale international war since 1815, and it dealt a heavy blow to the liberal optimism and the idea of progress which had dominated Western thinking since the French Revolution.

The war was triggered by a political act of terror. On June 28, 1914, in the town of Sarajevo, a young Serbian nationalist, Gavrilo Princip, assassinated Archduke Francis Ferdinand, the Hapsburg heir to the throne of Austria-Hungary, and his wife. It was an act of frustration, an attempt by a student to compel the Hapsburgs to grant autonomy to the people of Bosnia and to other Slavic peoples under their control. One member of the group to which Princip belonged described the rise of terrorism in this way:

Several years before the war, a little group of us, thirty-five in all, living in several Bosnian and Herzegovinian cities and villages, formed the Narodna Odbrana, the Secret Society, the aim of which was to work for freedom from Austria and a union with Serbia. . . .

We were not the only organization which plotted against Austrian rule. But we were the only one which went to the length of direct action—political crimes and demonstrations to inflame the hearts of the people. The others merely distributed nationalistic and revolutionary literature and by argument sought to prepare the ground for revolution. We were the extremists. All the organizations had a loose connection with each other, but none of them knew our plans or when we would strike. . . .

Coming up to the World War period, the men who were terrorists in 1914 in Bosnia embraced all classes. Most of them were students: youth is the time for the philosophy of action. There were also teachers, tradesmen, and peasants; artisans and even men of the upper classes were ardent patriots. They were dissimilar [in] everything except hatred of the oppressor.[1]

Tensions mounted in the European capitals as relations between Austria and Serbia deteriorated. After a month of negotiations, full of threats and promises, and attempts by the foreign offices of Europe to settle the problem peacefully, no satisfactory solution was found. Austria attacked Serbia and soon nearly all of Europe was in arms.

It would be misleading to suggest that the isolated act of terror by a youthful revolutionary brought about such a conflagration. To understand the origins of the First World War, one must understand the diplomatic relations between states in the years before 1914, and one must go back at least to the era of Bismarck to see how those relations developed.

THE IDEA OF BALANCE OF POWER

Diplomacy is the means of regularizing conduct between sovereign states. War occurs when diplomacy fails, unless, as in the practice of *Realpolitik*, a state sees an advantage in going to war and sets out to find a way to provoke another state to war while giving the appearance of being an innocent victim. In diplomatic relations between sovereign states, finding alternatives to war is essential if a resort to arms is to be avoided. In 1914, after the death of Francis Ferdinand, European diplomats were unable or unwilling to find alternatives to war.

The major concept which dominated diplomatic relations in Europe before 1914 was the balance of power. At that time Europe was the only continent in which so many states had considerable power, and in which no single state was capable of becoming dominant for a long period of time. Thus, when Napoleon I seemed on the way to creating a universal empire, a number of states, embracing different political ideologies, united against him in coalitions to protect their own interests and their own existence. The diplomats at the Congress of Vienna in 1814 and 1815 were generally agreed that it was in the interest of all states that no one state should dominate international affairs. Naturally, states attempted to gain advantages, but the notion of a "concert of Europe" in which there was a reasonable balance of power persisted.

But the European states had differing attitudes towards the balance of power. Britain supported it on the European continent in order to prevent any single power from dominating the area. Traditionally, the British had intervened actively in continental affairs when they felt one state, for example the France of Napoleon, was becoming too powerful. On the other hand, England admitted no equals in the battle for colonies and fought off all rivals to establish the greatest empire and the most powerful navy in the world. France, in contrast to England, had traditionally viewed the idea of a balance of power in Europe from a different perspective. The French thought, as Talleyrand said, that equality in power was dangerous. Europe should have Paris as its capital, with a benevolent France as the leading state. After 1815 the other powers were anxious to contain France and to prevent another outbreak of revolution and war. France continued to be the most important state on the continent until its defeat by Germany in 1871. After that the French saw European leadership go to the new German Empire with Berlin as the centre of power of the new Europe. Bismarck had established German supremacy, but once Germany was unified, the diplomatic policy of Bismarck coincided with the policies of Metternich and the Congress of Vienna. Revolution and war, Bismarck thought, were tied together. If Europe was going to survive, it must contain revolution and prevent all-out wars. Thus, in spite of his earlier belligerency in creating the new German Empire, Bismarck believed that a balance of power was essential for the maintenance of peace and the survival of European civilization.

TO THE CONGRESS OF BERLIN, 1878

The smashing victory of Germany over France in 1871 and the terrifying demonstration of German power made other states uneasy. The balance of power had changed and no one was certain about the future. There was deep hostility between Germany and France, and France yearned for revenge. Russia and Austria-Hungary were suspicious of each other, for each had interests in the Balkan peninsula, and each desired to expand in that area and to stop the other from gaining any advantage. Italy wished to become a major power, and Italians talked about the need to annex some Austro-Hungarian territories (often referred to as *Italia Irredenta*—"unredeemed Italy") which were populated by people who were Italian-speaking. England was without any territorial ambitions in Europe itself and concentrated on the expansion of its empire. The one unknown was Germany. What did Germany want? What position would the new giant take? In the early years of the new German Empire, to the Congress of Berlin in 1878, endless diplomatic soundings went on in an attempt to gauge Bismarck's intentions.

After 1871 Bismarck had declared that Germany was now "saturated" and did not desire any new territory. But statesmen were wondering whether to believe a man who had helped to create three limited wars within the last decade. France on its part managed to recover very quickly from its defeat in 1871, and by paying off a war indemnity imposed by Germany ended German occupation of France in 1874. France then passed a law indicating that its military forces would be increased considerably. Bismarck was unhappy about this development and made several remarks which seemed to indicate that Germany might take action. In the face of these belligerent statements, Russia and England both warned Bismarck that they would be quite unhappy with any German military move. Bismarck relented, protesting that his intentions were not to prepare for war. It is doubtful that Bismarck did wish to do anything other than scare France with words, but the episode is important for the speed with which other powers

A German cartoon of 1875 portraying Bismarck and Germany in control of Europe and North Africa (Kladderadatsch, Berlin, 1875)

declared their intention to maintain the balance of power.

The first major international crisis after 1871 occurred in the Balkans. The Ottoman Empire controlled some of the Balkan territory inhabited by Slavic peoples. In 1875 some of these peoples in Bosnia and Bulgaria rebelled against the Turkish rule. Russia, moved by pan-Slav elements and expansionist policies, took the side of the Slavs and the Russo-Turkish War began in April 1877. A Russian victory was certain, but speed was of the essence if Russia was to be successful in its new *Realpolitik* policy. Russia moved towards the Turkish capital of Constantinople, but was stopped by the Turks at the town of Plevna in July 1877. While the Russians tried to break through the Turkish lines, other states, particularly Britain and Austria-Hungary, moved to support Turkey, not out of love for the Turks, but out of fear of Russian expansion into the Mediterranean and into the Balkans. The Russians finally succeeded in breaking through Turkish lines in December 1877; they defeated the Turks, and imposed the Treaty of San Stefano on Turkey in March 1878.

The treaty gave Russia access to the Mediterranean, created a new state, Bulgaria, under Russian control, and gave both Rumania and Serbia their independence under Turkish rule. The British were unhappy because they felt their imperial interests in the Mediterranean threatened, and they began preparing for war with Russia. The treaty had upset the balance of power in a way unacceptable to England since Russia might now challenge English domination of the Mediterranean Sea. In the meantime Bismarck remained neutral and convened a European conference at Berlin to negotiate the differences between the powers.

The Congress of Berlin in 1878 was the most important diplomatic meeting in Europe since Vienna. It was also the most glittering. Bismarck was the host and, as he put it, the "honest broker." Among those also present were representatives of England, Russia, Austria-Hungary, and France. The meeting was a recognition of the fact that the Balkan peninsula was not just a Russo-Turkish problem but a European one. Any change in the balance of power affected all major states and therefore all those states had the right to their say.

At the Congress the major powers, especially England and Austria-Hungary, were determined to deprive Russia of the gains made from the victory in the Russo-Turkish War. Russia could do little to stop them—its armies exhausted, it could not face England and Austria-Hungary on the battlefield. By agreement of the Congress, the Balkan areas of Rumania, Serbia, and Montenegro became autonomous states. Russia obtained some small territory on the Black Sea. However, on the principle of "equivalent compensations"—that the balance of power should not be upset by giving one disputant too much more than another—England was given the island of Cyprus in the Mediterranean. Austria-Hungary also gained some territory. It was given permission to "occupy and administer," not to annex, Bosnia. Bismarck asked for nothing—his claim that Germany was "saturated" was borne out. Turkey was ignored. Russia had won the war, but lost the peace.

No one was particularly happy with the results of the Berlin Conference. All realized that the Balkans were a potential area of discord among the powers, and it was hoped that a settlement might be found which would be agreeable to all and would ensure peace in the area. Some historians have claimed that Berlin was a failure, that at the moment when the "Balkan problem" could have been solved the diplomats played the old game of trading off one thing for another, which only postponed the issue but did not settle it. That the question of establishing viable national states in the Balkans was not settled is clear; however, it is by no means certain that a peaceful solution to the problem was possible at the time.

IMPERIALISM: EUROPE OVERSEAS

It is difficult, perhaps futile, in the period 1871–1914 to separate imperial policy from European diplomatic affairs. They are both of a piece. From 1871 to 1914 Europe went round the globe, acquiring trading rights and territories with unparalleled rapidity and building great empires.

"Imperialism" generally refers to the quest for rights and possessions in other people's lands, but its late-nineteenth-century form had some special elements. In this period it meant control by the West of areas in Africa and in the East, with no intention of establishing any major Western settlement. Furthermore it involved whites controlling the territory of non-white people. As Europeans penetrated into the non-European world, both Westernization and industrialization began to occur, sometimes quickly, sometimes slowly. Along with traders came machines—extending the Industrial Revolution beyond the West. Imperial practices of the nineteenth century have gone far towards creating the "global village" of the twentieth century. In our time any imperialist activity is viewed with serious misgivings—suggesting an infringement on others' rights and a form of economic and human exploitation. In the nineteenth century, though imperialism was vehemently attacked by some on the same grounds, the term was not automatically associated with evils. It implied the extension of sovereignty, the opening of markets, the work of Christian missionaries, the acquisition of prestige and power. The impetus for imperialist activity included all these; it was diplomacy, business, and the spirit of the Crusades rolled into one.

Africa and China were the two major areas of imperialist activity in the decades prior to the First World War. The construction of the Suez Canal halved the journey from Europe to Asia. Opened in 1869 by the French, the canal came under the control of the English in 1875 when Disraeli purchased the shares of the indigent viceroy of Egypt. In this way England protected its position as the first power in the Mediterranean area. Control of the canal gave England a dominant position in northeast Africa. The French, thwarted in the northeast, moved into the northwest, and by the First World War Tunisia and Morocco were in the French imperial sphere.

The story of Stanley and Livingstone did much to focus attention on Africa. In 1871

An imperialist scene—British troops at the Egyptian pyramids in 1882   (Radio Times Hulton Picture Library)

the New York *Herald* sent a journalist, Henry Stanley, to central Africa to find a lost British missionary, Dr. David Livingstone. Stanley found Livingstone, and his reports on the economic possibilities of the region he explored aroused much interest in the area. In order to explore and examine the area, King Leopold II of Belgium founded a private company which gained international recognition of its sovereignty over the Congo. Other areas of Africa came under European control. France moved into an area west of the Belgian Congo; Italy moved into the east; Germany in 1884 began moving into areas in central and southwest Africa.

Bismarck was not eager to enter into any imperial activity, but in the face of public opinion and parliamentary pressure, he acquired some rights and territories in Africa. He did not wish to antagonize Germany's friends by entering into conflict over what

he considered the relatively unimportant areas of imperialist claims. Nor did Bismarck feel that the benefits of imperialism outweighed its dangers. For him, Europe came first.

Imperial tensions grew to the point where it was thought useful to call an international conference to meet in Berlin in 1885 to sort out differences and to deal with the partition and development of Africa. Attended by the United States and the European states, the conference agreed that a country which occupied a coastline had the right to the interior of a given territory. Occupation was to be "real," not simply on paper — a country claiming an area could not simply plant the flag and expect recognition of its sovereignty in the area. And each country was required to notify the others of areas it considered its own.

After the Berlin Conference the scramble for Africa was on. By 1914 all of Africa with

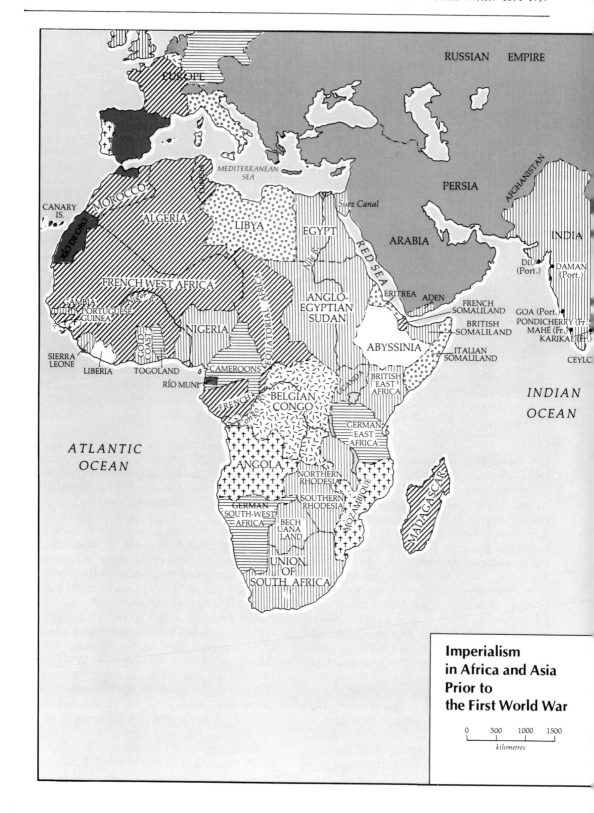

**Imperialism
in Africa and Asia
Prior to
the First World War**

0   500   1000   1500

kilometres

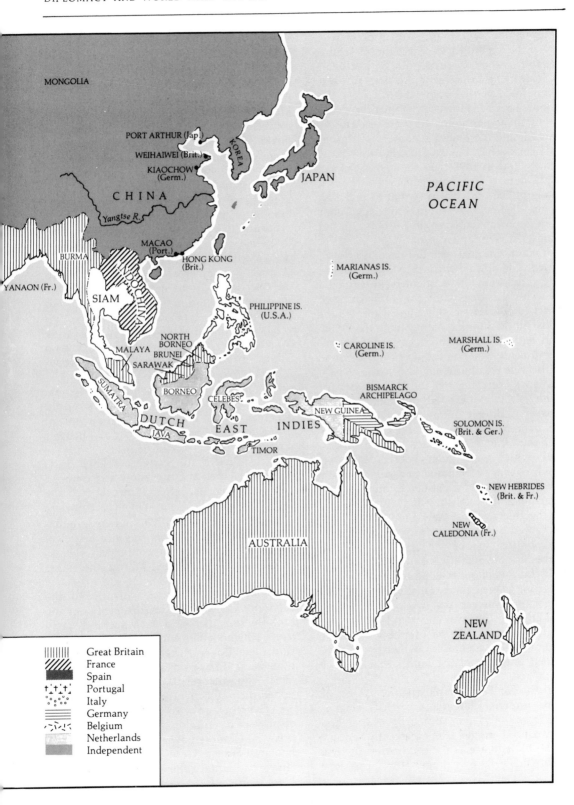

MONGOLIA

PORT ARTHUR (Jap.)
WEIHAIWEI (Brit.)
KIAOCHOW
(Germ.)

KOREA

JAPAN

*PACIFIC
OCEAN*

C H I N A

Yangtse R.

MACAO
(Port.)
HONG KONG
(Brit.)

MARIANAS IS.
(Germ.)

YANAON (Fr.)

BURMA

INDO-CHINA

SIAM

PHILIPPINE IS.
(U.S.A.)

NORTH
BORNEO
BRUNEI
SARAWAK

MALAYA

CAROLINE IS.
(Germ.)

MARSHALL IS.
(Germ.)

SUMATRA

BORNEO

CELEBES

BISMARCK
ARCHIPELAGO

DUTCH   EAST   INDIES

NEW GUINEA

JAVA

TIMOR

SOLOMON IS.
(Brit. & Ger.)

NEW HEBRIDES
(Brit. & Fr.)

NEW
CALEDONIA (Fr.)

AUSTRALIA

NEW
ZEALAND

‖‖‖‖‖	Great Britain
⁄⁄⁄⁄	France
	Spain
⸏⸏⸏	Portugal
∘∘∘	Italy
≡≡≡	Germany
⌁⌁⌁	Belgium
	Netherlands
	Independent

the exception of Ethiopia and Liberia was part of the imperial sphere of either Belgium, England, France, Germany, Italy, Portugal, or Spain. The Conference did help sort out claims and provide some control over the furious activity. However, hopes for peace among the imperial powers were not always realized, and there were a number of clashes and near clashes. England and France almost went to war in 1898 over the control of the headwaters of the Nile River. The French finally pulled out, realizing that to make an enemy of England would only hurt their more important interests in Europe directed against the German Empire.

A major colonial war did occur in South Africa. The normal entry into a territory involved dealing with local chiefs who ruled a pre-industrial society. On the southern tip of Africa, however, in the Cape Colony, the British in 1806 took territory from the Dutch who had colonized the area in the seventeenth century. Thus the authority prior to British rule was European and white, a people called "Boers," after the Dutch word for farmer. Many Boers left the Cape Colony when the British outlawed slavery in the area, and founded two neighbouring republics, the Orange Free State and the Transvaal, which were independent. However, the discovery of diamond and gold deposits in the two areas brought in a number of outsiders, mainly English, who were resented by the Boers. These new immigrants were prevented by the Boers from taking part in the political life of the area. The British wished to gain a political and economic foothold in the two areas and exerted every pressure against them. Finally, in 1899 war broke out between the two Boer republics and England. The war ended in 1902 with an English victory. The two republics became part of the British Empire, which by 1914 included one-fifth of the land surface of the earth.

In the Far East, China was the subject of many imperial claims and rivalries emanating from both Japan and Europe. Japan had modernized in the late nineteenth century and took its place as a world power. In 1894 Japan made its own imperialist thrust into

Korea, which China had long regarded as under its influence. The resulting Sino-Japanese War was won easily by Japan. The Treaty of Shimonoseki in 1895 ended the war, with Japan obtaining control over Manchuria, the Liaotung Peninsula, the southern tip of Formosa, and the Pescadores. Korea was granted independence by the Chinese. Shimonoseki startled Europe and awakened the world to the new power of Japan. Russia, France, and Germany promptly intervened and forced Japan to return the Liaotung Peninsula to China.

European incursions in the East prior to 1895 had been made into what had been recognized informally as areas under Chinese control. Russia, ever in search of ports to the east, moved into what is known as the Maritime Province and built the port city of Vladivostok in 1860. France began its involvement in Indo-China and in 1883 took over Annam, now a part of Vietnam, as a colony. Britain controlled Burma by 1886. After 1895 European nations sought concessions, licences, and privileges in China itself, hoping that these privileges would evolve into what was politely called a "sphere of influence," which meant control in fact, if not in name.

The United States sought to keep trade open in the area and not allow any power a dominant role in China. It proclaimed the "open door policy," in which all powers would be allowed equally to pursue economic interests in China, as the most efficient means of coping with conflicting claims. This policy was agreed to by the other powers in 1899.

Some Chinese reacted violently to the economic invasion of the Europeans, hating both the foreigners and the Manchu dynasty itself, which yielded concession after concession. The Boxer Rebellion in 1900 was a movement directed against Chinese Christians, who, the rebels thought, had abandoned their culture, and against the foreigners. The rebellion was crushed in an unusual display of international co-operation to uphold the Chinese government. Troops from England, France, Germany, Russia, Austria-Hungary, Japan, the United States, and

India joined together to end the rebellion in support of a government from which they had obtained many economic advantages. In the early twentieth century, as a nation-state, China was showing signs of political disintegration.

THE ALLIANCE SYSTEM TO 1890

Until the first Berlin Congress of 1878, Bismarck had relied on the congress system and traditional diplomatic relations to settle outstanding questions. After the Russo-Turkish War he had little faith in the concert of Europe. He felt it necessary to establish a treaty system in order to control events and prevent a minor crisis from breaking out into a major one. His system was to reflect Germany's new position as the major power on the European continent. The principle of the balance of power must be maintained, he thought, but he must try to be the major counterweight, the decisive influence in any division among the states. Bismarck had defeated Austria in 1866 and pushed it aside in the unification of Germany. Once having accomplished this, he saw Austria as a necessary ally and sought to heal the old wounds. Russia had to be controlled in the east, France had to be isolated from other powers, and Italy had to be prevented from creating a war situation with Austria over the *Irredenta*.

The key to his ability to manoeuvre freely was a tacit diplomatic understanding with England. Bismarck realized that his concept of the balance of power and the English concept could coincide. As long as England could extend its empire without serious challenges, it would not be unhappy with German domination of the European continent. Each had its "sphere of influence," and each understood not to encroach on the other. Hence Bismarck's reluctance to search for colonies, and hence Germany's late entry into naval building and the imperialist race. Germany was to have Europe; England the rest of the world. Bismarck, having achieved German unification and seeing his major problem as internal, continued his diplomacy of "limited gains." The

master of *Realpolitik* could be as realistic in peace as he had been in war.

The first of the major treaties prior to 1914 was made in 1879 between Germany and Austria. It was a *defensive* alliance, formed out of fear of Russian hostility after Russia's humiliation at Berlin in 1878. In this "Dual Alliance," each pledged that if either "one of the two Empires be attacked by Russia, the High Contracting Parties bind themselves to come to the assistance of each other with the whole military strength of their Empire and accordingly only to conclude peace in common and by mutual agreement."[2] If either was attacked by a fourth power, the other would maintain neutrality. In diplomatic language, the fourth power referred to France for Germany, and to Italy for Austria. Thus Germany and Austria would be protected from engaging in a war on two fronts. From this moment on Germany was committed to its alliance with Austria. This was a "secret treaty" in that its contents were never made public, though its terms were suspected.

Italy entered the Bismarckian system in 1882 as the Dual Alliance was enlarged to include it in a new "Triple Alliance." Germany and Austria agreed to support Italy if it were attacked by France. In turn, Italy agreed to go to war in support of its allies if either were attacked by two or more powers, or if Germany were attacked by France alone. By making this treaty Bismarck made himself the mediating and decisive party over any differences which might arise between Austria and Italy. He also continued to keep France isolated, one of the premises of his diplomacy. The Triple Alliance was known to exist in its general features; it, too, was a "secret treaty" in that its precise terms were not made public until well into the First World War.

In 1881 Bismarck took steps to prevent a war between Austria-Hungary and Russia over disputed territories in the Balkans. In order to accomplish this, he had to revive an informal agreement made in 1873 between the monarchs of Germany, Austria-Hungary, and Russia, and make it into a formal alliance. The Three Emperors' League, as it was called, agreed to co-operate on matters of mutual concern, fearful of any change on the European scene. No serious problems were discussed and Russia became disillusioned with the 1873 agreement when the other two countries failed to support Russian claims arising out of the Russo-Turkish War of 1877-78. In 1881 Bismarck succeeded in turning the League into a full-fledged Three Emperors' Alliance. The three powers agreed that "in case one of the High Contracting Parties should find itself at war with a fourth Great Power, the two others shall maintain towards it a benevolent neutrality and shall devote their efforts to the localization of the conflict."[3] They also agreed to consult on Balkan affairs. The Three Emperors' Alliance was renewed in 1884.

Continuing Austro-Russian hostility over Balkan affairs resulted in the expiration of the Three Emperors' Alliance in 1887. Yet Bismarck wished to keep an alliance with Russia, in part to be able to maintain some control over Russian policy in eastern Europe, in part to prevent Russia from seeking an agreement with France. Thus in 1887 he offered Russia another alliance. This was the "Reinsurance Treaty," aptly named because it stipulated in diplomatic language that should Austria attack Russia, Germany would remain neutral; should France attack Germany, Russia would remain neutral. There has been much discussion of the Reinsurance Treaty, of whether Bismarck in his anxiety to keep the link with Russia and effectively isolate France made a treaty which contradicted his obligations to Austria in the Dual Alliance of 1879. Certainly the treaty did not clarify anything, but it was a contradiction only if the 1879 Alliance is interpreted as an offensive one and not a defensive one. There is no doubt that Bismarck did not see the Dual Alliance as offensive but as a way of restraining Austria-Hungary in the Balkans by making sure that Germany had some control over Austrian policy.

Thus Bismarck had built his alliance system and accomplished what he wanted to do. There were no major wars from 1871 to 1890, and peace had been maintained in spite

of all the problems. Germany was now one of the great powers, with enormous prestige and a controlling influence in world affairs. But one of the dangers of treaties is that the purposes for which they are made are often no longer appropriate for the next generation and that the people called upon to implement them are often very different kinds of people from those who drew them up. It would remain for Bismarck's successors to try to pick up the somewhat tangled threads he left and to deal with the consequences of his policies. By 1914 the international situation and the diplomats had changed. Germany's agreement with Austria-Hungary was not interpreted as a defensive treaty but rather as an offensive one.

WILLIAM II AND GERMAN WELTPOLITIK

Bismarck's resignation from his post at the insistence of the young German Emperor William II was a turning point in German diplomacy. No two styles could have been more different. Where Bismarck was cautious, reserved, and quiet, William was unrestrained, flamboyant, and noisy. They were both conservatives, but Bismarck was a man of tradition, a throwback to the days of monarchs and powerful advisers, an aristocrat in an industrial world becoming more egalitarian. He believed in the monarchy as an institution, but thought the monarch should accept the advice of powerful ministers like himself. William's view of the monarch's position was different. He insisted on his right to rule and he enjoyed his role as leader of a prosperous German people. He tried to turn the myth of the power of the hereditary monarch into a reality. His diplomatic pronouncements were regarded as eccentric, but his eccentricities were not quaint; they were dangerous in a man who had so much power and believed in his own omniscience. Yet he often behaved as an adolescent in delicate situations. As it turned out, he was incompetent and psychologically insecure. It remained to be seen whether the system could function and survive under William, or if it needed a man of Bismarck's calibre to guide it.

William's first diplomatic act was to end the Reinsurance Treaty, to sever the diplomatic life-line between St. Petersburg, then the capital of Russia, and Berlin. Seeking to clarify Germany's commitments, William felt that the Dual Alliance with Austria-Hungary took precedence over the ambiguous and potentially dangerous agreement with Russia. He also believed that France and Russia would not be able to negotiate a union. William was wrong. France immediately saw its opportunity and began talks with Russia. The basics of an agreement were completed in 1892, though a treaty was not finally ratified until 1894. The union was frankly directed against the Triple Alliance. Each promised to mobilize if any member of the Triple Alliance mobilized. Each agreed to go to war if the other was attacked by Germany. Russia agreed to join France if Italy supported by Germany attacked France; France agreed to join Russia if Austria supported by Germany attacked Russia. Hence two of Bismarck's basic diplomatic foundations crumbled at once—France was no longer isolated and Germany no longer was the sole mediator in eastern Europe between Russia and Austria-Hungary.

William avidly pursued a policy of *Weltpolitik*, a "world policy," in which Germany aggressively sought colonies and challenged England's imperial leadership. It was not a co-ordinated policy, rather a kind of erratic diplomacy with a foray here and a sally there. While seeming to challenge England in Africa and the East, the Emperor did not have clear goals. Yet, when England indicated in 1898 the desire to negotiate differences with Germany, William refused.

What frightened England most, however,

A five-mark stamp issued during the reign of William II. The slogan of the new German Empire, "One people, one empire, one God", appears at the bottom. (Snark International)

was the new German naval policy inaugurated in 1898 under the direction of Admiral Alfred von Tirpitz, and with the enthusiastic support of the Kaiser. Germany began to build a navy, large enough, if carried through as planned, to challenge England's naval supremacy. England had a policy guideline that its navy must be larger than any two other naval powers combined, as the English believed that their existence depended on naval power. Bismarck had realized that England would not remain friendly if challenged on the sea, and he had carefully avoided any possible misunderstanding. Tirpitz, however, tried to build up the German navy to the point where England could no longer afford the funds to adhere to its own guideline. England continually tried to get Germany to stop, but with no success, and the result was an expensive naval race between the two countries.

Still it was not only the naval power of Germany, but also its industrial productivity and its successful competition in world markets which were of great concern to England. In view of Germany's new international activity, England, heretofore aloof from the continental alliance system, began searching frantically for allies. Whether correct or incorrect, the English foreign office interpreted Germany's actions as a conscious attack on English interests and the beginnings of an attempt on the part of Germany to establish a new universal empire. This interpretation led England to try to redress the balance of power.

The French government realized that the tension between England and Germany provided an opportunity to bring England and France together. It was necessary first to settle Anglo-French colonial rivalry, and an agreement was reached in 1904. This was the *Entente Cordiale*, a friendly understanding between the states. It was not a treaty such as the Dual or Triple Alliance, which committed the states to war in certain circumstances. It merely settled colonial differences, mainly in Africa. But it marked an end to Britain's policy of isolation from continental arrangements and opened the way to a broadening of Anglo-French co-operation in subsequent years.

The *Entente Cordiale* led to a similar agreement between England and Russia in 1907. France was eager to bring its two new friends together, and Russia, after its defeat in the Russo-Japanese War, was less hostile to a settlement of colonial claims. England wanted a clarification of spheres of influence in the Far East. The Anglo-Russian agreement of 1907 was mainly concerned with spheres of influence in Persia, but it had the side effect of bringing two powers hostile to German ambitions in much closer contact.

Now there was a loose Triple Entente between England, France, and Russia on the edges of Europe facing the Triple Alliance in central Europe. The Triple Entente was less formal than the Triple Alliance, but it meant that England, France, and Russia now began to work together as potential allies. Thus, after William's new policy, the balance of power had completely changed from Bismarck's day. Two armed camps now existed in Europe.

THE UNITED STATES AND JAPAN AS NEW WORLD POWERS

The nineteenth century was dominated by Europe—the twentieth century has seen that influence wane and the rising importance of both Western and non-Western states outside of Europe. At the turn of the century both the United States and Japan were becoming important industrial and military powers with large populations.

From the close of the Civil War in 1865, the United States was the dominant power in the western hemisphere. While the United States often pursued a policy of isolation from European affairs, the country in the 1890s came to regard the Monroe Doctrine as having a sort of Biblical sanction, and often intervened in Latin-American affairs when it decided it was in its best interest. A revolt in Cuba in 1895 against Spanish rule brought the United States and Spain into war by 1898. The Cuban revolt was directed against the arbitrary rule of Spain, and the Cubans gained great sympathy among the United States public.

Americans thought that both Cuba and the United States would be better off with

Cuba under United States influence than under the influence of Spain. Thus in 1898 the United States intervened and easily defeated Spain. The victory in the Spanish-American War resulted in Guam, the Philippines, and Puerto Rico being ceded by Spain to the United States. The Filipinos did not much like the idea and rebelled, but the United States crushed the rebellion. United States influence was now extended beyond the western hemisphere.

United States imperial policy continued during the administration of Theodore Roosevelt. He acquired land to build the Panama Canal by supporting a revolutionary movement in the Isthmus of Panama against Colombia, sent United States troops into the Dominican Republic, Cuba, and Nicaragua, and tried to extend United States influence in the Far East.

Once Japan industrialized, it acquired imperial ambitions like the Western powers and felt it needed markets for its goods. The Japanese had a particular interest in Manchuria. Russia, on the other hand, desired to build railways into Manchuria and to gain concessions in Korea, which Japan considered as part of its sphere of influence. The two countries tried to negotiate their differences but to no avail. In February 1904 Japan, unannounced, attacked Port Arthur, the Russian base in Manchuria. The Russo-Japanese War lasted sixteen months, during which Russia experienced serious domestic difficulties. The Japanese were successful, in part because Russia could not supply its navy and its troops, in part because of Russian military incompetence. However, the Japanese clearly demonstrated their military superiority. The world was astonished by the result.

The two parties agreed to let the United States act as mediator in an effort to make peace. With Theodore Roosevelt as intermediary the two parties met at Portsmouth in the state of New Hampshire in 1905 to hammer out an agreement. The Treaty of Portsmouth gave Japan Port Arthur and confirmed its interests in Korea, which became a protectorate of Japan.

Russians had not forgotten the military humiliation in the Crimean War and the diplomatic humiliation at the Berlin Congress of 1878 following the Russo-Turkish War. Russia's defeat at the hands of the Japanese and the Treaty of Portsmouth further diminished the Czar's prestige and lessened his control over the country. It contributed to a major uprising in 1905 and to the establishment of the first constitutional government in Russia.

The Spanish-American War and the Russo-Japanese War, though minor in themselves, were of major diplomatic significance. For the first time in the West, an offshoot of Europe, the United States, singlehandedly defeated a traditional European state, Spain. For the first time since the Renaissance, a non-European state, Japan, had been able to defeat a major European power, Russia. The actual balance of power was changed, and the concept of that balance had to be enlarged. No longer solely dependent on Europe, the balance of power now had to be considered on a world-wide basis. The victories of the United States and Japan were portents of things to come.

CRISES AND THE HOPES FOR PEACE: 1899-1912

In 1899 and 1907 two peace conferences to discuss the limitation of armaments and the peaceful settlement of disputes—the first called by Czar Nicholas II of Russia, the second by President Roosevelt—took place at The Hague in the Netherlands. No country was against peace, but no country was willing to lose any advantage diplomatically or to limit itself in the race for the production of armaments. In the absence of any international organization, the conferences did provide an opportunity for the powers to gather around a table and talk. Nothing concrete resulted and the nations blamed one another for the failure. The peace conferences were a revival of that old ghost, the congress system. They showed that the system so valued by Metternich and Bismarck no longer worked. The congress system had depended on restraint, diplomatic flexibility, and the determination of the major powers to maintain peace. These conditions no longer prevailed.

In this postcard portrait of William II in 1913 the major symbols of his reign are those reflecting military power. (Altonaer Museum in Hamburg)

Since Bismarck left the scene in 1890, military expenditures had risen at an alarming rate. In 1890 Germany spent $190 000 on her navy. By 1914, as a result of Tirpitz's and William II's naval ambition, the expenditure was $1 305 000. England responded between 1890 and 1914 by increasing its naval budget from $679 000 to $2 714 000. The cost per capita on military expenditures in 1870, 1890, and 1914 of the six European powers was as follows:

	1870	1890	1914
Germany	$1.33	$2.95	$8.52
Austria–Hungary	1.16	1.56	3.48
Italy	1.44	2.63	3.81
Britain	3.74	4.03	8.53
France	3.03	4.87	7.33
Russia	1.34	1.32	2.58

Diplomatic crises almost became normal in the early years of the twentieth century. The major crisis areas were North Africa, where French and German imperial ambitions confronted one another, and the Balkans, where Austria-Hungary and Russia continued to be rivals.

Two crises occurred over the status of Morocco in North Africa, where William II desired to extend the influence of Germany. In the *Entente Cordiale* of 1904 England had recognized Morocco as a French "sphere of influence." Piqued by this arrangement, William in 1905 challenged French influence in the area. The situation was made more difficult by the fact that German policy was not coherent, and no one was certain, including much of the German foreign office, what the Kaiser wanted. The British held to their agreement with the French. The British Foreign Minister, Sir Edward Grey, believed that the German intrusion in Morocco was yet another example of Germany's quest to dominate Europe. Whether this analysis was correct or not, from this moment on Grey strengthened his ties with France, both diplomatically and militarily. A second crisis over Morocco occurred in 1911. This time the Germans landed a gunboat at the Moroccan port city of Agadir as a way of getting "compensation" for the French domination of Morocco. England again supported France, and the Germans were bought off with a piece of the Congo belonging to France.

The Balkan crises were endemic. In 1908 war nearly broke out over Bosnia. Austria had occupied the area since the Congress of Berlin in 1878, but now feared that Turkey, which had undergone a revolution, would attempt to regain control. Russia, having given up its Far-Eastern ambitions for a time after the defeat in the Russo-Japanese War, turned back to the Balkans and the old question of opening the Straits to allow Russian warships easy access to the Mediterranean Sea. Austria-Hungary and Russia agreed secretly to support one another at a conference—Russia would have the opportunity to sail its ships into the Mediterranean, and Austria-Hungary would annex the Turkish provinces of Bosnia and Herzegovina in the Balkans. A major mix-up occurred: Austria, with the strong support of Germany, took over Bosnia, while Russia gained nothing, because it had no support from its allies in the Triple Entente for extending its power into the Mediterranean. Russian diplomacy was becoming desperate as Russia lost prestige again, this time among its fellow Slavs in the Balkans. In ruling Bosnia, Austria now faced more Russian belligerency as well as a fervent national independence movement.

Though Europeans may have had the impression that despite a succession of crises a European war between great powers would always be avoided, plans were being discussed and formulated for the possibility of an armed conflict. Apart from the decision to build a big fleet, German war plans changed after William II took control of affairs. Once the Russians were no longer tied to Germany, the Germans assumed that if war broke out they would be fighting on two fronts, against France in the west and Russia in the east. The German war plan, the Schlieffen Plan, assumed that Russia would mobilize slowly and that France must therefore be defeated quickly. The plan called for a rapid mobilization, the taking of Paris in six weeks by marching through neutral Belgium, and then turning to the east to face the slow-moving Russians. Its success depended on the precise timing and efficiency of the well-trained German army.

In the meanwhile from 1906, unknown even to the British parliament or most of the cabinet, the English and French general staffs were conducting military "talks." Not only was the British army given French military secrets, but by 1914 extensive plans for the deployment of the troops of both countries, in the event of a German attack on France, were in existence and ready to be put into operation. In addition, though England continually tried to get Germany to limit its navy, after the failure of a diplomatic mission in 1912, the English felt they would have to co-operate with the French on the seas as well. In the interests of military efficiency, the English and French agreed to coordinate naval operations—England would protect the North Sea, and France would move its navy into the Mediterranean.

By 1914 international relations were both complex and tense. The interpretation of the treaties and agreements which were designed to fit the world of the late nineteenth century was the subject of great speculation. All knew Germany had commitments, but no one was certain, even the Germans, what would be interpreted as defensive, and how far these commitments would be honoured. All knew England and France had ties, but no one was certain, even the French and the English, how intimate they were. Nor was it clear whether mobilization would be considered tantamount to war, or how one would determine "the aggressor" in a complex system of defensive alliances. And how often could countries, particularly Russia, afford to back down in the face of threats? Yet it is obvious that the powers were losing their freedom of action, and that alternatives were being reduced in a diplomatically complicated and insecure world.

THE BALKAN PROBLEM AGAIN:
1912-14

When war broke out in the Balkans in 1912, no one thought of it in terms of a large-scale affair. The Balkan countries—Bulgaria, Serbia, Greece, Montenegro—fought against Turkey and swept the Ottoman Empire out of Europe. Albania was created as an independent state and Serbia was given additional territory. In 1913 the victors argued about dividing the spoils, and Bulgaria, while still at war with Turkey, found itself fighting its former allies and Rumania. The major powers did intervene diplomatically. While Austria and Russia made noises about giving support to various Balkan countries, Germany and England acted as restraining forces on their allies and tried to sort out the problem. Then, in June 1914, the heir to the Austrian throne along with his wife paid a state visit to Sarajevo, the Bosnian city annexed by Austria and claimed by Serbia. They were both assassinated on June 28. Europe again was thrown into a crisis.

The Austrian reaction was twofold. It blamed Serbia for the killing, claiming that some Serbian officials had knowledge of the terrorist society which organized the deed,

"European Poker Game" by Eduard Thöny, 1912   (General Research and Humanities Division, The New York Public Library— Astor, Lenox, and Tilden Foundations)

and that Serbia had encouraged nationalist movements in Bosnia. Before taking any positive steps, Austria-Hungary checked with its German ally. On July 5 Austria-Hungary was informed by Germany that it could count on German support in any action taken against Serbia, even if Russia entered on the side of the Serbs. On July 23 Austria sent a set of demands to Serbia which, if agreed to, would virtually have deprived Serbia of its independence as a nation. Serbia's answer was conciliatory, but Austria had not sent the demands as a diplomatic manoeuvre; it had sent them as an excuse to go to war.

While all this was going on, the embassies and foreign offices of Europe were frantically trying to cool things down. Sir Edward Grey proposed yet another conference. The German foreign office was conciliatory, while the Germany military was preparing for mobilization. Russia was warning Austria not to attack Serbia. The diplomacy of the Bismarckian era was no longer able to cope with the problems that beset Europe. Great animosity now existed between England and Germany, and each had new commitments and a new policy. Austria was desperately anxious to maintain its empire intact in the face of nationalist demands. Russia, in the light of the military and diplomatic losses it suffered in the last decade, felt it necessary to support Serbian demands. France had few interests in the Balkans, but its ships now patrolled the Mediterranean as a result of military discussions with England, and it felt a need to maintain its Russian alliance. The diplomats could not cope with the realities of the day.

Austria declared war on Serbia on July 28, after stating that the Serbian response to Austrian demands was unacceptable. Russia mobilized on the next day but did not declare war. On July 30 the German general Helmuth von Moltke, without informing the civilian authorities, told Austria to reject all compromises and mobilize against Russia, and on July 31 Austria mobilized. Germany, fearful of losing its advantage of rapid mobilization, sent an ultimatum to Russia on July 31, warning Russia not to interfere in the Balkans. The Russians did not answer, and Germany declared war on Russia on August 1, 1914. Having declared war on Russia, the Germans at once put the Schlieffen Plan into effect. They sent their troops to defeat France by marching through Belgium. War was formally declared against France on August 3.

The one hope for moderation and conciliation was England. Though England was a member of the Triple Entente, the union brought with it no formal military commitments as did the Triple Alliance. Hence Germany had some hopes that England would remain neutral and let the war occur between two power blocs on the continent. Even the French were not certain on August 3 that England would enter the war. But did England have a moral commitment to France in the light of military agreements? Sir Edward Grey, Prime Minister Asquith, and the cabinet thought it did. Public opinion in England was repelled by the German invasion of Belgium, a breach of the treaty of 1839 guaranteeing Belgian neutrality. Moreover, in the light of English attitudes towards the balance of power and towards German imperial and naval activities of the last two decades, it had little choice but to join Russia and France. To allow the possibility of a German victory and the creation of a new universal empire on the European continent was to ignore British interests and British policy of the last few centuries. Once England sought continental allies as a counterweight to what it interpreted as a German attempt to supremacy, it had little choice but to support them when general hostilities broke out. Hence Grey made many attempts to preserve the peace while it seemed possible. But on August 4 the British government declared war on Germany, using the German violation of neutral Belgian territory to bring public opinion along.

Nearly everyone in Europe in August 1914, looking at the wars since the 1860s, thought this new conflict would be over within six months. Most people expected the decisive battles to occur in the first few months of the war. In every country the masses, including socialists, priests, and internationalists, were singing the song of nationalism. The war was viewed as a romantic, nationalist affair, a brief heroic excursion to defeat the enemy, an exciting interruption of the drabness of one's ordinary existence. It would soon be over, and then life would go on even better than before.

THE PROBLEM OF THE ORIGINS OF THE WAR

The question of the "origins" of the Great War has become one of the great historical problems of modern times. Even before the war was over, all the adversaries issued diplomatic documents and explanations of their actions to prove their innocence in starting the conflagration. All claimed to have acted out of motives of defence. The argument over responsibility goes on to this day. The reason the question of responsibility is so important is that the various interpretations of responsibility affected the making of the peace.

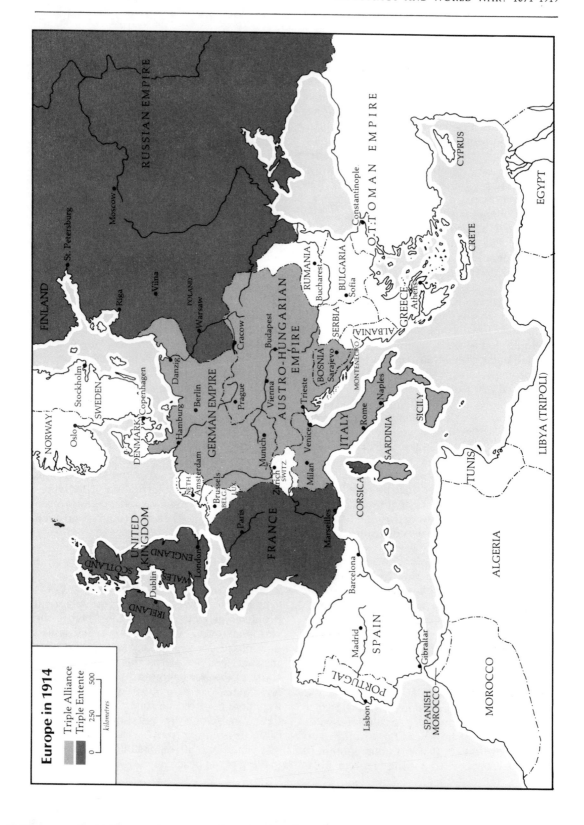

Europe in 1914

Triple Alliance
Triple Entente

0   250   500
kilometres

RUSSIAN EMPIRE

FINLAND

St. Petersburg

Moscow

Vilna

Riga

POLAND

Warsaw

NORWAY

Oslo

Stockholm

SWEDEN

DENMARK

Copenhagen

Hamburg

Danzig

Cracow

Berlin

GERMAN EMPIRE

Prague

Vienna

Budapest

AUSTRO-HUNGARIAN EMPIRE

Munich

SWITZ.

Zurich

Milan

Venice

Trieste

BOSNIA

Sarajevo

SERBIA

MONTENEGRO

ALBANIA

RUMANIA

Bucharest

BULGARIA

Sofia

OTTOMAN EMPIRE

Constantinople

GREECE

Athens

CRETE

CYPRUS

EGYPT

NETH.

Amsterdam

Brussels

BELG.

LUX.

Paris

FRANCE

Marseilles

ITALY

Rome

Naples

SICILY

SARDINIA

CORSICA

UNITED KINGDOM

SCOTLAND

ENGLAND

WALES

London

Dublin

IRELAND

Barcelona

Madrid

SPAIN

PORTUGAL

Lisbon

Gibraltar

SPANISH MOROCCO

MOROCCO

ALGERIA

TUNIS

LIBYA (TRIPOLI)

As soon as the war was over, the Allies—England, France, Italy (which had left the Triple Alliance and had entered the war on the side of the Allies in 1915), and the United States (which entered the war in 1917)—had a clear answer: Germany was responsible. Had Germany restrained Austria-Hungary in the final crisis, had William II not been so belligerent, the war would not have happened. Some went so far as to accuse Germany of wanting a war in 1914, of purposely heating up the Bosnian crisis to create an armed conflict. These interpretations seriously affected the peace treaty. In the 1920s many historians attacked and revised this view of the war. Some blamed Russia for its pan-Slav policy and its hostility to Austria-Hungary. Others pointed out that England might have played a role as arbiter between two camps but did not. Still others noted that France did its best to "isolate" Germany diplomatically as France had been isolated under Bismarck. Some writers blamed the war not on men but on "forces"—imperialism, secret treaties, military commitments, the armaments race, and competing ideologies.

It is possible to make a case that some powers were more responsible than others. In recent years some German historians have argued that Germany not only prepared for war but felt that it was essential to achieve the goals of its foreign policy and to open markets for its industry. These historians also state that conservatives in control of the German military and government thought that going to war would stem the trend towards liberalism and socialism in German domestic affairs. The Austrian diplomats, they claim, acted precipitously and with German backing launched a war which was bound to bring in Russia and Russia's ally, France. To the extent that some people wanted war, the two powers in central Europe, Germany and Austria-Hungary, were more responsible than the other states. Yet many historians have come to the conclusion that all the nations manoeuvring in an outmoded diplomatic system bear a collective responsibility for the conflagration.

THE WAR

The Great War bore little resemblance to what had been anticipated. It was not a romantic war; in fact, for the most part, it was brutal and ugly. It was a war among whole peoples, involving millions, both on the front lines and at home. Raymond Aron, the historian-sociologist, has described our time as "a century of total war." All are expected to participate. This is a continuation of the tradition of the French Revolutionary wars, but with enormously increased destructive powers as a result of the industrial revolution and mass production.

The German strategy was put into effect with great speed. Marching through Belgium and Luxembourg, the German soldiers were expected to destroy the French army in six weeks, and then turn to the east to face the Russians. The plan failed. In the Battle of the Marne, begun on September 6, 1914, the French managed to stop the German advance. This gave the Russians time to effect their mobilization. Now the Germans had to face a two-front war, something they had wished to avoid at all costs. The western front was established in France in late 1914. It would remain virtually the same for the next two and a half years.

On both fronts the fighting took on the aspect of a series of attempts to penetrate fixed trench positions. But, because of the length of the fronts, any offensive move had to be made directly against enemy lines, not from a flanking position. Thus hundreds of thousands of men were lost in attempts to advance a short distance. It was clear that the defenders were in a stronger position than the attackers, and the war often bogged down in the trenches, each side seeking an advantage against the deadly machine gun, the best defensive weapon of the time. Henri Barbusse, in his novel *Under Fire*, tried to realistically capture the feelings of men engaged in trench warfare. Here is his description of the experiences of one soldier at the Battle of Verdun of 1916, a battle in which the Germans tried to break through French lines to no avail, resulting in five hundred thousand deaths:

A shower of bullets spirts around me, increasing the number of those who suddenly halt, who collapse slowly, defiant and gesticulating, of those who dive forward solidly with all the body's burden, of the shouts, deep, furious, and desperate, and even of that hollow and terrible gasp when a man's life goes bodily forth in a breath. And we who are not yet stricken, we look ahead, we walk and we run, among the frolics of the death that strikes at random into our flesh.

The wire entanglements—and there is one stretch of them intact. We go along to where it has been gutted into a wide and deep opening. This is a colossal funnel-hole, formed of smaller funnels placed together, a fantastic volcanic crater, scooped there by the guns.

The sight of this convulsion is stupefying; truly it seems that it must have come from the center of the earth. Such a rending of virgin strata puts new edge on our attacking fury, and none of us can keep from shouting with a solemn shake of

the head—even just now when words are but painfully torn from our throats—"Ah, Christ! Look what hell we've given 'em there! Ah, look!". . .

A terrible volley bursts point-blank in our faces, flinging in front of us a sudden row of flames the whole length of the earthen verge. After the stunning shock we shake ourselves and burst into devilish laughter—the discharge has passed too high. And at once, with shouts and roars of salvation, we slide and roll and fall alive into the belly of the trench![4]

The entry of Japan on the side of the "Allies"—which put it alongside England, France, Russia, and other states fighting with them—in August 1914 and of Turkey on the side of Germany and Austria-Hungary in late 1914, and the switch of Italy to the Allies in 1915 did not change the course of the war. Japan spent nearly all its efforts on getting hold of German posses-

"Wounded, Fall 1916, Bapaume" by Otto Dix   (From The War, 1924. Etching and aquatint, 7¾" x 11⅜". Collection, The Museum of Modern Art, New York.   Gift of Abby Aldrich Rockefeller)

sions in the Far East and on gaining imperial concessions from China. Turkey harassed Russia in the Black Sea but was too weak to make a formidable difference in the balance of power. Italy abandoned the Triple Alliance in 1914, not wishing to go to war over the Balkans, claiming that the alliance was a defensive one, and that Austria-Hungary's actions towards Serbia were offensive. Both sides bargained with Italy, the Allies gaining it as a friend by the treaty of London of 1915, which promised much of the *Irredenta* to Italy should the Allies be victorious. The Italian front further helped to weaken the Austro-Hungarian Empire and hastened its demise.

Each country, however, had limited agricultural and industrial resources, and the war at sea determined the extent of additional resources available to each. Britain used its naval supremacy to attempt a blockade of German ports. The challenge to the big British ships lay in the ingenious submarine, used in great numbers by Germany. The use of the submarine raised a series of diplomatic questions for Germany—what to do about neutrals, particularly United States shipping. If Germany were to allow shipping from the United States to go unchallenged on the seas, it would mean allowing goods to go to the Allies.

The sympathy of the United States was clearly on the side of the Allies as the war went on. The question was whether the United States would continue to remain officially neutral and not bring its resources and fresh troops into the war against Germany. And there was also strong sentiment in the United States that it should continue its traditional policy of not becoming involved in European conflicts. The United States President, Woodrow Wilson (1913–20), continually tried to mediate between the powers and proposed many plans and conferences. He campaigned for a second term in 1916 on the slogan "He kept us out of war." However, the problem of German attacks on United States ships in British and neutral waters became in 1917 the major bone of contention between Germany and the United States.

The problem was a difficult one for the German high command. In 1915 Germany attempted a blockade of Britain and announced that shipping in these waters would be fired upon. Wilson was angered by this policy, and public opinion supported him. However, in May 1915 the British passenger ship *Lusitania* was destroyed by German submarines, resulting in approximately 1200 deaths, over one hundred of whom were Americans. The outcry in the United States was so great that Germany felt it wiser to retreat from such a policy, fearing that another incident of this sort would bring the United States into the war.

By 1917, however, the situation had changed for the Germans. They began to feel the shortage of resources as the English blockade was becoming more effective. They decided to gamble. In January 1917 Germany adopted a policy of unrestricted submarine warfare, knowing the United States would probably thus enter the war, but hoping that Germany would be able in this way to defeat England before the full effects of the United States entry would be felt.

The decision proved effective, as many tons of Allied shipping were sunk by Germany through the summer of 1917. However, United States policy and public opinion turned away from neutrality as United States ships were sunk by German submarines. By April, Wilson, the Congress of the United States, and the vast majority of the public felt there was no alternative. On April 6, 1917, the United States joined the Allies by declaring war against Germany.

The British, through a combination of escorted convoys and new weapons, managed by the end of 1917 to protect merchant vessels against the dreaded submarines. The vast productive power of the Allies, the introduction of the tank against the machine gun, the control of the seas, the attrition of German and Austrian forces, as well as the support of the United States meant that the Central Powers could not win. Germany made a last push in 1918 after Russia withdrew from the war, but it did not succeed. As the year wore on, mutinies occurred

A war poster (Public Archives, Canada)

in the Austrian army, and resistance weakened on the part of the Germans. In the summer the Allies broke through the German lines. Austria surrendered on November 3. In the middle of mutinies and rebellions, William II abdicated on November 9 and fled to Holland. On November 11, 1918, the Germans requested an armistice, and the war was over.

THE PEACE OF VERSAILLES

After the armistice a peace conference was called in Paris. The United States took its place among the great powers, and the hopes of the world for a just peace rested on the shoulders of its President. Woodrow Wilson had entered politics after a career as a professor of politics and president of Princeton University. Pledged to bring a "fair deal" to

all in the United States, he soon found himself deeply involved in diplomacy and war. He directed his efforts to make peace among the belligerent powers.

Wilson was greatly admired, even worshipped, by the people of Europe, and he occupied a unique position in world affairs in the first several months after the end of the war. In January 1918 he had issued a public statement of war aims in the Fourteen Points. Speaking for the United States, he prefaced the Fourteen Points in this way:

We entered this war because violations of right had occurred which touched us to the quick and made the life of our own people impossible unless they were corrected and the world secured once for all against their recurrence. What we demand in this war, therefore, is nothing peculiar to ourselves. It is that the world be made fit and safe to live in; and particularly that it be made safe for every peace-loving nation which, like our own, wishes to live its own life, determine its own institutions, be assured of justice and fair dealing by the other peoples of the world as against force and selfish aggression. All the peoples of the world are in effect partners in this interest, and for our own part we see very clearly that unless justice be done to others it will not be done to us.[5]

Some of the points dealt specifically with boundary disputes, such as the integrity of Belgium, the restoration of Alsace-Lorraine to France, the establishment of a new Poland, and a settlement of disputes in the Balkans, the Italian *Irredenta*, and Turkey. But most people were impressed with those points which enunciated principles. Wilson was convinced that secret diplomacy and secret treaties had contributed to the war. Thus he proclaimed the principle of "open covenants of peace openly arrived at." He called for freedom of the seas, the end of economic barriers between nations, and the reduction of armaments. Colonial disputes must be settled and the rights of colonial peoples protected. Above all, Wilson believed that in redrawing the map of Europe the principle of nationality must be the guiding force. He believed that national disturbances and international disputes arose out of the claims of nationalities against an empire or as a result of conflicting national interests. If only the map and the sovereignty of nations could be made to reflect the nationalist reality, he thought Europe would be able to evolve into a democratic society.

To establish a forum for expression of opinion and for negotiations to settle disputes, Wilson was convinced of the necessity of implementing his last point: "A general association of nations must be formed under specific covenants for the purpose of affording mutual guarantees of political independence and territorial integrity to great and small nations alike."[6] It was the congress system in a liberal-democratic twentieth-century guise.

Many nations were represented at the Paris Peace Conference. In addition to the major powers, some new European states—Poland and Czechoslovakia—were there, as well as Belgium and Greece. The British dominions had joined in the war and were present. Many Latin-American states were present, having entered the war after the United States came in. From the Far East came Japan, in the war since 1914, and Siam and China, both of which entered in 1917. From Africa came Liberia, which also joined the side of the Allies in 1917.

But there were some extremely important absentees. Russia had withdrawn from the fighting after the Bolshevik *coup d'état* in November 1917 and was in the midst of a civil war. It was not invited to attend. The defeated states—Germany, Austria-Hungary, Turkey, and Bulgaria (which joined the Central Powers in 1915) — were excluded from the negotiations while the victors decided their fate. Thus, unlike Vienna in 1814–15, the Paris Peace Conference represented the victors only. It did not represent all those who would have to keep the peace.

Nor was the peace made by all the victors combined. It was really the work of the representatives of the big powers. Wilson spoke for the United States. David Lloyd George, now the Prime Minister, represented England. He was concerned with English domestic affairs and wished to avoid having England committed to action on the European continent. He felt that the English were war-weary and wished to pick up where they had ended in 1914. The French Prime Minister was Henri Clemenceau, a man who had fought in the Franco-Prussian War, who had defended Dreyfus, and who wished, above all, guarantees against German resurgence. The Italian Prime Minister at the time was Vittorio Orlando, a statesman not unlike Wilson, but who was not a strong force in Italian affairs. It was these men who made the major decisions.

The victors' interpretation of the origins of the war was an important element in formulating the terms of the peace. No one on the winning side at Paris doubted that Germany and Austria were responsible, and the final treaty reflected this belief with a vengeance. A "war guilt" clause was written into the treaty stating that "war [was] imposed upon [the Allies] by the aggression of Germany and her allies,"[7] and Germany was to pay reparations for losses incurred by the Allies in the war.

The territorial settlement reduced the size of Germany. In the west, Alsace-Lorraine was given back to France, and France also received the right to use the rich coal mines in the Saar Basin for fifteen years as reparations for the destruction of some of its own mines. Poland was recreated as an independent state, and the "Polish Corridor," a strip of land giving Poland access to the Baltic Sea, was given to Poland. In addition, the city of Danzig, of mixed German and Polish population and located in the Corridor, was internationalized. Germany lost its colonies. They were to come under the authority of the League of Nations, which gave those in Africa mainly to England and France as mandates. South Africa and Belgium also received small pieces of territory there. Japan received mandates for most of Germany's former possessions in the Far East.

The military settlement was designed to keep Germany weak and to prevent it from playing a major role in world affairs. Germany was permitted a small navy and a professional army of 100,000 men. Certain weapons of an offensive nature were forbidden to be manufactured. In addition, the German Rhineland, the area west of the Rhine River, which is about 50 km wide, was demilitarized—German troops were forbidden to enter there—and the Allies were to occupy the area for fifteen years to make certain that Germany fulfilled its treaty obligations.

The League of Nations was written into the treaty. The League was given certain tasks—including the conducting of plebiscites, the handling of some colonial affairs, and the protection of minorities. Wilson tied his prestige and concept of peace to the League, hoping that once nations were forced to come to the conference table all would be well. Others were much less optimistic about the organization, pointing out that the League did not have arms or sovereignty, and that it therefore lacked the power to implement its decisions.

It is clear that the treaty was not an "open" covenant "openly arrived at." It was a peace hammered out by the major victorious states which, in the end, did not completely satisfy anyone. The French wanted an even weaker Germany; the Italians did not obtain what had been promised in the 1915 treaty which brought them into the war; the Japanese had counted on even more concessions in the Far East. Wilson had given the world the dream of a perfect peace; instead, it got a diplomatic compromise, arrived at in the old way. Moreover, many thought that the settlement with Germany was not based on justice but vengeance.

The treaty still had to be signed, and this event was to occur in the Hall of Mirrors at the Palace of Versailles. However, when the treaty was presented to the German representatives, they refused at first to accept it, asserting it was too harsh a settlement. Finally, after much discussion and threats of invasion of Germany by the Allies, a group of Germans from the Social Democratic Party and the Catholic Centre Party agreed to accept the document, including the war-guilt clause. In May 1919 the Treaty of Versailles was signed.

Other treaties followed with Germany's allies in the First World War—Austria, Bulgaria, Hungary, and Turkey. All were based on Versailles. New states were created on the basis of nationality. In addition to a new Poland, the map of eastern Europe now included Czechoslovakia, Yugoslavia, Lithuania, Latvia, Estonia, and Finland. Nationalism carried the day. For a moment it seemed that Mazzini's dream of a world made up of national states in which all people would be members of one family and in which a confederation of nations would maintain peace might come into existence.

THE CONSEQUENCES OF THE GREAT WAR

The war marked the beginning of the decline of Europe, though, paradoxically, it stepped

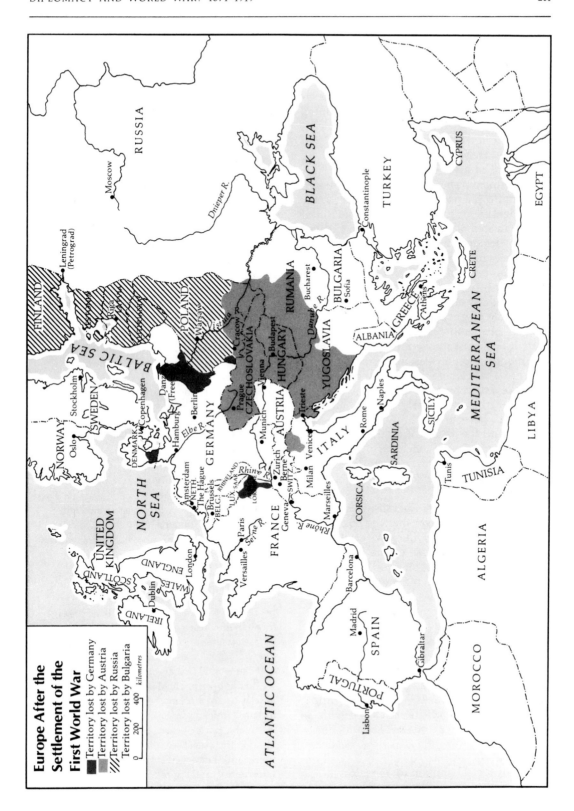

Europe After the Settlement of the First World War

- Territory lost by Germany
- Territory lost by Austria
- Territory lost by Russia
- Territory lost by Bulgaria

0   200   400   *kilometres*

up the Europeanization of the globe. Power no longer centred only in a small continent which had come to dominate the world since the late middle ages. Areas on the fringes—such as Japan, which had Westernized and industrialized, and the United States, which had industrialized—assumed a major role in world affairs.

Europe itself was drastically changed by the war. The great empires of Russia, Austria, Germany, and Turkey had been transformed. People returned from the war to new sovereignties, organized on national lines, and dedicated at least outwardly to furthering the democratic tradition. Though class differences remained, the *vox populi* was the reality more than ever before. After more than a century, the goal of the French Revolution was coming closer to being realized.

The role of governments in the everyday lives of people increased greatly during the war. It was up to governments to organize the mobilization of resources, and, in the midst of a war where the life of the state was at stake, there was less concern for the rights of the individual. Governments in large part determined the allocation of resources and the nature of industrial production. A complicated machinery grew up to manage the new organization, and the white-collar worker became an important element in all countries.

The old *laissez-faire* liberalism was dead. Few believed any longer that the business of the state was to play the role of the passive policeman. Liberals of the *laissez-faire* school were losing out all over the world to those who recognized the more central role of the state, sometimes to leftists and sometimes to rightists. Some writers have theorized that liberalism had nowhere to go in 1914; it had ceased to be a doctrine on the side of change.

The war itself, its terror and its destruction, changed people's attitudes towards themselves and towards Western civilization. It opened in high spirits; it closed with an almost universal cry against such madness. The total number of casualties—dead and wounded—is estimated at 37.5 million. Germany lost 1.8 million soldiers, Russia 1.7,

France 1.4, Austria-Hungary 1.2, and Great Britain 1 million. The number of wounded was more than double these figures. Many civilians were killed or injured, leaving few European families untouched. People wondered whether the optimism of the nineteenth century was nothing but a "grand illusion."

The war meant a profound change in cultural attitudes. The "crisis of culture" seen by a few before the war was intensified. The idea of progress lost credit. Doubt replaced certainty. Pessimism became more prevalent than optimism. The future was no longer seen as necessarily better than the past. Paul Valéry (1871-1945), French poet, essayist, and philosopher, wrote in 1919: "The swaying of the ship has been so violent that the best-hung lamps have finally overturned."[8] In 1922 he returned to this theme in an essay entitled "The European":

The storm is over, and yet we are still uneasy . . . anxious . . . . as though it were just now going to break. Nearly all human affairs are still in a state of terrible uncertainty. We ponder on what is gone, we are almost ruined by what has been ruined; we do not know what is to come, and have some reason to fear it. We hope vaguely, but dread precisely; our fears are infinitely clearer than our hopes; we recognize that pleasurable living and abundance are behind us, but confusion and doubt are in us and with us. There is no thinking person, however shrewd and experienced we imagine him to be, who can flatter himself that he is above this malaise, that he has escaped this sense of gloom, and can gauge the probable duration of this period of disturbance in the vital exchanges of humanity.

We are an unfortunate generation; it has befallen us to witness during our brief passage through life these great and terrifying events whose reverberations will fill the whole of our lives.

It can be said that everything essential in the world has been affected by the war, or more exactly by the circumstances of the war. Attrition has undermined something deeper than the renewable parts of man. You know of the great upset in the general economy, in the policies of States and the very lives of individuals: distress, uncertainty, and apprehension are everywhere.

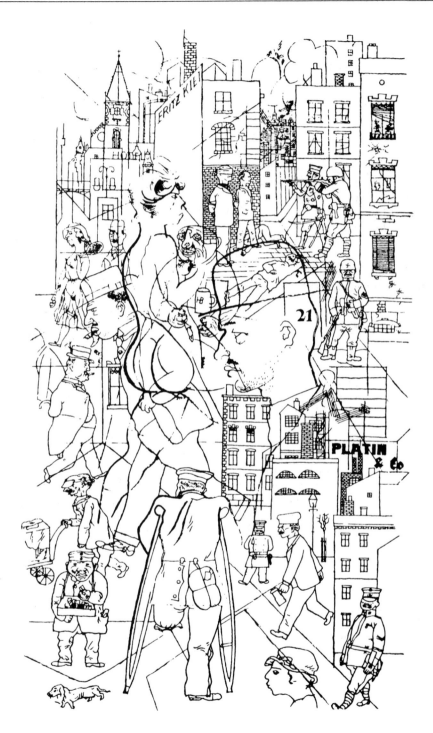

"Cross-Section" by George Grosz, 1920. A bitter statement reflecting the chaos, violence, and pessimism that followed the First World War   (Estate of George Grosz, Princeton, New Jersey)

The Mind itself has not been exempt from all this damage. The Mind is in fact cruelly stricken; it grieves in men of intellect, and looks sadly upon itself. It distrusts itself profoundly.[9]

Others feared the irrational and cynical attitudes that had been fostered by the experience of the war. The poet William Butler Yeats (1869–1939) wrote in "The Second Coming" in 1921:

> Things fall apart; the centre cannot hold;
> Mere anarchy is loosed upon the world,
> The blood-dimmed tide is loosed, and
>   everywhere
> The ceremony of innocence is drowned;
> The best lack all conviction, while the worst
> Are full of passionate intensity.[10]

All around, people of sensitivity were wondering what the twentieth century would be like.

THE LITERATURE OF THE WAR:
A NEW VIEW OF MAN

One of the most commonly shared experiences of people in the West in the twentieth century is war. Beginning with the Great War, poets and novelists have responded to the intensity and misery of the experience and have attempted to gain some insight into what occurs to people underneath the noise of the guns. While the literature of the First World War concentrates on the inhumanity of war, it is also a testament to the power of people to rise above their situation with "little" acts of heroism and kindness. Writers such as the Englishman Wilfred Owen, who died a week before the armistice in 1918, pondered the meaning of the slaughter:

I, too, saw God through mud,
> The mud that cracked on cheeks when
>   wretches smiled.
> War brought more glory to their eyes than
>   blood,
> And gave their laughs more glee than shakes
>   a child.

Merry it was to laugh there—
> Where death becomes absurd and life
>   absurder.
> For power was on us as we slashed bones
>   bare
> Not to feel sickness or remorse of murder.[11]

One of the characters in Ford Madox Ford's *No More Parades* reflected on the dilemma of the individual getting into war:

Intense dejection: endless muddles: endless follies: endless villainies. All these men given into the hands of the most cynically care-free intriguers in long corridors who made plots that harrowed the hearts of the world. All these men toys: all these agonies mere occasions for picturesque phrases to be put into politicians' speeches without heart or even intelligence. Hundreds of thousands of men tossed here and there in that sordid and gigantic mud-brownness of midwinter . . . by God, exactly as if they were nuts wilfully picked up and thrown over the shoulder by magpies. . . . But men. Not just populations. . . .[12]

Thus a new view of humanity and a new view of life: not orderly, but chaotic; not meaningful, but perhaps absurd; not rational, but intensely personal. The American poet Carl Sandburg attempted to get some perspective on the impact of war:

> Pile the bodies high at Austerlitz and
>   Waterloo.
> Shovel them under and let me work—
>   I am the grass; I cover all.
>
> And pile them high at Gettysburg
> And pile them high at Ypres and Verdun.
> Shovel them under and let me work.
> Two years, ten years, and passengers ask
>   the conductor:
>   What place is this?
>   Where are we now?
>
>   I am the grass.
>   Let me work.[13]

ANALYSIS AND DISCUSSION

1. "In 1914, after the death of Francis Ferdinand, European diplomats were unable or unwilling to find alternatives to war."
a) Illustrate both the incapacity and the unwillingness of the European leaders to avoid war in the crisis after the assassination at Sarajevo.
b) Explain why, after almost a century of avoiding major war, the European powers could not or did not want to do so any longer.

2. The concept of the balance of power was one of the most important factors governing the relationship among the European powers.
a) Define balance of power and illustrate its operation in the years 1871-1914.
b) How did the growing power of the United States and Japan affect the balance of power in Europe?

3. The Alliance System was designed to prevent major war. Trace the development of the Alliance System and explain how it came to limit the diplomatic alternatives available to statesmen in 1914.

4. At the outbreak of the war, the two sides appeared to be evenly matched. Outline the strengths and weaknesses of each side, and account for the eventual victory of the Allied forces.

5. The Treaty of Versailles was an attempt by statesmen to create a lasting settlement. Account for the criticism of the Treaty as one which failed to solve the diplomatic problems arising out of the First World War.

6. "The [First World War] marked the beginning of the decline of Europe, though, paradoxically, it stepped up the Europeanization of the globe." Discuss the reasons for this development in world affairs in the first two decades of the twentieth century.

SYNTHESIS AND EVALUATION   CHAPTERS 9 AND 10

1. As political philosophies, liberalism and Marxism have very different appeals:
a) If you had to choose, which of the two would you prefer? What values lie behind your choice?
b) Account for the greater appeal of Marxism in the less industrialized nations, and the preference for liberalism in many of the industrialized democracies of western Europe and North America.

2. "By 1914, the belief in a rational human nature no longer seemed tenable, and the optimism based on the idea of progress, which had characterized the West since the Enlightenment, was evaporating."
a) Is the idea of progress that is referred to in this statement a valid view of human history? Why or why not?
b) If you were an educated member of the European middle class in the early 1900s, how would you have reacted to the intellectual, social, and political changes of the time? Express your reactions in the form of a memoir, diary, or letter to a friend or relative.

3. Two opposing schools of thought about creative writing emerged in the nineteenth century. One, the "realist," claimed that writers should strive to be objectively, almost photographically, accurate in describing the human condition. The other, the "symbolist," claimed that reality went deeper than mere observation and that a writer should evoke the unconscious and profound in human nature.
a) Which view do you think is the more valid approach to creative literature? Why?
b) How does each of these approaches to literature reflect the changes going on in society?

4. "Freud's identification of the driving forces of the unconscious and the irrational took on a special meaning for the survivors of World War I." Discuss this statement with reference to both Freud's view of humanity and the new perceptions of human nature which emerged out of the First World War.

CHAPTER **11**

The Russian Revolution and the Spread of Communism

Russia and Europe

1856	Russia loses Crimean War
1861	Emancipation of the serfs
1856–81	Reign of Czar Alexander II
1881–94	Reign of Czar Alexander III
1894–1917	Reign of Czar Nicholas II
1898	Formation of Russian Social Democratic Party
1902	Lenin writes *What Is to Be Done?*
1903	Russian Social Democrats split into Mensheviks and Bolsheviks
1904–5	Russo-Japanese War
1905	Revolution in Russia; Czar promises to establish a Duma (parliament)
1914	First World War begins
March 1917	Revolution in Russia; Czar abdicates; Provisional Government
November 1917	Bolsheviks gain power
1918–20	Civil War in Russia
1919	Lenin forms Third International (Comintern)
1924	Death of Lenin
1927	Stalin in control of Communist Party
1928	Beginning of First Five-Year Plan
1934	Stalin's purges
1939	Russian-German Non-Aggression Pact

China

1900	Boxer Rebellion
1911	Manchu Dynasty falls; China becomes a Republic
1912	Kuomintang (National People's Party) founded
1921	Chinese Communist Party founded
1925	Death of Sun Yat-sen
1928	Chiang Kai-shek leads Kuomintang to power
1934–35	The Long March; Mao Tse-tung leader of Chinese Communists
1937	Japan invades China; Kuomintang and Communists form a United Front

I F THE FRENCH REVOLUTION OF 1789 was the most important historical event of the nineteenth century, the Russian Revolution has been of comparable significance for the twentieth century. The success of Vladimir Ilich Ulyanov ("Lenin") and his Bolshevik followers in taking control of the Russian state in November 1917 was an event of monumental importance for Europe and the world. A communist party had seized control of one of the major powers of Europe, and communism henceforth spread and became one of the leading political and social systems of the twentieth century. The form it took in Russia after the Bolsheviks consolidated their power was totalitarian and collective, a denial of the liberal, democratic, and individualist philosophies of the nineteenth century. Though all communists claimed inspiration from Marx, the intellectual and political guideposts of communism changed from time to time and from place to place. Like all dogmatic ideologies it was never without "orthodoxies," "heresies," and "splits." Yet in one form or another it has become both the political faith and the practice of over a billion people throughout the world.

The analogy between Russia in 1917 and France in 1789, however, should not be taken too far, lest it obscure the uniqueness of each revolution. In 1789 France was, and had been for some time, the leading political and intellectual force in the West. By the early twentieth century, although Russia was part of the West and was becoming increasingly industrialized, it stretched across Asia to the Pacific and had its own distinctive intellectual, social, and religious traditions. It was both part of the West and outside of it.

BETWEEN EAST AND WEST

Many Russians were Slavophiles, people who took pride in the uniqueness of their own culture and did not wish to adopt the values of the West. Instead of pursuing rationalist, scientific studies and the tradition of individualism in economics and politics, they emphasized the spiritual and collective unity of all Slav peoples under an ideal, autocratic czar and the Orthodox Church. The Slavophiles opposed the "Westerners" in Russia, whom they accused of undermining the unique qualities of Russia in favour of imported ideas. They rejected the technology, the materialism, and the economic relationships that had developed in the West, but were none the less influenced by Western nationalism and romanticism. As a result, they held up the Russian *mir*, the collective agricultural village community and a kind of extension of the Russian family, as a model for the ideal life.

Some Russian intellectuals, deeply moved by the plight of the peasants, rejected both the materialism of the West and the autocracy and bureaucracy of the czars. These men wound up as anarchists who challenged the very existence of the state. Though western European thinkers helped to develop anarchism, the most important anarchist, and one of Marx's greatest intellectual rivals in the latter part of the nineteenth century, was a Russian, Mikhail Bakunin (1814–76). Drawing on the political traditions of the Russian *mir* and a belief in the purity of peasant life, Bakunin became an important European figure, and his thoughts may be taken as an example of the anarchist position, though anarchists, both by definition and temperament, cannot be grouped together. Bakunin's anarchism gave philosophical form to a native Russian style, and for many Russians he had more appeal than Marx or the Slavophiles.

Bakunin believed in the goodness of people; he thought that political systems had corrupted people's basically humane nature. Growing up in provincial Russia, he used the present *mir* as his model of the good life. Bakunin preached the destruction of all authority by both the peasants and the proletariat. He saw "the State . . . as an inevitable negation and annihilation of all liberty, of all individual and collective interests." He believed that "the free organization of workers from below upward, is the ultimate aim of social development, and that every State . . . is a yoke, which means that it begets despotism on one hand and slavery on the other."[1] He claimed that Marx neglected the peasant and, by urging that the proletariat seize power from the *bourgeoisie*, was only substituting one authority for another. He broke with Marx over these questions.

In exile from Russia for most of his life, Bakunin could be found in the midst of revolutionary movements and conspiratorial activities, working for the destruction of authority and a return to a more primitive, happier social organization. Many Russian reformers and intellectuals, whatever their political views, generally believed that there was no hope for reform in the face of the autocratic rule of the czars, which allowed no political outlet for them to air their grievances. Touched by the suffering of the masses, they often became dreamers, utopians, and revolutionaries.

STABILITY AND CHANGE

To the Russian masses, the czar and the Church represented the continuity and the special quality of Russian life. The czar was seen as a paternal figure, a "father" to all Russians, who ruled benevolently on behalf of all of Russian society. Even when confidence in the czar was shaken, there was no thought of doing away with him. On Sunday, January 9, 1905, a crowd in St. Petersburg gathered to hand a petition to the Czar asking his help in reforming Russia:

All the people . . . are handed over to the discretion of the officials of the Government, who are thieves of the property of the State. . . . The Government officials have brought the country to complete destruction. . . . The people are deprived of the possibility of expressing their desires and they now demand that they be allowed to take part in the introduction of taxes and in the expenditure of them.

The workingmen are deprived of the possibility of organizing themselves in unions for the defence of their interests.

Sire, is [this] in accordance with divine law, by grace of which Thou reignest? . . . We are seeking here the last salvation. Do not refuse assistance to Thy people. . . . Give their destiny into their own hands. Cast away from them the intolerable oppression of officials. Destroy the wall between Thyself and Thy people, and let them rule the country together with Thyself.[2]

Most Russians felt that once the Czar was made aware of intolerable conditions, he would respond to their needs. However, after troops fired into the crowd which had gathered to present this petition, more radical demands were made. "Bloody Sunday," as the day became known, caused many Russians to wonder about the intentions of the Czar.

The czardom had a spiritual aura about it, supported as it was by the Church. The Russian Church was not Roman Catholic or Protestant, but an outgrowth of the Eastern Orthodox Church of the Byzantine Empire. By the early twentieth century it had become purely Russian, with its centre in Moscow, and had been controlled by the czars since the time of Peter the Great in the early eighteenth century. But, although it supported the regime, the Church was not an important political authority with power of its own. Furthermore, it had long ceased to be an important intellectual entity. The Church did not feel it had to respond to the challenge

Bloody Sunday, 1905. Russian troops fire on workers petitioning the Czar.   (Sovfoto)

of new ideas and thus it did not attract major intellectuals. The Church was so clearly identified with czardom that the end of czarist Russia would mean the end of the Church as a major influence in Russian affairs.

However, from the 1860s Russian life underwent important changes. The loss of the Crimean War in 1856 had demonstrated that Russia, which had witnessed continual expansion since the days of Peter the Great and had played a major role in the defeat of Napoleon, no longer ranked as one of the premier European powers. This failure motivated the new Czar, Alexander II (reigned 1855–81), to transform Russia's social structure in preparation for economic and military reform. In 1861 he issued an Emancipation Edict which freed the serfs and ended the authority of the nobles over the peasants. Emancipation did not mean that the peas-

ants were now legally equal to their lords, for the communal aspect of Russian life was retained—peasants were still legally members of a village group, which had some control over their lives. Moreover, peasant groups were required to make collective payments annually for forty-nine years in order to reimburse the lords for the land which the peasants received.

Other reforms followed emancipation. All Russians acquired the right to equality before the law, and the administration of justice was improved. Municipal councils and *Zemstvos*—local representative bodies in the cities and provinces—were established in 1864. Although the franchise for these bodies was based on property qualifications, this was the first time Russians could take part in a democratic political process. The military system was reorganized and the

A cartoon of 1900 issued by Russian socialists to express their view of the social structure of Czarist Russia   (Saltykov–Shchedrin Library, Leningrad)

army began to be shaped along Western lines. Since the new military techniques required that soldiers have some degree of literacy, the Russian army established an educational system for its troops. As a result, pamphlets of the Russian revolutionaries could now be read by a portion of the masses.

In 1881 Alexander II was assassinated. It was the deed of a terrorist group which felt that only revolution could transform Russia into a peasant socialist state. There had been various attempts at assassination since 1866, and towards the end of his rule Alexander II had imposed censorship and rigid control of what was being taught in Russian schools. His successor, Alexander III, who ruled until 1894, despised the radicals and reformers and was determined to strengthen the reactionary regime. He instituted an even tighter censorship, limited the rights of local autonomy granted by his father, and tried to stifle the universities. His successor, Nicholas II, who reigned from 1894 to 1917, was no more enlightened.

Though the czars tried to limit the effects of the changes begun in the 1860s, Russia was moving in the direction of industrialization along western European lines. Under the leadership of Count Witte (see Chapter VI), outside experts were brought into Russia in the 1890s, and modern industrial production was encouraged. This, too, contributed to the pressure for change, for the problems that had been faced by other countries in their early industrial phase—rapid urbanization, inadequate housing, poor factory conditions, the threat of machine production to the job security of craftsmen—began to complicate the already difficult domestic situation.

Nicholas II managed to contain the forces of change until 1905. However, the failure of Russia in the Russo-Japanese War increased the general desire for reform. "Bloody Sunday" in January 1905 only led to more protests in both the cities and the countryside. With the army tied up fighting Japan, the state simply did not have the resources to suppress this dissent, and Nicholas II did not seem to know how to respond to it. He did not want to grant concessions, nor did he wish to become a constitutional monarch. Hence he spoke of reform but then seemed to equivocate. Slowly the government lost control—outlawed groups met in the open, strikes grew in number and intensity, peasants disregarded the law and seized land, and on October 13 a committee of workers formed a soviet (council) in St. Petersburg to act as the spokesman for the workers. On August 19 Nicholas had promised to establish a Duma (parliament) and, when this did not quell the disturbances, he issued the "October Manifesto" on October 17, 1905.

The rioting and agitation in the capitals and in many localities of OUR Empire fills OUR heart with great and deep grief. The welfare of the Russian Emperor is bound up with the welfare of the people, and its sorrows are HIS sorrows. The turbulence which has broken out may confound the people and threaten the integrity and unity of OUR Empire.

The great vow of service [made] by the Tsar obligates US to endeavour, with all OUR strength, wisdom, and power, to put an end as quickly as possible to the disturbance so dangerous to the Empire. In commanding the responsible authorities to take measures to stop disorders, lawlessness, and violence, and to protect peaceful citizens in the quiet performance of their duties, WE have found it necessary to unite the activities of the Supreme Government, so as to insure the successful carrying out of the general measures laid down by US for the peaceful life of the state.

We lay upon the Government the execution of OUR unchangeable will:

1. To grant to the population the inviolable right of free citizenship, based on the principles of the freedom of person, conscience, speech, assembly, and union.

2. ... To include in the participation of the work of the Duma those classes of the population that have been until now entirely deprived of the right to vote, and to extend in the future ... the principles of the general right of election.

3. To establish as an unbreakable rule that no law shall go into force without its confirmation by the State Duma....[3]

The October Manifesto inaugurated a period of constitutional rule in Russia and became the basis of the 1906 constitution.

The constitution provided for an arrangement similar to that of the Germany of Bismarck. The Duma was to be elected by universal manhood suffrage and had to approve all laws and the budget. But government ministers were responsible to the czar, not the Duma. However, in the light of its history, this was an enormous step for Russia. It was a move towards the establishment of a liberal, constitutional monarchy.

However, the success of the new regime depended on the personality of the Czar and the willingness of his advisers to work with the Duma. Nicholas II, like his cousin William II of Germany, was not suited to his responsibilities. Though a well-meaning man, he was not the person to undertake and direct a basic reform of the system. Moreover, he did not give a great deal of time to government, for he was mainly devoted to his family. Thus he often appointed poor advisers and, when in doubt, behaved as an old-fashioned autocrat rather than a constitutional monarch. In fact, neither the Czar nor his advisers wished to see a strong, liberal Duma established. As revolutionary agitation died down after the October Manifesto and the granting of a constitution, the czarist regime began to reconsider its position on reform. It enforced a new electoral law in 1907 which limited the vote to those who had some property. And while the Duma continued to be elected and continued to meet, it frequently supported the Czar rather than taking an independent course, and parliamentary power began to erode.

THE RUSSIAN INTELLIGENTSIA AND THE RISE OF LENIN

In the eighteenth century the Russian intellectual class learned French, corresponded with the philosophers, and emulated the style of the French court. In the early nineteenth century many became "Westerners" and stood in opposition to the autocratic system. In the late nineteenth century intellectuals read deeply in political philosophy from Aristotle to Marx, became alienated from the existing system, and learned to be revolutionaries. Thus, in spite of the growth of the Slavophile idea, Russia was so deeply

affected by Western ideas that a good portion of its intellectual class became alienated from traditional values. Even the Slavophiles, who defended that which they felt to be both unique and good in the Russian tradition, did not defend the prevailing autocratic political system. In Russia by the late nineteenth century, the terms "intelligentsia" and "radical" meant the same thing for most people.

The first serious revolutionary movement emerged in the 1860s. Its slogan was "to go to the people." These "populist" revolutionaries were agrarian socialists, believing that by undertaking agricultural reform, Russia could transform itself into a socialist state with a contented peasant class. They undertook to go out to the villages and urge the peasants to overthrow the tyranny of the Czar. However, the peasants usually responded with bewilderment because they could not imagine a world without a czar. When the attempt to form a peasant mass movement failed, many intellectuals were disillusioned. Some, calling themselves "Socialist Revolutionaries," became anarchists and resorted to terrorist tactics. Attempts were made on the life of the Czar and on members of the aristocracy in the 1860s and 1870s, and in 1881 they succeeded in killing Alexander II. When political parties began developing in Russia, the Socialist Revolutionaries brought their concern for peasant socialism to the political arena. They were a popular party in the early twentieth century, because they had a program for peasant Russia which they had been advocating since the 1860s.

Socialism was the major ideological attraction for many Russian radicals. The first important Russian disciple of Marx was George Plekhanov (1857–1918), who was an orthodox Marxist, not a revisionist, and thus felt that Russia had to develop a bourgeois industrial society before it could advance towards the next stage, socialism. To those who wanted a socialist state immediately and viewed Russia as part of the larger international socialist movement, Plekhanov preached patience. He looked forward to the development of a bourgeois liberal democracy because, according to the Marxist pattern of history, it would be overthrown in turn by a proletarian revolution. Thus, to achieve his goals and help the process of social change, Plekhanov was willing to cooperate with liberal reformers. The Russian Marxists formed the Social Democratic Party, an underground group which had its first congress in 1898.

Another political organization, the Constitutional Democrats (or Cadets), adopted the liberal, constitutional ideas of the West. This was a more moderate group than the various socialist parties. Formed in 1905, the Cadet Party was linked to the small Russian middle class. It advocated universal manhood suffrage and parliamentary government and, though it also had a policy of land redistribution, was inclined to work with the Czar and his advisers hoping to reform Russia through constitutional means.

Lenin (1870–1924) became the leader of the second generation of Marxists. He is the most influential Marxist of this century and possibly the single most important political figure in the world in the period after the First World War. He came from a middle-class family—his father was a school inspector—but his older brother was a member of a Social Revolutionary terrorist group, and was hung by czarist authorities in 1887. His brother's death had a permanent affect on Lenin's life. Had Lenin been born in England, he might have become a politician or a professor; in Russia, partly as a result of his brother's execution, he became a revolutionary. His sense of alienation from Russian society may have been intensified because he was a member of the *bourgeoisie* in a land with a very small *bourgeoisie*. At any rate, he devoted himself to radical change, convinced that the existing system was so backward that it would have to tumble before anything positive could be built. Severely honest, Lenin had extraordinary zeal for his cause; it was the only thing that mattered. His capacity for work was enormous, but above all he had a fertile and exceptional mind. This combination of traits made him a dangerous revolutionary.

In eighteenth-century France there had been a generation of intellectuals who set the stage for revolution and a following generation of bourgeois revolutionaries who carried it out. In Russia and other "underdeveloped" countries of the twentieth century, the intellectuals have often been the revolutionaries. They create a new ideology, lead political and social movements, and establish a new regime.

In 1891 Lenin graduated in law from the University of St. Petersburg; in 1895 he joined a Marxist group in that city. After living for a brief period outside of Russia, he returned and was arrested by the authorities and exiled to Siberia. His exile, from 1897 to 1900, was not an especially difficult one; he lived comfortably, studied, and wrote. On his release he left Russia, joined fellow members of the Social Democratic Party abroad, and continued his revolutionary activities.

Lenin did not accept the political techniques of Plekhanov or the revisionist theories of men such as Bernstein, which were so popular in Europe at the turn of the century. Liberal democracy, he thought, could do nothing for the masses because it was a disguise for the tyranny of the middle class over the proletariat. But he also rejected democratic socialism because he felt it was a perversion of true socialist thought, a way of continuing capitalist rule while pretending to govern in the name of the people.

Lenin added a new ingredient to Marxism, one which was eventually to make socialism and communism quite distinct. Realizing that a successful revolution could be accomplished only by careful organization, Lenin insisted that a tight, well-disciplined group of people was needed to lead the revolution on behalf of the proletariat. This group would be made of loyal and committed revolutionaries, who could be intellectuals, members of the middle class, or workers. Lenin felt that one did not have to wait for history to create a spontaneous rebellion by the peasants or the proletariat; a revolution could be made by a "vanguard of the proletariat," acting in the name of the whole.

Lenin's concept of a small, elite party was outlined in his pamphlet *What Is to Be Done?*, written in 1902. He argued that the proletariat were not capable of organizing a successful revolutionary movement by themselves. They must be led by a well-disciplined party whose members shared absolute agreement on principles. Lenin stated that the "most imperative [principle is] to establish an *organization of revolutionists* capable of maintaining the energy, the stability and continuity of the political struggle."[4] This was to be a group of professional revolutionaries hostile to all other political groups. Lenin was not, then, building a political party in the traditional Western sense; he was creating a new ideology of action which demanded the total devotion of each member in the movement. The goal of this elite group was to seize political power, take over the machinery of the state, and eliminate all other political forces. Lenin thus invented an idea which has had a varied history in the twentieth century: the idea of a single totalitarian party, ruling the state on behalf of everyone.

In 1903, at a congress of the Social Democratic Party in London, Lenin split the party in two. While he argued that the party should be organized along the lines he had laid down in *What Is to Be Done?*, his opponents wanted a party with a broad democratic base. They claimed that to adopt Lenin's idea was to perpetuate the kind of elitism they were working to destroy. Lenin introduced a motion in support of his organizing principles, but lost. However, after some of his opponents left, Lenin's motion was reintroduced and passed. From this moment on, supporters of Lenin were known as Bolsheviks (or "the majority"), while those who supported his opponents were known as Mensheviks (or "the minority"). However, despite these labels, Lenin's group was, by its exclusive nature, very small; until 1917 the Mensheviks had the support of a majority of Russian Marxists. Despite the divisions of 1903, Mensheviks and Bolsheviks continued to work within the Social Democratic Party until 1912, when the Bolsheviks left to form their own group. But even then the Bolsheviks were just one of many small parties hoping to overthrow the czarist system.

Unlike so many socialists, Lenin was not carried away by the nationalist fervour which overtook most people in 1914. When the war broke out, he immediately condemned it as an "imperialist" venture, brought about because of the competition of capitalist nations for markets. In October 1914 he wrote:

The European war, for which the governments and the bourgeois parties of all countries have been preparing for decades, has broken out. The growth of armaments, the extreme intensification of the struggle for markets in the epoch of the latest, the imperialist, stage of capitalist development in the advanced countries, and the dynastic interests of the most backward East European monarchies were inevitably bound to lead, and have led, to this war. Seizure of territory and subjugation of foreign nations, ruin of a competing nation and plunder of its wealth, diverting the attention of the working masses from the internal political crises in Russia, Germany, England and other countries, disuniting and nationalist doping of the workers and the extermination of their vanguard with the object of weakening the revolutionary movement of the proletariat—such is the only real meaning, substance and significance of the present war.

On Social Democracy, primarily, rests the duty of disclosing this true meaning of the war and nationalist doping of the workers and the sophistry and "patriotic" phrase-mongering spread by the ruling classes, the landlords and the bourgeoisie, in defence of the war.[5]

During the war Lenin was in exile in Switzerland, defining his policies and working for revolution in Russia. The odds were overwhelmingly against such an exile ever succeeding in his program, for Lenin had only a few supporters, little money, and a policy which was opposed to Russian nationalist aspirations. His cause, at this time, looked hopeless; he appeared to be only one of many Russian revolutionaries out of touch with political and military reality.

RUSSIA AT WAR

The war went badly for Russia. Though Britain and France were Russia's allies, Russia was isolated geographically on Germany's eastern front. It was difficult to obtain any great resources from friends. Russia had been in this position in the past, and at times, such as in the war against Napoleon, had won glorious victories. However, in twentieth-century mechanized warfare, supplies, weapons, and food had to be moved quickly over great distances, and here the inefficient and incompetent czarist regime failed in its organization. Mobilization of troops was very slow, food shortages were ever present, and the soldiers were badly supplied.

The ravages of the war brought home to Russians the weaknesses of the czarist autocracy. By the end of 1915, it is estimated, over two million troops had been killed. People who had supported the regime now began to question its handling of the war. In 1915 the Duma, which was not composed of revolutionaries, demanded a larger share in the government but the Czar would not agree. Moderates, who still believed in Russia's cause and supported the war, ceased to believe in Nicholas II's ability to lead the country to victory.

Nicholas, like the czars of old, conducted the war as if it was a personal affair, and in September 1915 he went to the front to lead his troops. In his absence his wife, the Czarina Alexandra, conducted the government. She was a woman who loved her family, loathed the people, had contempt for any parliamentary form of government, and wanted Nicholas II to be another Peter the Great. Both she and the Czar were devoted to their son, the heir to the throne, who had hemophilia, a disease which caused him to bleed profusely as a result of the smallest cut and constantly threatened his health and life. She put great trust in the monk Rasputin, a spellbinding madman, who was the only person able to control the boy's bleeding. As a result, Rasputin had the total confidence of Alexandra and the two, in Nicholas's absence, appointed a series of unqualified men to the highest and most responsible positions in the state. By going to the front, Nicholas did not help the military effort, and his absence from the centre of power at the court hastened the deterioration of government. Commenting on one of

A Russian cartoon portraying Czar Nicholas and Czarina Alexandra in the control of Rasputin

Rasputin's recommendations in 1916, Nicholas wrote his wife:

Our Friend's opinions of people are sometimes very strange, as you know yourself—therefore one must be careful, especially with appointments to high office. . . . All these changes make my head go round. In my opinion, they are too frequent. In any case, they are not good for the internal situation of the country, as each new man brings with him alterations in the administration.[6]

Yet, within a month of writing this, Nicholas had agreed to Rasputin's suggestion.

The prestige of the Czar and his family was falling even among the more moderate and conservative of his followers. The Cadets in the Duma of 1916 began to ask whether Nicholas and his court were fit to govern. The aristocracy resented Rasputin's hold over the Czarina and his influence in government. In December 1916 he was assassinated by a group of nobles. When this failed to improve the quality of government, even those who ordinarily stood for the *status quo*, or moderate and peaceful change, began to think that extreme measures were necessary.

In early 1917 there seemed to be no centre of power in Russia—a Russia fighting for its very survival. The Czar was unable to govern, the court was corrupt and isolated, and the generals did not have the means to carry out successful campaigns. By now troops on the front, tired of fighting and lacking supplies, began to defect. In a time of crisis, the autocratic political regime was failing badly. And the Duma had no effective power.

THE MARCH REVOLUTION
OF 1917*

In March 1917 rioting broke out in Petrograd, renamed during the war because the older name, St. Petersburg, had a German connotation. Although it began among people who were short of food, the rioting spread to the factories and the troops. It became questionable whether the Czar could keep public order when his troops, sympathetic to the plight of the people, would not fire on the rioters. On March 4 the Czar dissolved the Duma, which had continued to be highly critical of his government, but its members decided to remain in session and public opinion supported them. The Duma asked the Czar to abdicate. Finding himself with little support, Nicholas vacated the throne, assuming that his brother Michael would succeed him. However, Michael refused to take the throne, and power was now placed in the hands of a Provisional Government that had been established by the Duma.

During the confusion of the March Revolution, the soviets, which had first been

* The Russian state did not adopt the Western calendar until February 1918. The old calendar is thirteen days behind the Western-style one. Hence, in Russia, what we refer to as the March Revolution is called the February Revolution. The November Revolution, November 7 in the new calendar, occurred on October 25 in the old-style calendar and is called the October Revolution.[8]

constituted in the revolution of 1905, reappeared. The most important of these, the Petrograd Soviet, was formed on March 12. Starting out as a workers' committee, it soon included soldiers, and called itself the Soviet of Workers' and Soldiers' Deputies. Though neither the Petrograd Soviet nor any of the others which appeared throughout the country had any legal standing, they were very powerful institutions. Workers looked to the soviets for leadership and saw them as protectors of their interests, while soldiers relied on these organizations to shield them from the incompetence and arbitrariness of the army commanders. Indeed, the Petrograd Soviet was soon issuing orders to soldiers and controlled much of the garrison stationed in Petrograd. Thus, although the Provisional Government had legal power, the soviets had become powerful forces in their own right.

The Provisional Government attempted to govern until a Constituent Assembly could meet, draw up a new constitution, and establish a new legal authority. Russia's allies recognized the Provisional Government immediately; secretly happy that the Czar had fallen, they hoped that the Provisional Government would be able to carry on the war effort more effectively than the old regime. The Provisional Government tried to do this, and under the leadership of Alexander Kerensky (1881–1970), a moderate socialist, it set out to win the war and reorganize Russia as a democratic state. Under the circumstances its task was extremely difficult.

Lenin learned of the March Revolution by reading about it in a Swiss newspaper, and he immediately set out for Russia. His return to his native country, however, was arranged in a very special way—via a sealed train through Germany. The Germans were quite happy to let one of the major critics of the war return to his native land to foment disorder. On his arrival in Petrograd, Lenin found that the Bolsheviks were supporting the Provisional Government. This he regarded as a mistake, and in April 1917 he laid down a program which has come to be called the April Theses. The war, he said,

A view of Lenin as hero, addressing workers and soldiers in 1917 (Drawn by P. N. Staronossow)

should not be continued, but should be stopped at once: "In our attitude towards the war . . . not the slightest concession is permissible." He analysed conditions in Russia in this way:

It is a specific feature of the present situation in Russia that it represents a *transition* from the first stage of the revolution—which, owing to the insufficient class-consciousness and organization of the proletariat, placed power in the hands of the bourgeoisie—to its *second* stage, which must place power in the hands of the proletariat and the poorest sections of the peasants.

This transition is characterized, on the one hand, by a maximum of legally recognized rights (Russia is *now* the freest of all the belligerent countries in the world); on the other, by the absence of violence in relation to the people; and, finally, by the unreasoning confidence of the people in the Government of capitalists, the worst enemies of peace and socialism.

This peculiar situation demands of us an ability to adapt ourselves to the *special* conditions of Party work among unprecedentedly large masses of proletarians who have just awakened to political life.[7]

Hence, he stated, the Bolsheviks should give no support to the Provisional Government. The true form of revolutionary government was the soviet, not the Duma, for the soviets were more directly representative of the people. Moreover, he demanded "nationalization of *all* lands in the country"; and the local soviets were to be given control of the land.

The slogan of the Bolsheviks thus became "all power to the soviets." But their real objective was to gain control of the soviets and

A demonstration in Petrograd, July 1, 1917 (Novosti Press Agency)

then, when the soviets had been given greater authority, of the state itself. Lenin did not care about majorities and mass opinion. Indeed, the Bolsheviks were a very small group in 1917; Lenin said there were 240 000 in mid-1917, but experts feel that even that number, which is relatively small for a country the size of Russia, was a great exaggeration. A figure between 20 000 and 40 000 is more likely. But Lenin believed that he understood the course of history and was prepared to lead the way to a com-

munist state, rather than wait on the will of a majority.

Almost all of the socialists, including many Bolsheviks, were shocked at Lenin's desire to do away so quickly with the "bourgeois revolution" (that is, the Provisional Government), which had been deemed a necessary stage in the communist revolution by Marx himself. But Lenin had revised Marx to deal with circumstances in Russia as he saw them, and the new ideology which he imposed on Russia should be called "Bolshevism," or "Leninism," rather than simply "Marxism."

THE NOVEMBER REVOLUTION OF 1917

As the military and internal situation deteriorated, Kerensky had great difficulty in governing. He was caught between the parties of the right, who wanted him to hold the line, and the parties of the left, who wanted him to make immediate changes. In September a representative of the right, General Kornilov, tried to bring about a *coup d'état*. Kerensky weathered the storm, but only with the assistance of the soviets and the parties of the left, who preferred him to a return to reaction. But Kerensky's continuation at the head of the Provisional Government was now dependent upon the support of the left, and he was beginning to lose his own followers. And, after September 1917, the Social Democrats and the Social Revolutionaries withdrew their support from the Provisional Government, demanding peace and a new division of land.

The Bolsheviks, hitherto a fringe group, began to gain seats in the elections to offices within the soviets. By November they had a majority in the Petrograd and Moscow soviets, and over 300 of the 650 delegates chosen for an All-Russian Congress of Soviets, scheduled to meet in November, were Bolshevik supporters. To understand the success of the Bolsheviks in these elections, we must not forget that by mid-1917, Lenin and his party were the only significant group which had consistently opposed the war. Now that this had become a widespread opinion, they were bound to gain popularity.

After he had returned to Russia in April 1917, Lenin had been joined by Leon Trotsky (1879–1940). Trotsky was an independent Marxist, had been a Social Democrat for some time, and on occasion had allied himself with the Mensheviks. He was well known in Petrograd, having been a president of the St. Petersburg Soviet in 1905. He had a "revolutionary" past, was one of the leading members of the Russian intelligentsia, and was an extraordinary orator. After the March Revolution he addressed the Petrograd Soviet and recommended that

the next step should be the handing over [of] all power to the Soviet of Workers' and Soldiers' Deputies. Only with the authority [concentrated] in one hand can Russia be saved. Long live the Russian Revolution as the prologue to the world revolution.[8]

Although Lenin was the leader of the Bolsheviks, Trotsky was much better known at the time and was more trusted by the lower classes. He gradually gained control of the Petrograd Soviet, becoming its head on October 3, and then began to organize the Soviet as a force against the Provisional Government. Trotsky was very careful not to say publicly that he now regarded the soviets as part of the Bolshevik machinery, to be used to seize power. The attack on the Provisional Government would be made in the name of the soviets, which could be shown to represent many of the Russian people, whereas the same could not be said of the relatively small and select Bolshevik Party.

The vital question that had to be considered by the Central Committee, the governing body of the Bolshevik Party, was when to attempt to overthrow the Provisional Government. At a meeting on October 23, Lenin said he was convinced that the moment had come. Several members wanted to wait, thinking that the Bolsheviks did not yet have enough support in the country. They feared that if the soviets took power, the Bolsheviks might not be able to control the soviets. Lenin, with Trotsky's support, persuaded the doubters that they should seize power when they could, and that their best chance was now.

In grappling with this issue, Lenin and his followers were faced with a practical problem that arose out of Marxist thought. According to the Marxist analysis, Russia had hardly gone through the bourgeois phase of its transformation to communism; how could it be ripe for a proletarian revolution? Lenin felt, however, that to be too devoted to theory in a time of revolutionary action would weaken any movement. He considered any tactic acceptable as long as it helped him attain the ultimate goal—control of the state in order to inaugurate a communist society. Faced with the possibility of gaining power, Lenin put revolutionary practice before socialist theory.

On November 7 an All-Russian Congress of Soviets was scheduled to meet in Petrograd, and Trotsky, who was organizing the seizure of power, judged it a good moment to strike. On November 6 the Bolsheviks, claiming that the parties of the right were organizing a revolution, overthrew the Provisional Government with the help of the military and the Petrograd Soviet. On November 7 the All-Russian Congress of Soviets declared that the Provisional Government was no more, and that power was now in the hands of a committee headed by Lenin.

On the afternoon of November 7, with Trotsky in the chair, Lenin addressed the Petrograd Soviet:

Comrades, the workmen's and peasants' revolution, the need of which the Bolsheviks have emphasized many times, has come to pass.

What is the significance of this revolution? Its significance is, in the first place, that we shall have a soviet government, without the participation of bourgeoisie of any kind. The oppressed masses will of themselves form a government. The old state machinery will be smashed into bits and in its place will be created a new machinery of government by the soviet organizations. From now on there is a new page in the history of Russia, and the present ... Russian revolution shall in its final result lead to the victory of Socialism.

One of our immediate tasks is to put an end to the war at once. But in order to end the war, which is closely bound up with the present capitalistic system, it is necessary to overthrow capitalism itself. In this work we shall have the aid of the world labor movement, which has already begun to develop in Italy, England, and Germany....

In the interior of Russia a very large part of the peasantry has said: Enough playing with the capitalists; we will go with the workers. We shall secure the confidence of the peasants by one decree, which will wipe out the private property of the landowners. The peasants will understand that their only salvation is in union with the workers.

We will establish a real labor control on production.

We have now learned to work together in a friendly manner, as is evident from this revolution. We have the force of mass organization which has conquered all and which will lead the proletariat to world revolution.

We should now occupy ourselves in Russia in building up a proletarian socialist state.

Long live the world-wide socialistic revolution.[9]

The Bolsheviks had carried out a successful *coup d'état* in the midst of a larger revolution and had thereby gained control of the Russian political machinery. It was not a very bloody uprising. The Provisional Government was in the process of collapse, few defended it, and Kerensky fled into exile. Not many people in Russia believed that this was the end of the transfers of power that had begun in March 1917. Although the Bolsheviks were being compared with the Jacobins of the French Revolution, they would, unlike the Jacobins, remain in power. Lenin's greatest accomplishment lay not in seizing power but in holding it.

LENIN'S RUSSIA

Lenin had no illusions about the nature of revolution. When a measure was proposed to repeal the death penalty for soldiers, Trotsky reported that Lenin exploded with rage:

That is madness.... How can we accomplish a revolution without shooting? Do you think you can settle with your enemies if you disarm?[10]

Above all, Lenin was determined that the Revolution should succeed. The tactics could change, but not the goals.

Few realized in November 1917 that Lenin intended to set up a one-party state. Soon, however, the meaning of Bolshevik control became clear. Freedom of the press was immediately curtailed, and a secret police, the CHEKA, was established in December 1918 in order to "suppress counter-revolution". Lenin sometimes regretted the stern measures which he considered necessary in order to create his proletarian revolution, but he regarded the first few years of control as a "transitional dictatorship of the proletariat," a time of upheaval when it was necessary to do evil in order to create the conditions out of which a true communist state would emerge. While he did not believe in repression, he felt that such steps were necessary at the time in order to achieve his ends.

The elections to the Constituent Assembly, which had been promised by Kerensky's government, were allowed to proceed in late November 1917. The Social Revolutionaries, not the Bolsheviks, were the victors, winning 370 out of approximately 700 delegates. Most Russians felt that the Social Revolutionary Party, with its long-standing concern for peasant Russia and its long history of opposition to czarist autocracy, best represented their views at the time. The Bolsheviks, a clear minority in the Constituent Assembly with approximately 168 delegates, stalked out of the first meeting of the Assembly on January 18, 1918. But the Assembly continued to meet without them. Lenin, however, would not tolerate another centre of power, or any other group claiming to be the legitimate representative of the people. When the Assembly tried to meet again the

next day, it was dissolved by troops under Bolshevik orders. This was the first and last freely elected assembly in Russia after Bolshevik rule.

Lenin was determined to put an end to Russia's participation in the war and sent Trotsky to negotiate with the Germans. Although the Germans laid down harsh conditions, Lenin was willing to give up much in order to end the hated war. On March 15, 1918, the Treaty of Brest-Litovsk was signed between Russia and Germany. On paper it was a disaster for Russia, which gave up twenty-six per cent of its territories, seventy-five per cent of its coal mines, and, in the Ukraine, its richest grain area. Having lost so much land on Russia's western border, Lenin moved his government into the interior of the country to the old capital of Moscow.

A civil war broke out in 1918 between the Bolsheviks, who came to be known as the "Reds," and a group of their opponents, styled the "Whites." The "Whites" were a mixed group, led by Social Revolutionaries, Cadets, and some members of the old privileged class. They were not reactionary but

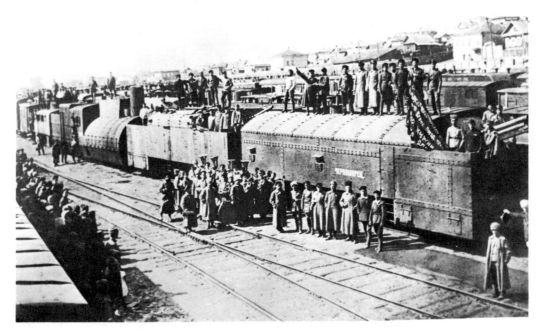

A Red Guard train carrying soldiers, 1918 (Novosti Press Agency)

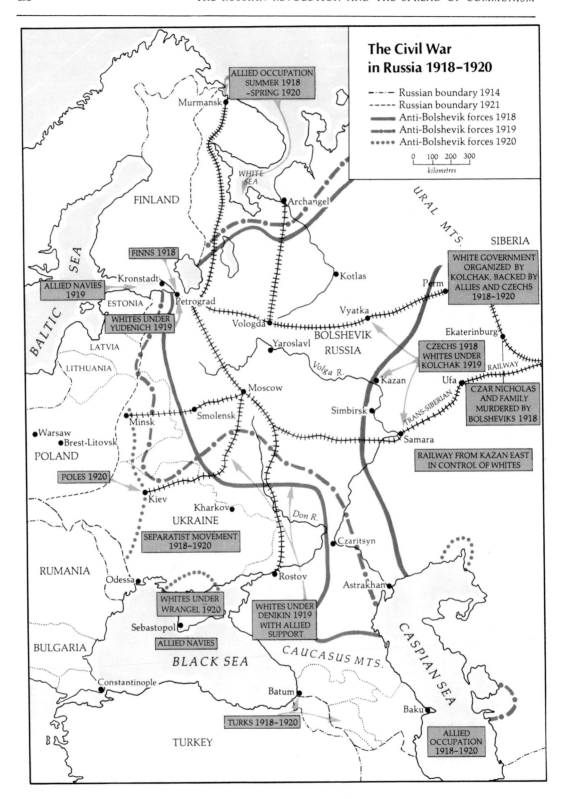

The Civil War in Russia 1918–1920

- –·–·– Russian boundary 1914
- – – – – Russian boundary 1921
- ▬▬▬ Anti-Bolshevik forces 1918
- ▬●▬●▬ Anti-Bolshevik forces 1919
- ●●●● Anti-Bolshevik forces 1920

0   100 200 300
kilometres

ALLIED OCCUPATION SUMMER 1918 –SPRING 1920

Murmansk

WHITE SEA

FINLAND

Archangel

FINNS 1918

Kronstadt

ALLIED NAVIES 1919

ESTONIA

Petrograd

WHITES UNDER YUDENICH 1919

LATVIA

LITHUANIA

Vologda

BALTIC SEA

Kotlas

Perm

SIBERIA

WHITE GOVERNMENT ORGANIZED BY KOLCHAK, BACKED BY ALLIES AND CZECHS 1918–1920

URAL MTS.

Vyatka

BOLSHEVIK RUSSIA

Ekaterinburg

Yaroslavl

Volga R.

CZECHS 1918 WHITES UNDER KOLCHAK 1919

RAILWAY

Moscow

Kazan

Ufa

Warsaw

Brest-Litovsk

Minsk

Smolensk

Simbirsk

CZAR NICHOLAS AND FAMILY MURDERED BY BOLSHEVIKS 1918

TRANS-SIBERIAN

POLAND

Samara

POLES 1920

Kiev

Kharkov

Don R.

RAILWAY FROM KAZAN EAST IN CONTROL OF WHITES

UKRAINE

SEPARATIST MOVEMENT 1918–1920

Czaritsyn

RUMANIA

Odessa

Rostov

Astrakhan

WHITES UNDER WRANGEL 1920

WHITES UNDER DENIKIN 1919 WITH ALLIED SUPPORT

CASPIAN SEA

Sebastopol

BULGARIA

ALLIED NAVIES

BLACK SEA

CAUCASUS MTS.

Constantinople

Batum

Baku

TURKS 1918–1920

ALLIED OCCUPATION 1918–1920

TURKEY

moderate, and most were supporters of the March Revolution. What united them was their hatred of Lenin and the Bolsheviks. They wanted an assembly elected by universal suffrage rather than a return to the old czarist regime.

Trotsky was the outstanding figure for the "Reds" during the Civil War. He organized the "Red Army" and gave it extraordinary mobility—at one point it held back its enemies on as many as sixteen fronts. He placed the economy of areas controlled by the Bolsheviks in the hands of the Central Committee of the party and put all people and goods at the service of the state. The Bolsheviks had to fight contingents of troops from foreign countries including Britain, Japan, Canada, and the United States, as well as Russians who were anti-Bolshevist. But by 1920 the main opponents of the Bolshevik regime had been defeated.

When the Civil War ended, Lenin rethought his economic program, called "war communism," which had originally attempted to centralize and nationalize all economic activity. A New Economic Policy (NEP) was introduced in 1921. Realizing that the human and economic costs of complete nationalization outweighed the advantages, he introduced a mixed economy combining some private enterprise with some state ownership. By 1923 the NEP was working reasonably well, and production and exports were rising.

One of the early acts of the Bolsheviks, in March 1918, had been to change their name officially to the Communist Party, thereby distinguishing their ideology from all other varieties of socialism—utopian, democratic, or revisionist. They believed their main task was to change the life style of the Russian people, and of a large part of the world. Bolshevism, following the behaviourist approach of Marx, assumed that if one changed the way people produce and live, one also changed their culture and civilization.

From the start, the Bolsheviks used propaganda and indoctrination in order to spread their beliefs. They tried to encourage a generation gap, a rift between older Russians brought up under the czars and the new generation being raised under communism.

They persecuted the Russian Orthodox Church, so closely tied with the conservative forces of the old state, and they deprived its clergy of their civil rights.

Like the Jacobins, the Bolsheviks tried to introduce a new "Republic of Virtue," in which the party and its ideology became a state religion. Party ideology and doctrine became dogma, free individual expression was impossible, and all who opposed or criticized bolshevism were regarded as enemies and punished. A cult of leadership grew up around Lenin, who was seen as the heir of Marx, the one true apostle amid many claimants. He was regarded with almost religious awe. As time went on and public education developed, the Bolsheviks had at their disposal a literate populace. Using both force and modern psychology, they were able to solidify their control over the Russian people.

In 1924 Russia officially became the Union of Soviet Socialist Republics. This title recognized how important the soviets had been in establishing communist rule. More significantly, by suggesting a federation of semi-independent units, the Union was a concession to the various "national" groups composing Russia. Hence the state recognized language and cultural differences and hoped to maintain Russian unity by giving each group some autonomy while retaining central control of all important affairs. There were separatist movements within the federation, most notably in the Ukraine, but these were for the time being extinguished.

Although a government apparatus existed, the major decisions were made by the Communist Party, not the state authorities. The Party had a Central Committee (its executive core) with a Secretariat to serve it. The Central Committee, in turn, had two major sub-committees—an Orgburo, which organized the civil service of the party, and a Politburo, which made party policy. Thus Russia had become a single-party state, with a small nucleus of party officials making government policy. No dissent was tolerated: Lenin's idea of a party elite creating the proletarian revolution continued to be a distinctive feature of bolshevism.

LENIN'S DEATH AND
THE PROBLEM OF SUCCESSION

Once revolutions are successful, the revolutionaries have to turn to the practical task of governing. But, since no one person can run everyday affairs, an organization is necessary for this purpose. This means that a bureaucracy must be established and revolutionaries turned into administrators. The main organizer of this transformation was Joseph Stalin (1879–1953), originally Joseph Djugashvili, a shrewd, methodical man from Georgia, a province on the Russian-Turkish border. Stalin was not a cosmopolitan like other revolutionaries—he had never been outside Russia—nor was he an intellectual like Lenin or Trotsky. But he did have great administrative talents; and by 1923 he was the man who had given many party functionaries their jobs.

Lenin had a cerebral hemorrhage in May 1922, the first of a series which partly incapacitated him until his death in January 1924. From the moment of his first illness, he was continually worried about the succession to power. It was clear to him that the choice lay between Stalin and Trotsky, and he had reservations about both. He believed that Trotsky was not only distinguished "by his remarkable abilities" but was also "very likely the ablest person in the present [group of leaders]. . . ."[11] Yet Lenin thought Trotsky lacked the qualities necessary for political leadership in a time of revolutionary transition. Of Stalin, Lenin wrote on January 4, 1923:

Stalin is too rude and this defect, although quite tolerable in our midst and in dealings among us Communists, becomes intolerable in a Secretary-General. That is why I suggest that the comrades think about a way of removing Stalin from that post and appointing another man in his stead who [is] . . . more tolerant, more loyal, more polite and more considerate to the comrades, less capricious, etc.[12]

To Lenin, Stalin represented all that worried him about the course of events since November 1917.

Having created bolshevism, Lenin began to fear it. Instead of freeing the proletariat, a bureaucracy had been created which seemed to imprison them. It had been necessary in the period after 1917 to have summary justice and to do evil in order, as he saw it, to prevent the greater evil of reaction. But now that Communist power was stabilized, Lenin was seriously troubled about the means that might be adopted to achieve Communist ends. The bureaucracy which had been created to achieve the proletarian revolution seemed to be developing a life of its own, to be functioning for its own ends. The human goals of the revolution seemed to be disappearing under a mountain of paperwork.

For all his human values and lack of personal vanity, Lenin left a strange legacy. He set out to create a spirited, zealous, revolutionary party, and he left a complicated ponderous party machine. His life was dedicated to freeing the masses from oppression, but he was instrumental in establishing an enduring totalitarian state run by an elite. He hated the czar's secret police, yet he established a secret service that was far more inhumane and efficient than its predecessor. His methods of achieving and consolidating power have been used by totalitarian dictators, both of the left and right, everywhere. And for all his self-effacement, he has been turned into a legend. Lenin's writings have become part of the permanent dogma of communism, and today in the Soviet Union, the most revered place is Lenin's tomb, which has become a "religious" shrine.

STALIN'S RUSSIA

Lenin's death left Trotsky and Stalin as the chief contenders for power. Trotsky came out for open elections to the party leadership, a loosening of the bureaucracy, and "permanent revolution," a policy of using Russia as a base in order to foment world communist revolutions. Stalin, in control of the bureaucracy, insisted that the better policy was "socialism in one country"—the development of industrialization in Russia and the firm establishment of a powerful socialist state there before pursuing an aggressive foreign policy. Stalin won because of his cunning and ability to organize various coalitions against Trotsky. But Trotsky contributed to his own defeat. Though he headed the army until January 1925, he did not use his position to place himself in power; he would not, he said, be a Napoleon. Trotsky was attached to Marxist theory, which assumed that the proletarian revolution was the inevitable outcome of the historical process. He was thus unwilling to attempt a new seizure of power, and this meant Stalin emerged the victor in the contest for leadership of the party. Under Stalin's direction, Trotsky was thrown out of the Communist Party in 1927 and exiled from Russia two years later. In 1940 he was assassinated at his home in Mexico by a Stalinist agent.

By the late 1930s Stalin was dictator of Russia, remaining firmly entrenched until his death in 1953. Many historians, accepting Trotsky's analysis of this development, have remarked upon the elements of continuity in Russian history: Stalin had become the new czar who completed the Westernization of Russia that had been started by Czar Peter the Great in 1696.

"Socialism in one country" was Stalin's early policy. The way to do this, he felt, was to replace Lenin's NEP with a rigidly planned economy. In 1928 he inaugurated Russia's First Five-Year Plan, hoping to develop heavy industry rapidly. The human cost was high: few consumers' goods were produced, and people were forced into labour against their will; nevertheless, the policy was thought to be essential. The First Five-Year Plan was followed by a second, from 1932 to 1937. In ten years iron and steel production expanded fourfold, while coal production rose by three and one-half. By the mid-1930s Russia had surpassed its 1913 production figures in iron, coal, and oil, which, until then, had represented a peak, production having declined during the world war and after Lenin's death. No country had ever industrialized so quickly, and the lesson was not lost on the rest of the world. Stalin's success became one of the motives for a turn to communism in underdeveloped countries. Using the methods of Communist Russia, these countries hoped to pass

from a pre-industrial society to a highly industrial state in one leap.

As part of his new policy, Stalin ordered that farms be collectivized. Communists felt that this would be more efficient and in accord with Marxist theory; Stalin wished to collectivize agriculture in order to control farm production and the millions engaged in it. With the resources of Russian agriculture at his disposal, he could divert capital formerly used for farming into his new industrial enterprises.

In 1929, as a result, collectivization was begun. The policy was directed mainly against people known as *kulaks*—peasants who had some land of their own, were well off, and produced enough surplus food to sell on the open market. In December 1929 Stalin spoke about his new agrarian policy:

The characteristic feature in the work of our Party during the past year is that we, as a party, as the Soviet Power:
a) have developed an offensive along the whole front against capitalist elements in the countryside;
b) that this offensive, as you know, has yielded and continues to yield very appreciable, *positive* results.

What does this mean? It means that we have passed from the policy of *restricting* the exploiting tendencies of the kulaks to the policy of *eliminating* the kulaks as a class. It means that we have carried out, one of the decisive turns in our whole policy. . . .

Today, we have an adequate material base [from which] to strike at the kulaks, to break their resistance, to eliminate them as a class, and to *replace* their output by the output of the collective farms and state farms.[13]

In effect, Stalin hoped to take land from people who had acquired it since 1861 or, in some cases, since 1917 and force all peasants to work for the state as part of a collective commune.

Many peasants, especially *kulaks*, resisted collectivization. When agents of the state came to expropriate lands, the peasants often fought them, and they slaughtered their own cattle rather than turn them over to the state authorities. None the less, Stalin persisted. People were relocated, many sent to forced-labour camps in Siberia, and millions were killed or died (estimates run from five to ten million) in a guerilla war between peasants and the state. To the extent that Stalin was determined to bring about collectivization, his policy succeeded. By 1934 over seventy per cent of the farms in Russia were collectivized, and the *kulaks* had been eliminated as a class. Many peasants, having been uprooted, went to the cities and became workers in factories.

Under Stalin, Russia was the most organized large state the world had ever seen. It was run by a single party, and the party was led by Stalin, who officially held the post of Party Secretary. As a result of this situation, a new elite emerged in the Soviet Union—the leaders of the party. As Milovan Djilas of Yugoslavia pointed out in the 1950s, a "new class" has appeared in our time—the managers, the people who organize and control a party and a state.

As noted previously, the party believed that it had a monopoly on truth and therefore suppressed dissent, sometimes ruthlessly. But in 1932 Stalin began a purge of the Communist Party itself. He thought it was necessary to eliminate all possible rivals and to make certain that his personal power was secure from attacks by critics—both the young who took Marx seriously and the old who had fought for the revolution and were appalled by Stalin's regime. Stalin was a highly suspicious man and feared even minor dissent. In 1934, in what many have called a modern "reign of terror," Stalin intensified his purge. One of the major party leaders, Sergei Kirov, had been recently assassinated, and, although it is probable that Stalin himself arranged the murder to eliminate a possible rival, he used the Kirov episode to set off a massive campaign against those whom he regarded as opponents of his program. On December 1, 1934, the Central Committee issued the following order:

1. Investigative agencies are directed to speed up the cases of those accused of the preparation or execution of acts of terror.

2. Judicial organs are directed not to hold up

the execution of death sentences pertaining to crimes of this category. . . .

3. The organs of the [secret police] are directed to execute death sentences against criminals of the above-mentioned category immediately after the passage of sentences.[14]

By 1938 the purge had resulted in the execution of a large number of the "old Bolsheviks" who had fought with Lenin for the revolution. It had also created an atmosphere of fear throughout the Soviet Union; people trembled lest the next knock on their door would be the secret police. "Trials" were conducted in which men who had been loyal to the party "confessed" to having betrayed the revolution. Though originally directed against Stalin's opponents, real or imaginary, within the ruling circles, the terror affected millions of people. Many were executed and large numbers were sent to prison or used as forced labour. By the end of this process Russia was a tight police state in which no opposition to Stalin in word, deed, or thought was tolerated.

One of the ordinary party members who was purged was Evgeniia Semyonovna Ginsburg, the wife of a Communist Party official. She stated in her memoirs that in 1934 "had I been ordered to die for the Party not once but three times . . . I would have obeyed without a moment's hesitation. I had not the slightest doubt that the Party's line was right." She described the atmosphere in the Soviet Union in early 1937:

After each trial, the screw was turned tighter. The dreadful term "enemies of the people" came into use. By some lunatic logic every region . . . had to have its own crop of enemies so as not to fall behind the others, for all the world as though it were a yearly campaign for deliveries of grain and milk.[15]

By mid-1937, "the agencies involved [with carrying out the purges] were inhumanly overworked. People were run off their feet; transport was insufficient; cells were crowded to bursting; the courts sat twenty-four hours a day."[16] Arrested along with many others, Mrs. Ginsburg underwent torture and terror. She was imprisoned for eighteen years and released in 1955, after the death of Stalin.

Under Stalin, communism, for all its international roots and aspirations, was becoming nationalized. His main interest was Russia, not world revolution, and he asked the Russian peasants and workers to produce for "mother Russia," not simply to prove the value of the communist system. In the 1930s Stalin painted Russia as the "Socialist Fatherland" which was "encircled" by capitalist countries, as a land which had to defend itself against its enemies at all costs. Stalin encouraged the study of Russian history and pictured some of the czars, such as Ivan the Terrible who helped to create the Russian state, as heroes. The propaganda machine of the state turned out materials which supported Stalin's policies and attempted to portray him as a figure larger than life, a kind of hero on a par with Marx, Lenin, and the great czars.

What did all this have to do with Marxism? Very little. To force people to work for the state was the very opposite of what the early revolutionaries had hoped to achieve. Perpetual terror was hardly the ultimate goal to which Marx had aspired. Elitism was not equality, nor did the establishment of a totalitarian society represent the withering away of the state. Stalin's communism, like Lenin's bolshevism, must be understood in its own terms and as it was practised. Stalin followed in the tradition of Ivan the Terrible or Peter the Great much more than in the footsteps of Marx or Engels, and his brand of communism is often called "Stalinism."

THE SPREAD OF COMMUNISM IN EUROPE

The aim of Marxism was world revolution, and to further this aim Lenin in 1919 had initiated the Third (Communist) International, known as the Comintern. Unlike the First and Second Internationals, the Comintern, from the start, was meant to bring together an international communist elite in order to help spread the world revolution. A clear distinction was made between socialists, whom Lenin accused of having capitulated to bourgeois states, and communists, whom he considered to be the leaders of the international proletarian movement. The Comintern was restricted to communists and led by Bolsheviks, and its organization was highly centralized. In this way the split which had been developing between democratic socialism and communism had now emerged in an international organization. Though leaders of both ideologies claimed to be the heirs of Marx, they differed on such fundamental issues as the means to be used to attain power, the role of the democratic process and the relationship of Marxists to parliamentary authority. According to the statutes of the Comintern, approved at its second meeting in 1920:

It is the aim of the Communist International to fight by all available means, including armed struggle, for the overthrow of the international bourgeoisie and for the creation of an international Soviet republic as a transitional stage to the complete abolition of the State. The Communist International considers the dictatorship of the proletariat the only possible way to liberate mankind from the horrors of capitalism. And the Communist International considers the Soviet power the historically given form of this dictatorship of the proletariat. . . .

The Communist International supports to the full the conquests of the great proletarian revolution in Russia . . . and calls on the proletariat of the entire world to take the same path. The Communist International undertakes to support every Soviet republic, wherever it may be formed.

The Communist International recognizes that in order to hasten victory, the Workingmen's Association which is fighting to annihilate capitalism and create communism must have a strongly centralized organization. The Communist International must, in fact and in deed, be a single communist party of the entire world. The parties working in the various countries are but its separate sections. The organizational machinery of the Communist International must guarantee the workers of each country the opportunity of getting the utmost help from the organized proletariat of other countries at any given moment.[17]

In its early years the leaders of the Comintern had hopes that other successful communist revolutions would come about outside Russia. In Munich, Germany, a socialist rebellion broke out in April 1919. German communists joined the small uprising and took over leadership of the movement. The German government, however, stepped in and put down the rebellion in a few weeks. In Hungary a communist, Bela Kun, took control of the government in March 1919, set up a soviet-type regime, and abolished private property. His supporters unleashed a terrorist campaign, emulating Lenin's policies after November 1917. Reaction soon followed the terror, and Kun's government could not maintain control. In August his regime ended, giving way to a moderate group, which was shortly replaced by a reactionary government.

In the 1920s communism did win support in many countries, but was not strong enough to take power anywhere outside Russia. Germany had a strong communist party, as did France and Italy, while many other states had political groups which, though not calling themselves communist, were sympathetic to Comintern policies.

Several attempts were made to bring together the parties of the left, including the many varieties of socialists and communists. By 1921 it was evident that no basis of agreement could be reached between such widely differing ideologies, and communists and socialists began to see each other as enemies. In many countries they launched bitter attacks against one another.

It became clear that world revolution was not imminent, and, after the struggle for power in the Soviet Union between Stalin and Trotsky had been resolved, the Comintern came firmly under the control of the Politburo of the Soviet Union and by 1930 had become an arm of Russian foreign policy. The leaders of the Comintern now insisted that all other communist parties obey its orders and asked European communists to take a longer view of events. Instead of trying to foment immediate revolution, they were to be concerned at this time with developing a strong core of devoted revolutionaries, as Lenin had done prior to 1917. Preparations for seizing power were to be made, but few open revolutionary acts were to be attempted. Communists in this period, acting under Comintern orders, regarded socialists as their most dangerous opponents and opposed socialists and all other democratic groups throughout Europe. In some cases, as in Germany, this deliberate splitting of the forces of the left contributed to the victory of reactionaries or fascists.

In 1934 Stalin changed Comintern policy once more. Fascism was now on the rise, and fascists had already seized power in Italy and Germany. Communists had originally interpreted fascism as the last gasp of capitalism, but they soon realized that it was an aggressive, ruthless mass movement. Until now, Stalin had opposed any collaboration between European communists and all other groups and had sought to avoid alliances between Soviet Russia and other countries. In order to counter the threat from fascism and the right, the Comintern supported international agreements between the Soviet Union and other countries, while its leaders advocated political co-operation between communists and other groups of the left, including socialists and members of the *bourgeoisie*.

This change was signalled in 1934 by the request of the Soviet Union to join the League of Nations and by the making of diplomatic agreements with Czechoslovakia and France. Moreover, "popular fronts" were encouraged throughout Europe, in which moderates, socialists, and communists either collaborated to win elections or, where rightist dictators were in power, joined forces against the existing government. In 1936 a popular-front group won an electoral victory in France and formed a government. During the Spanish Civil War, the Comintern was active against the Spanish fascists, led by General Franco.

But, despite all this activity, by 1939 many states were governed by fascist or rightist groups. Popular-front governments had not eradicated the right, and moderate parties, still wary of communists, would not let them take the lead in popular-front movements. Indeed, France and England, the major states of western Europe, were making concessions to fascist Germany, and Stalin feared that they would encourage Germany to move into eastern Europe, particularly Russia. Thus Stalin and the Comintern changed tactics again. In August 1939 Soviet Russia signed a non-aggression pact with fascist Germany, ending the period of communist collaboration with moderate elements. The Soviet Union, Stalin insisted, must be protected at all costs, and he expected communists everywhere to accede to this reversal of his former policy.

Though communism from 1917 to 1939 remained a minority movement outside of Russia, it had followers virtually everywhere. Communist parties were small, but composed of people who devoted their lives to the cause. It is estimated that in 1928 there were over three million members of communist parties outside the Soviet Union. When one remembers that the party was constructed as an exclusive group of dedicated people, and that many more individuals were sympathetic to communism, this is not an inconsiderable figure. Most communists were able to shift tactics with the Comintern until the 1939 pact between the Soviet Union and Germany. Stalin's pact with Hitler, the dictator of Germany, made it difficult for many communists to swallow the new line. There was unhappiness in the ranks of the party and great disillusionment among many sympathizers. Yet the hard core of party stalwarts did not fall away.

THE SPREAD OF COMMUNISM IN THE FAR EAST

Mao Tse-tung (1893–1976) has stated that "it was through the Russians that the Chinese found Marxism." Although at first communism made fewer gains in non-developed than in developed countries, China, the most populous land in the world, began to feel the impact of it in the 1920s. India and Indonesia also had sizable communist groups, while organized communist parties were established in the Philippines and Annam (today part of Vietnam) in 1930. Many Eastern intellectuals looked to Russia for leadership and to the Comintern for guidance, but, as in most of Europe, Eastern communists were at this time in a minority. In this period, it was only in China that communists developed a strong party which became a serious contender for national leadership.

In 1900 China was a weak nation, with authority nominally centralized in the Manchu dynasty, which had been in power since 1644. However, after losing a war with the British in 1839, the Manchus gradually lost their grip on China, which became dominated by the imperialists of the West. The increasing control of areas of China by Western states, the loss of the Sino-Japanese War, and the suppression of the Boxer Rebellion by Western troops (see Chapter VII) continued to undermine the power of the Manchus.

Following the Boxer Rebellion in 1900, the Manchus pursued a policy of reform. In the words of one of the leaders of the court, it was "in order to make up China's shortcomings." New schools were started under the auspices of the government; a military reorganization along the lines of Western armies was begun; and an attempt at administrative reform was made in an effort to centralize power. According to some historians, these reforms only hastened the collapse of the Manchus, for many Chinese nationalists, angry at the rulers who had weakened the state and allowed it to come under foreign domination, were brought together in this futile attempt by the dynasty to keep itself in power.

The Manchus fell in 1911. The rebellion which overthrew them began in central China over an incident involving the discovery of a revolutionary group by the Chinese authorities. The army of the area, now trained in modern warfare, refused to support the Manchus and many soldiers, in a fervour of nationalist sentiment, joined the revolutionaries. The incident thus became a signal for other groups to attack the government, which had few defenders. A few months later the Manchu emperor formally abdicated and China became a republic. The country remained in turmoil for decades, and power was seized in many areas by local warlords, while various individuals and parties contended for control of the central government.

The Kuomintang (National People's Party) became one of the unifying elements in the country. Founded in 1912 as a union of several groups opposed to the Manchus, it was led by Sun Yat-sen (1867-1925), often called the "father of the Chinese Revolution." Sun lived many years in exile before the fall of the Manchus and thus was familiar with Western ideology. He stressed the importance of China's ancient culture and the uniqueness of its needs and wanted to work out a distinctively Chinese ideology tied to the twentieth century. He believed that China must modernize but saw this as a means to an end. His major goals were the freeing of China from foreign domination, the unification of the country under a responsive government, and the continuation of an old and cherished culture. Like most Chinese who opposed the policy of the Manchus, he stressed nationalism and emphasized Chinese autonomy in the face of foreign encroachments.

Sun's policy, called the "Three Principles of the People," was accepted by Chinese of all political persuasions. He listed these principles as "People's Nationalism, People's Sovereignty, People's Livelihood." In 1924 he explained his doctrine in this way:

Western revolutions began with the struggle for liberty; only after war and [the] agitation of two or three centuries was the liberty realized from which democracy sprang. The watchword of the French Revolution was "Liberty, Equality, Fraternity." Our watchword is "People's Nationalism, People's Sovereignty, People's Livelihood." What relation do the two watchwords have to each other? According to my interpretation, our Nationalism may be said to correspond to their Liberty, because putting the People's Nationalism into effect means a struggle for the liberty of our nation. The Europeans fought for individual liberty, but today we have a different use for liberty. Now how shall the term "liberty" be

applied? If we apply it to a person, we shall become a sheet of loose sand; on no account must we give more liberty to the individual; let us secure liberty instead for the nation. The individual should not have too much liberty, but the nation should have complete liberty. When the nation can act freely, then China may be called strong. To make the nation free, we must each sacrifice his personal freedom. Students who sacrifice their personal liberty will be able to work diligently day after day and spend time and effort upon learning; when their studies are completed, their knowledge is enlarged and their powers have multiplied, then they can do things for the nation. Soldiers who sacrifice their personal liberty will be able to obey orders, repay their country with loyalty and help the nation to attain liberty. If students and soldiers talk liberty, they will soon have "unrestrained license," to use a Chinese phrase for liberty. Schools will have no rules and the army will have no discipline. How can you have a school without rules? What kind of army is that without discipline?

Why do we want the nation to be free?— Because China under the domination of the [Western] Powers has lost her national standing. She is not merely a semi-colony; she has indeed become a hypo-colony, inferior to Burma and Annam and Korea. They are each the protectorate of one nation, the slave of one master. China is the colony of all the nations and the slave of all. In fact, we are now slaves to over ten masters; our national freedom is terribly restricted. If we want to restore China's liberty, we must unite ourselves into one unshakable body; we must use revolutionary methods to weld our state into firm unity. Without revolutionary principles we shall never succeed. Our revolutionary principles are the cement. If we can consolidate our four hundred millions and form a mighty union and make the union free, the Chinese state will be free and the Chinese people will be really free. Compare the watchword of the French Revolution with that of ours. "Liberty" in the French revolutionary watchword and "People's Nationalism" in our watchword are similar. The People's Nationalism calls for the freedom of our nation. "Equality" is similar to our "Principle of the People's Sovereignty," which aims to destroy autocracy and make all men equal. "Fraternity" originally meant *brothers* and has the same significance as the Chinese word *t'ung-pao* (compatriots). The idea in "Fraternity" is similar to our "Principle of the People's Livelihood," which plans for the happiness of our four hundred millions.[18]

The Chinese Communist Party was founded in 1921, and was dedicated to a more fundamental revolution than Sun advocated, but in its early years it supported Sun Yat-sen, the great national hero. Moreover, since most Western powers were unwilling to give up the treaty rights they obtained from the Manchus, Sun Yat-sen turned to Russia for aid. Russia assisted the Kuomintang, and Chinese communists were thus allowed to join Sun's party.

The goal of the Kuomintang was to establish effective republican rule over all China. Hence it sought to eliminate the power of local warlords, and to rid the country of foreign control. When Sun died, his successor as head of the Kuomintang was Chiang Kai-shek (1887-1975). Though Chiang claimed to be the heir of Sun Yat-sen, many historians look upon him as a successful conservative warlord who followed a policy of nationalism without implementing the other parts of Sun's program. Under Chiang, the Kuomintang maintained close ties with the Chinese middle class and the personnel of the old civil service, and he was more interested in political control than social reform. Chiang was willing to sacrifice social change for political unity. In 1928 he established Kuomintang control over most of the country, though its authority was more theoretical than real, for local warlords still ruled in many areas. However, a national government now existed.

The Communists and the Kuomintang split in 1927. While the Kuomintang and most of the military had placed the nationalist issue before all others, the Communists had continued to talk about the need for class struggle and a continuation of economic and social revolution. The Communists, too, wished to make China stronger, but they were unwilling to concede too much of their program

in order to gain power. As a result of the split, fighting broke out between Kuomintang forces and the Communists, who went into exile or hid in the countryside, where they became a revolutionary force opposed to the growing power of the Kuomintang.

By the 1930s Mao Tse-tung had emerged as a major figure in the Communist Party in China. A leader of student radicals in the 1920s, Mao had risen to prominence in Hunan Province and become one of the founders of the Chinese Communist Party. While the Communists and the Kuomintang were co-operating, he divided his time between strengthening the local Communist organization and helping to transform the Kuomintang into a national revolutionary movement. A prolonged illness, however, forced him to return to his parents' estate to convalesce and gave him an opportunity to think through his political principles. He noticed, moreover, that the peasant farmers were becoming increasingly discontented with the chaos in China and were starting to take matters into their own hands.

Asked, on his recovery, to report on peasant unrest, Mao defended the peasants, who were killing their landlords and seizing control of local villages. He poured scorn on those who talk about "arousing the masses of people" and then "are scared when the people do arise." "A revolution," he asserted, "is not the same as inviting people to dinner." The peasants, he proclaimed, were the revolutionary class of China. This was a significant departure from the views of Russian Communists, who believed that the factory worker was the core of a Communist revolution. Mao did not apologize for this departure from orthodox Marxism. Marxism, he said,

can be translated into reality only through a *national form.* . . . There is no abstract Marxism, only concrete Marxism—i.e. Marxism in a national form. . . . Therefore there is the need to [make Marxism Chinese.][19]

As a Chinese patriot, Mao claimed, as did Chiang Kai-shek, to be the heir of Sun Yat-sen. Since his brand of Marxism had a distinctly Chinese orientation, it had a great appeal to those who felt that the Kuomintang, like the Manchus, had become too dependent on foreign interests.

Mao was a champion of classical Chinese culture. He became an important poet, and his poetry has a place of respect in Chinese literature. The following poem, "Loushan Pass," was written in January 1935, during one of the most difficult periods of Mao's life:

> Cold blows the west wind,
> Far off in the frosty air
>   the wild geese call
>   in the morning moonlight.
> In the morning moonlight
> Horses' hoofs ring out sharply
> And the bugle's note
>   is muted.
>
> Do not say
>   that the pass is defended with iron.
> This very day
>   at one step
>   we shall cross over it.
> We shall cross over it.
> The hills are blue like the sea,
> And the dying sun is like blood.[20]

When the Communists split with the Kuomintang, many Communist supporters established their base in southeast China and imitated the Russian revolutionaries by setting up soviets. Because the Communists had won peasant support and redistributed land in this territory, Chiang and the Kuomintang were eager to seize the area. By 1934 the Kuomintang attacks appeared to be successful, and victory over the Communists seemed within reach.

In one of the most audacious military manoeuvres of modern times, the Communists conducted a fighting retreat from their position in southeast China. On October 16, 1934, the Long March began— a trek on foot over a distance of 13 000 km that lasted a year. One hundred thousand people started out, and after crossing mountains, rivers, and plains, fighting Kuomintang forces as they went, twenty thousand arrived in an area in north-central China which the small group could defend and from which it could plan its revolution. By now, Mao had be-

come the most powerful leader among them. He had been elected chairman of the Politburo during the Long March, and by the time he and his fellow Communists settled in Yenan, his authority was unchallenged. He transformed the Long March, which had been difficult enough in reality, into an even greater myth, using it to foster the legend of the invincibility of the Chinese Communist Party. In 1935 Mao wrote:

We say that the Long March is the first of its kind ever recorded in history, that it is a manifesto, an agitation corps, and a seeding-machine. . . . For twelve months we were under daily reconnaissance and bombing from the air by scores of planes; we were encircled, pursued, obstructed and intercepted on the ground by a big force of several hundred thousand men; we encountered untold difficulties and great obstacles on the way, but by keeping our two feet going we swept across a distance of more than 20,000 *li* through the length and breadth of eleven provinces. Well, has there ever been in history a long march like ours? No, never. The Long March is also a manifesto. It proclaims to the world that the Red Army is an army of heroes and that the imperialists and their jackals, Chiang Kai-shek and his like, are perfect nonentities. It announces the bankruptcy of the encirclement, pursuit, obstruction and interception attempted by the imperialists and Chiang Kai-shek. The Long March is also an agitation corps. It declares to the approximately two hundred million people of eleven provinces that only the road of the Red Army leads to their liberation. Without the Long March, how could the broad masses have known so quickly that there are such great ideas in the world as are upheld by the Red Army? The Long March is also a seeding-machine. It has sown many seeds in eleven provinces, which will sprout, grow leaves, blossom into flowers, bear fruit and yield a crop in future. To sum up, the Long March ended with our victory and the enemy's defeat.[21]

Indeed, the group which settled in Yenan with Mao became the spearhead of the Communist Revolution in China.

In July 1937 Japan invaded China, and the Communists and the Kuomintang made an uneasy peace in the national interest. A "united front" against Japan had been encouraged by the Comintern in accordance with the policy of establishing popular fronts, and this coincided with the nationalism of the Chinese Communists. However, both Communists and members of the Kuomintang realized that their union was only temporary, a necessary tactic for both to survive against Japan. It was clear even during the national war with Japan that the two groups would again battle one another for control of China, if they managed to defeat the common enemy.

COMMUNISM IN 1939

Although communists were in control of only one major state in 1939, communism was one of the leading forces of the West and the world. Many intellectuals and politicians had been attracted by the Russian Revolution and looked upon it as a movement of the future. Moreover, the period from 1917 to 1939 was one in which fascist governments came into power, and the traditional Western democracies seemed to be in serious difficulty. Thus communism was often seen as the only alternative to fascism, and until 1939 Russia was the only power willing to take a strong stand against fascist dictatorships.

The distinction between communism and socialism became increasingly clear in these years. According to theory, both had similar ends, but the means they proposed to use were markedly different. Socialists believed in working within a democratic, parliamentary system, while communists followed Lenin's model and saw themselves as the "vanguard of the proletariat," a group of tough revolutionaries who would use any tactics to achieve their goals. In practice this meant the development of a totalitarian party and, when communists were in power, as in the Soviet Union, a one-party totalitarian state. Interestingly enough, Lenin's development of the one-party state made communism more appealing to "underdeveloped" countries than to "modernized," constitutional states. In the latter, universal suffrage and a constitutional government had already been established, and thus democratic socialism was possible and communism had limited mass appeal. On the other hand, in those states which had few or no parliamentary institutions and an authoritarian government, communism provided a technique and an inspiration for bringing about a revolution.

ANALYSIS AND DISCUSSION

1. "Revolutions are usually fought against ruthless tyrants, but often it is the weak and indecisive who are the victims." Discuss this statement with reference to the decline in power and prestige of Czar Nicholas II after 1905.
2. While Lenin was a devoted follower of Marxian theory, he felt free to adapt Marx's ideas to different circumstances and conditions. After examining Lenin's ideas and career, describe the main differences between Marxism and Leninism.
3. Stalinism, unlike Leninism, was not a theory, but rather the sum of the practices instituted under Stalin's regime. By examining the practices of Stalin's Russia, try to arrive at a definition of Stalinism.

4. "Stalin followed in the tradition of Ivan the Terrible or Peter the Great much more than in the footsteps of Marx and Engels." Account for Stalin's success as a communist leader. To what extent was his rule a rejection of the ideals of Marxism?
5. Re-read the excerpt from "Three Principles of the People" by Dr. Sun Yat-sen. Compare his ideas of liberty with those of Western liberal thinkers such as John Locke or John Stuart Mill.
6. Mao Tse-tung has stated that "There is no abstract Marxism, only concrete Marxism — i.e., Marxism in a national form. . . . Therefore there is the need to [make Marxism Chinese]." How did Mao make Marxism Chinese?

CHAPTER **12**

The Rise of Fascism:
1919-1939

IN HIS WORK *The Revolt of the Masses* (1930), the Spanish philosopher José Ortega y Gasset remarked that the nature of society in the twentieth century differed radically from anything the world had seen before. In the twentieth century, he said, "heap after heap of human beings have been dumped onto the historic scene at such an accelerated rate, that it has been difficult to saturate them with traditional culture. They have been hurriedly inoculated with the pride and power of modern instruments, but not with their spirit."[1] Thus the new masses of our time, according to Ortega, are technologically sophisticated but culturally primitive. He feared mass society because of its levelling qualities, and because it had the tools to wipe out all of the painfully achieved cultural advances of humanity. He wondered aloud whether the masses would demand so much that, in a crisis, they would follow any leader who promised a new utopia. At the same time, he saw political leadership falling into the hands of "primitive" people—people who exalted the mediocre, who disregarded what had been achieved in the past, and who abandoned the tradition of rational discourse in politics. If the masses are without a sense of tradition, he said, they will choose one of their own to lead.

The conditions Ortega was describing seemed to him to be applicable to the whole of the Western world. Like John Stuart Mill, he feared the mediocrity of the masses. Moreover, he believed that, in the twentieth century, they would want the economic and social benefits that had been advocated by nineteenth-century liberals, but without knowing or caring about the democratic process or the rights of the individual which the liberals had also championed. Ortega supported the liberal tradition but lamented that the nature of the twentieth century made it impossible to educate people in the self-restraint necessary for its continuation. Ortega's work was both an analysis of what was happening around him and a prophecy for the future.

When Ortega's book was published in 1930, two European countries seemed to have political systems which reflected his analysis most clearly—the Soviet Union and Italy. While the Soviet Union led the anti-democratic left, Italian fascism became the political and social style used as a model by the anti-democratic right and was shortly adopted by Germany and a number of eastern European states. All of these regimes, whether communist or fascist, claimed to speak for the masses, seized power in the midst of a national crisis, and adopted the one-party, totalitarian state pioneered by Lenin. Indeed, the totalitarian party and the totalitarian state turned out to be the most important political innovation of this century.

POST-WAR ITALY

From the time of the *Risorgimento* of 1859–60, Italy had had a constitutional democratic government. Universal manhood suffrage had been put into effect after the First World War. Yet in the 1920s and 1930s, it was not unusual in Italy to watch parades of men in black shirts, medals on their chests and fists in the air, marching down a street shouting slogans which glorified war and power, and proclaiming undying allegiance to *Il Duce*, their leader. These people called themselves "fascists"; the term was derived from the word *fasces*, an ancient Roman symbol consisting of bundles of rods with an axe and indicating the authority of Roman magistrates. The Fascist leader, Benito Mussolini (1883-1945), proclaimed that his movement stood for unity, strength, and justice. By 1926 Italy was virtually a dictatorship under Mussolini, and in 1928 his Fascist Party gained total control of the machinery of the Italian state. How had this come about?

In any consideration of the rise of fascism, whether in Italy or in other areas, the effects of the First World War must be taken into account. Italy entered the war on the side of the Allies in 1915, with promises of territorial gains after the victory. The Italians, however, did not win glorious victories, the war was extremely expensive, and the end of it brought extreme frustration. Italians were also disappointed with the Treaty of Versailles, which did not give them all the territorial gains they sought in Europe, nor did Italy obtain a mandate over any of the former German colonies. Moreover, the men who returned from the war faced the prospect of unemployment, for Italian industry was dismantling its war production. And although the wartime government had promised many economic and social reforms, none of these seemed forthcoming in 1919. In the north of Italy many strikes occurred as workers demanded better wages and working conditions. In the south peasants, tired of waiting for the government to act on its long-standing promises of land redistribution, took possession of land by force. All of this turmoil frightened the middle and upper classes.

In the November 1919 election, the Socialist Party gained the most representatives to parliament. Next came the Popular Party, and then the Liberals, who had been the traditional leaders of various government coalitions. No party obtained a majority of seats. The Socialists were divided among themselves, some applauding the Bolshevik Revolution in Russia, others deploring it. In January 1921 the group sympathetic to Lenin broke away from the Socialist Party and formed the Italian Communist Party. The majority of Italians were afraid to allow the Socialists to take power because they distrusted their Marxist orientation, and thus Italy continued to be ruled by a series of middle-of-the-road coalitions led by many of the same men who had governed prior to the First World War. Their response to most crises—whether inflation, strikes, the seizing of factories by workers in 1920, the seizing of land by peasants—was to do little. In the face of this impotence and signs that Italy was moving to anarchism and perhaps even communism, nearly everyone was unhappy with the *status quo*.

Solutions to the problems of the day were readily offered by various political groups, all of which promised to end all troubles, give people employment, and make Italy a great nation. Mussolini's followers were one of the groups offering an alternative to the ruling coalitions. Mussolini had been a socialist and a journalist before the war. Brought up as a Catholic, he was drafted in 1904 to perform his compulsory military service. After serving in the army, he joined the socialist movement and rose to prominence within the Italian Socialist Party. In 1912 he became a member of the executive committee of the party and was appointed editor of its newspaper *Avanti*. He broke with the Socialists in 1914 over whether Italy should enter the war. The leaders of the Socialists declared that Italy should not get involved in a "capitalist" war. However, though Mussolini was a socialist, he was, above all, a fervent Italian nationalist. In 1914, when Italy did enter the war, he went to the front to fight.

In response to the political turmoil and social dislocation in Italy that followed the end of the war, Mussolini organized a fascist group. He did not have a clear political program, but insisted that strong rule and action were required, and he promised "a radical transformation of the political and economic bases of the life of the community."[2] His group included mainly students and former soldiers who were unhappy with the conditions of Italian life and wanted drastic changes. Fascists took a strong nationalist position—they called for the creation of a powerful Italy and denounced the Treaty of Versailles and those who were responsible for it. They attacked communists, socialists, and liberals, both verbally and physically. Above all, in their early years the Fascists were identified in the eyes of Italians as unswerving opponents of communism and anarchism. Many Italian patriots, and people who feared chaos or a soviet-type society, were attracted to the Fascists and to the dynamic quality of Mussolini's personality.

In order to emphasize their solidarity and frighten their enemies, the Fascists wore uniforms, made use of colourful rituals, and adopted a special salute—the right fist in the air. They revelled in military pageantry and, because of their distinctive dress, were often called "black shirts." In addition, Fascist squads sometimes destroyed the offices of radical publications which disagreed with them; they helped businessmen break strikes; and they attacked socialists and others of the political left. To reinforce the Fascist sense of purpose, Mussolini appealed to the discontented in impassioned speeches and writings, urging them to take action and follow his leadership. Again and again, Mussolini promised order and *action*.

The Fascists were organized as a regular political party in November 1921, but they could claim only 35 seats in an Italian Chamber of Deputies which had over 500 members. At this time the violence of the Fascist squads was largely ignored by the army, local police, government leaders, and businessmen, all of whom saw the Fascists as allies in trying to put the country in order. But the opportunity to get away with many illegal acts only encouraged Mussolini and his black-shirted supporters, while the continuing stalemate in parliament convinced them of the weakness of democracy in Italy. They were further encouraged when, in the summer of 1922, the Socialists called a general strike. The Fascists responded with violence, and many conservatives and moderates commended the group for helping to maintain order, not realizing that in doing so they were preparing the way for Mussolini to gain control of the state.

In October 1922 Mussolini and his followers felt that their time had come to obtain power. Mussolini, however, did not wish to overthrow the state; he wanted to be appointed prime minister of Italy. By now 300 000 men belonged to the Fascist Party and one-tenth of them had gathered in Milan, the major city in northern Italy, ready to march south on Rome. In this crisis, the Prime Minister of Italy went to King Victor Emmanuel III and asked him to sign a declaration of martial law, giving the government the power to stop the Fascists. The King, however, refused to risk violence and civil war and would not sign the declaration. The parliamentarians, lacking the necessary legal authority, were reluctant to appeal to the army to move against the Fascists. And the public was sympathetic to Mussolini, for he seemed to offer a program of action which might help solve the problems of the nation. By now Mussolini had convinced Italians that the Fascists were the protectors of Italy against a communist revolution, and as a result devout Catholics and members of the middle class supported him, though as much for what he opposed as for what he wanted to accomplish.

On October 26, 1922, just before the march on Rome began, the Fascist leaders issued a statement:

Fascism . . . does not march against the police, but against a political class both cowardly and imbecile, which in four long years has not been able to give a Government to the Nation. Those who form the productive class must know that Fascism wants to impose nothing more than order and discipline upon the Nation and to help to raise the strength which will renew progress and prosperity. The people who work in the fields and in the factories, those who work in the railroads or in offices, have nothing to fear from the Fascist Government. Their just rights will be protected. We will even be generous with unarmed adversaries.

Fascism draws its sword to cut the multiple Gordian knots which tie and burden Italian life. We call God and the spirit of our five hundred thousand dead to witness that only one impulse sends us on, that only one passion burns within us—the impulse and the passion to contribute to the safety and greatness of our Country.

Fascisti of all Italy!

Stretch forth like Romans your spirits and your sinews! We must win. We will.

Long live Italy! Long live Fascism![3]

On October 30, 1922, the King invited Mussolini to become prime minister. It was all done "legally," but the threat of force had won the day, for the former prime minister had resigned when the authorities refused to resist the march on Rome. The whole affair was, in fact, a *coup d'état*.

In his first few years in power Mussolini proceeded slowly. He headed a coalition government which did end the recurring strikes, restored some order to the country, and saw some economic improvement. In 1923 he managed to get a new electoral law passed which stated that the party with the most number of votes in an election (and a minimum of twenty-five per cent of the total vote) would have two-thirds of the seats in the Chamber of Deputies. This measure appealed to those who insisted that Italy's problems since unification were a result of a succession of "weak" coalition governments.

Elections were next held in April 1924. The elections were "free" in the sense that other parties ran candidates, but the Fascists used open intimidation to secure votes. The result: sixty-three per cent of the voters supported the Fascists. While Mussolini now had a clear majority in parliament, at this point serious opposition arose in the Chamber against the Fascists, who were accused of violating the fundamental laws of the state. In May 1924 Giacomo Matteotti, a Socialist deputy, delivered a dramatic speech in the Chamber in which he catalogued many cases of illegal actions on the part of Mussolini's party. In June 1924 he was murdered by the Fascists, and this provoked the first strong public reaction against Fascism; from this time on, there were Italians both at home and in exile who worked to overthrow the Fascist regime. However, though Mussolini was shaken, the inertia of the King and of the moderates, and the support of the army, enabled him to remain in power.

MUSSOLINI'S ITALY

The pretence of constitutional government was soon ended by Mussolini. Beginning in November 1925, a series of laws were enacted which soon put the Fascists in control of much of Italian life. All organiza-tions, including political parties, were required to report their activities and membership to the police. The government was given the right to dismiss civil servants who disagreed with its policy—several university professors were the first to feel the effect of this statute. Newspapers were controlled. The government obtained the right to take away the citizenship of Italians who worked against the regime. In December 1925 Mussolini became "Head of Government" and was given the authority to take executive actions without being responsible to parliament. In the next month the government obtained the power to legislate by decree. And finally, in December 1928, the Fascist Party took full control of the state. The Fascist Grand Council, the executive of the Party, was by law declared "the supreme organ which co-ordinates all the activities of the regime" and Mussolini was made "the President of the Fascist Grand Council." In practice this meant that the Party and the government were merged, and that Mussolini, the head of both, was now a dictator ruling virtually by decree.

Mussolini's Fascism was a rejection of democracy, liberalism, capitalism, Marxism, and socialism. Arising out of a spirit of fierce nationalism, Fascism emphasized national power and solidarity above all else; the individual was submerged in the state. In 1929 Mussolini stated:

The Fascist State is not a night-watchman, [concerned] only [for] the personal safety of the citizens; nor is it organized exclusively for the purpose of guaranteeing a certain degree of material prosperity and relatively peaceful conditions of life, a board of directors would do as much. Neither is it exclusively political, divorced from practical realities and holding itself aloof from the [various] activities of the citizens and the nation. The State, as conceived and realised by Facism, is a spiritual and ethical entity for securing the political, juridical, and economic organisation of the nation. . . . The State guarantees the internal and external safety of the country, but it also safeguards and transmits the spirit of the people, elaborated down the ages in its language, its customs, its faith. The State is not only the present, it is also the past

Mussolini about to address a crowd in Rome in 1924   (Snark International)

and above all the future. Transcending the individual's brief spell of life, the State stands for the . . . . conscience of the nation. The forms in which it finds expression change, but the need for it remains. The State educates the citizens to [citizenship], makes them aware of their mission, urges them to unity; its justice harmonises their divergent interests; it transmits to future generations the conquests of the mind in the fields of science, art, law, human solidarity; it leads men up from primitive tribal life to that highest manifestation of human power, imperial rule. The State hands down to future generations the memory of those who laid down their lives to ensure its safety or to obey its laws; it sets up as examples and records for future ages the names of the captains who enlarged its territory and of the men of genius who have made it famous. Whenever respect for the State declines and the disintegrating and centrifugal tendencies of in-

dividuals and groups prevail, nations are headed for decay.[4]

In the Fascist state, real power was in the hands of *Il Duce*, who was revered as the supreme representative of the people, having achieved that distinction in some mystical way. *Il Duce* ruled because he felt called to the task, and his party was an elite of those most able to further the national purpose. Fascism had a religious spirit about it, and Fascists demanded belief, fervour, and a willingness to die for the cause.

Mussolini wanted to cast an image of power and self-assurance. In his *My Autobiography*, published in 1928, he wrote:

I love all sports; I drive a motor car with confidence; I have done tours at great speed, amazing not only to my friends, but also to old and experienced drivers. I love the airplane; I have flown countless times.

Even when I was kept busy by the cares of power, I needed only a few lessons to obtain a pilot's license. I once fell from a height of fifty metres, but that did not stop my flying.[5]

Comparing himself to other men, he asserted:

I never had any interval of uncertainty.... I understood that not only my prestige was at stake, but the prestige, the very name of the country which I love more than myself, more than anything else.[6]

Sometimes he spoke of himself as if he were super-human. Commenting on an unsuccessful attempt on his life, he said, "The bullets pass, Mussolini remains."

Mussolini never ceased to proclaim that it was action, rather than theory, that interested him, and once in control of the government he set out to reorganize the state. He established what he termed the "Corporate State"; this involved creating a series of institutions, called corporations or syndicates, to regulate the economy. Each labour group, industrial group, or professional group had its corporation, and each individual took part in the economic life of Italy by being a member of a corporation. Corporations would then bargain collectively under the authority of a central body to arrange contracts and settle disputes, with the government having the final say in any settlement. "Lockouts and strikes are abolished" stated one of the laws which established these institutions. As an extension of his nationalist policy, Mussolini's economic goal was "autarky"—self-sufficiency—but this was impossible in a country with the limited natural resources of Italy.

In theory the Corporate State opposed both class struggle and individual self-interest, but in practice it favoured the wealthy. The industrialists had supported Mussolini and their property was not in danger as long as they co-operated with the state. Thus, though Fascism gave the appearance of being deeply concerned with the problems of the masses, Mussolini did little to change the social structure of Italian life.

The "corporate" organization favoured the large industrialists and landlords, who were as well off under Mussolini as they had been under the non-interference policies of earlier Italian governments. The Fascist regime favoured those who had always been privileged, but all, rich and poor, were expected to serve the needs of the state.

Many traditional institutions were retained in the Fascist state. The King, Victor Emmanuel III, continued on his throne, and, more importantly, Mussolini made peace with the Roman Catholic Church, an enemy of the Italian state since the *Risorgimento*. The Lateran Agreements, in 1929, signed by Mussolini and Pope Pius XI, recognized "the full ownership and the exclusive and absolute dominion . . . of the Holy See over the Vatican,"[7] an independent territory of about forty-four hectares in the heart of Rome. All differences between Italy and the Vatican, such as the authority for the appointment of bishops, educational policy in Italy, and Italian marriage laws, were settled. In its turn, the Church recognized the existence of the Italian state. The Lateran Agreements were a great event for Mussolini—this was the first time the Papacy had recognized an Italian government since Italian unification. Though the Church and the State still had occasional conflicts in Fascist Italy, the agreements put the Papal stamp of approval on Mussolini's regime as far as Italy's many devout Catholics were concerned.

Though it used the rhetoric and the bureaucracy of a totalitarian state, the Fascist state in Italy was not as all-encompassing or terrifying as the regime of Stalin or the Third Reich of Hitler. While opposition was submerged, it was not entirely stamped out. And the Fascist bureaucracy was not especially efficient or ruthless. Moreover, some of the Italian courts were never taken over by Fascists, nor was the entire civil service. Political opponents of Mussolini may have been imprisoned, but, unlike Matteotti, few were killed. While many Italians opposed to Mussolini were forced underground or into exile, Benedetto Croce, the leading Italian philosopher and historian of the time, survived at home despite his political views. During the middle of the Fascist period, Croce published a work which has been translated into English as *History as the Story of Liberty*. Its major theme was the development of the idea of liberty both in thought and in practice. Though never mentioning Fascism, the work was frankly anti-Fascist in tone.

Once in control of the state, the Fascists, who had started as an action group without a political philosophy, sought to develop a doctrine of Fascism. The Fascist, said Mussolini, "conceives of life as duty and struggle and conquest." Mussolini demanded that the masses make sacrifices in the present in order to achieve a more powerful nation in the future; hence, he argued, the state required "authority, direction and order." Fascist doctrine always insisted on the necessity and virtue of unlimited expansion—the state must always go forward. Mussolini said:

Granted that the xixth century was the century of socialism, liberalism, democracy, this does not mean that the xxth century must also be the century of socialism, liberalism, democracy. Political doctrines pass; nations remain. We are free to believe that this is the century of authority, a century tending to the "right," a Fascist century. If the xixth century was the century of the individual (liberalism implies individualism) we are free to believe that this is the "collective" century, and therefore the century of the State.[8]

Above all, he said, Fascism was a "collective" idea. All people, in other words, have value only in so far as they work for the state and seek to enhance its future power.

What Mussolini achieved was more psychological than real. Roads were built and, as people said, the trains ran on time, but the Italian economy did not undergo any radical revival or transformation. Mussolini made many Italians feel that Italy was becoming a great power and that great innovations were occurring. Like Napoleon I, he managed to impose some order on chaos, but he lacked the Napoleonic genius in administration. Great emphasis was put on martial qualities and on the armed forces, but Mussolini did not really succeed in building a fine military machine.

However, as Fascism developed in Italy, many people in Europe, most especially conservatives and others who feared anything that smacked of communism or socialism, saw it as a real political alternative. Many regarded the depression of the 1930s as the beginning of the end for liberal democracy, and if forced to choose between fascism and communism, they preferred Mussolini's solution. But by the mid-1930s Mussolini was no longer the major spokesman for fascism. By then Germany was a fascist state and its leader, Adolf Hitler, was the most important person on the political right in Europe.

POST-WAR GERMANY: THE WEIMAR REPUBLIC

In February 1919 Germany's newly elected Constituent Assembly met in the town of Weimar. Its aims were to come to terms with the victorious Allies and to draw up a constitution for the new German state, which was to replace the Empire founded by Bismarck. The leaders of this Assembly signed the Treaty of Versailles, drew up the Weimar Constitution, and brought into being "the Weimar Republic," which lasted from 1919 to 1933.

The constitution established a liberal and democratic republic, consisting of a federation of various states, and gave the federal government strong central powers. A bicameral legislature was set up, consisting of a *Reichstag*, representing the people, and a *Reichsrat*, representing the states. A chancellor performed functions similar to those of a prime minister, and a president was elected to act as head of state. The president, however, had the right to step in and govern by decree in a time of emergency. Church and state were separated, "personal liberty" was declared "inviolable," and rights of speech, assembly, association, and property were guaranteed.

During the 1920s, governments in the Weimar Republic were formed by coalitions of various parties that were committed to the constitution and to parliamentary government. The most important group was the

Social Democratic Party, the heir of the revisionist socialists of pre-war times. They introduced moderate socialist legislation and continued to work through the ballot box to gain support for their aims. Other moderate elements were the Catholic Centre Party, which supported social and economic policies inspired by the Catholic Church, and the Democratic Party, which was liberal and individualist in orientation and lost support throughout the decade to other groups which pursued a policy of active state intervention in economic affairs.

Yet, as historians continually note, the Weimar Republic was in danger from its start. By signing the Treaty of Versailles, those who created the Republic seemed to be admitting, in the eyes of many Germans, the legitimacy of the war-guilt clause and the harsh peace. When various writers examined the origins of the war during the 1920s, they blamed the moderate parties which had made the peace for having signed away territory and colonies that properly belonged to the German nation. Some Germans claimed that Germany had not really lost the war— it had signed an armistice in November 1918, they said, in the belief that a "just peace" was to be negotiated on the basis of Wilson's Fourteen Points. Those who held this view accused the moderates of being the internal enemies of Germany.

In reality the Weimar Republic was a strange combination of the "new" and the "old" Germany. Many Germans were opposed to it from the start. The Communists on the extreme left and the Nationalists (representing Germany's aristocratic tradition) and the National-Socialists (Nazis) on the extreme right were against democratic government. But, while the parties of the right were handled leniently when they broke the law, the Communists were handled severely. This came about partly because the members of the civil service, the police, and the judiciary were often the same people who had performed these functions under the Emperor before the First World War. In addition, the army was still strongly nationalist and was led by the old Junker class, which belonged to the Nationalist Party.

Thus, behind the curtain of a new republican democracy, German society and daily life reflected the past.

In 1923 Germany suffered a severe economic upheaval. Because of its economic problems after the war, Germany had claimed that it could not meet its reparations payments. In retaliation the French occupied the Ruhr valley, a major German industrial area, in early 1923, and Germany, rather than meet French demands, declared a policy of passive resistance to the occupation. German currency had been declining in value, but now inflation broke loose and destroyed the value of the mark. The middle class saw its savings disappear, and people on fixed incomes and pensions became destitute. More and more people became disillusioned with republican government. The elections of May 1924 reflected this disillusionment as the moderates lost support to those parties which had always attacked the Republic.

None the less, the Weimar Republic did display some staying power. French troops left the Ruhr in 1924. Inflation was brought under control, and the parties at the centre of the political spectrum won back many of the voters. Germany stabilized its domestic affairs, and under the leadership of its foreign minister, Gustav Stresemann, began to play a more important role in world affairs. The reparations payments were reduced by agreement in 1924, foreign capital entered the country, border problems in the west were settled with France in 1925, and Germany was admitted to the League of Nations in 1926. From 1924 to 1929 it seemed that republicanism and democracy would survive in Germany, and the vast majority of voters rejected the anti-republican parties. Yet the far left and the far right continued to exist, both waiting for an opportunity to overthrow the regime; in the end, it was the extreme right—the Nazis—who finally succeeded.

HITLER: EARLY YEARS

Nazism can be classified as a form of fascism, though unlike Italian fascism it had a strong German racial orientation and was therefore not exportable as a real alternative to other

German devaluation, 1922–23. Inflation in Germany grew so rapidly that paper currency lost most of its value. The result was that ordinary purchases had to be made with vast quantities of paper money, often carried, as shown in the photograph, in laundry baskets and satchels. (top, Toronto Coin Centre Ltd.; bottom, Ullstein)

European forms of government. And its history in Germany was intimately tied up with the life of Adolf Hitler (1889-1945), the son of a minor customs official.

Hitler, who was born and raised in Austria, had a childhood which was marked by failure and deep frustration. A poor student, he dreamed of being an artist. He went to Vienna to try to make an artistic career, but was refused admission to the Vienna Academy of Fine Arts on the basis of a lack of talent. From 1909 to 1913 he lived in the streets of Vienna, a deeply bitter man. Temperamentally incapable of holding a regular job, he was a vagabond, hating Vienna and its intellectuals for rejecting him.

In the decades prior to 1914, the major issue in the Austro-Hungarian Empire was the unrest among some of the large national groups within the empire. Hitler became an ultra-German nationalist, believed in the superiority of all things German, and looked upon Slavs and other nationalities in the Austro-Hungarian Empire as inferior. He became a reader of the right-wing press and acquired a contempt for liberal and leftist philosophies. He also became a virulent anti-Semite. The Jews of Vienna, the city of Freud, had long been citizens of the empire, and were important in its intellectual and economic life. In Hitler's view, however, Jews were not Germans but a race apart to be hated and scorned. Thus by 1914, like many of his contemporaries, Hitler was ultra-nationalist, anti-democratic, and anti-Semitic.

The First World War gave Hitler something to do. When war broke out he obtained special permission to enlist in the German army, for he believed that the home of German nationalism was Germany, not Austria. He rose to the rank of corporal, fought on the western front and was decorated for valour. After the war he drifted to Munich, one of many veterans with little to do, harbouring a deep resentment over Germany's defeat and a hatred for the new Weimar Republic. Despite an abortive uprising, Munich was the centre of the "old" Germany, and Hitler in 1919 joined a tiny group called the German Workers Party.

In 1920 this group changed its name to the National Socialist German Workers Party, or the Nazis.

The combination of "nationalism" and "socialism" can be seen in the nature of the Party's program:

1. We demand the union of all Germans in one Great Germany by the right of self-determination of peoples.
2. We demand the equality of the German nation with all other nations and abrogation of the Treaties of Versailles and St. Germain [i.e. the peace treaty with Austria].
3. We demand land and territory (colonies) for the feeding of our people and for the settlement of our surplus population.
4. Only those who are members of the nation can be citizens. Only those who are of German blood, without regard to religion, can be members of the German nation. No Jew can, therefore, be a member of the nation.
5. He who is not a citizen shall be able to live in Germany only as a guest and must live under laws governing foreigners.
6. The right to decide on the leadership and on the laws of the state may belong only to citizens. Therefore we demand that every public office, of whatever sort...shall be filled only by citizens. We fight against the corrupting parliamentary system of filling offices with people chosen because of their party viewpoint without regard to character and ability.
7. We demand that the state be obliged, in the first instance, to provide the possibility of work and life for the citizen....
8. All further immigration of non-Germans is to be prevented. We demand that all non-Germans who have immigrated to Germany since the second of August 1914 shall be compelled to leave the Reich immediately.
9. All citizens must possess the same rights and duties.
10. The first duty of every citizen is to work productively with mind or body. The activities of individuals must not transgress the interests of the community but must be for the common good.

THEREFORE WE DEMAND:

11. The elimination of income which is acquired without labor or effort.

BREAKING OF THE INTEREST SLAVERY

12. Out of regard to the frightful sacrifice in goods and blood which every war demands from the nation, personal enrichment through war must be designated as a crime against the nation. We demand, therefore, summary confiscation of all war profits.
13. We demand the nationalization of all trusts.
14. We demand profit-sharing in large concerns.
15. We demand a large-scale extension of the old-age pension system.
16. We demand the creation of a sound middle class....
17. We demand land reform adapted to our national needs....
18. We demand the most ruthless campaign against everyone who injures the public interest by his actions.[9]

Other "demands" were made, designed to create a powerful state, a state-controlled system of education and a social-welfare program. The Nazi slogan was "public interest before private interest."

It was in Munich that Hitler first became prominent as a speaker. He discovered that he had extraordinary powers to arouse his audience. His success was sometimes a victory of style over content—it did not always matter what he said, but how he put it across, and he used the rhythm of his speech to create deep mass response out of an audience of individuals. But his popularity went beyond rhetorical tricks; for when his message was clear, it had tremendous appeal to frustrated and disillusioned Germans. In a speech in Munich in 1923, he said:

With the armistice [of November 1918 began] the humiliation of Germany. If the [Weimar] Republic on the day of its foundation had appealed to the country: 'Germans, stand together! Up and resist the foe! The Fatherland, the Republic expects of you that you fight to your last breath,' then millions who are now the enemies of the Republic would be fanatical Republicans. To-day they are the foes of the Republic not because it is a Republic but because

this Republic was founded at the moment when Germany was humiliated, because it so discredited the new flag that men's eyes must turn regretfully towards the old flag.

It was no Treaty of Peace which was signed, but a betrayal of Peace....

So long as this Treaty stands there can be no resurrection of the German people: no social reform of any kind is possible! The Treaty was made in order to bring 20 million Germans to their deaths and to ruin the German nation. But those who made the Treaty cannot set it aside. At its foundation our Movement formulated three demands:

1. Setting aside of the Peace Treaty.
2. Unification of all Germans.
3. Land and soil (Grund und Boden) to feed our nation.

Our Movement could formulate these demands, since it was not our Movement which caused the War, it has not made the Republic, [and] it did not sign the Peace Treaty.

There is thus one thing which is the first task of this Movement: it desires to make the German once more National, that his Fatherland shall stand for him above everything else. It desires to teach our people to understand afresh the truth of the old saying: He who will not be a hammer must be an anvil. An anvil are we today, and that anvil will be beaten until out of the anvil we fashion once more a hammer, a German sword![10]

Like many fringe parties in the 1920s, the Nazis adopted a semi-military organization. They wore uniforms, saluted, paraded and physically attacked their opponents, particularly the communists. Even though they were a small group, they viewed themselves as an elite destined to lead the German nation to greatness. They wanted to see an end to the Weimar Republic; Germany, they said, should be a great empire leading the world, not a weak republic which continued to have economic crises. They heaped scorn on those who had signed the Treaty of Versailles and proclaimed that Germany had not been defeated in war, but by traitors at home, particularly Jews and communists.

On the strength of his powers as a speaker and organizer, Hitler became the leader, the *Führer*, of the party in 1921 and thereby became the head of a self-constituted elite. To help protect the party from being attacked during its meetings and to threaten all those whom the Nazis viewed as enemies, the SA (after *Sturmabteilung*, or storm troopers) was organized in 1921. Like the squads of Italian Fascists, the SA was often tolerated by moderates who viewed it as an ally in the battle against communism.

In 1923 Hitler thought that the French occupation of the Ruhr and the inflation in Germany had so weakened the Republic that he could make a successful bid for power. His group was still centred in Munich, the major city of the state of Bavaria, and in collusion with General Erich Ludendorff, a German hero of the First World War, he hoped to overthrow the Bavarian and then the German governments. On November 8, at a meeting in a Munich beer hall attended by government officials, Hitler stood up, fired a shot in the air, and proclaimed his *coup d'état*. He won little support at the time, and the Beer Hall *Putsch*, as the incident has become known, ended the next day when the army dispersed a march of the SA led by Ludendorff and Hitler.

Taken into custody, Hitler was brought to trial. The trial provided him with vast publicity, and in conducting his own defence he became a prominent figure. He claimed that he had acted to protect Germany from the communists, and that, therefore, he was defending the national interest. Although he had in fact tried to overthrow the state, he was given only a five-year sentence and released in less than a year. Hitler used his time in jail to dictate *Mein Kampf* (*My Struggle*), a disorganized, hysterical work which became the Nazi Bible. Few outside the Nazi movement took it seriously until January 30, 1933, when Hitler came to power legally as Chancellor of Germany.

HITLER: RISE TO POWER

Hitler's promises of action and national glory, as proclaimed in his speeches and in *Mein Kampf*, became the basis of his appeal to the German nation. For Hitler, the key to understanding history was race or blood;

Germans, he asserted, were "Aryans,"* the race destined to rule the world. The German state, he said, must be a "folkish state," and all who were not Aryans must be given inferior positions and excluded from participating in government. A superior race proved itself by continually asserting and increasing its power. He explained Germany's defeat in the First World War as a "stab in the back" by enemies within Germany who had plotted against the German people. Echoing Mussolini, he insisted that a nation must continually struggle: greatness was not won easily, but only through a mass effort. Germany must expand to include all those who were Germans but were not yet part of the German state (for example, Austrians). But it must also find *Lebensraum*, "living space," for the superior race at the expense of inferior races, particularly the Slavs. Hitler viewed all history as a struggle between superior and inferior races and believed that the struggle was beneficial to the human species because it did away with, or subdued, the inferior.

Hitler singled out the communists and the Jews as the principle enemies of the Aryans, and he skilfully linked the two in the minds of the German people, despite the fact that a large number of German Jews were middle class, the very group attacked by communists. He called communism a "Jewish plot" and blamed all German failures, particularly the defeat in the war, on communists and Jews. Communists and Jews were also blamed for fostering liberalism and egalitarianism after the First World War, for Hitler despised these ideals as alien to the German spirit and as denying the importance of race and blood. Having catalogued

---

*"Aryan" was ordinarily used as a linguistic term and indicated a family of languages, known also as Indo-European or Indo-Germanic. When it was used as a noun, it denoted someone who spoke an Aryan language (which meant most European languages, as well as languages in Asia related to Sanskrit). Hitler used the term in a racial sense, implying that race and language are identical, although this viewpoint had been discredited by scholars. Often he simply meant those who spoke German and whose culture and "race" he presumed to be German.

the sins of these "enemies," Hitler promised to rid the state of them.

In *Mein Kampf* Hitler also enunciated his *Führerprinzip*, the "leadership principle." The Nazi Party, he claimed, would include only the best among the German people. As the Party would lead the people, so the *Führer* would lead the Party. Hitler asserted that the *Führer*—himself—was the embodiment of the will of the people; all were bound to carry out his will. He attempted to create a mystical aura around the leader as a special person who was somehow larger than life. That Hitler wrote *Mein Kampf* is not extraordinary; that many people followed him—eventually much of the German nation—is.

After he was released from prison in 1925, Hitler reorganized his party and made it a tight political organization devoted to seizing control of the state. The party recruited only those whom it felt would be absolutely loyal to its program and to Hitler. In addition to the SA, Hitler established in 1925 another military group, the SS (for *Schutzstaffel*, or defence corps), which was to be an elite group serving as his personal bodyguard. The large SA and the handpicked SS were dedicated to the leader and the party and were the military arm of an organization that was determined to destroy the Weimar Republic.

From 1925 to 1929 Germany enjoyed relative prosperity and played an important role in the diplomacy of Europe, and during this time the Nazis remained a small party. Hitler was joined by fanatic nationalists and by some fringe socialists who confused his program of state control and his speeches about the need to care for the people with socialism. He was also supported by some industralists and monarchists and was tolerated by people who viewed him both as a German patriot, albeit a misguided one, and an enemy of communism. Some politicians thought he could be used for their own purposes; eventually, however, he used everyone who associated with him for his own ends.

All revolutionaries thrive in a crisis. In good times Hitler had difficulty recruiting

George Grosz: "Hitler, the Saviour", 1925. This drawing captured much of the atmosphere surrounding Hitler and the National Socialist movement. (Estate of George Grosz, Princeton, New Jersey)

people and keeping himself in the public eye, but the depression of 1929 gave him his opportunity. Germany was in serious economic difficulty by 1930, and soon millions were unemployed. As in 1923, the politics of the Weimar Republic polarized, and the extreme parties, who were all opposed to the existence of the Republic, gained votes at the expense of the moderates. Beginning in 1930, a number of coalitions were formed in an attempt to produce a stable government.

After his failure in 1923, Hitler was determined to use the democratic system to his advantage and to come to power legally, and his campaign for votes met with reasonable success. The Nazis and the Communist Party both wanted control of the state and used their growing numbers in the *Reichstag* to make it difficult for others to govern. Stable government became impossible and this forced President Hindenburg, the German hero of the First World War, to use the emergency powers granted him in the constitution and rule by decree. Finally, those who wanted Hitler to come to power persuaded a reluctant Hindenburg to ask Hitler to attempt to form a government. By this time the army felt that Hitler was their best chance to establish firm conservative rule and its leaders were willing to support a Nazi regime. In addition, the Nationalist Party and several important people in the *Reichstag* were prepared to join in a coalition with the Nazis. On January 30, 1933, Hitler became Chancellor of Germany.

HITLER'S GERMANY

Having gained power legally, Hitler began to consolidate his rule over Germany. Like Mussolini, he claimed he was defending Germany from a communist revolution and used the supposed danger of communism to begin a systematic liquidation of all his political opponents. On February 27 the *Reichstag* building was burned down. Although responsibility for the act has never been clearly established, the Nazis blamed the communists, and a Dutch communist, who was clearly mentally retarded, confessed to having started the fire. But at the time many people felt that the Nazis were implicated in the act, and a number of historians still conclude that the evidence points to Nazi responsibility. In any case the German Communist Party was blamed, and the Nazis persuaded President Hindenburg that many of the civil liberties of the Weimar Constitution should be suspended for the sake of state security. The next day a decree was issued "as a protection against Communist acts of violence imperilling the state." It permitted "restrictions on personal freedom, on the right of free expression of opinion, including freedom of the press, and on the rights of association...."[11]

Elections had been scheduled for March 5, but the fire and the resulting suspension of civil liberties enabled Hitler to unleash the SA in order to suppress his opponents and intimidate the electorate. Still, the Nazis received only forty-four per cent of the votes, although the Nationalist Party's seats raised the total of the coalition to fifty-two per cent. Hitler arrested the communist deputies who had been elected and had them dismissed from the *Reichstag*. With the active support of the Nationalists, Hitler then introduced an "Enabling Act," which, in effect, suspended the Weimar Constitution and gave him dictatorial powers. The Social Democratic Party opposed the act, but the Catholic Centre Party went along when Hitler promised to respect the rights of the Catholic Church. On March 23 the *Reichstag* passed the Enabling Act and thus effectively ended the parliamentary and democratic constitution of the Weimar Republic. The new regime which Hitler then established was called the Third Reich. Hitler prophesied that it would last a thousand years. The name was chosen quite deliberately to recall the glories of the German past. Germans had always considered the Holy Roman Empire, which lasted from 962 to 1806, to have been the "First" German Empire and had called the state founded by Bismarck the "Second Empire." Hitler wanted them to think of his state as the "Third Empire," or *Reich*.

Hitler now began what has been called the *Gleichschaltung* (co-ordination or consolidation) of his power by giving his party effective control of all activities of the state. He still kept the *Reichstag* in existence because it provided the illusion of representative government and gave the acts of the Nazis a cloak of legality. In May the free activities of trade unions were ended, including the right to strike. In July a law was promulgated stating that "the only political party existing in Germany is the National Socialist German Workers' Party."[12] In December the Nazi Party was made "the custodian of the German national sentiment" and declared "indissolubly connected with the State."[13] By January 30, 1934, the first anniversary of his becoming Chancellor, Hitler felt secure enough to centralize power. A new law proclaimed that "the state legislatures are abolished,"[14] and that the powers of the states were given to the central government.

The burning of the Reichstag, February 1933 (Imperial War Museum, London)

Hence, with greater speed than either Lenin or Mussolini, Hitler established a totalitarian state. The symbol and the guardian of this authority was the *Gestapo* (from *Geheime Staatspolizei*), the secret police organization founded in 1933, which rooted out those suspected of opposition.

However, like most successful parties after they gain power, the Nazis were divided over policy. Those Nazis who had followed Hitler in the belief that he would introduce socialist legislation and change Germany's social structure wanted a "second revolution." One of these, Ernst Röhm, the leader of the SA, presented Hitler with a difficult problem. Hitler had come to power partly because the German army had agreed not to stand in his way, and he was anxious to retain the army's support for his regime. Röhm wanted the Nazi's "army," the SA, to replace the old aristocratic army as the basis for the new armed forces of Germany. Faced with dissident elements within his own party and the danger of the German army moving

against the Nazis as a result of the ambitions of Röhm and the SA, Hitler decided to purge his party. On "The Night of the Long Knives," June 30, 1934, Röhm and others were arrested and murdered by the SS and the *Gestapo*, and thus the "opposition" was wiped out. Several weeks later, the aged President Hindenburg died, and Hitler assumed the powers of the President, calling himself *Führer* and *Reichskanzler*. Members of the armed forces now took an oath of personal allegiance to Hitler, not to the constitution or the state:

I swear by God this holy oath: I will render unconditional obedience to the Fuehrer of the German Reich and People, Adolf Hitler, the Supreme Commander of the Armed Forces, and will be ready, as a brave soldier, to stake my life at any time for this oath.[15]

Hitler was now master of Germany.

Persecution of German Jews began almost immediately after the Nazis took power. Intimidation was officially encouraged, authorities ignored illegal acts committed against Jews by Nazis or other Germans, and several laws, including one regarding the ownership of newspapers, were directed against Jewish citizens. However, "legal" and systematic persecution began with the Nuremberg Laws of 1935. These deprived all Jews of German citizenship and forbade inter-marriage between Jews and other citizens. From this moment on, people whom the Nazis defined as Jews had no recourse to law. The Nazis took one step after another, first expelling Jews from the civil service, then from various professions and jobs, and ultimately from the cultural life of Germany. By the end of 1938 virtually all Jewish businessmen had been forced to shut down and all Jews had been excluded from the civil life of Germany. Some Jews, including Albert Einstein, emigrated.

But Jews were not the only people persecuted, nor were Jews the only inhabitants of German concentration camps. All opponents of the Nazi state were terrorized, and many, including Thomas Mann, Germany's greatest writer, went into exile. Those who

Oranienburg concentration camp near Berlin, 1933   (Ullstein)

stayed were arrested, imprisoned, and often killed. Terror became a way of life for the opponents of the Nazis, and all who openly disagreed with Nazi policies or were suspected of opposition were persecuted.

To most Germans, however, Hitler seemed a heaven-sent leader and they admired and loved him. He had saved Germany, many thought, from an imminent communist revolution and had stabilized the government. The people now had security and a strong collective identity. A "blemished past" was being wiped out in an onrush of nationalism and racism. Germany appeared once again to be on the brink of greatness.

The revival of the economy contributed to Hitler's popularity. Whereas six million Germans were unemployed in 1933, nearly all had found jobs by 1938. Soon after he came to power, Hitler pumped a great deal of money into the economy by inaugurating a public-works program, which increased employment and helped stimulate business. In 1935 he began a rearmament program which provided further employment and led to the expansion of the economy. As in Italy, labour was controlled through state organizations. A program called "Strength

through Joy" provided social activities and cheap vacations for groups of workers. Production rose steadily, and people felt that the Nazis had found a better way of organizing the economy than had the democratic governments of other countries.

In a totalitarian state, religious institutions that are not controlled by political authority cannot be tolerated. Hitler and the Nazis despised Christianity. They saw it as a religion of the meek, preaching love of one's fellow human beings and the equality of people before God. It was the opposite of Nazi racism and the exaltation of physical brutality. Moreover, the Jewish origins of Christianity disturbed the Nazi leaders. At the beginning of his rule, however, Hitler treaded softly in dealing with the churches. He made a Concordat with Pope Pius XI in July 1933, which guaranteed the Catholic Church the right to manage its own affairs in Germany. However, as with many of the Nazi agreements, this understanding was soon broken by Hitler. The Nazis, desiring complete control of education in order to indoctrinate children with the Nazi ideology, attacked Church schools. In addition, individual priests and Catholic organizations

*Berlin, January 30, 1938. A torchlight parade celebrates the fifth anniversary of the Nazis'
control of Germany.   (Barnaby's Picture Library)*

were challenged. In 1937 Pius XI in an encyclical strongly condemned the racist policy
of the Nazis. Some German Catholics risked
their position and criticized the regime;
some went into exile; most remained silent
or supported the Nazis. Nor did Pius XII,
who became Pope in 1939, make a clear
break with the Nazis. He preferred to deal
with them diplomatically, thinking he could
do more for the Church in this manner than
by speaking out publicly against Nazism.

The Protestants were the largest religious
group in Germany, and the Nazis attempted
to "co-ordinate" them by forcing all church
organizations into a central body controlled
by the state. The response was mixed—some
pastors went along, some protested meekly,
and others condemned Nazism outright. A
minority of pastors, vehemently opposed to
racism and any relationship between the
Nazis and Christianity, organized a "Confessional Church" to preach against Nazism. In
1937 over eight hundred "confessional" pastors were sent to Nazi concentration camps.

Although Nazism came to be a secular
religion, with a leader who wanted to be
looked upon as a messiah, with the swastika
as its emblem, and with rituals modelled on
pagan and Christian ceremonies, the Nazis
were not successful in replacing traditional
religion. However, they did much to silence
its spokesmen and to create an association in
people's minds between Christian institutions and the Nazi regime. Individual Christians protested, but after the arrest of the
"confessional" pastors, no organized movement against Nazism developed within the
churches.

In a totalitarian state, knowledge must serve the ends of the state. Once in power, therefore, the Nazis took control of the press, radio, and cinema. Books that presented ideas contrary to those of the regime were burned, beginning in May 1933, and "racial sciences," Nazi ideology, and the Nazi view of history were taught in the schools. Political tests were instituted for teachers, and the Nazis soon got rid of Jews and others who were considered "unfit" to teach. Most teachers, including university professors, remained in Germany and maintained silence.

Outside the schools other means were adopted to indoctrinate youth. The *Hitler-Jugend*, the Hitler Youth, had been established before 1933 in order to help recruit young people into the Nazi Party. When the Nazis gained control of Germany, millions of youths joined the *Hitler-Jugend*; they sang and marched and worked together, learning their duty to the Third Reich. All education, whether it was found in the schools, in such organizations as the Hitler Youth, or in the propaganda of the press and radio, was designed to submerge the individual in the group. Germans were taught to equate the Nazis with Germany and to believe that their mission on earth was to obey and follow Hitler.

Hitler believed that he had a true instinctive understanding of human nature. People, he felt, were irrational and motivated by fear; they did not wish to be free, but to be identified with a group. Thus he cultivated the myth of German superiority because he wanted all Germans to feel superior, but also to lose their individuality in the nation and depend on their *Führer* for guidance. Elaborate spectacles and pageants were organized to create a sense of comradeship among all Germans, and when Hitler spoke at these events he had a deep emotional impact on his audience.

Though many had fled the Nazi regime by 1939, most Germans supported Hitler and viewed him as one of the great men of history. There was no opposition to Hitler on the scale of the Italian underground or community-in-exile which opposed Musso-lini. By 1939 Jews were imprisoned or gone, Germany was "pure," and the Aryan nation was on the move and expanding its borders. Germany had in fact become a modern Sparta—self-sacrificing, devoted to the collective good, and united in a single, moral will.

THE GROWTH OF AUTHORITARIAN REGIMES: EASTERN EUROPE

In the peace settlements after the First World War, the diplomats had divided eastern Europe into a series of nation-states which included Poland, Czechoslovakia, Hungary, Rumania, and Yugoslavia. Ethnic differences remained within these states—for example, Czechoslovakia had large German and Hungarian minorities, and Yugoslavia contained Croats, Slovenes, and Serbs. In the creation of these new states, there had been strong differences of opinion over certain areas which could have been awarded to more than one state. Hungarians, for example, resented losing territory to Rumania and Czechoslovakia, while Pan-Slavs were angry that Rumania and Poland were given territory with Slavic minorities.

In addition to their ethnic problems, most of these new states were barely industrialized and lacked a substantial middle-class base. As a result, politics tended to be a battle between conservative, traditional elements representing the mass of the countryside, and a minority of liberal reformers usually based in urban centres. The western powers had thought they could establish regimes which had liberal-democratic tendencies, and some of the new states started out in this direction, for example Poland, Czechoslovakia, and Rumania. During the 1920s and 1930s, however, most of the eastern European states moved away from democracy towards some form of authoritarian rule.

Hungary was the first to turn authoritarian. In 1919 a conservative government had come into power after a brief period of communist rule under Bela Kun. Fear of internal revolution and an intense nationalism had then led to an inward-looking policy of reaction and order. The nationalists who dominated this government were anti-Semitic and anti-Marxist; they called themselves "right radicals" and wished to transform Hungary into a powerful, orderly state under strong government. From 1932 to 1936 Gyula Gömbös led the right radicals and ruled Hungary. In the early 1940s Ferencz Szalasi (1897-1944) dominated a Hungarian party that stood for a kind of racism not dissimilar from that of Nazi Germany and ruled a corporate state modelled on Mussolini's Italy.

In 1926 Poland became a military dictatorship under Marshal Joseph Pilsudski and, ten years later, Greece followed suit under General John Metaxas. By this time Rumania, Bulgaria, and Yugoslavia were governed by authoritarian kings. Austria had moved to the right in 1933 and by 1938 was absorbed into Hitler's Third Reich. Only Czechoslovakia retained a democratic government throughout this period, and it fell to Hitler by 1939.

This trend to authoritarianism reflects a disillusionment with liberal democracy during the inter-war period, as well as the difficulty of running a democracy in the atmosphere of these years, especially in states with no tradition or experience in democratic government. With limited economic resources, divisions between social classes, a fear of left-wing parties, highly nationalistic ideologies, and a desire for stability, all these states, with the exception of Czechoslovakia, moved of their own accord towards dictatorial rule. It should be noted, however, that though they had the trappings of totalitarianism, they were not totalitarian regimes in the sense that Germany was, for they lacked the technological base on which to organize a really effective totalitarian state. The churches in these states, whether Roman Catholic or Greek Orthodox, generally supported the regime, and the traditional ruling classes often continued in power. Fearing revolution above all, the governments of eastern Europe found enemies, even when they did not exist, in order to justify repression in the name of the nation and the preservation of national culture.

THE GROWTH OF AUTHORITARIAN REGIMES: PORTUGAL AND SPAIN

Portugal and Spain both turned to dictatorship in the 1930s after a period of republican government. In both states the Catholic Church was an extremely important and influential institution, industrialization had barely started, and leaders emerged who sought support among the traditional ruling classes, believing that they were defending traditional values against the onslaught of liberalism, socialism, and communism.

In 1926 General Antonio Carmona overthrew the Portuguese Republic which had existed since 1910. The Republic itself had been weak, beset by economic problems and corruption; it was the least developed state of western Europe. Carmona's assistant, Antonio Salazar (1889-1970), became Prime Minister in 1932, and his group, the National Union Party, was declared the only legal political organization. The Republic was formally ended in 1933 when a new constitution was drawn up, stating that Portugal was now a corporate state governed according to Catholic principles.

The corporate state in Portugal was, like Mussolini's version, designed to suppress all opposition and control the economic life of the country. Business and industry—what there was of it—continued as before, and nothing was done to improve working conditions. The Catholic Church was given a monopoly on education and continued to influence all areas of Portuguese life. Salazar believed that the *status quo* must be maintained if Christian principles were to triumph.

Francisco Franco (1892-1975) became dictator of Spain in 1939 at the end of the Spanish Civil War. After centuries of being ruled by a monarchy and a privileged class supported by the Spanish Catholic Church, Spain had become a republic in 1931. The Republic had introduced a reform program which limited the power of the Church and of the old landed elite, checked the authority of the military, attempted a program of public education, and granted local autonomy to several areas of the country. However, though most Spaniards wished an end to the authority of the monarchs, they could not agree on the nature of the new regime. The liberal republicans who governed the Spanish Republic were thus faced with opposition from the left, which wanted more extensive reforms and demanded a complete redistribution of land, and from the right, which formed the *Falange Española* in 1933 and resented the republicans' attacks on the Church, Spanish traditions, and the army.

In the election of 1936 Spain elected a Popular Front government—a union of liberals, socialists, and communists. The right, fearing the introduction of socialism, attempted a *coup d'état* with the support of much of the army. A civil war began when the government gave arms to its supporters to oppose this revolution of the right, and fighting broke out in many areas of the country. All Europe saw the Spanish Civil War as a test of the ability of democracy to defend itself against fascism, and many people from outside of Spain, full of idealism, volunteered to fight for the Republic. Hitler

Joan Miró did this illustration as the cover of a pamphlet soliciting support for the Republicans in Spain. The worker is clenching his fist in the traditional revolutionary salute.

and Mussolini intervened to help Franco's Nationalists, while Stalin aided the Republic. The western-European democracies, fearing that a European war would result if they intervened and uneasy about the communist elements in the Popular Front government, remained neutral.

After three years of intense fighting, the Nationalists succeeded in overthrowing the Republic. Spain became authoritarian once more, with the *Falange* as its fascist party. Franco, *El Caudillo* (the leader), established the trappings of a fascist state. He controlled the media and labour movements and inaugurated a police terror against his enemies. However, like Salazar's Portugal, Franco's Spain can better be described as an authoritarian dictatorship rather than a totalitarian state. The elements which had been in power in Spain prior to the Republic—the Church, the army, the landed nobility, and the leading businessmen—simply regained their privileged positions. Franco did not bring about an upheaval in Spain so much as a restoration of those groups which had ruled prior to 1931. Change was discouraged, although Franco attempted to revive Spain's economic life. On the other hand, in an attempt at an orderly succession, he arranged for the restoration of the monarchy after his death, which occurred in 1975.

THE GROWTH OF AUTHORITARIANISM IN THE FAR EAST: JAPAN

During the 1930s Japan became militarist, and by the end of the decade major political decisions were being influenced by its military leaders. However, the term fascism would be inappropriate for Japan. The traditions of the country were different from those of western Europe, and many Japanese felt that control by an elite was proper. Although Japan had a constitution and a Diet (parliament) since 1889, its government resembled that of Imperial Germany, because ministers of the government were responsible to the Emperor, not the Diet. The democratic state was not overthrown by a mass movement. Rather, military, industrial, and political elites combined to take over the country, ignoring the constitution.

They claimed, like the fascists, that their actions were necessary to further the national cause.

Democratic rule had continued into the 1920s in Japan, but, though the constitution was designed for an active, paternal Emperor, Hirohito, who became Emperor in 1926, felt that his position required him to remain isolated from the people and aloof from politics, as were the emperors of old. This meant that a good deal of the political power fell into the hands of his ministers. Although economic difficulties began for Japan in 1926, the world-wide depression which hit the country in 1930 was a more serious blow to its parliamentary development. The democratic political parties were blamed for the misfortunes of the country, and the prestige of party politics declined. In the 1930s ministers were often chosen who belonged to no party and who governed independently of both party and parliamentary control. Some of these ministers came from the army while others had its support, and Japan drifted into being governed by cabinets which became increasingly anti-democratic and pro-military in orientation. Throughout the period, democratic politicians continued their attempts to woo the voters, and the election of 1937 saw moderate democratic parties win the most votes. But this did not change the character of the government.

Japanese foreign policy contributed to the influence of the military. Japan had been an imperialist power in Asia since the late nineteenth century, and viewed with alarm the rise of Chinese nationalism and the apparent success of the Kuomintang in uniting China. The Japanese military was especially concerned about the security of Manchuria, which was within the Japanese sphere of influence, though still under Chinese sovereignty. Though the politicians urged that diplomacy be used to safeguard Japanese interests, several generals engineered an "incident" in 1931 that gave Japan the pretext to invade and seize control of the area. In 1932 a Japanese puppet state, Manchukuo, was established to replace Chinese sovereignty over Manchuria.

Full-scale war with China broke out in 1937 and this consolidated the control of the military over Japan. Maintaining that it needed to be independent in order to carry out the war effectively, the army slowly took control of government policy. The war, which became a great national cause, also silenced democratic opposition to the generals. From 1937 the military and the political right were allowed to pass laws which created an oligarchy to control the economy and enabled them to disregard the constitution when they felt this was necessary. The war became a holy cause, and few Japanese dared to challenge the authority of the ruling oligarchy.

By 1939, according to one historian, Japan was totalitarian, though not fascist. While the political right was in control, it was a right that represented a traditional elite. Nationalism was the major ideological cement that held the people together and made them accept the oligarchy, but it was not a nationalism that had arisen out of resentment over military or political defeat. The military controlled much of national policy, but it created no hero who promised the Japanese people a great future if they would only sacrifice the comforts of the present and follow him. The sense of community and the nation had always been extremely important in Japan, and it was reasserting itself in the face of what most Japanese saw as a time of economic, political, and military crisis.

FASCISM AND THE RIGHT IN 1939

In 1939 it looked as if fascism and authoritarianism was the wave of the future. In Germany, Italy, Spain, Portugal, eastern Europe, the Balkans, and Japan, the right was firmly in power. Though led by people who thought of themselves as above the common herd, and governed by elitist parties and groups which claimed to be the repository of national wisdom, these right-wing parties had much popular support. In the cases of Germany, Japan, and Italy, it is safe to say that, at least for a time, they did represent the will of the majority. Many people in these states thought that democracy was, as Mussolini styled it, an old-fashioned and empty idea. They loved their nation more than any political ideology and were willing to sacrifice individual freedom to see it win glory.

There were clearly many types of rightist politics in the two decades after the First World War. What unites them all is their aggressive nationalism and their nearly pathological fear of communism. These two features won tolerance for many rightist movements when they were in opposition, and offered a rationale for "emergency" and "enabling" laws once they had gained power. It should not be forgotten that Mussolini and Hitler made their revolution within legal bounds; they came to power by constitutional means, even though they then proceeded to transform the liberal-democratic states which had tolerated their actions.

Fear of communism won fascists much support from the middle class, especially from businessmen who felt threatened with the loss of their position and property should a soviet-type government be established. The old elite supported such groups to protect their traditional position and power. The military remained neutral as the fascists took power, as in Italy and Germany, or supported the right, as in Spain, or led the right, as in Japan. Such a union of business, traditional governing classes, and the military made for a powerful political force when it was combined with fierce nationalism.

Though they talked of great changes, right-wing parties actually shored up the power of traditional ruling groups. Whereas the Russian communists truly destroyed the old and built a new governing structure, the rightists embraced the old privileged groups. Nowhere did a right-wing regime change the old social structure radically. However "revolutionary" such states claimed to be, much of the old bureaucracy also remained intact, and certain institutions, such as the Church, were hardly touched.

Though the fascists did not achieve anything of permanence, they did provide internal stability and order where they came to power. Their ruthlessness and persecutions of political or racial opponents were overlooked—and often approved of—for the sake of national unity and glory. In the 1930s democracy was floundering and many in western Europe looked to fascist or authoritarian states as a model for solving their own economic and national difficulties.

ANALYSIS AND DISCUSSION

1. The causes of the rise of fascism in both Italy and Germany display remarkable similarities, in spite of some obvious differences. Analyse the rise of fascism in Italy and Germany.
2. The consolidation of power is often more difficult than the initial acquisition of it. Both Hitler and Mussolini accomplished the consolidation of their power with considerable success, although in somewhat different ways.
   a) Describe the methods employed by each dictator to consolidate his power.
   b) Which one do you think was more successful? Give the reasons for your choice.
3. "During and following World War II many observers tended to group the regimes of Benito Mussolini and Adolf Hitler as two ex-amples of the same type of government. On the contrary, the Italian and German models illustrate how different two brands of fascism could be!" Contrast Mussolini's style of fascist control with that of Hitler and the Nazis.
4. Compare the "philosophy" of the National Socialists (as outlined in items 1 to 10 on page 254) with their demands as stated in the next section. Discuss the reasons why this combination of objectives would have had such a widespread appeal in Germany.
5. "During the 1920s and 1930s, most of the eastern European states moved away from democracy towards some form of authoritarian rule." Explain why states such as Hungary, Poland, and Rumania, originally established as democracies after the Treaty of Versailles, eventually established authoritarian regimes.

6. ''In the 1930s, democracy was floundering and many in western Europe looked to fascist or authoritarian states as a model for solving their own economic and national difficulties.'' What economic and national difficulties did the authoritarian states try to solve, and how effective were they in solving them?

7. Account for Japan's turn to the right in the interwar years. Compare the Japanese experience with that of Italy, Germany, and Spain.

CHAPTER **13**

Democracy:
1919-1939

THE VICTORY OF THE ALLIES IN THE First World War was a triumph for the liberal democracies of the West. Britain, France, and the United States had defeated the German, Austro-Hungarian, and Turkish Empires, while Imperial Russia, which had been among the Allies at the beginning of the war, had collapsed under the stress of war and revolution. Woodrow Wilson, who seemed to personify the triumph of democracy, had seen the war as a battle between ideologies and he believed that the victory had made the world safe for democracy. Before going to the peace conference, he had toured Europe and everywhere received a hero's welcome. The treaties themselves all assumed the establishment of democratic regimes within the new nations that had emerged from the defeated empires. The statesmen who led their nations to victory and the masses who fought in the war expected that no war would again occur on the scale of 1914–18.

This optimism did not last very long. The period between the First and the Second World Wars, as we have seen, saw the rise and growth of both communism on the left and fascism on the right. The Great Depression, beginning in 1929, accelerated this trend and signalled a change in the morale of democratic states and those who defended democratic government. In 1919 most people felt that democracy had proven itself a viable form of government and that it represented the wave of the future. After the advent of the Great Depression, however, many became despondent about the prospects of democracy. Democratic states seemed unable to cope with their economic and social problems while fascist and com-

munist states appeared to be moving ahead with energy and conviction. Moreover, the diplomatic successes of the fascists and the vacillation of democratic politicians in the face of the fascist challenge only heightened the despair of democrats. According to the poet W. H. Auden, it was an "Age of Anxiety." Serious and intelligent people questioned the ability of democracy to survive, and many thought it was on the brink of extinction.

This chapter will examine the internal affairs of the major democratic states from 1919 to 1939. It should be kept in mind that external problems (to be discussed in the next chapter) contributed to the internal difficulties the democracies faced.

GREAT BRITAIN IN THE 1920s

After the armistice of November 11, 1918, the British wanted to get back to normal life, to pick up where they had left off in 1914. The troops and the public demanded a quick demobilization, and over four million persons returned to civilian status during the next year. In December 1918 the first general election since 1910 was held. During the war the country had been ruled by a coalition government of all major parties, led by the Liberal Lloyd George. After the armistice Lloyd George wished to continue the coalition, and, though the Labour Party and many Liberals would not go along, the Conservatives, led by Andrew Bonar Law, agreed to remain in the coalition. In the election of 1918 Lloyd George and his followers won an overwhelming victory, but most of Lloyd George's supporters were now Conservatives.

British workers repairing roads. The government sponsored such projects in Britain after the First World War to help relieve unemployment.   (Radio Times Hulton Picture Library)

The most serious issue of the immediate post-war years was unemployment. By mid-1921 over two million people were out of work, and England was in the midst of a mild depression. The goods produced by Britain's industries, such as cotton and coal, were less in demand than before the war and were facing stiff competition from other countries. While other nations were building new plants and producing new consumer goods, England tried to reinvigorate its old industries, but it was slow to replace old plants and machinery. The government did not come up with an effective consumer policy and clung to the traditional British position of free trade, even when other countries were protectionist. In the decade after 1921, ten per cent of England's labour force was ordinarily unemployed.

The Irish question, having been put aside in 1914 as a result of the outbreak of the First World War, came back to haunt the post-war government. During the war England had executed several young Irishmen who had engineered a rebellion which broke out Easter Monday, 1916, and as a consequence the bitterness between English and Irish increased. A group demanding complete independence from England, called the *Sinn Fein* (We Ourselves), entered candidates in the British parliamentary election of December 1918 and won nearly every seat in southern Ireland, which was predominantly Catholic. Six counties in the northeast, called Ulster, returned a Protestant majority that was "Unionist," that is, in favour of Ireland continuing as part of the United Kingdom. Members of the *Sinn Fein* refused to take their seats in the British Parliament; rather, in January 1919, they assembled in Dublin, constituted a parliament of their own, which they called the *Dáil Éireann*, and declared Ireland independent. The British responded with force, and guerrilla warfare broke out in the streets of Dublin and other cities.

In 1921 a treaty was negotiated between the British government and representatives of the *Sinn Fein* which made southern Ireland into a Dominion called the Irish Free State. Ulster was to remain part of the United Kingdom and was called Northern Ireland. The *Dáil Éireann* accepted this compromise by a small margin in January 1922 but then had to fight a civil war with extremist Irish nationalists, led by Eamon de Valera, who wished all of Ireland to be united and independent. In 1923 peace was restored in the Irish Free State, but agitation against the English and the partition of Ireland continued both in the Irish Free State and among the Catholic minority of Ulster. After the Second World War, the Irish Free State severed all links with England and declared itself the Republic of Eire. Violence between Catholics and Protestants in Ulster continued, and many of the Irish did not accept the partition as permanent.

Bedevilled by the problems of unemployment and of violence in Ireland, Lloyd George found it difficult to keep his coalition together. Not all Conservatives supported him, and many resented his leadership, and in October 1922 the Conservative Party caucus voted to withdraw from the coalition. A general election followed the next month in which the Conservatives, led by Andrew Bonar Law, gained a majority in parliament. However, the most startling consequence of the election was that the Labour Party won 142 seats, more than doubling its representation, and replaced the Liberals as the official opposition. The weakening of the Liberals had begun during the war when Lloyd George split the party in a struggle for leadership, and the division among the Liberals had become more pronounced in 1918 when he refused to endorse many Liberals for re-election. The Labour Party was able to attract many Liberal voters, and the Liberal Party never regained its former position as one of the two major parties of England.

Stanley Baldwin (1867-1947) soon replaced Bonar Law (who resigned because of ill health) as leader of the Conservatives and as Prime Minister. Baldwin was chosen Prime Minister by the King on the advice of some of the leaders of his party in preference to Lord Curzon, who many felt had a better claim. However, those who made the decision were consciously creating a constitutional precedent by choosing a member of the House of Commons over a member of the House of Lords. Baldwin introduced a quiet unassuming style onto the political scene, and, though he is still something of an enigma, it seems likely that this pipe-smoking, not-too-articulate man was a calculating and extremely clever politician.

Wishing to unite the Conservatives behind him and to tackle the persistent unemployment problem, Baldwin announced that he supported a policy of protective tariffs, a position contrary to the traditional *laissez-faire* attitude of his party. Then, against the advice of many of his supporters, he called an election in December 1923. The Conservatives won 258 seats but lost their majority, while Labour retained second place with 191 seats, and the Liberals, led by Herbert Asquith, won 158 seats. Asquith held the balance of power and decided to support the formation of a Labour government. In January 1924 the first socialist government in England took office when the King asked the leader of the Labour Party, Ramsay MacDonald, to form a cabinet.

MacDonald (1866–1937) was of lower-class origin but looked like an aristocrat. A socialist of long standing, his pacifism had made him unpopular during the war but was now an asset. He was a fine orator and made a favourable impression on statesmen throughout the world. Because he believed that society would move slowly towards socialism, he was always suspected by the left-wingers of his party of being insincere.

Working with a minority government, MacDonald's task was to prove to the electorate that Labour could govern. He proceeded cautiously in domestic affairs, for many Englishmen feared that Labour secretly wished to "bolshevize" England. His major innovation was in housing, where state subsidies for lower-class dwellings were introduced. In foreign affairs he recognized the Soviet Union and negotiated two economic agreements with the Bolshevik government. But, though MacDonald was a right-wing socialist with little sympathy for communism, the Liberals were fearful that relations between Labour and bolshevism were becoming too close, and hence with-

drew their support. In November of 1924 the Labour government fell.

The election which followed was complicated by the publication of a secret letter, allegedly written by a Comintern official to the British Communist Party and containing instructions on how to foment a revolution in England. Though the letter was suspected as a forgery almost at once, large numbers of voters backed the Conservatives, who emerged with 415 seats, while Labour was reduced to 152 seats, and the Liberals won only 42 seats in the House of Commons.

Baldwin's new government proved to be middle-of-the-road, with a mild interest in reform. It regulated the distribution of electric power, nationalized the British Broadcasting Company, and increased housing subsidies. None the less, unemployment remained high and British industry stagnated.

Worker discontent, particularly in the coal industry, led to the General Strike in 1926. In 1925 the mine owners, in desperate financial circumstances, announced longer hours and lower wages for workers. After much agitation the government began an investigation, the result of which satisfied neither side. The owners were particularly hard-headed, and the government seemed to support them against the miners. Finally, with the situation in deadlock and the government dragging its heels, the Trades Union Congress, representing the workers of many industries, called a General Strike in May 1926. One-sixth of England's workers were involved.

Some Englishmen feared revolution, as the government and many prominent figures called the strike illegal. The General Council of the Trades Union Congress was accused of wishing to overthrow the state. However, the following statement was issued to clarify the aims of the strikers:

The General Council does NOT challenge the Constitution.

It is not seeking to substitute unconstitutional government.

Nor is it desirous of undermining our Parliamentary institutions.

The sole aim of the Council is to secure for the

miners a decent standard of life.

The Council is engaged in an Industrial dispute.

In any settlement, the only issue to be decided will be an industrial issue, not political, not constitutional.

There is no Constitutional crisis.[1]

Though some violence did occur, there were no deaths and no attempt was made to overthrow the state. After the first few tense days, there was much good humour on both sides.

The General Strike ended after nine days. The government had persuaded many unions that their cause was hopeless, and when it insisted on unconditional surrender, the union effort, never intended to lead to revolution, collapsed. The miners were unhappy with the actions of their leaders and continued to strike for another half year, while the workers who returned to their jobs had to accept poor working conditions. In 1927, in what many saw as an act of vengeance, the government retaliated with the Trade Disputes and Trade Union Act. The act prohibited sympathy strikes and limited the political activities of unions.

The failure of the strike convinced many in the Labour Party that direct action would not work. Far from radicalizing the party, it united it behind moderates like MacDonald who urged reform through an appeal for votes and parliamentary activity. Moreover, the behaviour of Labour during the strike further convinced the electorate that the party and the movement were not revolutionary. The result was that the Labour Party pursued a moderate policy in an attempt to attract middle-class support, and these tactics were successful in the next election, held in 1929. Labour won 287 seats and became the largest party in parliament for the first time. The Conservatives obtained 261 seats and the Liberals had 59. Once again MacDonald was given the opportunity to lead a government and once again he needed Liberal support. The election proved that Labour could be re-elected into office, that most Englishmen no longer feared a socialist government, and that socialism was clearly distinguished from communism

(throughout the decade the communists never won more than two seats in a British election). By 1929 social democracy was no longer regarded as a great threat in England, and both major parties espoused it. The difference between the policies of Conservatives and Labour was one of degree, not kind. Both agreed on the form of government and both were in agreement in supporting the English constitutional tradition.

FRANCE IN THE 1920s

The rebuilding of a war-torn nation was the major domestic concern in French politics after Versailles. France had deeper political antagonisms than did England. The conservative parties on the right—those who were well disposed to big business, stressed nationalism and feared anything that appeared to resemble communism—united into a *Bloc National*. In the middle of the political spectrum was the Radical Party. The Radicals supported the political principles of the French Revolution of 1789 but did not extend these to the social or economic sphere. They espoused *laissez-faire* and relied for support on large numbers of small landowners, small businessmen, and the lower middle class. On the left was the Socialist Party, divided like most European socialist parties between those who were democratic socialists and those who were communists. However, after the war the temper of France was conservative, and in the election of 1919 the *Bloc National* won 433 seats in the Chamber of Deputies, while the Socialists got 104 and the Radicals 86.

No single party formed a government in France from 1919 to 1939; governments were made up of coalitions of parties and individual politicians, coalitions often united only temporarily against common enemies or for a specific program. Moreover, as in Germany, important elements in the country were against the very existence of the Republic itself. In 1920 the French Communist Party was founded, and after 1922 the labour movement in France was divided between the old *Confédération Générale du Travail*, which remained socialist, and the

Confédération Générale de Travail Unitaire, a Communist-dominated organization. The Communists often split the vote of the left between themselves and the Socialists and thus aided the victory of candidates of the right or the centre. At the opposite end of the political spectrum, among the rightist enemies of the Republic, was the fascist *Action Française,* an organization emanating from the Dreyfus affair. It was ultra-nationalist, bitterly anti-Semitic, rascist, and at this time associated with French Catholicism, even though it was attacked by Pope Pius XI. By the end of the decade the group had its own version of the stormtroopers, wearing special uniforms and engaging in activities similar to those in Germany. There were also other fascist organizations in France built more or less on the same model. In the 1920s, however, the anti-republican forces on the right did not make much headway. However, in the time of crisis that began in 1929, more Frenchmen tended to gravitate to the extremes of the political spectrum.

France recovered rapidly from the First World War. The area of the northeast that had been devastated by trench warfare was rebuilt, and French agriculture continued to be strong. But the major problem was obtaining enough capital to pay off war debts and to support the rebuilding process. The *Bloc National* expected that German reparation payments would provide the badly needed funds, and, when Germany did not keep up the payments, the French government, led by Raymond Poincaré, sent troops to the Ruhr. This only heightened Germany's economic difficulties and helped to reduce the value of the French franc on the world market. France gained nothing from the venture, and the *Bloc National* lost the confidence of its supporters.

Elections in 1924 were fought between a union of Radicals and Socialists called the *Cartel des Gauches,* and the rightist *Bloc National.* The *Cartel* won enough seats to enable the Radicals to form a government that would gain Socialist support. The Radical leader, Edouard Herriot, was not opposed to social legislation, but was not willing to increase taxes to pay for it. He wanted to help the peasants and the lower middle class, but his firm commitment to individual liberty and the rights of property meant that little was accomplished. As a result, the Socialist Party was disillusioned with the Radicals, government majorities became unstable, and cabinets had to be reshuffled continuously in order to placate important political groups. At the same time, inflation grew at an alarming rate in France, and by mid-1926 the French franc, worth twenty cents before the First World War, had fallen to two cents. Finally, the Radicals broke their union with the Socialists and joined with the moderate conservative parties, under the leadership of Poincaré, to form a government.

Poincaré, who had been President of France in the First World War, attracted moderate elements of both the right and left. Although a conservative who stood for financial stability, he was in no way identified with the far right. He was also associated with republicanism and the political principles of 1789. He had been responsible for the failure of the Ruhr expedition and realized that inflation could not be ended by grand gestures or by making others pay for France's difficulties. Above all, Poincaré was trusted by the financiers and the large middle class which resisted change and feared socialism. His leadership and the very existence of a conservative coalition helped to restore confidence in the French economy. None the less, few Frenchmen took a personal liking to this cold lawyer.

The Chamber of Deputies considered the financial crisis so acute and its trust in Poincaré was so complete that in 1926 it granted him the power to take measures by decree to end France's difficulties. This was the first time in the peacetime history of the Third Republic that such power had been given one person. Thus, in the face of the shifting majorities which could not keep together long enough to take any unpopular action, the Chamber resorted to the Napoleonic tradition and granted extraordinary powers to the Premier.

Poincaré acted at once. He reduced the cost of government, raised taxes, and made agreements on tariffs that were advantageous to France. In addition, he stabilized the franc at four cents, thereby doing what no "left" government could have done without serious opposition and cries of "communism," for this action meant that those who lived on fixed incomes, or depended on savings for their livelihood, in effect lost eighty per cent of their money. But the result was to make French goods competitive on world markets, to rid the state of many of its debts, and to restore French prosperity.

From 1926 to 1931 France experienced a rare period of stability and confidence. Industry flourished and was modernized, and the middle class solidly supported the government. In the elections of 1928 conservatives made gains, reflecting satisfaction with Poincaré's policies. The only group which did not make any headway was labour, divided between two unions and several political groups and ideologies. The government was not responsive to labour's demands and tended to look for support to the farmers and people in small businesses. Most Frenchmen were quite happy to support the Third Republic under the circumstances, and Poincaré remained Prime Minister of France for three years, the longest consecutive period for any holder of the office from 1919 to 1939. He retired because of ill health in July 1929, satisfied that he had stabilized the Third Republic and led it in a successful transition from war to peace.

THE GREAT DEPRESSION

European prosperity in the 1920s was dependent in great measure on world prosperity, for modern nations needed to trade with each other and to lend and borrow capital on the world money market. Employment and well-being all over the globe were, to a large degree, interconnected and were part of a single economy. Depression, when it came, was thus a world-wide phenomenon.

The signal that prosperity was at an end first came from the United States, when on "Black Thursday," October 24, 1929, the New York stock market took a spectacular drop. In the next three years industrial stocks decreased in value to one-fourth of their 1929 levels. Many historians feel that this financial crisis was the result of too much credit being extended to borrowers and of grossly inflated values for stocks. People had borrowed money to buy stocks that were quickly rising in value. This "orgy of speculation," as one historian has termed it, created a sense of false prosperity, and the United States government, following a policy of laissez-faire towards business, did not take measures to control the situation. Once the bubble was pricked and stocks began to fall, people were caught without money to pay their debts or even to cover the loans used to buy speculative stocks. Many became bankrupt, businesses failed or cut back production, and millions were thrown out of work. This was the beginning of the Great Depression, and its effects were soon felt throughout the world.

The United States was the major creditor nation after the First World War, having lent huge sums to the Allies for the war effort. It also exported a great deal more than it imported at this time because of its large industrial capacity and the tariff barriers it had erected against the goods of other countries. Other nations had borrowed from the United States to pay off internal and external debts and to buy American goods. This meant that the entire economic structure of the West was built on credit facilities in the United States.

World trade suffered as a result of the financial collapse in the United States. Agricultural areas felt the first blow. As agricultural production had grown after the First World War, farmers found, even during prosperous times, that they often had an oversupply of food, and that this kept prices low. Now, as prices fell again, farmers found that production costs were exceeding prices paid on the market. Industry fared no better. With loss of confidence in the economy, the shattering of credit facilities, and mounting unemployment, people no longer had money or credit to buy goods. Demand dropped, production slowed down, and industries collapsed.

By the end of 1932 the banking system of the United States was in a shambles. Five

"Breadline—No One Has Starved". A 1932 etching of the Great Depression by Reginald Marsh. (Prints Division, The New York Public Library—Astor, Lenox, and Tilden Foundations)

thousand banks had closed because their creditors could not repay loans, and there was thus not enough money to cover customers' deposits. Those financial institutions in the United States that had regularly loaned money to Europe no longer had the resources to continue. The drying up of American loans to Europe made it difficult for financial houses throughout the world to maintain their solvency. In May 1931 Austria's largest bank collapsed, while the government of Germany took emergency actions to meet a German financial crisis. In September 1931 Great Britain went off the gold standard and devalued its currency. By mid-1932 the French economy was in serious difficulty.

In terms of human misery and dislocation, the Great Depression had as much impact as the First World War. In 1932 unemployment had risen to twelve million in the United States and six million in Germany; other countries were equally hard hit. In the United States, Europe, and Japan, many of the unemployed left their families and roamed the streets. Many who occupied important positions were reduced to begging.

People who fell from prosperity often became disillusioned with the system itself, and sometimes with life. During these years, communism and fascism began to look good, as many decided that capitalism and democracy had failed. An English youth described his feelings and experiences:

Fits of depression and morbidness were the hardest things I had to fight against. But I attended gymnastic classes every morning, and gradually I shook off gloomy thoughts....

I became at this time a very rabid reader of social and anti-religious works. I marched in every demonstration that was organised in South London. Although interest in religious matters wanes amongst the unemployed, the study of politics spreads every day. People who have never given a thought to politics when in work wake up to the fact that something is definitely wrong and patronise all sorts of political meetings. I have never belonged to any trade union or co-operative movement, but I know men whom I have met at various political meetings, and unemployment seems to have stimulated interest in them to such an extent that they spend their spare time telling small knots of hearers what they would do if they were in charge of these movements, what drastic measures they would carry out and what social teachings they would impress upon the people.[2]

Economic misery created political crises throughout the world—in Germany, for example, it helped to bring the Nazis to power. Russia, with a controlled economy and more economic planning than any other country of the world, seemed unaffected. As democratic governments lost credit with the masses, a number of people decided that the Great Depression was the last chapter in the history of democracy—only authoritarian governments seemed capable of dealing with difficulties of this magnitude.

DEMOCRACY IN THE UNITED STATES: FRANKLIN ROOSEVELT AND THE NEW DEAL

On March 4, 1933, Franklin D. Roosevelt (1882–1945) took the oath of office as the new Democratic President of the United States. Conditions in the country were disastrous and the mood of the people was bitter. The previous Republican government had followed a policy of allowing business to find its own way out of the dilemma. In a speech on the day of his inaugural, Roosevelt said:

First of all, let me assert my firm belief that the only thing we have to fear is fear itself—nameless, unreasoning, unjustified terror which paralyzes needed efforts to convert retreat into advance. In every dark hour of our national life a leadership of frankness and vigor has met with that understanding and support of the people themselves which is essential to victory. I am convinced that you will again give that support to leadership in these critical days.

In such a spirit on my part and on yours we face our common difficulties. They concern, thank God, only material things. Values have shrunken to fantastic levels; taxes have risen; our ability to pay has fallen; government of all kinds is faced by serious curtailment of income; the means of exchange are frozen in the currents of trade; the withered leaves of industrial enterprise lie on every side; farmers find no markets for their produce; the savings of many years in thousands of families are gone.

More important, a host of unemployed citizens face the grim problem of existence, and an equally great number toil with little return. Only a foolish optimist can deny the dark realities of the moment. . . .

We do not distrust the future of essential democracy. The people of the United States have not failed. In their need they have registered a mandate that they want direct, vigorous action. They have asked for discipline and direction under leadership. They have made me the present instrument of their wishes. In the spirit of the gift I take it.[3]

The new President, a cousin of former President Theodore Roosevelt, was a member of a patrician family in New York State. He was a lawyer and had been governor of New York State from 1929 to 1933. In the 1920s he had suffered from polio, which left his legs partly paralysed, and his struggle for recovery from illness, against great odds, helped him to identify with people in difficulty. Despite the fact that he was sometimes in a wheelchair, he exuded strength. A very magnetic figure who was despised and called a "demagogue" by those who opposed him, he offered hope to many who were in despair. Like other popular leaders of the age, he became a master at using the new medium of radio to get his thoughts across to the masses. Roosevelt was not attached to any ideology; he was a pragmatist who would follow a hands-off policy when he thought it would achieve a desired end, or would take decisive action when he felt it necessary. Willing to experiment at a time when people were groping for answers, he promised "a New Deal for the American people."

The New Deal was a whirlwind of legislation and executive action, all designed to end the stagnation of the preceding few years. It was a heady contrast to the policy of his predecessors, who believed in *laissez-faire* except when it came to protective tariffs. Roosevelt closed all banks and re-opened them under government supervision, started a public-works program which employed 300 000 people by the end of the summer and took the United States off the gold standard, thus helping to stimulate trade with other nations. In addition, federal money was given to local authorities for relief programs, agricultural programs were inaugurated to help the plight of farmers and control production, and the stock exchange was placed under federal regulation. Roosevelt also arranged for government assistance to industry, imposed further regulations on wages and hours, guaranteed workers the right of collective bargaining, and introduced a scheme for old-age pensions. The scope of all this social legislation was unprecedented in United States history. It is calculated that by 1936 over eight billion dollars had been spent for relief and public works by the Roosevelt administration.

Unemployment began to decline and was reduced to less than ten million by mid-1935. More importantly, Roosevelt gave the people hope and a belief in the future—both essential ingredients for renewed confidence in the economy. In the election of 1936 he won an electoral victory of unprecedented proportions, securing a majority of votes in forty-six of the forty-eight states. Though the recovery was slow, the fact that the economy of the United States was once again gaining strength gave an impetus to the economies of other countries.

Roosevelt was hated by the very class he saved—the capitalists of the United States. They despised the regulations and restrictions on business which he introduced. Yet he restored confidence in both democracy and capitalism by demonstrating that the capitalist system was not helpless in a time of economic crisis, and that democratic states could produce leaders of great energy. Other critics, however, levelled a more serious charge, for they felt that the vast network of power created by new government agencies and the bureaucracy established to implement Roosevelt's programs meant the erosion of the liberty of the individual. Some accused Roosevelt of being a totalitarian in democratic clothes, a man who knew how to deal with an emergency, but who concentrated a vast amount of power in the federal government, particularly in the hands of the President. There is no doubt that this occur-

red, but to equate Roosevelt's America with Mussolini's Italy is to miss the point. Roosevelt always worked within the democratic process, even when he behaved in a high-handed manner. Despite Roosevelt's bureaucracy, authority in the nation was still very much dispersed among various levels of state and local government. Viewed from the perspective of the 1930s when democratic states were in great turmoil and when the West seemed to be abandoning democracy for totalitarianism, Roosevelt's program and his policy of clear action within the framework of the democratic process represented for many the last hope for the survival of democracy. European supporters of democracy now looked to the United States for leadership and inspiration.

GREAT BRITAIN IN THE 1930s

The Second Labour government led by Ramsay MacDonald took office on June 4, 1929. Within a short time it was faced with a mounting economic crisis. Unemployment grew worse as the effects of the Depression spread to Europe, and by 1931 over two and a half million were out of work. Exports, on which the life of England depended, had dropped by 1931 to nearly half the level of 1929 as a result of shrinking world markets and increases in protective tariffs. MacDonald, to the disappointment of many members of his party, resorted to traditional rather than innovative measures. Despite the growing need of welfare funds for the unemployed, he tried to economize and to balance the budget. The gold standard—which reduced England's power to export because it gave the pound an artificially high value—was maintained, and no large-scale program of public works was begun. As the leader of a minority government, MacDonald knew that he could be put out of office if he offended the political views of his Liberal supporters. On top of that, however, he was a man of conservative temperament and was still trying to prove to Englishmen of all classes that Labour could be trusted to govern.

By 1931 the British economy was in grave difficulty. A parliamentary committee reported in July that the budget deficit would reach record levels and recommended that the British tighten their belts further—taxes should be raised, while unemployment benefits, on which many families depended, should be cut down. Meanwhile, British gold reserves were decreasing, and the Bank of England was finding it increasingly difficult to support the official value of the pound. The government needed loans to carry on its business, but foreign bankers would only lend money on the condition that it reduce unemployment benefits. For a Labour government, supported by working-class voters and elected on promises to raise the standard of living, this was a difficult measure to accept. When MacDonald put the matter to his cabinet, it split on the issue. MacDonald then accepted the resignation of his cabinet. It was assumed that the King would call on a leader from one of the other parties to form a government, but to the surprise of most of the Labour Party, MacDonald remained Prime Minister. He formed a National Government, a coalition in which the Conservative leader, Stanley Baldwin, was second-in-command, and members of all three parties were admitted to the cabinet. While most of MacDonald's party disowned him, he claimed that he was trying to save the country in a national emergency.

MacDonald continued as Prime Minister, supported by a majority in parliament that was mainly Conservative. Labour opposed the new government and expelled MacDonald and all those members who supported him from the party. The government cut unemployment benefits, raised taxes, and, in the face of mounting pressure on the pound, took Britain off the gold standard.

Housing in Britain. During the inter-war years the housing shortage was acute.   (Greater London Council Photograph Library)

As a result, the pound dropped in value from $4.86 to $3.40.

After adopting these measures, the coalition called an election in order to obtain a clear mandate for its policies. The National Government won over 550 supporters, while Labour dropped from 287 seats to 46. The electorate clearly had spoken in favour of the National Government and against any drastic or revolutionary measures. In fact, the election of 1931 was a great victory for the Conservatives who won 472 seats.

The National Government did adopt some measures aimed at producing economic recovery, but did nothing as spectacular as Roosevelt's New Deal. It aided farmers with price supports and under the impetus of Neville Chamberlain, a leading figure in the cabinet, built houses. In 1932 it introduced a protective tariff, thereby losing the support of many Liberals, who clung to their hard-line policy of free trade. Unemployment did begin to decline after 1933, but it continued to be a major problem. The gradual recovery of world trade produced a parallel revival in Britain.

MacDonald retired as Prime Minister in 1935, and Baldwin took over as leader of the National Government. He soon called a general election. This was only a few weeks after Mussolini had invaded Abyssinia, and while he took a strong stand in favour of the League of Nations, he was careful to point out that Britain was not thinking of going to war. The electorate gave Baldwin strong support; the Conservatives won 387 seats, Labour recovered some of its strength by winning 154 seats, and the Liberals won only 21. This turned out to be the last election before the end of the Second World War in 1945.

In 1937 Baldwin went to the House of Lords, after spending most of 1936 presiding over the abdication of King Edward VIII, who wished to marry Mrs. Wallis Simpson, a twice-divorced American. Baldwin remained Prime Minister until the coronation of Edward's brother, George VI, and then stepped aside in favour of Neville Chamberlain.

An intelligent, cold, and angular man who had been one of the active members of the lethargic cabinets of the thirties, Chamberlain now became preoccupied with diplomacy. Germany was rearming and had combined with Italy and Japan in an alliance called the "Axis." At the same time, the League of Nations had been weakened by inaction and defection, the Spanish Civil War was raging, German troops were in the Rhineland, and the Treaty of Versailles was being ignored. Nations were rearming and aggression went unchallenged. In this atmosphere, war became a real possibility, and as a result domestic problems were increasingly relegated to the background. Chamberlain's main interest and experience had been in internal affairs; now he was increasingly occupied with foreign policy.

Throughout the 1930s the National Government had charted a middle course and had won overwhelming public support, despite its failure to deal adequately with the Depression. There was never any great danger that political extremists would take over the government of Britain. The "respectability" of the Labour Party had already been established through the governments of 1924 and 1929–31. The General Strike of 1926 had been orderly and not at all revolutionary, and the vast majority of Labour supporters advocated democracy and parliamentary government. Few Englishmen were afraid that the Labour Party or the British workers would undermine the traditional British process of government.

The British were not without their fascists and communists. Sir Oswald Mosley, by turns a Conservative and a socialist, had formed the British Union of Fascists after failing to get the Labour Party to adopt more dramatic policies. Using Mussolini's Fascists as a guide, his small group organized rallies, wore uniforms, "protected" Mosley as he delivered speeches, and fomented violence. The British generally reacted to the fascist style and brutality with disgust, and Mosley's group never achieved a single electoral victory.

Although British communism attracted some distinguished followers, it made little headway with the public, never winning more than two seats in any election. Some intellectuals admired the Soviet system, believing that capitalism was dying and that a planned society was necessary if western Europe was going to pull out of the Depression. The Communists argued that the Labour Party had sold out to the capitalists, and that a temporary dictatorship of the left was necessary in order to transform England into a true socialist state. As the thirties wore on, as economic recovery began, and as more information about the workings of Stalin's system came out of Russia, communism lost its appeal.

The weakness of the extreme right and left in Britain does not mean that there was any great enthusiasm for the National Government. Despite its overwhelming electoral support, the government did not excite admirers. It was not hostile to labour and did adopt moderate measures to deal with social and economic problems, but it lacked inspiration. No decisive program, such as the New Deal, was inaugurated.

FRANCE IN THE 1930s

The Great Depression affected France later than any other major industrial country, a testament to the diversity of the French economy. However, by 1932 an economic slump had set in, and by 1933, 1 300 000 were unemployed. For the rest of the decade the country was in serious economic difficulty. Elections in 1932 were fought between the *Cartel des Gauches* — Socialists — and the parties of the right. The parties of the *Cartel* won 334 seats in the Chamber of Deputies, the right won 257, and the Communists 10. The Radicals, led by Edouard Herriot, formed a government which won the support of the Socialists, but as in the earlier decade this coalition government proved to be ineffective in the midst of a crisis. Herriot pursued a policy of budget cuts and deflation—public works were stopped, salaries slashed, expenditures cut. This policy tended to aggravate rather than alleviate the crisis, and it infuriated his Socialist supporters. Herriot's government fell in December 1932.

During the next fifteen months four prime ministers of the *Cartel* took office; none was able to keep it, as majorities in the Chamber shifted. More energy was spent creating governments than in finding solutions for the problems of France. As a result, confidence in the *Cartel* declined and with it confidence in the Republic. No reform program was inaugurated because it was impossible to get a majority of deputies to support any legislation which changed the *status quo*. Despite France's economic difficulties and the threat from a resurgent Germany, the Chamber of Deputies behaved like a club that was mainly concerned with the private interests of its members.

Disillusionment with the Republic increased with the Stavisky affair, which broke in the newspapers in late 1933. Serge Stavisky was a financier who had manipulated an issue of worthless bonds for his own enrichment. When his fraud was discovered, he left Paris and was found dead in January 1934. The right and much of the French press claimed that the police had killed Stavisky and made his death appear as suicide, in order to protect prominent members of the government from exposure. The government denied the charges but bungled the investigation, and in an atmosphere already charged with suspicion these events further undermined faith in the Republic. The scandal became intensified as it was revealed that Stavisky had links with prominent men in and out of government, who seemed to have protected him for years from prosecution.

The Stavisky affair was a signal for an attempted coup by the fascist right. The *Action Française* and other rightist leagues prepared for action. These leagues were ultra-nationalist, anti-socialist, anti-Semitic, and anti-republican, and they enjoyed the support of several newspapers. On February 6, 1934, the *Action Française* issued the following statement:

After the closing of the factories and offices [the people] will meet before the Chamber tonight and crying "Down with the Thieves!" they will tell the Government and its parliamentary supporters that they have had enough of this putrid régime.[4]

Accordingly, the fascists gathered in the

Place de la Concorde in Paris to demonstrate against the Republic and to march on the Chamber of Deputies. The police fired on the crowd; eleven demonstrators and one policeman were killed, and several hundred people were injured. Not since 1871 had blood been shed in a political clash between Frenchmen. Although this challenge to the Republic failed, the presence of the far right continued to be a menace.

The growing strength of the rightists throughout Europe, particularly the fascists in Italy and Germany, helped to bring together the French left after 1934. At the same time, the Comintern reversed its policy of demanding that communists oppose social-ists and ordered them to join with other parties in "popular fronts" that would op-pose fascism. After much negotiation the Radicals, Socialists, and Communists put forth a common program in January 1936. The political demands of this "Popular Front" movement included the "dissolution of semi-military formations" and the "appli-cation and observance of trade union rights for all." The group supported the League of Nations and collective security. It called for controls on exports and the arms trade, and asked for tax reform in France. Among its "economic demands" were:

1. The establishment of a national unemploy-ment fund.
2. Reduction of the working week without reduction of the weekly wage.
3. Drawing young workers into employment by establishing a system of adequate pensions for aged workers.
4. The rapid carrying out of a scheme of large-scale works of public utility.[5]

In addition, agricultural supports were to be put into effect and banking and credit organ-izations were to be regulated. The Popular Front program was a comprehensive scheme designed to attract the support of moderates as well as leftists.

In May 1936 the Popular Front, particu-larly the Socialists, won an unprecedented electoral victory. It could count on the sup-port of about 380 deputies, while the com-bined right had 237 seats. Moreover, the

coalition was much more "leftist" than similar coalitions in the past. The Commu-nists had increased their strength from 10 to 72 seats, while the Radicals lost 43 seats and were replaced as the dominant party by the Socialists, who gained 39. With a resounding electoral victory and a coherent political program, the most important Popular Front movement in Europe formed a government that included Socialists and Radicals and could count on Communist support in the Chamber of Deputies.

Léon Blum (1872-1950) became the Prime Minister of the new government. With a firm loyalty to democratic socialism, Blum had demonstrated his commitment to the Third Republic during the early 1920s when com-munism had drawn many socialists away from his party. He had become the leader of the Socialist Party through his undoubted intellectual ability. Business feared Blum because of his socialism, and the Fascist Leagues hated him because he was a Jew as well as for his politics. Although he was bitterly attacked, Blum was a moderate during a time when French politics was turn-ing to the extremes of fascism and com-munism.

Immediately on taking office, Blum faced a series of strikes by workers who felt that the election of the Popular Front meant that factories would be turned over to labour. The strikes were passive and no violence occurred, but business and the right only grew more suspicious and spread rumours of a communist takeover. Blum personally presided over the negotiations between the workers and owners at the Hôtel Matignon, the residence of the Prime Minister, and on June 7 representatives of employers and em-ployees made what was called the Matignon Agreement. Workers received the right to collective bargaining, wages were raised by seven to fifteen per cent, and the forty-hour work week and paid holidays came into effect. The Agreement was a major break-through for French labour and represented Blum's greatest success.

Blum's government also reorganized the Bank of France, gave aid to French agricul-ture, and devalued the franc. However, the

In this French cartoon of 1937, the symbol of France is caught between Communism and Hitler.   (Snark International)

economy continued to decline, despite such government intervention, while new strikes hindered exports, and the government's social policy proved to be quite expensive. Moreover, while the aim of the Front was to transform France internally, it had to put some of the government's revenues into an arms program in order to counter German rearmament. No miracles were produced by the Front, and disillusionment soon set in. By March 1937 Blum felt that further reform would have to be postponed. His followers were divided—the Radicals believed he had gone too far, while the Communists felt he had not gone far enough. The Communists wanted to pursue a more aggressive foreign policy. Finally, in June 1937, faced with defections from his supporters, pressures from labour, and antagonism from business, Blum resigned.

The dissolution of the Popular Front put the French state once again at the mercy of shifting majorities in the Chamber of Deputies. After the fall of the Blum government, parliamentary institutions were increasingly discredited. Many workers became communist, convinced that under the Third Repulic it was impossible for a government of the left to survive. In the meantime the French right demanded a strongly nationalist and authoritarian regime, arguing that Blum and the Popular Front were the wedge opening the way to a Communist government in France. They reviled Blum as a Jew and were privately afraid that he would be successful and strengthen the Republic, to which they had no loyalty. Their slogan, "Better Hitler than Blum," served to undermine the Blum government and was an indication of the fragility of French democracy in the late thirties. Indeed, in the summer of 1940 they got their wish: France was conquered by Germany, and Hitler and his troops marched down the *Champs Elysées*. The Third Republic collapsed and was replaced by an authoritarian regime.

DEMOCRACY IN 1939

The major democratic states, reeling from the effects of the Depression and easily exposed to public criticism by virtue of their democratic systems, seemed to be doing badly in comparison with the various authoritarian regimes. No democratic politician denied that there was a crisis, but apart from Roosevelt, who was willing to experiment boldly, no one seemed able to get a reform program underway. Although the worst effects of the Depression were over by the middle of the decade, none of the major democratic states had thoroughly recovered by 1939.

Some of the smaller democracies retained their parliamentary system in spite of the general trend to authoritarianism. Canada, Australia, New Zealand, and the Union of South Africa, all dominions within the British Empire, looked to the British tradition for guidance. Though all were badly hit by the Depression, they rode out the storm without any grave challenge to their democratic systems. At the same time, they continued to move towards a greater degree of independence from Great Britain. In 1926 the dominions were defined as "autonomous communities within the British Empire, equal in status, in no way subordinate to one another in any aspect of their domestic or external affairs, though united by a common allegiance to the Crown, and freely associated as members of the British Commonwealth of Nations."[6] In 1931 the Statute of Westminster formalized this arrangement.

Belgium, Holland, and Switzerland also continued as democratic states and were usually governed in this period by conservatives. In Belgium the major problem was the division of the country into two nearly equal linguistic groups—those who used French and those who used Flemish, a language related to Dutch. French had been the major language, but Flemish-speaking people obtained equal language rights by the early 1930s. A small fascist movement called the Rexists, closely tied to Hitler and Mussolini, grew up in the 1930s. While it never had political power, the movement did influence the Belgian government to weaken its ties with England and France. In Holland and Switzerland the central government obtained more power while preserving the

traditional democratic system, but neither country experienced serious political difficulties, even in times of economic crisis.

Democratic socialism made great headway in the Scandinavian states of Norway, Sweden, and Denmark. Each of these countries was small and had a democratic tradition. Their socialist parties resembled the Fabians of England and the revisionists of western Europe rather than the dogmatic Marxists. Thus, while they were not afraid to intervene in the economy of the country, these parties were careful to preserve civil and political rights. When the Depression hit, the Scandinavian governments took decisive action. In contrast to the orthodoxy of Labour in Britain and the Radicals in France, the Scandinavians subscribed to the "new economics," going into debt in order to pump money into the economy. They did what their leaders thought necessary but kept within the existing constitutional framework without being wedded to any economic slogan and without polarizing the issue between free enterprise and socialism. By 1939 Scandinavians had the most comprehensive social insurance plans in the world. The result was a rough economic equality among citizens, freedom of action within the limits of community organization, and the most successful response of any of the democracies to the crisis of the inter-war years, particularly the Depression.

No one individual or government had any clear way out of the Great Depression. In England and France the resort to national coalitions obscured the inability of politicians to come up with effective programs. Indeed, the charge has been made that the British House of Commons and the French Chamber of Deputies functioned during these decades as private clubs in which members jockeyed for power within the small select group. Certainly, though Labour and the French left formed several governments, conservatives were in the main in control of both parliaments. The Popular Front in France of 1936-37, a government led by Socialists, came to power too late and was too much dependent on its coalition parties for effective action. Even the more successful politicians of northern Europe and the United States admitted that many of their experiments were shots in the dark.

One of the features of democratic states is that governments are, to a great extent, accountable to the public-at-large. While a government will try to put itself in the best light possible, it cannot indefinitely suppress or openly distort the truth. Moreover, freedom of the press and opinion are normally protected in democratic states. Hence the misery of the Great Depression in the United States, England, France, and Weimar Germany became a matter of public record, and public debate exposed these conditions to the world. In fascist and communist regimes, news and opinion were under state control and it was possible to cover up and distort failure, even when millions of lives were lost. Italy fared no better in the Depression than other states, but Mussolini substituted rhetoric for accomplishment, and many believed him. Germany pulled out of the Depression with a policy of massive public expenditure, but the price was Hitler's dictatorship, concentration camps, and the end of freedom. Stalin managed to collectivize and industrialize at a terrible human cost.

But as far as most outsiders were concerned, the authoritarian states had firm programs and were successfully managing their economies while the democratic states were proving indecisive. Many of the people who attacked Roosevelt and Blum as enemies of democracy voiced their admiration for the "systems" of Hitler and Mussolini. Many on the left who called Roosevelt a fascist and Blum a lackey of capitalism found virtue only in Stalin. The flaws in the democratic regimes and the indecision of many of their leaders were matters of public knowledge. In a time of crisis simple answers became attractive and the façade of success presented by dictators was often taken for the real thing.

Critics of democracy found further reason for dissatisfaction for not only were the democratic states in trouble at home, but their foreign policies lacked vigour and conviction. Their position in the world appeared to be diminished. Hitler was rearming and openly flouting the Treaty of Versailles; Mussolini talked about empire and invaded Abyssinia; and militarists in Japan were pushing for a policy of expansion. Communists believed their movement to be the wave of the future. Only the democratic states seemed to be in retreat. The authoritarian regimes declared that democracy was in decay; it was, they said, an old-fashioned way of organizing people and its days were numbered. During the late 1930s many people expected that the ultimate confrontation would be between fascism and communism, a confrontation which would take place after the final defeat of the democracies.

ANALYSIS AND DISCUSSION

1. "The period from 1919 to 1939 was, according to the poet W. H. Auden, an 'Age of Anxiety.' Serious and intelligent people questioned the ability of democracy to survive, and many thought it was on the brink of extinction."
a) What common problems did the democracies share in this period? Illustrate your answer with references to France, Britain, the United States, and Scandinavia.
b) How did each democracy attempt to solve its problems? Which do you think were most successful? Why?

2. "European supporters of democracy looked to the United States for inspiration and leadership."
a) Explain the reasons for the pre-eminence of the United States among the Western democracies at this time.
b) In what ways was Franklin Roosevelt a more effective leader than the leaders of the European democracies in this period?

3. Despite their difficulties, the old democracies survived the period between the wars. What factors account for this survival?

CHAPTER **14**

Diplomacy and War: 1919-1945

THE WAR TO END ALL WARS CAME TO a close in November 1918; hardly two decades later, in September 1939, the Second World War began. After the First World War many people were hopeful that statesmen, through open diplomacy, would solve contentious issues between nation-states, and that the world would witness a trend towards democracy. These hopes and beliefs soon faded away. The Treaty of Versailles created almost as many national and international problems as it solved, and European politics began to move in an authoritarian direction. In the 1930s economic distress put the democracies in a difficult position, and they found it hard to compete with both fascist and communist states.

Moreover, in 1919 not all the major powers were prepared to defend the Versailles settlement. Neither Russia nor Germany participated in the negotiations for the peace—the former claimed to be supporting "revolutionary" movements all over the world, while the latter accepted the treaty only under threat and rejected the blanket condemnation of Germany's responsibility for the war. Japan and Italy were both on the side of the victors in the First World War, and both helped to make the treaty, but they felt "cheated" out of the spoils of victory. Only the United States, England, and France could be said to favour the *status quo* resulting from the treaty; yet there was some doubt about the willingness of the United States and England to become involved in continental European affairs, should that prove necessary to defend the treaty. The settlement of 1919 could only be as fixed as those who made it and had the power to enforce it wanted it to be. As events in the next

two decades were to make clear, the treaty would not be the basis of a new order.

THE LEAGUE OF NATIONS

The Covenant of the League of Nations was incorporated in the Treaty of Versailles at the insistence of Woodrow Wilson, who hoped that an international organization would help to keep the peace and rectify any injustices contained in the settlement itself. The League of Nations was, for Wilson, an integral part of the post-war settlement. He was willing to bargain over many things at the peace conference, but the idea of the League was for him sacred, and he was determined to see it realized.

The League, as set up, had two chambers—an Assembly and a Council. The Assembly included all member states and met annually to consider the important issues of peace and war. The Council, which had executive functions, was composed of the five big powers—the United States, England, France, Italy, and Japan—and four (later six) other states elected by the Assembly. The Covenant said that "the Council may deal at its meetings with any matter within the sphere of action of the League or affecting the peace of the world." A Secretariat, which formed the corps of a new international civil service, ran the day-to-day business of the organization. Many international bureaus, such as the International Labour Organization, were associated with the League, though not part of it.

The League was an attempt to co-ordinate the efforts of sovereign states to maintain peace, and to further international co-operation. In effect it was a more formal expression of the "congress system" established after the Napoleonic Wars, when powerful states met in times of crisis to negotiate differences and maintain peace. By setting up an Assembly and a Council, the founders of the League of Nations tried to balance the interests of both the smaller and the larger states. Moreover, as envisioned by Wilson, the League was to be a worldwide organization—all states were to be members.

It was generally recognized that the League did have some authority to enforce its will, and Article 10 of the Covenant stated:

The members of the League undertake to respect and preserve as against external aggression the territorial integrity and existing political independence of all Members of the League. In case of any such aggression or in case of any threat or danger of such aggression the Council shall advise upon the means by which this obligation shall be fulfilled.[1]

Other articles provided for the compulsory arbitration of international disputes and for the "severance of all trade or financial relations" between League members and any state which resorted to war to settle a dispute. With the power to impose such "sanctions," the League was a much more coherent idea than the old congress system.

When the great powers of the world were in agreement, the League functioned well and did play an important role in dealing with a number of international problems. As a diplomatic alternative to war, it provided a way of settling colonial disputes through international commissions. The League Covenant established a Permanent Court of International Justice which could deal with legal problems which arose among nations. The International Labour Organization, associated with the League, helped to establish international guidelines for conditions of labour. Also associated with the League were international agencies that dealt with such international problems as health, finance, and the settlement of refugees. On such issues it was evident that it was in the interests of all states to co-operate.

The question of membership was among the many problems facing the League at its inception. The original members were the European Allies who had won the war, many of the eastern European states that had been created by the peace treaties, the Latin-American states, Japan, China, Siam, and several small states. Of the countries defeated in the First World War, Austria and Bulgaria joined in 1920, Hungary in 1922, Germany in 1926, and Turkey in 1932. Russia joined in 1934 when its foreign policy shifted from diplomatic isolation to one of co-operation with other states against fascism. But in 1920 at the League's initial meeting in Geneva, Germany and Russia were not present. However, the greatest void was the United States. Although Wilson had signed the Treaty, the United States Senate, in March 1920, refused to ratify it, and as a result, though the United States often co-operated with the League, it never belonged to it. Thus three of the major powers whose co-operation was necessary to maintain peace were not members of the League of Nations in 1920.

The question of national sovereignty was another thorny problem for the League. While all member nations believed in international co-operation, few were willing to give any independent power to the League. In an age of nationalism, when national self-interest was considered a sufficient justification for nearly any action, it was difficult for any state to do more than promise voluntary co-operation. Hence, though "sanctions" could be voted against an aggressor, there was no mechanism for making each state in the League abide by the decision of the organization. Nor did any state wish such a mechanism to exist, for they were all jealous of their sovereign rights. Each state thus adhered to the League and its policies only to the extent that it wished. In a crisis, when national self-interest conflicted with League policy, the League was usually ignored.

Yet another difficulty for the League in the years between the wars was that even the democratic states, which had placed much of their hopes in the organization, came to doubt that the League could ever be very useful in keeping the peace. By the 1930s democracies were in the minority in the

League, and those nations which had rejected democracy seemed to be getting stronger. By the time Hitler challenged the very basis of the Treaty of Versailles in the mid-1930s, few nations were prepared to put much faith in the effectiveness of the League. In the end the League, like all associations of sovereign states, worked as well as those who had power wanted it to work. People, however, often judged the League against Wilson's utopian ideal and found it wanting. In fact, the League served as a ready forum for the discussion of international problems, and it helped to foster co-operation in many areas. In the context of the times, it could do no more. In the 1920s, however, many people in the democratic countries placed too much faith in the League, and the result was that, in the difficult and turbulent 1930s, they became thoroughly disillusioned with it.

THE SEARCH FOR SECURITY: 1919-24

The balance of power of 1914 no longer existed by 1919, but no one was certain how the new power relationships would be sorted out. For the moment, among the old powers, Germany and Austria had ceased to count. Russia was in the midst of being transformed into the Soviet Union, and the Russian communists were too busy consolidating their power to play any large diplomatic role in the world. Among the victors in the war, Italy and Japan were unhappy with the treaty but were not strong enough to revise it by themselves.

The United States, England, and France were the dominant powers in the world in 1919. However, both the United States and England placed limits on their diplomatic commitments, and the unwillingness of the United States Senate to ratify the Treaty of Versailles in 1920 was the beginning of a period of American withdrawal from European affairs. Wilsonian internationalism was replaced by isolationism, a feeling that in times of peace the United States ought to be mainly concerned with developments in its own hemisphere. English policy, on the other hand, was unclear. While the British wished to prevent a revision of Versailles

and to make certain that no new war occurred, they seemed more concerned with domestic affairs and were unwilling to devote too much energy to upholding the international *status quo* of 1919. Of the major powers, only France was vitally concerned with diplomatic problems. France thus dominated the diplomatic scene in the first years after Versailles, not because it was all-powerful, but because it was the only big power willing to act to ensure the continuation of the situation created by the Treaty.

The French continued to fear Germany. Ever since the Franco-Prussian War, Frenchmen had looked to Germany as their major rival and enemy. Now, with a population only two-thirds that of Germany, with the memory of millions of their countrymen killed in the trenches, and a bitterness resulting from the belief that Germany had started the First World War, the French felt they must be certain there would be no German resurgence. French insecurity was heightened by American isolationism and by English reluctance to make clear commitments to defend France against future German attacks. In its search for allies, France turned to the new states created by the peace settlement. In 1921 France and Poland signed a treaty in which each was committed to help the other in the event of either being attacked. Later in the decade "understandings" were reached with Czechoslovakia, Rumania, and Yugoslavia, who had organized a "Little Entente" in 1920 and 1921 to preserve the boundaries of the post-war settlement. Unable to get firm commitments from the big powers, France looked to these smaller states of eastern Europe for support in the event of German aggression.

France's sense of insecurity was heightened when the two outcasts of Europe—Germany and Russia—came together in 1922. A European economic conference had been held at Genoa in April to discuss general problems, and Russia and Germany had been invited. But no economic understandings were reached because the Russians would not recognize the debts contracted by the czarist regime, and this position had infuriated the French. Moreover, while the conference was proceeding, German and Russian diplomats signed an agreement of friendship at the nearby town of Rapallo. The Treaty of Rapallo was not important so much for its contents—it merely asserted that the two countries would settle their differences "on a basis of reciprocity"—as for the fact it was signed at all. For both countries, it was the first voluntary agreement made with any other power since the end of the war, and it meant that each was no longer alone. No one underrated the combined power of the two, and France was in panic. French diplomatic efforts to isolate and encircle Germany had received a serious setback.

In its quest for allies against Germany, France had strongly supported the collective security machinery of the League and insisted on a rigid application of the terms of Versailles. One of the most difficult prob-

"Hands off the Ruhr!" proclaims a German poster of 1923. "France" is shown as a usurper grimacing in pain as a result of the occupation. (Internationaal Instituut voor Sociale Geschiedenis, Amsterdam)

lems arising out of Versailles, however, was reparations. The section of the treaty dealing with reparations began with the war-guilt clause, which declared that Germany and its supporters had caused the war and hence must reimburse the Allies for damages. The treaty then stated that Germany would pay a sum determined by a Reparations Commission. In 1921 the Commission reported that Germany was to pay $33 billion altogether and fixed a schedule of payments. Germany made one payment in money and several other payments in goods. Though some Western economists claimed that the Commission erred in making the payments so large that Germany could not possibly make them, others felt that Germany was reluctant to pay. The German mark was declining in value in any case, and in mid-1922 the German government requested a two-year moratorium on the payments. The English were willing to go along, but the French insisted that the payments continue. Finally, in January 1923, when no payments were forthcoming, France sent troops to occupy the industrial area of the Ruhr in Germany.

German inflation became severe. While German workers in the Ruhr adopted a policy of "passive resistance," refusing to mine the rich coal area, the German government printed money twenty-four hours a day. The mark, worth 62 to the dollar in May 1921, was worth 100 000 to the dollar in June 1923, and 4 trillion, 200 billion to the dollar in November 1923. People used wheelbarrows to carry enough money to buy a loaf of bread.

It was clear that the reparations problem had to be reconsidered. In 1924 a committee chaired by Charles G. Dawes of the United States drew up a plan that was accepted by both Germany and the Allies; it reduced the amount of payments, provided for a loan which helped to stabilize the German currency, and led to the withdrawal of French forces from the Ruhr in November 1924.

Two major attempts were made to strengthen the powers of the League of Nations in the event of international war or lesser disputes. In 1923 a Treaty of Mutual

Assistance was considered by the Assembly of the League. It provided that all members of the League would be obligated to give military assistance to any state which the Council declared to be a victim of aggression. This meant that sanctions against an aggressor would be compulsory, rather than voluntary. France and its allies supported this agreement, but many nations, including England, refused to commit themselves to compulsory sanctions. The measure was defeated.

In 1924 the first British Labour government proposed the Geneva Protocol. Designed to clarify the arbitration procedures of the Covenant of the League, it provided for compulsory binding arbitration in the event of international disputes which could not be settled in other peaceful ways. The French supported this proposal, only to see it fail when the British Conservatives, who formed a new government in November 1924, turned down the agreement. As a result, France was frustrated in its search for allies or for international guarantees in a world which seemed hostile or indifferent to its diplomatic interests.

THE LOCARNO SPIRIT

The settlement of the reparations issue between France and Germany and the revival of Germany's economy, led the way to negotiations among European powers about Germany's frontiers. While England was unwilling to sign agreements that called for compulsory action or arbitration in the event of international quarrels, it was willing to consider the specific question of the border between France and Germany. Negotiations went on for much of 1925, and in October, at the Swiss city of Locarno, agreement was reached on a series of treaties which were formally signed by the individual nations in December 1925.

In the Locarno treaties, Germany accepted its eastern and western borders as fixed, and arbitration procedures were agreed upon in the event of a dispute. The major agreement, however, was a treaty of mutual guarantee signed by Germany, Belgium, France, England, and Italy. The treaty stated that

The High Contracting Parties collectively and severally guarantee . . . the maintenance of the territorial *status quo* resulting from the frontiers between Germany and Belgium and between Germany and France and the inviolability of the said frontiers as fixed by . . . the Treaty of Peace signed at Versailles. . . .[2]

But, although England, Belgium, and Italy had thus guaranteed the western frontier of Germany, they did not do the same in the east. France therefore took it upon itself to support its eastern European allies and made agreements with Poland and Czechoslovakia to aid them in the event of a violation of their frontiers. England refused to sign such a commitment.

In the long run Locarno served to weaken the post-First World War settlement. The distinction made between the eastern and western boundaries of Germany indicated that the major European powers were less willing to counter German expansion in the east than they were in the west. Moreover, the fact that the Locarno treaties were signed at all implied that Versailles was somehow not quite binding—that Germany had to reaffirm it in order to make it a solid commitment.

Although these agreements made no *real* difference to European security, they had a profound psychological effect. They marked the re-entry of Germany onto the international scene as an equal power among the other states. They gave birth to the "spirit of Locarno," heralded in its day as a time of co-operation. Germany entered the League of Nations in 1926, and for the next few years, while prosperity and internal stability continued in most states, there was optimism that international problems could be solved and that the prospects for peace had been enhanced.

Several attempts were made during the 1920s to reduce or limit armaments. The most successful was the Washington Conference of 1921–22, dealing with naval disarmament. The conference resulted in a ten-year agreement on capital ships in accordance with the following ratio: the United States 5,

England 5, Japan 3, France 1.67, and Italy 1.67. This meant that for every five capital ships (battleships, aircraft carriers, or cruisers) possessed by the United States and England, Japan would have three and France and Italy would have 1.67. The agreement was meant to maintain a constant ratio among the fleets of these nations and avoid a costly ship-building competition. Very little further progress on limiting arms and weapons was made at naval disarmament conferences at Geneva in 1927 and at London in 1930.

Although it was difficult to bring about a real limitation of arms, it was not hard to obtain an agreement to outlaw war in the optimistic atmosphere following Locarno. In 1927 the French Foreign Minister, Aristide Briand, suggested to the United States that both countries agree to outlaw war between each other. The United States Secretary of State, Frank Kellogg, wished to enlarge the pact so that all nations could sign. The French agreed, and in 1928 the Pact of Paris (sometimes referred to as the Kellogg-Briand Pact) was signed by some fifteen states. It was eventually agreed to by sixty-five.

1. The High Contracting Parties solemnly declare in the names of their respective peoples that they condemn recourse to war for the solution of international controversies, and renounce it as an instrument of national policy in their relations with one another.

2. The High Contracting Parties agree that the settlement or solution of all disputes or conflicts of whatever nature or of whatever origin they may be, which arise among them, shall never be sought except by pacific means.

3. ... This Treaty shall ... remain open as long as may be necessary for adherence by all the other Powers of the world. . . .[3]

Though many people have suggested that the Pact of Paris was the equivalent of a document on the virtues of motherhood, it was the first international agreement signed by most sovereign states which stated that war was not a legitimate method of settling international disputes.

The Pact of Paris may have been an illusion, but it was one which people could at least entertain during the Locarno honeymoon. The Great Depression ended the mood which gave birth to this kind of agreement, and by the early 1930s states were being torn apart by domestic problems. The most important new figure on the international scene was Adolf Hitler, and the spirit of *Mein Kampf* replaced the spirit of Locarno.

GERMAN REARMAMENT AND THE ESTABLISHMENT OF THE "AXIS"

Hitler had outlined his aims frequently in the years before he came to power. He was an ardent nationalist and a believer in German racial superiority; he insisted that Germany must have *Lebensraum* for the expansion of the German people; he demanded the unification of all those of the "master race" under one German state; and he promised to make Germany the "hammer," not the "anvil," in international affairs. In the years prior to the Second World War his foreign policy was successful largely because he mastered the psychology of his potential enemies just as he continued to understand and exploit the mood of the German people. In the 1930s most countries had serious domestic concerns and were unwilling to go to war or to stop German aggression. Moreover, Hitler linked all his acts with a condemnation of the Treaty of Versailles and a defence of the idea of national self-determination. Some people in France, and more especially in England, could not help agreeing that Versailles had been a dictated peace; they even welcomed a revision if they thought it would right the balance of power and eliminate grievances. In an age of nationalism Hitler's plea—that he only wished to bring all Germans under one sovereignty—won some sympathy. He knew what ideas would produce the desired effect, and in addition he had the uncanny ability to time his moves exactly right.

The 1930s began in a mood of pacifism. Many in the West felt that war was an abomination, and all were disillusioned with the destruction and the after-effects of the First World War. One of the most popular books of the decade was Erich Maria Remarque's *All Quiet on the Western Front* (1929), a novel condemning the mindlessness and emptiness of war and its destruction of humane values. Hitler realized that this pacifist mood, combined with his attacks on Versailles and claims of national self-determination, would allow him to achieve his ends without serious challenge. Whenever he changed the *status quo*, whether repudiating the disarmament clauses of Versailles in 1935 or demanding a part of Czechoslovakia at Munich in 1938, Hitler continually insisted that his latest demand was the final "revision." He claimed that, like Bismarck, he was a man of restraint and could be satisfied once he achieved his limited ends. A Europe and a world anxious for peace believed him until it could do so no longer.

That Hitler was determined to upset the international *status quo* was made clear in his first year in power. In October 1933 he withdrew from the League of Nations and took Germany out of a disarmament conference then under way in Geneva. He then set out to destroy France's elaborate treaty structure in eastern Europe. To that end he negotiated a ten-year, non-aggression pact with Poland, signed in January 1934. Germany, Hitler claimed, would take its rightful place in the world, the place denied it by the vengeful victors of the First World War.

In March 1935 yet another revision of Versailles was announced. Hitler proclaimed that Germany would henceforth ignore the disarmament clauses of the treaty. In his proclamation he claimed that the treaty required that all states disarm, but, while Germany had been forced to do so, others had not. According to Hitler:

That means: the High Contracting Parties of the former victor States have one-sidedly divorced themselves from the obligations of the Versailles Treaty.

Not [only] did they refrain from disarming. . . . No. Not even was there a halt in the armaments race, on the contrary, the increase of armaments . . . became evident. . . .

The world . . . has again resumed its cries of war, just as though there never had been a World War nor the Versailles Treaty. In the midst of these highly-armed, warlike States . . . Germany was, militarily speaking, in a vacuum, defencelessly at the mercy of every threatening danger. . . .

What the German Government, as the guardian of the honour and interests of the German nation, desires is to make sure that Germany possesses sufficient instruments of power not only to maintain the integrity of the German Reich, but also to command international respect and value as co-guarantor of general peace.

For in this hour the German Government renews before the German people, before the entire world, its assurance of its determination never to proceed beyond the safeguarding of German honour and the freedom of the Reich, and especially does it not intend in rearming Germany to create any instrument for warlike attack but, on the contrary, exclusively for defence and thereby for the maintenance of peace.

In so doing, the German Reich's Government expresses the confident hope that the German people, having again reverted to their own honour, may be privileged in independent equality to make their contribution for the pacification of the world in free and open co-operation with other nations and their Governments. . . .[4]

In a law announced the same day, Germany adopted universal military service. Several of the other powers, notably France, protested this action, but most people took Hitler's words at face value—they agreed that the victors of the First World War had not disarmed, and that Germany did have the right to defend itself. Far from viewing this as an aggressive action, many welcomed it as a realistic measure in the light of power politics, and hence as a contribution to maintaining peace.

The League of Nations was in no position to challenge Hitler, even if it wanted to do so. As an instrument for peace it had been weakened by its failure to deal with aggression. When Japan invaded Manchuria in 1931, the Chinese brought the act to the attention of the League. A commission, under Lord Lytton of England, was created to investigate the situation. The Lytton report, issued in 1932, condemned Japanese actions. The Assembly of the League adopted the report in February 1933, along with a series of recommendations for settling the problem. Japan ignored the report and the recommendations, withdrew from the League the next month, and continued fighting in China.

An Italian invasion of Abyssinia (Ethiopia) in 1935, as part of Mussolini's quest for empire, brought a plea for help from the aggrieved country. The Abyssinian Emperor, Haile Selassie, went to the League and asked that Italy's aggression be stopped. In October 1935 the League declared Italy the aggressor and invoked economic sanctions: no member of the League was to sell arms or raw materials to Italy. However, coal and oil, which Italy needed more than any other supplies, were not included in the sanctions, and the result was that, while Mussolini was denied some materials, not enough was done to stop him. The British and French, who continued to ship oil to Italy, and who wanted both to support the League and to avoid getting Mussolini too angry at them, succeeded only in driving him into an alliance with Hitler. In May 1936 Italian troops marched into the capital of Abyssinia, Addis Ababa, and the king of Italy was proclaimed emperor of Ethiopia. Thus, in the cases of both Japan and Italy, two crucial instances when a big power was clearly in violation of the League Covenant, the League had failed to take effective action.

German troops marched into the Rhineland in March 1936. This area of Germany had been demilitarized by the treaties of Versailles and Locarno, but Hitler counted on the reluctance of the League and the Western powers to risk war in the defence of these treaties. The Germans in the area, declaring their nationalism, welcomed the troops as a sign that the bitter memories following the First World War were being erased. But Hitler's generals had opposed this act—the army was still weak, and they would have retreated if France had taken action against this direct violation not only of the "dictated" Versailles Treaty, but of the "negotiated" Locarno Pact. However, France was in the midst of internal difficulties, and it did not receive any encouragement from its consultations with England. As a result, there were the usual protests, but no action. Hitler had taken a major gamble and won. German troops remained in the Rhineland, and Hitler's control over the German nation was stronger than ever.

The fascist states drew together in 1936 and 1937. Italy had been condemned by all nations except Germany for its invasion of Abyssinia; Germany had been condemned by all nations but Italy for its remilitarization of the Rhineland. Both saw Britain and France blocking their ambitions; both proclaimed that democracy was all but buried, and that fascism was the wave of the future. The Spanish Civil War, which broke out in July 1936, cemented this ideological and diplomatic relationship, for both countries sided with Franco from the outset. Said Hitler:

According to the English there are two countries in the world today which are led by adventurers: Germany and Italy. But England too, was led by adventurers when she built her empire. Today she is governed merely by incompetents.[5]

A pact of co-operation between Italy and Germany was signed in October 1936, and Mussolini announced the agreement on November 1:

The Berlin conversations have resulted in an understanding between our two countries over certain problems which had been particularly acute. But these understandings, which have been sanctioned in fitting and duly signed agreements—this Berlin-Rome line—is not a diaphragm but rather an axis, around which can revolve all those European states with a will to collaboration and peace.[6]

This was the birth of the "Rome-Berlin Axis."

Japan joined the "Axis" at the end of November by signing an Anti-Comintern Pact with Germany. Although outwardly directed against the Russian Comintern, the agreement opened the way for co-operation between Germany and Japan in revising the map of the world. Italy initialled the Anti-Comintern pact in 1937 and the union of the

An artist's view of the Spanish Civil War. (*Picasso, Pablo.* Guernica Studies and *"Postscripts": May 9, 1937. Mother with Dead Child.* Ink on white paper, 9½" x 17⅞". On *extended loan to* The Museum of Modern Art, New York, *from the estate of the artist.*)

major fascist and militarist states was completed. By 1937 the world of the late 1920s had completely changed—the Treaty of Versailles had been shattered; no one had much faith in the League; Locarno was dead both in spirit and reality; and the Pact of Paris was a dream of another era. Germany, Japan, and Italy had been successful in open aggression. There was little left of the hope of peace and of the building of a better world that had come in the wake of the First World War. A new era of aggression had begun.

ANSCHLUSS, APPEASEMENT, AND MUNICH

There were many Germans outside the boundaries of the Third Reich who, Hitler claimed, belonged under the protection of Germany. Hitler had always looked upon his native land, Austria, as part of the German nation and believed it would eventually be incorporated into Germany in an *Anschluss* (union). Austria had a Nazi party as early as 1930, and in 1934 Austrian Nazis murdered a hostile chancellor in an attempt to take control of the state. The new chancel-lor, the conservative Kurt von Schuschnigg, maintained friendly relations with Germany while attempting to retain Austrian independence. In 1936, as a result, Hitler and Schuschnigg signed an agreement in which Austria promised to pursue its foreign affairs along lines parallel with those of Germany. In exchange Germany declared that it would never interfere with Austrian independence.

Hitler meanwhile did nothing to discourage the Austrian Nazis from agitating against the government, and in early 1938 he felt the time was ripe to make his move. He accused Schuschnigg of having pursued a foreign policy that violated the 1936 agreement. Summoning the Austrian chancellor to his mountain home at Berchtesgaden in February 1938, Hitler harangued him for long hours on his errors and, after threatening to invade Austria, browbeat Schuschnigg into agreeing to let several Nazis into his cabinet, including the appointment of one of the Nazi leaders as head of internal security. This meant the end of an independent Austria, for now the Nazis were in charge of the police. In early March, however, Schuschnigg called for a plebiscite on the question of whether Austria should maintain its independence, hoping that an overwhelming vote against Hitler would discourage the German dictator. Hitler then mobilized his troops against Austria, got Austrian Nazis to create disorder, and forced Schuschnigg to resign. One of the Nazi ministers in Austria then asked for German troops to enter the country to prevent disorder, thereby providing Hitler with the cloak of legality to carry out his plans. On March 12 German troops entered Austria and marched on Vienna, the city which had rejected Hitler in his youth. By March 13 Austria was no longer a state but a part of the Third Reich. Not all Austrians were unhappy with the *Anschluss*; many cheered the German soldiers and welcomed the union with Germany.

The response of England and France to this union was to pursue a policy of appeasement. It is important to note that appeasement was regarded as a means of dealing with a difficult situation, not simply a cowardly refusal to do anything. Though it is now agreed that it was the wrong policy for the democracies to pursue in the 1930s, it might have been the correct one in different circumstances. Those who were in power in England and France were sympathetic to Hitler's demand for national self-determination for all Germans. Faced with an economic depression, they were not prepared to go to war over parts of middle Europe, and, being afraid of communism in Russia, they were willing to tolerate fascism if it seemed the only alternative. They had been through the First World War and recoiled in horror at any suggestion that another war of such magnitude might be the only way of halting fascist aggression. Moreover, while most of them disliked Hitler's racism (although some even accepted this), many admired Mussolini, who seemed to be free of such prejudice. In the end, however, appeasement was based on one basic calculation—that, like Bismarck, Hitler would be satisfied with adjustments in the *status quo*, that he was a man who could be content with limited gains. It took Neville Chamberlain, the British Prime Minister and leading advocate of

appeasement, a full year after the *Anschluss* to recognize that there was no way for Hitler to be content, and that Hitler would exploit appeasement by taking territory a bit at a time, rather than attempt an all-out conquest of Europe with his armies.

Opposition to appeasement came from many quarters and grew stronger as the decade neared its end. The French never wholly supported appeasement, although they hoped it would succeed; they could not stop fascism alone. The Soviet Union never adopted the policy; in 1934 it switched its policy from a blanket opposition to all democratic states and parties to a policy of co-operation with democracies against fascism. In the Spanish Civil War, the Soviet Union was the only country to aid the Spanish Republic against the fascists. But, though Russia periodically called for concerted action against fascism, few leaders in the democratic states trusted Stalin or were willing to deal with the Soviet Union.

In the United States, Franklin Roosevelt began to abandon isolationism in 1937. Ahead of public opinion in his country, he saw fascism as a great danger and slowly began to shift from an isolationist position to one of co-operation with other democratic countries. In the West as a whole, the Spanish Civil War caused many intellectuals to reconsider their pacifist attitude. Some went to Spain to aid the Republic; at home they urged opposition to the fascism and racism of Hitler. In England, the most notable opposition to appeasement at this time came from Anthony Eden and Winston Churchill. Eden had been Foreign Minister but resigned in February 1938, unhappy with appeasement and determined that England must prepare to resist fascism. Churchill, a former cabinet minister, was out of office throughout the decade.

After Austria, Hitler turned to Czechoslovakia. A stable democracy since its creation after the First World War, Czechoslovakia was part of the "Little Entente" allied with France. It was a multi-national state, with Czechs, Slovaks, Hungarians, Ruthenians, and three million German-speaking inhabitants living within its borders. The Germans were in the area of the Sudetenland, on the long German-Czech frontier. Hitler and those who supported him in the Sudetenland stirred up discontent among this German-speaking population, and, as in Austria, Hitler used the local Nazis to provide a convenient excuse for entering the country. When disorders occurred in the Sudetenland in the summer of 1938, Hitler began making military preparations. Chamberlain sent a British negotiator to act as mediator between the Germans and the Czechs, but no agreement could be reached. Czechoslovakia prepared to stop any invasion, and war seemed to be on the way in September.

At this point Chamberlain took matters into his own hands. He asked for a meeting with Hitler in Berchtesgaden on September 15 to discuss the situation with him. This itself was an extraordinary concession. "I was astonished," said Hitler, recalling his reaction when he heard that Chamberlain wished to fly to see him. At the ensuing meeting, Hitler was firm in insisting that all areas in Czechoslovakia with a German majority— virtually the whole Sudeten area, a mountainous region essential to the defence of Czechoslovakia—must be annexed to his empire. A memo of the conversation, made by the Germans, states that Hitler insisted "that in every place where there was a majority for Germany, the territory in question would have to go to Germany."

Chamberlain accepted the logic of this, based as it was on the concept of national self-determination. The French agreed and the two then confronted Czechoslovakia with the plan, informing the Czechs that if they were not in accord neither Britain nor France would be able to help them against Germany. Without other allies and with much of their territory negotiated away by

Munich, October 1938. From the left, Chamberlain, Daladier, Hitler, Mussolini, and Italy's Minister of Foreign Affairs, Count Ciano (Imperial War Museum, London)

their friends, the Czechs had no alternative but to capitulate. Chamberlain then went to see Hitler on September 22 at Bad Godesberg to inform him that an accord could be reached. Hitler changed his terms, demanding that Germany be allowed to send in troops at once to occupy the Sudetenland. Chamberlain was upset, and, though Hitler delayed the date of occupation to October 1, the English Prime Minister had little hope that a peaceful settlement could be made.

Informed by Chamberlain of the conversation at Bad Godesberg, the Czechs insisted that Hitler's proposal to occupy the Sudetenland immediately was "wholly unacceptable." They mobilized their forces and the Western democracies feared a general war. The French called up some of their reserves, and the English mobilized the navy on September 28. Hitler began making war speeches. However, one last attempt was made to keep the peace—this time at a four-power meeting suggested by Chamberlain and involving Britain, France, Germany, and Italy.

The meeting—the third encounter between Hitler and Chamberlain—occurred at Munich on September 29. The powers agreed that the proposal made at Bad Godesberg was the only one which was workable. While the Czechs waited outside the conference room, their country was split up by the leaders of the democracies and the fascist states. This was the "Munich Agreement." Chamberlain felt that for the sake of peace the concessions made to Hitler were worth it. When he flew back to London he announced: "I believe it is peace for our time." He was cheered by most of his countrymen for finding a way of avoiding war. As for the Czechs, Chamberlain wrote in a letter of October 2, 1938: "I am sure that someday the Czechs will see that what we did was to save them for a happier future. And I sincerely believe that we have at last opened the way to that general appeasement which alone can save the world from chaos."[7]

TO WAR

Munich was the ultimate test of the policy of appeasement. Hitler had said once more that he wanted no more territory and had promised to respect the integrity of what remained of Czechoslovakia. On March 15, 1939, however, German troops marched into what was left of Czechoslovakia, and it became clear to all that Chamberlain had badly miscalculated—Hitler could not be appeased. As in Austria, Hitler used internal disorders and bullying to make the invasion seem "legal," but the invasion of Austria and Czechoslovakia differed in significant ways. In annexing Austria, Hitler could claim to be creating a national union of Germans on the principle of Versailles. In marching into Czechoslovakia in March 1939, he was in clear violation of the Munich Agreement. Britain and France now had no illusions and they began preparing for war in earnest.

Chamberlain now made pledges of support to areas where it seemed Nazi aggression was imminent—Poland, Greece, Rumania, and Turkey. As fascism grew in power— the Spanish Civil War ended with Franco's victory in March 1939; Italy invaded Albania and annexed it to the Italian Empire in April 1939—the Western democracies were no longer willing to give in to Hitler's demands in the hope that he would be satisfied. They had become aware there was no stopping German fascism with promises and treaties.

Both the Axis powers and the democracies realized that the balance of power in Europe might depend on the attitude of Russia. Were Russia to join with Britain and France, Hitler would be forced to fight a two-front war; were Russia to stay neutral, Hitler could concentrate on the west. Both camps entered into negotiations with Russia. But Stalin and Communist Russia had been distrusted equally by both sides. The democracies saw communism as a great menace to their existence, and, even when Stalin abandoned isolationism for a policy of popular fronts against fascism, few in power in England or France wished to be associated with him. On the other hand, communists and fascists were sworn enemies, and the mutual hatred was intensified by the fact that they were on opposite sides in the Spanish Civil War. In the end, however, Stalin abandoned ideological concerns to do what he thought was best for Russia. He was tired of dealing with a western Europe which thoroughly distrusted him, and he wished to avoid war at all costs, until, at least, he felt that Russia was prepared for it. He probably hoped that the democracies and the fascist states would also fight each other to exhaustion and leave Russia alone. Thus, on August 23, 1939, Stalin and Hitler signed a non-aggression treaty, meant to last for ten years. A secret addition to the treaty provided for the division of spheres of influence in the Baltic states, Bessarabia, and Poland.

The Nazi-Soviet Pact was the most shocking turnabout in a decade of surprises. No one truly expected the two hostile powers to draw together, but national self-interest was for both more important than ideological concerns. The pact meant that Hitler had finished his diplomatic preparations for war. With Russian neutrality guaranteed and a statement from Mussolini that he would support Germany but was not prepared to give immediate military assistance, Hitler sent German troops into Poland on September 1, 1939. Britain notified Hitler that he must withdraw. Hitler refused, and on September 3 Britain and France formally declared war on Germany. What some have called "the twenty years' truce" ended; the Second World War began.

AXIS OFFENSIVES: 1939-41

The strategy of Hitler in the Second World War was based on the *Blitzkrieg*, the "lightning war." Having begun rearmament in the 1930s, the German war machine in September 1939 was more modern and better equipped than any other. While others prepared their defences, attack was the important element in the German plan. Airplanes were used to knock out industry and supply lines and to terrorize civilian populations; tanks were employed to break through static defences and to make way for motorized infantry. Hitler did not want a protracted war of attrition like the First World War. The *Blitzkrieg* suited the circumstances.

The invasion of Poland, launched on September 1, was enormously successful for the German army. In a few weeks Warsaw, the Polish capital, was surrounded by German troops. Russia entered the war on September 17 in order to lay claim to the Polish territories promised it in the Nazi-Soviet Pact of August. The two armies—the German from the west, the Russian from the east— crushed Polish resistance. Poland, brought into existence as a modern nation-state at Versailles, was again partitioned, and on September 28 it ceased to exist as a sovereign entity.

Russia then began negotiations with Finland regarding border changes which would help Russia defend itself against any future German attack. Stalin was aware that Germany might eventually attack his country, and that the Nazi-Soviet pact would only last as long as each of the two powers thought it useful. But the Finns were unwilling to meet Russia's demands and the Russians attacked on November 30. The Finns put up a surprisingly strong resistance through the winter of 1939-40, and, although vastly outnumbered, the Finnish army did not finally give up until March 1940. The Winter War, as it was called, brought great sympathy for the Finns (but no aid) from western Europe. The inability of the Russians to defeat the Finns quickly led to a belief in Europe that Russia was weak, and that the Russian soldier could not fight on equal terms with the soldiers of other European powers.

The Winter War was the only serious action for several months after the partition of Poland. The winter of 1939-40 was a time of waiting for most of Europe—Germany was strangely holding back, and Hitler, for propaganda purposes, was continually offering to make peace with Britain and France. Within the German high command there was some hesitation about attacking to the west. In Britain and France people were puzzled. They were at war; people were mobilized; but little was happening. This was called the "phony war," a *Sitzkrieg* instead of a *Blitzkrieg*.

The lull ended on April 9, 1940, with the German invasion of Denmark and Norway. Britain saw Norway as a strategic territory—

it gave Germany many naval bases and allowed ore from neutral Sweden to be shipped to Germany as raw material for armaments. Though Britain and France sent a moderate amount of aid to Denmark and Norway, Germany had little difficulty overrunning the two Scandinavian countries. In Norway the Germans set up a puppet government under Vidkun Quisling, a Norwegian who had supported the Nazi cause; the Norwegian King and government fled to England, where they set up a government-in-exile. Denmark was conquered so rapidly that its King and government remained at home, resisting the German occupation as best they could.

Prime Minister Chamberlain's conduct of the war was under continual attack in Great Britain. His policy of appeasement had failed, and there was little confidence in his ability to lead a British government in a time of crisis. The loss of Norway and Denmark was the final blow to his prestige. In May 1940 he resigned as Prime Minister. He was replaced by Winston Churchill (1874–1965), probably the most able war leader of this century. Author, journalist, sailor, soldier, imperialist, and parliamentarian, Churchill had held various ministries in both Liberal and Conservative governments since 1906. In the 1930s he was no longer near the centre of power, but continuously urged that England should ally itself with other countries to stop Hitler. Though his judgment had been challenged in the 1930s, he was considered a prophet in 1940.

Churchill was a great orator and a fine writer, and his speeches gave hope to those who fought the Nazis. He urged the British to fight on, to remain calm in the midst of crises, and to steel themselves for any eventuality. On June 4, 1940, he told the House of Commons:

I have, myself, full confidence that if all do their duty, if nothing is neglected, and if the best arrangements are made, as they are being made, we shall prove ourselves once again able to defend our island home, to ride out the storm of war, and to outlive the menace of tyranny, if necessary for years, if necessary alone. . . . Even though large tracts of Europe and many old and famous States have fallen or may fall into the grip of the Gestapo and all the odious apparatus of Nazi rule, we shall not flag or fail. We shall go on to the end, we shall fight in France, we shall fight on the seas and oceans, we shall fight with growing confidence and growing strength in the air, we shall defend our island, whatever the cost may be, we shall fight on the beaches, we shall fight on the landing grounds, we shall fight in the fields and in the streets, we shall fight in the hills; we shall never surrender. . . . [8]

Pugnacious and dedicated, Churchill provided inspiring leadership at a very difficult time.

As Churchill was assuming his new post, Hitler struck in the west. On May 10 German troops invaded the Netherlands and Belgium in order to get at the French and British armies. The Germans bombed the Dutch city of Rotterdam, killing an estimated 40 000 civilians, and on May 14 the Dutch surrendered, their Queen and government leaders escaping to England. The Belgians, victims of the initial German thrust of the First World War, had built up their defences in the east, but by May 28 the Belgians had surrendered.

The German thrust into Belgium and Holland also brought disaster to England and France, for their armies had rushed into Belgium on the first day of the German attack and were thus cut off by the German advance. The French had built the Maginot Line, a strong series of fortifications in the areas of German penetration in the First World War. Instead of attacking the Maginot Line, however, the Germans had gone around it to the north, through territory that was thought to be impassable. As one person put it, the French had prepared very well for the last war. The German armies then moved quickly towards the English Channel to close the net on the British and French soldiers. At the end of May and in early June the British tried to evacuate as many Allied soldiers as possible. All British vessels, from navy ships to yachts to fishing boats, were asked to go to Dunkirk to evacuate troops across the English Channel. While the rearguard held off the Germans, 335 000 soldiers were rescued.

Now German troops moved on Paris. Mussolini, always ready to make gains on the cheap, entered the war on June 10, hopeful that Italy would benefit from the defeat of France. Italian troops were sent to attack France in the south, but advanced slowly. It was Germany alone which drove France out of the war. Paris was taken by mid-June, and the Prime Minister of France, Paul Reynaud, resigned. He was replaced by Marshal Henri Pétain, aged eighty-four, a hero of the First World War, and a strong supporter of the French right. Pétain signed an armistice with Germany on June 22, 1940. The Battle of France was over.

The fall of France startled the world. France was considered a great power, and no one thought any single state could defeat France in so short a time. Frenchmen who were unsympathetic to the Republic blamed democratic statesmen and institutions for weakening the French military. Although historians still disagree on the reasons for the French defeat, many think France simply could not compete with the German military machine. It was no longer the era of Napoleon, and, while the French had stubbornly fought the Germans in the Franco-Prussian War and in the First World War, by this time German power simply overwhelmed the French very quickly.

The armistice with Germany divided France in two. The northern two-thirds of the country was to be occupied by Germany; the southern one-third was to be left unoccupied. Paris was in the hands of Hitler, and the French government was moved to Vichy in southern France; hence it was styled the "Vichy Régime." Pétain, who led the Vichy Régime, was a French nationalist of the right, not a fascist, although he was surrounded by many persons who were most sympathetic to fascism. He calculated that he could best help France by working against the Nazi occupation from within. However, as the war went on, Vichy France lost whatever independence it had at its beginning, and it increasingly came to collaborate with the Nazis. There were many Frenchmen in exile in London and North Africa, and a resistance movement developed in France itself. The leadership of the "Free French" was assumed by General Charles de Gaulle, who had been one of a number of junior officers who took exception to the military strategy devised in the inter-war period, but whose opinions were not valued. De Gaulle organized from London a group of volunteers which the Allies recognized as a kind of "free" government-in-exile.

Churchill responded to the defeat of France in his characteristically tough and idealistic manner. On June 18, 1940, he told the House of Commons,

the Battle of France is over. I expect that the battle of Britain is about to begin. Upon this battle depends the survival of Christian civilization. Upon it depends our own British life, and the long continuity of our institutions and our Empire. The whole fury and might of the enemy must very soon be turned on us. Hitler knows that he will have to break us in this island or lose the war. If we can stand up to him, all Europe may be free and the life of the world may move forward into broad, sunlit uplands. But if we fail, then the whole world, including the United States, including all that we have known and cared for, will sink into the abyss of a new dark age made more sinister, and perhaps more protracted, by the lights of perverted science. Let us therefore brace ourselves to our duties, and so bear ourselves that, if the British Empire and its Commonwealth last for a thousand years, men will still say, 'This was their finest hour.'[9]

Hitler, during the summer, gave several hints that an armistice could be negotiated between Germany and England. No one in the British government gave it any serious consideration.

Hitler called his projected invasion of England "Operation Sea Lion." The plan was to send a fleet across the English Channel to invade and occupy Britain. To protect the fleet while it crossed, the German air force, the *Luftwaffe*, had to establish control of the air. Preparations for "Operation Sea Lion" began in July 1940 when German planes were sent to attack English ports. In August and September the targets were broadened to include English airfields and the city of London. But the Royal Air Force managed to

London, 1940. Londoners sleep in the Underground train stations to protect themselves from German air attacks.   (Imperial War Museum)

A destroyed German bomber in the English countryside   (Miller Services)

inflict heavy losses on the *Luftwaffe*—over one thousand German planes were shot down—forcing the Germans to change from daytime to night raids. Moreover, the invention of radar, and its use by the British, enabled the Royal Air Force to gain an immense strategic advantage. Hitler had calculated that bombing would create panic among the British people; however, the morale of the British did not crack, and many of them lived in air-raid shelters during this period. Finally, Germany could not stand any more heavy losses, and in mid-September Hitler cancelled "Operation Sea Lion." The Battle of Britain was over; Germany had failed in its attempt to subdue England in 1940.

Although Hitler was still planning to defeat England after the summer of 1940, he began to turn his attention eastwards in his quest for universal empire and for badly needed raw materials. In September he concluded a Tripartite Pact with Italy and Japan which divided Africa and Asia among the Axis powers. He offered Russia a sphere of influence in the east, but Stalin was unwilling to enter into any pact which did not recognize Russian interests in the Balkans. Hitler, in fact, had other plans for Russia: preparations for the German invasion of Russia—"Operation Barbarossa"—began in December 1940. Hitler decided Russia would have to be defeated quickly because time was on Russia's side. The plan called for a characteristic *Blitzkrieg* which had worked so well in western Europe.

The Russian invasion was an important part of Hitler's world plan. Hitler talked about securing territory in the east for the expansion of the German race; orders were issued on certain fronts not to take prisoners, but to "exterminate" members of an "inferior race"; and a great propaganda campaign was launched emphasizing the hostility between fascism and bolshevism. Germany counted on capturing the rich territories of the Ukraine in order to provide food and raw materials for the Third Reich. The stakes were extraordinarily high; if Russia were not defeated within a limited time period, Germany risked a two-front war and the possibility of losing a war of attrition to the Allies.

On June 22, 1941, German troops invaded Russia. At first the Germans advanced quickly and by the end of the summer had captured the Ukraine. As in the Napoleonic wars and the First World War, Russia retreated, forcing the enemy to extend its lines of supply, hoping for "General Winter" to do what the Russian army alone could not accomplish. The German army, having captured several major centres, reached the outskirts of Moscow in late November. Stalin remained in the city, and in savage fighting the Russians held fast. On December 8, 1941, with Moscow, Leningrad (formerly St. Petersburg), and Stalingrad (formerly Czaritsyn, now Volgograd) still in Russian hands, Hitler halted operations for the year, realizing that the Russian winter would not permit him to go on.

At the very moment that Hitler was suspending military operations on the Russian front, the United States entered the war, and the Second World War became truly a global affair. On December 7, 1941, Japan launched an air attack on the United States naval base of Pearl Harbor, Hawaii. Nineteen American ships were sunk or disabled, and over two thousand people were killed in the attack. The United States declared war on Japan, and the next day England and its dominions followed suit. Germany and Italy joined Japan by declaring war on the United States.

The attack on Pearl Harbor brought the United States into the war, but the Americans had been edging into the fray before then. President Franklin Roosevelt had moved out of isolation by the time he was elected President for an unprecedented third term of office in November 1940. From 1937 onwards the United States had aided the Chinese government of Chiang Kai-shek against the Japanese invaders. When the Second World War broke out, there was a growing sympathy in the United States for the Allies, and Roosevelt himself was prepared to do anything short of war to help them. In 1940, just as France was falling,

Roosevelt shipped arms to Britain. In the summer of that year he sent fifty over-age destroyers to Britain in exchange for the right to use bases in Newfoundland and the Caribbean. In March 1941 the Lend-Lease Act was passed by the United States Congress, a law which enabled the Americans to send war materials and food to Britain. The first peacetime conscription in the history of the country was organized, and, after Hitler's invasion of Russia, goods were sent to the Soviet Union under the Lend-Lease arrangements. Hence, even before December 1941, the "neutral" United States was clearly against the Axis.

However, the invasion of Pearl Harbor and the active entry of the United States did much to change the balance of forces in the war. From the fall of France in June 1940 to Hitler's invasion of Russia in June 1941, Britain fought alone in Europe. By the end of 1941 the Soviet Union and the United States had joined Great Britain in what Churchill called "the Grand Alliance."

THE SECOND WORLD WAR: THE MIDDLE YEARS: 1941-43

Even before Pearl Harbor, the United States and Great Britain were co-ordinating their efforts against the Axis. Lend-Lease was one element of this co-operation. In addition, the United States helped to protect the Atlantic shipping lanes from attack by Axis vessels. As part of this mutual understanding, the two nations conducted discussions about the shape of the post-war world. Meeting on a ship in the Atlantic Ocean in August 1941, Roosevelt and Churchill signed the Atlantic Charter:

First, their countries seek no [gains], territorial or other;

Second, they desire to see no territorial changes that do not accord with the freely expressed wishes of the peoples concerned;

Third, they respect the right of all peoples to choose the form of government under which they will live; and they wish to see sovereign rights and self-government restored to those who have been forcibly deprived of them;

Fourth, they will endeavor, with due respect

An aircraft factory in the United States in 1940. The planes on the production line are Flying Fortresses.   (Library of Congress)

for their existing obligations, to further the enjoy-ment by all States, great or small, victor or vanquished, of access, on equal terms, to the trade and to the raw materials of the world which are needed for their economic prosperity;

Fifth, they desire to bring about the fullest collaboration between all nations in the economic field with the object of securing, for all, improved labor standards, economic adjustment and social security;

Sixth, after the final destruction of the Nazi tyranny, they hope to see established a peace which will afford all nations the means of dwelling in safety within their own boundaries, and which will afford assurance that all the men in all the lands may live out their lives in freedom from fear and want;

Seventh, such a peace should enable all men to traverse the high seas and oceans without hindrance;

Eighth, they believe that all of the nations of the world, for realistic as well as spiritual reasons, must come to the abandonment of the use of force.[10]

Hence it is not surprising that the two countries quickly came together after December 1941 and co-ordinated their war efforts. The Atlantic Charter soon was signed by representatives of twenty-six other nations, some of these representing governments-in-exile; it can be viewed as the beginning of the formation of the United Nations.

The United States and Britain, in co-ordinating their plans, agreed to give priority to Europe and the defeat of Germany. Japan was to be contained, but the major effort would be directed towards the defeat of Hitler. In an arrangement unprecedented in the history of modern diplomacy and warfare, the United States and the British Commonwealth joined their commands and fought virtually as one army for the rest of the war. The United States also agreed to co-operate with the Soviet Union, though neither Britain nor the United States would come as close to the Soviet Union as they did to one another.

In 1942–43 the British were locked in battle with German and Italian troops for the control of North Africa. In 1940 Italian troops had attempted to take the Suez Canal, but the British managed to contain them and to move into Italian-held Libya. In 1942 the Germans had sent aid to the Italians, and, under the leadership of General Erwin Rommel, the Germans moved on Egypt by mid-1942. But the German general was operating with extended supply lines. He was, in addition, short of the supplies he needed to continue his advance, because Hitler was more concerned with the European continent. In October 1942, under General Bernard Montgomery, British and Commonwealth troops launched a counterattack and began driving Rommel back into Libya. A second Allied force landed in November 1942 in the French territories of Morocco and Algeria and attacked the Axis troops from the rear. Finally, in May 1943 the Axis force surrendered; 250 000 German and Italian soldiers were taken prisoner by the Allies.

The North African campaign, while successful for the Allies, was questioned by Stalin and others; it seemed to them it was the right battle in the wrong place. Stalin wanted Britain and the United States to open a "second front" in western Europe in order to relieve the Russians of the full burden of the German onslaught. This was a matter of some contention among the Allies. Britain and the United States finally decided that an invasion of France at this time would be premature. The United States was already doing the major share of fighting in the Pacific against Japan (the Soviet Union and Japan were not at war at this time) and felt it could not yet risk an invasion of Europe.

Once the North African campaign was won, the Allies decided to move directly to an attack on what Churchill styled the "soft under-belly of Europe"—an assault on Italy via the Mediterranean. In July 1943 Sicily was invaded. German and Italian resistance was overcome and the island was occupied by the Allies.

The success of the invasion helped bring about the fall of Mussolini. On July 25 the Fascist Grand Council, led by Marshal Pietro Badoglio, overthrew Mussolini and took him prisoner. Badoglio, formerly a supporter of fascism, was appointed head of a new government by King Victor Emmanuel III, the same monarch who twenty-one years earlier had called upon Mussolini to form a government.

Badoglio began to negotiate for peace, but he found himself caught between the intransigence of Hitler, who demanded that Italy fight on, and the policy of the Allies, who would not accept anything but unconditional surrender. In September, as Allied troops were moving across the Straits of Messina from Sicily to the Italian mainland, Badoglio surrendered unconditionally to the Allies. Though the Axis was broken, Hitler did not give up Italy without a desperate fight. Mussolini was freed from prison by the Germans on September 12, 1943, and was made the head of a regime in northern Italy loyal to Hitler. The Allies pressed on to Naples and by the end of September captured it. However, the Germans decided to defend Rome and established strong positions around the city. In the winter of 1943–44 Rome remained in German hands as the Italian campaign bogged down in trench warfare. Not until June 1944 did Rome fall into the hands of the Allies.

In eastern Europe the German drive in Russia had been resumed in the spring of 1942. Hitler felt he was on the verge of success, even though the Russians had made some small gains in the winter. The key point of the struggle became the city of Stalingrad, which was reached by German troops in August 1942. Hitler staked his military reputation on its capture, while Stalin was determined to hold it, not only because it was a major centre, but because Russia would be demoralized if the city named after the chief architect of Russia's defence was taken by the enemy. By September the Germans and Russians were fighting

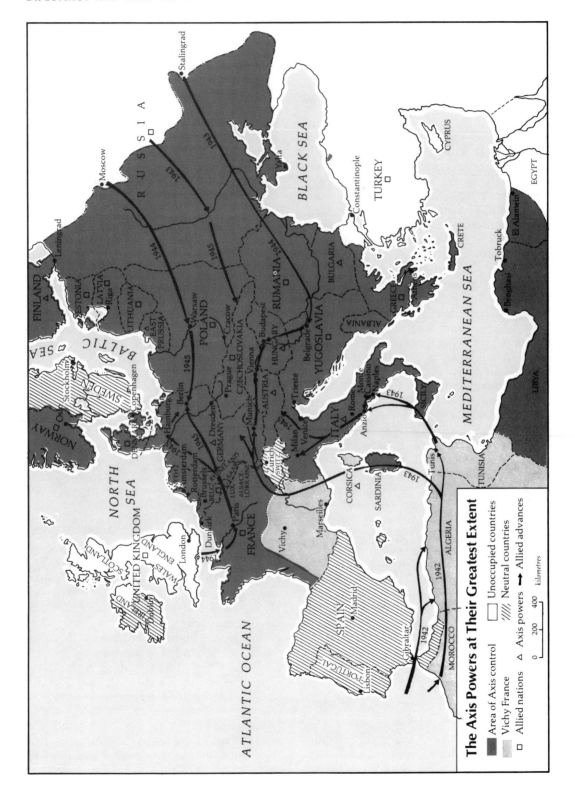

The Axis Powers at Their Greatest Extent

Area of Axis control
Vichy France
☐ Allied nations
☐ Unoccupied countries
Neutral countries
△ Axis powers
→ Allied advances

0   200   400
kilometres

from house to house in Stalingrad. Once the Germans had been halted, Stalin ordered the Russian troops to advance under General Georgi Zhukov in a pincers movement north and south of the German positions at Stalingrad, a strategy designed to entrap the Germans. As the pincers closed it became apparent that the Germans would have to retreat, but Hitler ordered his troops to fight on. With the coming of winter, the Germans had lost the battle, and by February 1943, when the struggle was finally over, more than 300 000 German troops had died. Russia had successfully stopped the German advance. The tide in Europe, to use Churchill's metaphor, now turned in the direction of the Allies.

By 1943 the position of the Allies in the Pacific was also improved. After Pearl Harbor, Japan immediately attacked Singapore, Malaya, and many islands in the Pacific, including Midway and Wake. Singapore was captured by Japan in February 1942, and Burma was taken in May. However, two Allied victories in the summer of 1942 stopped Japanese expansion. The American and Japanese fleets clashed in May in the battles of the Coral Sea. American carrier-based planes halted the Japanese advance which was directed towards Australia; in the process they sank a Japanese carrier and damaged two others. In June the Japanese lost another four carriers in the battle of Midway, and the Japanese were thus prevented from expanding in the direction of Hawaii.

In August 1942 the United States felt secure enough to go on the offensive in the Pacific. Troops were landed on the island of Guadalcanal in the Solomon Islands. After many sea and land engagements, the Japanese abandoned the area on February 9, 1943. The American strategy, as directed by General Douglas MacArthur, became one of "island hopping" across the Pacific, in order to reach Japan and force the enemy to surrender unconditionally.

ALLIED VICTORY IN EUROPE: 1944–45

By mid-1944 Germany was under pressure on three fronts—Italy, western Europe, and eastern Europe. Rome fell to the Allies on June 4, 1944, after heavy fighting and many casualties. Aided by an active Italian resistance movement, Allied soldiers then moved north quickly. The government of Marshal Badoglio collapsed in the face of the unwillingness of the resistance leaders and other Italians returning from political exile to work with him. A democratic Italian government was formed which the Allies recognized; in effect, Italy now fought on the side of the Allies against Germany. Under the protection of the Nazis, Mussolini continued his claim to be the ruler of Italy until he was captured by Italian partisans on April 27, 1945. The next day he was assassinated.

The United States and Britain accumulated their resources for "Operation Overlord," the invasion of France. Led by General Eisenhower of the United States, the organization for the invasion surpassed anything of its kind in warfare. The Allies had decided to land on a sixty-mile stretch of the Normandy coast in France and then move from these beaches to Paris and eventually Berlin; the specific plans were kept secret until the last moment, and elaborate moves were made in order to outwit the Germans. Over 4000 ships and 11 000 airplanes were involved. On "D-Day," June 6, 1944, over 150 000 soldiers were taken across the English Channel; in the first week, over 300 000 Allied troops were in Normandy; and in the first month almost 1 000 000 were part of the invasion force. Over 500 000 tons of supplies and about 170 000 vehicles were landed in Europe in that first month. The Allied armies overcame stubborn German resistance and, breaking through German lines, raced into France, aided by a strong French resistance group.

In a second invasion, on August 15, 1944, Allied forces landed in southern France and drove north. With Paris about to be liberated, General de Gaulle took "free French" troops from England to help free the city. On August 26 Paris was in the hands of the Allies, and de Gaulle began to group the various resistance leaders around him. British and Canadian troops liberated the Belgian cities of Brussels and Antwerp on

September 4, and Luxembourg was liberated on September 11.

Russia in the meantime was making advances in the east. In the summer of 1943 it had smashed the German armies in the greatest tank battle of the war, at Kursk, and by 1944 Russian troops moved into Poland. In the Balkans, Bulgaria was defeated in September, and by the summer of 1945 the Russians had established political or military control by communists in all Balkan states, with the exception of Greece. Both from the east and the west, the Allies were moving in on Berlin.

Though by the end of the summer of 1944 it was clear that Germany would be defeated, there seemed to be no possibility of an armistice. The Allies, having learned from the errors of Versailles, demanded unconditional surrender, but Hitler was determined to fight to the end. In Germany there was no active resistance movement to act as a fifth column for the Allies. However, in July 1944 a group of high-ranking Germans, mainly but not exclusively composed of people who had served Hitler for years, decided that it was foolish to fight to the end now that the Normandy invasion was successful. They set about to assassinate Hitler and seize control of the German government. On July 20 a bomb was planted at a meeting which Hitler was attending. The bomb exploded but failed to kill Hitler, and the conspirators were rounded up and executed. Now there was no serious opposition among the German élite to a continuation of the war.

Facing almost certain defeat, Hitler hung on, hoping that new weapons and possible dissension among the Allies might turn the tide. In September the V-2, a rocket-propelled missile, was launched against London and Antwerp, causing damage and disorder. But

Hitler in 1945, decorating German youth for their role in the defence of the Third Reich (Ullstein)

Canada entered the Second World War in 1939. On top, new Canadian troops set sail for Europe.
The pictures at the bottom show women and soldiers involved in the war, as the conflict deeply
changed people's lives.   (Top: A.E. Armstrong/DND/Public Archives Canada/PA-114805; Left:
H.G. Aikman/DND/Public Archives Canada/ PA-132851; Right: H.G. Aikman/DND/Public
Archives Canada/PA-142245)

the missiles did not alter the outcome of the war, and their launching pads were soon overrun by Allied troops. One last German counter-offensive, the Battle of the Bulge, was begun in the west in December. A German thrust at Allied lines pushed American troops back 80 km, but by the new year this advance had been halted and the Allies were moving forward again.

Nothing stopped the advances in the east and the west—Marshal Zhukov led the Russians into Vienna in April, and American and Russian troops met at the River Elbe on April 25. On April 30, two days after Mussolini was killed, Hitler committed suicide in his bunker in Berlin. By May 2 Berlin surrendered, and on May 8 Germany accepted the terms of unconditional surrender. The war in Europe was over.

THE END: THE ATOM BOMB AND ALLIED VICTORY IN THE PACIFIC

A new weapon determined the outcome of the war in Japan. On behalf of a number of distinguished scientists, Albert Einstein had signed a letter in August 1939 to be sent to President Roosevelt:

Sir: Some recent work by E. Fermi and L. Szilard, which has been communicated to me in manuscript, leads me to expect that the element uranium may be turned into a new and important source of energy in the immediate future. Certain aspects of the situation seem to call for watchfulness and, if necessary, quick action on the part of the administration. I believe, therefore, that it is my duty to bring to your attention the following facts and recommendations.

In the course of the last four months it has been made probable—through the work of Joliot in France as well as Fermi and Szilard in America—that it may become possible to set up nuclear chain reactions in a large mass of uranium, by which vast amounts of power and large quantities of new radium-like elements would be generated. Now it appears almost certain that this could be achieved in the immediate future.

This new phenomenon would also lead to the construction of bombs, and it is conceivable—though much less certain—that extremely powerful bombs of a new type may thus be constructed. A single bomb of this type, carried by boat or exploded in a port, might very well destroy the whole port together with some of the surrounding territory. However, such bombs might very well prove to be too heavy for transportation by air. . . .

In view of this situation you may think it desirable to have some permanent contact maintained between the administration and the group of physicists working on chain reaction in America. One possible way of achieving this might be for you to entrust with this task a person who has your confidence and who could perhaps serve in an unofficial capacity. His task might comprise the following:

a) To approach government departments, keep them informed of further developments, and put forward recommendations for government action, giving particular attention to the problem of securing a supply of uranium ore for the United States.

b) To speed up the experimental work which is at present being carried on within the limits of the budgets of the university laboratories, by providing funds, if such funds be required, through his contacts with private persons who are willing to make contributions for this cause, and perhaps also by obtaining the cooperation of industrial laboratories which have the necessary equipment.[11]

As a result of a proposal by Einstein and others, the United States, England, and Canada agreed in 1941 to conduct joint research into atomic weapons at the University of Chicago. This secret investigation was called the "Manhattan Project." The first atomic chain reaction was produced in 1942, and the atom bomb was successfully developed in 1945. It was a kind of irony that the Allies were able to make the bomb partly as a result of the work of scientists who were exiled from fascist states. Germany had also been working on a nuclear bomb, but failed to produce it.

Harry Truman, who had become President of the United States on the death of Roosevelt on April 12, 1945, decided to use the new weapon against Japan in order to shorten the war in the Pacific. He gave orders to drop the first atomic bomb on the city of Hiroshima on August 6, 1945. This bomb killed

70 000 of the 200 000 people in the city, maimed many others, and through its radio-active fallout it is likely to have affected unborn generations. Still the Japanese refused to give up. On August 9 a bigger bomb was dropped on Nagasaki. This time the Japanese surrendered unconditionally, signing an armistice on September 2, 1945.

THE DIPLOMACY OF WAR AND PEACE

No new Congress of Vienna, no new Versailles, was held when the Second World War ended. A peace settlement was brought about slowly by a combination of wartime agreements, negotiations with countries on whose territory occupation troops were stationed, and diplomatic activity at the United Nations. Preparations for peace had gone on throughout the war, and there had been consultations among the Allies, especially towards the end of the fighting when victory was only a matter of time.

At the first major meeting between Churchill, Roosevelt, and Stalin, at Teheran in December 1943, it was agreed that "unconditional surrender" would be the Allied policy towards the Axis. Clearly, no one wanted to see repeated the confusion of the armistice of 1918 and the thorny problems of the Versailles settlement.

But Churchill disagreed with Roosevelt and his advisers about the approach to a peace settlement in the Balkans and the other territories of eastern Europe. Churchill suspected that Russia would not be willing to relinquish hold of the countries of eastern Europe once it had troops occupying them, and that Russia would attempt to set up a series of dependencies (referred to as a *cordon sanitaire*) in eastern Europe as a buffer zone to protect Russia against attack from the west. Hence Churchill tried early in 1944 to persuade Roosevelt to seek agreement with Stalin on a peace plan for eastern Europe. Roosevelt refused to discuss this question, claiming, as did Eisenhower in drawing up Allied military plans, that victory in the war was the prior consideration and diplomatic questions were best discussed afterwards. Roosevelt judged at the time that

Allied unity was more important than diplomatic considerations, and did not want to do anything to antagonize Stalin, whose country was bearing the major brunt of the European war.

However, by 1945, with the military superiority of the Allies clearly established, the question of the post-war world could not be ignored. Two meetings between the three major Allied powers, one held at Yalta (February 4–11, 1945) and the other at Potsdam (July 17–August 2, 1945), proved to be of great significance for the post-war world. At Yalta agreement was reached on some procedural questions related to the United Nations Organization. In addition, Roosevelt got Stalin to agree to enter the war in the Far East soon after victory in Europe was achieved. In return, Russia was to receive territories in the area lost since the Russo-Japanese War in 1905.

The major bone of contention at Yalta was eastern Europe. The Russians had taken control of much of the territory through which they moved on the way to Berlin. Poland now had a government which was virtually controlled by Moscow. Churchill and Roosevelt thought this trend must be stopped. At Yalta Polish boundaries were fixed, giving Russia some territory which had been in Poland's hands before the war, and compensating Poland with some German territory to the north and west. It was agreed by the three powers that free elections be held in Poland and that its government would be reorganized on a more democratic basis. While it was clear that there were differences among the Allies regarding the shape of the post-war world, relations remained cordial, for the Allies still focussed on defeating Germany. Stalin gained some concessions in exchange for his pledges to enter the war in the Far East and to allow elections in Poland. Few at the time realized that he was intending to control all of eastern Europe.

At Potsdam relations between the Allies were considerably more strained. Truman now represented the United States, and in the middle of the conference Clement Attlee, leader of the British Labour Party, replaced

Churchill, for Labour had just won the British elections. Stalin continued to speak for the Soviet Union. Now both the United States and Britain were suspicious of Stalin's motives, while Stalin wanted guarantees that Russia would never again be threatened by Germany. Agreement was reached on the demilitarization and disarmament of Germany and on a "de-Nazification" program. Nazi leaders were to be arrested and tried, and Germany's war potential was to be eliminated.

Though peace treaties were eventually made with Germany's allies—Italy, Rumania, Bulgaria, Hungary, and Finland— no formal peace was concluded with Germany. After Potsdam the wartime coalition of Britain, the United States, and Russia began to fall apart, ruptured by the mutual distrust of the post-war period. What was thought of as a temporary arrangement for the occupation of Germany became, in fact, the *status quo*. Agreements made from 1943 to 1945 had divided Germany into four parts, to be administered by Russia, the United States, Britain, and France. But occupied Germany became two states—the Russian part known as East Germany, the American-British-French part known as West Germany. The city of Berlin, located in the midst of East Germany, had been given a four-power occupation, and it too was divided between east and west. Though in the first two decades the German arrangement created diplomatic problems between Russia and the other Allies, the perennial "German problem" of modern world diplomacy was largely solved in a strange way by this arrangement. East Germany came under rigid Soviet control, while West Germany developed under the watchful eyes of the United States, Britain, and France. There were now two Germanies (in addition to a reconstituted, independent Austria), each part of a system in which it was not the leader.

The settlement with Japan was a good deal simpler. After the unconditional surrender, the Japanese islands were occupied by American troops. The country was placed under the authority of General MacArthur, who supervised the dismantling of Japan's war effort and the transition to a constitutional monarchy organized along Western lines.

Thus the Second World War ended. The Axis was defeated; Germany and Japan were occupied. Fifteen million soldiers had died, nearly half of them Russian, and many more civilians had been killed as a direct result of the war. Countless millions were maimed and wounded; other millions had been victims of German atrocities. The power structure of the world had changed, and neither Britain nor France were now first-rate powers. The United States and the Soviet Union were the undisputed leaders of the world, but the wartime union between them quickly disintegrated as both the United States and the Soviet Union tried to make the world safe for themselves. The hot war was over; the cold war was soon on.

THE PROBLEM OF GUILT: NUREMBERG AND BEYOND

Only when the Allies entered German territory towards the end of the war and saw the death camps did the full magnitude of the horrors of the Nazi regime become apparent. The "new order" of Nazism was seen as a nightmare of terror, sadism, wholesale execution, and genocide.

Upon conquering a territory, the Germans under Hitler had behaved towards the subject peoples according to the primitive Nazi racial ideology. There was great contempt for all Slavic peoples, and many were sent into forced labour or summarily executed. And from 1941 onwards, Hitler's Germany followed a policy of systematically killing Jews. Concentration camps — models of efficiency and technology — were built to house Jews destined to be put to death. The largest of the concentration camps was at Auschwitz in Silesia, and after the war its commandant, Rudolf Höss, reported:

I estimate that at least two and a half million victims were executed and exterminated at Auschwitz by gassing and burning and that at least another half million succumbed to starvation and disease, making a total of about three million dead. This figure represents about seventy to eighty per cent of all persons sent to Auschwitz as prisoners, the remainder having been selected and used for slave labour in the concentration-camp industries. . . . The total number of victims included about a hundred thousand German Jews, and great numbers of citizens, mostly Jewish, from Holland, France, Belgium, Poland, Hungary, Czechoslovakia, Greece or other countries. We executed about four hundred thousand Hungarian Jews alone at Auschwitz in the summer of 1944. . . .

The "final solution" of the Jewish question meant the complete extermination of all Jews in Europe. I was ordered to establish extermination facilities at Auschwitz in June, 1941. At that time there were already three other extermination camps in the Government General: Belzek, Treblinka and Wolzek. I visited Treblinka to find out how they carried out their extermination. The Camp Commandant told me that he had liquidated eighty thousand in the course of one half year.[12]

In all, six million Jews, about one-third of the Jewish population of the world, were killed by the Germans. There were also at least five million victims of the camps who were not Jewish.

The rise of fascism and totalitarianism had raised enormous ethical problems in the West. The major question was: how responsible is the individual in a totalitarian state for the activities of his government? The problem revolved particularly about the Nuremberg trials, conducted at the close of the war. The trials were held in 1945 and 1946 in the German city of Nuremberg by the four major victorious powers of the Second World War—the United States, the Soviet Union, Great Britain, and France. Twenty-two Nazi leaders were indicted on four counts:

1) Conspiracy to commit the crimes alleged in the other counts;
2) Crimes against peace;
3) War crimes;
4) Crimes against humanity.[13]

A catalogue of Nazi deeds was drawn up and the world was shocked. Nineteen men were found guilty; eleven of those were sentenced to hang and eight received prison sentences. These people were tried, not for obeying the state, but for committing acts repulsive to all human dignity. It was thus tacitly assumed that individuals are answerable for their actions before a universal ethical system, and that this code supersedes the laws of sovereign states.

Many people had serious reservations about such a trial. Some felt the trials were simply a case of the victors passing judgment on the defeated. Moreover, in a relativist world, many people did not want to play judge. Yes, they said, these were evil people, but when traditional values had crumbled, when there were few secure guideposts to human actions, who were we to execute them? Were we not in fact behaving like the men on trial? None the less, the trials of "war criminals" were carried out.

The state of West Germany (brought into existence in 1949 by uniting the occupied zones of the United States, England, and France) also put on trial some of the major Nazi figures, and these trials have continued to our own day. But West Germany too was questioned about the validity of its trials. Did not all citizens take part in the activities of the Nazis, if only by their silence? Is it just to try only the worst offenders, and not all the others who co-operated?

In 1963 *The Deputy*, a play by Rolf Hochhuth, spoke of the silent acquiescence of the Catholic Church to Nazi atrocities. Specifically, Hochhuth blamed Pope Pius XII for not intervening to save Jewish lives during the Second World War. The Pope, according to Hochhuth, should have denounced Nazism to the world. A storm of protest arose around the theme of the play, and many claimed that the Pope did more by using diplomacy than could have been accomplished by public condemnation.

The new state of Israel was interested in the activities of former Nazis. In 1961 Adolf Eichmann, who had been responsible for the killing of many people in German concentration camps, was captured by Israeli agents in South America and placed on trial in Jerusalem. The Eichmann trial was a major world event, and it was discussed by many of the leading intellectuals in the West. Eichmann was a Nazi functionary whose orders were to operate concentration camps and to kill people efficiently. His defence was not a denial of the act, but rather the denial of personal responsibility for the act. His counsel claimed Eichmann was a soldier and that he was simply obeying orders. The duty of the soldier demanded that he not question his superiors, but carry out his orders. Thus, in Eichmann's own eyes, he would have been guilty had he *not* done his job well, for he had made his own personality a function of the collective philosophy of Nazism. He looked upon himself as the little man who had been drafted by the state to do a job and had done his duty. What, after all, made him any different from a British soldier who had carried a gun and obeyed his orders?

The prosecution adopted a position emanating from existentialist philosophy. The existentialists—Jean-Paul Sartre and Albert Camus among them—have claimed that, though there is no absolute guilt, each person finds definition in the midst of life's situations. Each person makes personal choices, and these commitments are made as universals—we make them for all people when we make them for ourselves. We define what we mean by justice, for example, through the actions of our everyday lives. Acting, or not acting, matters.

Eichmann, contended the prosecution, was guilty because he had a choice, because he was a human being. In the midst of his situation he chose to ignore his humanity; he chose not to face the problem of evil. His accusers stated that he even went beyond his duty and demonstrated his zeal in the way he carried out his orders—he could have been less ruthless without any risk to his own person.

Thus the trial raised some of the most important issues about human nature in the twentieth century. On the one hand, we have the collective mentality—the attitude that people are not responsible for their acts. In the words of Erich Fromm, people have chosen an "escape from freedom" by joining a collective. Some have argued that the burden of freedom is too much for people; they should not be seen as free beings. On the other side, we have the view that to be human is to make choices; life is not easy, but it must be faced by each individual—every person is a responsible being. The decision made by Eichmann—a decision to obey—was a decision to act on his own responsibility. By doing what he did, Eichmann, according to this reasoning, committed himself to inhumanity.

A contemporary social philosopher, Hannah Arendt, has commented on totalitarianism and human nature in the modern age:

It is chiefly . . . for the sake of complete consistency that it is necessary for totalitarianism to destroy every trace of what we commonly call human dignity. For respect for human dignity implies the recognition of my fellow-men or our fellow-nations . . . as builders of worlds or co-builders of a common world. No ideology which aims at the explanation of all historical events of the past and at mapping out the course of all events of the future can bear the unpredictability which springs from the fact that men are creative, that they can bring forward something so new that nobody ever foresaw it.

What totalitarian ideologies therefore aim at is . . . the transformation of human nature itself. The concentration camps are the laboratories where changes in human nature are tested, and their shamefulness therefore is not just the business of their inmates and those who run them according to strictly "scientific" standards; it is the concern of all men. Suffering, of which there has been always too much on earth, is not the issue, nor is the number of victims. Human nature as such is at stake. . . .[14]

In dealing with the problem of individual responsibility, some thinkers have made the distinction between a state which commits criminal acts and a criminal state. States, it is understood, can never be perfect. The real question is in terms of the aspirations of states and their fundamental laws. For example, there may be a state which aspires to justice, but which still commits isolated, unjust acts. But in our time there have also been criminal states—states based on racism and other fundamentally "criminal" principles. The duty of the individual in this kind of state, many suggest, is to rebel, because to obey the orders of a criminal state is to be a criminal yourself. Thus, according to this position, those who performed the deeds of the Nazi state were guilty of letting things happen, or not resisting, and this made them criminals.

ANALYSIS AND DISCUSSION

1. The League of Nations was created, in the words of Woodrow Wilson, "for the purpose of affording mutual guarantees of political independence and territorial integrity to great and small nations alike."
a) Describe the strengths and weaknesses of the League as an instrument for maintaining collective security.
b) List the problems faced by the League at its inception and explain why it was unable to deal with them effectively.
2. In addition to the League, security was sought by means of a number of pacts and treaties designed to limit or eliminate war. Describe these agreements and explain why, in each case, they were ineffective.
3. The following series of events includes some of the most significant steps in the progress towards the outbreak of the Second World War. For each event listed, explain how it contributed to peace or war:
a) Japan invades Manchuria, 1931.
b) Hitler proclaims the rearmament of Germany, March 1935.
c) Mussolini invades Abyssinia, 1935.
d) Germany militarizes the Rhineland, March 1936.
e) Hitler and Mussolini sign a pact of cooperation (the Rome-Berlin Axis), October 1936.
f) Hitler annexes Austria, March 1938.
g) Czechoslovakia dismembered; Germany acquires the Sudetenland, September 1938.
h) Stalin and Hitler sign a non-aggression pact, August 1939.
4. "Between 1936 and 1940 the French and British were paralyzed by a Maginot Line complex. Unwilling to relive the horrors of World War I, the allies hoped that a show of defensive strength would persuade the Nazis of their military might and convince them to strike elsewhere." Evaluate the allied willingness to sacrifice Eastern Europe as a product of this war weariness.
5. "From the Fall of France to the attack on Pearl Harbor, Britain's only strategy was to hold on, with its allies, until the United States could be actively drawn into the conflict." Discuss this statement with reference to the British/Commonwealth strategy from the summer of 1940 until the end of 1941.
6. At the beginning of the Second World War, the "Axis" powers (Germany, Italy, and Japan) experienced phenomenal success, but within six years their power had been totally destroyed. Account for both the initial success and eventual defeat of the "Axis" powers.
7. The peace settlement after the Second World War was the result of a series of wartime agreements and several conferences. Discuss the shape of the settlement in 1945, and account for the absence of a large conference or major treaties, as had been the case after other worldwide hostilities in the past.
8. "Some historians feel that the dropping of the atomic bombs was not to demonstrate their destructive power to the Japanese but rather to the Russians." Evaluate the idea that the explosions at Hiroshima and Nagasaki may not have been the last shots in World War II but rather the first shots of the Cold War.
9. "Considering the studied neglect of the realities of the Nazi racial policy and the holocaust between 1933 and 1945 perhaps all of Western Civilization should have been on trial at Nuremburg." Discuss this hypothesis in terms of the actions and attitudes prevalent during the period.

SYNTHESIS AND EVALUATION   CHAPTERS 11–14

1. The two great revolutions of the modern world, the French and the Russian, provide fertile ground for comparisons. Compare the revolutions within the following framework.

a) The French and Russian Revolutions were both preceded by periods of intellectual ferment. For some observers, the ideas produced in these periods were the most important cause of the revolutions. What role did ideas play in bringing about these revolutions? Using both revolutions as examples, assess the importance of ideas as a cause of revolution.

b) Crane Brinton, in his *Anatomy of Revolution*, suggests that revolutions can be compared to a fever and progress through the following stages: (i) prodromal signs, or indications that a disease is on the way, (ii) arrival of full symptoms, indicating the presence of the disease, (iii) a crisis, worked up to through a series of advances and retreats and frequently accompanied by delirium, (iv) convalescence, often marked by a relapse or two, (v) recovery, with the patient changed and perhaps strengthened in some ways by his experience. Apply this scheme to the French and Russian revolutions and determine to what extent it fits.

c) Violence or the threat of violence is an essential component of every revolution, whether it is spontaneous violence or deliberately planned. Compare the role of violence in the French and Russian revolutions. In which revolution was it more important?

2. Some observers regard totalitarianism as a unique contemporary phenomenon, while others see it as simply a modern adaptation of the kind of authoritarian regimes which have existed throughout history. In what ways, and to what extent, do you see modern totalitarianism as unique to the twentieth century? Support your ideas with evidence from Stalin's Russia, Mussolini's Italy, and Hitler's Germany.

3. The *Führerprinzip*, or leader principle, was an important element of fascist ideology, as evidenced by the use of the word "leader" as a title in fascist states (*El Caudillo*—Franco; *Il Duce*—Mussolini; *Der Führer*—Hitler). Using Hitler and Mussolini as examples, assess the importance of the leader in acquiring and consolidating power in the fascist states of the 1920s and 1930s.

4. Mussolini stated that the nineteenth century was the century of socialism, liberalism and democracy but that the twentieth century was the century of the state. Evaluate this idea in terms of the events of the period between the two world wars.

5. "The League of Nations tried to be a democratic institution in an anti-democratic world." Account for this viewpoint in terms of the failure of the League to preserve the peace.

6. "In the final analysis, the Western powers felt that Eastern Europe was expendable. This attitude would not be forgotten when the war was over." Discuss this statement with reference to the actions of the Western allies in the late 1930s and their possible effects on postwar attitudes.

7. "If Vienna struck a 'concert of Powers', and Versailles proclaimed the 'self-determination of peoples', Potsdam divided a world." Compare the changing focus of the "peace process" from 1815 to 1945.

CHAPTER **15**

Europe and the West Since 1945

CONTRARY TO POPULAR FEELING IN 1945, Europe was not dead. However, the dominant powers were now the Soviet Union and the United States, and the world looked to them for leadership. Europe was still an important continent for both its culture and its productivity, but Europeans no longer determined the course of world affairs as they had before the Second World War.

The process of "decolonization" got under way after the Second World War, and the result was the formation of a number of new states in Africa and Asia. While European forms and institutions were often adopted by these new states, the European empires of another age were dismantled.

Perhaps the most significant feature of the post-war period was the persistence of the idea of nationalism. Though ideas of internationalism were strong, a large number of new national states emerged after the war. In many countries there was tension between the attractions of nationalism and the ideals of internationalism.

A. THE POST-WAR WORLD

THE BEGINNING OF THE COLD WAR

The United States and the Soviet Union emerged from the Second World War as the new "super-powers." Their economic and military strength far exceeded that of any other countries, and the result for the next decade was a "bi-polar" world, a system in which each great power led an alliance of states organized around itself.

Russia, having lost many millions in two world wars, desired above all the protection of its borders. The kind of insecurity which led Stalin to conduct his purges in the 1930s governed his foreign policy after the war.

In eastern Europe a pattern of Russian policy emerged. After Russian troops freed a country from the Germans, a coalition government, including local communists, was established. Then the communists took over the entire government and established a regime modelled on Stalin's government and loyal to the Soviet Union. Poland, Hungary, Rumania, and Bulgaria all followed this course in the first few years after the war. Stalin openly violated treaty obligations, such as his promise at Yalta to have free elections in Poland. In February 1948 he encouraged Czechoslovakian communists to move against their own government and establish a one-party state. It became clear that the Soviet Union would not give up control of those areas it had marched through in the Second World War on the way to Berlin. A group of "satellites"—buffer states whose policies would be co-ordinated with the Soviet Union—was being set up in eastern Europe.

American policy was, in part, a response to Stalin's unwillingness to abide by his treaty obligations and his interference in the internal affairs of other nations. George Kennan, an American diplomat, suggested in 1946 that Russia would follow its traditional policy of expansion unless it was made clear that the United States would defend, with arms, what it regarded as its own sphere of influence. Kennan thus proposed an aggressive policy of "containment" in place of the traditional isolationism of the United States. To a generation which had witnessed the failure of appeasement against Germany, this seemed a reasonable policy.

Elements of isolationism, however, still existed in the United States, and it was questionable whether the country would abandon its old peacetime posture of no world entanglements. But after much frustration in trying to negotiate with Russia, President Truman decided there was no turning back. Russian support of communist rebels in Greece led him to ask the United States Congress, in March 1947, for funds to aid the Greek government. In his message to Congress, he said:

To ensure the peaceful development of nations, free from [outside] coercion, the United States has taken a leading part in establishing the United Nations. The United Nations is designed to make possible lasting freedom and independence for all its members. We shall not realize our objectives, however, unless we are willing to help free people to maintain their free institutions and their national integrity against aggressive movements that seek to impose upon them totalitarian regimes. This is no more than a frank recognition that totalitarian regimes imposed on free peoples, by direct or indirect aggression, undermine the foundations of international peace and hence the security of the United States.[1]

The "Truman Doctrine" was accepted by Congress, and the United States undertook to support an active foreign policy and a large program of foreign aid.

Western Europeans no longer saw Germany as the potential aggressor, and began to unite against the Soviet Union. In March 1948 England, France, and the Benelux countries (Belgium, the Netherlands, and Luxembourg) signed the Brussels Treaty, an agreement for mutual defence in the event of outside aggression. However, western Europe could no longer depend on its own resources and looked to the United States for assistance in a policy of collective security. The result was the Atlantic Pact of April 4, 1949, a treaty signed by the states of the Brussels Pact, as well as by the United States, Canada, Norway, Denmark, Iceland, Portugal, and Italy. The aims of the groups were:

To safeguard the freedom, common heritage, and civilization of their peoples, founded on the principles of democracy, individual liberty, and the rule of law.

. . . to promote stability and well-being in the North Atlantic area.

. . . to unite their efforts for collective defense and for the preservation of peace and security.[2]

The major clause said: "The parties agree that an armed attack against one or more of them in Europe or North America shall be considered an attack against them all."[3]

The North Atlantic Treaty Organization (NATO) was established by the treaty. A common defence system with a unified command was set up, and each country contributed some of its resources. Greece and Turkey joined NATO in 1952, and West Germany became a member in 1955. The United States shipped enormous quantities of arms to Europe—in 1949 and 1950 the United States Congress authorized four and one half billion dollars for military assistance, and American and Canadian troops were permanently stationed in Europe as part of the agreement.

While the Soviet Union had mutual assistance agreements with most of its satellites by 1948, it was not until 1955, with the making of the Warsaw Pact, that the armed forces of eastern European countries began to be integrated. Albania, Bulgaria, Czechoslovakia, East Germany, Hungary, Poland, and Rumania joined the Soviet Union in a defence agreement. At the same time, both the United States and Russia supported other governments which backed their policies. Thus, within a few years of the end of the Second World War, world power was polarized in two spheres, each with its own interests, its own commitments, and its own ideology. A "cold war" developed between the two parties. They regarded each other with deep suspicion and contended for the allegiance of uncommitted countries. While each sought to protect its interests, neither wanted to resort to a ruinous "hot war."

As early as March 1946, Winston Churchill, in a speech given in the United States, underlined the division in Europe: "From Stettin in the Baltic to Trieste in the Adriatic, an iron curtain has descended across the Continent." He went on:

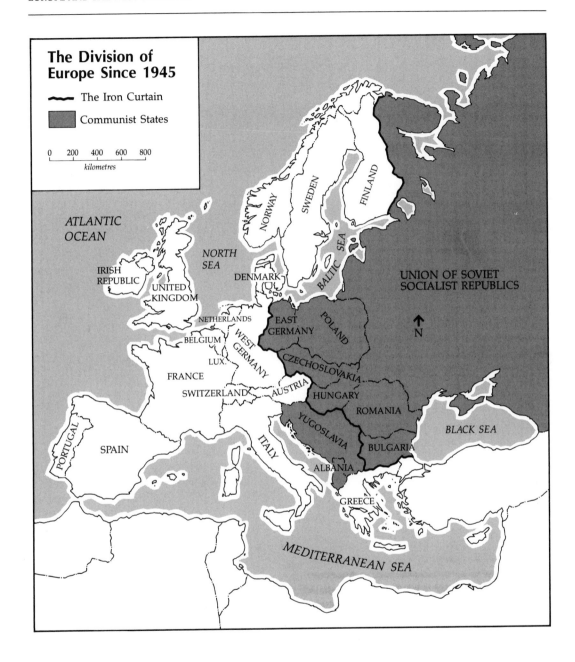

**The Division of
Europe Since 1945**

〜〜〜 The Iron Curtain

▨ Communist States

0   200   400   600   800
kilometres

ATLANTIC
OCEAN

NORTH
SEA

IRISH
REPUBLIC

UNITED
KINGDOM

DENMARK

NORWAY

SWEDEN

FINLAND

BALTIC SEA

UNION OF SOVIET
SOCIALIST REPUBLICS

↑
N

NETHERLANDS

BELGIUM

LUX.

WEST
GERMANY

EAST
GERMANY

POLAND

CZECHOSLOVAKIA

FRANCE

SWITZERLAND

AUSTRIA

HUNGARY

ROMANIA

BLACK SEA

PORTUGAL

SPAIN

ITALY

YUGOSLAVIA

BULGARIA

ALBANIA

GREECE

MEDITERRANEAN SEA

Behind that line lie all the capitals of the ancient states of central and eastern Europe. Warsaw, Berlin, Prague, Vienna, Budapest, Belgrade, Bucharest and Sofia, all these famous cities and the populations around them lie in what I might call the Soviet sphere, and all are subject, in one form or another, not only to Soviet influence but to a very high and in some cases increasing measure of control from Moscow. . . .

The communist parties, which were very small in all these eastern states of Europe, have been raised to pre-eminence and power far beyond their numbers and are seeking everywhere to obtain totalitarian control.

. . . I repulse the idea that a new war is inevitable; still more that it is imminent. It is because I am sure that our fortunes are still in our hands, in our own hands, and that we hold the power to save the future, that I feel the duty to speak out now. . . .

I do not believe that Soviet Russia desires war. What they desire is the fruits of war and the indefinite expansion of their power and doctrines. . . .

Last time I saw it all coming, and cried aloud to my own fellow-countrymen and to the world, but no one paid any attention. Up till the year 1933 or even 1935, Germany might have been saved from the awful fate which has overtaken her and we might all have been spared the miseries Hitler let loose upon mankind. . . .

We surely, ladies and gentlemen, I put it to you, but surely we must not let that happen again.[4]

The idealism which followed the First World War was absent after 1945. On both sides of the "iron curtain," there was a war psychology. The world was becoming once again a tense armed camp.

ECONOMIC RECONSTRUCTION

All states involved in the war, especially those on whose soil it was fought, regarded economic reconstruction as the first priority after 1945. There had been enormous destruction, and initially recovery was very slow. In 1947 European coal and steel production was below that of 1939; food was scarce in most areas, and rationing was still in effect; even advanced equipment was lacking. The United States was now by far the richest sovereignty in the world. Its industrial production had nearly doubled since 1939, and it produced huge surpluses of food. Hence it was logical that other nations battered by war should look to the United States for assistance.

The Secretary of State of the United States, George C. Marshall, in June 1947 inaugurated the European Recovery Program, known as the Marshall Plan.

In considering the requirements for the rehabilitation of Europe, the physical loss of life, the visible destruction of cities, factories, mines, and railroads was correctly estimated, but it has become obvious during recent months that this visible destruction was probably less serious than the dislocation of the entire fabric of European economy. For the past ten years conditions have been highly abnormal. . . .

Our policy is directed not against any country or doctrine but against hunger, poverty, desperation and chaos. Its purpose should be the revival of a working economy in the world so as to permit the emergence of political and social conditions in which free institutions can exist. Such assistance, I am convinced, must not be on a piecemeal basis as various crises develop. Any assistance that this Government may render in the future should provide a cure. . . .

Any government that is willing to assist in the task of recovery will find full cooperation, I am sure, on the part of the United States Government. . . .

. . . It would [not] be . . . fitting . . . for this government . . . to draw up unilaterally a program designed to place Europe on its feet economically. This is the business of the Europeans. The initiative, I think, must come from Europe. The role of this country should consist of friendly aid in the drafting of a European program and of later support of such a program so far as it may be practical for us to do so. The program should be a joint one, agreed to by a number, if not all European nations.[5]

France and Britain responded by calling for a European conference. But the proposal had been announced only a few months after the introduction of the Truman Doctrine, and the Soviet Union was suspicious and hostile, seeing the Marshall Plan as part of an effort by the United States to dominate all of Europe. Several eastern-European countries indicated their interest, but the Soviet Union intervened and prevented them from participating. As a result, the Marshall Plan became entangled in the diplomacy of the cold war, and its participants were mainly those countries in western and southern Europe already aligned with the United States.

The aid sent via the Marshall Plan was extremely valuable in helping western Europe to recover. Between 1948 and 1952 the United States sent twelve billion dollars to Europe, mainly to England, France, and Germany. By 1951 industrial production in the Marshall Plan countries was fifty per cent above the figure of four years earlier. The deficit in their balance of payments was reduced from eight billion in 1947 to one billion in 1950. Europe experienced a boom which in turn aided the American economy.

Eastern Europe had its own organization for economic recovery. A Communist Information Bureau (Cominform) was established in October 1947 to replace the Comintern, which had been dissolved by Stalin in 1943 in order to pursue his policy of co-operation with his wartime Allies. The Cominform agreement was made by the communist parties of the Soviet Union, Yugoslavia, Bulgaria, Rumania, Hungary, Poland, France, Czechoslovakia, and Italy. The organization was clearly a political and propaganda response to the Marshall Plan. The signatories stated:

Two opposite political lines have crystallized: on the one extreme the U.S.S.R. and the democratic countries aim at whittling down imperialism and the strengthening of democracy. On the other side the United States of America and England aim at the strengthening of imperialism and choking democracy. . . .

. . . The Truman-Marshall Plan is only a farce, a European branch of the general world plan of political expansion being realized by the United States . . . in all parts of the world. The plan of the economic and political subjugation of Europe through American imperialism is complemented by plans for the economic and political subjugation of China, Indonesia and South America. The aggressors of yesterday—the capitalist tycoons of Germany and Japan—are being prepared by the United States of America for a new rôle—as tools of the imperialistic policy in Europe and Asia of the United States.[6]

The Cominform did little but issue propaganda statements and serve as a vehicle for Moscow's increasing hold over the affairs of eastern European countries. By 1956 the Russians no longer thought it useful and it was dissolved.

The lasting and economically more important organization linking eastern Europe has been the Council for Economic Mutual Assistance (COMECON), established in 1949, and including most of the eastern European states. Little was accomplished in its early years, and during the 1950s the contrast between the economic vitality of western Europe and the difficulties of the less developed states in eastern Europe was striking. From 1956 onwards, attempts were made to integrate the economy of these states in order to provide an efficient and more prosperous division of labour. Each country was to supply its raw materials—Russia provided oil, ore, and cotton; Czechoslovakia and East Germany built machinery; Poland contributed sulphur and coal; Rumania had oil. Each country was to specialize in various industrial activities. Huge electric power systems were built to link the whole area, and what had been, until 1960, largely an agricultural area developed a good deal of industry. By the end of the 1960s, much of the austerity in consumers' goods in the area had ended. Yet some of the participating states resented the Russian domination of COMECON, and a few, such as Czechoslovakia, made efforts to trade with western Europe as well.

One of the most extraordinary developments of the post-war period was the rapid recovery of West Germany and Japan, aided by their former enemy the United States. West Germany's "economic miracle" in a short time transformed a country whose productive capacities had been destroyed into one of the major industrial regions of the world. After becoming a sovereign state in 1948, West Germany adopted a policy of free trade; in four years a favourable balance of trade had been achieved, and by 1961 prosperity was so great that the German mark had to be revalued upwards. Japan experienced even greater growth. Its industrial expansion was the greatest in the world in the 1950s, and in the year 1960 the economy grew an astounding seventeen per cent. Both countries benefited from having few military expenses in comparison with other large states.

THE UNITED NATIONS

The League of Nations faded away with the start of the Second World War. However, the Allies, beginning with the Atlantic Charter, stressed future peacetime co-operation among the various states. It was understood in wartime discussions between the United States, Britain, and the Soviet Union that a new international organization would be established. At Yalta and Potsdam, agreement was reached on the creation of the United Nations.

The United Nations came into existence, officially, in April 1945. It was designed as a forum for dealing with international disputes, and only the most optimistic thought it was possible to establish a strong organization. Thus fewer hopes were placed in the United Nations than in the League, and no one was disappointed when it failed to solve all of the problems of the cold war.

The members of the United Nations included all the victorious powers of the Second World War. Neutrals such as Sweden, Eire, Spain, and Portugal and such former Axis powers as Italy and the Balkan states joined soon after its inception. Many of the new states of the post-war period, including Israel, Jordan, and Indonesia, also became members.

The United Nations took over responsibility for the work of some of the pre-war international agencies, such as the International Labour Organization. It set up the World Health Organization and the United Nations Relief and Rehabilitation Administration. It fostered international co-operation in economics, social welfare, aid to underdeveloped areas, and atomic energy. The United Nations was not expected to have political sovereignty but rather to provide a diplomatic forum, and given its limited aims it has had a degree of success.

It was organized into two main bodies. The General Assembly was composed of all member nations—it met yearly and discussed and voted on issues of general importance. A Security Council was also established, composed of five permanent member states—the United States, the Soviet Union, Britain, France, and China—and six other members (now eight) elected by the Assembly for two-year terms. The Security Council was to be the crisis body, dealing with threats to world peace. On all important matters, the five permanent members had to agree before action could be taken; each thus had a veto over the actions of the Council.

A Secretariat, an international civil service, was created, with a Secretary-General at its head. However, as the United Nations undertook peacekeeping operations in the Belgian Congo and the Near East, the functions of the Secretary-General became more diplomatic than administrative. Thus the Secretary-General has been able, on occasion, to influence world affairs in a considerable way, and sometimes member nations have sought to weaken the power of the office.

THE KOREAN WAR

Tensions in the post-war years were not confined to Europe. Guerrilla movements in Asia—Burma, French Indo-China, Malaya, Indonesia, the Philippines—sought to overthrow existing governments and put communist regimes in power. In 1949 Mao Tse-tung achieved a great victory for communism by overthrowing Chiang Kai-shek and his followers and establishing the Chinese Peoples' Republic on the mainland. But, while all these movements were to some degree sponsored by Russia, they should not be thought of as instigated and controlled by the Soviet Union. They were more often nationalist than communist, in the sense that they opposed the policies of the United States and the colonial powers of Europe.

In Korea open warfare broke out. After the Second World War, the pattern of partition used in Germany was followed in Korea. It was divided into two zones, the north under Soviet control, the south under American control, and it was agreed that elections would be held as soon as possible in order to

American soldiers in Korea, 1950.   (The Photo Source)

end the temporary occupation and create a single nation-state. As in Germany, the territories became two sovereignties, for the Russians refused to entertain the possibility of a vote. In 1948 North Korea and South Korea were formally created as separate states, divided at the thirty-eighth parallel. At the same time, the United States announced that it was extending its policy of containment of communism to Asia, and that it would aid its allies there as well.

The North Koreans invaded the south in June 1950 in an attempt to create a unified, communist Korea. Truman decided to consult the United Nations before taking decisive action. At that moment the Soviet Union was boycotting the organization because the

General Assembly had refused to replace the Chinese delegation of Chiang Kai-shek with that of Mao Tse-tung, and thus the Soviet Union was not present to veto the decision of the Security Council to send troops under the United Nations flag to defend South Korea. Most of the soldiers were from the United States, although Australia, Canada, and Britain also participated. Chinese "volunteers" entered the war to aid North Koreans in 1951.

Korea was the first "limited war" in the post-Second World War world. Like Bismarck's wars, it was limited in its objectives—in this case, pushing North Korea back to the thirty-eighth parallel. But it was also controlled in a new sense, for it was

fought with less than the maximum armaments available. The United States had the
atom bomb, but it did not use it in Korea,
fearing a world war. It also did not use all
of the power it had even for a non-nuclear,
or "conventional" war.

Domestic concerns in the United States
affected the conduct of the war. Truman's
policy of limited war as well as the policy of
containment became enormously controversial issues. Many right-wing politicians
in the United States suspected a "communist conspiracy" behind every action of the
Truman government. Led by Senator Joseph
McCarthy, this element created an atmosphere of fear by accusing individuals of
sedition and by persecuting many innocent
people. On the other side, there were those
who questioned whether it was feasible or
moral for the United States to attempt to
police the world.

Truman decided not to enter the presidential contest of 1952, and in November Dwight
Eisenhower (1890–1968), the former Commander of Allied forces in the Second World
War and a former head of NATO, became the
first Republican president elected since
1928. As a military hero, Eisenhower was
relatively immune from attack by the right,
and thus in the summer of 1953 he established a truce in Korea which acknowledged
a military stalemate and the sovereignty of
both North and South Korea.

One effect of the Korean War was the
formation of a NATO-like organization, the
Southeast Asia Treaty Organization (SEATO).
Established in 1954, SEATO included Australia, New Zealand, Britain, France, the
United States, Pakistan, Thailand, and the
Philippines. Cambodia, Laos, and South
Vietnam were also associated with the
group. Not as structured as NATO, the agreement none the less committed its members to
respond collectively against aggression,
both external and internal. SEATO clarified
the commitments of the United States and
gave notice that its European policies were
now formally extended to Asia. Through
NATO and SEATO the United States believed
that it had taken the necessary action to contain
communism.

POLAND AND HUNGARY: COMMUNISM IN CRISIS, 1956

In 1956 crises in eastern Europe and in the old
colonial world resulted in a sorting out of
spheres of influence and in a reaffirmation of
the supremacy of the Soviet Union and the
United States in world affairs.

Several of the Soviet satellites resisted Russian control and attempted to achieve some
autonomy in their domestic and foreign affairs.
This turn of events was related to changes
occurring in the governance of the Soviet
Union after the death of Stalin. Nikita Khrushchev, the new Soviet leader, attacked the
rigidity of the old Soviet system (see pages
234–237). Meetings between the leaders of Yugoslavia and Russia in June 1956 culminated
in a communiqué which proclaimed that there
were a number of ways to achieve socialism
which were acceptable to the Soviet Union:
"the ways of socialist development vary in
different countries and conditions," it stated.
Yugoslavia under Marshall Tito had retained
a considerable amount of autonomy, when
compared with other eastern European states.
These events seemed to indicate a willingness on the part of the Soviet Union to permit
some latitude in other communist states. Poland and Hungary, in late 1956, tested the
limits of this freedom.

In Poland, after Stalin's death, there had
been some change from the rigid controls
which had been imposed on intellectuals since
the end of the Second World War. Wladislaw
Gomulka, a communist who was associated
with nationalist aspirations in Poland and who
believed that national communist parties
should direct their own countries, began to
gain popularity in the face of a loss of confidence among Polish writers and political
leaders in the leadership of the Soviet Union.
In June 1956 a workers' strike in the city
of Poznan was broken up by the military.
Gomulka became the leader of the dissidents,
as public protests against rigid controls became more open. The Stalinist Polish authorities were forced out of governmental positions, and in October Gomulka became a
member of the Polish Politburo, the major
committee dominating Polish political life.

Rebels in Hungary during the 1956 uprising against Soviet domination. (Erick Lessing, Magnum)

Russia became anxious over events in Poland and the prospect of Gomulka's leadership. In an extraordinary move, a group of Soviet leaders, including Khrushchev, flew to Poland to discuss the new policies with Gomulka and the new Politburo. Simultaneously, Russian troops began movements which seemed to be directing large contingents of soldiers towards Poland. Gomulka managed to convince the Russians that he was a loyal Marxist and that he continued to believe in Leninist principles of centralized communist leadership. Moreover, he reaffirmed that Poland would remain a loyal member of the Warsaw Pact, thereby indicating an acceptance of the framework of foreign and military poli-

cies supported by the Russians. Given these reassurances of Gomulka's loyalty, Russia accepted his election in late October as General Secretary of the Polish communist party.

Hungarians saw the events of Yugoslavia and Poland as a signal to seek greater liberalization of their own rigid communist regime. Dissent centered in universities and among intellectuals, but soon spread to the general populace. This resulted on October 23 in a huge demonstration in front of the Polish Embassy in the Hungarian capital of Budapest. The demonstrators called for the resignation of the government in Hungary; the symbolic statue of Stalin in the city park was destroyed; and students made attempts to take over the radio station in order to broadcast appeals for support of the dissenters. Russian troops opened fire.

In the midst of this rebellion, Imre Nagy, a Hungarian communist associated with liberal and national causes, was appointed prime minister by the communist leadership, in an attempt to appease the dissent. Nagy was in a difficult position, because he feared Russian intervention, yet had a mandate from his own people to bring about change. He appointed some of the opposition to official posts in the government and liberalized the leadership, and, initially, he was supported by many non-communists. At the end of October Nagy announced that Hungary would now have a political system with a number of political parties and that it was the intention of the country to withdraw from the Warsaw Pact. The revolution seemed to be pointing towards a democracy of the western European sort, and it received encouragement from radio broadcasts from the West. The symbol of the new Hungary became Cardinal Mindszenty, a Catholic priest freed from prison, who had great moral authority and who supported the new direction in Hungary.

Russia viewed the events in Hungary with great anxiety, fearing a serious break in the communist bloc. In late October, at the request of Nagy, Soviet troops had been withdrawn from Budapest. On November 4, however, Russian troops reentered the city and controlled it by nightfall. The few days of Hungary's attempt at a national revolution were ended with a reassertion of authoritarian control. Cardinal Mindszenty sought refuge at the American embassy, where he was given political asylum. Nagy asked for asylum at the embassy of Yugoslavia, but he was returned to the new Soviet-imposed leadership in Hungary. He and a number of other communists who had joined him were executed. Many Hungarian citizens fled the country in late 1956 to emigrate to western Europe and North America.

THE SUEZ CRISIS, 1956

Western Europe's difficulties with areas it had controlled in the nineteenth and early twentieth century were also increasing. This can be seen in the Suez Crisis of 1956, which occurred at roughly the same time as the events in Poland and Hungary.

Nationalism was an element in the politics of the Near East after the Second World War. This is shown by the establishment of the new state of Israel in 1948, and by a revolution in Egypt in 1952 in which army officers overthrew the Egyptian king and organized a new government with nationalist goals. In Egypt the new government negotiated with the Conservative government in Britain in 1954 for a withdrawal of British troops from Egypt and from the Suez Canal. Britain was guaranteed passage through the important waterway and assured that it would continue to control the canal through a holding company.

In July 1956 the Egyptian leader, Gamal Abdel Nasser (1918–70), who was determined to become the spokesman for Arab nationalism and self-determination, announced that Egypt was nationalizing the Suez Canal. The British government, headed by Prime Minister Anthony Eden, was determined to maintain its traditional powerful role in the Suez area and to resist Nasser, as a way of checking the growing nationalism of the Arab world. France and Israel joined Britain in military manoeuvres against Egypt; France as a means of cutting off Egyptian supplies to Algerian rebels; Israel as a way of guaranteeing its right to use the canal (from which it had been barred by Egypt) and to increase its influence over a strategic border area.

Though the combined forces of Britain, France and Israel demonstrated they could easily defeat Egypt, the three allies had failed to shore up their military efforts with necessary diplomacy. After some vacillation, the United States decided to oppose the invasion. In a rare display of co-operation after the Second World War, the United States and the Soviet Union, on November 3, 1956, used the United Nations to stop the advancing armies and to get Eden and his allies to leave the canal area and withdraw. A United Nations force entered the canal zone to monitor the peace.

Britain's influence in the Near East was diminished by Suez, as the world's response was overwhelmingly against the restoration of the old imperial style of rule and supportive of national autonomy. Ironically, Suez became a major chapter in certifying that European imperialism was now on the wane and that European nations were not able to maintain their old control over areas in other parts of the globe.

BERLIN

In Europe, East and West met in Germany and, more specifically, in the old German capital of Berlin. After the Second World War Germany was divided among the four occupying powers: the United States, Great Britain, France, and the Soviet Union, each with its own zone. The city of Berlin was entirely enclosed in the Soviet zone, and it too was divided into four parts. In 1948 the Soviet Union blockaded the Western part of Berlin, halting all rail and road communication. The Western powers broke the blockade with an airlift to bring in supplies. An agreement in 1949 ended the blockade. The two western European powers and the United States continued to co-operate, and their areas of Germany were united in 1949 to form the German Federal Republic or, as it is known, West Germany, with its capital in the city of Bonn. The Soviet area became the German Democratic Republic or East Germany. Each of the two German states was dependent upon its sponsor states in the first years of its existence.

For the first two decades after the creation of West Germany and East Germany, one of the major issues was the legality of both new states; many still thought about the possibility of a new unification of the German nation. Berlin became the focus of the diplomatic differences between East and West. In 1958 Khrushchev stated that Berlin should be made into a free city and be demilitarized. The Russians seemed to be suggesting that the West must accept such a solution to the Berlin problem within six months, or else the Soviets would sign a peace treaty with East Germany and turn over to them all transportation and communication links to the city. This would involve the West in having to recognize the existence of East Germany and would thus force the West to abandon its position that its

goal was the unification of Germany.

Diplomatic talks between foreign ministers were held throughout 1959, as the Russians postponed the implementation of their threat. The West German government was pleased that its allies, the United States, Britain, and France, were determined to support it, though it was unhappy the West would enter into any negotiations which might adversely effect the long-term possibility of German unification. The United States, Britain, and France to a lesser extent, were not as concerned with unification as much as with protecting an ally, West Germany, and territory they regarded as part of their sphere of influence. Negotiations continued into 1961, on and off, at various levels. Khrushchev kept the issue open, trying to gain an advantage.

In May 1961 Khrushchev and the new president of the United States, John F. Kennedy (1917–63), held a summit conference in Vienna. Khrushchev blustered and continued to demand that Berlin be a free city. He intimated he would sign a separate treaty with the East Germans and turn over the Russian part of the city and access to West Berlin to them. Kennedy responded to the unhappy tone of the meeting by increasing the strength of American troops in West Germany. The West German government also announced troop increases. Then, after having made a display of power, the Western states made it clear to Khrushchev they would negotiate, if the Soviets were willing to do so.

The tensions in Berlin and the authoritarian regime in East Germany had resulted in a wave of emigrants from the East who used Berlin as an escape route to the West. Over two million East Germans fled to the West between 1950 and 1961, with over 30 000 East Germans fleeing to the West in July of 1961 and 22 000 in early August.

On August 13, 1961, East Germany and the Soviet Union announced the closing of the border between the two Berlins. A barbed wire fence was erected. The fence was soon turned into a wall, sealed and heavily guarded. East Berliners and East Germans were forbidden to enter West Berlin. The West used a great deal of rhetoric to condemn the wall, which became for them a symbol of totalitarian

The Berlin Wall. Children in West Berlin are seen in front of a local grocery store, as the wall divides the city.   (Canapress Photo Service)

authority. But no Western power tried to dismantle it, for fear of turning the issue into one which would result in a general war. The West again signalled it would defend West Germany, and the wall became a line of demarcation between the powers. In 1963, in a visit to West Berlin, Kennedy proclaimed: *"Ich bin ein Berliner"* (I am a Berliner), a statement calculated to make clear the determination of the United States and NATO to act, if necessary, in defense of West Germany.

The wall, in a strange manner, actually stabilized the German situation. It meant the dream of reunification was replaced by the reality of two Germanies after the Second World War. It forced both Germanies eventually to recognize the existence of the other as a permanent entity. It made clear the lines of defense in Europe. Not everyone in the West was unhappy about the turn of events. Many saw a united Germany as a force for instability in Europe and viewed the two-Germany solution as a better way of maintaining the balance of power and the peace.

THE CUBAN MISSILE CRISIS

Hungary, Poland, and East Germany were seen by the Soviet Union to be in its backyard, and therefore it had a special interest in their loyalty. Similarly, the United States viewed its special area as the western hemisphere — North and South America. Since the early nineteenth century, with the articulation of the Monroe Doctrine, the United States has warned other powers to refrain from getting involved in the hemisphere.

The island of Cuba has posed difficult problems for the United States since 1959, when Fulgencio Batista, one of the most authoritarian and arbitrary Latin-American dictators, was overthrown by a revolutionary movement led by Fidel Castro. The Batista regime had been supported by the United States. The new Cuban government, though recognized by the United States, openly criticized the policies of its huge neighbour, and Castro, soon after coming into power, began to confiscate American property in Cuba. Castro announced he intended to extend his political revolution into the economic and social areas, and, in some of his policies, began emulating the Soviet political style. In 1960 he negotiated a trade agreement with the Soviet Union. The United States responded by banning the importation of Cuban sugar, an attempt to beat Cuba into the ground economically. Russia only increased its support of Cuba, delighted to have a client state only 115 kilometres from the United States. Castro continued his anti-American policy, viewing the United States as an imperialist power which supported right-wing dictatorships in Latin America.

In January 1961, just before his term of office ended, President Dwight D. Eisenhower of the United States broke off diplomatic relations with Cuba. Kennedy, his successor, decided to follow up on an initiative begun by Eisenhower. The United States had been training anti-Castro Cuban exiles and was supplying them with weapons with which to invade Cuba and establish a pro-United States government. Kennedy authorized the invasion. It went ahead in April, the invaders landing at the Bay of Pigs on the southern coast of Cuba. Castro's forces were aware of the invasion and were prepared for it. They easily defeated the force and the United States was humiliated. The invasion only pushed Castro further into the hands of the Soviet bloc, and it made the United States appear little different from those regimes in the communist bloc which it regularly condemned.

In addition to sponsoring the building of the Berlin Wall in 1961, the Soviet Union resumed the testing of nuclear weapons in the atmosphere. The United States then believed it had to respond in kind, or it would fall behind in the military and diplomatic quest for advantage in the arms race. Therefore, the U.S. resumed testing in April 1962.

In 1962 Khrushchev precipitated what is agreed to have been the most dangerous confrontation of the cold war between the two major powers. In October 1962 Kennedy learned that, in addition to having sent conventional weapons and airplanes to Cuba along with Soviet military advisers, the Soviet Union was shipping medium-range nuclear missiles and launching pads. Kennedy mobilized United States and world public opinion. On television he stated that the installation of missiles "is a deliberately provocative and unjustified change in the status quo which cannot be accepted. . . ." He announced a "quarantine," really a blockade, of Cuba, noting "all ships of any kind bound for Cuba from whatever nation or port will, if found to contain cargoes of offensive weapons, be turned back." He called the Soviet Union the instigator of the crisis and warned that any missile launched from Cuba would be viewed as coming from the Soviet Union and that the United States would retaliate.

Kennedy resisted advice to attack Cuba immediately. For several days the world watched the diplomats trying to seek a way out. Khrushchev bargained. He claimed the missiles had been placed only to defend Cuba. Finally, he backed away from a nuclear confrontation over the island. Khrushchev withdrew the missiles in exchange for an end to the blockade and a United States pledge not to support any invasion of Cuba. The crisis ended, seemingly with a United States victory. But Kennedy wisely knew the United States "won" only because the Soviet Union did not see Cuba as essential to its national welfare. Had the crisis come over an area which the Soviets believed to be in their sphere of influence, the United States would not have been able to be so firm. The result was a "thaw" after the crisis, a realization that the United States and the Soviets had actually come dangerously close to nuclear war. In July 1963 both countries negotiated a ban on the testing of nuclear weapons in the atmosphere, signed by all the major powers except China and France.

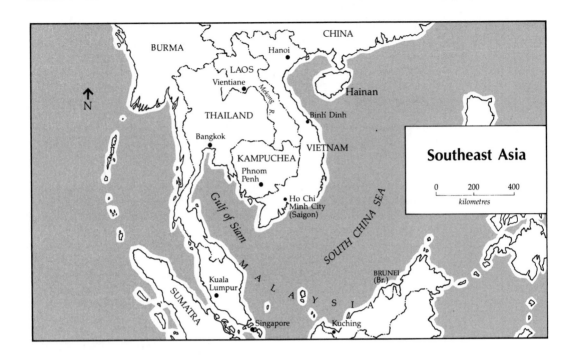

SOUTHEAST ASIA: WAR IN VIETNAM

When the Vietminh under the leadership of Ho Chi Minh defeated France in 1954, the United States came to the aid of South Vietnam, applying to Asia the policy of containment which had worked in Europe. In the late 1950s the United States sent in "military advisers" to train South Vietnamese troops, and, while it did not approve of President Ngo Dinh Diem's authoritarian temperament or the slowness of economic reform, the United States supported him as its only alternative to a communist government.

Meanwhile South Vietnam was fighting a civil war. An organization called the Viet Cong, composed mainly of South Vietnamese who, like Ho Chi Minh, adopted the banner of communism for nationalist as well as ideological reasons, tried to overthrow the Diem government. Supported by Ho Chi Minh in the North, the Viet Cong were very successful at guerilla warfare and in taking control of some of the rural areas of the South.

In 1961 President Kennedy sent in more advisers and shipped huge amounts of equipment to support Diem's regime. However,

Diem continued to lose support in the countryside. In addition, the Buddhists of Vietnam were persecuted by Diem, himself a Catholic, and they agitated against his government. Finally, in 1963 Diem was assassinated. This did not result in the installation of a stable government, nor did it halt the gains being made by Ho and the Viet Cong. In 1964 President Lyndon B. Johnson (1908–72) of the United States began the bombing of North Vietnam by American planes.

Johnson, in August 1964, extended his mandate in Vietnam. In that month American destroyers battled with North Vietnamese gunboats in the Gulf of Tonkin. It was later revealed the United States ships were helping South Vietnamese raiders. At the time, however, Johnson struck a posture of innocence, and he went to the United States Congress in order to obtain authority to "take all necessary measures to repel any armed attack against the forces of the United States and to repel any further aggression." American troops began to extend their role in the war. They had been "advisers" to the South Vietnamese. Soon they were coming to the aid of South Vietnamese troops when the latter were under enemy fire. By the middle of 1965 the United States was actively in the war. Its troops were carrying out "search and destroy missions" designed to "liberate" villages held by the North.

Conscription in the United States provided the army for the war. The escalation undertaken by Johnson meant that by 1967 a half-million American soldiers were in Vietnam, and the North was now being systematically bombed. United States troop casualties rose rapidly; by the end of 1968 more than 30 000 United States soldiers had died and over 100 000 were wounded.

The United States became engaged in a war which was different from anything it had known. The North Vietnamese fought a guerrilla war on familiar territory, using the terrain and their national aspirations to their advantage. Johnson and his advisers continued to believe that much was at stake for the United States. They talked about halting communism and used the media to build a spirit of patriotism. Yet, many Americans felt that the remoteness of Vietnam did not warrant such a heavy expenditure of lives and resources. Many also came to agree with the analysis that the United States had foolishly involved itself in a foreign civil war. Atomic weapons were ruled out, but the United States' generals seemed to believe that, given enough conventional weapons, they would eventually win. By 1968 it became apparent they had miscalculated badly, and that a European-type war made no sense in the villages of southeast Asia.

The policy of the United States government in Vietnam resulted in domestic turmoil and anger. Protests against the war began in the universities in 1965 with a teach-in at the University of Michigan, criticizing the government policy. The movement spread among young people, many of whom found it impossible to see what was happening in Vietnam as a clear cause for which lives should be risked as in the Second World War and even in Korea. The war divided the United States into "hawks" and "doves," those who defended the aggressive policy of Johnson, and those who claimed it was misguided and foolish to turn a civil war in Vietnam into a defense of

Western democracy. The United States was seen by the doves as a foolish, arrogant imperialist power, pursuing a futile war at enormous cost, while misreading the nationalist politics of Asia. Johnson withdrew from the race for the presidency in 1968 because of the large protest movement. Though he had been a successful vote-getter, there was strong opposition to him even in his own political party.

Richard Nixon (1913–   ), who headed the Republican ticket, was elected president in 1968. He, too, had favoured an aggressive foreign policy, and had built a career on a position of virulent anti-communism. He began a policy of "Vietnamization" in 1969, in an effort to build up the South Vietnamese troops to permit a United States withdrawal. Massive aid went to the government of the South, but it was never able to mobilize its people, as did the North. Nixon then pursued a policy of withdrawal, alternately pulling out troops and massively bombing the North, hoping for a negotiated solution which would satisfy his militant supporters. Anti-war protests continued in the United States, major ones in 1970, after it became clear that United States troops on occasion deliberately killed innocent people in their quest for control of villages. The United States had also conducted an invasion of Cambodia in order to destroy North Vietnamese bases there.

In 1973 a settlement between the United States and North Vietnam was finally negotiated. The North retained some areas it had controlled in the South, United States prisoners of war were returned, and the United States withdrew. In the end, The United States intervention proved totally futile. The war between North and South continued until, in the spring of 1975, the South collapsed.

Vietnam was a source of contention between East and West, but the United States and the Soviet Union did negotiate arms control agreements during this period. In an effort to reduce tensions, Nixon, in 1972, visited both Peking and Moscow in order to try to construct better relations between the United States and its major adversaries. Gerald Ford, who became president in 1974 following Nixon's resignation over the Watergate affair, continued his predecessor's foreign policy.

THE SOVIET UNION AND CZECHOSLOVAKIA, 1968

Events in Czechoslovakia in 1968 again tested the willingness of the Soviet Union to permit its satellites in eastern Europe to develop a measure of autonomy. Czechoslovakia in the 1950s and 1960s had pursued Stalinist policies of centralization of governmental authority. This angered minority national groups in the country, such as the Slovaks, and students and intellectuals, who were aware of liberalized policies in other eastern European countries.

In January 1968 a change of leadership occurred. A group within the communist party, led by Alexander Dubček, a Slovak, succeeded in defeating the old conservative leaders and took control of policy matters. Censorship was immediately relaxed, and many political prisoners were released. Dubček announced that the party would become more democratic, and a federal system was proposed for Czechoslovakia.

The period from January to August has become known as the "Prague Spring," a time of hope and rebirth for the country. Dubček talked about giving socialism a "human face," and of making the political process within the communist party more democratic. Czech intellectuals were eager to support Dubček and urged him to move further in the direction of democracy and freedom of expression.

Dubček, aware of the history of intervention in eastern Europe, attempted to reassure the Soviet Union. He constantly proclaimed the loyalty of Czechoslovakia to the Warsaw Pact, hoping that this orthodoxy in foreign affairs might persuade the Russians to permit Czechoslovakia some latitude in its domestic life. Dubček also indicated that the communist party would retain centralized control, but the Russians viewed him with suspicion.

Moscow was not happy with the Czech developments, and cautioned Dubček about going too far; it was especially concerned when Dubček began to talk about seeking trade and credits with West Germany and other western European states. Dubček was attempting to walk the fine line of Tito—Czechoslovakia was to remain a single-party communist state, but the party would be more responsive to needs of the people, and the Czechs were to have the final say over their own internal affairs. The "Czech experiment" with a liberalized communist state was looked upon with interest and encouragement by the West, and by such eastern European states as Rumania and Yugoslavia.

Finally, after much cajoling and many threats, Russia took action. It feared that if Dubček were successful in creating a more independent state, other eastern European states would likely move in the same direction as Czechoslovakia. On August 10, 1968, Russian troops, supported by soldiers from Hungary, Bulgaria, Poland, and East Germany, invaded Czechoslovakia. The reform program was ended, the liberal leaders were ousted, and by the next year Czechoslovakia was in the hands of a government more responsive to Moscow.

The invasion of Czechoslovakia was a signal of the end of the internal liberalization of eastern European governments. Earlier, as in Hungary in 1956, Russia had invaded only when the Warsaw Pact seemed to be at stake. Now it was invading to prevent Czechoslovakia from experimenting with the model of communism which the Soviets had formerly accepted. This became apparent in November 1968 when Leonid Brezhnev (1907–82), Khrushchev's successor, articulated what became known as the Brezhnev Doctrine. Brezhnev claimed, as Metternich had done a century earlier under different circumstances, that the domestic policy of states in the Soviet bloc was the concern of all members, and would be monitored. When communism (Brezhnev called it "socialism") was seen to be in danger in any country, he claimed it was "not only a problem of the people of the country concerned, but a common problem and concern of all socialist countries."[7] A warning was being issued. It was one which frightened some, and caused communist parties in western Europe, for example in Italy and France, to shift their policies away from the Soviet Union.

Neither the Soviet Union nor the United States have hesitated to intervene in the domestic affairs of other nations when they believed their interests to be at stake. In 1979 the Soviets invaded Afghanistan to support a puppet government and remained to be involved in a guerrilla war in that country. In 1983, the United States sent troops to the tiny Caribbean island of Grenada for the purpose of deposing a Marxist government. In Latin America the United States gives aid to various embattled regimes or, as in the case of Nicaragua, aids and trains revolutionaries.

In the 1960s there was talk of "detente," a relaxation of tensions, among the superpowers. Some say this period ended in the 1980s. Yet, there was continuity in the acknowledgment by both superpowers that each has a clearly defined sphere of influence. While one power or the other might try to undermine its rival, the areas of control have usually been carefully respected. In 1968 the Czechoslovaks knew the United States would not actively help; and Latin-American insurgents might get material aid from the Soviet Union, but no troops. Both countries, in the old tradition of political sovereignty, have worked to pursue their self-interest; both have also worked to avoid serious and disastrous confrontation.

ARMS CONTROL AND THE COLD WAR

It is in the area of arms control that those involved in the cold war have come to acknowledge the new reality of the twentieth century — the possibility of nuclear destruction — which changed the nature of warfare and provided an imperative to control national ambition and even to consider disarmament. The prospects of a nuclear war were so grim that all agreed on the need to limit weapons and to avert the possibility of a war occurring through accident or misunderstanding.

John Kennedy delivered the most important diplomatic speech of his presidency in June 1963, after the events of the Cuban missile crisis quieted down. Kennedy talked about the need to seek a "genuine peace." Total war, he claimed, "makes no sense in an age when the deadly poisons produced by a nuclear exchange would be carried by wind and water and soil and seed to the far corners of the globe and to generations yet unborn." Kennedy acknowledged the differences between the United States and the Soviet Union, but praised the Soviet people for their "many

achievements"; he recalled that the two countries had been allies, and that Russia had suffered deeply in the Second World War.

. . . both the United States and its allies, and the Soviet Union and its allies, have a mutually deep interest in a just and genuine peace and in halting the arms race. Agreements to this end are in the interests of the Soviet Union as well as ours — and even the most hostile nations can be relied upon to accept and keep those treaty obligations, and only those treaty obligations, which are in their own interest.

So let us not be blind to our differences — but let us also direct attention to our common interests and the means by which those differences can be resolved. And if we cannot end now our differences, at least we can help make the world safe for diversity. For, in the final analysis, our most basic common link is that we all inhabit this small planet. We all breathe the same air. We all cherish our children's future. And we are all mortal.[8]

Kennedy's signal was taken up by the Soviet Union. Khrushchev praised the speech publicly and the Russian media gave it extensive coverage. Several weeks after, Khrushchev offered a limited test ban treaty, which was signed in August by the nuclear powers, the United States, Great Britain, and the Soviet Union. The parties to the treaty agreed "to prohibit, to prevent, and not to carry out any nuclear weapon test explosion, or any other nuclear explosion, at any place under its jurisdiction or control: . . . in the atmosphere; beyond its limits, including outer space; or underwater. . . ."[9] This is probably the most important arms control agreement since the Second World War, as it slowed the arms race at a time when it was escalating. It was also an opening to other arrangements between the major powers. This treaty had been under discussion and negotiation since 1961; it was Kennedy's speech and Khrushchev's response which made it a reality.

The issue of arms control became more complicated in the 1960s because of the spread of nuclear weapons to other states. France and China had them by the middle of the decade.

Japan, West Germany, and Canada, with advanced technological capabilities, could develop such weapons if they chose to move their research in that direction. Yet other states, including Brazil, India, and Israel, would soon be able to do so. There was a sense among many states that the possibilities of nuclear war would soon increase dramatically, especially because of the potential for a local dispute to escalate into nuclear confrontation. There was seen to be a need for an agreement which would limit the number of countries which had nuclear weapons and which would prevent nuclear powers from giving such weapons to allies.

The United States and the Soviet Union negotiated such an agreement and then submitted it to the United Nations in order to obtain broader approval. The result was the Treaty on the Nonproliferation of Nuclear Weapons, approved by the General Assembly of the United Nations in June 1968. The first article states:

Each nuclear-weapon State Party to the Treaty undertakes not to transfer to any recipient whatsoever nuclear weapons or other nuclear explosive devices or control over such weapons or explosive devices directly, or indirectly; and not in any way to assist, encourage, or induce any non-nuclear-weapon State to manufacture or otherwise acquire nuclear weapons or other nuclear explosive devices, or control over such weapons or explosive devices.[10]

An inspection system was part of the agreement. Countries which did not have nuclear weapons were required to accept inspection of their nuclear energy installations. The treaty went into effect in March 1970, without the signatures of France or China. Moreover, other countries which did not sign included Argentina, Brazil, Cuba, Egypt, India, Israel, Pakistan, Portugal, South Africa, Spain and Uruguay.

Separate from the nonproliferation agreement the United States and the Soviet Union, in 1969, began bilateral Strategic Arms Limitation Talks (SALT). The first part of these talks resulted in two agreements in 1972. The first agreement limited strategic offensive weapons, those which have a range, usually called intercontinental, which permit one of the powers to strike directly at the other. This was a freeze on intercontinental ballistic missiles (ICBMs). At that time, each country had roughly equal strength in ICBMs. The idea was to institute a freeze as a way of beginning to talk about further arms limitations.

The second treaty undertook to limit antiballistic missile (ABM) systems: "Each Party undertakes not to deploy ABM systems for the defense of the territory of its country and not to provide a base for such a defense. . . ."[11] The limitation on ABMs meant that, given the technology at the time, each country left its population open to nuclear attack. This was an acknowledgment that in nuclear weaponry offensive capability was overwhelmingly in advance of defensive capability, and that there was no guarantee of protection. Simply, there was no defense against hundreds of missiles; nuclear war would mean destruction for all parties.

These SALT I pacts were followed by the SALT II agreement in 1979, a United States-Soviet Union treaty on the limitation of intercontinental offensive nuclear weapons. SALT II, though signed by the executives of both countries, was never ratified by the United States Senate, and is thus not formally binding. However, both countries have been abiding by its conditions. It set ceilings on nuclear arms and provided for parity in quantities of arms. SALT II did not limit weapons as much as regulate how rapidly weapons development would proceed. It was an agreement about development and direction.

Other arrangements were made since the 1960s to limit warfare and its effects, all made possible by the openings provided by the Partial Test Ban Treaty of 1963 and the Nonproliferation Treaty of 1968. In 1963 a "hot-line," a direct communications link between the United States and the Soviet Union, was established. This was a result of the demonstrated need for quick links between heads of government during the Cuban missile crisis of 1962. In 1971 a more advanced communications link was put into place. The hot-line has been used regularly and has been found to be valuable in dealing with responses to crises in

November 1985. Mikhail Gorbachev and Ronald Reagan greet one another at the Geneva ''summit meeting.''   (Sygma)

other parts of the globe, as a way of clarifying policies and interests.

In 1972 the United Nations sponsored the Biological Weapons Convention, which prohibits the development, production, or stockpiling of biological weaponry. In 1977 an agreement was made not to employ new scientific advances to produce arms which use techniques of environmental modification. In 1979 a treaty was signed prohibiting the development of radiological weapons.

Relations between the United States and the Soviet Union deteriorated in the early 1980s with the election of Ronald Reagan (1911–   ) to the presidency of the United States. Reagan was a conservative Republican whose rhetoric was highly anti-communist, viewing the Soviet Union as the instigator of all events in

the world which were seen to be contrary to the interests of the United States. He emphasized the need for a strong defense, and redirected United States resources towards building up its armed capabilities. At the time Reagan's presidency began, in 1981, the Soviet Union was coping with a lack of stability in its chief leadership. Brezhnev was very ill and died in 1982. He was replaced by an ill Yuri Andropov, who died in 1984. In turn, Andropov was succeeded by the ailing Constantin Chernenko, until his death in 1985. All three men were of the older Russian generation. During this period Soviet policy did not change towards the United States, and Reagan's hostility did not encourage new departures.

In 1984 the United States announced that it

was beginning research into a nuclear Strategic Defense Initiative, the development of what has come popularly to be called "Star Wars," a system of nuclear weapons designed for defense, to be placed in space. This upset the Soviets. In 1985 with the rise to Soviet leadership of Mikhail Gorbachev, who was only fifty-six and who initiated a reopening of discussions, new possibilities were opened up. Reagan agreed to begin arms talks again, and, later in the year, the two leaders met in Geneva. Both countries wished to have a rough parity of weapons with adequate inspection, and both did not want nuclear weapons to fall into others' hands. As a result, some progress was made toward a new agreement on arms limitations.

B. EUROPE AND NORTH AMERICA SINCE 1945

THE UNION OF SOVIET SOCIALIST REPUBLICS

Russia suffered more destruction than any of the other Allies in the Second World War, but it came out of the war as the greatest power of Europe. Many millions were killed in Russia, and more were left homeless because of the war. During the invasion, the Germans destroyed a good deal of Russian industry and systematically killed livestock and ruined land. However, the Russian capacity for recovery was extraordinary. Motivated by fear of outsiders and by a determination to make Russia a great nation, the government set about rebuilding the country.

In 1946 Stalin inaugurated a new Five-Year Plan for Russia; it was designed to move production beyond pre-war levels. Like the three plans before it, it concentrated on the development of heavy industry, virtually ignoring the consumer sector of the economy. It was Stalin's belief that only by building huge plants and running them efficiently could Russia be a great power. The plan achieved its aim. In 1950 steel production was fifty per cent above the 1940 level and coal production was up sixty per cent. Electricity was extended throughout the country. Moreover, Stalin continued to

emphasize the development of Russia's frontier, the lands to the east which were underdeveloped and underpopulated but had vast natural resources.

The fifth Five-Year Plan, launched in 1951, was again successful in the development of heavy industry and the exploitation of raw materials. Iron, coal, steel, and oil production rose dramatically. However, the Russians did not achieve the same dramatic rise in agricultural production and in the consumer sector. The vast number of agricultural collectives was reduced to eighty thousand, and it was hoped that farming would, in this way, be more efficient. While agricultural production grew, it nowhere matched the impressive results of industrial growth, and in bad crop years Russia had to import grain and other commodities. But, as Russia became more industrialized, there was a rising demand among the population for better housing, clothing, and consumers' goods. This demand was acknowledged by Russia's leaders, and priorities were gradually shifted in the mid-1950s to satisfy it.

Stalin's strong hold over the Communist Party and the Russian state continued after the war. Although the Russian system was seemingly run by committees giving orders to other committees, the word of Stalin was virtually law. He headed both the party and the government and kept his supporters in power. Censorship was still rigid, culture was still under state control, and people still feared the secret police. Extremely suspicious in nature and hostile to everything that deviated from his own ideas and persuasions, Stalin, like some of the czars of old, crushed all opposition.

On March 4, 1953, Stalin died of a stroke. Russia was again faced with a succession problem, for no provision had been made for a new leader during Stalin's regime. After much manoeuvring, a "collective" leadership was established. Within the Soviet system there was a struggle for the control of policy-making between "liberals" and "conservatives," with Nikita Khrushchev (1894–1970) a major figure among the former, and Lavrenti Beria the leader of the latter.

Beria was a devoted Stalinist, and as head of the secret police he had enforced many of Stalin's decisions. Most of the other leaders banded against him out of fear that his organization would begin a new purge if Beria himself was not stopped. At the end of 1953 Beria was arrested on charges of treason, tried, and shot. The collective leadership continued for a time, though there was much jockeying for power between those who wished to follow Stalin's old policies and those who wished to pursue a less harsh course. Beria's death was the last execution of a deposed political leader in the Soviet Union.

In 1956, at the Twentieth Congress of the Communist Party, Khrushchev astounded the delegates of over fifty countries by denouncing Stalin. Speaking for the Central Committee of the Party, the most important political entity in the Soviet Union, Khrushchev said:

Stalin acted not through persuasion, explanation, and patient cooperation with people, but by imposing his concepts and demanding absolute submission to his opinion. Whoever opposed this concept or tried to prove his viewpoint, and the correctness of his position was doomed to removal from the leading collective and to subsequent moral and physical annihilation. . . .

Stalin originated the concept "enemy of the people." This term automatically rendered it unnecessary that the ideological errors of a man or men engaged in a controversy be proven; this term made possible the usage of the most cruel repression, violating all norms of revolutionary legality, against anyone who in any way disagreed with Stalin, against those who were only suspected of hostile intent, against those who had bad reputations.

This concept "enemy of the people" actually eliminated the possibility of any kind of ideological fight or the making of one's views known on this or that issue, even those of a practical character. In the main, and in actuality, the only proof of guilt used, against all norms of current legal science, was the "confession" of the accused himself; and, as subsequent probing proved, "confessions" were acquired through physical pressures against the accused.

This led to glaring violations of revolutionary legality, and to the fact that many entirely innocent persons, who in the past had defended the party line, became victims. . . .

Possessing unlimited power, he indulged in great willfulness and choked a person morally and physically. A situation was created where one could not express one's own will. . . .

Comrades! In order not to repeat [the] errors of the past, the Central Committee has declared itself resolutely against the cult of the individual. We consider that Stalin was excessively [praised].[12]

When this speech was made public in the West, most people interpreted it as the beginning of a less rigid and totalitarian style in the Soviet Union. By 1958 it was clear that Khrushchev, now Secretary of the Communist Party, was the leading political figure in Russia.

After Stalin's death, a "thaw" occurred in the cultural sphere, which resulted in the relaxation of censorship. Works critical of the system (though not works attacking the system itself) were published in Russia, and people were no longer as fearful of arbitrary arrest for making critical remarks about the state. A major work published after Khrushchev's speech was Vladimir Dudintsev's *Not By Bread Alone*, which attacked the massive bureaucracy, ideological rigidity, and lack of personal freedom and self-expression in the Soviet Union. Yevgeny Yevtushenko's poem "Babi Yar," an attack on anti-Semitism in Russia, was a major work of the 1960s.

However, there have been clear limits to what is acceptable. Works by two winners of the Nobel Prize for Literature have not been published in Russia. Boris Pasternak's *Dr. Zhivago*, a best-seller in the West, which was a nostalgic, romantic work, critical of the Soviet Revolution and the collective mentality, was attacked by communist authorities. Much of the work of Aleksandr Solzhenitsyn, whom most critics consider Russia's best modern novelist, and who has likened Soviet society to a "cancer ward," has never been published in the Soviet Union. Solzhenitsyn was exiled from the Soviet Union in 1974, after the publication in

Europe and the United States of the *Gulag Archipelago*, a work which was a personal history of terrorist activities of the Soviet state and its prison system. It is still not unheard of for writers who attack the regime to be arrested and sent into exile in a distant part of the country.

Despite the "thaw," the ideal of "socialist realism" is still advocated by the state. The concept of "socialist realism" is defined in the following way by the Union of Soviet Writers:

Socialist Realism is the fundamental method of Soviet literature and criticism: it demands of the artist a true, historically concrete representation of reality in its revolutionary development. Further, it ought to contribute to the ideological transformation and education of the workers in the spirit of socialism.[13]

What this means is that art must serve politics and the state, that individual expression is severely limited, and that the value of a work of art will be judged by what it contributes to the "proper" intellectual development of the people. It means that certain forms of individual expression—most especially abstract art, free-form poetry, and attacks on the system as a whole—are unacceptable. The result can be seen in the development of dance in Russia. Classical ballet and "folk" dance programs flourish, but modern dance is frowned upon in the Soviet Union. Similarly, in art, glorifications of proper heroes and themes are encouraged, but abstraction is discouraged.

Economic development after the death of Stalin more closely reflected the needs and wishes of the people. Khrushchev decentralized industrial planning in an effort to do away with much unnecessary bureaucracy. Attempts were made to alleviate the housing shortage in the cities, to provide more meat in people's diets, and to respond to the demand to produce more consumers' goods. From this point on, the Soviet economy began to resemble more that of the United States and western Europe in its style of production and in its response to consumers' needs. By now a new "middle class" had

appeared in the Soviet Union—a large number of people who wished to live a life not unlike that of the traditional Western *bourgeoisie.*

In October 1957 Russia startled the world when it placed "sputnik," a satellite, into orbit around the earth. This was a great technical accomplishment, and it meant that in this area Russia was ahead of the United States. The Americans made a major effort to catch up, and manned space flights by both Russia and the United States followed in the 1960s.

The Khrushchev years also saw a thaw in the cold-war mentality. Serious negotiations were begun with the United States on disarmament, limitations on nuclear testing, and a relaxation of tensions in Europe. While both the United States and Russia were still hostile to one another, discussions could now proceed without the rancour of the Stalin period. In the late 1950s the Soviet Union did reduce its troops from about 5 million to about 3.7 million, a response to internal economic needs as well as the more subdued international atmosphere. In 1962, after an attempt to place Soviet missiles in Cuba, Khrushchev retreated in the face of an American blockade and threats of nuclear war from the United States. In 1963 both countries signed a treaty limiting the testing of atomic weapons.

Khrushchev never had the power or authority of Stalin. He ruled initially through his ability to put together groups of people to support his policies. Temperamentally he was not dictatorial, but paternal. He enjoyed playing the role of the folksy politician, full of adages and ancient wisdom, hiding his intelligence and shrewdness behind a politician's mask. However, the one area in which he could not make gains was in his specialty, agriculture. His accomplishments fell short of his projections, and a massive "virgin lands" program meant to open new agricultural land failed to live up to expectations. Moreover, there was a growing resentment that he was beginning to conduct government business and foreign policy without proper consultation with other party members. In 1964, as a result, they forced him to resign his posts and go into retirement. Russia again was governed collectively. The dominant personalities proved to be Leonid Brezhnev, who held the most important post, that of Secretary of the Communist Party, and Alexsei Kosygin, who became premier.

The new leaders were not revolutionaries, but technicians who were practical people. They had regular dealings with western Europeans and North Americans, and did not fear economic and social relationships, provided that the communist political system was not challenged. Kosygin in 1965 moved the Soviet economy to a more liberal stance: individual plants were encouraged to shift to a system which would reward efficiency and productivity. The collective style of the economy was not changed, but aspects of it became more liberal.

Russia had also been dealing with the West in the area of agriculture. The Soviet Union had difficulties in growing enough grain to feed its people, primarily because of the concentration on the development of industry, and on urbanization, security, and defense. In years when the crops fell short of needs, 1972 and 1976 for example, Russia imported grain, mainly from the United States and Canada. There is still concern about the efficiency and productivity of the agricultural sector of the economy.

In the late 1970s the Soviet leadership, in an effort to increase production, began again to centralize the economy, but without much success. The annual growth was a disappointing one and one-half per cent in the early 1980s. Problems cited by the Soviet leadership included low productivity of workers and excessive absenteeism from jobs. Some observers blamed the slowdown in the Soviet economy on the leadership style of the older generation, which remained in authority until Mikhail Gorbachev came to power in 1985. Others believed the Soviet economy paid a price for the rigid ideological politics of the Soviet Union: there was an inability to absorb new ideas and an unwillingness to dissent from authority out of fear of the consequences.

It is true, however, that the people of the Soviet Union and its orbit of states in eastern Europe were far better off in their standard of living than they had been before the Second World War. The people of the eastern bloc, in fact, resembled western Europeans and Americans more than they did their own grandparents. They were educated in technological skills, worked in one of the most highly developed areas of the world, and desired a measure of freedom, leisure, and consumers' goods. Basically, though, the political structure remained authoritarian.

Political dissent in the Soviet Union existed in an underground of magazines and newsletters. Dissenters, such as Andrei Sakharov, a Jewish scientist of prominence, were often exiled from major centers, deprived of freedom of movement, and not given the opportunity to pursue their professional work. National identity in the Soviet Union was not discouraged — it is, after all, the Union of Soviet Socialist Republics — but strong national groups which assert their right to some cultural or political autonomy, such as those in Estonia, Latvia, Lithuania, and the Ukraine, were punished. Churches associated with separate national identities found it difficult to obtain the means to support their institutional structure. Jews in Russia were prevented from openly teaching their heritage to their children and were regularly punished for practicing their religion. In 1971 Jews were permitted to emigrate in large numbers, a decision made as part of the policy of pursuing better relations with the United States and western Europe. During the decade of the 1970s over 200 000 Jews left, some to Israel, others to Western countries, mainly the United States and Canada. As relations with the West deteriorated in the early 1980s, permission to emigrate was seldom given; human rights groups in the West have tried to publicize the difficulties of Soviet dissidents of all sorts.

While it experienced much international tension and several changes of leadership, the Soviet Union remained internally stable. It is a dictatorship practising political repression, and while it is still safest to be a political conformist, the Soviet Union is now a society run by professionals and technocrats whose tastes and needs are not unlike those of similar classes in every other country. The totalitarian state under Stalin now seems remote.

POLAND: DISSENT AND AUTONOMY IN THE 1980s

In the 1980s Poland became the scene of dissent from the Soviet system, and Poles have been participating in an attempt to transform a traditional Soviet Union-style communist regime into a more liberal polity. This change has focussed on Solidarity, the workers' union in Poland, which also had support from the Polish Catholic Church, as well as intellectuals and students.

Poland experienced various economic difficulties in the 1970s, mainly in the area of agriculture. Food was imported, prices continued to rise, shortages became the norm, and lines at the shops were long. The Polish communist party, which many Poles saw as a group of managers with special privileges, but unable to govern well, was blamed for the continuing crisis. During this time the regime was forced to try to keep wages low in order to earn money to import food; the state also borrowed from banks in the West.

In August, 1980, in response to rising prices and a government demand for a stabilization of wages, the shipyards at the Polish city of Gdansk (formerly Danzig) were taken over by workers, led by the Solidarity leader Lech Walesa. The workers wanted Solidarity to be a union with authority to choose leaders and to negotiate with the government. Solidarity became the focus of the general discontent in the country. The Polish Catholic Church supported the workers and wanted increased rights of freedom of worship; intellectuals, acting as advisors, collaborated with Solidarity and sought a liberalization of the regime, including freedom of speech and the right to publish.

At the end of August a temporary agreement was reached between the state and Solidarity. The new union was given permission to exist, but it was agreed it would not ''play the role of a political party.'' The union acknowledged the political authority of the state. But this arrangement did not solve the crisis. In the next year the state again tried to limit the freedom of the workers, while Solidarity leaders talked of the need for elections and human rights. Many strikes occurred in various centers of Poland, and the economy was

Solidarity leader Lech Walesa in 1982, in a discussion with the press in which he expressed his determination to continue to work for the goals of the Polish labour movement. (Canapress Photo Service)

in even more difficult circumstances. In the West, Lech Walesa became a political hero. Western political leaders supported change in Poland, and Western banks did not press for payments of their loans to Poland, trying not to destabilize the new economic and political arrangements.

Solidarity's challenge in 1981 went even further. Some of its leaders began to deny the legitimacy of the rule of the communist party of Poland, claiming that the workers were better and more democratically represented by the union movement. They called for a pluralist political system, free elections, and an end to censorship, among other reforms traditionally associated with democratic socialism.

The Soviet response to this change in Poland was to monitor it carefully and to warn the people through various meetings with Polish leaders that Poland was expected to remain a loyal ally as part of the Soviet bloc. In February 1981, while the Soviet Union threatened invasion, the former defence minister, General Wojciech Jaruzelski, at Soviet insistence, became head of government. He was expected to restore order, and troops began to be used to break up demonstrations and strikes. Yet, Solidarity continued its pressure, asking for a part in making economic policy. In response to pressures from within and without, Jaruzelski's government, in December 1981, declared martial law: civil rights were suspended, union activity was ended, and leaders were arrested and imprisoned. Poland was now under military rule.

This action may well have prevented Soviet intervention, but it meant the suppression of a popular movement and the existence of a permanent group of dissidents. Supported by Pope John Paul II, himself a Pole, the leaders of the workers' movement continued to press for rights. In 1983, though Solidarity had grown weaker, Lech Walesa was awarded the Nobel Peace Prize. He would not leave Poland to accept it, fearing he would not then be permitted to reenter the country. The leaders of the Polish opposition remained restricted in their rights, and had to tread the fine line that separates acceptable dissent from the kind that gets one imprisoned. In 1984 the Jaruzelski regime tried to make conditions more normal — ending martial law, granting an amnesty to some political prisoners, and trying to negotiate a settlement. However, in October 1984 a Polish priest, Jerzy Popieluszko, who was a prominent supporter of the workers, was kidnapped by authorities and murdered. The subsequent trial implicated the whole system of authoritarian repression.

The leaders of Solidarity were aware that they would continue to obtain encouragement from the West, but no military support. They were also aware that, like Hungary and Czechoslovakia before them, they faced Soviet intervention if they went too far. Still, they were eager to remain a dissident force, and to keep their organization intact in the face of government hostility. Adam Michnik, one of the leaders, wrote in 1985:

. . . Radicals and exiles typically delude themselves that dictatorships are based exclusively on coercion. This is not true. Long-lived dictatorships engender their own characteristic subculture and peculiar normalcy. They create a type of man unused to freedom and truth, ignorant of dignity and autonomy. Rebels are a tiny minority in such dictatorships; they are seen as a handful of desperate men who live like a band of heretics. For every dictatorship, the critical moment arrives with the reappearance of human autonomy and the emergence of social bonds that do not enjoy official sanction. As a rule such moments are short—temporary tremors marking a crisis in the dictatorial power structure.

In [the Communist system] such loss of balance never lasted longer than a few months. But in Poland the structures of independent civil society have been functioning for several years. . . . So long as these structures exist side by side with totalitarian power which attempts to destroy all independent institutions, the stream of people flowing to prisons will not cease. Poles will stop going behind bars only when they succeed in their struggle for democratic reform of public life. But if they let their independent institutions be destroyed, the whole country will become a prison.

. . . We live in truly interesting times. We witness the barren twilight of the old world of totalitarian dictatorship. We, the people of Solidarity, have been put to a difficult trial. But even if it becomes an ordeal by fire, fire cleans and purifies what it cannot consume. I am not afraid of the generals' fire. There is no greatness about them: lies and force are their weapons, their strength stems from their ability to release the darkest and basest instincts in ourselves. I am sure that we shall win. Sooner or later, but I think sooner, we shall leave the prisons and come out of the underground onto the bright square of freedom. But what will we be like then?

I am not afraid of what they will do to us, but of what they can make us into. For people who were outlaws for a long time feed on their own traumas and emotions which, in turn, strangle their reason and ability to recognize reality. Even the best people can be demoralized by years of persecution and the shock of regaining their lost stature. I pray that we do not return like ghosts who hate the world, cannot understand it, and are unable to live in it. I pray that we do not change from prisoners to prison guards.[14]

Moving from an authoritarian to a free system is not without its own complications.

INTEGRATION IN WESTERN EUROPE:
THE COMMON MARKET

The states of western Europe began to integrate their economic plans after the initial success of the Marshall Plan and the establishment of NATO. Most states realized that alone they could not compete with the vast industrial enterprise of the United States. Moreover, modern technology and industry require vast amounts of capital to create new products. Specialization is also necessary in order to produce cheaply. Only by uniting their economic resources could Europeans hope to achieve as high a level of prosperity as that of the United States.

After the success of the Marshall Plan, a number of western European countries coordinated their coal and steel production. The scheme was the idea of the French economist Jean Monnet who was the leading figure in the post-war effort to unite Europe, and Robert Schuman, the French Foreign Minister. The European Coal and Steel Community (ECSC), formed in 1952, involved France, West Germany, Italy, and the Benelux countries. It made the western part of the European continent into a single market for coal and steel.

Success in coal and steel led to discussions about the possibility of creating a customs union for these countries—one large market—by lowering or doing away with tariffs. In 1957 the ECSC group took a major step in this direction with the Treaty of Rome, which established a European Economic Community, known as the Common Market. The plan was to move slowly towards a common tariff policy and an integrated economic community. Each country sent representatives to Common Market offices in Brussels. The political implications of the Treaty of Rome were obvious to its founders, many of whom hoped that it was a prelude to political union.

Economically, the Common Market was spectacularly successful. Five years after the Treaty of Rome, trade between member nations had risen seventy-three per cent, and production had risen by more than a third. Tariff barriers came down, and workers immigrated from southern Europe to West Germany and the Netherlands to make up for a shortage of labour in the latter countries. While advances were not as spectacular after the mid-1960s, the Common Market helped to revitalize Europe. It became clear that a united western Europe could compete successfully with both the Soviet Union and the United States.

When the Common Market was being formed, Britain was invited to join. But the British declined because of their traditional ties with the Commonwealth and because, as importers of food, they did not think it would be economically advantageous to be tied in with nations that had a large farm production and hence relied on high agricultural prices. Instead, Britain sponsored another economic union, the European Free Trade Association (EFTA), allying itself with Denmark, Norway, Sweden, Austria, Portugal, and Switzerland. The "Seven," as the EFTA was often called, had a looser tariff system than the "Six," the group composing the Common Market. Britain maintained close links with countries in the Commonwealth, and agriculture was not included in the tariff system of the "Seven."

The success of the economic policy of the Common Market, and its considerable political power, soon led many in Britain to regret their earlier unwillingness to join. In contrast to the rest of western Europe, the British economy continued to stagnate, and in 1961 Prime Minister Harold Macmillan decided to apply for membership in the Common Market. Much depended on the attitude of West Germany and France, the two leading members of the "Six," who by this time had begun to draw close together. West Germany was willing to welcome Britain, but Charles de Gaulle, President of France, was worried that Britain's entry would weaken French influence on the continent and that England would open the door to greater American influence and investment in Europe. De Gaulle believed in European integration, but only so long as France would continue to lead the group. The result was a long series of negotiations, which were abruptly broken off by de Gaulle in 1963.

Pressure continued for greater economic

The back of a special issue of fifty pence coins in Great Britain, done in 1973 to commemorate its entry into the Common Market. (The Press Association Ltd.)

integration within the market. De Gaulle was not reluctant to see an industrial union, but he demanded large subsidies from other members of the Common Market for French farmers before he finally agreed in 1966 to an agricultural policy common to all of the countries of the "Six." In 1968 all internal industrial tariffs within the Common Market area were ended, and a system of common external tariffs was introduced. Hence in eleven years a large portion of western Europe had become virtually a single economic entity.

Britain continued to press for entry into the Common Market. After de Gaulle resigned as President of France in 1969, negotiations were carried on by his successor, Georges Pompidou, and the British Prime Minister, Edward Heath, who took office in June 1970. Finally, an agreement was reached in 1971. Britain officially joined the Common Market on January 1, 1973. Denmark and Eire also entered the group at that time. Greece joined in 1981 and Spain and Portugal in 1986. In the 1980s the Common Market has been seen to have stagnated, as national interests have superceded regional ones. Some countries have questioned the economic benefits of union.

GREAT BRITAIN

The first post-war election in Britain was held in July 1945. Even though Churchill was universally revered as a great wartime leader, the British voted overwhelmingly for the Labour Party, which won 393 seats to 213 for the Conservatives. The mandate was clear—the economy was to be restructured, the class system modified, and a strong welfare program introduced.

Clement Attlee (1883–1967) became Prime Minister in the first Labour government to rule with a majority. He tried to deal with the huge balance of payments problems—Britain now regularly imported more than it exported—which was alleviated only temporarily by a devaluation of the pound and by Marshall Plan aid. Labour had preached for decades that industries vital to the public interest should be nationalized in order to eliminate excess profits, and that these industries should be made responsive to public needs. In 1946, as a result, the Bank of England and the coal mines were nationalized, while in 1947 the British Transport Commission took control of trucking, canals, railways, and the London transportation system. Electricity, which had been partly nationalized in 1926, was fully taken over, and in 1949 a bill was passed to nationalize iron and steel production.

The life of Britishers was greatly changed by the introduction of comprehensive social welfare measures. There had been a degree of social security in Great Britain since the early twentieth century, but the program was now expanded to protect the individual from the cradle to the grave. In 1948 the National Health Service Bill was passed. It provided a national plan for health needs: all medical care, drugs, dental care, and various para-medical aids were to be free. The Labour government also embarked on large housing and education schemes.

The program of Labour, however, was more ambitious than its resources could handle. Economic problems, for example the price of imported lumber, made the building of housing difficult. Nationalization, on more than one occasion, turned out not to be a panacea, but (as the Soviet Union learned) the substitution of one bureaucracy for another. Moreover, many businessmen were fiercely opposed to the Labour program. The shortage of medical supplies and trained personnel rendered the National Health Service less effective than it could have been in a more prosperous time. However, many aspects of the Labour program achieved a fair degree of success.

In the election of 1950 Labour retained a narrow margin, but its popularity was eroded by disputes within the party on how far social welfare should go. The 1951 election turned the tables. The Conservatives won 321 seats and Labour obtained only 295, and Churchill, at the age of seventy-six, again became Prime Minister. Little that Labour had done was reversed, however, in spite of veiled threats by many Tory politicians. Iron, steel, and some parts of the trucking industry were denationalized, but the rest of Labour's program, including the vast welfare program, was retained. By 1954, when food rationing was ended, British prosperity, to the extent that it existed, had filtered further down the social scale than ever before.

Churchill resigned in 1954 and was succeeded by Anthony Eden, who was in turn replaced by Harold Macmillan in 1957. The Conservatives governed pragmatically, facing economic crisis after crisis with "stop-and-go" policies designed to patch together a faltering economy. Although Britain retained considerable influence in foreign affairs, the development of the Common Market and the inability of the British economy to keep pace with competition in world markets suggested that new opportunities were needed. After years of struggle to enter the Common Market, a Conservative government negotiated successfully with the member countries for Britain's entry, which took place on January 1, 1973. The Labour Party returned to power in 1974. It conducted a referendum on the Common Market in 1975 in which the electorate reaffirmed Britain's participation in the economic union.

British unions represent a powerful constituency, and are intimately associated with the Labour Party. In 1973–74 the Conservative

prime minister, Edward Heath, decided to try to limit wage rises. Coal miners went on strike against the government in the winter. Heath lost the election of 1974 to the Labour Party as a result of the difficulties caused by the strike, which were aggravated by an Arab oil boycott. The new Labour government then made an agreement with workers which permitted gradual pay rises.

Inflation, which was serious throughout the economies of the West in the 1970s, was in part the result of the success of the union movement in negotiating wages. Great Britain's economy was stagnating and only the discovery of oil reserves in the North Sea gave much new hope. The Labour Party followed a policy of attempting to keep unemployment as low as possible, and this contributed to the protection of industries that were no longer profitable. This policy was blamed for some of the continuing inefficiency and backwardness of British industry.

In the election of 1979, the Conservatives won a majority under the leadership of Margaret Thatcher (1925–). The new prime minister, a staunch conservative by temperament and social philosophy, was determined to change the trend of the British economy and British social policy since 1945; she sought to limit government spending on social welfare, to end the nationalization of industry, and to foster private economic development. Public spending was decreased and wages were held down. The percentage of resources allocated to education, the national health service, and public housing was cut, in some cases severely. Inflation continued for a time, then began to slow down, as was the case in the United States and the rest of the West. Unemployment, which in Great Britain had been at 5.6 per cent in 1979, was over eleven per cent in 1981. By 1983, three million were unemployed.

There were labour riots in several cities in 1981, and unions agitated for relief from Conservative policies. In 1984 a miners' strike which lasted a year broke out as a result of the attempt of the Conservative government to close some mines and redeploy workers. The government in this case managed to get public opinion on its side, as the radical union leaders flirted with support from the Soviet Union and Libya, and openly advocated illegal and violent behaviour.

Thatcher's right-wing conservatism and the radicalism of some of the unions and Labour Party members resulted in a polarization of political life. This led moderates in the Labour Party to break away in 1982 and form a new political party of the center — the Social Democratic Party. They united with the small Liberal Party in an attempt to gain the support of those who were uncomfortable with the state of British politics. They won seats in the House of Commons in the 1983 election and became a third major party in Britain.

One aspect of right-wing conservatism was the encouragement of a strong nationalist sentiment. In 1982 an incident between Britain and Argentina in the Falkland Islands (a group of islands 400 kilometres off the southeast coast of Argentina, which Britain had acquired in its imperialist heyday) permitted the Conservatives to tap nationalist support and to derive political benefits in the process. These islands were inhabited by British settlers who did not wish to live under the sovereignty of Argentina. In May, when Argentine troops invaded the Falklands, Thatcher sent troops to recapture the islands, portraying the event in nostalgic imperial terms, as Great Britain upholding civilization against an evil foe. Britain won the tiny war, which nevertheless cost a number of lives, and the British electorate responded in the next year by giving the Conservatives an increased majority in the House of Commons.

In spite of the policies and hopes of the Conservatives, Britain remained a social democracy with extensive welfare services. Its empire had been liquidated after the Second World War and, while it had strong ties to the Commonwealth, observers recognized that Great Britain was no longer one of the major powers of the world. Britishers still had to come to terms with their new role as a less important, and relatively less wealthy, state. Because of the welfare state, the working class received a larger share of the national prosperity. But class divisions were an ongoing reality in the institutional and social structure of Great Britain and these continued to produce discord.

FRANCE

The France which emerged from the war was a country with mixed attitudes about its past and future. Defeated in 1940, France lived through the war partly under the Nazis, partly under a subservient French government—Vichy—which many regarded as treasonous. The Third Republic was a thing of the past, but the future was uncertain. The Fourth Republic did not have a constitution until 1946. After the "liberation" in 1944, Charles de Gaulle (1890–1970) was head of a provisional government and governed France with the aid of a Consultative Assembly. De Gaulle's main concern was to make France the equal of the three major Allied powers, to turn the defeat of 1940 into a victory after 1945.

In 1940 de Gaulle had defiantly refused to admit defeat and organized a "free French" movement from London which, along with the large French resistance movement within France, fought against the Nazis. Aloof, conservative but not reactionary, coldly intelligent, a believer in social democracy and political aristocracy, and with a mystical love of France and a belief in its greatness which recalled the old monarchs, de Gaulle was a man in the Bonapartist tradition.

The first election for a National Assembly, in October 1945, saw three parties gain support. The Communists, who admired the Russian system, won 151 seats; the Socialists, a democratic constitutional party, won 142 seats; the new Mouvement Républicain Populaire (MRP), a Catholic democratic group of the centre which was mildly socialist, also won 142 seats. The most significant result of the election was the absence of a strong right, so notably in evidence throughout the 1930s.

The Assembly elected de Gaulle as President of the Republic, but de Gaulle had a different view of the role of the president from the majority of those in the Assembly. He wished to have a strong presidency, in order to avoid the bickering, the coalitions, and the consequent paralysis of many of the governments of the Third Republic. However, the Assembly—mainly the Communists and Socialists—favoured a strong parliament with a figurehead president. The result was that in January 1946 de Gaulle resigned as president.

The early post-war governments of the Fourth Republic inaugurated a welfare state in France, not unlike that proposed by the Popular Front of pre-war years. Major banking, insurance, and credit institutions were nationalized, as were the coal mines, gas producers, and electricity companies. A large social-security system was begun. Moreover, a plan created by Jean Monnet for controlling government resources and developing industry was adopted. This plan helped to bring about recovery and the modernization of French industry, and, in spite of the instability of French politics in subsequent years, Monnet's plan remained the basis for French economic and social developments.

While the French were overwhelmingly in favour of a new constitution, they had difficulty in agreeing on one. In October 1946, after defeating one proposed constitution, they approved another by a slim margin. It provided for a strong National Assembly and resembled the structure of the Third Republic. Many of the old problems thus reappeared immediately: governments were unstable (there were twenty-five between 1947 and 1958) long-term plans were difficult to develop, policies changed abruptly, and response to agricultural crises or rampant inflation was slow.

These governments also floundered badly in conducting foreign affairs. France became involved in a colonial war in Indo-China, while attempting to retain control of its possessions there. On May 7, 1954, the French were defeated at Dien Bien Phu. A vigorous new premier, Pierre Mendès-France, managed to pull France out of the war, but his government fell before he could initiate a far-sighted economic program.

A colonial war in Algeria became the last crisis of the faltering Fourth Republic. In 1954 Algerians rebelled against French rule and attacked the *colons*, the European settlers in Algeria. In the midst of a civil war in Algeria between Algerians and *colons*, the French government tried to be moderate. But in 1958 a group of French military men formed a "Committee of Public Safety" to hold Algeria against the rebels and declared themselves to be the governing authority in the territory. The Fourth Republic had thus lost control over its own army, and the Assembly turned to the one person in France who might save the situation—Charles de Gaulle. It gave de Gaulle authority to rule by decree for six months, to write a new constitution, and to end the war in Algeria. In effect, the Assembly ended the Fourth Republic.

De Gaulle proposed a new constitution tailored to his own beliefs. The president was to have great powers as head of state, for he appointed the premier and the cabinet, was the commander-in-chief of the armed forces, and could dissolve the Assembly. Proportional representation in the Assembly was abandoned in favour of a system of voting by districts. Eighty per cent of those who voted in a referendum in September 1958 approved his constitution and, in so approving, inaugurated the Fifth Republic. De Gaulle was chosen the first President of the Fifth Republic and ruled until 1969.

De Gaulle's main concern was France's position in the world. He ended the war in Algeria, while retaining the support of most of the army and bringing it under civilian control. He had France build its own atom bombs, largely as an item of international prestige. Resenting the close ties between Britain and the United States, he began to loosen France's involvement in NATO; and turning eastwards he developed excellent relations with both West Germany and the Soviet Union. His concern with maintaining France's independence and its power in Europe led him to veto English attempts to join the Common Market. Believing in the "greatness" of France, he behaved as if he were above politics and represented the true spirit of the nation.

The economy of France was aided by its Common Market association and the growth of its population. Industrial production rose twenty-five per cent from 1958 to 1962, and energy capacity, due to the development of new oil fields, hydro-electric, and nuclear power plants, grew substantially. While France produced a good deal more agricultural products than it could consume, generous Common Market subsidies helped French farmers maintain a high standard of income.

De Gaulle resigned in 1969 after the French people, in a referendum, rejected his plan for the reorganization of the governmental structure of the country. He believed the referendum was a blow to his own prestige and amounted to a vote of non-confidence. Georges Pompidou succeeded de Gaulle as President of the Fifth Republic. Pompidou had been associated with de Gaulle and continued many of his policies, while at the same time he helped to steer Great Britain into the Common Market.

Upon Pompidou's death in 1974, French politics began to move in a more traditional direction. Gaullism was abandoned by the French people, and some believed that this proved the earlier contention of critics of de Gaulle that his policies and the stability he gave to France were more dependent upon his person than on a new system of government. The two final candidates for President were Valéry Giscard d'Estaing, a conservative who had been associated with a financial policy helpful to entrepreneurs, and François Mitterand, a democratic socialist who managed to unite the left behind him. In this new battle between the traditional two sides of French politics, Giscard d'Estaing won by a narrow margin. His policies were moderate in economics, and he carried out the work of his office in a less regal, more democratic style than his predecessors.

France had similar economic difficulties as other major industrial states in the late 1970s — high inflation and rising unemployment — which Giscard could not control. In the presidential election of 1981, Mitterand ran again for the Socialists and this time defeated Giscard. Socialists, allied with the small French Communist Party, also won a majority in the elections to the French Assembly.

Mitterand soon nationalized certain major industries, among them telecommunications and electronics, and the remaining private banks in France. His policies resulted in greater government debt and inflation. In 1982 he took a more moderate course and devalued the franc and froze wages and prices, relying now solely on his Socialist supporters, as the more left-wing Communist group could no longer support him. Mitterand has seen his task as restoring France's economy without dismantling its social program. France continued following a moderately independent foreign policy, building its own nuclear arsenal and remaining a member of NATO, while keeping closer ties to the Soviet Union than did most other Western powers.

OTHER DEMOCRATIC STATES

West Germany

West Germany, officially called the German Federal Republic, was created in 1948 by a union of the occupation zones of the United States, Britain, and France. As a political and economic entity, it was still large and powerful, even though it was separated from East Germany, which the Soviet Union continued to control.

In 1955 West Germany was accepted into NATO. Its population was fifty million people, and by 1960 its industrial capacity was large enough to make it the major industrial country of western Europe. It adopted all the welfare and social legislation that has come to mark the social democracies of western Europe.

In West Germany a democratic constitution with a federal parliamentary form of government was approved in 1949. Two major parties developed, the Christian Democratic Party and the Social Democratic Party. The Christian Democratic Party was the group which led all governments until 1969. It was a center party, cautious in its politics, devoted to economic growth and to legitimatizing the place of West Germany in world affairs. Its first leader was Konrad Adenauer (1876–1967), who stressed domestic stability, cultivated excellent relations with de Gaulle, and presided over the reintegration of West Germany into European diplomacy. The Social Democratic Party was the heir of the old German socialists of the Weimar Republic. Somewhat to the left of the Christian Democrats in their approach to social policy, the Social Democrats formed their first ministry in 1969 under the leadership of Willy Brandt.

Brandt pursued a policy of reconciling the new West Germany with the post-Second World War European political scene. His "Ostpolitik" (politics of the East), was an initiative designed to end the old policy of not having diplomatic relations with any country which recognized East Germany, and to achieve better relations with the Soviet Union and its satellites. In 1970 an agreement was reached between West Germany and Russia which recognized the post-war frontiers of both West and East Germany. Later, Polish-West German border issues were cleared up, and West Germany officially recognized the existence of East Germany. During Brandt's term in office the new Europe was acknowledged to be a stable entity. Brandt and his successor as chancellor, Helmut Schmidt, were concerned with social reform and economic strength. Helmut Kohl, who followed Schmidt, was a conservative, as West Germany in the 1980s, like the United States and Great Britain, moved to the right politically. Brandt, Schmidt, and Kohl, like many others in the West, extended the role of the state in the affairs of the whole community. They attempted to strengthen the Common Market, seeing in trade the basis of a healthy economy.

Italy

The major post-war party in Italy was also a Christian Democratic Party, led in its initial years by Alcide de Gasperi (1881–1954). Italy became a republic in 1946 and in 1947 approved a new constitution. Like others in western Europe, the new constitution provided for political and social rights and a parliamentary form of government. Although Italy had a strong Communist Party, de Gasperi adopted a middle-of-the-road approach to domestic policy and a foreign policy that stressed alignment with western Europe. He accepted Marshall Plan aid and joined in the European Coal and Steel Community (ECSC). Industrial growth was stressed and agricultural reform was attempted.

The Italian Socialist Party, the second largest political force, split in 1947 between a group that wished to collaborate with Social Democratic politicians and a group to the left, led by Pietro Nenni, that was closer in policy to the Communists. In 1966 the two groups reunited as the Nenni wing moved away from the Communists in support of more moderate Christian Democratic policies. Italy had difficulty obtaining stable governments late in the 1960s and early 1970s, and there were signs of a resurgence of the political right.

The Communist Party continued to be strong and by the mid-1970s had secured the support of nearly a third of the Italian voters. Italian Communists, however, have shown themselves to be increasingly independent of the Soviet Union.

Benelux and Scandinavian countries

The Benelux and Scandinavian countries continued their pre-war democratic course. In the Benelux countries, the major development was the integration of their economy and defence with that of the rest of western Europe. All these countries had center and moderate socialist parties vying for power and all continued their strong constitutional traditions.

The Scandinavian countries went furthest towards socialism of all the countries of western Europe. Democratic socialism under strong constitutional traditions had been a feature of Scandinavian life before the Second World War, and the willingness of Danes, Norwegians, and Swedes to support this pragmatic brand of socialism continued. All these countries had many co-operatives and strong social-welfare programs, and were models of political democracy. While each state had owned industries before the Second World War, nationalization was carried further, pension systems were improved, and education was upgraded and extended.

In Europe as a whole since the Second World War, the communist states have moved towards granting a moderate degree of freedom, and the democratic states have moved in the direction of socialism. They have all encouraged economic development and growth as the key to a secure and prosperous future, and all governments now direct the economy in some measure. The West has settled for "mixed" economics—a combination of public and private ownership depending on what seems feasible. In the East the state-run economy, organized by a central bureaucracy, is no longer the fashion; now local authorities have some autonomy and consumer demand is given greater consideration. Although the political rhetoric of eastern and western Europeans is very different, and occasionally vituperative, and although real differences do exist, eastern and western Europe, having integrated within their separate blocks, are now closer to each other than at any time since the beginning of the cold war. The major difference between East and West, however, remains the degree of political and social freedom in each area.

THE UNITED STATES AND SOCIAL MOVEMENTS

The West was no longer led by European nations after the Second World War. In foreign policy and in economics the United States was the major power in the North Atlantic political community and in the world. In bringing about European recovery and the development of the United Nations it was the acknowledged forerunner. Its economy was the most important in the world, its culture and technology the pacesetters.

In its domestic life the United States had occasional stormy moments, but it remained a stable, committed federal democracy. In 1974, after President Nixon was revealed to have sanctioned illegal acts during his election campaign of 1972, he was forced to resign in the face of a Congress which would have impeached him. Americans were riveted by the "Watergate" scandal, as it is called, but they also felt that their system of checks and balances and constitutional legality demonstrated that their democracy was working.

The main domestic issue which affected the United States after the Second World War was civil rights. It involved the legal and social status of black Americans (over ten per cent of the population of the United States), who had been subject to discrimination and separate treatment since their emancipation from slavery in 1864. In many southern states schools for blacks and whites were segregated, as were many public facilities. Local authorities often made it difficult for blacks to vote, and educational opportunities were limited. Only after the Second World War was the armed forces of the United States integrated.

In 1954 the Supreme Court of the United States, dealing with the question of segregation in the schools, declared the idea of "separate but equal," on which those who wished to maintain school segregation based their case, to be unconstitutional. Lawyers for black organizations submitted evidence based upon psychological and sociological studies which showed that to be denied equal rights meant being denied equal opportunities. The Court stated: "separate educational facilities are inherently unequal," and it ordered desegregation at a measured pace.

Blacks, and many other Americans who supported their cause, began to pursue equal status in an organized manner. They boycotted bus lines which had forced blacks to sit in separate areas in the rear. They "sat-in" at lunch counters which refused to serve blacks; they applied for entry to segregated universities in the south; and they demanded the vote.

The leadership of the United States civil rights movement was taken by a young Baptist minister from the southern state of Georgia, Martin Luther King (1929-68). King organized the Southern Christian Leadership Conference, and many sit-ins, demonstrations, and "freedom rides" took place. He was an integrationist who had taken up the ministry and who had been highly influenced by the non-violent doctrines of the Indian leader Mohandes K. Gandhi. King combined the social role of the southern black churches with sophisticated legal weapons and a determined non-violent moral stance. His movement and others attracted support from many whites in the United States, especially after the newspapers and television reported and showed the

Little Rock, Arkansas, United States, 1957. Black students enter Central High School, protected by troops sent to defend them from local violence against integration.   (Popperfoto)

violence of the segregationists. Occasionally arrested, King would cite the idea of civil disobedience of the nineteenth century American philosopher Henry David Thoreau as part of his heritage.

In 1963, while in jail for demonstrating in the state of Alabama, King wrote his ''Letter from Birmingham Jail,'' his statement to moderates who had criticized him for demonstrating in support of integration in the city of Birmingham.

We know through painful experience that freedom is never voluntarily given by the oppressor; it must be demanded by the oppressed. Frankly, I have yet to engage in a direct-action campaign that was 'well timed' in the view of those who have not suffered unduly from the disease of segregation. For years now I have heard the word 'Wait!' It rings in the ear of every Negro with piercing familiarity. This 'Wait'

has almost always meant 'Never'. We must come to see, with one of our distinguished jurists, that 'justice too long delayed is justice denied'.

We have waited for more than 340 years for our constitutional and God-given rights. The nations of Asia and Africa are moving with jetlike speed toward gaining political independence, but we still creep at horse-and-buggy pace toward gaining a cup of coffee at a lunch counter. Perhaps it is easy for those who have never felt the stinging darts of segregation to say, 'Wait'. But when you have seen vicious mobs lynch your mothers and fathers at will and drown your sisters and brothers at whim; when you have seen hate-filled policemen curse, kick and even kill your black brothers and sisters; when you see the vast majority of your twenty million Negro brothers smothering in an airtight cage of poverty in the midst of an affluent society; . . . then you will understand why we find it so difficult to wait. There comes a time when the cup of endurance runs over, and men are no longer willing to be plunged into the abyss of despair. I hope, sirs, you can understand our legitimate and unavoidable impatience.

. . . One has not only a legal but a moral responsibility to obey just laws. Conversely, one has a moral responsibility to disobey unjust laws. I would agree with St. Augustine that 'an unjust law is no law at all'.[15]

King's eloquence moved many. In August 1963 a march to Washington on behalf of civil rights was organized. Two hundred thousand people gathered to hear King proclaim that it was time for the American dream to become a reality.

Great headway was made in this area. In 1964 the Civil Rights Act was passed. Blacks could now vote unhampered by restrictive local laws, and public segregation and discrimination in the workplace was made illegal. Other laws were passed to enforce legal status for blacks and other minority groups. King's own career ended when he was assassinated in 1968.

Some blacks became more militant than King. They demanded "black power" and an end to white participation in black movements. Many took pride in their African heritage and were determined to reconstitute a history which had been taken away when their ancestors became slaves. Moreover, some blacks saw their people as caught in a cycle of poverty, both in the rural South and in the urban North. Riots occurred in black ghettos in Los Angeles, Detroit, Chicago, and Newark in the 1960s.

While integration has had many successes, American blacks remain in an ambiguous position, for much remains to be done and poverty still prevails. Moreover, blacks wish to better their lot while retaining black identity and demand that the United States pass more legislation to achieve full equality. The civil rights movement has forced the United States to acknowledge a difficult and unfortunate part of its history. The institutions of the country are under strain in an attempt to right past injustices.

American immigration has also been a source of major change since the Second World War. Immigration had traditionally been mainly from western Europe, and immigration acts passed in 1917, 1924, and 1952 supported this policy with restrictive clauses. In 1965, as part of the reform which can be attributed to a new consciousness raised by the civil rights movement, the United States adopted a new immigration act, permitting large-scale immigration from the Third World. Now immigrants included large numbers of people from the Philippines, Korea, China, and India. Special refugee acts in response to international developments since the 1960s have brought many immigrants from Kampuchea, Laos, Vietnam, and Cuba. The result has been to change the tone and mix of United States society, and to reinvigorate its tradition of being a haven for oppressed people.

Other social movements prominent in the United States have had broader implications for the West. In France, in 1949, the noted philosopher Simone de Beauvoir published *The Second Sex*, a long work seeking to emancipate women from being defined by their relationships with men. She wanted women to feel free to choose and benefit from "an independent existence." De Beauvoir demanded, polemically, that "we abolish the slavery of half of humanity, together with the whole system of hypocrisy that it implies...."[16] The theme articulated by de Beauvoir was taken up by the American Betty Friedan, in 1963, in her highly influential *The Feminine Mystique*. Friedan argued that in women in the United States "there was a strange discrepancy between the reality of our lives as women and the image to which we were trying to conform, the image that I . . . call the feminine mystique." She wanted a new sense of self:

Who knows what women can be when they are finally free to become themselves? Who knows what women's intelligence will contribute when it can be nourished without denying love? Who knows of the possibilities of love when men and women share not only children, home, and garden, not only the fulfillment of their biological roles, but the responsibilities and passions of the work that creates the human future and the full human knowledge of who they are? It has barely begun, the search of women for themselves. But the time is at hand when the voices of the feminine mystique can no longer drown out the inner voice that is driving women on to become complete.[17]

Feminists founded many organizations, including, in the United States, NOW (National Organization for Women) in 1966. Using the methods of the civil rights movement, supporters lobbied and demonstrated on behalf of equal pay, changes in marriage and divorce laws, and equal rights. NOW released a "bill of rights" for women, asking for statutes protecting equality under law regardless of sex, equal opportunity laws, help with child care, and reforms which it believed would enable women to obtain equality in society.

Students and youth led social movements in universities in the 1960s in support of ending the Vietnam War, bringing about racial equality, and reducing poverty. Students demanded power in a society which they believed treated them as children, and which was itself full of unfairness and contradictions. The first student riots occurred at the University of California at Berkeley in 1964. Students organized sit-ins and stopped the institution from functioning, demanding on the one hand an end to university involvement in weapons and war research, and on the other hand student participation in the governance of the university. The riots spread as students advocated university reform throughout much of the country.

French students in Paris rioted in 1968, demanding changes in the rules of the university. The situation grew violent as public authorities tried to stop the students. Over 400 were arrested. The French student movement had the support of the unions and a general strike was called in May. The government placated the workers with higher wages, and by the summer life in Paris was calm again. The two events, Berkeley in the United States and Paris in Europe, were emulated throughout both continents by discontented students, some wanting university reform, others demanding major changes in government policies, many supporting peace causes.

These movements have made their impact on American and Western legal and social structures. Yet, the response of the majority

in the United States, and most everywhere, has been a shift to the right, towards conservatism and nationalism. In the United States in the 1980s the popular president Ronald Reagan took office on a program of helping private industry, reducing taxes, balancing the budget to rid the country eventually of its mounting deficit, eliminating much government spending, and cutting social programs. He emphatically supported a nationalist, jingoist foreign policy. In his speeches Reagan stressed traditional values: family, religion, the nation.

In his first Inaugural Address, in January 1981, Reagan articulated what many Americans believed: "In this present crisis, government is not the solution to our problem; government is the problem. . . . It is time to reawaken this industrial giant, to get government back within its means and to lighten our punitive tax burden."[18] In one area, however, Reagan enlarged the activity of government: he promised to increase the military might of the United States, to face its various foes, all of which he associated with the Soviet Union.

Domestic programs were cut, and spending on the military grew much higher; new nuclear initiatives were also taken. Reagan cut taxes, especially for the well off, but ran higher government deficits than any administration in United States history. His cuts in student loans, housing subsidies, and public service jobs did not hurt his overall popularity; nor did the negative response of black America and feminists. Reagan opposed an equal rights for women amendment to the United States Constitution. He advocated prayers in public schools, in contradiction to traditional church-state relations, and won the support of wealthy fundamentalist groups. In his second presidential election in 1984 Reagan won over sixty per cent of the popular vote and had a majority in forty-nine of the fifty states. The United States, and much of the West, opened the 1980s far more conservative than it had been for some time.

CANADA: POLITICS, NATIONAL IDENTITY, AND CULTURAL AUTONOMY

Canada is a federal state with two major founding cultural groups, the English and the

French. Its Constitution was intended to protect the French minority as well as the English majority. However, from the 1960s Canada experienced a serious separatist movement, a movement of French Canadians in the province of Quebec to withdraw from the Canadian confederation and to become a sovereign state.

Quebec is more than eighty per cent French Canadian, and though there are also French Canadians in other provinces it is here that the cultural issue translated itself into political terms. In Canada, including Quebec, the language of business had been English, the control of the federal government was largely in English-Canadian hands, and the English managed much of the Quebec urban economy. Many people in Quebec feared that French culture would be absorbed into an ''English sea'' in North America if the province did not obtain political sovereignty of some sort. ''*Maîtres chez nous*'' (masters in our own home) became a provincial slogan.

In 1968 French Canadians formed the Parti Québécois, a provincial political party whose platform included the idea of obtaining sovereignty within an economic union in Canada, what came to be called sovereignty-association. The leader of the party was a prominent journalist and uncompromising democrat, René Lévesque (1922–   ), who believed in a Quebec national state, and wished to obtain it by gaining control of the provincial National Assembly and then submitting separatism to a general referendum. He said:

Essentially, to be ourselves means to maintain and develop a personality that has lasted for three-and-a-half centuries.

At the heart of this personality is the fact that we speak French. Everything else is tied to this essential element, derives from it or brings us back to it, without fail.

. . . Until recently, our difficult survival has depended on a certain type of isolation. We were fairly well protected by a rural society where there was a consensus and where poverty limited progress as well as ambition.

We are descended from this society, in which our 'habitant' fathers or grandfathers were still the crucial citizens. We are also the heirs to a

René Lévesque, the founder of the Parti Québécois. (Canapress Photo Service)

tremendous adventure in which America, at first, was almost entirely French. We are, to an even greater extent, heirs to the collective stubbornness which has enabled us to keep alive this part of French America known as Quebec.

All this lies at the heart of our personality.[19]

Quebeckers in support of sovereignty used images drawn from the Third World and oppressed peoples. They claimed to have been a ''colony'' of the English-speaking people since 1759, and to be similar in many ways to blacks in the United States seeking to be free and searching for their identity.

During this period the prime minister of Canada was another French Canadian, Pierre Elliot Trudeau (1919–   ). The leader of the federal Liberal Party, Trudeau was a lawyer whose record on civil rights had been unblemished when he became prime minister in 1968. He had earlier been associated with a group of reformers in Quebec seeking modernization of the economy of the province and an end to local corruption. He believed that a strong central government was necessary to direct the economy and to protect Canadians of all backgrounds, including newer immigrants and Native peoples. Trudeau entered federal politics as a way of showing that Quebeckers did not need special status; rather, he believed that once French as a language was protected throughout the country, and French Canadians were treated equally, French Canada would be loyal to the confederation. Trudeau saw the Parti Québécois as a narrow movement, one which was dangerous to the welfare of French Canada in the long term. During his years in office, he made the federal government and its civil service bilingual, attracted many French Canadians into federal government service, and encouraged closer ties between Quebec and the rest of the country. This did not endear him to many English Canadians, particularly those in the western provinces of Canada who believed they were being ignored, but Trudeau weighed that political risk and took it.

In 1976 the Parti Québécois was elected into office in Quebec. The Lévesque government's first measure was Bill 101, a new language act. French was declared to be the official language of Quebec, to be used in the government, the courts, and in business in the province. In education all children were required to attend French-language schools with the exception of children of English-speaking parents who were themselves educated in Quebec. Immigrants were not excepted; their children were to go to French schools. In its economic policy, the Parti Québécois was competent and cautious, trying to reassure the international community that it was a responsible and safe government.

A referendum which asked voters for authorization to negotiate sovereignty-association with the rest of Canada was held in 1980.

Quebeckers, voting sixty per cent against the proposal, showed that they wanted change in the federal system, but not separation.

Trudeau used the Quebec issue to try to reform federalism in Canada. He had wanted to repatriate Canada's Constitution from Great Britain, and to make new constitutional arrangements with the provincial governments. Several meetings between the federal and provincial governments had occurred since the early 1970s, but without agreement. Trudeau then tried unilateral action. In 1981 he introduced a resolution for a Canadian Constitution which retained the existing distribution of powers between the federal and provincial governments, but included a Charter of Rights and new amending procedures. The Supreme Court of Canada ruled that the resolution was legal but in violation of custom. In further negotiations, agreement on a new Constitution was achieved in 1982 between Trudeau, representing the federal government, and nine of the ten Canadian provinces. Quebec would not agree and has yet to sign the constitution. The constitution contained a strong Charter of Rights protecting minorities and civil liberties. Lévesque retired as leader of the Parti Québécois in 1985, and in November of that year the Liberal party defeated the Parti Québécois at the polls.

Canada has always had an "identity problem," founded as it was by both English and French, who, despite their differences, generally were able to find a compromise that enabled them to live together. Collectively, Canadians tended to be more concerned with sharing a continent with the United States, a powerful neighbour with ten times the population. Identity and nationhood continue to be major issues in this large, underpopulated, and regionally-divided country.

ANALYSIS AND DISCUSSION

1. "[Had we acted sooner] Germany might have been saved from the awful fate which has overtaken her and we might all have been spared the miseries Hitler let loose upon mankind. . . . We must not let that happen again." Analyse Churchill's statement in terms of Western defence policy in the late 1940s and early 1950s.

2. Comment, from the Soviet point of view, on the claim in the late 1940s that Germany and Japan were being rebuilt to act as aggressive foreign bases for the United States.

3. Describe the organization and operation of the United Nations and then comment upon the following statements:

a) "The UN can solve any problem (as long as it doesn't concern the Great Powers)!"

b) "The early disillusionment with the United Nations can be seen in the rapid formation of a series of regional alliances."

c) "Hungary, Suez and Berlin. Three strikes and the UN was out of the picture!"

d) "The true worth of the UN lies not in its role as a peacekeeper but rather as the conscience of the world."

4. "The preservation of South Korea led the United States to believe that it could wage limited wars for the containment of communism elsewhere in Asia." Discuss this statement as an explanation for American involvement in Vietnam during the 1950s.

5. "Johnson fought in Vietnam to 'win' while Nixon fought to get out!" Comment on this statement as a reflection of changing American priorities in the war in Vietnam.

6. "The division of spoils at Yalta and Potsdam did not involve territory but rather spheres of influence." Evaluate this statement with reference to events in areas such as Poland, Hungary, Czechoslovakia, Afghanistan, Cuba, Chile, and Central America from 1945 to the present.

7. Trace the history of arms negotiations between the Soviet Union and the United States and comment on the current state of negotiations between the two superpowers.

8. "Continuity of leadership does not necessarily mean the development of long-term policy." Comment on this statement with reference to the evolution of Soviet leadership since World War II.

9. "The Soviet Union is now a society run by professionals and technocrats. . . . The totalitarian state under Stalin now seems remote." Evaluate this quotation in terms of Soviet response to internal protest in the 1970s and external dissent in Poland in the 1980s.

10. Select one of the Western European democracies and analyse its response to the political, economic, and military realities of the modern world.

11. "The greatest challenge to the North American democracies in the post-war world has been in the area of the preservation and extension of human rights. All in all they can be proud of their record." Evaluate this statement with reference to the social and political response to such issues as civil rights, anti-war protest, feminism, separatism, and Native rights.

CHAPTER **16**

The West and the World Since 1945

SINCE THE NINETEENTH CENTURY LARGE POR-
tions of Asia and Africa had been tied to
the West as parts of European empires. After
the First World War the empires of the losers
were broken up and sometimes distributed
among the winners. There was also some agitation on the part of the colonial peoples for
self-determination. After the Second World
War, though not without some reluctance on
the part of the European powers, the empires
of the victors, as well as of the defeated, were
largely broken up. While Churchill claimed
he had not become Prime Minister ''to preside
over the dissolution of the British Empire,''
by the time of his death in 1965 the British
Empire, in the old sense — as well as the
French, the Dutch, and the Belgian empires—
was very much a thing of the past.

THE PROCESS OF DECOLONIZATION: ASIA,
AFRICA, AND THE FORMATION OF NEW
STATES

In 1947 the Indian sub-continent was broken

Jawaharal Nehru and ''Mahatma'' Gandhi, in India   *(Canapress Photo Service)*

into two independent states, India and Pakistan, based roughly on the distinction between the Hindu and Moslem areas. The Indian nationalist movement was led by Mohandas K. Gandhi (1869–1948), whose tactics of non-violence and non-co-operation have had great influence in the modern age. Living simply, and adopting a spirituality which enabled him to appeal to religious individuals as well as those who believed in his politics of liberation, he became known throughout India as the "Mahatma" (Great Soul) and gained world-wide support for his cause and his tactics of civil disobedience. Ironically, he was killed by an assassin at the very time his dream was being realized. Upon achieving independence in 1947, India, led by Jawaharal Nehru (1889–1964), an English educated nationalist who had joined Gandhi in the 1920s, was one of the largest states in the world (it had a population of 350 million in 1947), as well as one of the poorest.

In the Dutch East Indies, in 1948, a nationalist movement led by Achmed Sukarno (1902–69) defeated the Dutch, who were reluctant to leave the area. The nationalist victory resulted in the establishment of the state of Indonesia. The British granted independence to Malaysia in 1955.

The French, however, attempted to retain control of Indo-China. While they had been in the area since the 1880s, a native nationalist movement had grown up in Vietnam during the Second World War, under the Japanese occupation. Under the leadership of Ho Chi Minh (1890–1969), this group became known as the Vietminh. The French tried to force the Vietminh to join a federation which would include all of Vietnam, Laos, and Cambodia. Although it was communist, the Vietminh became the focus of nationalist sentiment, and, after the French installed a puppet government in the capital city of Saigon, war broke out between the Vietminh and the French. This war was being fought at the time of the Korean War, and many in the NATO states interpreted it as a war between communism and democracy, instead of as a struggle between nationalism and colonialism. The United States gave considerable aid to the French.

In 1954 the Vietminh defeated the French in the battle of Dien Bien Phu, and a truce was made on the Korean model—Vietnam was divided in two at the seventeenth parallel: North Vietnam, with its capital at Hanoi, was communist and led by Ho Chi Minh; South Vietnam, with its capital at Saigon, was allied with the western democratic states and led by Ngo Dinh Diem. Exhausted by the war, their morale shattered and distracted by the civil war in Algeria, the French pulled out of the area. The United States, however, moved in to support the regime in South Vietnam as part of its policy for the containment of communism in Asia. Though it was agreed, as part of the truce in 1954, that elections would be held to unite Vietnam under one sovereignty, the partition, like that of Germany and Korea, became fixed. No elections were held and North and South faced each other with hostility. As two Vietnams came into being, the United States became increasingly involved in a war supporting the South. In 1973, the United States, having failed in its objective, withdrew, and in 1975 Vietnam was united under the leadership of the North.

Colonialism began to be understood in a new way after the Second World War. Frantz Fanon, a black French psychiatrist, in his book *The Wretched of the Earth* (1961), stated that imperialism and colonialism were racist in character and violent in their application and their psychic consequences. He claimed that the colonial world was always divided into two zones, settlers and natives, and that natives were seen as objects under colonial rule. Hence, though expected to be passive, the native was taught violence as a value by the West, "the violence with which the supremacy of white values is affirmed." The only solution for the native was to struggle for identity and liberation; to Fanon, this meant negating the West and finding one's own roots. Fanon claimed that the native knew that in his desperate condition of economic and personal exploitation there was only one solution: taking the place of the colonizers by violent means.

Fanon advocated violence as a necessity. Decolonization, he stated, was "a program of

"Boat-people." Vietnamese refugees on a freighter off the coast of Malaysia. (Canapress Photo Service)

complete disorder'' and the natives must be violent in order to create new active personalities out of the passivity of colonialism. He suggested that the West would preach nonviolence to natives, even while it had uprooted whole tribes, destroyed tradition, and controlled others for centuries. Violence was necessary, for otherwise the blacks in Africa would create a middle class, and adopt Western values. ''The colonized man finds his freedom in and through violence.'' Fanon turned the West's power and wealth into its problems, for he, and many others, believed that the West obtained a portion of its wealth by exploitation. ''The wealth of the imperial countries is our wealth too. . . . Europe is literally the creation of the Third World.''[1]

Fanon's analysis was written in the context of North African battles for independence from French colonial rule. While France granted independence to Tunisia and Morocco in 1956, Algeria posed a much more difficult problem. Approximately one out of nine people in Algeria was European French. Algeria had cultural ties to France dating back many generations and had been incorporated as part of France after 1871. But in 1954 a war broke out between Algerian nationalists and the French *colons*, who were supported by the French army and the political right. The war was extraordinarily fierce, with torture and terror on both sides. It seriously affected French domestic politics, for any government which suggested an end to the war faced a possible revolt by the army. De Gaulle, who became ruler of France during the height of the crisis, ended the war and suppressed the power of the army. Some of the army leaders were arrested when they tried to defy the policy of the French state, and in 1962, after a referendum in Algeria, the country became independent.

During the 1960s, Africa south of the Sahara became a mosaic of independent states. In the British territories, Ghana led the way to independence in 1957 and Nigeria followed in 1960.

In the area of the Belgian Congo, the Belgians were determined to continue their colonial rule in a system in which no local leaders were given authority and no blacks were permitted in the senior civil service. In 1959, in the capital of Leopoldville, there was a riot in which unemployed blacks destroyed European shops and schools sponsored by missionaries. A local leader, Patrice Lumumba (1925–61), came to the forefront and formed a national party in an effort to unite various local tribal and provincial interests into a single political entity. Local riots broke out all over the large colony in 1959, and the Belgians had difficulty maintaining order.

The Belgians now reversed their old policy and, though their unenlightened rule had not resulted in the training of a native civil service or professional class, they announced in January 1960 that in six months they would withdraw. Lumumba managed to form a government after elections in May. On independence

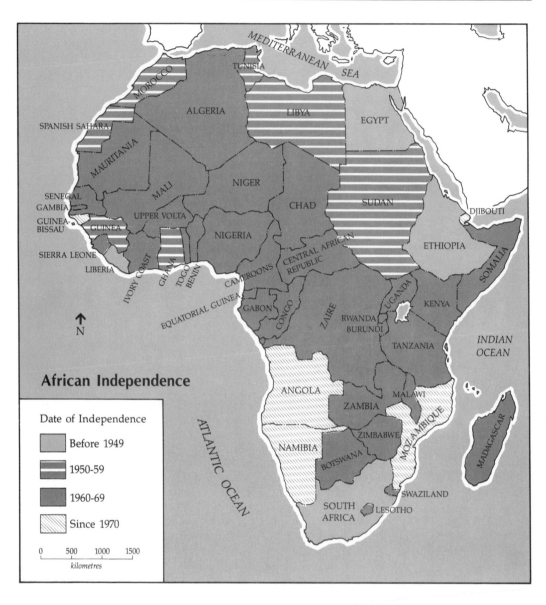

African Independence

Date of Independence

Before 1949

1950-59

1960-69

Since 1970

0   500   1000   1500
         kilometres

day in June, in response to an imperialist-style speech from the Belgian king, he proclaimed: ''We are no longer your monkeys.'' In the new country, renamed Zaire, there was civil war between regions and tribes over who would rule. An army officer, Joseph Mobutu, seized power in September, and Lumumba was executed in January 1961.

After independence the United Nations had sent in troops to maintain order, but Zaire became caught in cold war politics. Lumumba

had asked the Soviet Union for assistance, and the United States came to back his rival Mobutu. After the United Nations troops withdrew in 1963, Mobutu became the dictator of the country, and tried to identify himself with nationalist aspirations. In the 1970s Zaire relied heavily on United States aid and became an important ally of the United States in the politics of the African continent.

Those areas south of the Sahara with large white populations had generally been part of the British Empire, for the British, unlike other European nations, had encouraged white settlement in their colonies. After defeating a terrorist movement directed against colonial rule, the British granted independence to Kenya in 1963. Though tension continued among various racial groups (including a large number of Indians), Kenya managed to establish a stable government which maintained the constitutional rights of its multi-racial population.

South Africa, which has been independent since 1910, resisted pressure to make political concessions to native Africans. It pursued a policy of *apartheid*, which is defined as sepa-

rate development of the races. A number of areas have been set aside as self-governing areas for blacks. In fact, this has meant white supremacy, white control of the economy and the best lands, and a legal system which favours the whites.

In 1948 an election in which only whites participated gave power to the Nationalist Party which pursued racist policies. Blacks were persecuted by "legal" acts which were enforced by the military and the police. What civil rights blacks had were withdrawn, political protest became illegal, and all blacks were required to carry "passes," which were permits for residence, travel, and work. In 1952

Apartheid. A bridge in Capetown, South Africa.   (Canapress Photo Service)

the African National Congress, an organization which had long protested the treatment of blacks, led a movement of passive resistance against these laws. In response, the government of South Africa in 1953 enacted yet further legislation, giving itself power to declare a state of emergency, to arrest people who were engaging in non-violent protest, and to ban individuals from certain areas.

Some resistance continued. In 1960 police fired on a crowd at a peaceful demonstration in the black town of Sharpville, killing sixty-seven and wounding 186. The leaders of the blacks began to organize terror and sabotage. Many were arrested and imprisoned for life. Then the South African government began a policy of "separate development," which was an attempt to turn African reserves into segregated areas of black population, eventually, it was said, to develop them into separate states. Many blacks were uprooted from their homes and transferred into the segregated areas, which the government calls "homelands."

In industrial and urban areas there was still resistance among blacks. In 1972 and 1973 mass strikes won blacks higher wages. Black students founded consciousness movements. In 1976 in Soweto, the largest black urban area in the state, students boycotted the schools in protest of a law which required them to be taught in the Afrikaans language of the white ruling minority. Police shot at student groups, killing more than 200 and wounding many.

Apartheid was viewed by all of black Africa and most of the rest of the world as a system founded on injustice and racial oppression. South African whites were determined to maintain their authority, but protests continued and violence increased. In the mid-1980s the political situation became very tense: blacks engaged in organized protest, resulting in clashes with the authorities and many deaths. There have been attempts from outside South Africa to pressure the government into taking a more balanced position. South African black literature is openly revolutionary; much of South African white literature records an inner awareness that the privileged life lived by the whites is in its last phase. There is a sense that great changes will occur.

The new nations of Africa and Asia have faced staggering problems. Many of these countries, for example India, Togo, and Gabon, have no industrial base. Their problems begin at the level of sustenance—how to feed their people. Most of them have sought outside technical aid in an effort to become industrialized; some of them do not have the human or natural resources for a balanced economy and have been dependent on foreign aid. In order to organize their economies, all have accepted the idea of state direction and control. Most of these new states, such as Tanzania, do not worry about labels such as capitalism, socialism, or communism; they are concerned with the practical issues of industrial and agricultural development.

The tribal, regional, and religious differences within these new states often pose the gravest difficulties. Many of these countries were formerly European colonies which cut across traditional tribal, regional, and religious groups. Malaysia incorporates peoples of different racial and religious traditions. Many African states include peoples from different tribes. The center of loyalty for many of the people in these states often *is* the tribe, the region, the religion — not the state. Many problems have arisen as a result of the adoption of a Western form, the nation-state, by peoples who have traditionally oriented themselves in other ways.

The most glaring case of tribal differences arose in Nigeria, a union created out of three tribes in 1960. With great natural resources and a population more literate than that of most African states, Nigeria was referred to for some years after its independence as the most stable and democratic state of the new Africa. But the Ibos, a minority tribe in Nigeria, claimed that the state was systematically excluding them from participation in political affairs, arbitrarily imprisoning them, and following a policy of genocide. In 1967 the Ibo tribe broke away from the central state and proclaimed the new nation of Biafra. In the civil war which ensued, the Ibos were defeated, and attempts have since been made to integrate them again into the larger Nigerian entity.

In the early 1960s decolonization and the

establishment of new states was discussed in cold-war terms: would a new state become communist or democratic? This kind of question was in fact an imposition of European categories on the rest of the world. Most of the new states wanted above all to solve the problems arising out of their internal differences, to provide reasonable economic sustenance for their peoples, and to retain their independence. They took aid wherever they could get it, with as few strings attached as possible. "The Third World," as Asians, Africans, and Latin Americans sometimes refer to themselves, was usually neither Russian nor American in political orientation.

THE FAR EAST: THE CHINESE REVOLUTION AND THE DEMOCRATIZATION OF JAPAN

The two major political groups in China— the Kuomintang led by Chiang Kai-shek and the Communists led by Mao Tse-tung— had formed an alliance after the Japanese invasion of China in 1937. During the Second World War they fought against the Japanese as separate groups, the Communists being especially effective at guerilla warfare in rural areas. The Kuomintang, though supported by the Allies, did little to aid the war effort and in fact lost control of their industrial base to the Japanese. Led by mandarins and industrialists, the Kuomintang claimed to be democratic but represented the interests of the wealthy and those in high social positions. Both the Communists and the Kuomintang, moreover, hoped ultimately to eliminate one another.

Thus, when the Second World War ended, a civil war broke out in China. The United States supported Chiang Kai-shek with a great deal of money and equipment. The forces of Mao received some aid from the Soviet Union, but also made use of arms captured from the Japanese during the war and American arms captured from defeated Kuomintang soldiers. The Communists were victorious in 1949; Chiang and many other Kuomintang supporters escaped to the island of Formosa (Taiwan) and established a government there. On the mainland, Mao

proclaimed the People's Republic of China.
In a speech in 1949 Mao said:

After their political régime is overthrown the reactionary classes and the reactionary clique will also be given land and work and a means of living; they will be allowed to re-educate themselves into new persons through work, provided they do not rebel, disrupt, or sabotage. If they are unwilling to work, the people's state will compel them to work. Propaganda and educational work will also be carried out among them, and, moreover, with care and adequacy, as we did among captured officers. . . . but we shall never forgive their reactionary acts and will never let their reactionary activity have the possibility of a free development.

Such re-education of the reactionary classes can only be carried out in the state of the people's democratic dictatorship. If this work is well done the main exploiting classes of China—the landlord and bureaucratic capitalist classes— will be finally eliminated. . . . There [remains] the national bourgeoisie among many of whom appropriate educational work can be carried out at the present stage. When socialism is realized, that is, when the nationalization of private enterprises has been carried out, they can be further educated and reformed. The people have in their hands a powerful state apparatus and are not afraid of the rebellion of the national bourgeois class.[2]

The regime Mao established had the familiar Leninist trappings: a single leader, a devoted party, and a totalitarian state.

China went through a period of isolation that was both voluntary and imposed. The Communists wished first to establish internal control, and the country was closed to most outsiders, especially those from the West. The United States refused to recognize Mao's regime and kept it out of the United Nations, thus enabling a representative of Chiang's regime in Formosa to continue to speak for all China. Meanwhile China made enormous strides in science and agriculture. By the mid 1960s mainland China was producing large amounts of foodstuffs. In 1964 China succeeded in developing atomic weapons.

Towards the end of 1966 Mao feared that

opposition to his policies was developing within China. He felt that China was losing its revolutionary zeal in developing a new society, and in response to this he conducted a purge of the highest ranks of the party, the military, and the government. Students were encouraged to carry out their own purges. This new movement became known as the "cultural revolution." For some time there was serious dislocation in the country— universities closed, riots occurred, "revolutionaries" fought "reactionaries," and "revolutionaries" battled among themselves. At the same time Mao began to build a cult around himself: he was worshipped and his words had the force of holy writ. The events of the "cultural revolution" solidified the hold of Mao and his followers on China. By the end of 1968 the "cultural revolution" had ended.

China has only recently begun to come out of its isolation and has encouraged the establishment of diplomatic relations with many states in the West. In 1971 the United Nations voted to replace the seat of the Formosan representative with that of the People's Republic of China, and in 1972 Richard Nixon, the president of the United States and a politician long associated with right-wing, anti-communist policies, visited China on a diplomatic mission. In 1972 China and Japan restored diplomatic relations, and in 1979 the United States and China agreed to have normal diplomatic relations.

Internally, major efforts were made to increase economic production: to improve the yield in agriculture, and to foster industry and technology. China is now attempting to modernize without abandoning its ideology and its culture, or giving up any autonomy.

When the Communist revolution in China was successful in 1949, the Soviet Union anticipated yet another satellite entering its orbit and looked upon China as the spearhead of communism in Asia. But as the Chinese Communists began to consolidate their rule, they made it clear that they would be independent of the Soviet Union. The two countries continued to have border difficulties, and in the late 1950s they developed serious ideological differences. While the Soviet Union, after

A 1949 Russian poster. ''Glory to the great Chinese people!'' is the caption, as the Russians celebrated Mao's victory. (From the Royal Museum of the Army, Brussels)

Stalin's death in 1953, began to modify its totalitarian society and to seek better relations with other countries, China still followed the hard Stalinist line. By 1960 Russia and China were competing for the allegiance of various communist movements in the world, and Russia ceased giving aid to China. In the early 1960s the European state of Albania successfully moved out of the Russian orbit and developed close ties with China.

The developments in China meant that a third great power was on the world scene, one which now competed with Russia as well as with the United States. Russia now began to build up its border defences in Asia. In the late 1960s border incidents between Russia and China flared up, and even the fiction of co-operation among communist states disappeared from the propaganda of both countries. Thus "polycentrism" appeared in Asia as it had in Europe. Communist states were more concerned with national development than with a uniform ideology.

Japan, the other major power in the Far East, has moved from the military control of politics in the 1930s to a democratic style in the post-war period. Defeated in the Second World War largely by American forces, Japan was occupied by the United States and put under the authority of General MacArthur, who instituted a policy of demilitarization and democratization. A new constitution was written which made the emperor a constitutional monarch and established a parliamentary government with two houses of parliament. The constitution also contained clauses on human rights and the renunciation of military aims.

Major land reforms were undertaken in Japan: in 1945 nearly half the land was in the control of wealthy owners who rented it out to small farmers; by 1950 only eight per cent of the arable land was rented. After the Second World War industrialization moved ahead very quickly, and by the mid-1950s the gross national product was growing at a rate of seven per cent a year. When the Japanese found markets in China closed to them in 1949, the United States became Japan's major trading partner.

As China grew in power, the United States was eager to build Japan into a counterweight in the Far East. In 1952 the United States and Britain negotiated a treaty with Japan which formally brought to an end Japan's old colonial empire and restored independence to the country.

Though the Japanese in 1952 were happy about regaining their independence, they were sceptical about another arrangement with the United States which went into effect at the same time. The United States was given the right to deploy troops throughout Japan for defence purposes and for protection against civil war. Though in 1960 the Japanese obtained some control over the use of these troops, many Japanese opposed all agreements of this sort. As the victims of the first atomic bombs in 1945, many Japanese developed a strong pacifist sentiment, opposing armaments and security treaties. This revulsion was heightened in 1954 when a Japanese fishing crew contracted radiation sickness as a result of the testing of American atomic weapons in the Pacific.

Japan became the economic wonder of the modern age. After the Second World War it made great strides in the new technology and industrialization. By 1980 this group of crowded islands, which needed to import much of its food, became one of the half-dozen most wealthy countries in the world. Japan has been a world leader in cameras since the 1950s, automobiles and shipbuilding since the 1960s, electronics since the 1970s, and computer technology since the 1980s. In the 1970s average industrial growth exceeded ten per cent a year. Japan has continued to be a major part of the Western alliance. The country has been guided domestically by conservative democratic leadership which pursued political compromise and consensus. Japan's traditional culture, though changing, still exists alongside its Westernized economy, and there is an attempt to preserve the traditional style in the face of the demands of an industrial society.

THE NEAR EAST: THE ARAB STATES AND ISRAEL

The area of Palestine in the Near East had been administered by Britain as a League of Nations mandate from the end of the First World War. The region contained both Arabs and Jews. At the end of the nineteenth century, a Zionist movement had arisen in Europe to encourage Jewish immigration to Palestine with the idea of eventually establishing a homeland for the Jewish people. The British supported Zionist aspirations with the Balfour Declaration of 1917:

His Majesty's Government view with favour the establishment in Palestine of a National Home for the Jewish people, and will use their best endeavours to facilitate the achievement of this object, it being clearly understood that nothing shall be done which may prejudice the civil and religious rights of existing non-Jewish communities in Palestine, or the rights and political status enjoyed by Jews in any other country.[3]

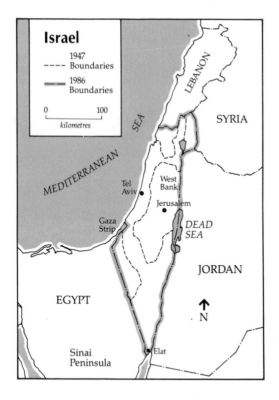

The Arab states viewed this policy as a form of Western imperialism, and as time went on the British adopted an attitude which was more sympathetic to Arab wishes.

None the less, after the Second World War many Jews who had survived the Nazi persecution began to come to Palestine in great numbers. They demanded the right to establish a national state and conducted a guerrilla campaign against the British. World public opinion, with the memory of the concentration camps so close, was at the time strongly in favour of the establishment of a Jewish homeland. In 1947 the United Nations accepted a plan for the partition of Palestine into a Jewish state, an Arab Palestinian state (which never came into being), and the internationalization of the city of Jerusalem, a holy place for the Moslem, Jewish, and Christian religions. The British decided to withdraw from the territory, and the state of Israel was proclaimed in May 1948. Jerusalem became a city divided between Israel and Jordan.

Unwilling to accept the existence of Israel,

several Arab states—Egypt, Syria, Lebanon, and Iraq—formed an Arab League which sought to destroy the new state. But the Arab forces failed; Israel survived, and the new state was admitted into the United Nations in 1949 and recognized by most of the international community. However, tens of thousands of Arabs fled Israeli territory and became refugees in Arab lands. The Arabs continued their policy of total hostility to Israel and called for a religious and national crusade against the enemy.

The major leader of Arab nationalism after the Second World War was the Egyptian President, Gamal Abdel Nasser (1918–70), who came to power in a *coup* in 1952 and established a military government. Wishing to use the big powers to help build his country, he obtained aid from both sides in the cold war. But in 1956 Egypt and the United States quarrelled, and the latter withdrew its aid. Nasser then seized the Suez Canal, a vital transportation link at the time, and prepared for a war with Israel. Britain, France, and Israel combined in an attack on Egypt, but pressure from the United States and the Soviet Union stopped them from taking control of the canal. Nasser retained power and agreed to let the ships of all nations use the waterway. However, he subsequently barred Israeli shipping. A United Nations force was stationed on the border between Egypt and Israel to help keep the peace.

The Arab states continued to do everything in their power to harass Israel. Terrorist activities became commonplace on the borders, and the Soviet Union began to supply large quantities of arms to Nasser and his allies. In May 1967 Nasser again precipitated an international crisis. He announced he was barring Israeli shipping from the Gulf of Aqaba, an area off the Red Sea which had become Israel's lifeline to the east. Arab forces began to mobilize, and border incidents increased in spite of the presence of the United Nations' peacekeeping force. Fanning Arab nationalism to its peak, Nasser publicly announced his intention of exterminating Israel. Open warfare broke out in early June, and Syria and Jordan joined Egypt.

One comment on the Arab-Israeli conflict. The two are kept fighting by trans-fusions of arms from Nixon, representing the United States, and Brezhnev, repre-senting the Soviet Union.
(Les Gibbard)

The war was an Arab rout. Israel quickly destroyed the Arab air force and won in six days; it now occupied the Sinai Peninsula, all of Jerusalem, all of the area on the west bank of the Jordan River, and some hills on the Israel-Syria border which had been used by Syria to shell Israeli positions and communities. A diplomatic stalemate resulted as Israel refused to discuss major issues unless the Arab states would negotiate face to face, and the Arab states refused to recognize the existence of Israel.

Yet another war broke out in October 1973. This time the Arabs took Israel by surprise with Egypt and Syria attacking simultaneously on Yom Kippur, a fast day and the most sacred of Jewish holidays. In a bloody war which lasted less than two weeks, the Arab states fared better on the battlefield and at the diplomatic tables of the West. Moreover, the Arab states realized they had a valuable economic weapon to help them achieve their aims, for much of the West, especially western Europe, relied on supplies of oil from Arab states. The Arabs refused to supply oil to those states supporting Israel and also raised the price of their oil by a substantial margin. The result was great pressure for a settlement as well as the flow of much more wealth to the Arab states. Israel was able to turn the tide on the Arabs on the battlefield, but in the peace negotiations the Arabs continued to retain their advantages.

After the 1973 war the Arab world led the Organization of Petroleum Exporting Countries (OPEC), a group which, through its control over the major part of the world's supply of oil, became a powerful diplomatic and economic force for the remainder of the decade. By limiting supply, the Arabs made economic and political gains, and the policies of OPEC were considered to be a major factor causing the combination of inflation and recession in the West in the late 1970s and early 1980s. The West has increased its own oil resources and engaged in efforts to develop alternative sources of power. By the mid-1980s the members of OPEC were in disagreement with one another, oil prices had fallen, and OPEC's influence was much reduced.

Another factor of growing importance in the Near East was the Palestine Liberation Organization (PLO), founded as a terrorist and underground organization supported by many Arab states. Its program was to destroy Israel and to form a state including the Palestinians residing in Israel and in refugee camps. The PLO increased its activities after the 1973 war, and was recognized by most Arab countries as the representative of the stateless Palestinians. Its main headquarters in the 1970s was in Lebanon, a country to the north of Israel with much internal strife and an inability to achieve control over all of its territory.

In 1977 the new Egyptian president, Anwar Sadat (1918–81), startled the world by stating in his Assembly that he would travel to Jerusalem in order to establish peace between Egypt and Israel. The Israelis immediately accepted his offer, and in November for the first time an Arab leader arrived in Israel and addressed the Israeli Parliament in Jerusalem. In a dramatic atmosphere Sadat stated that he wished a peace between Israel and all of the Arab states. "We used to reject you. . . . Yet today I tell you, and I declare it to the whole world, that we accept living with you in permanent peace based on justice. We do not want to encircle you, or be encircled ourselves, by destructive missiles ready for launching, nor by the shells of grudges and hatred." Sadat ended with the following:

Peace is not a mere endorsement of written lines. Rather it is a rewriting of history. Peace is not a game of calling for peace to defend certain whims, or hide certain ambitions. Peace, in its essence, is a joint struggle against all and every ambition and whim. Perhaps the examples and experience taken from ancient and modern history teach us all that missiles, warships and nuclear weapons cannot establish security. Rather, they destroy what peace and security build. . . . For the sake of civilization made by man, we have to defend everywhere against the rule of the force of arms, so that we may endow the rule of humanity with all the power of the values and principles that promote the sublime position of mankind.[4]

The Israeli Prime Minister, Menachim Begin (1913–   ), in his reply expressed the hope of a "full, real peace with complete reconciliation between the Jews and the Arab peoples."

In mid-1978, however, the negotiations seemed at an impasse. President Jimmy Carter of the United States personally intervened, and in September 1978 the three heads of government met at Camp David near Washington. An agreement was reached. The Camp David Agreement was called "A Framework for Peace in the Middle East." It included such principles as "respect for sovereignty, territorial integrity and political independence of every state in the area."[5] It arranged a set-

tlement of all outstanding territorial and military issues between Israel and Egypt, stipulating that Israel would give up the Sinai Peninsula to Egypt. The final peace treaty was signed in March 1979.

The hoped for peace for all of the area did not occur. The PLO continued its terrorist activities. Israel and its other neighbours, especially Syria and Jordan, remained in a state of non-recognition and hostility. When Sadat was assassinated in 1981, Israelis wondered about the stability of the arrangements with Egypt, but though relations have at times been cool, the peace between Israel and Egypt has held.

In June 1982 Israel launched an attack into Lebanon to the north. Israel's stated aim was to destroy the PLO's military bases in the areas which were being used to shell settlements in Israel and as a safe haven for terrorists. It also wished to prop up the Lebanese government so that the Lebanese could control and stabilize their own territory.

The Israeli thrust was initially successful. Its military campaign against the PLO and Syrian forces which had been based in the area was rapid and managed to weaken both. However, when it became evident that the government of Lebanon could not bring together its own battling factions, Israel decided to go further into Lebanon and occupy the southern part of the country. Successful in forcing the evacuation of the PLO from Beirut, the capital of Lebanon, Israel could not provide stability in the area, and it became an occupying power in the eyes of the world instead of a beleaguered country defending its borders. In Israel itself, public opinion was deeply divided on the occupation. Prime Minister Begin, in a state of depression, resigned in 1983. In 1985 Israel moved out of Lebanon, but that country has become the scene of much internal destruction as warring elements within continue to seek advantage. It has become a pawn in the Near East, caught between the conflicting goals of Syria, Israel, Jordan, and the PLO.

Peace remains tenuous in the Near East, as border incidents and terrorism by Arab guerrilla groups continue to be part of daily life. The refugee problem remains unsolved.

THE AMERICAS

The power of the United States is an inescapable reality for every other country in North and South America. The attitude represented by the Monroe Doctrine still persists in the United States, which views the two continents as its special sphere of influence. Moreover, the United States dominates the hemisphere economically. While interference in the internal affairs of other nations of the hemisphere is not as open or bold as it was during the days of Theodore Roosevelt, the United States uses its considerable economic weight as a lever of diplomatic policy, and on occasion, such as when control over the Panama Canal was threatened, it has openly intervened.

The Organization of American States (OAS) was founded in 1948, including all the hemispheric countries except Canada, and was designed to deal with common problems. While it has served as a forum to help resolve disputes, the OAS is distrusted by the leftist politicians in Latin America as a vehicle for American influence. Most Latin-American countries want more control over their economies; they wish to break free of their inevitable dependence on the United States, but they also do not wish to hurt the interests of their people in the process. In Peru and other countries, corporations owned by American interests have been nationalized, and relations between these countries and the United States have at times been strained.

A revolution in Cuba resulted in its complete break with the United States. In 1959 Fidel Castro overthrew a right-wing dictatorship, began to socialize the Cuban economy, and announced that he was accepting aid from the Soviet Union. When it appeared that Castro was establishing a communist regime, the United States trained Cuban exiles to overthrow him. However, an attempt in 1961 by a group of these to invade Cuba with American help was unsuccessful, and open hostility developed between the United States and Cuba. The implications of Castro's revolution, his ability to survive, and his restructuring of the economy and society of Cuba went beyond his island. His success encouraged a more independent posture towards the United States on the part of other Latin-American states.

The controversial sovereignty of the United States over the Canal Zone was ended in 1977 when, under President Carter, the United States signed two treaties with Panama. The United States had taken control of the territory in 1903 when the Panama Canal was created, in what was an imperialist intervention. By the middle of the twentieth century, the original agreement, which gave the United States control of the Canal Zone in perpetuity, angered many Latin-Americans, who felt the arrangement was an unfair remnant of an unhappy past. There was much agitation for renegotiation, but strong opposition in the United States to a surrender of the Canal. The new treaty left control of the Canal to the United States until 2000. Then, the Panamanians would take over, guaranteeing the United States the right to use and defend the important waterway. Carter was seen by many Americans to be giving up too much, but he believed that in the long run it was in the interest of the United States to withdraw as gracefully and as responsibly as possible.

After 1981 the administration of Ronald Reagan took an aggressive stance in Latin America, especially in Central America. Reagan saw the hand of the Soviet Union everywhere, not distinguishing between outside influence and internal differences. He was also eager to encourage and support regimes openly loyal to the United States. In El Salvador Reagan supported the existing dictatorial regime, and claimed that local revolutionaries represented "a virus imported from eastern Europe." Opponents of United States policy charged that it was ignoring local conditions and circumstances, and that the United States seemed to be propping up any government which would support its foreign policy. In Nicaragua, the United States, unhappy with the leftist government, helped train guerrillas, whom it called "freedom fighters," to support a rebellion. In 1984 the media revealed that the United States government was secretly aiding Nicaraguan revolutionaries to mine the harbours of the country. In the Caribbean, Reagan dispatched United States troops to Grenada in 1983 to stop a Marxist coup. In the 1980s United States policy in Latin America has been clear: it considers the area to be in its sphere of influence, and it will intervene to maintain that position.

Relations between Canada and the United States were usually more cordial than those between the United States and other countries in the hemisphere. The two states cooperated and were interdependent in many areas — NATO, North American defense, the building and administration of the St. Lawrence Seaway, water policy, energy, and the administration of a very long and serene border. Both countries were part of the same industrial community and were highly developed. They were each others' best trading partner.

In the 1970s, under the Liberals, there was a widespread belief in Canada that the power of American corporations in the Canadian economy and the close cultural and political ties between Canada and the United States were eroding Canadian identity and sovereignty. Prime Minister Pierre Elliot Trudeau likened the relationship to that of a mouse living next to an elephant, and followed a policy of trying for greater independence for Canada in its economy and culture. In the mid-1980s this policy was all but abandoned under the Conservatives, led by the new prime minister, Brian Mulroney (1939–   ). His Conservative government was more in tune with the economic policies of the Reagan administration and it welcomed greater American investment and participation in the Canadian economy.

In spite of some significant differences there were few major issues separating Canada and the United States. They had a similar legal tradition and a common language; they were each others' best customers; they had fought as allies in several wars and had largely integrated their defense systems; they participated in the same hockey and baseball leagues; they watched the same television shows and listened to the same music. But most Americans know little, if anything, about Canada, while most Canadians know much about the United States. Canadians continue to work to maintain a national and cultural identity in the face of so powerful a neighbour.

THE RICH AND THE POOR

The old aristocracy has virtually come to an end in the West, though in some places titles persist. In democratic countries the middle class remains in power, but it has lost a considerable amount of social control and economic freedom since the days of *laissez-faire*. Within most states, opportunities have become more widespread. There are now fewer economic or social privileges, and the progressive income tax alone has done much to reduce economic discrepancies among people. Communist countries have established a high degree of equality, though they have by no means eliminated economic and social distinctions.

However, with the development of technology, the gap between the rich nations and the poor nations continues to widen. Those countries which have resources, or are able to industrialize, or both, can produce surpluses. The others fall further behind. One of the reasons for this disparity seems to lie in population growth in underdeveloped countries. The birth rate of poor areas is higher than that of areas already rich, and, as a result, a country such as India must run very fast to stay in the same place. In order to produce more goods to feed a greater population, underdeveloped countries are unable to raise per capita income. It is extraordinarily difficult for a poor area to thrust forwards. Lack of wealth is usually accompanied by lack of power; the rich industrial nations are capable of building sophisticated armaments, while the poor and unindustrialized nations can only secure these from the rich.

Though class distinctions have been reduced over the centuries, even the industrialized states have not conquered the problem of poverty. In the United States, it has been estimated that one-fifth of the population is still living in poverty, and pockets of extreme poverty exist in virtually every industrial country. While the wealthier states are capable of producing food in abundance, none has solved the problem of

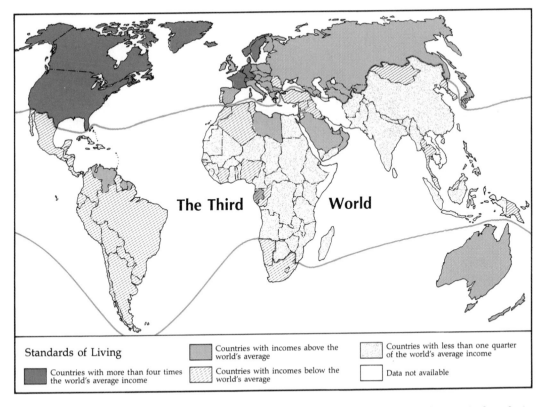

The Third   World

Standards of Living

Countries with more than four times the world's average income

Countries with incomes above the world's average

Countries with incomes below the world's average

Countries with less than one quarter of the world's average income

Data not available

distribution in a way that eliminates hunger and want. Countries with high industrial and agricultural productivity generally spend far more on armaments than on the welfare of their citizens.

Poverty in the underdeveloped world is a part of the reality of everyday life. The countries most developed industrially had in 1981 an average Gross National Product (GNP) of $11 120 per capita.* These include Japan, Australia, Denmark, Canada, and the United States. Low income countries, including India, Zaire, Ghana, and Afghanistan, had an average of $270 GNP per capita. In the middle are such moderately developed places as Ecuador ($1180), Malaysia ($1840), Brazil ($2220), Israel ($5160), and Singapore ($5240).

Many poor countries have taken loans from the wealthy countries to tide them over difficult times. But inflation in the late 1970s and early 1980s, in the main a result of a rise in the price of oil forced by OPEC, combined with a

*All figures in United States currency.

severe recession during that period, only increased the debt burden. Many countries are unable to pay back loans in the foreign currency in which they were borrowed. Their debts were incurred for purposes of development, but this did not happen as rapidly as optimists had predicted. Indebtedness is especially serious in Latin America and Africa, and it often means that countries there, for example Mexico and Brazil, Nigeria and Gabon, spend much of their resources simply paying interest to highly developed countries. The total Latin-American debt in 1985 was $350 billion; the African debt was $150 billion. Both continents move closer to financial collapse every year. The real dilemma is that many governments now are unable to undertake further social and economic development because so much of their already meager resources is used to repay loans. African countries in 1985 were paying on the average twenty-five per cent of their foreign currency, which they earn through exports, as interest on debts; the principal remains the same.

*Rio de Janeiro, Brazil. The famous statue
of Jesus the Redeemer dominates the
landscape, while* favelas, *shacks
inhabited by the urban poor, ring the
mountain below. (Popperfoto)*

The World Bank concluded in 1983:

It has been estimated that even with an annual
. . . growth rate of 5 to 6 percent between 1975
and 2000, more than 600 million people will
remain below the poverty line in developing
countries in the year 2000, unless the pattern of
growth is modified to put more emphasis on
poverty alleviation. The current projections clearly
suggest more moderate growth prospects and
thus reinforce the need for policies not only for
stimulating growth but also for curbing
population growth and meeting basic needs.[6]

While political imperialism is nearing its end,
there is a sense among low-income countries
that they are economically controlled by the
rich, and there is anger over a system in which
the poor find themselves in a position of seemingly endless and hopeless debt. Whatever

the level of aid by the West and whatever
adjustments are made in the loan repayment,
the only way out of poverty for many countries lies in rapid development and control of
their own products and resources.

With poverty goes hunger and, in some
cases, starvation. Even in wealthy countries
there is the extraordinary anomaly of bread
lines and malnutrition. In the underdeveloped
world, especially in Africa in the mid-1980s,
there was the spectre of masses of people dying
from lack of food.

In the 1970s there was some hope that a
"green revolution" would help to alleviate
hunger by increasing food productivity in a
great leap. This was the result of experiments
in genetics which permitted the cultivation of
hardier and greater yielding crops of grains,
rice, and wheat. In some areas the situation
improved for a time, but the food plants required great amounts of fertilizer and very
moist soil, and this did not permit them to be
grown in dry climates without very expensive and sophisticated irrigation systems.

In 1985, in an area of drought in Africa below
the Sahara Desert, called the Sahelian zone, it
was brought to the attention of the West that
people in Ethiopia, the Sudan, and elsewhere
were starving to death. The media showed
pictures of the horror, and much aid was
committed to these areas. Many experts claim
that charity from the West is not a long-term
answer: programs must be developed locally
which give people control over their own lives
and their own food; changes must be made in
the market price structure of the West, which
keeps food prices at a level beyond the power
of the underdeveloped countries to acquire
in sufficient quantities.

In our world there are rich nations and poor
nations, and there are rich and poor within
both types of nations. Poverty, hunger, and
discrimination remain potent forces in the lives
of countless millions.

THE CONTEMPORARY WORLD

International developments since 1945 have
shown that the diplomatic scene is very
fluid. The rigidity and simplicity of the
world divisions of the cold-war years has
ended, and realignments on the basis of new

power realities have taken place. The relative power of both the United States and the Soviet Union has declined while China and Europe have become more important. The emerging nations can also influence events. It is thus a more complex world than the one that came into existence immediately after the Second World War. An indication of the new flexibility and practicality in world affairs is the success in 1972 of West German Chancellor Willy Brandt's non-aggression treaties with Poland and the Soviet Union.

Nationalism remains the most important of modern ideologies. Even the emerging nations have organized themselves as nation-states, and most people would still agree with Mazzini's definition of a nation (see pages 117–18). While international political organizations have not been successful in challenging national sovereignty, international economic organizations considerably influence world events. The most successful, the European Common Market, may possibly point the way to a supranational parliamentary organization.

A number of fundamental problems are still a long way from being solved—how to feed, clothe, and shelter people in a world in which economic production and consumption are unevenly distributed, and malnutrition and starvation are the lot of large numbers of people. However, one should not be totally pessimistic about Europe, about the West, or about the world. From the ashes of the Second World War, Europe has become economically viable and politically stable; the West has divested itself of some of the less happy features of its influence—imperialism and colonialism—while in culture and economics Europe and the West continue to have enormous strength and influence. This is not the best of all possible worlds—but it is also not the worst that human beings have created in the course of their long history.

ANALYSIS AND DISCUSSION

1. "Frantz Fanon provided an intellectual denouncement of colonialism and Social Darwinism. His exhortations to violence were an attempt to throw off the remnants of superior white culture." Apply Fanon's philosophy as an explanation of the process of "decolonization" in Africa.

2. "Mao was a revolutionary, not a ruler." Evaluate this hypothesis in terms of Mao Tsetung's policies as Chairman.

3. "In 1948 the odds that Israel would survive, as a nation, were minimal. Forty years later it is the most successful state in the Middle East." Chronicle the history of modern Israel and account for its survival and expansion in the face of continued hostility.

4. Many critics would argue that the political imperialism of the nineteenth century has been replaced by economic and technological imperialism in the twentieth. In what ways would this account for Third World resentment of the policies of both the Soviet Union and the United States?

CHAPTER **17**

Europe and the West Since 1945: Intellectual and Artistic Movements

THE CULTURE OF THE WEST IN THE TWENTIETH century, and particularly since 1945, has not been as optimistic as it was during the Enlightenment. The idea of progress has been questioned, science is viewed as a two-edged sword, and concepts of human nature have been revised in light of the chaotic and destructive experiences of two world wars. In philosophy and theology there has been an attempt to regain the bearings of the West, to look for new starting points to approach the eternal questions about the meaning of life.

A decline in optimism has not resulted in despair. There has also been great creativity and a search for new forms. Artists are experimenting with new modes of communication; popular culture is vital; dramatists are introducing new kinds of theatrical experience; and Western culture, while less arrogant about its powers and less sure of itself than at the opening of the modern age, is displaying flexibility and great vitality.

SCIENCE, TECHNOLOGY, AND SOCIETY

In the twentieth century, scientific knowledge has grown at an unprecedented rate, and science and scientists have had a greater effect than ever before in shaping human life. Modern technology and medicine are dependent on a large army of scientists engaged in highly specialized research. Governments employ scientists as advisers, to help make policy decisions about the allocation of resources and future development. Scientists daily help to determine the kinds of weapons of war that are produced, the types of agricultural activity stressed, and the priorities in the exploration of space.

It has none the less become clear in recent years that industrial countries have achieved their high standard of living at a heavy ecological price. The "nature" described by Wordsworth and the Romantics has become, in some heavily industrialized areas, a nightmare of pollution. Moreover, the environmental "balance" has often been disturbed. Some species can no longer survive in many former breeding places, for industrial wastes have been dumped into rivers, streams, and oceans, changing the environment in a way Darwin could never have imagined.

Scientific development is no longer automatically equated with progress. In many industrial states there have been movements, particularly among the young, which have attempted to turn their back on science and technology. A number of "communes" have been set up in the countryside to live the "simple" life. Crafts have been revived in an effort to undo the depersonalization of mass production. A new interest in things of the spirit—sometimes related to traditional Western religions, sometimes based on Eastern religious philosophy (such as Zen Buddhism), sometimes associated with the occult—has grown in the West as part of a rejection of science.

The threat to the environment and the development of highly destructive armaments have given some contemporary thinkers a sense of impending disaster. The production of nuclear weapons in the United States and the Soviet Union has given each of these countries the power to destroy the earth many times over. As nuclear power spreads—to Britain, France, China, and to other countries—a number of thinkers believe that catastrophe is likely, for ethical standards are weak and national self-interest still reigns supreme.

It was once thought—by Descartes, by Condorcet, by Comte—that scientific and technological developments would help create an ideal world. Now many serious thinkers fear the uses to which scientific creativity may be put. Aldous Huxley in *Brave New World* (1932) and George Orwell in *1984* (1949) wrote of societies in which totalitarianism was so complete and the techniques of brain control were so advanced that people no longer had the possibility of being free. People were "programmed" by a system which was simple and all-pervasive. Huxley, Orwell, and others feared that scientific accomplishments would be used for inhuman ends.

Sir Julian Huxley predicted in 1969 that in the future people may be unable to cope with the world created by their own technology. Modern technology "has created a life of its own," he stated, and, by letting technology get out of hand, the human species "has imperilled the welfare of the earth and [its] own tenure on it."[1] The logic of unrestrained technological growth is no longer accepted by all social philosophers and economic planners. Questions about the quality of life have become as important as questions about the quantity of production.

It has been suggested by the economist John Kenneth Galbraith that life is now more influenced by industrial development than by political forms. Both in democratic and communist countries, technology has imposed a common way of life. The isolated inventor and entrepreneur have been replaced by the community of "technocrats" who make decisions about what people will eat and wear *before* production starts. According to Galbraith, large business enterprises are no longer run as the private concern of owners; they are now run by professional managers, with the co-operation and regulation of government. The days of the entrepreneur are over. It is the managers who make the vital decisions and control industrial enterprises. While democracies and communist states claim they are different from one another, they seem to be remarkably similar in their economic organ-

ization and in the way decisions are made about production and consumption.

In recent years a number of writers have argued that the West is now in a post-technological age. It has gone beyond the Industrial Revolution and the goal of ever-increasing production, they claim, and is moving towards controlled production, new religiosity and romanticism, and a new appreciation of the "natural" life. Some writers insist that the real issue now is to make certain that individuals do not become mere functions of the technology which is supposed to serve them, but that they learn to use in a creative way the freedom gained from abundance.

SPACE, WEAPONS, AND PEACE

Science became a major part of the cold war when, on October 4, 1957, the world learned that the Soviet Union had launched into space the first artificial satellite, Sputnik I. Less than a month later Sputnik II went up carrying a dog which was fitted with instruments that transmitted physiological data. In April 1961, a Soviet cosmonaut became the first human being to orbit the earth.

The implications of the Soviet accomplishment were not at first clear to the West. Sputnik meant that Soviet science, in this area, was in advance of that of the NATO countries. The United States and its allies undertook a review of their scientific programs and their educational goals. Whether military issues were at stake was an open question, but the United States viewed its own image and its national prestige as damaged. It began an intensive program of space research. In May 1961 President Kennedy announced a new national goal: to land a human being on the moon and to have that person return to earth safely.

The space race was on, though the Soviets declined to join in the race to the moon. The United States was successful. On July 20, 1969, in what was to many the realization of humanity's quest since ancient times and an actualization of much speculative science-fiction, an astronaut from the United States landed on the moon. Even more unusual, perhaps, television showed the landing and the surface of the moon to the world. People in their homes saw pictures of the moon and, indeed, pictures of the earth from outer space.

As other space ships, equipped with scientific instruments, were sent to explore the solar system, knowledge of space was greatly increased. United States crafts flew by Venus in 1962, 1965, and 1974, Mars in 1964, 1969, and 1971, Mercury in 1974, Jupiter in 1973, and Saturn several years later. Both the United States and the Soviet Union tried new types of spacecraft. By the mid-1970s it became clear that the value of the space missions was in the main long-term and related to pure scientific knowledge, and both countries began to cut down their costly programs.

Scientific research in other directions continued apace. While some of this activity was for peaceful purposes, research for the purpose of war and defence produced new and deadlier weapons. The capability of these weapons was so great that some countries with nuclear military power had the capacity to destroy the earth many times over. In the 1960s concerns over the future of humanity led to attempts by governments to halt the spread of nuclear weapons (see pages 335–338). The question arose of the means to harness science and to work for peace in the wake of an era that had known two world wars and that now had developed the capacity to destroy the planet.

Peace movements arose which attempted to end the production of nuclear weapons. In Great Britain the aged Bertrand Russell (1872–1970), one of the most distinguished mathematicians and philosophers of the twentieth century, led marches in favour of unilateral disarmament which gained world-wide attention. Russell published articles warning that the ''continued existence of the human race [is] in jeopardy,'' because of nuclear weapons. He publicized the destructive capabilities of nuclear power and warned that ''a world war would result, not in the victory of either side, but in the extermination of both.'' Russell wished to go beyond the politics of the cold war to speak on behalf of the whole species.

As geological time is reckoned, man has so far existed only for a very short period — 1,000,000 years at the most. What he has achieved,

The first space shuttle of the United States, launched in 1981.   (NASA)

especially during the last 6,000 years, is something utterly new in the history of the cosmos, so far at least as we are acquainted with it. For countless ages the sun rose and set, the moon waxed and waned, the stars shone in the night, but it was only with the coming of man that these things were understood. In the great world of astronomy and in the little world of the atom, man has unveiled secrets which might have been thought undiscoverable. In art and literature and religion, some men have shown a sublimity of feeling which make the species worth preserving. Is all this to end in trivial horror because so few are able to think of man rather than this or that group of men? Is our race so destitute of wisdom, so incapable of impartial love, so blind even to the simplest dictates of self-preservation, that the last proof of its silly cleverness is to be the extermination of all life of our planet?[2]

In the 1950s and 1960s peace movements grew up all over the globe. Disarmament and the prevention of the spread of nuclear weapons became a cause which often attracted vocal minorities, especially among the young. Numerous articles and books were written to publicize the possibility of nuclear catastrophe, to point out the vulnerability of the planet, and to warn of the improbability of recovering after a nuclear war.

THE BIOLOGICAL SCIENCES

Great achievements have been made in the biological sciences since the Second World War. In genetics James Watson and Francis Crick, in 1953, analysed deoxyribonucleic acid (DNA), the chemical structure in gene cells, and proposed that DNA was structured as a "double helix," a spiral-shaped set of four different kinds of molecules. The way these molecules were arranged in a pattern determined the character of the genes and of the organism. This led within a decade to a much deeper understanding of hereditary diseases and an ability to control some of them.

New drugs were introduced to cure and control illness. Penicillin, discovered by Alexander Fleming before the Second World War, was the first of the antibiotics, and was used extensively along with others to control infectious diseases. Vaccines have been developed to prevent measles and polio. In 1955 the first tranquilizers were introduced, designed to help in the treatment of those with certain mental disorders.

Many drugs, including tranquilizers, have been used as means of altering the mental state of individuals, and have been regarded as potentially very dangerous by health experts. In the affluent countries, heroin, cocaine, and marijuana were used regularly, and tranquilizers were sold in pharmacies in great quantities. Drug cultures of two sorts arose in the West: the first, prominent in the 1960s, was made up of a group of social and political dissenters from the mainstream, who experimented with illegal drugs as part of their alienation from society; the second includes ordinary citizens who become dependent on one drug or another. There is an extensive illegal drug trade throughout the West.

The new developments in the biological sciences have raised thorny questions of medical ethics in the contemporary world. Genetics has given scientists the capability of changing life forms, as well as curing disease. Should this genetic engineering be done, and, if so, how should it be controlled? Medical advances have prolonged life, in some cases by using machines to continue the function of vital organs of individuals who will exist in a permanent state of unconsciousness. At what point is death reached, and how should decisions about life and death be made?

COMPUTERS AND COMMUNICATIONS

Technological advances have resulted in new developments which have changed the way we work and communicate. The computer has become part of everyday life, and it is transforming the way information is handled and communicated.

The first electronic computer was assembled in 1946. Called the Electronic Numerical Integrator and Calculator (ENIAC), it worked on the decimal system, filled up a huge room, had 18 000 tubes, and used an enormous amount of power. At a public demonstration in 1946 it was given the problem of multiplying the number 97 367 by itself five thousand times. It did this in one-half of a second, and was described by one journalist as being "faster than thought." Computers continued to be developed which were smaller and which could do more, much faster. Their memories were expanded, and the silicon chip enabled hundreds of thousands of electronic circuits to be placed on a piece of plastic the size of a dime. Microcomputers came into homes in the 1980s.

The new technology received momentum in three ways. During the days of the space race there was a need to develop smaller and more efficient machines; the military uses of the computer were many, from helping with planning to controlling vast inventories; and its commercial uses were quickly realized by the developed countries. Computers have aided in the development of industrial robots, which are transforming the workplace in major manufacturing countries.

Television, which comes close to being a universal presence in the West, has transformed the mode of communications. In some respects, it has created a single culture, where people in one country, and sometimes around the world, are watching the same thing and absorbing the same information. Its implications are exciting — in permitting education to reach millions not heretofore able to obtain it, and distressing — in catering to the lowest common denominator in taste.

We live, it has been said, in a "post-industrial" age, a new form of society in which a professional class which understands the new technology has come to the fore. Rapid change has become commonplace, and a theory of "future-shock," suggesting that reality changes so quickly that the world is never stable and the ordinary person is lost in the chaos, has become popular in recent times. Some writers have cast doubt on the human benefits of ever-increasing industrialization, and have called for a rethinking of our dedication to economic growth.

SCIENCE AS A NEGATIVE VALUE: THE FRANKENSTEIN PROBLEM

Frankenstein was written in 1816 and 1817 by Mary Shelley, a young woman of nineteen. In the book it is Dr. Frankenstein, the scientist, who tampers with the laws of nature and creates life. But his creation, seen as a monster, is left to die by the scientist, who is incapable of dealing with the consequences of his knowledge. However, the new being survives and blames his creator for his monstrousness. Dr. Frankenstein is haunted and stalked by the creature until his own death. Thus, humanity is punished for attempting to emulate the role of the deity.

The Frankenstein story has become a modern myth because of its appropriateness to many of the problems of science in the contemporary world. Science is seen both as enormously beneficial and as coldly inhuman and destructive. No longer is science perceived, as it once was almost universally, as a positive

force. It is human nature which is in question now, and some believe that our nature is incapable of handling the consequences of our creativity. The result is a fear of scientific progress, something new to the West. No country wants to give up its scientific accomplishments, but the "price of progress," is now being considered more carefully. The focus is now on questions raised by Mary Shelley: should we engage in certain types of science without first understanding the ethical issues which are raised by its development? Are we capable of handling our own creativity? How does science relate to the dark side of human nature? Many scientists now try to retain control over the uses to which their inventiveness will be put.

NEW PHILOSOPHICAL PATHS

In the contemporary West there have been two major philosophical movements. The first, Logical Positivism, is an effort to apply scientific analysis to philosophical thinking. The other, Existentialism, is a concern with human beings, their identity, and their behaviour in an age of uncertainty and ambiguity.

Logical Positivism began in Vienna in the 1920s under the leadership of Rudolf Carnap. Many of Carnap's colleagues—the most notable was Ludwig Wittgenstein—went to England and the United States. Logical Positivists believed that the *method* of philosophy should be "scientific"—that it should be both logical and verifiable by the senses. Thus they said that philosophy ought to get back to the basics. "Essentially a philosophy is a system of definitions," one Logical Positivist stated, "or, only too often, a system of descriptions of how definitions might be given."[3] The main purpose of philosophical inquiry, insisted followers of this school of thought, was to clarify the meaning of questions and to make philosophical investigation precise. Until this was accomplished, Logical Positivists believed, it was useless to try to answer traditional queries about ethics or beauty or truth. Hence, they directed their attention to the method rather than the content of philosophy. In discussing the role of philosophy in relation to science, Carnap wrote:

. . . it consists in the clarification of the statements of empirical science; more specifically, in the decomposition of statements into their parts (concepts), the step by step reduction of concepts to more fundamental concepts and of statements to more fundamental statements. This way of setting the problem brings out the value of logic for philosophical enquiries. Logic is no longer merely one philosophical discipline among others. . . . Logic is the method of philosophizing.[4]

Logical Positivists began their inquiry with an analysis of language—how do we communicate and when do we say that something has meaning? Applying the tests of mathematical logic and experience, the Logical Positivists concluded that many traditional questions were meaningless. For example, to say "I have two apples" is to make a statement which can be verified through sense experience. But to say "these apples are beautiful" is a meaningless statement because the concept of beauty involves a subjective, not a wholly objective, experience. Soon the Logical Positivists began relegating questions involving beauty, ethics, and metaphysics (such as: does God exist? what is "good"?) to the meaningless category.

In a sense, however, the concern of the Logical Positivists reflected the relativist world which humanity faces in the twentieth century. They believed that the inherited philosophical tradition was not adequate to deal with large questions. Indeed, the attempt of the Logical Positivists to go back to the elements of philosophy and build a new foundation is a denial of much of the inherited wisdom of the West. But, though Logical Positivists have been accused of ignoring too many important issues in their quest for precision, they have imposed clarity on many muddled questions and have made important contributions to the problem of knowledge.

Many philosophers continued to address themselves to ethical questions in an age in which tradition is seldom looked upon as a reliable guide. Existentialism was a label for the ideas of a number of philosophers whose concern was human beings and their behaviour in a world without norms. "Existence precedes essence," wrote Jean-Paul

Sartre (1905–80), one of the leading existentialist philosophers.

. . . man first of all exists, encounters himself, surges up in the world—and defines himself afterwards. If man as the existentialist sees him is not definable, it is because to begin with he is nothing. He will not be anything until later, and then he will be what he makes of himself. Thus, there is no human nature, because there is no God to have a conception of it. Man simply is. Not that he is simply what he conceives himself to be, but he is what he wills. . . . Man is nothing else but that which he makes of himself. That is the first principle of existentialism.[5]

Some thinkers have been concerned that the sense that the world is incoherent and meaningless—which is one of the basic assumptions of existentialism—would make people immobile and lead to a rejection of life. This view has been refuted by Albert Camus (1913–60). Camus argued that to recognize that life might be absurd need not lead to despair, for people can now be free from the gods and systems which inhibit them, and which are often the source of suffering. Though a person may choose wrongly, being human is being conscious of the dignity of choice and creating one's own values. Awareness of what Camus called "the benign indifference of the universe"[6] frees one to make decisions for oneself, to be a responsible person.

Sartre has stated that "the first effect of existentialism is that it puts every man in possession of himself as he is, and places the entire responsibility for his existence squarely upon his own shoulders."[7]

IDEAS IN THE MODERN THEATRE

A "theatre of the absurd" evolved after the Second World War, concerned with using various new theatrical techniques to try to portray what was regarded as the essential existential loneliness and absurdity of the human condition. Samuel Beckett's (1906–   ) *Waiting for Godot*, first performed in 1953, was the landmark play of the type, and Beckett's whole work has come to be seen as a profound commentary on the tragedy and hope inherent in the modern human condition. *Waiting for Godot*

"Vladimir," in a production of Waiting for Godot. *(Canapress Photo Service)*

is played on a nearly bare stage on which its characters seem to be living aimless lives full of despair. Yet, they wait for the enigmatic Godot — could it be God? — not knowing who or what he is. One character, Vladimir, asks his friend Estragon: "What are you insinuating? That we've come to the wrong place?"

Estragon: He should be here.
Vladimir: He didn't say for sure he'd come.
Estragon: And if he doesn't come?
Vladimir: We'll come back to-morrow.
Estragon: And then the day after to-morrow.
Vladimir: Possibly.
Estragon: And so on.
Vladimir: The point is —
Estragon: Until he comes.
Vladimir: You're merciless.
Estragon: We came here yesterday.
Vladimir: Ah no, there you're mistaken.
Estragon: What did we do yesterday?
Vladimir: What did we do yesterday?

Estragon: Yes.
Vladimir: Why . . . (Angrily.) Nothing is certain when you're about.[8]

Although Beckett's main characters seem to be leading meaningless lives, they take refuge in friendship and a willingness to hope in the midst of a possibly empty universe. Beckett's language catches the essential emptiness of daily existence, and yet the play is full of hope and has a softness about it because of the small displays of kindness of his two main characters. Two wanderers without a home, who represent all of us, they do make commitments to one another and to life in spite of the seeming void in which they find themselves. Beckett's theatre speaks to the audience in metaphor and enigma. It rejects the attempts of the traditional theatre to show life on the stage as it is in society, because it is Beckett's belief that new means have to be devised to speak to contemporary human beings.

Another type of philosophical theatre, often using existential themes, is the "theatre of cruelty," which attempts to use theatrical productions to display pain and evil to the audience in ways which resemble primitive rituals. It, too, abandons traditional modes of theatrical naturalism in order to try to communicate to the audience in essential psychological terms.

Peter Weiss' (1916–1982) play, *Marat/Sade** (1964) is set in Napoleonic times, and is seemingly a play within a play about the French Revolution and Napoleon. However, all of the events and characters are metaphors for issues which Weiss regards as important to his own time. The play is set in an asylum, and the players are inmates who, as a form of therapy, are putting on a play for the keeper of the asylum and his guests, the audience. The asylum becomes a statement about our own times. Weiss suggests that the world might well be a madhouse; in his play the inmates are more sensitive than their "normal" keepers. The play becomes a dialogue between rationality and sensuality, both sides of human nature. The world of Napoleon is por-

Marat/Sade is the short title: the full title is *The Persecution and Assassination of Marat as Performed by the Inmates of the Asylum of Charenton under the Direction of the Marquis de Sade.*

trayed as close to our world, in which ordinary people commit unspeakable horrors in the name of the defense of civilization. The chorus, ironically extolling Napoleon, sings:

> All men want to be free
> If they don't
> never mind
> we'll abolish all mankind.[9]

At the close of the play the inmates irrationally destroy the asylum, with the implication that the reality of the modern world has become inverted, that the audience is itself at least as mad and certainly more corrupt than those whom it incarcerates.

Existentialism insisted on a rigorous examination of self. This philosophy, in assessing humanity, refused to begin with assumptions either holy or sublime. Yet, it was not pessimistic; there was a hopefulness in the demand for commitment and in an insistence that life must be examined and choices consciously made.

RELIGIOUS THOUGHT

As part of the questioning of traditional religious beliefs and as a result of the events of the Second World War, particularly the destruction of millions in death camps, the post-war world has seen an intellectual controversy centering on the "death of God." Is God dead? The question has many meanings and the answers have been varied.

Paul Tillich (1886–1965), a Protestant theologian, suggested that the metaphors used in the West to understand what is meant by God—for example, that God is above, that God predestines events—are inadequate in the modern age. Instead of worrying about the nature of God, Tillich thought that people should worry about their own values and human relationships, and that through these they can then participate in sacred acts. Many theologians, like the existentialists, stressed human behaviour, and they moved away from what they regarded as false and sentimental religious notions that are unrelated to people's lives.

A number of Protestant thinkers stressed a "demythologization" of religion, empha-

sizing human experience rather than prayer. The emphasis has been on a Jesus-centered rather than a God-centered theology. Some theologians have "bracketed" metaphysical questions about the nature of God as being unanswerable at this time and have looked to the lives of holy people for religious guidance. Dietrich Bonhoeffer, a Protestant minister who died in a concentration camp in the Second World War, wrote while in prison:

> The Church is her true self only when she exists for humanity. As a fresh start she should give away all her endowments to the poor and needy. The clergy should live solely on the free-will offerings of their congregations, or possibly engage in some secular calling. She must take her part in the social life of the world, not lording it over men, but helping and serving them. She must tell men, whatever their calling, what it means to live in Christ, to exist for others. And in particular, our own Church will have to take a strong line with the blasphemies of *hybris*, power-worship, envy and humbug, for these are the roots of evil. She will have to speak of moderation, purity, confidence, loyalty, steadfastness, patience, discipline, humility, content and modesty. She must not underestimate the importance of human example, which has its origin in the humanity of Jesus.[10]

Martin Buber (1878–1965), a Jewish theologian, called for a concern with human beings and the human community as the only way to participate in a religious life. Buber felt that one is closest to God when one is closest to one's fellow human beings, when one treats others as "thou" and not "you." Tillich, Bonhoeffer, and Buber did not seek God solely through mysteries, nor did they concern themselves much with institutions. They claimed that everyone must seek God in one's own fashion, that one's behaviour will demonstrate how serious a person is in this quest.

The Catholic Church underwent considerable changes after the Second World War, starting with the Second Vatican Council, called by Pope John XXIII in 1962. This Council was very different from the First Vatican Council held a century earlier, for it attempted a reconciliation with the modern world and a decentralization of authority. It encouraged greater participation by laymen in services and in the governance of the Church. John XXIII's encyclical *Pacem in Terris* (1963) was a plea for international co-operation and for social action. John XXIII cared less about papal and Italian politics than about the ethical role of the Church.

The concentration camps of the Second World War and the Holocaust have become the focus of theological concern. Among believers the issue has been that of a reaffirmation of faith and identity in the face of having to deal theologically with the possibility of abandonment. The Jewish novelist Elie Wiesel (1928–   ) experienced the concentration camps as a young boy. The fact of having been in the center of the Holocaust changed his religious perception of the world. He has raised the issue of having to cope with a radical transformation of the role of God in the world, and he has tried to understand the meaning of human suffering. In his autobiographical work *Night* (1958) he wrote:

. . . Never shall I forget the little faces of the children, whose bodies I saw turned into wreaths of smoke beneath a silent blue sky.

Never shall I forget those flames which consumed my faith forever.

Never shall I forget that nocturnal silence which deprived me, for all eternity, of the desire to live. Never shall I forget those moments which murdered my God and my soul and turned my dreams to dust. Never shall I forget these things, even if I am condemned to live as long as God Himself. Never.[11]

Wiesel has stated: "I had the impression . . . of being present at the death of God. I have remained haunted by it. God died in each one of those deported children. I survived, but not completely."[12] The "death of God" is a concept which was raised by many theologians.

One of the initial responses to the Holocaust was a special kind of silence, a sense that words could not describe the experience; to try and articulate it would debase it and make it ordinary. Many works about the Holocaust, such as Jerzy Kosinski's *The Painted Bird*, (1965) deal with the event by indirection, and use silence as part of their plot and as a device to describe the overwhelming power of the event. Kosinski and Wiesel both use characters who lose their capacity to speak or refuse to do so, who are mute in the midst of what the existentialists term "the void." Fear of trivializing what many have thought to be one of the major theological events in Western history has led to this posture.

But after a time silence turned into a need to bear witness. Jewish thinkers insisted that the fact of the Holocaust must be confronted or else Nazism and racism would obtain a "posthumous victory." Hence, there has been an attempt to incorporate the Holocaust into religious dialogue and thought. One of the values which Jewish theologians have asserted is that of survival. There is a belief that to give in to inhumanity by despairing is implicitly to adopt a position accepting death and destruction. Hence, there is a reevaluation of values which has come as a statement about our shared humanity and the importance of our links with time and history.

Some Christian theologians have demanded that their faith confront the fact that the Holocaust occurred in Christian civilization, and was institutionalized by people who claimed to be believing Christians. Gregory Baum, a Roman Catholic priest, has stated: "The message of the Holocaust to Christian theology . . . is that at whatever cost to its own self-understanding, the church must be willing to confront the ideologies implicit in its doctrinal tradition."[13] Both Protestant and Catholic theologians have attempted to reformulate and re-examine traditional beliefs in the light of the events of the twentieth century. The implications of such a reexamination include reflections on concepts of the demonic, the holy, the sacred, and humanity's relationship to God.

THE FINE ARTS

Artists in the West in the twentieth century have broken with the past radically. Many have abandoned the perspective and representational art, which had been the goal of the artistic enterprise for over four hundred years,

NU DESCENDANT UN ESCALIER

◁ *Marcel Duchamp, "Nude Descending a Staircase, No. 2", 1912. Duchamp was asked: "How did that painting originate?" He replied:*

> *In the nude itself. To do a nude different from the classic reclining or standing nude, and to put it in motion. There was something funny there, but it wasn't at all funny when I did it. Movement appeared like an argument to make me decide to do it.*
>
> *In the "Nude Descending a Staircase", I wanted to create a static image of movement: movement is an abstraction, a deduction articulated within the painting, without our knowing if a real person is or isn't descending an equally real staircase. Fundamentally, movement is in the eye of the spectator, who incorporates it into the painting.*

Pierre Cabanne, Dialogues with Marcel Duchamp, *ed. Robert Motherwell, trans. Ron Padgett   (The Viking Press, 1971)*

Wassily Kandinsky, unnamed improvisations, ▷ *1914.   Kandinsky said:*

> *Painting is a thundering collision of different worlds, destined to create a new world. Technically, every work comes into existence as the universe comes into existence, namely through catastrophes. Yet in the end the chaotic discord of the instruments makes for a symphony which we call music of the spheres.*

A. Neumeyer, The Search for Meaning in Modern Art, *trans. R. Angress   (Prentice-Hall, Inc., 1965)*

STÄDTISCHE GALERIE IM LENBACHHAUS, MÜNCHEN

Pablo Picasso, "Three Musicians", 1921. In 1923, Picasso discussed this new style of cubism:

Many think that cubism is an art of transition, an experiment which is to bring ulterior results. Those who think that way have not understood it. Cubism is not either a seed or a foetus, but an art dealing primarily with forms, and when a form is realized it is there to live its own life.....

Cubism has kept itself within the limits and limitations of painting, never pretending to go beyond it. Drawing, design and color are understood and practiced in cubism in the spirit and manner that they are understood and practiced in all other schools. Our subjects might be different, as we have introduced into painting objects and forms that were formerly ignored. We have kept our eyes open to our surroundings, and also our brains.

The Arts, *New York, May 1923. (Statement made by Picasso to Marius de Zayas, translated into English and published in* The Arts *under the title "Picasso Speaks".)*

Paul Klee, "The Ships Depart", 1927.   In a lecture "On Modern Art" (1924), Klee stated:

. . . the artist must be forgiven if he regards the present state of outward appearances in his own particular world as accidentally fixed in time and space. And as altogether inadequate compared with his penetrating vision and intense depth of feeling.

And is it not true that even the small step of a glimpse through the microscope reveals to us images which we should deem fantastic and overimaginative if we were to see them somewhere accidentally, and lacked the sense to understand them?

Your realist, however, coming across such an illustration in a sensational magazine, would exclaim in great indignation: "Is that supposed to be nature? I call it bad drawing."

Does then the artist concern himself with microscopy? History? Paleontology?

Only for purposes of comparison, only in the exercise of his mobility of mind. And not to provide a scientific check on the truth of nature.

Only in the sense of freedom.

In the sense of a freedom, which does not lead to fixed phases of development, representing exactly what nature once was, or will be, or could be on another star (as perhaps may one day be proved).

But in the sense of a freedom which merely demands its rights, the right to develop, as great Nature herself develops.

From type to prototype.

Modern Artists on Art: Ten Unabridged Essays, *ed. R. L. Herbert   (Prentice-Hall, Inc., 1964)*

Joan Miró, "Woman and Bird in the Night",
1945.   In 1939, Miró stated:

> *If the interplay of lines and colors does not lay*
> *bare the conflict of their creator, it is no more*
> *than a bourgeois amusement; forms . . . should*
> *reveal the movement of a spirit who is trying to*
> *escape from present reality, which is par-*
> *ticularly disgusting today, approach fresh*
> *realities and finally offer other men the chance*
> *of elevating themselves. What rottenness has*
> *to be swept away before a habitable world can*
> *be discovered.*

Quoted in Pierre Guégen, "The Enchanted
Humor of Miró", XXe Siècle Review, *No. 8,*
(January 1957).

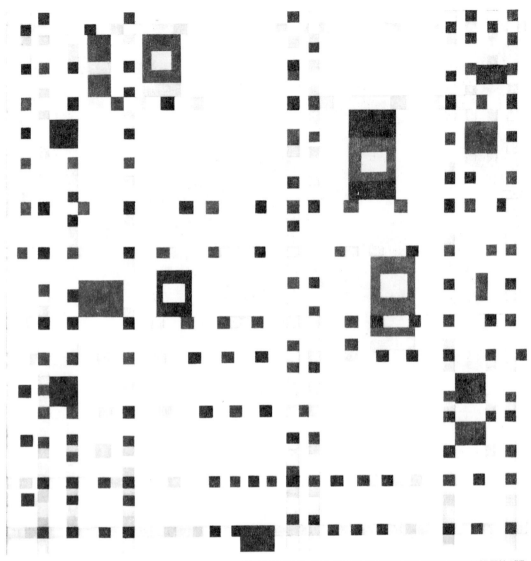

MONDRIAN, PIET. *BROADWAY BOOGIE WOOGIE*. 1942-43. OIL ON CANVAS, 50″ X 50″. COLLECTION, THE MUSEUM OF MODERN ART, NEW YORK

Piet Mondrian, "Broadway Boogie Woogie", 1942–43. Several years prior to painting "Broadway Boogie Woogie", Mondrian wrote:

For pure art then, the subject can never be an additional value, it is the line, the color, and their relations which must "bring into play the whole sensual and intellectual register of the inner life, ..." not the subject. Both in abstract art and in naturalistic art color expresses itself "in accordance with the form by which it is determined", and in all art it is the artist's task to make forms and colors living and capable of arousing emotion. If he makes art into an "algebraic equation" that is no argument against the art, it only proves that he is not an artist.

Modern Artists on Art: Ten Unabridged Essays, ed. R. L. Herbert,   (Prentice-Hall, Inc., 1964)

Robert Motherwell, ''Wall Painting III'', ca. 1952. Motherwell related abstract art to the modern world:

''I think that abstract art is uniquely modern—not in the sense that word is sometimes used, to mean that our art has 'progressed' over the art of the past; though abstract art may indeed represent an emergent level of evolution—but in the sense that abstract art represents the particular acceptances and rejections of men living under the conditions of modern times. If I were asked to generalize about this condition as it has been manifest in poets, painters, and composers during the last century and a half, I should say that it is a fundamentally romantic response to modern life—rebellious, individualistic, unconventional, sensitive, irritable. I should say that this attitude arose from a feeling of being ill at ease in the universe, so to speak—the collapse of religion, of the old close-knit community and family may have something to do with the origins of the feeling. I do not know.

''But whatever the source of this sense of being unwedded to the universe, I think that one's art is just one's effort to wed oneself to the universe, to unify oneself through union.... If this ... is true, then modern art has a different face from the art of the past because it has a somewhat different function for the artist in our time. I suppose that the art of far more ancient and 'simple' artists expressed something quite different, a feeling of already being at one with the world....''

Herschel B. Chipp, ed., Theories of Modern Art, (University of California Press, 1968)

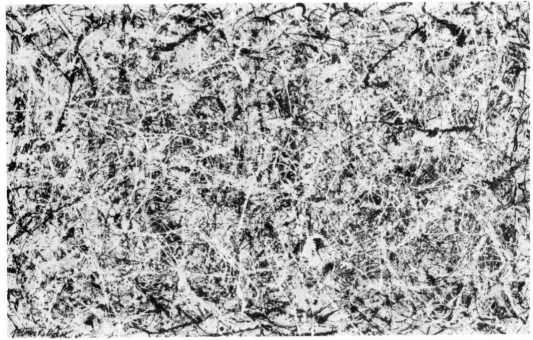

Jackson Pollock, ''Number 1'', 1949. Two years earlier, Pollock stated:

''My painting does not come from the easel. I hardly ever stretch my canvas before painting. I prefer to tack the unstretched canvas to the hard wall or the floor. I need the resistance of a hard surface. On the floor I am more at ease. I feel nearer, more a part of the painting, since this way I can walk around it, work from the four sides and literally be in the painting. This is akin to the method of the Indian sand painters of the West.

''I continue to get further away from the usual painter's tools such as easel, palette, brushes, etc. I prefer sticks, trowels, knives, and dripping fluid paint or a heavy impasto with sand, broken glass, and other foreign matter added.

''When I am in my painting, I'm not aware of what I'm doing. It is only after a sort of 'get acquainted' period that I see what I have been about. I have no fears about making changes, destroying the image, etc., because that painting has a life of its own. I try to let it come through. It is only when I lose contact with the painting that the result is a mess. Otherwise there is pure harmony, an easy give and take, and the painting comes out well.''

Herschel B. Chipp, ed., Theories of Modern Art, (University of California Press, 1968)

Alexander Calder, ''Three Arches'', 1963. In 1951, Calder recalled:

''My entrance into the field of abstract art came about as the result of a visit to the studio of Piet Mondrian in Paris in 1930.

''I was particularly impressed by some rectangles of color he had tacked on his wall in a pattern after his nature....

''I think that at that time and practically ever since, the underlying sense of form in my work has been the system of the universe, or part thereof. For that is a rather large model to work from.

''What I mean is that the idea of detached bodies floating in space, of different sizes and densities, perhaps of different colors and temperatures, and surrounded and interlarded with wisps of gaseous condition, and some at rest, while others move in peculiar manners, seems to me the ideal source of form.''

Herschel B. Chipp, ed., Theories of Modern Art, (*University of California Press, 1968*)

*Willem de Kooning, ''Excavation'',
1950. The next year de Kooning
discussed abstract art:*

''Personally, I do not need a movement.
What was given to me, I take for granted.
Of all movements, I like Cubism most. It
had that wonderful unsure atmosphere
of reflection—a poetic frame where
something could be possible, where an
artist could practice his intuition. It
didn't want to get rid of what went
before. Instead it added something to it.
The parts that I can appreciate in other
movements came out of Cubism. Cubism
became a movement, it didn't set out to
be one. It has force in it, but it was no
'force movement'....
''If I do paint abstract art, that's what
abstract art means to me.''

Herschel B. Chipp, ed., Theories of
Modern Art, (University of California
Press, 1968)

in a quest to find new meaning in artistic shapes, forms, and colours. Artists outside the communist countries no longer feel obliged to depict the "realistic" world "out there," nor do they expect to deliver an allegory or a moral tale. Form and colour have their own meaning in art, and for many the relationship between shapes and colours themselves is exciting and creative.

The result has been the springing up of a number of schools and styles since the beginning of the twentieth century, as innovation has replaced tradition, and artists have felt free to experiment. This new freedom of expression first appeared among a group of artists dubbed by one critic as the *fauves*, or wild beasts. The name stuck and Fauvism, which was inaugurated early in the twentieth century, came to mean an explosion of colour on the canvas, as artists such as Henri Matisse (1869–1958) painted ordinary objects in an attempt to capture mood and emotion. Now the artist expected the audience to work at their own understanding of the canvas.

Cubism, developed by the master artist of the twentieth century, Pablo Picasso (1881–1973), as well as by Georges Braque (1882–1963), did to form what Fauvism had done to colour. Picasso from 1906 to 1914 experimented with form, trying at first to develop a symbolic and stylized artistic language which sought to express the essential of what was being painted rather than its externals. Then, he and Braque tried to synthesize what we see, by using the geometry of form to depict many things at once. Cubist paintings became complicated statements about what the eye sees and about reality. The artists attempted to change the way painting is executed and how it is understood. So radical that viewers sometimes rejected it outright, Cubism successfully challenged our perceptions of the world and demanded and achieved a reevaluation of the meaning and aims of art.

An international movement called Dada grew in the interwar years, which reflected the disillusionment that set in after the First World War. Dada meant nothing, and the members of the movement flippantly challenged the social values of their society and its art. Described as a "state of mind," Dadaism was rebellious and anti-establishment. One of the artists associated with Dada, Jean Arp, said:

Philosophies have less value for Dada than an old abandoned toothbrush, and Dada abandons them to the great world leaders. Dada denounced the infernal ruses of the official vocabulary of wisdom. Dada is for the senseless, which does not mean nonsense. Dada is senseless like nature. Dada is for nature and against art.[14]

Artists wanted to challenge the complacency of their times, to shock people into perceiving reality differently, to demand a break with traditional perceptions and modes of seeing things.

Surrealism began as an outgrowth of Dada. It is an attempt by artists, including Joan Miro and Salvadore Dali, to get to the world of the unconscious, not unlike what Freud had tried to do through psychoanalysis. Surrealists claimed that our imagination and our inner life is a world understood through symbols and signs, sometimes through our dreams and fantasies. Their paintings totally abandon representation and they ask viewers to interpret them via their inner lives. Paintings of surrealists often have unusual shapes and juxtapositions in an effort to depict our inner world.

After the Second World War the main influence in art in the West came from New York rather than Paris. The major new development in the 1940s was Abstract Expressionism. Begun as a style called automatism, and developed in its most powerful form by Jackson Pollock, it used colour freely and expressively in non-objective art which, at its beginnings, had the quality of spontaneity. Artists dripped and splattered paint on a canvas, trying to challenge all of the old self-conscious artistic styles. Imagery was usually absent, and, as the school developed, its canvases got larger and larger. Abstract Expressionism actually demanded a new critical understanding of what a painting was, and what could be considered a work of art.

Abstraction and non-objective art are the keynotes of painting in the twentieth century. Since 1945 other styles have developed, including: Pop Art, which uses popular imagery;

Op Art, concerned with form and illusion; Minimalism, a reductionist attempt to get the canvas to incorporate only essentials; and Conceptual Art, which puts its emphasis on information and ideas. The range of styles and types of art is extraordinary as artists attempt to develop a new visual language to depict the inner and outer worlds, and to speak to and for the modern age.

THE POPULAR ARTS

The cinema since the Second World War has, in many ways, challenged the novel as the major art form that reaches most people. "Realistic" films made after the Second World War, such as those of Roberto Rossellini (*Rome — Open City*) and Vittorio de Sica (*The Bicycle Thief*), depict poverty and despair, greyness and slums, but also testify to the strength of the human character in trying to overcome limitations of environment. The poetry and mysticism of Ingmar Bergman, a Swedish film director whose major works include *The Seventh Seal*, have pointed out the vast potential for symbolism and allegory in the cinema. Michaelangelo Antonioni's *Blow-Up* was a film capturing the tone of middle-class culture in the 1960s, while at the same time asking important questions about the nature of reality and illusion.

In a world in which cinema and television have become major forms of mass communication, it has been suggested, particularly in the works of Marshall McLuhan, that we are now moving out of an era of printing and are in a period in which people understand and perceive things "visually," rather than "linearly." Certainly cinema and television are powerful influences in shaping public opinion and public taste. Whether visual culture will replace a culture based on printing is highly debatable; it is likely they will complement one another in the quest for insights into human nature and the human condition.

HISTORY AND THE HUMAN CONDITION

People in the West think historically and use the past to discuss and comprehend their own nature and their community. History has been used by people in the West to determine their identity and to make decisions on social and political action; history has been used to rationalize both tradition and revolution, and to justify both war and peace in the names of nationalism, liberalism, conservatism, socialism, and communism. Human beings today are historical animals, and without history, their memory as it were, they would be lost. While in the twentieth century people have had less confidence in grand systems of historical interpretation, such as the nineteenth-century systems of Marx and Comte, historical thinking continues to be an integral part of the intellectual life of people in the West.

Oswald Spengler's *Decline of the West*, the first volume of which appeared in 1917, had a great impact in the first decade after the First World War. As its title suggests, Spengler's message was hardly optimistic— the West was in decay, it was due for a time of "Caesarism" in politics, and not science nor rationality nor industrialization could save it. The popularity of Spengler's work was related to its message of doom—he spoke to a generation which had gone from optimism to despair, from a belief in progress to the trenches of the First World War, from a faith in science to uncertainty about the future of humanity.

Arnold J. Toynbee's multivolume *A Study of History*, begun in 1934, was a more scholarly work. Toynbee believed that the West was in a "time of troubles," but he was much less fatalistic than Spengler. According to Toynbee, the West has a good deal of vitality left if it renews itself through a revival of its own values and through contact with other cultures and civilizations. Decay sets in, stated Toynbee, when old responses are made to new challenges. Individuals in the West must constantly renew their creativity. In his later writings, Toynbee has suggested that one of the ways the West can move away from its "time of troubles" is to help to create a universal religion by fusing Western and Eastern forms.

The Marxist tradition continued to be a powerful force in the world, and large populations look to the Marxian analysis as a guide for understanding the course of human history. Marx's stress on the importance of economics, his belief that people must make an effort to end the alienation in their lives, his plea that people must take action to end an oppressive system—all these have great appeal in an age where poverty and riches exist side by side and where technology seems to be its own justification. However, as Marx has been interpreted more and more rigidly in eastern European states, the subtlety of his analysis has often been lost in the justifications of policy by authoritarian communist regimes.

Prophecies about the future continue to be popular in an age in which people wonder about the direction of life. An "apocalyptic" trend in historical analysis has appeared in some quarters in the West since the Second World War. Some writers feel that the West is on the threshold of "a great event" which will launch humanity into a new era. Others predict that human beings will permanently end their history. There have been a number of suggestions that a nuclear catastrophe will destroy culture and civilization as we know it and introduce a new dark age. Writers such as Walter Miller in *A Canticle for Leibowitz* have speculated that human beings might be doomed to repeat their history indefinitely until a mutation occurs leading to a new species. Works of science-fiction, including Arthur C. Clarke's *Childhood's End* and the film *2001*, have asked about the future of the human species in a universe which is seen as interstellar and which might be guided by some form of life unknown to us. Human beings are seen by Clarke as possibly becoming other creatures with very different natures and hence life on earth as we have known it would end.

The apocalyptic trend is also related to those who wonder whether our technology has mastered our lives rather than the reverse. This trend has resulted in reflections on whether human beings will soon destroy their environment, so that within a short period of time, they will be unable to live on the planet in any great numbers.

Speculations about the extent of human freedom remain near the center of reflections about the past and future of humanity. Some writers are convinced that people in the modern world have proven that they are incapable of dealing with freedom, for the burden of making choices is too difficult to bear. Totalitarian systems, taking a rigid and deterministic view of history, offer to relieve people of the uncomfortable burden of making their own destiny. To accept this view of historical inevitability is to look upon people as incapable of moulding themselves and their future. It suggests that people may even choose not to be free.

Some thinkers continue to emphasize that human freedom, honest inquiry, and the making of rational choices are central to the Western tradition, and that this legacy can and must be preserved. Camus has said:

It is not true that culture can be, even temporarily, suspended in order to make way for a new culture. Man's unbroken testimony as to his suffering and his nobility cannot be suspended; the act of breathing cannot be suspended. There is no culture without legacy and we cannot and must not reject anything of ours, the legacy of the West.[15]

According to this outlook everyone makes one's own history, and it is up to us to do with it as we wish. In his *Gulag Archipelago*, Aleksandr Solzhenitsyn challenged the right of the state to manipulate the past for its own ends by ignoring or changing the truth. There is no possibility of a reasonable future, implied Solzhenitsyn, without having first faced the truth about the past. Solzhenitsyn quoted a Russian proverb which has two parts. "Don't dig up the past! Dwell on the past and you'll lose an eye" says the first part. But the proverb continues: "Forget the past and you'll lose both eyes."[16]

ANALYSIS AND DISCUSSION

1. Writers such as Aldous Huxley in *Brave New World* and George Orwell in *1984* envisioned a future world in which science and technology had produced frightening and repressive totalitarian states.
a) What evidence is there in modern society to indicate we are moving towards the kind of world they envisioned?
b) What evidence is there in our society to indicate that science and technology are improving rather than degrading the contemporary world?

2. "The real danger in the post-industrial world is that individuals become mere functions of the technology which is supposed to serve them." Analyse this statement and comment on the role of the individual in the modern world.

3. Camus wrote that a person who was aware of the "benign indifference of the universe" was able to act on the basis of free choice. In what ways would such existential sentiments challenge the social and political institutions of Western society?

4. Assess the impact of existentialist thought upon such Jewish and Christian theologians as Paul Tillich, Dietrich Bonhoeffer, and Martin Buber.

5. Select one of the paintings in the chapter. Discuss the comments made by its artist in relation to the work.

6. Evaluate and compare the following two views of the impact of film upon the mass culture of the twentieth century:
"Film is the one truly great art form of the twentieth century."
"Film is passive garbage. It hides behind illusion, glorifies violence and sacrifices meaning for popularity. The only thing worse is television!"

SYNTHESIS AND EVALUATION   CHAPTERS 15–17

1. The United States and the U.S.S.R. emerged from the Second World War as "super-powers" and have dominated world affairs since 1945. Compare the history of these two nations since 1945 under the following headings: (i) growth and development, (ii) problems, (iii) strengths and weaknesses.

2. One of the major developments of the post-Second World War period has been the emergence of the "Third World." What is the "Third World" and what significance does it have in contemporary society?

3. The establishment of the United Nations was a continuation of the search for collective security begun with the League of Nations.
a) In what respects is the United Nations an improvement over the League?
b) To what extent does the United Nations share the weaknesses of the League?

4. While Britain and France have been greatly overshadowed by the super-powers since 1945, their cultures can still be described as "vibrant" and "vital." What improvements in their societies did these two nations bring about after 1945? In what ways and to what extent do they still exert an important influence on the world?

5. "In many ways Berlin is a microcosm for the entire Cold War in Europe." Evaluate the importance of Berlin as a symbol of the differences between East and West.

6. The process of decolonization has often involved the "liberation" of people from Western values. Examine the nature of this process as illustrated in such countries as Vietnam, China, Iran, or South Africa.

7. "The greatest single threat to Western society in the post-war world is not the nuclear peril but rather the terrorist threat. To the humanist and rational citizen of the democracies

the ideas of irrational attack and political mar-
tyrdom are incomprehensible.'' Study the
growth of terrorism as a political force in the
modern world and assess its effectiveness.
8. ''Escapism in the early years of the twentieth century meant retreat into a 'golden past'.
In the post-war world fearful citizens have
looked to a utopian future. Nowhere in modern society is this faith in the eventual supremacy of science and reason more evident
than in the widespread popularity of science
fiction.'' Assess science fiction writing in terms
of the basic western faith in science and technology existing since the Scientific Revolution.
9. Re-read Solzhenitsyn's quote which closes
the book. After studying the history of the
past three hundred years, which version of
the proverb do you prefer?

Select Bibliography

(**Note:** *All titles are paperback books to facilitate acquisition for a classroom library.*)

Chapter 1

ASHLEY, MAURICE. *Louis XIV and the Greatness of France*. Free Press.

BUTTERFIELD, HERBERT. *The Origins of Modern Science*. Free Press.

GOUBERT, P. *Louis XIV and Twenty Million Frenchmen*. Random House.

HALL, A.R. *The Scientific Revolution, 1500–1800*. Beacon Press.

HAZARD, PAUL. *The European Mind: The Critical Years, 1680–1715*. Peter Smith.

KUHN, THOMAS S. *The Structure of Scientific Revolutions*. University of Chicago Press.

LEWIS, W.H. *The Splendid Century*. Morrow.

NUSSBAUM, F.L. *The Triumph of Science and Reason, 1660–1685*. Harper and Row.

RANUM, OREST. *Paris in the Age of Absolutism*. Indiana University Press.

Chapter 2

BECKER, CARL. *The Heavenly City of the Eighteenth-Century Philosophers*. Yale University Press.

GAGLARDO, J.G. *Enlightened Despotism*. AHM Publishers.

GAY, PETER. *The Enlightenment: An Interpretation*. Knopf.

GERSHOY, LEO. *From Despotism to Revolution, 1763–1789*. Harper and Row.

HAMPSON, NORMAN. *The Enlightenment*. Penguin.

KRIEGER, LEONARD. *Kings and Philosophers, 1689–1789*. Norton.

PALMER, R.R. *The Age of the Democratic Revolution, Volume I*. Princeton University Press.

RITTER, GERHARD. *Frederick the Great: A Historical Profile*. University of California Press.

Chapter 3

BRINTON, CRANE. *A Decade of Revolution, 1789–1799*. Harper Torchbooks.

CHURCH, WILLIAM F., ed. *The Influence of the Enlightenment on the French Revolution*. D.C. Heath.

COBBAN, ALFRED. *The Social Interpretation of the French Revolution*. Cambridge University Press.

GERSHOY, LEO. *The Era of the French Revolution, 1789–1799*. Anvil Books.

GOODWIN, ALBERT. *The French Revolution*. Harper and Row.

HAMPSON, NORMAN. *A Social History of the French Revolution*. University of Toronto Press.

LEFEBVRE, GEORGES. *The Coming of the French Revolution*. Vintage Books.

PALMER, R.R. *The Age of the Democratic Revolution, Volume II*. Princeton University Press.

THOMPSON, J.M. *The French Revolution*. Oxford University Press.

Chapter 4

BRUUN, GEOFFREY. *Europe and the French Imperium, 1799–1814*. Harper and Row.

CONNELLY, OWEN. *The Epoch of Napoleon: France and Europe*. Krieger.

HEROLD, J. CHRISTOPHER, ed. and trans. *The Mind of Napoleon*. Columbia University Press.

HOLTMAN, ROBERT B. *The Napoleonic Revolution*. J.B. Lippincott.

KISSINGER, HENRY. *A World Restored: Metternich, Castleraegh, and the Problem of Peace, 1812–1822*. Houghton-Mifflin.

MARKHAM, FELIX M.H. *Napoleon and the Awakening of Europe*. Macmillan.

NICOLSON, HAROLD. *Congress of Vienna*. Harcourt Brace Jovanovich.

Chapter 5

ASHTON, THOMAS S. *The Industrial Revolution, 1760–1830*. Oxford University Press.

HALSTED, JOHN B., ed. *Romanticism*. Harper and Row.

HENDERSON, W.O. *The Industrialization of Europe, 1780–1914*. Harcourt Brace Jovanovich.

HOBSBAWM, ERIC. *Industry and Empire: 1750 to the Present Day*. Pantheon.

KOHN, HANS. *Absolutism and Democracy, 1814–1852*. Anvil Books.

LANDES, DAVID S. *The Unbound Prometheus*. Cambridge University Press.

LICHTHEIM, GEORGE. *Origins of Socialism*. Weidenfeld & Nicolson.

0

STEARNS, PETER N. *European Society in Upheaval: Social History Since 1750.* Macmillan.

TALMON, J.L. *Romanticism and Revolt: Europe, 1815–1848.* Harcourt Brace Jovanovich.

TAYLOR, PHILIP A., ed. *The Industrial Revolution in Britain: Triumph or Disaster.* D.C. Heath.

Chapter 6

(**Note:** *Most of these also apply to Chapter 5.*)

ARTZ, FREDERICK B. *Reaction and Revolution, 1814–1832.* Harper and Row.

BREUNIG, C. *The Age of Revolution and Reaction, 1789–1850.* Newton.

DROZ, JACQUES. *Europe Between Revolutions, 1815–1848.* Harper and Row.

HOBSBAWM, ERIC J. *The Age of Revolution, 1789–1848.* New American Library.

KOHN, HANS. *Nationalism: Its Meaning and History.* Anvil Books.

LANGER, W.L. *Political and Social Upheaval, 1832–1852.* Harper and Row.

SCHAPIRO, J. SALWYN. *Liberalism: Its Meaning and History.* Anvil Books.

SCHWARZ, HENRY F., ed. *Metternich: The Coachman of Europe, Statesman or Evil Genius?* D.C. Heath.

VIERECK, PETER. *Conservatism.* Anvil Books.

Chapter 7

BRUUN, GEOFFREY. *Revolution and Reaction, 1848–1852.* Anvil Books.

BURN, W.L. *The Age of Equipoise.* Norton.

DUVEAU, GEORGES. *Eighteen Forty-Eight: The Making of a Revolution.* Random House.

EYCK, ERICH. *Bismarck and the German Empire.* Norton.

FASEL, GEORGE. *Europe in Upheaval: The Revolutions of 1848.* Rand McNally.

HAMEROW, THEODORE S., ed. *Otto von Bismarck: A Historical Assessment.* D.C. Heath.

———. *Restoration, Revolution, Reaction.* Princeton University Press.

PASSANT, ERNEST J. *A Short History of Germany, 1815–1945.* Cambridge University Press.

PFLANZE, OTTO. *Bismarck and the Development of Germany, 1815–1871.* Princeton University Press.

RICH, NORMAN. *The Age of Nationalism and Reform, 1850–1890.* Norton.

ROBERTSON, PRISCILLA. *The Revolutions of 1848: A Social History.* Princeton University Press.

SALVADORI, MASSIMO. *Cavour and the Unification of Italy.* Anvil Books.

STEARNS, PETER N. *1848: The Tide of Revolution in Europe.* Norton.

ZELDIN, THEODORE. *The Political System of Napoleon III.* Norton.

Chapter 8

BERLIN, ISAIAH. *Karl Marx: His Life and Environment.* Oxford University Press.

BRIGGS, ASA. *Victorian Cities.* Penguin Books.

HALE, ORON J. *The Great Illusion, 1900–1914.* Harper and Row.

HAYES, CARLETON J.H. *A Generation of Materialism, 1870–1900.* Harper and Row.

HOOK, SIDNEY. *Marx and the Marxists: The Ambiguous Legacy.* Anvil Books.

KOHN, HANS. *The Hapsburg Empire, 1804–1918.* Anvil Books.

LASKI, HAROLD J. *The Rise of European Liberalism: An Essay in Interpretation.* Humanities Press.

ROSENBERG, ARTHUR. *Imperial Germany: The Birth of the German Republic, 1871–1918.* Oxford University Press.

SCHORSKE, CARL E. *German Social Democracy, 1905–1917.* Russell.

SEDGWICK, A. *The Third French Republic, 1870–1914.* T.Y. Crowell.

THOMSON, DAVID. *Democracy in France Since 1870.* Oxford University Press.

TUCKER, ROBERT C. *The Marxian Revolutionary Idea.* Norton.

Chapter 9

BAUMER, FRANKLIN L. *Modern European Thought.* Macmillan.

CLARK, RONALD W. *Einstein: The Life and Times.* Avon Books.

HIMMELFARB, GERTRUDE. *Darwin and the Darwinian Revolution.* Norton.

HUGHES, H. STUART. *Consciousness and Society: The Reorientation of European Social Thought, 1890–1930.* Random.

IRVINE, WILLIAM. *Apes, Angels, and Victorians: The Story of Darwin, Huxley, and Evolution.* McGraw-Hill.

KOHN, HANS. *Nationalism and Realism, 1852–1879.* Anvil Books.

ROAZEN, PAUL. *Freud and His Followers.* New American Library.

STROMBERG, ROLAND N. *European Intellectual History Since 1789*. Appleton.

Chapter 10

BETTS, RAYMOND F. *Europe Overseas: Phases of Imperialism*. Basic Books.

FALLS, CYRIL. *The Great War: 1914–1918*. Putnam.

FISCHER, FRITZ. *Germany's Aims in the First World War*. Norton.

FUSSELL, PAUL. *The Great War and Modern Memory*. Oxford University Press.

GOLLWITZER, HEINZ. *Europe in the Age of Imperialism*. Thames & Hudson.

HOBSON, J.A. *Imperialism: A Study*. University of Michigan Press.

LAFORE, LAWRENCE D. *The Long Fuse: An Interpretation of the Origins of World War One*. Harper and Row.

LEDERER, IVO J., ed. *The Versailles Settlement: Was It Foredoomed to Failure?* D.C. Heath.

LEE, DWIGHT E. *The Outbreak of the First World War: Who or What Was Responsible?* D.C. Heath.

THORNTON, A.P. *Imperialism in the Twentieth Century*. University of Minnesota Press.

TUCHMAN, BARBARA. *The Guns of August*. Bantam.

TURNER, L.C.F. *Origins of the First World War*. Norton.

Chapter 11

CARR, EDWARD H. *The Bolshevik Revolution: 1917–1923*. 3 vols. Penguin Books.

CH'EN, JEROME. *Mao and the Chinese Revolution*. Oxford University Press.

CURTISS, JOHN SHELTON. *The Russian Revolutions of 1917*. Anvil Books.

HILL, CHRISTOPHER. *Lenin and the Russian Revolution*. Penguin.

KENNAN, GEORGE F. *Russia and the West under Lenin and Stalin*. New American Library.

RABINOWITCH, ALEXANDER. *The Bolsheviks Come to Power*. Norton.

SHUB, DAVID. *Lenin*. New American Library.

ULAM, ADAM B. *Expansion and Coexistence: Soviet Foreign Policy, 1917–1973*. Praeger.
_____ . *Bolsheviks*. Macmillan.

VON LAUE, THEODORE H. *Why Lenin? Why Stalin?* Lippincott.

WOLFE, BERTRAM D. *Three Who Made a Revolution*. Dell.

Chapter 12

ARENDT, HANNAH. *The Origins of Totalitarianism*. World Publishing.

BRACHER, KARL DIETRICH. *The German Dictatorship*. Praeger.

BULLOCK, ALAN. *Hitler: A Study in Tyranny*. Bantam Books.

CARSTEN, F.L. *The Rise of Fascism*. University of California Press.

CASSELS, ALAN. *Fascist Italy*. T.Y. Crowell.

EYCK, ERICH. *History of the Weimar Republic*. Harvard University Press.

HALPERIN, S. WILLIAM. *Mussolini and Italian Fascism*. Anvil Books.

NOLTE, ERNST. *The Three Faces of Fascism*. Holt, Rinehart and Winston.

SCHOENBAUM, DAVID. *Hitler's Social Revolution: Class and Status in Nazi Germany, 1933–1939*. Doubleday.

SHIRER, WILLIAM L. *The Rise and Fall of the Third Reich: A History of Nazi Germany*. Simon and Shuster.

WEBER, EUGEN. *Varieties of Fascism*. Anvil Books.

WISKEMANN, ELIZABETH. *Fascism in Italy*. St. Martin.

Chapter 13

BURNS, JAMES M. *Roosevelt: The Lion and the Fox*. Harcourt, Brace, Jovanovich.

GALBRAITH, JOHN K. *The Great Crash, 1929*. Sentry.

GRAVES, ROBERT, and HODGE, ALAN. *Long Weekend: A Social History of Great Britain, 1918–1939*. Norton.

GREENE, NATHANAEL. *From Versailles to Vichy: The Third Republic, 1919–1940*. AHM Publishing Corp.

MITCHELL, B. *Depression Decade: From New Era through New Deal*. Harper and Row.

SHANNON, DAVID A. *The Great Depression*. Spectrum.

TAYLOR, A.J.P. *English History, 1914–1945*. Oxford University Press.

THOMSON, DAVID. *England in the Twentieth Century*. Penguin Books.

Chapter 14

CARR, EDWARD H. *Twenty Years' Crisis, 1919–1939*. Harper and Row.

DAVIDOWICZ, LUCY S. *The War Against the Jews, 1933–1945*. Bantam.

DIVINE, ROBERT A. *Roosevelt and World War II*. Penguin.

HENIG, RUTH B. *The League of Nations*. Barnes & Noble.

HILBERG, R. *The Destruction of the European Jews*. Harper and Row.

JACKSON, GABRIEL. *The Spanish Republic and the Civil War*. Princeton.

PAXTON, ROBERT O. *Vichy France: Old Guard & New Order, 1940–44*. Norton.

SONTAG, RAYMOND J. *A Broken World, 1919–1939*. Harper and Row.

TAYLOR, A.J.P. *The Origins of the Second World War*. Atheneum.

WISKEMANN, ELIZABETH. *Europe of the Dictators*. Harper and Row.

WRIGHT, GORDON. *The Ordeal of Total War, 1939–1945*. Harper & Row.

Chapter 15

ARENDT, HANNAH. *The Human Condition*. University of Chicago Press.

DEUTSCHER, ISAAC. *Stalin: A Political Biography*. Oxford University Press.

GRAEBNER, NORMAN A., ed. *The Cold War*. D.C. Heath.

LACQUER, WALTER. *Europe Since Hitler*. Penguin.

LUKACS, J. *A New History of the Cold War*. Doubleday.

NOVE, ALEC. *The Soviet Economic System*. Allen Unwin.

REES, DAVID. *The Age of Containment: The Cold War, 1945–65*. Macmillan.

SMITH, H. *The Russians*. Ballantine.

WILLIS, F. ROY. *Europe in the Global Age: 1939 to the Present*. Harper and Row.

Chapter 16

BAIROCH, PAUL. *The Economic Development of the Third World Since 1900*. University of California Press.

BELL, DANIEL. *The End of Ideology*. Free Press.

BLACK, CYRIL E. *The Dynamics of Modernization*. Harper and Row.

EMERSON, R. *From Empire to Nation: The Rise to Self-Assertion of Asian and African Peoples*. Harvard University Press.

FITZGERALD, C.P. *The Birth of Communist China*. Penguin.

HERRING, GEORGE C. *America's Longest War: The United States and Vietnam*. Wiley.

OLIVER, ROLAND, and FAGE, J.D., eds. *A Short History of Africa*. Penguin Books.

REISCHAUER, E.O. *Japan: The Story of a Nation*. Knopf.

SCHRAM, STUART. *Mao Tse-tung*. Penguin Books.

SHONFELD, A. *Modern Capitalism*. Oxford University Press.

Chapter 17

GAMOW, GEORGE. *Thirty Years That Shook Physics*. Doubleday.

STROMBERG, ROLAND N. *After Everything: Western Intellectual History Since 1945*. St. Martin.

GENERAL

BRINTON, CRANE. *The Anatomy of Revolution*. Vintage Books.

BRODIE, BERNARD, and BRODIE, FAWN M. *From Crossbow to H-Bomb*. Indiana University Press.

HOOK, SIDNEY. *The Hero in History*. Beacon Press.

LEIDEN, CARL, and SCHMITT, KARL. *The Politics of Violence: Revolution in the Modern World*. Spectrum.

McNEILL, WILLIAM H. *The Rise of the West: A History of the Human Community*. Mentor.

SNYDER, LOUIS LEO. *Fifty Major Documents of the Nineteenth Century*. Anvil Books.

_____ . *Fifty Major Documents of the Twentieth Century*. Anvil Books.

TRUEMAN, JOHN H. *The Anatomy of History*. Dent.

WESTERN, JOHN RANDLE. *The End of European Primacy, 1871–1945*. Blandford Press.

Sources of Quotations

CHAPTER 1

1. Stillman Drake, ed. and trans., *Discoveries and Opinions of Galileo* (Garden City, New York: Doubleday and Company, 1957), pp. 174, 182, 183.
2. John Donne, *Complete Poetry and Selected Prose* (London: The Nonesuch Library, 1955), p. 202.
3. Isaac Newton, *The Mathematical Principles of Natural Philosophy*, trans. Andrew Motte (London: Dawsons of Pall Mall, 1968), Volume II, pp. 388–390.
4. Alexander Pope, *Selected Works*, ed. Louis Kronenberger (New York: Random House, Inc.), p. 330.
5. Francis Bacon, from *Novum Organum*, in Charles Hirschfeld, ed., *Classics of Western Thought*, Volume III (New York: Harcourt Brace and World, Inc., 1964), p. 9.
6. Pope, *op. cit.*, pp. 107, 127.
7. Saint-Simon, quoted in Orest and Patricia Ranum, eds., *The Century of Louis XIV* (New York: Harper and Row, 1972), p. 87.

CHAPTER 2

1. Immanuel Kant, "What is Enlightenment?," in Carl J. Friedrich, *The Philosophy of Kant* (New York: The Modern Library, 1949), p. 138.
2. Thomas Hobbes, *Leviathan* (New York: Bobbs-Merrill, 1958), p. 107.
3. John Locke, *Two Treatises of Government* (London: George Routledge and Sons, n.d.), pp. 193–4.
4. Jean-Jacques Rousseau, *The Social Contract* and *Discourse on the Origin of Inequality*, ed. Lester G. Crocker (New York: Washington Square Press, 1967), pp. 3, 200.
5. Rousseau, *Ibid.*, p. 22.
6. Pierre Bayle, *Historical and Critical Dictionary* (New York: Bobbs-Merrill, 1965), p. 53.
7. John Hope Mason, *The Irresistible Diderot* (London: Quartet Books, 1982), p. 83.
8. Denis Diderot, et al, *Encyclopedia*, trans. Nelly S. Hoyt and Thomas Cassirer (Indianapolis: Bobbs-Merrill, 1965), p. 284.
9. Voltaire, *Candide and Other Writings*, ed. Haskell M. Block (New York: The Modern Library, 1956), p. 328.

10. *Ibid*, pp. 222, 312.
11. A.R.J. Turgot, "A Philosophical Review of the Successive Advances of the Human Mind," in Ronald L. Meek, ed., *Turgot on Progress, Sociology and Economics* (Cambridge: Cambridge University Press), p. 41.
12. Voltaire, *op. cit.*, p. 202.
13. *Ibid.*, p. 357.
14. Jean-Jacques Rousseau, *Emile*, ed. and trans. by William Boyd (New York: Teachers College Press, Columbia University, 1956), p. 11.
15. Jonathan Swift, *Gulliver's Travels*, ed. Robert A. Greenberg (New York: W.W. Norton and Company, Inc., 1970), p. 264.
16. *Ibid.*, pp. 107, 110.
17. William Butler Yeats, *The Collected Poems of W.B. Yeats* (New York: The Macmillan Company, 1959), p. 241.
18. George L. Mosse, et al, eds., *Europe in Review* (Chicago: Rand McNally and Company, 1957), p. 111.
19. *Ibid.*, pp. 111–12.
20. Adam Smith, *An Inquiry into the Nature and Causes of the Wealth of Nations* (London: J.M. Dent and Sons Ltd., 1910), Volume 1, p. 431.
21. *Ibid.*, Volume II, p. 155.
22. *Ibid.*, Volume II, p. 180.
23. Thomas Paine, *Common Sense* (Garden City, New York: Anchor Books, 1973), p. 41.
24. Bernard Bailyn, et al, *The Great Republic*, 3rd ed. (Lexington, Massachusetts: D.C. Heath and Company, 1985), appendix, pp. v–vi.
25. *Ibid.*, appendix, pp. xi, xvi.
26. Johann Joachim Winkelmann, in Lorenz Eitner, *Neoclassicism and Romanticism, 1750–1850* (Englewood Cliffs, New Jersey: Prentice-Hall, Inc., 1970), Volume I, p. 6.
27. Edward Gibbon, *Autobiography* (London: Oxford University Press, 1907), p. 180.
28. Edward Gibbon, *The Decline and Fall of the Roman Empire* (New York: The Modern Library, n.d.), Volume II, pp. 90, 439.
29. Gibbon, *Autobiography, op. cit.*, p. 177.
30. Gibbon, *The Decline and Fall of the Roman Empire, op. cit.*, Volume II, pp. 442–3.
31. *Ibid.*, Volume II, p. 444.

CHAPTER 3

1. Voltaire, as quoted in Thomas C. Mendenhall et al., *The Quest for a Principle of*

Authority in Europe, 1715 to the Present (New York: Holt, Rinehart & Winston, Inc., 1960), pp. 17-18.

2. Antoine-Nicolas de Condorcet, *Sketch for a Historical Picture of the Progress of the Human Mind*, trans. June Barraclough (London: Weidenfeld and Nicolson, 1955), pp. 163, 168.

3. *Ibid.*, pp. 201-2.

4. E. L. Higgins, *The French Revolution* (Cambridge, Mass.: Houghton Mifflin Company, 1938), p. 74.

5. Philip Dawson, ed., *The French Revolution* (Englewood Cliffs, N.J.: Prentice-Hall, Inc., 1967), p. 31.

6. *Introduction to Contemporary Civilization in the West: A Source Book*, vol. 1 (Columbia University Press, 1946), pp. 1077, 1080, 1081.

7. Higgins, *French Revolution*, p. 100.

8. Georges Lefebvre, *The Coming of the French Revolution*, trans. R. R. Palmer (Princeton: Princeton University Press, 1947), pp. 221-3.

9. Thomas Paine, *The Rights of Man* (London: J. M. Dent and Sons, n.d.), p. 24.

10. F. M. Anderson, *The Constitution and Other Select Documents Illustrative of the History of France, 1789-1901* (Minneapolis: H. W. Wilson Company, 1904), p. 184.

11. George Rudé, ed., *Robespierre* (Englewood Cliffs, N. J.: Prentice-Hall, Inc., 1967), p. 61.

CHAPTER 4

1. R. M. Johnston, *The Corsican: A Diary of Napoleon's Life in His Own Words* (New York: Houghton Mifflin, 1910), p. 74.

2. *Ibid.*, p. 166.

3. *With Napoleon in Russia: The Memoirs of General de Caulaincourt*, abridged, edited, and translated by George Libaire (New York: William Morrow and Co., Inc., 1935), pp. 223-4, 259.

4. Johnston, *Corsican*, pp. 475, 499.

CHAPTER 5

1. *The Works of Jeremy Bentham*, vol. 1, ed. J. Bowring, reproduced from the Bowring Edition of 1838-43 (New York: Russell & Russell, Inc., 1962), p. 33.

2. "The Sadler Report", as quoted in John L. Beatty and Oliver A. Johnson, *Heritage of Western Civilization*, 2nd ed., vol. 2 (Englewood Cliffs, N.J.: Prentice-Hall, Inc., 1966), pp. 257-8.

3. Arnold Toynbee, *Lectures on the Industrial Revolution in England* (London: Rivingtons 1884), p. 93.

4. T. S. Ashton, "The Standard of Life of the Workers in England, 1790-1830", *Journal of Economic History* 9 (1949): 36-7.

5. *Henri Comte de Saint-Simon (1760-1825): Selected Writings*, ed and trans. F. M. H. Markham (Oxford: Blackwell & Mott, Ltd., 1952), pp. 74-5.

6. *Ibid.*, p. 78.

7. Julia Franklin, trans., *Selections from the Works of Fourier* (London: Swan Sonnenschein & Co., Ltd., 1901), p. 164.

8. Voltaire, *Candide and Other Writings*, ed. Haskell M. Block (New York: The Modern Library, 1956), p. 346.

9. Ernest Bernbaum, ed., *Anthology of Romanticism*, 3rd ed. (New York: Ronald Press Company, 1948), p. 189.

10. Author's translation from René de Chateaubriand, *Génie du Christianisme*, vol. 1 (Paris: Garnier-Flammarion, 1966), p. 57.

CHAPTER 6

1. G. de Bertier de Sauvigny, *Metternich and His Times*, trans. Peter Ryke (London: Darton, Longman and Todd, 1962), p. 87.

2. *The Letters of Queen Victoria*, vol. 1, eds. A. C. Benson and Viscount Esher (London: John Murray, 1907), p. 451.

3. Sir Charles K. Webster, *The Foreign Policy of Castlereagh, 1815-1822* (London: G. Bell and Sons, 1963), p. 521.

4. G. de Bertier de Sauvigny, *Metternich*, p. 19.

5. *Memoirs of Prince Metternich, 1815-1829*, vol. 3, ed. Prince Richard Metternich, trans. Mrs. Alexander Napier (London: Richard Bentley & Son, 1881), pp. 455, 462, 465-6, and 469.

6. *Annual Register, 1819* (London: Baldwin, Cradock, and Joy, 1820), pp. 159, 162.

7. *The Works of Jeremy Bentham*, vol. 9, ed. J. Bowring, reproduced from the Bowring

Edition of 1838–43. (New York: Russell & Russell, Inc., 1962), p. 5.

8. David Thomson, *England in the Nineteenth Century* (Harmondsworth, Middlesex: Penguin Books, 1950), p. 87.

9. *Annual Register, 1830* (London: Baldwin and Cradock, 1831), p. 366.

10. *Ibid.*, 1831, pp. 371, 373.

11. Herbert H. Rowen, ed., *From Absolutism to Revolution, 1648–1848* (New York: Collier-Macmillan, 1963), p. 266.

CHAPTER 7

1. George Woodcock, ed., *A Hundred Years of Revolution, 1848 and After* (London: Porcupine Press, 1948), pp. 161-2.

2. *Ibid.*, pp. 169-70.

3. Edward Hertslet, *The Map of Europe by Treaty, showing the various political and territorial changes which have taken place since the June Peace of 1814*, vol. 2 (London: Butterworths, 1875), p. 1255.

4. E. N. Anderson et al., eds., *Europe in the Nineteenth Century*, vol. 1 (New York: Bobbs-Merrill, 1961), pp. 122-3.

5. *Annual Register, 1860* (London: J. & F. H. Rivington, 1861), pp. 281-2.

6. T. C. Mendenhall et al., eds., *The Quest for a Principle of Authority in Europe, 1715–Present: Select Problems in Historical Interpretation* (New York: Henry Holt & Co., 1948), p. 220.

7. C. G. Robertson, *Bismarck* (London: Constable & Co., 1919), pp. 496-7.

8. *Ibid.*, p. 496.

9. Lord Durham, *The Report of the Earl of Durham, Her Majesty's High Commissioner and Governor General of British North America* (London: Methuen & Co. Ltd., 1902), p. 8.

10. Ryūsaku Tsunoda, William Theodore de Bary, and Donald Keene, comps. *Sources of the Japanese Tradition* (New York: Columbia University Press, 1958), p. 644.

CHAPTER 8

1. John M. Robson, ed., *John Stuart Mill: A Selection of His Works* (New York: The Odyssey Press, 1966), pp. 13-14.

2. *Ibid.*, p. 145.

3. *Ibid.*, p. 147.

4. Karl Marx and Friedrich Engels, *Selected Works*, vol. 1 (Moscow: Foreign Languages Publishing House, 1962), p. 34.

5. *Ibid.*, pp. 34-5.

6. *Ibid.*, p. 54.

7. *Ibid.*, p. 52.

8. *Ibid.*, p. 65.

9. *Ibid.*, p. 246.

10. Karl Marx and Friedrich Engels, *Selected Works*, vol. 2 (Moscow: Foreign Languages Publishing House, 1962), p. 153.

11. Eduard Bernstein, *Evolutionary Socialism: A Criticism and Affirmation*, trans. Edith C. Harvey (London: Independent Labour Party, 1909), pp. x, xi-xii.

12. Nicholas Halasz, *Captain Dreyfus* (New York: Simon and Schuster, 1955), pp. 134-5.

13. Paul Sabatier. *Disestablishment in France*, trans. Robert Dell (London: T. Fisher Unwin, 1906), pp. 139, 140.

14. G. A. Kertesz, *Documents in the Political History of the European Continent, 1815–1939* (Oxford: Clarendon Press, 1968), p. 266.

15. Alfred Rambaud, *History of Russia from the Earliest Times to 1882*, vol. 3, trans. L. B. Lang (London: Sampson, Low, Marston, Searle, and Rivington, n.d.), p. 221.

CHAPTER 9

1. Charles Darwin, *On the Origin of Species by Means of Natural Selection, or The Preservation of Favoured Races in the Struggle for Life* (London: Cassell and Company, Ltd., 1909), p. 413.

2. Herbert Spencer, *Social Statics* (London: Williams and Norgate, 1868), p. 94.

3. Excerpt from "The White Man's Burden" taken from Rudyard Kipling, *The Five Nations* (London: Methuen & Co. Ltd., 1948), p. 79.

4. Heinrich von Treitschke, *Politics*, trans. Blanche Dugdale (New York: The Macmillan Company, 1916), pp. 24, 33-4, 65.

5. Henry Bettenson, ed., *Documents of the Christian Church* (London: Oxford University Press, 1963), pp. 383-4.

6. Honoré de Balzac, *Old Goriot*, trans. Marion Ayton Crawford (Harmondsworth, Middlesex: Penguin Books, 1968), p. 28.

7. Honoré de Balzac, *Eugénie Grandet*, trans. Henry Reed (New York: New American Library, 1964), pp. 180-1.
8. Eugen Weber, ed., *Paths to the Present: Aspects of European Thought from Romanticism to Existentialism* (New York: Dodd, Mead and Company, Inc., 1960), p. 165.
9. *Ibid.*, p. 167.
10. Max Weber, *The Methodology of the Social Sciences*, trans. and eds. E.W. Shils and H.A. Finch (New York: The Free Press, 1949), p. 57.
11. Angel Flores, ed., *An Anthology of French Poetry from Nerval to Valéry in English Translation with French Originals*, New Revised Edition (Garden City, N.Y.: Doubleday and Company, 1958), pp. 21-2.
12. Friedrich Nietzsche, *Beyond Good and Evil*, trans. Marianne Cowan (Chicago: Henry Regnery Company, 1955), p. 4.
13. Werner Heisenberg et al, *On Modern Physics* (New York: C.N. Potter, 1961), p. 12.

CHAPTER 10
1. *The New York World*, June 29, 1924.
2. *British and Foreign State Papers*, vol. 121, part I (1925), pp. 1014-15, as quoted in *Documents in the Political History of the European Continent, 1815-1939*, selected and ed. G. A. Kertesz (Oxford: Clarendon Press, 1968), p. 209.
3. A. F. Pribram, *The Secret Treaties of Austria-Hungary, 1879-1914*, ed. Archibald Cary Coolidge, trans. Denys P. Myers and J. G. D'Arcy Paul (Cambridge: Harvard University Press, 1920), vol. 1, p. 37.
4. Henri Barbusse, *Under Fire: The Story of a Squad*, trans. Fitzwater Wray (New York: E. P. Dutton & Co., 1917), pp. 258, 259.
5. *Congressional Record* 56 (1918): 680-1.
6. *Ibid.*
7. *The Treaty of Peace between the Allied and Associated Powers and Germany* (Ottawa: J. de Labroquerie Taché, Printer to the King's Most Excellent Majesty, 1919), p. 82.
8. Paul Valéry, *The Outlook for Intelligence*, trans. Denise Folliot and Jackson Mathews (New York: Harper & Row, Publishers, 1962), p. 26.

9. Paul Valéry, *History and Politics*, trans. Denise Folliot and Jackson Mathews, vol. 10 of *The Complete Works of Paul Valéry*, Bollingen Series 45 (Princeton, N.J.: Princeton University Press, 1962), pp. 307-8.
10. "The Second Coming" from *The Collected Poems of W. B. Yeats* (London: The Macmillan Company, 1933).
11. Excerpt from "Apologia Pro Poemate Meo" taken from *The Collected Poems of Wilfred Owen* (London: Chatto & Windus, 1963).
12. Ford M. Ford, *No More Parades* (New York: Albert & Charles Boni, 1925), p. 9.
13. "Grass" from Carl Sandburg, *Cornhuskers* (New York: Holt, Rinehart & Winston, 1918).

CHAPTER 11
1. Mikhail Bakunin, *The Political Philosophy of Bakunin: Scientific Anarchism*, ed. G. P. Maximoff (New York: The Free Press, 1953), pp. 268, 288.
2. A. J. Sack, *The Birth of the Russian Democracy* (New York: Russian Information Bureau, 1918), pp. 100-1.
3. F. A. Golder, ed., *Documents of Russian History, 1914-1917*, trans. E. Aronsberg (New York: The Century Press, 1927), pp. 627-8.
4. V. I. Lenin, *What Is To Be Done?* (New York: International Publishers, 1929), p. 99.
5. V. I. Lenin, *Selected Works in Two Volumes*, vol. 1, part 2 (Moscow: Foreign Languages Publishing House, 1952), p. 397.
6. *The Letters of the Tsar to the Tsaritsa, 1914-17*, trans. A. L. Hynes (London: John Lane, The Bodley Head Ltd., 1929), pp. 256-7.
7. V. I. Lenin, *Selected Works in Three Volumes*, vol. 2 (London: Lawrence and Wishart, n.d.), pp. 45-8.
8. Golder, *Documents of Russian History*, p. 358.
9. *Ibid.*, pp. 618-19.
10. Leon Trotsky, *Lenin* (New York: Minton, Balch and Company, 1925), p. 133.
11. V. I. Lenin, *Collected Works*, vol. 36 (Moscow: Progress Publishers, 1966), p. 595.
12. *Ibid.*, p. 596.

13. J. V. Stalin, *Works*, vol. 12 (Moscow: Foreign Languages Publishing House, 1955), pp. 172-3, 175.

14. *The Anti-Stalin Campaign and International Communism: A Selection of Documents* (New York: Columbia University Press, 1956), p. 25.

15. Evgeniia S. Ginsburg, *Into the Whirlwind*, trans. Paul Stevenson and Manya Harari (Harmondsworth, Middlesex: Penguin Books, 1968), p. 27.

16. *Ibid.*, p. 114.

17. *The Communist International, 1919–1943: Documents*, vol. 1, selected and ed. by Jane Degras (London: Oxford University Press, 1956), pp. 163-4.

18. Dr. Sun Yat Sen, *San Min Chu I: The Three Principles of the People*, trans. F. W. Price (Shanghai: China Committee, Institute of Pacific Relations, 1927), pp. 212-14.

19. Jerome Ch'ên, ed., *Mao* (Englewood Cliffs, N.J.: Prentice-Hall, Inc., 1969), p. 18.

20. Jerome Ch'ên, *Mao and the Chinese Revolution* (with Thirty-seven Poems by Mao Tse-tung translated from the Chinese by Michael Bullock and Jerome Ch'ên) (London: Oxford University Press, 1965), p. 334.

21. *Ibid.*, pp. 199-200.

CHAPTER 12

1. José Ortega y Gasset, *The Revolt of the Masses* (New York: W. W. Norton and Company, Inc., 1957), p. 51.

2. Count Carlo Sforza, *Contemporary Italy*, trans. Drake and Denise de Kay (New York: E. P. Dutton & Co., Inc., 1944), p. 295.

3. Benito Mussolini, *My Autobiography*, trans. Richard Washburn Child (New York: Charles Scribner's Sons, 1928), p. 177.

4. Benito Mussolini, *Fascism: Doctrine and Institutions* (New York: Howard Fertig, 1968), pp. 27-8.

5. Mussolini, *My Autobiography*, p. 204.

6. *Ibid.*, p. 206.

7. *British and Foreign State Papers*, vol. 130, part I (1929), pp. 791-814, as quoted in *Documents in the Political History of the European Continent, 1815–1939*, selected and ed. G. A. Kertesz (Oxford: Clarendon Press, 1968), p. 398.

8. Mussolini, *Fascism: Doctrine and Institutions*, p. 26.

9. W. E. Rappard et al, *Source Book on European Governments* (New York: D. Van Nostrand Company, 1937), pp. IV 9-IV 13.

10. *The Speeches of Adolf Hitler, April 1922 to August 1939*, vol. 1, ed. Norman H. Baynes (London: Oxford University Press, 1942), pp. 56-7.

11. *British and Foreign State Papers*, vol. 136 (1933), pp. 7-9, as quoted in *Documents in the Political History of the European Continent, 1815–1939*, selected and ed. by G. A. Kertesz (Oxford: Clarendon Press, 1968), p. 421.

12. *British and Foreign State Papers*, vol. 136 (1933), pp. 10-15, 22-3, as quoted in *Documents in the Political History of the European Continent, 1815–1939*, selected and ed. by G. A. Kertesz (Oxford: Clarendon Press, 1968), p. 423.

13. *Ibid.*

14. Rappard et al, *op. cit.*, p. IV 16.

15. Alan Bullock, *Hitler: A Study in Tyranny* (London: Odhams Press Limited, 1952), p. 282.

CHAPTER 13

1. C. L. Mowat, *The General Strike, 1926* (London: Edward Arnold Ltd., 1969), p. 50.

2. *Memoirs of the Unemployed*, ed. H. L. Beales and R. S. Lambert (London: Victor Gollancz Ltd., 1934), pp. 79-80.

3. From Franklin D. Roosevelt's Inaugural Address, March 4, 1933.

4. Alexander, Werth, *France in Ferment* (London: Jarrolds, 1934), p. 143.

5. G. Fraser and T. Natanson, *Léon Blum* (London: Gollancz, 1937), p. 310.

6. R. K. Webb, *Modern England* (New York: Dodd, Mead and Company, 1971), p. 529.

CHAPTER 14

1. *The Treaty of Peace between the Allied and Associated Powers and Germany* (Ottawa: J. de Labroquerie Taché, Printer to the King's Most Excellent Majesty, 1919), p. 11.

2. *League of Nations Treaty Series*, 54 (1926/27): 291-7, as quoted in *Documents in the Political History of the European Continent, 1815–1939*, selected and ed. by G. A. Kertesz (Oxford: Clarendon Press, 1968), p. 465.

3. *League of Nations Treaty Series*, 94 (1929): 59-64, as quoted in *Documents in the Political History of the European Continent, 1815–1939*, selected and ed. by G. A. Kertesz (Oxford: Clarendon Press, 1968), p. 469.

4. *Documents on International Affairs, 1935*, vol. 1, eds. John W. Wheeler-Bennett and Stephen Heald (London: Oxford University Press, 1936), pp. 60-1, 63-4.

5. *Ciano's Diplomatic Papers*, ed. Malcolm Muggeridge, trans. Stuart Hood (London: Odhams Press Ltd., 1948), p. 57.

6. Ivone Kirkpatrick, *Mussolini: Study of a Demagogue* (London: Odhams Books Ltd., 1964), p. 328.

7. Sir Keith Feiling, *The Life of Neville Chamberlain* (London: Macmillan & Co. Ltd., 1946), p. 375.

8. *The War Speeches of the Rt. Hon. Winston S. Churchill*, vol. 1, comp. Charles Eade (London: Cassell & Co. Ltd., 1951), p. 195.

9. *Ibid.*, pp. 206-7.

10. Louis L. Snyder, ed., *Fifty Major Documents of the Twentieth Century* (New York: D. Van Nostrand Company Inc., 1955), pp. 92-3.

11. Excerpt from letter of August 2, 1939, from Dr. Albert Einstein to President Roosevelt, now in the Franklin D. Roosevelt Library collection.

12. Bullock, *Hitler*, p. 642.

13. Snyder, *Fifty Major Documents*, p. 127.

14. Hannah Arendt, *The Origins of Totalitarianism*, 2nd ed. (New York: Meridian Books, 1958), p. 458.

CHAPTER 15

1. Arthur P. Mendel, ed., *The Twentieth Century, 1914–1964* (New York: The Free Press, 1965), p. 163

2. Alexander Baltzly and A. William Salomone, eds., *Readings in Twentieth-Century European History* (New York: Appleton-Century-Crofts, Inc., 1950), p. 608.

3. *Ibid.*, p. 609.

4. *Current History* 10, no. 56 (April 1946): 358-60.

5. *The New York Times*, June 6, 1947.

6. *The New York Times*, October 6, 1947.

7. Brezhnev, as quoted in H. Stuart Hughes, *Contemporary Europe: A History*, 4th ed.

(Englewood Cliffs, N.J.: Prentice-Hall, Inc., 1976), p. 556.

8. Kennedy, as quoted in Gwyn Prins, ed., *Defended to Death* (Harmondsworth, England: Penguin Books, Ltd., 1983), p. 123.

9. Trevor N. Dupuy and Gay M. Hammerman, *A Documentary History of Arms Control and Disarmament* (New York: R.R. Bowker Company, 1973), p. 525.

10. *Ibid.*, p. 561.

11. *Ibid.*, p. 604.

12. *The New York Times*, June 5, 1956.

13. Eugen Weber, ed., *Paths to the Present: Aspects of European Thought from Romanticism to Existentialism* (New York: Dodd, Mead and Company, Inc., 1960), pp. 395–6.

14. Adam Minchnik, ''Letter from the Gdansk Prison,'' *New York Review of Books*, Volume XXXII, Number 12 (18 July 1985), pp. 42, 48.

15. Martin Luther King, Jr., *Why We Can't Wait* (New York: Harper and Row, 1963), pp. 82–4 *passim*.

16. Simone de Beauvoir, *The Second Sex* (New York: Vintage Books, 1974), pp. 813, 814.

17. Betty Friedan, *The Feminine Mystique* (New York: W.W. Norton and Company, Inc., 1963), pp. 9, 378.

18. *Presidential Papers of the Presidents of the United States: Ronald Reagan, 1981* (Washington: United States Government Printing Office, 1982), p. 1.

19. René Lévesque, *Quotations from René Lévesque*, ed. Jean Cote and Marcel Chaput (Montreal: Editions Heritage, 1977), pp. 14–16.

CHAPTER 16

1. Frantz Fanon, *The Wretched of the Earth* (New York: Grove Press, 1963), pp. 43, 83, 102.

2. *A Documentary History of Chinese Communism*, eds. Conrad Brandt, Benjamin Schwartz, and John K. Fairbank (New York: Atheneum Publishers, 1966), pp. 457-8.

3. Rt. Hon. the Earl of Balfour, *Speeches on Zionism*, ed. Israel Cohen (London: Arrowsmith, 1928), pp. 19–20.

4. Itamar Rabinovich and Jehuda Reinharz, eds., *Israel in the Middle East* (New York: Oxford University Press), pp. 322–4.
5. *Ibid.*, p. 325.
6. The World Bank, *World Development Report 1983* (Oxford University Press, 1983), p. 39.

CHAPTER 17

1. *The New York Times*, October 12, 1969.
2. Bertrand Russell, *The Basic Writings of Bertrand Russell* (Herts, England: Allen & Unwin, 1961), pp. 726, 732.
3. Frank P. Ramsey, ''Philosophy,'' in A.J. Ayer, ed., *Logical Positivism* (New York: The Free Press, a Division of Macmillan, Inc., 1959), p. 321.
4. Rudolf Carnap, ''The Old and the New Logic,'' in A.J. Ayer, *op. cit.*, p. 133.
5. Jean-Paul Sartre, *Existentialism and Humanism*, trans. Philip Mairet (London: Methuen & Co. Ltd., 1948), pp. 28, 29.
6. Albert Camus, *The Outsider*, trans. Stuart Gilbert (Harmondsworth, Middlesex: Penguin Books, 1973), p. 120.
7. Sartre, *Existentialism*, p. 29.
8. Samuel Beckett, *Waiting for Godot* (New York: Grove Press, Inc., 1959), pp. 10–11.
9. Peter Weiss, *The Persecution and Assassination of Marat as performed by the Inmates of the Asylum of Charenton under the Direction of the Marquis de Sade* (London: Calder and Boyars, Ltd., 1965), p. 104.
10. Dietrich Bonhoeffer, *Letters and Papers from Prison*, 2nd ed., ed. Eberhard Bethge, trans. Reginald H. Fuller (London: SCM Press Ltd., 1956), pp. 180–1.
11. Elie Wiesel, *Night* (New York: Avon Books, 1960), p. 44.
12. Elie Wiesel, quoted in Ellen S. Fine, *Legacy of Night* (Albany: State University of New York Press, 1982), p. 28.
13. Gregory Baum, quoted in A. Roy Eckardt, with Alice L. Eckardt, *Long Night's Journey into Day* (Detroit: Wayne State University Press, 1982), p. 111.
14. Nikos Stagnos, ed., *Concepts of Modern Art*, 2nd ed. (New York: Wittenborn Art Books, Inc.), p. 114.
15. Albert Camus, *Resistance, Rebellion and Death*, trans. Justin O'Brien (New York: The Modern Library, 1963), pp. 206–7.
16. Aleksandr I. Solzhenitsyn, *The Gulag Archipelago*, trans. Thomas P. Whitney (New York: Harper & Row, 1974), p. x.

Index